DELIA'S COMPLETE HOW TO COOK

Originally published in three volumes:
Delia's How To Cook Book One
Delia's How To Cook Book Two
Delia's How To Cook Book Three

5 7 9 10 8 6 4

Published in 2009 by BBC Books, an imprint of Ebury Publishing.
A Random House Group Company

The Random House Group Limited Reg. No. 954009

Addresses for companies within the Random House Group can be found at
www.randomhouse.co.uk

A CIP catalogue record for this book is available from the British Library.

ISBN 978 0563539070

The Random House Group Limited supports The Forest Stewardship Council (FSC), the leading international
forest certification organisation. All our titles that are printed on Greenpeace approved FSC certified paper carry
the FSC logo. Our paper procurement policy can be found at www.rbooks.co.uk/environment

Jacket design by Vanessa Holden
Book design by Flo Bayley
Printed and bound in the UK by Butler Tanner & Dennis Ltd

DELIA'S
COMPLETE
HOW TO COOK

Photographs by Miki Duisterhof

Conversion tables

All these are approximate conversions, which have either been rounded up or down. In a few recipes it has been necessary to modify them very slightly. Never mix metric and imperial measures in one recipe, stick to one system or the other. All spoon measurements used throughout this book are level unless specified otherwise; all butter is salted unless specified otherwise.

Weights

½ oz	10 g
¾	20
1	25
1½	40
2	50
2½	60
3	75
4	110
4½	125
5	150
6	175
7	200
8	225
9	250
10	275
12	350
1 lb	450
1 lb 8 oz	700
2	900
3	1.35 kg

Volume

2 fl oz	55 ml
3	75
5 (¼ pint)	150
10 (½ pint)	275
1 pint	570
1¼	725
1¾	1 litre
2	1.2
2½	1.5
4	2.25

Dimensions

⅛ inch	3 mm
¼	5 mm
½	1 cm
¾	2
1	2.5
1¼	3
1½	4
1¾	4.5
2	5
2½	6
3	7.5
3½	9
4	10
5	13
5¼	13.5
6	15
6½	16
7	18
7½	19
8	20
9	23
9½	24
10	25.5
11	28
12	30

Oven temperatures

Gas mark 1	275°F	140°C
2	300	150
3	325	170
4	350	180
5	375	190
6	400	200
7	425	220
8	450	230
9	475	240

Contents

Introduction

If you would like to know how to cook, the very first step is to learn. The reason so many people don't cook is because they haven't been taught and they are afraid. Cooking is not an innate gift we're all born with; it has to be learnt and practised like any other skill.

In my day there were cookery classrooms in schools, equipped with worktops, ovens, fridges and equipment. Then the government ordered the removal of both cookery classes and equipment, which meant that a whole generation of young people left school without any knowledge of the subject.

Fast-forward to the 21st century and we are in an age of ready meals, takeaways and all-day grazing on wall-to-wall snacks and confectionery. The result is that we now have a government concerned with obesity and health and nutritional problems! Added to which we find ourselves faced with a world economic crisis and all of a sudden money is an issue: buying two cappuccinos and a couple of sandwiches that cost nearly twice as much as a home-cooked meal is no longer viable for the majority of people.

If there really is no gain without pain, then there has never been a better time to learn how to cook at home. What is on offer here is a helping hand: someone to stand beside you and remove the fear. This book will guide you through the basics and, once you have mastered them, give you the confidence to move on to enjoy a lifetime not just of preparing and eating good food but of sharing it with others too.

You don't need to be a great chef or make people gasp at your culinary accomplishments. If you are able to invite friends and loved ones to sit round a table and share a home-cooked meal, it will never fail – for you or them – to be one of life's richest and most pleasurable experiences.

Delia Smith
March 2009

For an update on ingredients for the 2009 edition go to
www.deliaonline.com

1

All about eggs

If you want to learn how to cook, start with eggs. That's my advice. Eggs are, after all, a powerful symbol of something new happening – new life, a new beginning. But there is another reason. Somehow eggs have become an equally negative symbol. When someone says, 'Oh, I can't even boil an egg,' what they are actually saying is, 'I can't cook anything at all.'

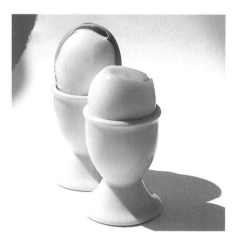

It's the amount of air in the pocket at the wide end of the egg – which in turn depends on the egg's freshness – that will determine how best to use the egg

That's why anyone wanting to make a start should begin by understanding eggs. Yes – even how to boil them. By cracking egg cookery (sorry about the pun) and simply knowing how to boil, poach, scramble, make an omelette and so on, you're going to give your cooking confidence a kick-start and ensure you will never go hungry. You'll also be able to offer your friends and loved ones a very quick but pleasurable meal. But that's not all: eggs are a supremely important ingredient in the kitchen, serving the cook in any number of ways. They can thicken soups and sauces, set liquids and baked dishes, they can provide a glorious airy foam to lighten textures and will also, quite miraculously, emulsify oils and butter into a rich smoothness.

What we have to do first and foremost, though, before we even begin cooking, is to try and understand what eggs are and how they work.

Understanding eggs

A hen's egg is, quite simply, a work of art, a masterpiece of design and construction with, it has to be said, brilliant packaging! It is extremely nutritious, filled with life-giving protein, vitamins and minerals. It has a delicate yet tough outer shell which, while providing protection for the growing life inside, is at the same time porous, meaning the air can penetrate and allow the growing chick to breathe.

It's the amount of air inside the egg that the cook needs to be concerned with. If you look at the photograph above left, you'll see the construction of the egg includes a space for the air to collect at the wide end, and it's the amount of air in this space that determines the age and quality of the egg and how best to cook it. In newly laid eggs, the air pocket is hardly there, but as the days or weeks pass, more air gets in and the air pocket grows; at the same time, the moisture content of the egg begins to evaporate. All this affects the composition of the egg, so if you want to cook it perfectly it is vital to determine how old the egg is. Now look at the photograph at the top of the opposite page and see what the egg looks like when it is broken out. What you start off with, on the left, is an egg at its freshest, with a rounded, plump yolk that sits up proudly. The white has a thicker, gelatinous layer that clings all around the yolk, and a thinner outer layer. After a week, on the right, the yolk is flatter and the two separate textures of white are not quite so visible.

Now all is revealed! You can see very clearly why you may have had problems in the past and why an egg needs to be fresh if you want to fry or poach it, because what you will get is a lovely, neat, rounded shape. Alas, a stale egg will spread itself more thinly and what you will end up with if you are frying it is a very thin pancake with a yellow centre. If you put it into water to poach, it would probably disintegrate, with the yolk and white parting company. Separating eggs is yet another hazard if the eggs are too old, because initially the yolk is held inside a fairly tough, transparent membrane, but this weakens with age and so breaks more easily.

The inner membrane within the shell begins as a taut, stretched skin; with age, however – and the inclusion of more air – this skin slackens

A fresh egg, far left, is distinguished by its plump, rounded yolk and distinctive two-layer white. A week-old egg, however, is characterised by a flatter yolk and a more even-textured white, left

So far, so good. But we haven't quite cracked it yet because, just to confuse matters, a very fresh egg isn't always best. Why? Because we have another factor to take into consideration. If we get back to the presence of air, what you will see from the photograph below left is that inside the shell is an inner membrane, a sort of safety net that would have protected the chick if the egg had been fertilised. When the egg is fresh, this is like a taut, stretched skin; then, as more air penetrates the egg, this skin slackens. This explains why, if you hard-boil a really fresh egg, peeling off both the shell and the skin is absolute torture. But if the egg is a few days or even a week old, the skin will become looser and the egg will peel like a dream.

What all this means is, yes, you can cook perfect eggs every time, as long as you know how old they are.

How to tell how old an egg is

How to tell how old a raw egg is while it is safely tucked away in its shell could seem a bit tricky, but not so. Remember the air pocket? There is a simple test that tells you exactly how much air there is. All you do is place the egg in a tumbler of cold water: if it sinks to a completely horizontal position, it is very fresh; if it tilts up slightly or to a semi-horizontal position, it could be up to a week old; if it floats into a vertical position, then it is stale. The only reason this test would not work is if the egg had a hairline crack, which would allow more air in. That said, 99 per cent of the time the cook can do this simple test and know precisely how the egg will behave. To sum up, the simple guidelines are as follows:

1 For poaching and frying, always use eggs as spanking fresh as you possibly can.

Below, left to right: a very fresh egg will sit horizontally when placed in a glass of water; one that lies semi-horizontally is generally up to a week old; and one that floats in a vertical position is stale

2 For separating egg yolks from whites, use eggs that are as fresh as possible, though up to a week old is fine.

3 For peeled hard-boiled eggs, about a week old or up to a fortnight is okay.

4 For scrambled eggs and omelettes, the fresher the eggs the better, but up to two weeks is fine.

5 For baked dishes, such as quiches or for home baking and so on, eggs more than two weeks old can be used.

6 In my opinion, all eggs should be used within two weeks if at all possible. An extra week is okay, but three weeks is the maximum keeping time.

How to buy and store eggs

Number one on the list here (unless you happen to know the hens) is to buy your eggs from a supplier who has a large turnover. Boxes now (and sometimes the eggs themselves) carry a 'best before' date. What you should know is that this date, provided the egg box is stamped with the lion mark, corresponds precisely to 21 days after laying (not packing), so you are, therefore, able to work out just how fresh your eggs are.

Although it is now being recommended that eggs should be stored in the refrigerator, I never do. The reason for this is that for most cooking purposes, eggs are better used at room temperature. If I kept them in the fridge I would have the hassle of removing them half an hour or so before using them. A cool room or larder is just as good, but if, however, you think your kitchen or store-cupboard is too warm and want to store them in the fridge, you'll need to try and remember to let your eggs come to room temperature before you use them. My answer to the storage problem is to buy eggs in small quantities so I never have to keep them too long anyway.

The very best way to store eggs is to keep them in their own closed, lidded boxes. Because the shells are porous, eggs can absorb the flavours and aromas of other strong foods, so close the boxes and keep them fairly isolated, particularly if you're storing them in the fridge.

There is, however, one glorious exception to this rule. My dear friend and great chef Simon Hopkinson once came to stay in our home. He brought some new-laid eggs in a lidded box, which also contained a fresh black truffle. He arrived on Maundy Thursday, and on Easter Sunday made some soft scrambled eggs, which by now had absorbed all the fragrance and flavour of the truffle. Served with thin shavings of the truffle sprinkled over, I have to say they were the very best Easter eggs I have ever tasted!

What about cholesterol?

Eggs, I am very happy to report, are out of the firing line on the cholesterol front. It is now believed that the real culprits on this one are saturated fat and partially hydrogenated fat, which eggs, thankfully, are low in. There is more good news, too: even if you are on a low-fat diet, eating up to seven eggs a week is okay. Hooray!

The porosity of eggs' shells isn't always a bad thing: here a fresh black truffle is kept with the eggs, which in turn absorb its flavour and fragrance, adding an unexpected dimension to the finished dish

How safe are they?

Poor old eggs; just as they recover from one slur, along comes another. Eggs, as we know, can harbour a bacterium called salmonella. Cases of food poisoning, or even death, from eating eggs are isolated but do occur. Therefore, the only way we can be absolutely certain of not being affected is by only eating eggs that are well cooked, with hard yolks and no trace of softness or runny yolk at all. Ugh!

What we all need to do is consider this very seriously and be individually responsible for making our own decisions. Life, in the end, is full of risks. The only way I can be absolutely sure I won't be involved in a car accident (and statistically this is a far greater risk than eating eggs) is to never ride in a car. But I am personally willing to take that risk – as I am when I eat a soft-boiled egg. So it's a personal decision. As a general practice, though, it is not advisable to serve these to vulnerable groups, such as very young children, pregnant women, the elderly or anyone weakened by serious illness.

Some general egg information

1 Is there any difference between brown and white shells?
   None whatsoever. The colour of the shell is determined by the breed of the hen that laid it. Aesthetically speaking, white denotes a sophisticated kind of purity, while brown is full of rural wholesomeness.

2 Size. Having gone through a couple of decades of numbering eggs, we are now back to size descriptions, which are as follows: very large, large, medium and small. Please note that in this book the eggs used in all recipes are large.

3 The eggs now available on a large scale commercially are as follows: free-range means the hens have continuous daytime access to open-air runs that contain vegetation; barn or perchery means the hens are enclosed but have floor space covered in straw or other materials. Eggs labelled organic are produced in the same way as free-range, but, in this case, the hens' habitat is land that has been certified as free from herbicides and pesticides (as is the land on which their feed has been grown). The remaining eggs are all produced in battery units.

4 There are, of course, other types of eggs. I have included recipes and timings for commercially produced eggs (ie, hens' and quails' eggs), but if you have access to and want to cook other types of eggs (goose, turkey, duck), then allow extra time for size. If you are baking, the best way to measure is by comparing the eggs you are using weight for weight with hens' eggs to give you a guideline. Gulls' eggs are pretty rare and exclusive, but they should be boiled like quails' eggs, peeled, and are traditionally served with a sprinkling of celery salt.

How do you boil eggs?

A pinprick made in the rounded end of an egg will allow steam to escape while it boils, thus avoiding cracking

The answer to this is carefully. Even the simplest of cooking tasks demands a degree of care and attention. But in the end all it involves is first knowing the right way to proceed and then happily being able to boil perfect eggs for the rest of your life without even having to think about it. What we need to do first of all, though, is memorise a few very important rules.

1 Don't ever boil eggs that have come straight from the refrigerator, because very cold eggs plunged straight into hot water are likely to crack.

2 Always use a kitchen timer. Trying to guess the timing or even remembering to look at your watch can be hazardous.

3 Remember the air pocket? During the boiling, pressure can build up and cause cracking. A simple way to deal with this is to make a pinprick in the rounded end of the shell, as left, which will allow the steam to escape.

4 Always use a small saucepan. Eggs with too much space to career about and crash into one another while they cook are, again, likely to crack.

5 Never have the water fast-boiling; a gentle simmer is all they need.

6 Never overboil eggs (you won't if you have a timer). This is the cardinal sin because the yolks will turn black and the texture will be like rubber.

7 If the eggs are very fresh (less than four days old), allow an extra 30 seconds on each timing.

Soft-boiled eggs – method 1

Obviously every single one of us has a personal preference as to precisely how we like our eggs cooked. Over the years I have found a method that is both simple and reliable, and the various timings set out here seem to accommodate all tastes. First of all have a small saucepan filled with enough simmering water to cover the eggs by about ½ inch (1 cm). Then quickly but gently lower the eggs into the water, one at a time, using a tablespoon. Now switch a timer on and give the eggs exactly 1 minute's simmering time. Then remove the pan from the heat, put a lid on it and set the timer again, giving the following timings:

> 6 minutes will produce a soft, fairly liquid yolk and a white that is just set but still quite wobbly
>
> 7 minutes will produce a firmer, more creamy yolk with a white that is completely set

Don't boil eggs in too large a saucepan: the less room they have to move about in the simmering water, the less likely they are to crack

Soft-boiled eggs – method 2

I have found this alternative method also works extremely well. This time you place the eggs in the saucepan, cover them with cold water by about ½ inch (1 cm), place them on a high heat and, as soon as they reach boiling point, reduce the heat to a gentle simmer and give the following timings:

> 3 minutes if you like a really soft-boiled egg
>
> 4 minutes for a white that is just set and a yolk that is creamy
>
> 5 minutes for a white and yolk perfectly set, with only a little bit of squidgy in the centre

Hard-boiled eggs

Some people hate soft-boiled eggs and like to eat them straight from the shell, hard-boiled. All well and good, but if you want to use hard-boiled eggs in a recipe and have to peel them, this can be extremely tricky if the eggs are too fresh. The number one rule, therefore, is to use eggs that are at least five days old from their packing date. The method is as follows: place the eggs in a saucepan and add enough cold water to cover them by about ½ inch (1 cm). Bring the water up to simmering point, put a timer on for 6 minutes if you like a bit of squidgy in the centre, 7 minutes if you want them cooked through. Then, the most important part is to cool them rapidly under cold running water. Let the cold tap run over them for about 1 minute, then leave them in cold water till they're cool enough to handle – about 2 minutes. Once you've mastered the art of boiling eggs you can serve them in a variety of ways, and one of my favourites is in a curry, as in the recipe on the following page.

Clockwise from top: a very soft-boiled egg has a liquid yolk and a white that is still wobbly; a soft-boiled egg has a creamy yolk and a white that is just set; in a medium-boiled egg, both the white and yolk are set

Peeling hard-boiled eggs

The best way to do this is to first tap the eggs all over to crack the shells, then hold each egg under a slow trickle of running water as you peel the shell off, starting at the wide end. The water will flush off any bits of shell that cling on. Then back they go into cold water until completely cold. If you don't cool the eggs rapidly they will go on cooking and become overcooked, then you get the black-ring problem.

Quails' eggs

Quails' eggs for boiling should, again, not be too fresh, and these are best cooked by lowering them into simmering water for 5 minutes. Then cool them rapidly and peel them as above.

The distinctive colouring of quails' eggs makes them a beautiful alternative to hens' eggs, and they're just as simple to cook

Egg and Lentil Curry with Coconut and Pickled Lime

This is one of my very favourite store-cupboard recipes. If you always keep a stock of spices and lentils handy and a pack of creamed coconut stashed away in the fridge, you can whip this one up in no time at all. It also happens to be inexpensive and highly suitable for vegetarians.

Serves 2

4 large eggs
3 oz (75 g) green lentils
3 oz (75 g) creamed coconut
1 rounded teaspoon lime pickle
juice and grated zest ½ fresh lime
1 large onion
1 small red chilli (preferably bird eye)
2 fat cloves garlic
1 inch (2.5 cm) piece root ginger
3 cardamom pods, crushed
1 teaspoon cumin seeds
1 teaspoon fennel seeds
1 dessertspoon coriander seeds
2 tablespoons groundnut or other
flavourless oil
1 rounded teaspoon turmeric powder
1 teaspoon fenugreek powder
salt

To serve:

5 fl oz (150 ml) rice, cooked
(see page 200)
a little extra lime pickle

You will also need a medium frying pan with a lid.

Start off by getting everything prepared and ready to go. First peel the onion, cut it in half and then into thin slices. Next deseed and finely chop the chilli, peel and chop the garlic as well, then measure out the lime pickle and chop that quite finely. Now peel and grate the ginger – you need a good heaped teaspoonful. The creamed coconut should be shredded with a sharp knife and placed in a heatproof measuring jug. At this stage put the kettle on to boil.

Now place the frying pan over a medium heat and, as soon as it gets hot, measure the whole spices (cardamom, cumin, fennel and coriander) straight into it. What they need to do now is dry-roast, and this will take 2-3 minutes. Shake the pan from time to time to toss them around a bit and, as soon as they start to jump, remove them from the heat and tip them straight into a mortar.

Now place the pan back over the heat, turn it up high and add the oil. As soon as it is really hot, add the onions and, keeping the heat highish, let them sizzle and brown and become quite dark at the edges, which will take about 4 minutes. After that, turn the heat back down to medium and add the chilli, ginger, garlic and lime pickle, along with the turmeric and fenugreek. Now crush the roasted spices finely with a pestle, add these to the pan as well, then stir everything together. See to the coconut next: all you need to do here is pour boiling water up to the 1 pint (570 ml) level in the jug containing the coconut, then whisk it all together.

Now stir the lentils in to join the rest of the ingredients, add the grated lime zest and the coconut liquid, stir again and, as soon as it reaches simmering point, turn the heat down. Put the lid on and let the mixture simmer as gently as possible for 45 minutes, stirring it now and then (don't add any salt at this stage).

About 10 minutes before the end of the cooking time, place the eggs in a saucepan of cold water, bring them up to a gentle simmer and time them for 6-7 minutes, depending on how you like them. When they're ready, let the cold tap run on them until they're cool enough to handle. When the sauce is ready, season it well with salt and add the lime juice. Now peel the eggs under cold running water, slice them in half and pop them on top of the sauce, giving everything a couple more minutes' cooking with the lid on. Serve the egg curry with rice, some more lime pickle and perhaps some mango chutney to add a touch of sweetness.

Open-Faced Egg, Chive and Spring Onion Sandwiches

Serves 2
3 small bread rolls, warmed,
halved and buttered

For the topping:
3 large eggs, hard-boiled as
described on page 17
1 rounded tablespoon fresh
snipped chives
4 spring onions, very finely chopped
(including most of the green as well)
½ teaspoon butter
1 tablespoon mayonnaise
salt and freshly milled black pepper

To garnish:
1 box fresh cress

My next-door neighbour Dot keeps me well supplied with delightful home-made grainy brown rolls. As supper at home on Sundays is almost always a snack meal, we love to eat them warmed, halved and buttered, then spread with one of these yummy egg toppings.

As soon as the eggs are cool enough, peel them, discard the shells and place the eggs in a bowl with the rest of the topping ingredients. Now take a large fork and mash like mad until the eggs are thoroughly blended with the rest of the ingredients. Then pile it on to the rolls and sprinkle each one with the cress before serving.

For an egg and bacon topping

Grill six rashers of streaky bacon until crispy, chop four of these into small pieces and add these to the egg mixture (minus the spring onions and chives). Top the rolls with this and garnish with the other two rashers, as in the photograph, right.

For an anchovy and shallot topping

Add six drained and finely chopped anchovies to the egg mixture (minus the spring onions and chives), and add a very finely chopped shallot and a dessertspoon of finely chopped parsley. Pile this on to the rolls and garnish each one with another anchovy fillet wrapped around a black olive, as in the photograph, right.

Opposite, clockwise from top:
Open-Faced Egg and Bacon Sandwich;
Open-Faced Egg, Chive and Spring
Onion Sandwich; Open-Faced Egg,
Anchovy and Shallot Sandwich

How to poach eggs

The key to a well-poached egg is to keep the water at a bare simmer throughout the cooking

Before we begin to talk about how to poach eggs, I think it is appropriate to clear up a few myths and mysteries that surround the whole subject. I met someone recently who said they had been to six leading kitchen shops and not one of them sold an egg poacher. My reaction was, 'What a great leap for mankind.' Egg poachers not only came out of the ark, but they never did the job anyway. What they did was to steam and toughen the eggs, not poach them – and did you ever try to clean one afterwards? The dried-on toughened egg white was always hell to remove.

Then came professional chefs, who passed their exams only if they created a strong whirlpool of simmering water using a whisk and then performed a sort of culinary cabaret act by swirling the poached egg back to its original shell shape. At home we can now relax, throw out our egg poachers and poach eggs simply and easily for four or even six people. The method below is not at all frightening or hazardous, but bear in mind that for successful poaching the eggs have to be really fresh (see page 13). You will need:

4-6 large, very fresh eggs (under four days old)
a suitably sized frying pan (according to the number of eggs)
boiling water from the kettle
a draining spoon and a folded wodge of kitchen paper

Place the frying pan over a gentle heat and add enough boiling water from the kettle to fill it to 1 inch (2.5 cm). Keep the heat gentle, and very quickly you will see the merest trace of tiny bubbles beginning to form over the base of the pan (above left). Now carefully break the eggs, one at a time, into the water and let them barely simmer, without covering, for just 1 minute. A timer is essential here because you cannot guess how long 1 minute is.

After that, remove the pan from the heat and let the eggs sit calmly and happily in the hot water, this time setting the timer for 10 minutes. This timing will give perfect results for a beautifully translucent, perfectly set white and a soft, creamy yolk. Now remove each egg by lifting it out of the water with the draining spoon and then letting the spoon rest for a few seconds on the kitchen paper, which will absorb the excess water. As you remove the eggs, serve them straight away. (For the toast, see page 83.)

There are now dozens of ways that you can use your new-found skill in egg poaching. For someone on a strict budget (or not), baked beans on toast topped with a poached egg (or two) is one of the world's cheapest but greatest nutritional combinations. If you're not on a budget, wholefood shops sell baked beans that taste almost home-made, in a sauce that does not contain any sugar. More expensive but very good.

Another fast but comforting supper dish is to poach smoked haddock in a frying pan of water. Drain well and keep it warm while you slip a couple of eggs into the same water to poach. Serve the haddock with the eggs on top and buttered chunks of brown Irish soda bread.

Warm Spinach Salad with Poached Eggs, Frizzled Kabanos and Bacon

This is actually a delightful combination of sausage, egg, bacon and mushrooms. Sorry about the chips – but you won't miss them because the salad leaves, crisp, crunchy croutons and the sherry dressing make this much more special.

Serves 2 as a light lunch or supper
4 oz (110 g) ready-washed young leaf spinach, plus a few sprigs of watercress
4 large, very fresh eggs
3 oz (75 g) smoked kabanos sausage
4 rashers smoked back bacon or 8 streaky rashers
1 small onion, peeled
2 oz (50 g) open mushrooms
2 slices white bread, crusts removed
3 tablespoons extra virgin olive oil
3 tablespoons dry sherry
1½ tablespoons sherry vinegar
freshly milled black pepper

You need to begin this by preparing everything in advance. The onion, mushrooms and bacon rashers need to be finely chopped into ¼ inch (5 mm) pieces; the sausage should also be chopped, but fractionally larger. Then cut the bread into ¼ inch (5 mm) cubes (croutons) and arrange the spinach and watercress on two large plates, removing any large stalky bits first.

Now poach the eggs as described on the previous pages, and, while they're sitting in the hot water, take a medium-sized, heavy-based frying pan and heat 1 tablespoon of the oil in it until it's very hot and gives off a fine haze. Then fry the croutons, tossing them around in the pan, until they're crisp and golden brown – about 1-2 minutes – and after that remove them to drain on some kitchen paper.

Now add the rest of the oil to the pan and, again, let it get really hot before adding the prepared bacon, onion and sausage. Toss them all around, keeping the heat high to make everything brown and toasted at the edges.

After 4 minutes, add the chopped mushrooms and toss these around, still keeping the heat high, for about 2 minutes. Finally, season with freshly milled black pepper, add the sherry and sherry vinegar to the pan, giving it a few seconds to bubble and reduce. Then transfer the eggs to sit on top of the spinach and watercress, pour the contents of the pan over everything and sprinkle the croutons on top.

Eggs Benedict

Can there be anybody who doesn't drool at the thought of Eggs Benedict? Soft, squidgy, lightly toasted bread, really crisp bacon and perfectly poached eggs which, when the yolks burst, drift into a cloud of buttery hollandaise sauce. It's certainly one of the world's great recipes. Although originally it was meant to be served at breakfast or brunch (and still can be), I think it makes a great first course, particularly in winter. A light version of this can be made using Foaming Hollandaise on page 71, which also has the advantage that it can be prepared ahead.

Poach the eggs as described on page 22. When the pancetta is cooked, keep it on a warm plate while you lightly toast the split muffins on both sides. Now butter the muffins and place them on the baking tray, then top each half with two slices of pancetta. Put a poached egg on top of each muffin half and then spoon over the hollandaise, covering the egg (there should be a little over 1 tablespoon of sauce for each egg).

Now flash the Eggs Benedict under the grill for just 25-30 seconds, as close to the heat as possible, but don't take your eyes off them – they need to be tinged golden and no more. This should just glaze the surface of the hollandaise. Serve straight away on hot plates.

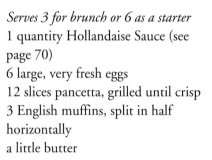

Serves 3 for brunch or 6 as a starter
1 quantity Hollandaise Sauce (see page 70)
6 large, very fresh eggs
12 slices pancetta, grilled until crisp
3 English muffins, split in half horizontally
a little butter

You will also need a grill pan and rack and a 10 x 14 inch (25.5 x 35 cm) baking tray.

Pre-heat the grill to its highest setting.

How to fry eggs

A perfectly fried egg is a glory to behold – crispy edges and a wobbly pinkish yolk. One of my treasured memories of eating fried eggs is on the beautiful Caribbean island of Barbados, where I have been lucky enough to spend several holidays. For me it's the best place on earth for an early morning dip in the sea, and as you swim and look back at all that beauty, the evocative smell of bacon and eggs cooking is sheer heaven. Afterwards, at breakfast, there's always a happy, smiling Bajan wielding an old, blackened frying pan, enquiring how you like your eggs fried.

When considering a recipe for fried eggs, this is the pertinent question – how *do* you like them? It's very personal, but my own method, below, can be adjusted to suit most tastes. So here goes.

You will need:

2 large, very fresh eggs
1 dessertspoon of fat left from frying bacon (or groundnut or grapeseed oil)
1 small heavy-based frying pan
1 slotted kitchen slice
some kitchen paper

Basting the egg while cooking, top, will help it to cook evenly, resulting in a perfectly fried egg: crispy edges and a wobbly pinkish yolk, above

First place the pan over a high heat and, as soon as the fat or oil is really hot (with a faint shimmer on the surface), carefully break the eggs into the pan. Let them settle for about 30 seconds, then turn the heat down to medium and carry on cooking them, tilting the pan and basting the eggs with the hot fat so that the tops of the eggs can be lightly cooked, too. After about 1 minute the eggs will be ready, so remove the pan from the heat, then lift the eggs out with the slice. Let them rest on the kitchen paper for a couple of seconds before putting them on a plate, then lightly blot up any excess fat with kitchen paper and eat them as soon as possible.

This method will provide a fried egg with a slightly crispy, frilly edge; the white will be set and the yolk soft and runny. If you prefer not to have the crispy edge, use a medium heat from the beginning and, if you like your eggs more cooked, give them a little longer.

Note: If you would like to fry your eggs in butter, then you need to use a gentler heat and give them a bit longer so the butter doesn't brown too much.

For fried eggs and bacon, fry the eggs as above but fry the bacon first. To do this, make a few nicks with a pair of scissors along the fat edge of some back bacon (this stops it frilling while it's cooking), then add a tiny spot of groundnut oil (about a teaspoon) to a fairly hot frying pan and fry the rashers until they are crisp and golden. Transfer them to a warm plate, blotting them with kitchen paper, and keep them warm while you fry the eggs in the fat left from the bacon.

Corned-Beef Hash with Fried Eggs

I love New York and, in particular, New York delis, where I always order a hot pastrami sandwich on rye bread and my husband always orders corned-beef hash with a fried egg. Although we don't have the same type of corned beef here, our humble, modest tinned version makes a mean old hash and, what's more, at an amazing price.

Start this off by cutting the corned beef in half lengthways, then, using a sharp knife, cut each half into four ½ inch (1 cm) pieces. Now chop these into ½ inch (1 cm) dice, then scoop them all up into a bowl. Combine the Worcestershire sauce and mustard in a cup and pour this all over the beef, mixing it around to distribute it evenly.

Now peel and halve the onion, cut the halves into thin slices and then cut these in half. The potatoes need to be washed and cut into ½ inch (1 cm) cubes, leaving the skin on, then place the cubes in a saucepan. Pour enough boiling water from the kettle to almost cover them, then add salt and a lid and simmer for just 5 minutes before draining them in a colander and then covering with a clean tea cloth to absorb the steam.

Now heat 2 tablespoons of the oil in the frying pan and, when it's smoking hot, add the sliced onions and toss them around in the oil to brown for about 3 minutes altogether, keeping the heat high, as they need to be very well browned at the edges.

After that, push all the onions to the edge of the pan and, still keeping the heat very high, add the potatoes and toss these around, too, because they also need to be quite brown. Add a little more oil here if necessary. Now add some seasoning, then, using a pan slice, keep turning the potatoes and onions over to hit the heat. After about 6 minutes, add the beef and continue to toss everything around to allow the beef to heat through (about 3 minutes).

After that, turn the heat down to its lowest setting and, in the smaller frying pan, fry the eggs as described left. Serve the hash divided between the two warm plates with an egg on top of each and don't forget to have plenty of tomato ketchup on the table.

Note: There's now a tomato ketchup available in wholefood shops that does not contain sugar and has a real tomato flavour.

Serves 2

7 oz (200 g) tinned corned beef
2 large, very fresh eggs
2 tablespoons Worcestershire sauce
1 rounded teaspoon grain mustard
1 large onion
10 oz (275 g) Desirée or King Edward potatoes
2-3 tablespoons groundnut or other flavourless oil
salt and freshly milled black pepper

You will also need a heavy-based frying pan approximately 8 inches (20 cm) in diameter, a slightly smaller frying pan for the eggs and two plates placed in a warming oven.

Chorizo Hash with Peppers and Paprika

This, if you like, is a more sophisticated version of the previous recipe, with red peppers as well as onion and potato. It's brilliant, but only worth making if you get genuine chorizo, available at deli counters and specialist food shops.

First the onion needs to be peeled, sliced in half and then each half sliced as thinly as possible so you end up with little half-moon shapes. Next halve and deseed the red pepper, slice it, then chop it into ½ inch (1 cm) pieces. After that, peel the skin off the chorizo sausage and cut into pieces roughly the same size as the pepper.

The potatoes need to be washed and cut into ½ inch (1 cm) cubes, leaving the skin on. Then place them in a saucepan and pour enough boiling water from the kettle to almost cover them, then add salt and a lid and simmer for just 5 minutes before draining them in a colander and covering with a clean tea cloth to absorb the steam.

Next heat 2 tablespoons of the oil in the frying pan and, when it's fairly hot, add the onion, pepper and garlic and cook for about 6 minutes, until softened and tinged brown at the edges. Then push these to the side of the pan, add the chorizo and, keeping the heat fairly high, cook for about 2 minutes, again, till nicely browned at the edges. Next, add the paprika and stir everything together, then remove the whole lot to a plate. Now add the last tablespoon of oil to the pan and, still keeping the heat high, add the potatoes and seasoning. Toss them around in the hot pan for about 3 minutes, keeping them moving, until they begin to crisp and brown at the edges, then return the chorizo, onion and pepper to the pan and, using a pan slice, keep turning the mixture over. Carry on cooking the whole thing for 5-6 minutes, until it's all really brown and crispy. Then turn the heat down to its lowest setting and, in the other pan, fry the eggs as described on page 28. Serve the hash divided between the two warmed plates with an egg on top of each, as shown on page 29, and have plenty of tomato ketchup on the table.

Serves 2

5 oz (150 g) chorizo sausage
1 small red pepper
1 rounded teaspoon hot paprika
1 medium onion
10 oz (275 g) Desirée or King Edward potatoes
3 tablespoons olive oil
1 fat clove garlic, peeled and crushed
2 large, very fresh eggs
salt and freshly milled black pepper

You will also need a heavy-based frying pan approximately 8 inches (20 cm) in diameter, a slightly smaller frying pan for the eggs and two plates placed in a warming oven.

How to make softly scrambled eggs

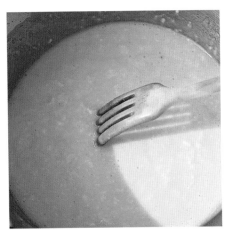

Add the beaten eggs to the butter in the pan and scramble until three-quarters of the egg is a creamy mass. Off the heat, add the rest of the butter and finish scrambling

I learnt how to make scrambled eggs for the very first time by following a recipe by the famous French chef Auguste Escoffier, and I still think his is the best version of all. However, during the past 30 years, since the first *Cookery Course* was published, there has been an enormous move away from butter, which in some ways is right because at one stage we were all far too heavy-handed with it, and it sometimes obscured the delicate flavour of fresh vegetables and so on. But let's never forget what a beautiful ingredient butter is and what a great affinity it has with eggs. For this reason I am sticking with Escoffier on scrambled eggs.

To begin with, there's only one rule, and that is not to have the heat too high; if you do, the eggs will become flaky and dry. The trick is to remove the pan from the heat while there's still some liquid egg left, then this will disappear into a creamy mass as you serve the eggs and take them to the table.

Scrambled Eggs for One

For more people, just multiply the ingredients accordingly. The method remains the same, but more eggs will obviously take longer to cook.

2 large eggs
½ oz (10 g) butter
salt and freshly milled black pepper

First of all, break the eggs into a small bowl and use a fork to lightly blend the yolks into the whites, whisking gently. Add a good seasoning of salt and freshly milled black pepper.

Now take a small, heavy-based saucepan and place it over a medium heat. Add half the butter to the pan and swirl it around so that the base and about 1 inch (2.5 cm) of the sides of the pan are moistened with it. Then, when the butter has melted and is just beginning to foam, pour in the beaten eggs. Using a wooden fork or a wooden spoon with a point, start stirring briskly using backwards and forwards movements all through the liquid egg, getting into the corners of the pan to prevent it from sticking. Don't, whatever you do, turn the heat up: just be patient and keep on scrambling away until you calculate that three-quarters of the egg is now a creamy, solid mass and a quarter is still liquid.

At this point, remove the pan from the heat, add the rest of the butter and continue scrambling with the fork or spoon. The eggs will carry on cooking in the heat from the pan. As soon as there is no liquid egg left, serve the scrambled eggs absolutely immediately. The secret of success is removing the pan at the right stage, because overcooking makes the eggs dry and flaky. Once you've mastered the art of allowing them to finish cooking off the heat, you will never have a problem. If you like you can add a little double cream or crème fraîche as well as the butter. Either way, soft clouds of perfectly scrambled eggs are one of life's special joys. Serve on buttered toast or bagels.

Slimmers' Scrambled Eggs

This recipe is devised for people on a diet or for those who have to cut down on fat. Nevertheless, it's extremely good, and on diet days I like to spread it on to sesame Ryvitas. I like it best made with Quark, which is a skimmed-milk soft cheese, but it also works well with cottage cheese.

Serves 1
2 large eggs
1 tablespoon milk
1 heaped dessertspoon Quark or cottage cheese
1 tablespoon fresh snipped chives
salt and freshly milled black pepper

You will also need a small non-stick saucepan and a wooden fork.

Begin by beating the eggs in a bowl, together with a good seasoning of salt and pepper. Now place the saucepan over a gentle heat, then add the milk to moisten the pan, whirling it around the edges. Add the eggs and, using a wooden fork or pointed wooden spoon, briskly stir backwards and forwards through the liquid egg. Keep on scrambling until three-quarters of the egg is a creamy, solid mass and a quarter is still liquid. Now add the Quark or cottage cheese and chives and continue to scramble, then remove the pan from the heat and continue scrambling until no liquid egg is left.

Scrambled Eggs with Smoked Salmon and Brioche

This has to be one of the most sublime combinations: soft, creamy scrambled eggs, together with the subtle, smoky flavour of the salmon. Some restaurants serve the scrambled eggs topped with slices of smoked salmon, but what a waste: soaking strips of salmon in cream and incorporating them into the scrambled eggs is in another league altogether.

Serves 2
4 large eggs
4½ oz (125 g) traditional smoked salmon trimmings
4 tablespoons single cream
2 all-butter brioche buns
½ oz (10 g) butter
salt and freshly milled black pepper

To garnish:
a little fresh dill

The salmon needs to be chopped fairly small for this, so if you're using offcuts you might still need to chop some of the larger pieces. I say chop here, but very often I use scissors. Either way, place all the salmon pieces in a small bowl, pour in the cream, give it all a good stir, cover the bowl and leave it aside for 30 minutes.

When you are ready to make the scrambled eggs, pre-heat the grill to its highest setting. Slice the top off each brioche, then carefully scoop out and discard half the bread from inside, then place each one, alongside its lid, under the grill, and lightly toast on both sides.

Now melt the butter in a medium-sized saucepan over a very gentle heat. While it's melting, break the eggs into a bowl and beat them lightly with a fork, seasoning with a little salt and freshly milled black pepper. When the butter has melted and begins to foam, swirl it around the edges of the pan, then pour in the beaten eggs. Increase the heat slightly and, using a wooden fork or a wooden spoon with a point, stir continuously backwards and forwards, getting right into the corners of the pan.

As soon as the eggs begin to solidify – after about 1 minute – and when you have about 50 per cent solid and the rest still liquid, quickly add the salmon and cream, then keep on stirring like mad until almost all the liquid has gone, which will take 3-4 minutes. Then remove the pan from the heat and continue stirring until the eggs become a soft, creamy mass. Taste to check the seasoning and spoon into the toasted brioche buns. Top with a little dill, replace the lids and serve immediately.

Gratin of Eggs with Peppers and Chorizo

This is a variation on oeufs sur le plat, and the name means, literally, eggs cooked on a plate, and a plate can indeed be used, provided it's heatproof. Best, though, are shallow gratin dishes measuring 6 inches (15 cm) in diameter, which have enough space for one or two eggs. This recipe has a Basque element, as the eggs are baked on a base of onions, garlic, peppers and chorizo sausage. The whole thing is topped with bubbling cheese, and it makes a perfect lunch or supper dish, taking hardly any time to prepare.

Begin by preparing all the ingredients. Remove the skin from the chorizo and slice it into ¼ inch (5 mm) rounds. The onion needs to be peeled, sliced in half and then each half sliced as thinly as possible so you end up with little half-moon shapes. Remove the stalk from the pepper and then halve it, scooping out the seeds. Slice it first into quarters and then each quarter into thin slices. The tomatoes need to be skinned, so pour boiling water over them, leave for 30 seconds, then drain and slip off their skins. Slice each tomato in half, squeeze each half gently to remove the seeds, then chop the flesh into small cubes. Peel and finely chop the garlic.

Next take a large, heavy-based frying pan, place it over a high heat and add the olive oil. When the oil is really hot, brown the chorizo pieces, tossing and turning them around until they turn slightly brown at the edges. Using a slotted spoon, transfer the chorizo from the pan to a plate. Next add the onion and pepper to the pan and toss these around, keeping the heat high, until they're nicely tinged brown at the edges and softened, which will take 5-10 minutes. Now add the tomatoes and garlic and cook for 1 minute more, then return the chorizo to join the rest of the ingredients. Finally, give everything a good mix and season with salt and freshly milled black pepper.

Then remove the pan from the heat and divide the mixture between the two gratin dishes. Carefully break two eggs side by side on top of the mixture in each dish, season them, then sprinkle them with the grated cheese. Place the dishes on the baking sheet on the top shelf of the oven to cook for 12-15 minutes (or a little longer, depending on how you like your eggs). I think this needs some quite robust red wine and some warm crusty baguette served alongside.

Serves 2
4 large eggs
1 small red or green pepper
3 oz (75 g) chorizo sausage
1 medium onion
3 medium tomatoes
1 fat clove garlic
1 tablespoon olive oil
2 oz (50 g) Gruyère, grated
salt and freshly milled black pepper

You will also need two round, 6 inch (15 cm) diameter gratin dishes moistened with a few drops of olive oil, and a baking sheet measuring 14 x 11 inches (35 x 28 cm).

Pre-heat the oven to gas mark 4, 350°F (180°C).

Eggs en Cocotte

This is another special way of cooking and serving eggs. The classic French name for this type of egg dish is oeufs en cocotte, and it is named after the dishes in which the eggs are cooked, which are called ramekins and look like mini soufflé dishes with enough space for baking one egg. The following recipe will give you the basic method of baking eggs in ramekins, including several variations.

First boil some water. Break an egg into each ramekin, season, then put a knob of butter on top of each yolk. Place the dishes in the baking tin, then pop it on the centre shelf of the oven and pour enough boiling water into the tin to come halfway up the sides of the dishes. Now let the eggs bake for 15 minutes if you like them soft and runny, or 18 minutes if you like them more set. Either way, bear in mind that they go on cooking in the dishes as they leave the oven and reach the table.

There are several variations, too. Instead of a knob of butter, pour in a tablespoon of double cream, soured cream, crème fraîche or, for a lower-fat version, Greek yoghurt works superbly. In addition, you could sprinkle a dessertspoon of grated cheese on top of the cream. Other ingredients that can be included under the egg are lightly cooked asparagus tips or cooked, chopped leeks. You could also use chopped smoked salmon or lightly cooked flakes of smoked haddock.

Serves 2 as a starter
2 large, fresh eggs
about 1 oz (25 g) butter
salt and freshly milled black pepper

You will also need two ramekins with a 3 inch (7.5 cm) diameter, 1½ inches (4 cm) deep, well buttered, and a baking tin measuring 11 x 8 inches (28 x 20 cm), 2 inches (5 cm) deep.

Pre-heat the oven to gas mark 4, 350°F (180°C).

Eggs en Cocotte with Morel or Porcini Mushrooms

I love to make this with dried morels, which are available in some supermarkets as well as specialist food shops, but dried porcini will also be excellent.

Serves 4 as a starter
4 large, very fresh eggs
½ oz (10 g) dried morels or porcini
5 fl oz (150 ml) boiling water
3 shallots, peeled and finely chopped
4 oz (110 g) dark-gilled flat mushrooms, roughly chopped
¼ whole nutmeg, grated
1 oz (25g) butter
3 rounded tablespoons crème fraîche, half-fat crème fraîche or Greek yoghurt
salt and freshly milled black pepper

You will also need four ramekins with a base diameter of 3 inches (7.5 cm), 1½ inches (4 cm) deep, well buttered, and a baking tin measuring 11 x 8 inches (28 x 20 cm), 2 inches (5 cm) deep.

Start by soaking the morels or porcini about 30 minutes ahead of time. Place them in a bowl with the boiling water and leave them aside to soak. After that, strain them in a sieve and squeeze them to get rid of any surplus water. (You can reserve the soaking water, which can be frozen and is great for soups and sauces.) Set aside 4 pieces of the morels or porcini and put the rest in a food processor, along with the shallots, flat mushrooms, nutmeg and salt and freshly milled black pepper. Process until finely chopped.

Heat the butter in a small saucepan. When it starts to foam, add the chopped mushroom mixture and, keeping the heat low, let it cook very gently, without a lid, for 25-30 minutes; the idea is that any excess liquid will evaporate and leave a lovely, dark, concentrated mixture.

All this can be prepared in advance, but when you're ready to cook the eggs, start by pre-heating the oven to gas mark 4, 350°F (180°C) and boil a kettle. Gently re-heat the mixture and, stirring in 1 rounded tablespoon of the crème fraîche or yoghurt, divide it between the ramekins, making a small indentation where the egg will be placed. Now break an egg into each one and season. Stir the rest of the crème fraîche or yoghurt around to loosen it, divide between the dishes, then spread it gently over the eggs using the back of the spoon or a small palette knife. Place a piece of the reserved morels or porcini on top of each ramekin, then place the ramekins in the baking tin, pop the tin on the centre shelf of the oven and add enough boiling water to the tin to come halfway up the sides of the dishes. Bake for 15-18 minutes. These are lovely served with slices of wholemeal bread and butter.

2 The art of the omelette

'Egg may be dressed in a multiplicity of ways but seldom more relished in any form than in a well made, expeditiously served omelette.'
(Eliza Acton)

So says Eliza, and things have not changed. She has said everything I want to say. If I can teach you how to master the 'well made, expeditiously served omelette' then I will have served you well, because you'll never be short of one of life's simplest, quickest and most pleasant dishes.

However, the art of the omelette begins not, as you might think, in the kitchen but in the high street. 'First catch your frying pan' is the optimum expression here. In all my years of attempting to teach cooking, buying the right frying pan has always been a tricky business. Yes, I was there when the non-stick revolution arrived in the shops, and the number of miserable, peeling, scratched and worn non-stick pans that have passed through my kitchen since is legion.

The problem is that there are strict rules, and the rules have to be obeyed: thou shalt never place the pan over direct heat without anything in it; thou shalt never turn the heat higher than medium; thou shalt never, ever use metal utensils. My problem with non-stick is that I *can't* stick to the rules. I like to heat the pan before I put the butter in; I can't sear a steak unless the pan is scorching hot, and I simply cannot make an omelette without a metal spoon. Then, having made a glorious, open-faced flat omelette to be served in wedges, I'm not allowed to use a sharp knife to cut it.

Yes, I know there are special non-metal tools, but wood simply sticks to the food, and plastic is not for people with busy lives who leave it in the pan when the phone rings and then find it's melted down into the food. I am not against non-stick if carefully handled – it is a useful piece of equipment – it's just that I am not careful enough.

My last warning is beware of the 'I'm only here for my looks' brigade. Stainless steel never was a good conductor of heat, and pans made only of stainless steel, however good they look, are to be avoided.

There I'll rest my case, but the good news is that after years of testing omelette pans I have discovered a little gem: the humble, unglamorous but utterly reliable British-made, heavy gauge aluminium pan. Yes, I know red lights are flashing, 'What about the safety of aluminium?' I have done my homework and discovered that, like most health scares, this was unproven. Extensive tests have concluded that aluminium is perfectly safe for all cooking, except for very acidic fruits and vegetables, such as plums, tomatoes and rhubarb, where the acid can attack the metal. This type of pan is also one of the cheapest quality pans on the market and, if you season it properly, it becomes virtually non-stick and will serve you for a lifetime of happy omelette-making.

Size is crucial

First of all, the size of the pan is vital: too small and the omelette will be thick, spongy and difficult to fold; too large and the eggs will spread out like a thin pancake and become dry and tough. When you buy a pan, take a tape measure and measure the base (not the top), because that's where the cooking happens. I have found the pan recommended above best for either a two- or three-egg omelette, which is average for a folded omelette. The base measures 6 inches (15 cm) in diameter. Pans with an 8 inch (20 cm) base are suitable for tortillas or open-faced omelettes.

How to season a new frying pan

Please, please, whatever pan you buy, don't forget to do this. All you do is coat the base of the pan with about ½ inch (1 cm) of any old cooking oil (something lurking in the back of the cupboard, past its use-by date would be ideal). Make really sure the sides and the whole surface of the pan are well oiled, then just put it on the lowest heat possible for about eight hours. Do keep an eye on it, don't go out and leave it, and check from time to time that the oil is barely warm. The best frying pan is a well-used one, so what this is doing is the equivalent to about six months of cooking. You can use the pan for any kind of frying; the more you use it the better it will be. After use, wash it in mildly soapy hot water with a dish cloth. Dry it and then rub a little oil round the inside surface.

Making a folded omelette

Before you begin, have everything ready: bowl, eggs, omelette pan, fork, tablespoon, salt and pepper, butter and oil. Put the plates in a warm oven.

1 *Eggs*

    One omelette will serve one person and, because it is so quick to make, it's not worth cooking a large one for two. So, according to how hungry you are, use two or three large eggs per person. Just break the eggs carefully into a bowl, add a seasoning of salt and freshly milled black pepper, then gently combine the yolks and whites with a fork – don't overbeat them, combine is the word you need to think of here. Under-rather than overbeating the eggs seems to make a fluffier omelette.

2 *Oil or butter?*

    You can use either, but remember that butter burns very easily on a high heat. Some oil will prevent this from happening so, if you like a buttery flavour, I would recommend that you use half a teaspoon of each. For extra butteriness or creaminess you could add a teaspoon of melted butter or double cream to the eggs in the bowl.

3 *Heat*

    Heat is a vital element in omelette-making because the essence of success is speed. Begin by turning the heat to medium, place the pan over the heat and let it get quite hot (about half a minute). Now add the butter and oil and, as soon as it melts, swiftly swirl it round, tilting the pan so that the base and the sides get coated. Turn the heat up to its highest setting now – when I first demonstrated this on television I remember saying, 'hot as you dare', and that still stands.

4 *Cooking the omelette*

    When the butter is foaming, pour the eggs into the pan, tilting it to and fro to spread the eggs evenly over the base. Then leave it on the heat without moving it for a count of five.

5 *Working with a spoon*

    After 5 seconds a bubbly frill will appear round the edge. Now you can

When making an omelette, begin by heating the oil or butter on as high a heat as you dare; next, pour the eggs into the pan, tilting it so they cover the base; using a spoon, start to draw the edge of the omelette into the middle so the liquid egg runs into the space, continuing until almost all the liquid egg has cooked

tilt the pan to 45° and, using a tablespoon, draw the edge of the omelette into the centre. The liquid egg will flow into and fill the space. Now tip the pan the other way and do the same thing. Keep tilting it backwards and forwards, pulling the edges in with the spoon and allowing the liquid egg to travel into the space left – all this will take only half a minute. Soon there will be just a small amount of liquid left, just on the surface, so now is the time to start folding. Tilt the pan again and flip one side of the omelette into the centre, then fold again. Take the pan to the warm plate, and the last fold will be when you tip the omelette out on to the plate.

6 Remember, an omelette will go on cooking, even on the plate, so serve it immediately. For this reason it is important to have some liquid egg left before you start folding, but if you have left too much, leave it to set on the plate before eating. The perfect omelette is one just tinged with gold on the surface and very soft and squidgy on the inside.

Omelettes with fillings

Now you have mastered the art of a plain omelette you can begin to think about fillings.

Fontina, Gruyère (pictured) and Taleggio make a great melted-cheese omelette, particularly with the addition of ham

To make a *straightforward cheese omelette*, add 1½ oz (40 g) of grated mature Cheddar to the egg mixture and sprinkle some Parmesan over the finished omelette before it goes to the table.

For a *blue cheese and onion omelette*, add 1½ oz (40 g) of crumbled Stilton, Roquefort or Gorgonzola, plus 2 finely chopped spring onions, to the egg mixture, then cook as described.

For a *melted-cheese omelette*, first pre-heat the grill, then take 2 oz (50 g) of a good melting cheese, such as Fontina, Gruyère or Taleggio, slice it thinly, lay the slices all over the omelette at the stage where it is almost set but still liquid (you could also add some ham now if you like), then flash the omelette pan under the pre-heated grill to melt the cheese quickly. Then turn it out as described earlier and this will produce a melted cheese centre that oozes out when you take your first forkful.

For a *Swiss omelette*, pre-heat the grill and add ½ oz (10 g) of grated Gruyère to the egg mixture. Have ready another ½ oz (10 g) of grated Gruyère mixed with 1 tablespoon of double cream. After folding and turning out the omelette, spoon this mixture over the folded omelette and flash it under the hot grill to form a cheesy, creamy glaze. Not good for the waistline but…

On a diet? Yes, you can still have a *cheese omelette*. Grated Parmesan (Parmigiano Reggiano) has a wonderful flavour and not too high a fat content. Just ½ oz (10 g) – half in the egg mixture and half sprinkled over the top after turning out – will set you back only 39 calories and 2.8g of fat.

For a *mushroom omelette* for one person use 4 oz (110 g) of chopped mushrooms. Very gently stew them, uncovered, in 1 teaspoon of oil or butter for 20 minutes, until all the excess moisture has evaporated and the flavour is concentrated. Scatter them over the omelette before folding.

For a *fines herbes omelette*, combine 1 tablespoon of chopped parsley and 1 tablespoon of fresh snipped chives (or any herb combination you choose). Stir the herbs into the mixed eggs 30 minutes before making the omelette to allow the flavours to develop.

For a *smoked salmon omelette*, soak 2 oz (50 g) of smoked salmon trimmings in 1 tablespoon of cream or milk for 30 minutes, then add this to the egg mixture before making the omelette.

Open-Faced Flat Omelettes

While the French folded omelette described earlier is probably the ultimate 'fast food' in the home, it does make certain demands on the cook in that it all has to happen fairly swiftly, which is great for one or two people but not so easy when you're doing a kind of production line for four or more. The open-faced omelette, on the other hand, gives you time to play with. Here, the whole thing is much more laid back – you can even pop one on the stove to cook while you sip an aperitif and chat, and then serve even six people with absolute ease.

Tortilla (Spanish Omelette)

I sometimes marvel how it is that three basic, very inexpensive ingredients – eggs, onions and potatoes – can be transformed into something so utterly sublime. Yet it's simply the way the Spanish make their omelettes. A Spanish omelette, or tortilla, is not better than a French one, and it certainly takes longer to make, but in this age of complicated, overstated, fussy food, it's a joy to know that simplicity can still win the day. A well-made tortilla served with a salad and a bottle of wine can give two or more people a luxury meal at any time and at a very low cost.

Serves 2-3
5 large eggs
1 medium onion, about 4 oz (110 g)
10 oz (275 g) small Desirée potatoes
3 tablespoons olive oil
salt and freshly milled black pepper

Potatoes and onions are cooked until they are gently stewed; every now and then the edge is drawn in gently with a palette knife, giving the tortilla a rounded edge

First some points to note. The size of the frying pan is important: a base measurement of 8 inches (20 cm) diameter is about right for two to three people. If using a larger pan for more people, it should not be too heavy because you need to turn the omelette out using both hands. Use a non-stick pan if you don't have a well-seasoned frying pan. An enormous asset here is a flat saucepan lid or large plate that fits the pan.

Tortilla can be served as a main course or, because it is good served cold, it makes excellent picnic food cut into wedges and wrapped in clingfilm. In Spain they serve it as tapas, cut into small cubes and speared with cocktail sticks – lovely with chilled amontillado sherry. The Spanish also serve tortilla sandwiched between chunks of crusty bread – sounds yummy but very fattening!

First of all, peel and cut the onion in half, then thinly slice each half and separate the layers into half-moon shapes. Now thinly pare the potatoes using a potato peeler and slice them into thin rounds – you have to work pretty quickly here because you don't want the slices to brown. When they are sliced, rub them in a clean tea cloth to get them as dry as possible.

Next, heat 2 tablespoons of the olive oil in the frying pan and, when it's smoking hot, add the potatoes and onions. Toss them around in the oil to get a good coating, then turn the heat right down to its lowest setting, add a generous sprinkling of salt and pepper, put a lid on the frying pan and let the onions and potatoes cook gently for 20 minutes, or until tender. Turn them over halfway through and shake the pan from time to time, as they are not supposed to brown very much but just gently stew in the oil.

Meanwhile, break the eggs into a large bowl and, using a fork, whisk them lightly – it's important not to overbeat them. Finally, add some seasoning. When the onions and potatoes are cooked, quickly transfer them to the eggs in the bowl.

Put the frying pan back on the heat, add the rest of the oil and turn the heat back up to medium. Then mix the potato and eggs thoroughly before pouring the whole lot into the frying pan and turning the heat down to its lowest setting immediately. Now forget all about French omelettes and be patient, because it's going to take 20-25 minutes to cook slowly, uncovered. Every now and then draw the edge in gently with a palette knife, as this will give it a lovely rounded edge. When there is virtually no liquid egg left on the surface of the omelette, place a flat lid or plate over the pan, invert it, turning the pan over, and put it back on the heat and use the palette knife to gently ease the omelette back in. Give it about 2 minutes more, then turn the heat off and leave it for a further 5 minutes to settle. It should then be cooked through but still moist in the centre. Serve hot or cold, cut in wedges, with a salad and a glass of Rioja – it's brilliant.

How to make an Italian frittata

This is Italy's version of an open-face omelette, and while the tortilla is golden brown, the frittata is cooked even more slowly and should not be too coloured on the outside. The Italian word here is *lentamente* – very slowly; the eggs cook through gradually and the finished omelette should be very moist. For this reason it is better not turned over but rather quickly flashed under a hot grill so that the top only just sets. It then has to be served immediately, otherwise it goes on cooking and loses its soft creaminess.

Melted Cheese Frittata with Four Kinds of Mushroom

Serves 4
8 large eggs
4 oz (110 g) Fontina or Gruyère
12 oz (350 g) mixed mushrooms
(3 oz/75 g of each)
1 tablespoon olive oil
salt and freshly milled black pepper

You will also need a 10 inch (25 cm) frying pan and the oven pre-heated to its lowest setting.

I like to use Fontina cheese for this, but Gruyère is also a good melting cheese, so you could use that instead. The mushrooms can be whatever is available, though I love the contrasting textures and colours of a mixture of oyster, shiitake, black dark-gilled mushrooms and the vibrant pied de mouton. However, none of this is vital: if you use only one type of mushroom it will still be extremely good.

First of all chop the mushrooms into roughly 1 inch (2.5 cm) chunks – it's going to look an enormous quantity at this stage, but they will lose approximately half their volume in the initial cooking. Now heat a teaspoon of the olive oil in a frying pan and, when it's hot, throw in the mushrooms and toss them around by shaking the pan. Don't worry that there is so little oil, because the mushrooms give off masses of juice once the heat gets to them. Season with salt and pepper, then turn the heat down to very low and just let the mushrooms cook gently, uncovered, so that all the juice evaporates and the flavour of the mushrooms becomes more concentrated. Leave them like that for 30 minutes, stirring them around once or twice.

While they are cooking, cut two-thirds of the cheese into ¼ inch (5 mm) cubes and grate the other third on the coarse blade of the grater. After that, break the eggs into a large bowl, whisk lightly with a fork and season well with salt and pepper. Then add three-quarters of the cooked mushrooms to the eggs, together with the cubed cheese. Place the rest of the mushrooms in a bowl covered with foil and keep them warm in the oven.

Now wipe the pan clean with some kitchen paper and put it back on a medium heat, add the rest of the olive oil and, when it's hot, swirl it around the pan. Turn the heat down to its lowest setting and pour the egg mixture into the pan, scattering the grated cheese all over the surface. Now all you have to do is leave it alone and put a timer on for 15 minutes.

When 15 minutes have passed, turn the grill on to its highest setting and see how the omelette is cooking – it will probably take about 20 minutes in total to cook, but there should still be about 10 per cent of liquid egg left on the top. At that stage transfer the pan to the grill – not too close – and cook briefly to allow the liquid egg to set. This will take 20-30 seconds. Scatter the remaining cooked mushrooms over the top of the frittata and cut it into four wedges. Transfer the wedges to warm plates and serve immediately, because the egg will continue cooking even though the frittata is no longer in contact with the heat. I like to serve this with two salads – a plain, green-lettuce salad and a tomato and basil salad.

The initial quantity of mushrooms for this frittata will seem like an awful lot to begin with, but they will lose about half their volume during the initial cooking

A Soufflé Omelette with Three Cheeses and Chives

Though making a soufflé proper can be a stressful experience, particularly if you've had no practice, making a soufflé omelette is a doddle. It takes no more than five minutes and honestly tastes every bit as good as the oven-baked variety. This one has three cheeses, but you can make it with just one, or even four if you happen to have them hanging around. I've included this in the omelette section, but if you are unsure of beating up the egg whites, read the notes in the next chapter on page 56.

Serves 1
3 large eggs
1 oz (25 g) mature Cheddar,
finely grated
1 oz (25 g) Parmesan (Parmigiano
Reggiano), finely grated
1 oz (25 g) Gruyère, finely grated
1 heaped tablespoon finely
snipped chives
½ oz (10 g) butter
salt and freshly milled black pepper

You will also need a medium
solid-based frying pan with a base
diameter of 7 inches (18 cm).

Pre-heat the grill to its highest setting
for 10 minutes and have a warm
plate ready.

First separate the eggs – yolks into a small bowl and whites into a squeaky-clean large bowl; it helps if you separate the whites singly into a cup first before adding them to the bowl, then if one breaks, it won't ruin the rest. Now beat the egg yolks with a fork, seasoning well with salt and pepper. Next put the pan on to a low heat to warm through.

While that's happening, whisk the egg whites with either an electric hand whisk or a balloon whisk, until they form soft peaks. Next add the butter to the pan and turn the heat up. Then, using a large metal spoon, quickly fold the egg yolks into the egg whites, adding the Cheddar, half the Parmesan and the chives at the same time.

Then, when the butter is foaming, pile the whole lot into the pan and give it a good hefty shake to even it out. Now let the omelette cook for 1 minute exactly. Then slide a palette knife round the edges to loosen it, sprinkle the grated Gruyère all over the surface and whack the omelette under the grill, about 4 inches (10 cm) from the heat. Let it cook for 1 more minute, until the cheese is melted and tinged golden. Next, remove the pan from the heat, then slide the palette knife round the edge again. Take the pan to the warmed plate, then ease one half of the omelette over the other and tilt the whole lot out on to the plate. Scatter the rest of the Parmesan all over and serve immediately.
Note: If you want to make this omelette for two, that's okay if you double everything. Just use a 9 or 10 inch (23 or 25.5 cm) diameter pan and give each stage more time, then divide the omelette into two.

3

Separate ways with eggs

For me, the talent of the egg as an ingredient seems infinite. It could be thought of as rather humdrum and everyday, but when closely examined, the humble egg becomes an absolute star turn in the kitchen. Though we've already discovered its potential for providing endless combinations of delightful and nutritious meals that can be made in moments, in addition, eggs are essential for making batters, baking puddings and cakes and for setting the fillings of tarts and quiches.

For now, though, I want to introduce you to yet another dimension of egg cookery, namely what happens when you separate the yolk from the white. While, as whole eggs, they can make puddings, batters, cakes and so on, once separated, they move on to being two quite unique and essential components in cooking.

If you want to separate the yolk from the white of an egg, the egg has to be as fresh as possible. The protective membrane that encloses the yolk weakens with age and breaks more easily, and this can cause problems, because if even one speck of yolk gets into the white, it won't be suitable for whisking. So with eggs as fresh as possible there's much less chance of that happening.

How to separate eggs

To separate yolks from whites, all you do is hold the egg over one bowl and have another bowl beside it. Crack the egg on the side of the bowl, round about its centre, then, using both hands, break it into two halves, one in each hand. Now slip the yolk back and forth from one half-shell to the other, tilting it as you do so and letting the white trickle down into the bowl while you hang on to the yolk. When there is no white left in the shells, pop the yolk into the other bowl.

Egg whites whipped to the soft-peak stage

Leftover whites and yolks

One query that often comes up in your letters is what I do with leftover whites if I'm only using yolks, and vice versa. The good news here is that eggs freeze very well, so pack them in small containers and don't forget to label them with the amount – trying to guess how many egg whites you have is not a good idea.

Egg whites

In the *Complete Cookery Course* I wrote: 'The secret of beating egg whites is knowing when to stop.' Twenty years and many more egg whites under my belt, I would add another proviso: you also need to know when *not* to stop.

I have to say in all honesty that getting whisked egg whites precisely right is an acquired skill, no doubt about it. But all skills can be acquired, and it does help if, a) someone (hopefully me) explains it properly so you know precisely what you're supposed to do and why, and, b) you are prepared to practise enough, because nothing beats experience.

So let's begin with egg whites.

… and to the stiff-peak stage

Egg whites

What happens when you whisk egg whites?

First of all, the most important ingredient is not the egg white but the air, because the whisked egg white is going to provide aeration for soufflés, meringues, cakes and the like. In whisking them, what you're actually doing is incorporating air, and as you do so, the original volume of the egg white can actually be increased by up to eight times.

As you whisk in the air, tiny air bubbles are formed. It might help to think of what happens when you blow up balloons here: too little air and the balloon will not be buoyant and bouncy, too much air and it will burst and the air will be lost. Therefore the cook has to whisk to precisely the right degree and then stop: too little and the egg white will be flabby, too much and the bubbles will burst, releasing the precious air (and it will still be flabby!).

When do you stop?

Knowing the right moment to stop is tricky, and all the cook can do is follow the tried and trusted guidelines, namely, to stop when you reach the stage at which the egg white stands up in well-defined peaks. If the egg white is for a cake, mousse or soufflé, where it has to be folded into other ingredients, the peaks should be soft (so that when you lift the whisk the peaks drop slightly); if it is for a meringue, where sugar is going to be incorporated, it should stand up in stiff peaks. In this book I will always indicate whether stiff or soft peaks are called for (see the photographs on page 55).

Grease: the enemy

The one thing that will prevent egg whites from reaching their full-blown potential is even the tiniest presence of grease. That's why the merest trace of egg yolk in the white means you are done for. But I'm afraid that's not all: you also have to be scrupulously careful about the bowl and whisk, which must also be grease-free. So always wash them in mild soapy water, rinse in very hot water, then dry them with an absolutely clean tea cloth. Just to make quite sure, run a slice of lemon round the whisk and the bowl.

Which equipment?

A balloon whisk is said by chefs to be the best, but it is too much like hard work for me. If you're young and more energetic, by all means go for it. A free-standing mixer or processor may be used, but I have always felt that the whites are not exposed to enough air this way. Others disagree, and you might find it best for you. An electric hand whisk is my personal favourite, as I can feel and see everything and the motor actually does all the work for me.

How to whisk egg whites

Before you begin, make sure that the mixing bowl is as large as you can get, which means as much air as possible can circulate around the egg whites as you whisk them.

Separate the eggs one at a time, placing each white in a cup or small bowl before adding it to the beating bowl. This means that if an accident occurs with, say, the third egg, and you break the yolk, the other two are safe. Switch the whisk on to a slow speed first of all and begin whisking for about 2 minutes, until everything has become bubbly (this timing will be right for two to three egg whites; you'll need slightly more time for four, five or six). After that, switch to a medium speed for a further minute, then whisk at the highest speed and continue whisking through the soft-peak stage until stiff peaks are formed.

Fear not

Always remember that a cake, or even a soufflé, with less or more air in it will not be a disaster. If the egg whites are not quite right, the finished dish will still taste good. If you're cooking with natural, fresh ingredients, who cares what it looks like? It's bound to taste good. I have often got egg whites wrong but still enjoyed the not-quite-so-puffy pavlova. Of course, we should always endeavour to get things right, but cooking, like life, isn't always perfect.

How to make meringue

I think one of the best ways to start practising whisking egg whites is to make meringues.

Meringue must be the most popular egg-white recipe of all, whipped with fine sugar into tall, stiff, shining peaks, then very lightly baked so that the surface is crisp and the centre is soft and chewy. The tricky bit is whisking the egg whites (see the method above), but the way it is cooked is important, too. My own method of baking has stood the test of time and, provided your oven temperature is correct, it will never let you down. The secret, I think, is allowing the meringue to remain in the closed oven after the heat is turned off so that it partly bakes and then slowly dries out.

Egg whites, whipped with sugar into stiff, glossy peaks, are the basis of all meringues

Petits Monts Blancs

When I first worked in a restaurant kitchen in the early 1960s, this recipe was on the menu and I became totally addicted to the sweetened chestnut purée. Chestnut has an amazing affinity with meringue and whipped cream, but in this modern version I have replaced the cream with Mascarpone and fromage frais; this way you get the flavour and creamy richness of the Mascarpone but lightened by the fromage frais.

Serves 8

For the meringues:
2 large egg whites
4 oz (110 g) white caster sugar

For the topping:
9 oz (250 g) Mascarpone
7 fl oz (200 ml) 8 per cent fat fromage frais
1 rounded dessertspoon caster sugar
1 teaspoon vanilla extract

To finish:
2 x 250 g tins crème de marrons de l'Ardèche (sweetened chestnut purée), chilled
a little icing sugar

You will also need a 16 x 12 inch (40 x 30 cm) baking sheet lined with silicone paper (parchment).

Pre-heat the oven to gas mark 2, 300°F (150°C).

To make the meringues, place the egg whites in a large bowl and, using an electric hand whisk on a low speed, begin whisking. Continue for about 2 minutes, until the whites are foamy, then switch the speed to medium and carry on whisking for 1 more minute. Now turn the speed to high and continue whisking until the egg whites reach the stiff-peak stage. Next, whisk the sugar in on fast speed, a little at a time (about a dessertspoon), until you have a stiff and glossy mixture.

Now all you do is spoon 8 heaped dessertspoons of the mixture on to the prepared baking sheet, spacing them evenly. Then, using the back of the spoon or a small palette knife, hollow out the centres. Don't worry if they are not all the same shape – random and rocky is how I would describe them (see the photograph below left). Next, pop them on the centre shelf of the oven, immediately reduce the heat to gas mark 1, 275°F (140°C) and leave them for 30 minutes. After that, turn the oven off and leave the meringues to dry out in the warmth of the oven until it is completely cold (usually about 4 hours) or overnight. The meringues will store well in a tin or polythene box, and will even freeze extremely well.

Whisk the topping ingredients together. To assemble the Monts Blancs, spoon equal quantities of the crème de marrons into each meringue, followed by equal quantities of the topping. A light dusting of icing sugar is good for a snowcapped-mountain image.

Meringue nests before cooking…   *and afterwards*

Meringues with Passion Fruit

This is a variation of the Petits Monts Blancs recipe on the previous page, and all you need is the same amount of meringue and Mascarpone filling, together with 6 passion fruit and a little icing sugar.

To assemble the 8 meringues, spoon the seeds from half a passion fruit into the bottom of each meringue nest. Then, mix the seeds from the other 2 passion fruit into the Mascarpone mixture. Spoon this mixture on top of the nests, dust with icing sugar and serve.

Meringues with Summer Fruit

The two previous meringue fillings are perfect for the winter months, but in the summer soft fruit make the perfect filling, as their sharp acidity contrasts beautifully with the sweetness of the meringue. For 8 meringue nests, use the same quantity of Mascarpone cream as for the Petits Monts Blancs, together with 1 lb (450 g) of strawberries, raspberries or, my favourite, a mixture of redcurrants, raspberries and strawberries. Then dust the fruit with icing sugar before serving. Nice made with a sauce of puréed fresh raspberries sweetened with a little icing sugar.

The yolks of eggs fulfil three main functions in cooking. One is turning liquids into solids, as in a baked custard or quiche. The second is as a thickening agent for liquids. What happens here is that when the yolks are whisked into liquids over heat, the thickening agent in the yolk gets distributed to make a smooth, thick sauce or soup. They are also a powerful emulsifier that can bind and thicken oil- or butter-based sauces such as mayonnaise or hollandaise.

How to handle egg yolks

The problem the cook has when dealing with egg yolks is that if they are not treated carefully, and in the right way, they can 'split', or curdle, a mixture. In parting company with the whites they have lost some of their stability, as egg whites are great stabilisers. This often causes problems and stress for beginners, but there is some good news here. Over the years I have spent cooking and developing recipes and trying to help busy people cook at home without undue stress, I have developed various ways of using egg yolks in all the traditional recipes without the worry of curdling and spoiling a recipe. On this subject, I have to part company with the purists. I'm perfectly aware that there are people who simply don't mind standing over things for ages, nurturing them along and whisking till the cows come home (as my Welsh grandmother would say), but not me – I don't want to be confined to the kitchen, missing out on a conversation.

Therefore, I am here to tell you that you need never be afraid to use egg yolks in a custard. If you add just a small amount of cornflour there will never be any danger of it curdling, and even if it looks guilty of it, it will soon whip back to an amazing smoothness, because that tiny amount of cornflour will stabilise the eggs.

No more whisking!

If you do exactly the same making lemon curd, sabayon sauce or zabaglione, it will mean (as with custard) that the time you spend carefully whisking will be 2 minutes instead of 20. So here's an end to boring whisking sessions over bowls of barely simmering water, because life is short enough as it is! Similarly, I have discovered that when trying to make a lighter version of hollandaise sauce (for health reasons – not quite so much butter), adding whisked egg whites not only makes it go twice as far but also stabilises it perfectly. This means no last-minute fuss, that you can make it two days ahead if you want to re-heat it, and you can even freeze it so that if you only want a small amount, you can have some tucked away.

Traditional
English Custard

This is the ultimate custard, perhaps <u>the</u> traditional British sauce. I offer it here as it has been made down the centuries – with thick double cream, but you can, if you wish, modify this extravagance by using single cream or creamy whole milk. These last two might be better if the custard is for pouring, but for a trifle for a special occasion I recommend going the whole hog! It's now fashionable to split a vanilla pod and incorporate the seeds into the sauce – this reduces the time it needs to infuse in the hot cream. But I can also recommend pure vanilla extract, which is a wonderful store-cupboard stand-by.

Serves 6-8
1 vanilla pod
1 pint (570 ml) double cream
6 large egg yolks
1 dessertspoon cornflour
2 oz (50 g) golden caster sugar

Begin by splitting the vanilla pod lengthways and using the end of a teaspoon to scoop out the seeds. Then place the pod and the seeds in a small saucepan, along with the cream. Now place the pan over a gentle heat and heat it to just below simmering point. While the cream is heating, whisk the egg yolks, cornflour and sugar together in a medium bowl using a balloon whisk. Next remove the vanilla pod from the hot cream. Then, whisking the egg mixture all the time with one hand, gradually pour the hot cream into the bowl. When it's all in, immediately return the whole lot back to the saucepan using a rubber spatula. Now back it goes on to the same gentle heat as you continue whisking until the custard is thick and smooth, which will happen as soon as it reaches simmering point. If you do overheat it and it looks grainy, don't worry, just transfer it to a jug or bowl and continue to whisk until it becomes smooth again. Pour the custard into a jug or bowl, cover the surface with clingfilm and leave to cool. To serve it warm later, remove the clingfilm and sit the bowl over a pan of barely simmering water.

The very finest ingredients make a truly indulgent traditional English custard

Though the vanilla pod is removed from the cream, its distinctive seeds remain

Whisking the custard over a low heat ensures a smooth, creamy finish

Butterscotch and Banana Trifle with Madeira

There are endless variations on the trifle theme, and this is the latest Delia version. It's wickedly rich and quite wonderful – not for an everyday event, but perfect sometimes for those really special days. The best way to measure the syrup is to first weigh the saucepan on its own, keep it on the scales, then add a 5 oz (150 g) weight and pour the syrup straight in.

Serves 6-8
3 medium bananas
5 fl oz (150 ml) Madeira
8 trifle sponges

For the butterscotch sauce:
5 oz (150 g) golden syrup
2 oz (50 g) butter
3 oz (75 g) soft brown sugar
2 oz (50 g) golden granulated sugar
5 fl oz (150 ml) double cream
a few drops vanilla extract

For the topping:
1 quantity Traditional English Custard
(see page 62)
2 oz (50 g) pecan nuts
10 fl oz (275 ml) double cream

You will also need a 3 pint (1.75 litre) glass trifle bowl.

First of all make the butterscotch sauce, and to do this place the golden syrup, butter and sugars in a small saucepan. Then place over a gentle heat and allow to slowly melt and dissolve, giving it a stir from time to time, which will take 5-7 minutes. Let it continue to cook for about 5 minutes, then gradually stir in the double cream and vanilla extract until well combined. After that, let it cool. While it's cooling, make the custard.

To assemble the trifle, begin by first of all splitting the trifle sponges in half lengthways, spread each half with butterscotch sauce, then re-form them into sandwiches. Cut each one across into three and arrange the pieces in the base of the glass bowl. Now make a few stabs in the sponges with a sharp knife and carefully pour the Madeira all over them, distributing it as evenly as you can. Then set aside to allow the sponges to soak it all up – about 20 minutes.

Now peel and slice the bananas into chunks about ¼ inch (5 mm) thick, scatter these all around the sponges, then pour the remaining butterscotch sauce as evenly as possible all over. Pour the custard in next, then cover the bowl with clingfilm and let the whole lot chill in the fridge to firm up.

Meanwhile, pre-heat the grill, line the grill pan with foil and toast the pecan nuts carefully for about 4 minutes, watching them all the time, as they burn easily. After that, whip the double cream to the floppy stage, spread it all over the trifle, scatter the toasted nuts on top, re-cover and chill till needed.

Note: This is best made the day you want to serve it. I used to scatter the nuts on just before serving, but forgot them so many times that I now put them on directly after the cream.

Hot Lemon Curd Soufflés

Serves 4

For the soufflés:
3 large eggs
grated zest and juice 1 medium lemon
(2 tablespoons juice)
2 oz (50 g) golden caster sugar and
1 dessertspoon golden caster sugar

For the quick-method lemon curd:
grated zest and juice 1 small lemon
1 large egg
1½ oz (40 g) golden caster sugar
1 oz (25 g) cold unsalted butter, cut
into small cubes
1 teaspoon cornflour

To serve:
a little sifted icing sugar

You will also need four ramekins with
a base diameter of 2½ inches (6 cm),
a top diameter of 3 inches (7.5 cm),
2 inches (5 cm) deep, lightly buttered,
and a small, solid baking sheet.

Pre-heat the oven to gas mark 3,
325°F (170°C).

On the television series I called these 'everlasting', and yes, it's true, because unlike traditional soufflés, they never collapse. They will shrink down when they come out of the oven, but they will still be light and soufflé-like 15 minutes later. And just to prove my point, the soufflé in the small picture was actually a day old – not brimming up over the edge, but still a soufflé: soft and squidgy and very lemony. The quick lemon curd rounds the whole thing off.

First of all make the lemon curd by lightly whisking the egg in a medium-sized saucepan, then add the rest of the lemon curd ingredients and place the saucepan over a medium heat. Now whisk continuously using a balloon whisk until the mixture thickens; this won't take long – about 3 minutes in all. Next, lower the heat to its minimum setting and let the curd gently simmer for 1 further minute, continuing to whisk. After that, remove it from the heat and divide the curd between the bases of the ramekins. (This can all be done well in advance, but cover and leave at room temperature.)

When you're ready to make the soufflés, separate the eggs, putting the yolks into a medium-sized bowl and the whites into a spanking-clean larger one. Now, using an electric hand whisk, whisk the whites to the stiff-peak stage, which will take 4-5 minutes – start on a slow speed, gradually increasing to medium and then high. Then add the dessertspoon of caster sugar and whisk on a high speed for 30 seconds more. Next add the zest and lemon juice and the remaining 2 oz (50 g) of sugar to the yolks and mix them together briefly. Now take a tablespoon of the whites and fold them into the yolks to loosen the mixture, then fold the rest of the whites in using a light cutting and folding movement so as not to lose the precious air. Spoon the mixture into the prepared ramekins, piling it high like a pyramid, then run a finger round the inside rim of each one.

Next place them on the baking sheet and put this in the oven on the centre shelf for 15-17 minutes or until the tops are golden. Then remove them and let them settle for about 5 minutes to allow the lemon curd to cool. They will sink a little, but that's normal. Just before serving, place them on smaller plates and give them a light dusting of icing sugar.

Twice-Baked Roquefort Soufflés

The obvious advantage of twice-baked soufflés is that they can be done and dusted the day before you need them. Then they rise up again like a dream, with a brilliantly light texture and flavour.

Serves 6

6 oz (175 g) Roquefort
8 fl oz (225 ml) milk
¼ inch (5 mm) onion slice
1 bay leaf
grating of nutmeg
6 whole black peppercorns
1½ oz (40 g) butter
1½ oz (40 g) plain flour
4 large eggs, separated
5 fl oz (150 ml) double cream
salt and freshly milled black pepper

To garnish:
6 sprigs watercress

You will also need six ramekins with a 3 inch (7.5 cm) diameter, 1½ inches (4 cm) deep, lightly buttered, an 11 x 8 x 2 inch (28 x 20 x 5 cm) baking tin, and a 14 x 10 inch (35 x 25.5 cm) baking tray.

Pre-heat the oven to gas mark 4, 350°F (180°C).

Begin by heating the milk, onion, bay leaf, nutmeg and peppercorns in a medium-sized saucepan till it reaches simmering point, then strain the milk into a jug, discarding the rest now. Rinse out the saucepan, then melt the butter in it. Add the flour and stir to a smooth, glossy paste, and cook this for 3 minutes, still stirring, until it turns a pale straw colour. Then gradually add the strained milk, whisking all the time, until the sauce is thick and cleanly leaves the sides of the pan. Then season lightly and cook the sauce on the gentlest heat possible for 2 minutes, stirring now and then.

Next remove the pan from the heat and let it cool slightly, then beat in the egg yolks one at a time. Now crumble 4 oz (110 g) of the cheese into the mixture and stir until most of it has melted – don't worry if some cheese is still visible. Put a kettle on to boil and, in a spanking-clean large bowl, whisk the egg whites to the soft-peak stage, then fold a spoonful of egg white into the cheese sauce to loosen it. Now fold the sauce into the egg white using a large metal spoon and a cutting and folding motion.

Divide the mixture equally between the ramekins. Put them in the baking tin, place it on the centre shelf of the oven, then pour about ½ inch (1 cm) of boiling water into the tin. Bake the soufflés for 20 minutes, then transfer them to a cooling rack (using a fish slice) so they don't continue cooking. Don't worry if they sink a little as they cool, because they will rise up again in the second cooking.

When they are almost cold, run a small palette knife around the edge of each ramekin and carefully turn the soufflés out on to the palm of your hand, then place them the right way up on a lightly greased, shallow baking tray. They can now be stored in the fridge for up to 24 hours, lightly covered with clingfilm.

When you are ready to re-heat the soufflés, pre-heat the oven to gas mark 4, 350°F (180°C) and remove the soufflés from the fridge so they can return to room temperature. Dice the remaining Roquefort into ¼ inch (5 mm) pieces and sprinkle it on top of the soufflés, then place them in the oven, on the shelf above centre, for 30 minutes.

Then, 2 or 3 minutes before serving, spoon a tablespoon of cream over each soufflé and return them to the oven while you seat your guests. Serve the soufflés immediately on warm plates and garnish each with a sprig of watercress.

Hollandaise Sauce

This great classic butter sauce from France can be tricky if it gets too much heat, so great care is in order here. However, since the advent of blenders and processors, the risk is not as large as it used to be with hand whisking over hot water. It has to be said that a blender is best, but a processor works well, too. My own problem has always been how to keep it warm, as I always like to make it in advance, and overheating will make it curdle. There are two possible answers for this: either use a wide-necked Thermos flask rinsed with boiling water, or to make a lighter, more stable version, see right.

Serves 4
2 large egg yolks (reserve the whites if you want to make Foaming Hollandaise)
1 dessertspoon lemon juice
1 dessertspoon white wine vinegar
4 oz (110 g) butter
salt and freshly milled black pepper

Begin by placing the egg yolks in a small bowl and season them with a pinch of salt and pepper. Then place them in a food processor or blender and blend them thoroughly for about 1 minute. After that, heat the lemon juice and white wine vinegar in a small saucepan until the mixture starts to bubble and simmer. Switch the processor or blender on again and pour the hot liquid on to the egg yolks in a slow, steady stream. After that, switch the processor or blender off.

Now, using the same saucepan, melt the butter over a gentle heat, being very careful not to let it brown. When the butter is foaming, switch the processor or blender on once more and pour in the butter in a thin, slow, steady trickle; the slower you add it the better. (If it helps you to use a jug and not pour from the saucepan, warm a jug with boiling water, discard the boiling water and then pour the butter mixture into that first.) When all the butter has been incorporated, wipe around the sides of the processor bowl or blender with a spatula to incorporate all the sauce, then give the sauce one more quick burst and you should end up with a lovely, smooth, thick, buttery sauce.

Once the egg yolks are blended, add the hot lemon juice and white wine vinegar to the processor in a slow, steady stream

Next, melt the butter in the same pan used for the lemon juice and vinegar and add it in a thin, even trickle

When the butter has been incorporated you will end up with a beautifully smooth, thick Hollandaise Sauce

Foaming Hollandaise

Foaming Hollandaise

I tend nearly always to make this one now. What happens here is that the 2 reserved egg whites are whisked to soft peaks and folded into the sauce as soon as it's made. The advantages are legion: firstly it lightens the sauce, so not quite so many calories, and you get a greater volume, so it goes further. It will never curdle because the egg whites stabilise the whole thing, which means you can happily keep it warm in a bowl fitted over simmering water. That's not all: you can also re-heat it in the same way, which means you can make it the day before. Finally, it will even freeze, which means that anything left over can be stored for a rainy day.

Either version of this supremely wonderful sauce can be used for serving with asparagus or artichokes, or with any kind of grilled or poached fish (see page 626). And served with Eggs Benedict (see page 27), it's a positive star.

4
Rediscovering bread

'Wherefore do ye spend money on that which is not bread?' When the late Elizabeth David was struggling to find the words to introduce her masterpiece *English Bread And Yeast Cookery*, these words, spoken by the prophet Isaiah in 600 BC, said all she wanted to say about the state of commercially made British bread. That was over 30 years ago, and I am here to say that not a lot has changed. It is a sad fact that whilst there has been some improvement, 'that which is not bread' is still what a vast number of people consume.

Small high street and village bakers struggle to produce quality, but it gets harder and harder as they can't possibly compete on price with the larger commercial factories, who can always undercut price for quality. Thus in buying cheaper bread we may well be richer by the money saved, but in truth we are infinitely poorer because, if you think about it, few people could deny that having really good bread on a daily basis would instantly and inexpensively improve the quality of life.

Instead, the majority choose the dull option; perhaps it's because we don't value ourselves enough to feel we deserve the best – who knows? All I know is that 'that which is not bread', ie, the average packed and sliced loaf (although there are, of course, exceptions), compared with what bread should be, is extremely dull and poor quality; a flat, pappy, tasteless kind of blotting paper. Take a close look at a slice: it will be slightly damp and clammy; if you squeeze it in your hands it will emerge looking like an elongated piece of rough dough with the indentations of your fingers all along it. Do you really want to consume it?

It's a kind of downward spiral of 'how low can you go?' Millers mill their flour to provide for larger factories that bake mass-produced bread. Retailers sell it, then large retailers get involved in price wars. Something has to give in order to cut prices, so quality is what has to give. The factory can't afford to provide quality if the retailer can't afford to pay for it, because he has to keep his prices competitive. So quality cutting goes back to the factory, then to the miller and even the farmer. And what do we get?

I once heard modern bread given a sort of job description by a flour miller, who said that it was merely required to be a carrier. Isn't that a sad statement? In other words, it's what goes in or on the bread that's more important. If I can achieve anything at all in this whole *How To Cook* project it will be to persuade the younger generation to make and taste some real bread, just so they know what it's really like.

That which *is* bread

That which *is* bread is both astoundingly simple (after all, the main ingredients are merely flour and water), but at the same time gloriously luxurious because of its rarity. It's a strange paradox – here we are, a nation that spends a fortune on food and restaurants (you could say on the 'food experience'), yet give anyone at all a slice of real home-made bread and you might as well be giving them the moon. When we were filming the bread programme for the television series that accompanied this book, absolutely everyone was drooling, so enthusiastic and so appreciative, and forever wanting just one more slice. So why is it that home-made bread has so much going for it?

I would put flavour as number one on the list – the real, pure, natural flavour of the wheat, which is somewhat enhanced and intensified by the yeast, which also adds its own subtle flavour. Number two on my list would be texture: in a white loaf this is very soft, aerated and silky fine. Number three is the crust, which is very crisp and crunchy but at the same time light, and a well-baked crust is always fairly dark as this darkness creates extra flavour. Freshly baked white bread with good butter is one of the simplest pleasures in life. I love eating it with soft-boiled eggs (see page 16).

Wholemeal bread

This is not as delicate as white bread, but has other charms. Here we have all the flavour of whole, ripe wheat berries crushed so the germ and the bran are present. It therefore has a more gutsy and robust flavour. It also has a crisp and crunchy crust on the outside and is moist and mealy within.

But how can busy people find time to make bread?

I'm afraid it's a myth that breadmaking takes time. True, the bread itself needs its own time, but it will take only about 6-10 minutes of your *actual* time. I have come to the conclusion that it takes me less time than travelling to a really good baker and back. It is also a myth that breadmaking is difficult. One of the joys of making bread is that it needs so few ingredients; in fact, for a straightforward loaf, only four are required.

1 Flour

What the cook needs to know is that there are three types of wheat grain – hard, medium and soft – and the flour they yield will contain something called gluten. In order not to get too technical, gluten can be described as something like chewing gum. Soft grains produce ordinary chewing gum, which will stick somewhat, but hard grains produce something more like bubble gum, which means air can be incorporated and the gluten will stretch and expand into bubbles. Thus, when it comes to baking pastry, biscuits or cakes, what you need are very light-textured, soft grains containing the chewing-gum variety, but in bread, when the action of the yeast needs to raise the dough, you need hard wheat – the bubble-gum variety.

In our country plain flour is always made from soft grains, so this is the one for cakes, pastry and so on, whilst the one labelled strong flour, which has a high gluten content, is the one needed for most types of bread, although for something like a pizza dough, where you don't need the dough to rise as much, a soft ordinary plain flour is, I think, better. So just think chewing gum or bubble gum and you've got your gluten sorted.

Flour milling

What happens here is the wheat grains are crushed and ground between either traditional milling stones or modern automatic rollers, but it's the human skill of the miller – not the method – that determines the quality of the flour. A grain of wheat is made up of three components: the protective layers of outer casing called bran, the white starchy endosperm, and the germ, which contains oils, vitamins and protein.

Flours and meals

Originally the whole wheat berries were ground into the flour, which, more correctly, should be called meal, hence wholemeal. Flour is the fine white powdery part that has had the bran layers and germ removed. Wholefood enthusiasts will say that white flour, having much of the goodness removed, is a refined product and not a so-called healthy, whole one.

However, in my opinion we need both types, and thankfully the so-called healthy brown era, with its heavy brown pastries, cakes, pizzas et al has moved on and given way to a more balanced view on what is or isn't healthy. So now both can be enjoyed equally and combined at times in certain recipes to give the required flavour and texture.

Top row, from left: grains of durum wheat, hard wheat and English soft wheat
Second row: whole meal
Third row: fine semolina and medium semolina
Fourth row: plain white flour, wheatgerm and bran

Self-raising flour This is simply a term used to describe soft flour to which raising agents have been added by the manufacturer.

Semolina This word comes from the Italian, meaning semi milled, and it is, as you can see in the photograph, not ground to fine flour, meaning the grains are coarser. Semolina is what is used for traditionally made pasta – milled from hard wheat grain to a texture specified by the pasta maker so that the finished product will be rough-textured to enable the sauce to cling sufficiently (see page 216). Semolina, from softer wheat, has also played a part in British cuisine, where it has been used in puddings and cakes.

2 Liquid

This is usually water, though milk and buttermilk are sometimes used. The water should always be hand-hot, meaning you can hold your finger in it without discomfort. If the water is too hot it will kill the yeast.

3 Yeast

For beginners this is now blissfully simple, because it's powdered into something called easy-blend: no mixing, no waiting for frothy heads and so on. All you do is sprinkle it in with the flour, and that's all. Don't forget to inspect the date stamps, though, because if it's too old it won't do its work.

4 Salt

Salt is an important ingredient in bread, but don't use too much as it slows down the rising. But if you like a little more than I have included in my recipes, then allow a little extra rising time.

Kneading

There are two schools of thought on this: one is 'what a bore', because 3 minutes is a long time in a busy life. Alternatively, some people find the whole operation extremely therapeutic. I am in both camps here: resentful if I'm short of time, but it also has to be said that kneading and daydreaming are a pleasant occupation if time permits.

Kneading in a processor

On busy days it's all perfectly simple. If you use a processor with a dough hook attached, the whole thing – mixing and kneading – really is very little trouble.

How to knead dough

For bread dough that has to be kneaded, simply place it on a flat work surface then stretch it away from you, using the heel of one hand to push from the middle and the clenched knuckles of your other hand to pull the other half of the dough towards you (both hands should move simultaneously to stretch out the dough). Then lift the edges over and back to the middle. Give it a quarter turn and repeat the process. It soon becomes a rather rhythmic operation, and the dough will then start to become very elastic. What happens here is you begin to feel the magic – the dough literally begins to spring into life as you push it away and it defiantly springs back to challenge you. When it's become very smooth, springy and begins to appear blistery on the surface, which takes about 3 minutes, it's then ready to rise.

Rising

We don't need to go into the science of breadmaking, but when flour, water and yeast are introduced to each other, let's say something magical occurs, and the mixture (which started out being a heavy lump of dough), if given the correct amount of time, will stretch and expand to twice its original volume. This process can be speeded up if the dough is put in a warm place, but the longer you leave it to rise naturally at room temperature, the better the bread. I now prefer to just leave it to rise naturally. One point, though: bread will also rise at a cold temperature, so if it's more convenient, pop it in the lowest part of the fridge and let it rise overnight, ready to bake in the morning.

Bread dough, which starts off as a heavy lump, stretches over time and expands to twice its original volume

Once the dough has risen, the air is knocked out – just use your fist – and then left to rise again, this time in its tin

What is knocking back and proving?

White bread dough is better if it has a second rise, as this gives a more even texture. So now what happens is you punch, or knock out, all the air using your fist, shape the dough, place it in a tin and give it a second rise, which will be much quicker. The word 'prove' refers to this second rise, because you're actually testing, or proving, that the yeast is still (we hope) alive and kicking.

Bread tins and cooling trays

Good old-fashioned bread tins with pleated corners are thankfully still available (see the photograph on page 72) in 2 lb/900 g (7¼ x 4½ x 3½ inches/ 18.5 x 11.5 x 9 cm) and 1 lb/450 g (6 x 3¾ x 2¾ inches/15 x 9.5 x 7 cm) sizes. Grease them well with butter first. Then, when the bread is cooked, it's most important to remove it from the tin to cool on a wire cooling tray. If you leave it in the tin or place it on a flat surface, it will become steamy and soggy. A cooling tray allows the air to circulate and ensures the crust stays crisp and crunchy.

Is it cooked?

The way to test this is to turn the loaf out, holding it in a cloth, then give the underneath a sharp tap with your knuckles: if it's cooked it will sound hollow and not dense. Remember, it's always better to overbake rather than underbake bread. Because I like an extra crunchy crust, I always put the loaf back in the oven without its tin for 5-10 minutes to crisp up the underneath and sides, so if you do this it will ensure the loaf is cooked through.

Once this second rising, or 'proving', is done, the loaf is ready to be baked in the pre-heated oven

To test whether the loaf is cooked, hold it in a cloth and tap the underneath with your knuckles – it should sound hollow

Plain and Simple White Bread

A good, old-fashioned, English, white, crusty loaf, soft inside and lightly textured, is still hard to beat – it's my own favourite for soldiers to go with softly boiled eggs, and the next day or the day after it always makes divine toast. Made either by hand or with the help of a food processor, it couldn't be easier, and the pleasure of eating it is difficult to match.

Makes 1 large or 2 small loaves
1 lb 8 oz (700 g) strong white bread flour, plus a little extra for the top of the bread
1 tablespoon salt, or less, according to taste
1 teaspoon easy-blend yeast
1 teaspoon golden caster sugar
about 15 fl oz (425 ml) hand-hot water

You will also need two 1 lb (450 g) loaf tins or one 2 lb (900 g) loaf tin, well buttered.

Pre-heat the oven to its lowest setting.

Begin by warming the flour in the oven for about 10 minutes, then turn the oven off. Sift the flour, salt, yeast and sugar into a bowl, make a well in the centre of the mixture, then add the water. Now mix to a dough, starting off with a wooden spoon and using your hands in the final stages of mixing, adding a spot more water if there are any dry bits. Wipe the bowl clean with the dough and transfer it to a flat work surface (you may not need to flour this). Knead the dough for 3 minutes or until it develops a sheen and blisters under the surface (it should also be springy and elastic). You can now either return the dough to the mixing bowl or transfer it to a clean bowl; either way, cover it with clingfilm that has been lightly oiled on the side that is facing the dough. Leave it until it looks as though it has doubled in bulk, which will be about 2 hours at room temperature.

After that, knock the air out, then knead again for 2 minutes. Now divide the dough in half, pat each piece out to an oblong, then fold one end into the centre and the other in on top. Put each one into a buttered tin, sprinkle each with a dusting of flour, then place them side by side in an oiled polythene bag until the dough rises above the tops of the tins – this time about an hour at room temperature. Alternatively, place all the dough in the one tin. Meanwhile, pre-heat the oven to gas mark 8, 450°F (230°C).

Bake the loaves on the centre shelf for 30-40 minutes, or 35-45 minutes for the large loaf, until they sound hollow when their bases are tapped. Now return them, out of their tins, upside-down to the oven to crisp the base and side crust for about 5-10 minutes, then cool on a wire rack.

White bread using the processor

Although making bread as above is not hard, it can be even easier if you make the whole thing in a processor. To do this you fit the dough hook on to the processor (some also have a special bowl), then all you do is sift the dry ingredients into the bowl, put the lid on and switch it on to a low speed or the one recommended in the manufacturer's handbook for use of the dough hook. Now pour the water through the feeding tube, then leave the processor to 'knead' the dough for about 3 minutes – but don't go away, because the machine can sometimes stick and slide about. Then transfer the dough to a clean bowl and cover it with clingfilm that has been lightly oiled on the side facing the dough. Leave it until it looks as though it has doubled in bulk – about 2 hours at room temperature. You can now return the dough to the food processor and let it 'knead' it again for 1 minute, still at a low speed. Then simply continue to make the loaves as above.

Quick and Easy Wholemeal Loaf

The poet Pam Ayres once said, when describing her home-made wholemeal bread, that it was like 'biting into a cornfield', and that's it – the very best description I've ever come across. A crisp, crunchy crust and then all the flavour of the wholewheat grain – take a bite, close your eyes and you'll know just what she meant. Then, when you've grasped how easy wholemeal bread is to make, you'll probably never stop making it. The recipe here is adapted from Doris Grant's famous loaf in her book Your Daily Bread, for which I continue to give thanks.

Makes 1 large or 2 small loaves
1 lb 4 oz (570 g) 100 per cent organically produced wholewheat flour, plus a little extra for the top of the bread
2 teaspoons salt
1 teaspoon soft light brown sugar
2 teaspoons easy-blend yeast
about 14 fl oz (400 ml) hand-hot water

You will also need either a 2 lb (900 g) loaf tin or two 1 lb (450 g) loaf tins, well buttered.

Pre-heat the oven to its lowest setting.

Begin by warming the flour slightly in the oven for about 10 minutes, then turn the oven off for now. Next, tip the warm flour into a large mixing bowl and all you do is simply sprinkle on the salt, sugar and easy-blend yeast, mix these together thoroughly, make a well in the centre and pour in the hand-hot water. Then take a wooden spoon and begin to mix the warm liquid into the flour gradually to form a dough: the exact amount of water you'll need will depend on the flour. Finish off by mixing with your hands until you have a smooth dough that leaves the bowl clean – there should be no bits of flour or dough remaining on the sides of the bowl and, unlike pastry, it is better to have too much water than too little.

Now transfer the dough to a flat surface and stretch it out into an oblong, then fold one edge into the centre and the other over that. Now fit the dough into the tin, pressing it firmly all round the edges so that the top will already be slightly rounded. Next, sprinkle the surface with a generous dusting of flour, then cover the tin with a damp, clean tea cloth and leave to rise in a warm place for 30-40 minutes or at room temperature for about an hour. If you're making two loaves, divide the dough in half before following the steps above and folding it into the two tins.

Meanwhile, pre-heat the oven to gas mark 6, 400°F (200°C). When the dough has risen to the top of the bread tin or tins, bake the bread for 40 minutes for the 2 lb (900 g) loaf tin or 30 minutes for the 1 lb (450 g) loaf tins. When the bread is cooked, turn it out on to a cloth to protect your hands – it will sound hollow when rapped underneath with your knuckles. Then return the bread, out of its tin, upside-down to the oven for a further 5-10 minutes to crisp the base and sides. Cool the bread on a wire rack, and never put it away or freeze it until it is absolutely cold.

Toast

*A friend of mine invented the term 'wangy', a very accurate word
to describe what 90 per cent of the world's catering establishments call
toast. It's a good word because we're all absolutely familiar with what
it's saying – cold, leathery, bendy little triangles that arrive at breakfast
when you are asked, 'Would you like some toast?'*

So I've been thinking, as this is a basic cookery course, why not give the
world the definitive recipe for perfect toast? To begin with, I am not a
disciple of automatic toasters. The ones I've experienced all seem to be
a bit hit and miss, and if you're rather inept at slicing bread (like me),
then they're not very helpful at all because if the bread is slightly wonky,
a) it probably won't go in the toaster at all, and, b) if it does, one bit ends
up not being toasted at all while the other bit is giving off nasty black
smoke signals!

1 The key to slicing bread is to use gentle, rapid sawing movements with
   the knife and not to push down too hard on the loaf. For toast, cut the
   bread into slices of about ½ inch (1 cm) thickness. The crusts can be
   on or off, depending on how you like them.
2 Pre-heat the grill for at least 10 minutes before making the toast,
   turning it to its highest setting.
3 Place the bread on the grill rack and position the tray 2 inches (5 cm)
   from the heat source.
4 Allow the bread to toast on both sides to your own preferred degree of
   pale or dark golden brown.
5 While that is happening, keep an eye on it and don't wander far away.
6 When the toast is done, remove it immediately to a toast rack. Why a
   toast rack? Because they are a brilliant invention. Freshly made toast
   contains steam, and if you place it in a vertical position, in which the
   air is allowed to circulate, the steam escapes and the toast becomes crisp
   and crunchy. Putting it straight on to a plate means the steam is trapped
   underneath, making it damp and soggy. If you don't possess a toast rack
   you really ought to invest in a modest one. Failing that, stand your
   slices of toast up against a jar or something similar for about 1 minute
   before serving.

*A toast rack is absolutely necessary if you
want to avoid soggy toast; failing that,
prop the slices up against a jar for a
minute or so before serving*

7 Always eat toast as soon as possible after that, and never make it ahead
   of time.
8 Never ever wrap it in a napkin or cover it (the cardinal sin of the catering
   trade), because the steam gets trapped and the toast gets soggy.
9 Always use good bread, because the better the bread, the better the toast.
   It is also preferable if the bread is a couple of days old.

Goats' Cheese, Onion and Potato Bread with Thyme

Don't make this if you are on a diet – it's so wonderful that it's impossible to stop eating it. It's also great for a packed lunch or journey because you've got the bread and cheese all in one. It must also be the quickest, easiest home-made bread on record.

Makes 1 loaf, to serve 4-6
1 x 4 oz (110 g) round firm goats' cheese
4 spring onions, finely sliced
1 medium red potato weighing approximately 6 oz (175 g)
1 rounded teaspoon chopped thyme leaves, plus a few small sprigs
6 oz (175 g) self-raising flour, plus a little extra for the top of the loaf
1 teaspoon salt
⅛ teaspoon or generous pinch of cayenne pepper
1 large egg
2 tablespoons milk
1 heaped teaspoon grain mustard

You will also need a small, solid baking sheet, very well greased.

Pre-heat the oven to gas mark 5, 375°F (190°C).

Start off by taking your sharpest knife, then pare the rind from the cheese and cut it into ½ inch (1 cm) cubes. Then sift the flour, salt and cayenne into a big, roomy mixing bowl, holding the sieve up high to give the flour a good airing. Then thinly pare off the potato skin using a potato peeler and grate the potato straight into the flour using the coarse side of the grater. Then add the spring onions, chopped thyme and two-thirds of the cheese. Now take a palette knife and blend everything together thoroughly.

After that, beat the egg gently with the milk and mustard, then pour the mixture into the bowl, just bringing it all together to a loose, rough dough, still using the palette knife. Next transfer it on to the baking sheet and pat it gently into a 6 inch (15 cm) rough round. Now lightly press the rest of the cheese over the surface, dust with a little flour and scatter the small sprigs of thyme over.

Bake the bread on the middle shelf of the oven for 45-50 minutes or until golden brown. Then remove it to a cooling rack and serve it still slightly warm if possible (but I have to say it's still divine a day later, warmed through in the oven).

Feta Cheese, Potato and Rosemary Bread

This is a delicious variation on the recipe above, using a different cheese and a different herb. Simply substitute the goats' cheese for the same amount of cubed Feta cheese, a quarter of a red onion, peeled and finely chopped, instead of the spring onions, and use rosemary instead of thyme. Before baking, scatter over a quarter of an onion, sliced into half-moon shapes, along with some small sprigs of rosemary and a few halved olives.

Goats' Cheese, Onion and Potato Bread with Thyme, right; Feta Cheese, Potato and Rosemary Bread, left

Parsnip, Parmesan and Sage Bread

In this loaf the potatoes in the previous recipe are replaced with parsnips – a great alternative. I love to serve this with the Curried Parsnip and Apple Soup from the Winter Collection, as it extends the parsnip flavour, but it's also good with tomato or any other soup, or for a snack with crisp apples and celery and a soft, ripe, creamy cheese such as Brie, Camembert or Dolcelatte.

Makes 1 loaf, to serve 4-6
6 oz (175 g) parsnips (peeled weight)
2 oz (50 g) Parmesan (Parmigiano Reggiano), cut into ¼ inch
(5 mm) cubes
1 rounded tablespoon chopped fresh sage
8 oz (225 g) self-raising flour
1½ teaspoons salt
2 large eggs, lightly beaten
1 tablespoon milk

For the topping:
1 oz (25 g) Parmesan (Parmigiano Reggiano) shavings
a few whole small sage leaves
a little extra flour for dusting
1 teaspoon olive oil

You will also need a small, solid baking sheet, very well greased.

Pre-heat the oven to gas mark 5, 375°F (190°C).

First of all sift the flour and salt into a large, roomy bowl. Then put a grater in the bowl and coarsely grate the parsnips into the flour, then toss them around. After that, add the cubes of Parmesan and chopped sage and toss that in. Now lightly beat the eggs and milk together, then add this to the bowl a little at a time, mixing evenly with a palette knife. What you should end up with is a rough, rather loose, sticky dough, so don't worry what it looks like at this stage. Transfer this to the baking sheet and pat it gently into a 6 inch (15 cm) rough round, then make a cross with the blunt side of a knife. Now scatter the Parmesan shavings over the surface, followed by a sprinkling of flour. Finally, spoon the olive oil into a dish, dip each sage leaf in the oil and scatter them over the bread. Now it should go into the oven on a high shelf to bake for 45-50 minutes, by which time it will be golden and crusty. It then needs to go on a wire rack, then either serve it still warm or re-heat it later.

Irish Oatmeal Soda Bread

This is the real thing – proper Irish bread. As it bakes in the oven and the aroma reaches you, close your eyes, picture the beauty of the Irish landscape and dream you're there. It's heaven just spread generously with butter and good jam, or, now that we can buy good Irish cheeses, a chunk of Cashel Blue or Milleens with this bread, as well as a glass of Murphy's, will give you a little taste of that wonderful country, even though you're not there.

This could not be easier. Begin by placing the dry ingredients in a large, roomy bowl, mix to combine, then beat the egg and buttermilk together and add them to the dry ingredients. Start mixing, first with a fork, then finish off with your hands to form a smooth dough. All you do now is transfer the dough to the loaf tin and level the top. Alternatively, shape into a round about 6 inches (15 cm) across and make a deep cut across it three times, but don't cut all the way through. Sprinkle with flour and bake in the centre of the oven for 50-60 minutes, then turn it straight out on to a wire rack to cool. This is best eaten fresh, but fear not, because the next day or the day after, it makes wonderful toast.

Makes 1 loaf, to serve 4-6
6 oz (175 g) wholemeal flour
2 oz (50 g) plain flour
2 oz (50 g) pinhead oatmeal
1 oz (25 g) wheatgerm
1 teaspoon bicarbonate of soda
1½ teaspoons salt
1 teaspoon sugar
1 large egg
10 fl oz (275 ml) buttermilk
a little extra flour for dusting

You will also need a 1 lb (450 g) loaf tin, well greased.

Pre-heat the oven to gas mark 5, 375°F (190°C).

Cornmeal and Mixed-Seed Bread

This is another very quick and easy loaf, but with lots of varying textures. And don't worry if the sunflower seeds turn green during baking – it actually looks very attractive.

Makes 1 small loaf

5 oz (150 g) polenta (cornmeal)
6 oz (175 g) strong white bread flour
1 rounded teaspoon salt
1 teaspoon bicarbonate of soda
1 oz (25 g) pumpkin seeds
1 oz (25 g) sunflower seeds
1 oz (25 g) poppy seeds, reserving
1 teaspoon for the top of the loaf
1 oz (25 g) pinhead oatmeal
1 rounded teaspoon golden caster sugar
1 large egg
10 fl oz (275 ml) buttermilk

You will also need a 1 lb (450 g) loaf tin, lightly oiled.

Pre-heat the oven to gas mark 5, 375°F (190°C).

Begin by sifting the flour, salt and bicarbonate of soda together into a large bowl, then add the polenta, all the seeds, the oatmeal and caster sugar and give everything a good mixing. Next, whisk the egg and buttermilk together, add this to the bowl and gradually stir with a wooden spoon until the mixture forms a soft and slack dough. Now just transfer the dough to the prepared loaf tin, scatter the reserved poppy seeds over and bake the loaf on the middle shelf of the oven for 50-60 minutes. The loaf is cooked when after you've turned it out it sounds hollow when you tap the underneath with your knuckles. Return it to the oven upside-down, without its tin, for 5 minutes to give it a final 'crunch', then cool it on a wire rack.

Crostini Lazio

Italian in origin, crostini are 'little crusts'. In France they are called croutons, but both are little rounds or squares of bread brushed with olive oil or butter, and sometimes crushed garlic, then baked in the oven.

For the crostini, drizzle the olive oil over the baking tray, add the garlic, then, using your hands, spread the oil and garlic over the surface of the baking tray. Now place the bread on top of the oil and turn them over so that both sides are lightly coated. Now bake them in the oven for 10-15 minutes, until crisp and crunchy, but put a timer on, as they soon overbake.

For the topping, just peel the rind off the goats' cheese using a sharp knife, then cut the cheese into four pieces. Next place all the ingredients, including the reserved oil, into a liquidiser or processor and blend until the mixture is smooth. If making this ahead, cover and chill in the refrigerator till needed, then remove it half an hour before serving and spread it on top of the crostini, topped with a caper berry (if using). Don't assemble them until the last minute, though, or the bread loses some of its crispness.

Makes 12, to serve 4-6
For the crostini:
1 small, thin French stick cut into 12 slices about 1 inch (2.5 cm) thick, or 3 slices from a thick sliced loaf, cut into quarters
3 tablespoons olive oil
1 fat clove garlic, peeled and crushed

For the topping:
4 oz (110 g) firm goats' cheese
4 oz (110 g) tuna in oil – the best quality you can buy – drained, reserving 1 tablespoon of the oil
1 tablespoon salted capers or capers in vinegar, thoroughly rinsed and drained
1 tablespoon finely grated Parmesan (Parmigiano Reggiano)
1 dessertspoon lemon juice

To garnish:
12 caper berries (optional)

You will also need a baking tray measuring 14 x 10 inches (35 x 25.5 cm).

Pre-heat the oven to gas mark 4, 350°F (180°C).

Bruschetta

Bruschetta is a very special type of toasted bread, pronounced brusketta. When I first tasted the real thing in Tuscany, it was one of the most memorable eating experiences of my life. Italian country bread is toasted on both sides over hot, fragrant coals, then slashes are made along the surface of each piece of bread, which is then rubbed with an open clove of garlic. After that, peppery Italian extra virgin olive oil is poured over quite generously so that it runs into the bread, making little pools all around the base of the plate. The pleasure and joy in its utter simplicity are indescribable.

Given that few of us have hot coals handy (though don't forget bruschetta during the barbecue season), the next best thing is a cast-iron ridged griddle or, failing that, an ordinary domestic grill.

First pre-heat the ridged griddle over a high heat for about 10 minutes. When it's really hot, place the slices of bread – on the diagonal – and grill them for about 1 minute on each side, until they're golden and crisp and have charred strips across each side. (Alternatively, toast them under a conventional grill.) Then, as they are ready, take a sharp knife and quickly make about three little slashes across each one, rub the garlic in and drizzle about half a tablespoon of olive oil over each one. Serve straight away, sprinkled with a little rock salt.

Makes 12, to serve 4-6
1 ciabatta loaf, cut in 12 thin slices
1 clove garlic, peeled and rubbed in a little salt
about 6 tablespoons extra virgin olive oil
rock salt

You will also need a cast-iron ridged griddle.

Bruschetta with Tomato and Basil

Good bread, good olive oil – what more could you want? Just two things: very red, ripe plum tomatoes and basil leaves. It's perhaps the best bruschetta of all, and perfect for serving with drinks before a meal instead of serving a starter.

Prepare the tomatoes before toasting the bread. All you do is place them in a bowl, pour boiling water over them and leave for exactly 1 minute before draining them and slipping off the skins (protect your hands with a cloth if they are too hot). Then chop them finely.

When the bruschetta are made (as above), top with the tomatoes and basil leaves, season with salt and freshly milled black pepper and sprinkle a few more drops of olive oil over before serving. It's hard to believe that something so simple can be so wonderful.

Makes 12, to serve 4-6
6 red, ripe plum tomatoes
a few torn basil leaves
a few drops extra virgin olive oil
rock salt and freshly milled black pepper

Bruschetta with Tomato and Basil

Croque Monsieur

Serves 1
2 large slices good-quality white
bread, buttered
2 oz (50 g) Gruyère, finely grated
2-3 slices smoked cooked ham, Parma
ham or wafer-thin ham
½ oz (10 g) butter, melted
1 dessertspoon finely grated Parmesan
(Parmigiano Reggiano)
salt and freshly milled black pepper

Pre-heat the grill to its highest setting.

This is my version of the toasted cheese and ham sandwich of café society fame, and just thinking about it and imagining atmospheric, crowded pavement cafés makes me long to be in Paris and eat it there. But, that not being possible, it's one of the nicest snack meals for one that I know.

This could not be simpler. On one slice of the buttered bread, spread half the grated Gruyère, then cover that with the slices of ham, folding them if need be to fit the size of the bread. Now sprinkle the rest of the Gruyère on top of the ham, season, then press the other slice of bread on top of that and press it down very firmly. You can at this stage cut off the crusts, but I think they add extra crunchiness. Now brush half the melted butter on the top side of the sandwich, sprinkle it with half the Parmesan and press it in. Now transfer the sandwich to the grill pan and grill it for about 2 minutes, 2 inches (5 cm) from the heat. When it's golden brown, turn it over, brush the other side with the remaining melted butter, sprinkle the rest of the Parmesan all over and grill for another 2 minutes. Then remove it from the grill, cut it into quarters and eat it while it's still crunchy.

Toasted Cheese and Chilli Relish Sandwich

This is the vegetarian version of Croque Monsieur. You can use the ready-made relish normally served with burgers, or my own home-made version on page 188.

Serves 1
2 large slices good-quality white bread,
buttered
2 heaped teaspoons tomato chilli relish
2 oz (50 g) Gruyère, finely grated
½ small onion, peeled and sliced
into thin rings
½ oz (10 g) butter, melted
1 oz (25 g) Parmesan (Parmigiano
Reggiano), finely grated
salt and freshly milled black pepper

Pre-heat the grill to its highest setting.

Start off by spreading both slices of bread with a heaped teaspoon of relish each. Now sprinkle the Gruyère on one of the slices, then sprinkle the onion rings over, season with salt and pepper and then place the other piece of bread on top.

Next, brush the top of the sandwich with half the melted butter and sprinkle over half the Parmesan, lightly pressing it down. Then place the sandwich on the grill rack and grill it 2 inches (5 cm) from the heat until the top of the sandwich is golden brown – about 2 minutes. Then turn the sandwich over and brush the top with the rest of the melted butter and Parmesan, then return the sandwich to the grill for another 2 minutes. Finally, cut it into quarters and eat it pretty quickly.

Basic Pizza Dough

Pizza dough is made in almost the same way as the white bread on page 80 – by hand or using a food processor, except that you add olive oil and a little sugar to the flour mixture and there isn't a second rising. You might consider making double the quantity and freezing half to make another pizza at a later stage. Just pop the dough, after knocking out the air, into a polythene bag, seal and freeze.

Makes a 10 inch (25.5 cm) base pizza – serves 2

6 oz (175 g) plain white soft flour (see page 75)
1 teaspoon salt
1 teaspoon easy-blend yeast
½ teaspoon golden caster sugar
1 tablespoon olive oil
4 fl oz (120 ml) hand-hot water

To roll out:
2-3 tablespoons cornmeal (polenta)

You will also need a pizza stone or solid baking sheet measuring 14 x 11 inches (35 x 28 cm).

Pre-heat the oven to its lowest setting.

Left to right: once the dough has doubled in bulk, remove the clingfilm; now tip the dough on to the work surface and knock out the air; finally, knead briefly using the cornmeal and shape into a ball

Begin by warming the flour slightly in the oven for about 10 minutes, then turn the oven off. Sift the flour, salt, yeast and sugar into a bowl and make a well in the centre of the mixture, then add the olive oil and pour in the water. Now mix to a dough, starting off with a wooden spoon and using your hands in the final stages of mixing. Wipe the bowl clean with the dough, adding a spot more water if there are any dry bits left, and transfer it to a flat work surface (there shouldn't be any need to flour this). Knead the dough for 3 minutes or until it develops a sheen and blisters under the surface (it should also be springy and elastic). You can now either leave the dough on the surface covered by the upturned bowl or transfer the dough to a clean bowl and cover it with clingfilm that has been lightly oiled on the side that is facing the dough. Leave it until it looks as though it has doubled in bulk, which will be about an hour at room temperature.

Having made the dough and left it to rise, pre-heat the oven to gas mark 8, 450°F (230°C), along with the pizza stone or baking sheet. The next stage is to tip the dough back on to a work surface that has been sprinkled generously with cornmeal to prevent it from sticking. Knock all the air out of the dough and knead it for a couple of seconds to begin shaping it into a ball. Then dust your rolling pin with cornmeal and roll the dough out to a circle that is approximately 10 inches (25.5 cm) in diameter. Then finish stretching it out with your hands, working from the centre and using the flat of your fingers to push the dough out; it doesn't need to be a perfect round, but you want it to be a fairly thin-based pizza, with slightly raised edges. Now you can top the pizza with one of the toppings that follow.

This is the classic version of one of the most wonderful combinations of bread and cheese imaginable. You can, of course, vary the cheeses, but the ones I've chosen here are a truly magical combination.

First make the pizza base as described opposite. Then, using a thick oven glove, very carefully lift the baking sheet or pizza stone out of the oven and sprinkle it with cornmeal. Now carefully lift the pizza dough on to the stone or baking sheet and quickly arrange teaspoonfuls of Ricotta here and there all over. After that, scatter the Mozzarella and Gorgonzola pieces in-between and, finally, scatter the Parmesan over. Bake the whole thing on a high shelf for 10-12 minutes, until the crust is golden brown and the cheese is bubbling. You can lift the edge up slightly to check that the underneath is crisp and brown. Carefully remove the baking sheet or pizza stone from the oven, again using a thick oven glove, and serve the pizza on hot plates straight away.

Sufficient for a 10 inch (25.5 cm) base pizza – serves 2

1 basic pizza base (see opposite)
2½ oz (60 g) Ricotta
2 oz (50 g) Mozzarella, cut into 1 inch (2.5 cm) slices
2 oz (50 g) Gorgonzola Piccante, cut into 1 inch (2.5 cm) slices
1 oz (25 g) Parmesan (Parmigiano Reggiano), grated
a little cornmeal (polenta) for dusting

Pre-heat the oven to gas mark 8, 450°F (230°C).

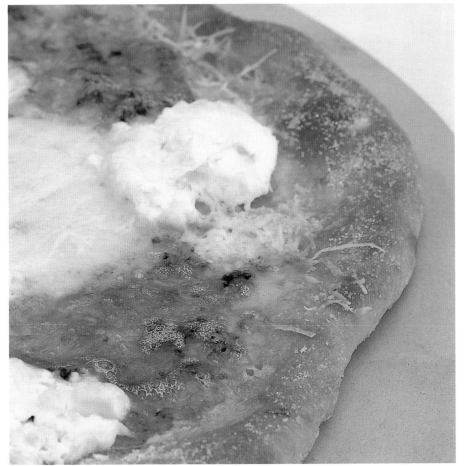

Four Seasons Pizza

Sufficient for a 10 inch (25.5 cm) base pizza – serves 2
1 basic pizza base (see page 94)
1 heaped tablespoon sun-dried tomato paste
3 oz (75 g) Parma ham (about 4 slices)
5 oz (150 g) Mozzarella, cubed
4 oz (110 g) small tomatoes, thinly sliced (approximately 3 tomatoes)
2 oz (50 g) small open mushrooms, thinly sliced
1 rounded tablespoon salted capers or capers in vinegar, rinsed and drained
8 pitted black olives, halved
4 anchovy fillets, drained and split in half lengthways
a few basil leaves, dipped in oil and torn, plus a few extra leaves to garnish
2 tablespoons olive oil

Pre-heat the oven to gas mark 8, 450°F (230°C).

Originally the toppings were placed on this pizza in four sections, representing each season, but because this pizza serves two, it's better to distribute them around more evenly.

Begin by making the pizza base as described on page 94, then spread the sun-dried tomato paste up to the edges of the pizza dough. Carefully lift it on to the hot baking sheet or pizza stone, then first lay the slices of Parma ham over, folding them, then simply scatter the cubes of Mozzarella, the tomatoes, mushrooms, capers and olives all over. Finally, decorate with the anchovy fillets in a criss-cross pattern and the basil leaves. Now drizzle the olive oil over and bake on a high shelf for 10-12 minutes, until the crust is golden brown, then scatter the whole basil leaves over before serving.

Four Seasons Pizza; uncooked, above, and cooked, right

Puttanesca Pizza

Puttanesca has always been one of my favourite pasta sauces – strong and gutsy, with lots of flavour – then one inspired day I decided to try it on a pizza base instead. The result is brilliant, with the added charm of pools of Mozzarella and crusty bread.

First make the pizza base as described on page 94. For the sauce, heat the oil in a medium saucepan, then add the garlic and chilli and cook briefly until the garlic is pale gold. Then add all the other sauce ingredients, stir and season with a little pepper – but no salt because of the anchovies. Turn the heat to low and let the sauce simmer very gently without a lid for 40 minutes, by which time it will have reduced to a lovely, thick mass with very little liquid left. Spread the filling over the pizza base, taking it up to the raised edge, then carefully lift it on to the hot baking sheet or pizza stone. Now scatter the Mozzarella over, then dip the basil leaves in the olive oil and place them here and there on top. Bake the pizza on a high shelf for 10-12 minutes, until the crust is golden brown and crusty. Use an oven glove to remove it from the oven, then garnish with the extra basil.

Sufficient for a 10 inch (25.5 cm) base pizza – serves 2
1 basic pizza base (see page 94)

For the sauce:
1 tablespoon olive oil
1 clove garlic, peeled and finely chopped
½ red chilli, deseeded and finely chopped
1 heaped teaspoon chopped fresh basil
8 oz (225 g) fresh tomatoes, skinned and chopped
1 oz (25 g) anchovies, drained and cut in half lengthways
3 oz (75 g) black olives, pitted and chopped small
1 dessertspoon salted capers or capers in vinegar, rinsed and drained
freshly milled black pepper

For the topping:
5 oz (150 g) Mozzarella, cut into 1 inch (2.5 cm) slices
a few small whole fresh basil leaves, plus a few extra to garnish
a little olive oil

Pre-heat the oven to gas mark 8, 450°F (230°C).

Puttanesca Pizza; cooked, left, and uncooked, above

Steamed Panettone Pudding with Eliza Acton's Hot Punch Sauce

Yes, this is a bread recipe. Panettone is an Italian fruit bread that's sold here mostly in the autumn and around Christmas time in beautifully designed boxes with carrying ribbons. If you would like a light but quite delectable alternative to Christmas pudding, this is it. I've tried making it in advance, freezing and then re-heating it, and it works beautifully. But don't confine it to Christmas, as it's a truly great steamed pudding to serve at any time, particularly with Eliza's extremely alcoholic citrus sauce.

Serves 6
For the steamed panettone pudding:
3 x 100 g panettone cakes or the same amount from a 500 g panettone cake
6 oz (175 g) dried mixed fruit, soaked in 3 tablespoons rum overnight
2 oz (50 g) whole almonds with their skins left on
2 oz (50 g) candied peel, finely chopped
grated zest 1 orange
grated zest 2 lemons
2 oz (50 g) molasses sugar
10 fl oz (275 ml) milk
5 fl oz (150 ml) double cream
3 large eggs

For Eliza Acton's hot punch sauce:
1 large orange
1 lemon
4 oz (110 g) caster sugar
10 fl oz (275 ml) water
1 oz (25 g) plain flour
2 oz (50 g) unsalted butter, softened
2 tablespoons rum
2 tablespoons brandy
6 fl oz (175 ml) medium sherry

You will also need a 2 pint (1.2 litre) pudding basin, well buttered, and either a double pan steamer or a large saucepan with a fan steamer and a tight-fitting lid, and some foil and string.

You need to begin this by soaking the dried mixed fruit in the rum overnight. The next day, toast the almonds. To do this, pre-heat the grill to its highest setting for 10 minutes, then place the almonds on some foil and toast them under the grill for 2-3 minutes, but don't go away, as they will burn very quickly. When they look nicely toasted and browned on one side, turn them all over and toast the other side, then remove them from the grill and leave them aside to cool.

Next, cut the panettone into 1 inch (2.5 cm) chunks and place them in a large mixing bowl, along with the candied peel, orange and lemon zests and the soaked dried mixed fruit and any drops of rum that didn't get soaked up. Now chop the almonds into thin slivers and add these. Now give it all a really good stir to distribute everything evenly.

Then, in another bowl, whisk together the sugar, milk, cream and eggs and pour this all over the panettone, giving everything another good mix. Now pour the mixture into the buttered pudding basin and press everything down to pack it in. Now cover the top of the pudding with a double sheet of foil measuring about 10 inches (25.5 cm) square and tie it securely with the string round the top of the basin, then make a string handle by taking a length of string over the top of the pudding basin and attaching it to each side – this will help you lift the pudding into the steamer. Now boil a kettle and pour the boiling water into the saucepan, about half-full, place it on a medium heat and, when it comes back to the boil, fit the steamer over the top.

Now pop the pudding in, put the lid on and steam the pudding for exactly 2 hours. After 1 hour, check the water level in the saucepan and, if necessary, top it up with boiling water. If you are using a fan steamer, put in enough water to just reach the steamer, and you'll need to top it up two or three times.

Meanwhile, make the hot punch sauce. First prepare the orange and lemon zests, and to do this it's best to use a potato peeler and pare off the outer zest, leaving the white pith behind. What you need is four strips of each zest measuring approximately 2 x 1 inch (5 x 2.5 cm). Then, using a sharp knife, cut the strips into very thin, needle-like shreds. Now pop these into a medium-sized saucepan, along with the sugar and water, bring everything up to a slow simmer and let it simmer as gently as possible for 15 minutes.

While that is happening, squeeze the juice from the orange and lemon, and in a separate bowl, mix the flour and butter together to form a paste.

When the 15 minutes is up, add the orange and lemon juice, along with the rum, brandy and sherry, and bring it all back up to a gentle heat. Now add the paste to the liquid in small, peanut-sized pieces, whisking as you add them, until they have dissolved and the sauce has thickened. Serve the sauce hot in a warmed serving jug, and if you make it in advance, re-heat it gently without letting it come to the boil.

To serve the pudding, remove the foil and string and let it stand for 5-10 minutes, then slide a palette knife all round to loosen it and turn it out on to a warmed plate. Pour some of the hot punch sauce over the pudding and carry it to the table, with the rest of the sauce in a jug to hand round separately.

5

First steps in pastry

If you can't make pastry, or don't even know how to start, the very first thing you need to do is forgive yourself and not feel guilty – please understand it isn't because you're inadequate or not born to such things, it's probably because no one's ever actually taught you how. In the age we now live in, cooking skills are rarely learnt from watching mother, because working mothers have little time for home baking. So now we have to think differently. But teaching is essential: someone had to teach you to swim, ride a bike or drive a car, things that are now second nature to you.

With pastry it is precisely the same: someone (hopefully me) has to show you how, then, with a bit of practice, pastry-making will also become automatic, something you do without having to think about it.

What I want to do here is show you how to make two basic types of pastry, and, if you master these, you can have a lifetime of happy pastry cooking without having to worry.

What is pastry?

Originally pastry was an inedible paste used to seal in juices and aromas, but there must have been a time when some clever person thought, 'What a waste,' added some fat and made it deliciously edible in its own right, so that now the pastry crust itself is every bit as important as what it encases or surrounds.

But what should it be like? What are the constituents of a really good pastry crust? Firstly it should be crisp, but the word that has been adopted to describe perfect pastry is 'short' (meaning meltingly light). It should also be well baked and offer a character and flavour in its own right so that it complements whatever it is partnering.

I have a theory about how to make good pastry at home, and that's to keep it simple. Professional pâtissiers have years of training and great skills, and we can all be dazzled by what they can produce. The trouble is that if we have busy lives, we can't do the same at home, so we should enjoy their expertise whenever we can. But at home, learn to master simple pastry well. It's also important not to fall into the trap of some chefs by adding too much fat, because sometimes the pastry gets so rich that it begins to compete with and not complement the filling.

The case for shortcrust

Not fashionable, not clever, not over-rich, but for my money the humble shortcrust is one of the best pastries of all. What it provides is a light, crisp, melting crust, which has all the important flavours of the wheat – all that you imagine home-made pastry to be. It is made, quite simply, from flour, fat and water, with nothing else added. But a well-made, thinly rolled shortcrust provides a discreet 'melt in the mouth' presence, a perfect backdrop to the richness, intensity or even delicacy of filling and ingredients. But first let's take a look at what is needed to make a good pastry.

Ingredients

Flour

This should always be plain and made from soft wheat (ie, not strong bread flour). Note the date stamp when you buy it and be careful of how long you store it: flour can lurk in the back of cupboards long after its shelf life has ended, and I have found that stale flour does not make the best pastry. In my opinion, self-raising flour does not make good shortcrust, and neither does 100 per cent wholemeal – witness those stodgy 'brown' creations that are offered in the name of healthy eating. A mixture of half wholemeal and half soft plain flour, however, does work well and gives a nutty flavour.

Fat

The type you use is your choice, and can depend on whether or not you are a vegetarian or have anything against animal fats. Whipped vegetable fats and margarines can be used, but after years of cooking and side-by-side tests and tastings, my opinion is that, in most cases, the very best flavour and texture I've obtained with shortcrust pastry is when equal quantities of lard and butter are used. Generally speaking, the amount of fat in shortcrust is half the amount of flour: thus for 4 oz (110 g) of flour you use 2 oz (50 g) of fat. People sometimes add more fat because they think this will produce a 'shorter' texture; I do not agree with this and feel the result is actually heavier and too rich and fatty.

Fat temperature is the single most important rule to remember. Fat should be at room temperature and soft enough for a knife to make an indentation straight through it in a second. This is because it needs to be incorporated into the flour as quickly as possible – if it's too cold, you will have to rub it in for twice as long, making the fat oily with the warmth of your hands and the pastry difficult to roll out. One tip here: leave a note on the fridge the night before you want to make the pastry saying, 'Don't forget to remove fat!'

But help! I forgot! Don't worry – so do we all, but don't panic. Put the cold fat, cut into lumps, in a processor, together with the flour, and process with the pulse button till you have a crumbly mixture (see page 106).

Salt

I've changed my mind on this over the years and now think that pastry, like bread, needs some salt, even if it is to be used in sweet dishes.

Keep cool

This means you yourself, psychologically, as well, because keeping things as cold as possible is important. If the fat, as I mentioned earlier, becomes oily because the rubbing takes longer and everything is too warm, what happens is it coats more flour grains than it should. This means the flour is unable to absorb enough water and the pastry will crumble and be difficult to roll out. I always make pastry by an open window, as a bit of a draught coming in seems to keep things nicely cool.

Liquid

In shortcrust pastry don't use milk or egg – just add plain water, and leave the tap running to get the water as cold as possible. Remember, too, that exact amounts can never be specified in recipes, because the amount of water that flour absorbs varies. Start with about 1 tablespoon, sprinkling it evenly all round, then add more little by little. Too much water will make the pastry stick and too difficult to roll out, and when it's baked it will be hard; too little water, on the other hand, will also make rolling out a problem, and the cooked result will be too crumbly. However, don't be afraid – if you follow the precise directions given below and on page 106, it's easy to get just the right amount.

Air

Believe it or not, air is the most important ingredient in pastry. So, rule number one is to sift the flour into the bowl, holding the sieve as high up as possible, so that the flour gets a really good airing before you begin.

Rubbing in

Once the flour is sifted into the bowl, add the fat, cut into smallish lumps, then take a knife and begin to cut the fat into the flour. Go on doing this until it looks fairly evenly blended, then begin to rub the fat into the flour using only your fingertips and being as light and gentle as possible. Being light with your fingers is not a special gift, it's just a conscious decision, a signal the brain gives to the fingertips, and then a bit of concentration.

As you lightly rub the fat into the flour, lift it up high and let it fall back down into the bowl, which again means that air is being incorporated all the time, and air is what makes pastry light. Speed is also what's needed here, so don't start daydreaming and go on rubbing all day, but just long enough to make the mixture crumbly with a few odd lumps here and there.

Adding the water and mixing

Sprinkle 1 tablespoon of cold water in, then, with a knife, start bringing the dough together, cutting and turning and using the knife to begin to make it cling together. Then discard the knife and, finally, bring it all together with your fingertips. When enough liquid is added, all the bits of flour and fat should be incorporated and the pastry should leave the bowl completely clean. If this hasn't happened, then add a spot more water (sometimes it really only needs your fingers dipped into water once or twice to bring it together).

Processing pastry

I have found it impossible to make shortcrust pastry in a processor alone, as you can't gauge how much water the pastry needs without feeling it. But it is possible to process the flour and fat in a processor, and the advantage is that you can take the fat straight out of the fridge. Be careful not to over-process: just 1-2 minutes on a low speed is enough. Then tip it into a bowl and add the water as described earlier.

Resting

All pastries must be rested before rolling out. If you're in a hurry, this can seem like an awful bore, but I promise you resting the pastry will, in fact, save you more time in the end. Why does it need to be rested? Flour contains something called gluten (see page 75), and gluten reacts to water in a way which – if it's given time – makes the dough more elastic in texture, so that when you come to roll out the pastry, this elasticity makes the dough roll out like a dream. Without this resting time rolling can be a nightmare, because the pastry won't have enough stretch so it will break and crack. So, as the pastry is made, place it in a polythene bag and leave it in the fridge for 30 minutes.

Surface

A flat surface is all you need to roll out – a pastry board is not absolutely necessary – a scrubbed kitchen top will do. If, however, you want to go on making pastry, you might like to invest in a piece of granite or marble. It is expensive and very heavy, but it will last a lifetime and can be purchased from a stonemason or marble supplier. The ideal size is approximately 18 x 18 inches (46 x 46 cm).

Rolling out

Rolling out, as I've said, is easy if the pastry has been rested. Use a rolling pin that is absolutely straight – handles can get in the way if you want to roll out large quantities. Place the dough on a lightly floured surface and place the pin, also dusted with flour, in the centre of it, then place the flat of your hands lightly on each end of the pin and begin to roll, re-dusting the pin and surface lightly with flour if you need to stop the pastry from sticking.

If you want to roll it out to a round, give it quarter turns as it expands and, provided you roll backwards and forwards, it will roll out into a round shape. Don't be tempted to roll from side to side, unless for some reason you want to roll out a map of the UK! If you can concentrate on only going backwards and forwards, you will end up with a better rounded shape. If you want an oblong, just knock the sides gently with the rolling pin to keep it in shape; if you want a square, give quarter turns – as for a round – and then square it up using the rolling pin to knock the edges into shape.

Storing pastry

Making pastry in advance is perfectly all right – it will keep for up to three days in a polythene bag in the fridge – but don't forget to remove it and let it come back to room temperature before rolling it out. Raw pastry also freezes extremely well for up to three months.

Basic Shortcrust Pastry

4 oz (110 g) plain flour, plus a little
extra for dusting
pinch of salt
1 oz (25 g) softened lard
1 oz (25 g) softened butter
a little cold water

Begin by sifting the flour and pinch of salt into a large bowl, holding the sieve as high as possible, so that they get a really good airing before you begin. Now add the lard and butter, cut into smallish lumps, then take a knife and begin to cut the fat into the flour. Go on doing this until it looks fairly evenly blended, then begin to rub the fat into the flour using your fingertips only and being as light as possible. As you gently rub the fat into the flour, lift it up high and let it fall back into the bowl, which again means that all the time air is being incorporated, but do this just long enough to make the mixture crumbly with a few odd lumps here and there.

Now sprinkle 1 tablespoon of water in, then, with a knife, start bringing the dough together, using the knife to make it cling. Then discard the knife and, finally, bring it together with your fingertips. When enough liquid is added, the pastry should leave the bowl fairly clean. If this hasn't happened, then add a spot more water. Now place the pastry in a polythene bag and leave it in the refrigerator for 30 minutes to rest.

Note: This will make 6 oz (175 g) finished weight of pastry, which will be enough to line a 7 or 8 inch (18 or 20 cm) flan or quiche tin.

Begin by sifting the flour and salt into a large bowl, then add the soft fat; if the fat is too cold, it won't rub in effectively

Starting with a knife, cut the fat into the flour, then lightly rub it in with your fingertips until the mixture looks crumbly

Add the liquid by sprinkling it all over the mixture, then use a knife again to start bringing the dough together

The final stage is to bring the pastry together with your hands, adding a little more liquid if necessary

How to line the flan tin

Once the pastry is rolled out to the correct size, place the rolling pin in the centre, fold the pastry over and lift it on to the pin. Then transfer it to the flan tin, laying it down evenly and carefully. Now, using your hands, gently press the pastry into the tin to line the base and sides. (If, while you were lifting the pastry, you found it stretched, don't worry – as you line the tin, ease the stretchiness back, especially round the edges.) When you've pressed it all round with your fingers, try to ease the pastry that is sticking up above the edges back down, so what you're in fact doing is reinforcing the edge, because if it gets stretched too much, it will shrink during cooking. When you've lined the tin, trim off any excess around the edges with a knife, but press the edges again so you have ¼ inch (5 mm) above the edges of the tin.

Pre-baking

Forget about baking beans – it's really all too much bother. Provided you've lined the tin correctly, as above, all you now need to do is prick the base all over with a fork, as this will release any trapped air, which is what causes the centre to rise up. Then brush the base and sides all over with beaten egg, which will provide a sort of waterproof coating so that the pastry stays beautifully crisp even after the filling has gone in. Normally this small amount of beaten egg can be taken from the egg used for the filling in the recipe.

The oven

This needs to be pre-heated and, at the same time, you should pre-heat a good, solid baking sheet on the centre shelf. Then pop the pastry case in to pre-bake for 20-25 minutes or until the pastry is turning golden brown. It's a good idea to have a peep halfway through – if the pastry is bubbling up a bit, just prick it with a fork and press it back down again with your hands.

To remove the flan tin, place the tart on a tin or jar, loosen the pastry all round with a small knife or skewer and ease it down

Now pop the pastry in a polythene bag and refrigerate for 30 minutes, which will make rolling it out far less trouble

Once rolled out, transfer the pastry to the tin by rolling it over the pin, then gently ease it into the tin using your hands

Finally, prick the base all over with a fork to release any trapped air, then brush the base and sides with the beaten egg

Leek and Goats' Cheese Tart

This is what I call a wobbly tart – creamy and soft-centred. Leeks and goats' cheese have turned out to be a wonderful combination, and the addition of goats' cheese to the pastry gives it a nice edge.

Serves 6 as a starter or 4 as a main course
For the pastry:
1 oz (25 g) firm goats' cheese (rindless)
4 oz (110 g) plain flour, plus a little extra for dusting
pinch of salt
1 oz (25 g) softened lard
1 oz (25 g) softened butter
a little cold water

For the filling:
1 lb 6 oz (625 g) leeks, ie, 12 oz (350 g) trimmed weight (see instructions in the method)
6 oz (175 g) firm goats' cheese (rindless)
½ oz (10 g) butter
3 large eggs, beaten
7 fl oz (200 ml) crème fraîche or double cream
4 spring onions, trimmed and finely sliced, including the green parts
salt and freshly milled black pepper

You will also need a 7½ inch (19 cm) diameter fluted quiche tin with a removable base, 1¼ inches (3 cm) deep, very lightly buttered, and a small, solid baking sheet.

First sift the flour with the pinch of salt into a large bowl, holding the sieve up high to give it a good airing. Then add the lard and butter and, using only your fingertips, lightly rub the fat into the flour, again lifting the mixture up high all the time. When everything is crumbly, coarsely grate the goats' cheese in and then sprinkle in some cold water – about 1 tablespoon. Start to mix the pastry with a knife and then finish off with your hands, adding a few more drops of water, till you have a smooth dough that will leave the bowl clean. Then pop the pastry into a polythene bag and let it rest in the refrigerator for 30 minutes. Meanwhile, pre-heat the oven to gas mark 5, 375°F (190°C) and pop the baking sheet in to pre-heat on the centre shelf.

Now prepare the leeks. First take the tough green ends off and throw them out, then make a vertical split about halfway down the centre of each one

and clean them by running them under the cold-water tap while you fan out the layers – this will rid them of any hidden dust and grit. Then slice them in half lengthways and chop into ½ inch (1 cm) slices.

Next, in a medium-sized frying pan, melt the butter over a gentle heat and add the leeks and some salt. Give it all a good stir and let them cook gently, without a lid, for 10-15 minutes or until the juice runs out of them. Then you need to transfer them to a sieve set over a bowl to drain off the excess juice. Place a saucer with a weight on top of them to press out every last drop.

By this time the pastry will have rested, so remove it from the fridge and roll it out into a circle on a lightly floured surface. As you roll, give it quarter turns to keep the round shape and roll it as thinly as possible. Now transfer it, rolling it over the pin, to the tin. Press it lightly and firmly over the base and sides of the tin, easing any overlapping pastry back down to the sides, as it is important not to stretch it. Now trim the edges and press the pastry up about ¼ inch (5 mm) above the rim of the tin all round, then prick the base all over with a fork. After that, paint some of the beaten egg for the filling over the base and sides. Now place the tin on the baking sheet and bake for 20-25 minutes or until the pastry is crisp and golden. Check halfway through the cooking time to make sure that the pastry isn't rising up in the centre. If it is, just prick it a couple of times and press it back down with your hands.

Leek and Goats' Cheese Tart; cooked, above, and uncooked, left

While the pastry case is pre-baking, crumble the goats' cheese with your hands, then gently combine it with the leeks in the sieve. Now, in a jug, mix the beaten eggs with the crème fraîche or double cream, seasoning with just a little salt (there is some already in the leeks) and a good grinding of freshly milled black pepper. As soon as the pastry case is ready, remove it from the oven, arrange the leeks and cheese all over the base and then sprinkle the spring onions over the top. Now gradually pour half the cream and egg mixture in to join them, then put the tart back on the baking sheet with the oven shelf half pulled out, then slowly pour in the rest of the mixture. Gently slide the shelf back in and bake the tart for 30-35 minutes, until it's firm in the centre and the surface has turned a lovely golden brown. Next, remove it from the oven and allow it to settle for 10 minutes before serving. This 10 minutes is important as it will be much easier to cut into portions. The best way to remove the tart from the tin is to ease the edges from the sides of the tin with a small knife, then place it on an upturned jar or tin, which will allow you to carefully ease the sides away. Next slide a palette knife or wide fish slice underneath and ease the tart on to a plate or board ready to serve, or simply cut it into portions straight from the tin base.

Smoked Fish Tart with a Parmesan Crust

This tart is not as wobbly as the previous one, as it has a substantial amount of filling. The various smoked flavours of the fish are quite sensational partnered with the hint of piquancy in the gherkins and capers.

Serves 6-8 as a starter or 4-6 as a main course

For the pastry:
1 oz (25 g) finely grated Parmesan (Parmigiano Reggiano)
4 oz (110 g) plain flour, plus a little extra for dusting
pinch of salt
1 oz (25 g) softened lard
1 oz (25 g) softened butter
a little cold water

For the filling:
8 oz (225 g) undyed smoked haddock (skinned raw weight)
4 oz (110 g) kipper fillet (skinned raw weight)
9 oz (250 g) smoked salmon trimmings
2 fl oz (55 ml) milk
1 bay leaf
pinch of ground mace
2 large eggs, plus 2 egg yolks
a little ground nutmeg
7 fl oz (200 ml) crème fraîche or double cream
1 dessertspoon salted capers or capers in vinegar, well rinsed and drained
2 cocktail gherkins (cornichons), finely chopped
freshly milled black pepper

You will also need a 7½ inch (19 cm) diameter fluted quiche tin with a removable base, 1¼ inches (3 cm) deep, very lightly buttered, and a small, solid baking sheet.

First of all sift the flour with the pinch of salt into a large bowl, holding the sieve up high to give them a good airing. Then add the lard and butter and, using only your fingertips, lightly and gently rub the fat into the flour, again lifting the mixture up high all the time to give it a good airing. When everything is crumbly, add the Parmesan and then sprinkle in some cold water – about 1 tablespoon. Start to mix the pastry with a knife and then finish off with your hands, adding more drops of water till you have a smooth dough that will leave the bowl clean. Then pop the pastry into a polythene bag and let it rest in the refrigerator for 30 minutes.

Meanwhile, pre-heat the oven to gas mark 5, 375°F (190°C) and pop the baking sheet in to pre-heat on the centre shelf.

After that, roll the pastry out into a circle on a surface lightly dusted with flour, and as you roll, give it quarter turns to keep the round shape, rolling it as thinly as possible. Now transfer it, rolling it over the pin, to the tin. Press it lightly and firmly all over the base and sides of the tin, easing any overlapping pastry back down to the sides, as it is important not to stretch it too much. Now trim the edges and press the pastry up about ¼ inch (5 mm) above the rim of the tin all round. Then prick the base all over with a fork and, after that, brush some of the beaten egg for the filling all over the base and sides. Now place the tin on the baking sheet and bake it for 20-25 minutes or until the pastry is crisp and golden. Check halfway through the cooking time to make sure that the pastry isn't rising up in the centre. If it is, just prick it again a couple of times and press it back down again with your hands.

When the pastry is cooked, remove the tin from the oven and lower the temperature to gas mark 3, 325°F (170°C).

For the filling, put the haddock and kipper in a medium-sized saucepan, along with the milk, bay leaf and mace. Now bring it up to simmering point, cover with a lid and poach gently for about 2 minutes, then remove the fish from the milk. Discard the bay leaf, but reserve the milk.

Then lightly whisk the eggs and egg yolks together with a seasoning of black pepper and nutmeg, but no salt, as the fish will be fairly salty. Then heat the reserved milk, whisking in the crème fraîche or double cream. Then, when it has come to simmering point, pour it over the beaten eggs, whisking well. Now divide the cooked haddock and kipper into flakes about ½ inch (1 cm) in size and arrange them in the cooked pastry case, along with the smoked salmon trimmings. Next scatter the capers and gherkins all over and slowly pour half the cream and egg mixture in, allowing the liquid to settle between each addition. Then place the baking sheet in the oven, gradually add the remainder of the filling and cook for 30-35 minutes or until the surface is golden brown and feels firm in the centre.

When you have removed it from the oven, let it rest for 10 minutes, then ease it away from the edges using a small knife and place it on a suitable-sized jar, which will allow you to carefully ease the sides away. Then slide a palette knife or wide fish slice underneath and ease the tart carefully on to a plate or board ready to serve, or simply cut it into portions straight from the tin base.

Smoked Fish Tart with a Parmesan Crust; cooked, left, and uncooked, below

Pumpkin Pie

This recipe uses another version of shortcrust pastry that is used for sweet open-faced flans and tarts. It's richer than shortcrust, but very crisp, and the eggs give it a shortbread quality. Nuts can sometimes be added; here there are toasted pecans, although walnuts or hazelnuts can be used, or the pastry can be made without nuts if you prefer. In autumn I love the velvet texture of pumpkin, but this tart could be made with butternut squash.

Serves 8
For the pastry:
1½ oz (40 g) pecan nuts
6 oz (175 g) plain flour, plus a little extra for dusting
½ oz (10 g) icing sugar
pinch of salt
3 oz (75 g) softened butter
a little cold water
1 large egg yolk

For the filling:
1 lb (450 g) prepared weight pumpkin flesh, cut into 1 inch (2.5 cm) chunks
2 large eggs plus 1 yolk
(reserve the white)
1 tablespoon molasses
3 oz (75 g) soft dark brown sugar
1 teaspoon ground cinnamon
½ teaspoon freshly grated nutmeg
½ teaspoon ground allspice
½ teaspoon ground cloves
½ teaspoon ground ginger
10 fl oz (275 ml) double cream

You will also need a 9 inch (23 cm) diameter fluted flan tin, 1½ inches (4 cm) deep, with a loose base, lightly greased, and a medium-sized solid baking sheet.

Pre-heat the oven to gas mark 4, 350°F (180°C).

To begin this you need to toast the pecan nuts. First of all, when the oven has pre-heated, spread the nuts out on the baking sheet and toast them lightly for 8 minutes, using a timer so that you don't forget them. After that, remove them from the oven to a chopping board (turning the oven off for now) and let them cool a little. Then either chop them really finely by hand or in a processor using the pulse action. Be careful here, though, because if you overdo it they will go oily.

For the pastry, first of all sift the flour, icing sugar and the pinch of salt into a large bowl, holding the sieve up high to give them a good airing. Then add the butter and start cutting it into the flour using a knife, then, using only your fingertips, lightly and gently rub it into the flour, again lifting the mixture up high all the time to give it a good airing.

When everything is crumbly, add the chopped nuts, then sprinkle in about 1 tablespoon of water and the egg yolk. Start to mix the pastry with a knife and then finish off with your hands, lightly bringing it together (you may need to add more water) until you have a smooth dough that will leave the bowl clean. Then pop it into a polythene bag and let it rest in the refrigerator for 30 minutes.

Meanwhile, pre-heat the oven to gas mark 4, 350°F (180°C) with the baking sheet inside. Now place a steamer over a pan of simmering water, add the pumpkin, put a lid on and steam for 15-20 minutes, until the pieces feel tender when tested with a skewer. After that, place a large, coarse sieve over a bowl and press the pumpkin through it to extract any seeds or fibres.

By this time the pastry will have rested, so now remove it from the fridge. Roll it out into a circle on a surface lightly dusted with flour, and as you roll, give it quarter turns to keep the round shape. Roll it into a circle approximately 12 inches (30 cm) in diameter, as thinly as possible. Now transfer it, rolling it over the pin, to the tin. Press it lightly and firmly all over the base and sides of the tin, easing any overlapping pastry back down the sides, as it is important not to stretch this bit too much. Now trim the edge, leaving ¼ inch (5 mm) above the rim of the tin all round. Then prick the base all over with a fork and brush it and the sides with the reserved egg white, lightly beaten. Now place the tin on the pre-heated baking sheet on the centre shelf of the oven and bake it for 20-25 minutes, until the pastry is crisp and golden. Check halfway through the cooking time to make sure that the pastry isn't rising up in the centre. If it is, just prick it again a couple of times and press it back down again with your hands.

Now for the filling. First lightly whisk the eggs and extra yolk together in a large bowl. Next measure the molasses (lightly greasing the spoon first, as this makes things easier), then just push the molasses off the spoon with a rubber spatula into a saucepan. Add the sugar, spices and the cream, then bring it up to simmering point, giving it a whisk to mix everything together. Then pour it over the eggs and whisk it again briefly. Now add the pumpkin purée, still whisking to combine everything thoroughly, then pour the filling into a jug. When the pastry case is ready, remove it from the oven on the baking sheet using an oven glove. Then pour half the filling in, return it to the oven, then, with the shelf half out, pour in the rest of the filling and slide the shelf back in. Bake the pie for 35-40 minutes, by which time it will puff up round the edges but still feel slightly wobbly in the centre. Then remove it from the oven and place the tin on a wire cooling rack.

I prefer to serve this chilled (stored loosely covered in foil in the fridge) with some equally chilled crème fraîche, but warm or at room temperature would be fine. In America, ice cream is the preferred accompaniment.

Old-Fashioned English Custard Tart

This old-fashioned Custard Tart needs a thick, wobbly filling, so I've used a round tin with sloping sides and a rim, which gives a good depth. The nutmeg is very important to the flavour, so always use it freshly grated and grate it on to a piece of foil, which helps when you have to sprinkle it on quickly when it goes into the oven.

Serves 6
For the shortcrust pastry:
5 oz (150 g) plain flour, plus a little extra for dusting
pinch of salt
1 oz (25 g) softened lard
1½ oz (40 g) softened butter
a little cold water

For the filling:
1 pint (570 ml) single cream
3 large eggs, plus 2 large egg yolks, lightly beaten
2 oz (50 g) caster sugar
½ teaspoon vanilla extract
1½ whole nutmegs, freshly grated
1 teaspoon softened butter

You will also need a 2 inch (5 cm) leaf cutter, a tin that has a rim and sloping sides (1½ inches/4 cm deep, with a 7 inch/18 cm base and a ½ inch/ 1 cm rim), lightly greased, and a medium-sized, solid baking sheet.

To make the pastry, first of all sift the flour with the pinch of salt into a large bowl, holding the sieve up high to give it a good airing. Then add the lard and butter and, using only your fingertips, lightly and gently rub the fat into the flour, again lifting the mixture up high all the time to give it a good airing.

When everything is crumbly, sprinkle in about 1 tablespoon of cold water. Start to mix the pastry with a knife and then finish off with your hands, adding a few more drops of water, till you have a smooth dough that leaves the bowl clean. Then pop the pastry into a polythene bag and let it rest in the refrigerator for 30 minutes. Meanwhile, pre-heat the oven to gas mark 5, 375°F (190°C) and pop the baking sheet in to pre-heat on the centre shelf.

After that, roll the rest of the pastry out into a circle, giving it quarter turns to keep its round shape; it's a good idea at this stage to put the tin lightly on top of the pastry – the size needs to be 1 inch (2.5 cm) bigger all round. Now transfer it, rolling it over the pin, to the tin, and press it lightly and firmly around the base, sides and rim. Now take a sharp knife and trim the overlapping pastry. Then press the rim of the pastry so that about ¼ inch (5 mm) overlaps the edge. Next, roll the trimmings and cut out about 24 leaves, making veins in them with the blunt side of the knife. Now brush the whole surface of the pastry case with some of the beaten eggs, arranging the leaves all around the rim, overlapping them. Brush these, too, with beaten egg. Now prick the base of the tart with a fork, then place it on the baking sheet and bake on the centre shelf for 20 minutes, until the pastry is crisp and golden. Check after 4 minutes to make sure that the pastry isn't rising up in the centre. If it is, prick it again a couple of times, pressing it back down with your hands. After 20 minutes, remove it from the oven, leaving the baking sheet there, and reduce the temperature to gas mark 3, 325°F (170°C).

Now place the cream in a saucepan and bring it up to a gentle simmer, then whisk the beaten egg mixture and sugar together in a large heatproof jug using a balloon whisk – but not too vigorously because you don't want to make bubbles. Then pour the hot liquid over the beaten eggs, add the vanilla extract and half the nutmeg and whisk briefly again.

Now place the pie tin back on the baking tray with the oven shelf half out and have ready the rest of the grated nutmeg on a piece of foil. Carefully pour the filling into the pastry case (it will be very full) and scatter the rest of the nutmeg all over, then dot with the softened butter and bake in the oven for 30-40 minutes, until the filling is golden brown, firm in the centre and slightly puffed up. Serve either warm or, as I actually prefer it, cold.

Apple and Raisin Parcels

This is yet another version of a good old apple pie, but the great thing about this recipe is that it bakes into individual portions, so it's much easier when you come to serve it. Raisins are a good winter addition, but in autumn you could replace them with 4 oz (110 g) of blackberries or, in summer, make the whole thing with 1 lb (450 g) of gooseberries, adding 3½ oz (95 g) sugar.

Serves 8
For the shortcrust pastry:
12 oz (350 g) plain flour
pinch of salt
3 oz (75 g) softened lard
3 oz (75 g) softened butter
a little cold water

For the filling:
8 oz (225 g) Bramley apples (unpeeled), cored and cut into ½ inch (1 cm) dice
4 oz (110 g) Cox's apples (unpeeled), cored and cut into ½ inch (1 cm) dice
3 oz (75 g) raisins, soaked overnight in 4 fl oz (120 ml) dry cider
8 teaspoons semolina
16 whole cloves
2 oz (50 g) golden caster sugar, plus an extra teaspoon for sprinkling
1 egg white, lightly beaten

You will also need a non-stick baking tin measuring 10 x 6 inches (25.5 x 15 cm) and 1 inch (2.5 cm) deep.

Start this recipe the night before by soaking the raisins in the cider. The next day, start the pastry, and to do this sift the flour with the pinch of salt into a large bowl, holding the sieve high. Add the lard and butter and, using your fingertips, lightly rub the fat into the flour, lifting the mixture up to give it a good airing. When the mixture is crumbly, add about a tablespoon of cold water. Start mixing the pastry with a knife, then finish off with your hands, adding a little more water, till you have a smooth dough that leaves the bowl clean. Now pop it in a polythene bag and chill for 30 minutes.

Meanwhile, pre-heat the oven to gas mark 6, 400°F (200°C). Remove the pastry from the fridge, then divide it into four pieces. Dust your work surface lightly with flour, then roll each into a length about 10 x 5 inches (25.5 x 13 cm) and trim each piece into two 5 inch (13 cm) squares. Working with two squares at a time, scatter a teaspoon of semolina over each pastry square, then mix both varieties of apple together and add 2 tablespoons of chopped apples, 2 cloves, 2 teaspoons of sugar and some drained raisins to each square. Now brush the edges of each square with some of the beaten egg white, then loosely fold the corners over. Then, using a fish slice to help you, lift each parcel into the tin, tucking them neatly into the corners, and repeat with the remaining squares so that they all fit snugly in the tin. If you have any fruit left over, carefully lift the corners of each parcel and add some more apples and raisins. Now either leave the parcels open or squeeze the pastry corners together a little more (for the closed version see the photo on page 100). Next brush the pastry with the remaining beaten egg white and scatter the rest of the sugar over, along with the extra teaspoon of sugar. Bake in the oven on the shelf just above centre for 50 minutes, then serve warm with cream, ice cream or Traditional English Custard (see page 62), and don't forget to warn your guests that there are a few whole cloves lurking.
Note: If you're using blackberries, gooseberries, rhubarb or blackcurrants, use a level dessertspoon of semolina in each parcel to absorb the extra juice.

Quick and easy flaky pastry

Clever chefs and professional pâtissiers make proper puff pastry and sometimes call it *millefeuille* (meaning 'thousand leaves'). It involves rolling and folding the pastry several times to trap the air, and letting it rest between rollings. It is a labour of love and dedication – and can be therapeutic if you have time to lock yourself away for a few hours – but it is not something for the fraught cook, trying to juggle this with the rest of life happening outside the kitchen. Yet all is not lost because there is a quick and easy version – crisp, light and, if you close your eyes, you won't know whether you are eating 50 or 1,000 leaves, because the taste will be the same.

Quick flaky pastry is really a cheat's version, because it doesn't involve the turning, rolling, resting and all the palaver that go into the real thing. The advantage is that what you get is a home-made pastry made purely with butter, which gives a texture and flavour that are quite unique and special but, at the same time, doesn't involve either a lot of time or – believe it or not – a lot of skill. The secret is grating partly frozen butter, then mixing it with flour (so no boring rubbing in). It really does involve the minimum of skill but, at the same time, produces spectacular results.

What should perfect flaky pastry be like? Answer: as light as possible, wafer-thin and so crisp it eats like a whisper so that you hardly know it's there. So if you don't believe that it's incredibly easy to achieve, here are the detailed instructions. I promise you will be so pleased with the results that you will probably make four more batches to put in the freezer for a rainy day.

Flour should always be soft, plain and sifted, lifting the sieve high as you do so and letting it fall into a large, roomy bowl. I have said it before, but there is no harm in underlining that the most important ingredient in pastry is air. Sifting the flour like this gives it a good airing.

Butter Because the butter is going to be coarsely grated, it needs to be almost frozen. So measure it out, then wrap it in foil and place it in the freezer or freezing compartment of the fridge for 30-45 minutes. If it is too soft, it won't grate properly.

Resting Like all pastries, quick flaky pastry must be rested after it has been mixed – that means putting it in a polythene bag in the refrigerator and leaving it there for 30 minutes.

Baking Because this pastry has a high fat content, it's essential to have a high oven temperature, which is important if you want to achieve that lovely light, crisp effect, so do be sure to pre-heat the oven before baking the pastry.

Texture Quick flaky pastry is not puff pastry, so don't expect it to rise up like a thousand leaves. It is light-textured and flaky, though, and will puff and rise fractionally when it is cooking.

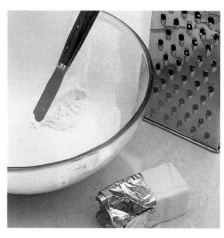

Your secret weapons in this cheat's flaky pastry are frozen butter and a grater…

To begin the recipe, first of all remove a pack of butter from the fridge, weigh out 4 oz (110 g), then wrap it in a piece of foil and return it to the freezer or freezing compartment of the fridge for 30-45 minutes.

Then, when you are ready to make the pastry, sift the flour and salt into a large, roomy bowl. Take the butter out of the freezer, fold back the foil and hold it in the foil, which will protect it from your warm hands. Then, using the coarse side of a grater placed in the bowl over the flour, grate the butter, dipping the edge of the butter on to the flour several times to make it easier to grate. What you will end up with is a large pile of grated butter sitting in the middle of the flour. Now take a palette knife and start to distribute the gratings into the flour – don't use your hands yet, just keep trying to coat all the pieces of fat with flour. Now sprinkle 2 tablespoons of cold water all over, continue to use the palette knife to bring the whole thing together, and finish off using your hands. If you need a bit more moisture, that's fine – just remember that the dough should come together in such a way that it leaves the bowl fairly clean, with no bits of loose butter or flour anywhere. Now pop it into a polythene bag and chill for 30 minutes before using. Remember, this, like other pastries, freezes extremely well, in which case you will need to defrost it thoroughly and let it come back to room temperature before rolling it out on a lightly floured surface.

For the pastry:
4 oz (110 g) butter
6 oz (175 g) plain flour
pinch of salt
a little cold water

All you do is grate the frozen butter into the flour using the coarse side of the grater

Once the butter is distributed, add water and use a palette knife to combine

Finish off with your hands, adding a little more water if the pastry needs it

Tomato and Goats' Cheese Galettes

Galettes are very thin discs of pastry which, unlike conventional tarts, have no sides. The concept is a good one because the pastry is barely there, yet it gives a light, very crisp background to all kinds of toppings, both savoury and sweet. There's no limit to what you can put on top of them – the combinations are endless, and you can serve them for a light lunch, as a first course, on a picnic or for a dessert. What I often do is freeze the pastry circles raw, interleaved with foil or greaseproof paper, so you can just whip some out for an impromptu meal any old time at all. If you don't have the right-sized cutter, just cut around a saucer of the same size.

The first of my recipes for galettes calls for lovely ripe red tomatoes for colour, and the preferred cheese in our house is Crottin de Chavignol, but any firm goats' cheese will do.

*Serves 3 as a light lunch
or 6 as a first course*
quick flaky pastry made with 6 oz (175 g) plain flour and 4 oz (110 g) butter (see page 119)
12 medium tomatoes
7 oz (200 g) firm goats' cheese
18 large basil leaves, plus 6 sprigs for garnish
a little olive oil, for drizzling
salt and freshly milled black pepper

You will also need two solid baking sheets measuring 14 x 11 inches (35 x 28 cm), lightly greased, and a 6 inch (15 cm) plain pastry cutter.

Pre-heat the oven to gas mark 7, 425°F (220°C).

Make the pastry as described on page 119 and chill for 30 minutes in the fridge. Meanwhile, you need to skin the tomatoes, so pour boiling water over them and leave for exactly 1 minute before draining and slipping off the skins (protect your hands with a cloth if they are too hot). Next, on a lightly floured surface, roll out the pastry very thinly to ⅛ inch (3 mm), cut out six 6 inch (15 cm) discs and place these on the baking sheets.

Now scatter the large basil leaves over the pastry, tearing them first if they're very large. Next, thinly slice the tomatoes and arrange them in circles overlapping each other on top of the basil. Peel the goats' cheese and crumble it over the tomatoes, then pour some olive oil on to a saucer and dip the reserved basil leaves in it, placing one on each tart. Then season well and drizzle each one with a little extra olive oil. Now bake the galettes in the oven, one tray on a high shelf, the other on the next one down, for 10-12 minutes or until the tomatoes are tinged brown and the cheese is bubbling, swapping the baking sheets over halfway through. Serve warm straight from the oven, or they're still excellent cold, cooled on a wire tray.

Feta Cheese, Spinach and Pine Nut Galettes

This is a very Greek combination where, authentically, the filling gets wrapped in pastry parcels. I now prefer this version, though, which has less pastry and is much prettier to look at.

Make the pastry as described on page 119 and chill it for 30 minutes in the fridge. Meanwhile, cook the spinach by placing it in a saucepan with a lid on, then place it over a medium heat. Just let it collapse down into its own juices, timing it for 2-3 minutes and turning it over halfway through. Drain the spinach in a colander, pressing it with a saucer to extract every last bit of juice, then season with a little nutmeg. Next roll out the pastry on a lightly floured surface to ⅛ inch (3 mm), cut out six 6 inch (15 cm) discs and place these on the baking sheets. Finely chop the spinach and divide it between the pastry circles, spreading it out towards the edges of the pastry but leaving a small uncovered rim around the edge. Next scatter the Feta over the spinach, then sprinkle over the pine nuts. Now cook the galettes for 10-12 minutes, one tray on the high shelf, the other on the next one down, until golden brown, swapping the baking sheets over halfway through. Remove from the oven, sprinkle the Parmesan over and serve warm, or cool on a cooling tray.

Serves 3 as a light lunch or 6 as a first course

quick flaky pastry made with 6 oz (175 g) plain flour and 4 oz (110 g) butter (see page 119)
4½ oz (125 g) Feta cheese, chopped into small cubes
8 oz (225 g) young leaf spinach
1 oz (25 g) pine nuts
a little freshly grated nutmeg
1 oz (25g) Parmesan (Parmigiano Reggiano), finely grated

You will also need two solid baking sheets measuring 14 x 11 inches (35 x 28 cm), lightly greased, and a 6 inch (15 cm) plain pastry cutter.

Pre-heat the oven to gas mark 7, 425°F (220°C).

Tomato and Goats' Cheese Galette, far left; Feta Cheese, Spinach and Pine Nut Galette, left

Apricot Galettes with Amaretto

Serves 6
quick flaky pastry made with 6 oz
(175 g) plain flour and 4 oz (110 g)
butter (see page 119)
27 ready-to-eat dried apricots
6 teaspoons amaretto liqueur
18 whole blanched almonds, toasted
and cut into slivers (optional)
6 heaped teaspoons demerara sugar

To serve:
a little icing sugar, sieved
7 fl oz (200 ml) crème fraîche

You will also need two 12 x 10 inch
(30 x 25.5 cm) solid baking sheets,
lightly greased, and a 4 inch (10 cm)
plain pastry cutter.

Dried apricots are great for this in the winter, but in summer it's also good with fresh apricots, in which case you'll need the same quantity of small apricots, halved and stoned.

Make the pastry as described on page 119 and chill for 30 minutes in the fridge. Then roll the pastry out on a lightly floured surface to ⅛ inch (3 mm), cut out six 4 inch (10 cm) discs and place these on the baking sheets. Meanwhile, pre-heat the oven to gas mark 7, 425°F (220°C).

Now cut the apricots in half, then place nine apricot halves on each round of pastry, topped by a few almond slivers (if using). Sprinkle a teaspoon of amaretto over each one, then sprinkle them all with the demerara sugar. Bake for 10-12 minutes in the oven, one tray on the highest shelf, the other on the next one down, until the pastry is crisp and brown and the apricots have browned and caramelised a little at the edges, swapping the baking sheets over halfway through. Serve straight from the oven, sprinkled with icing sugar and the chilled crème fraîche, or leave to cool.

Prune and Apple Galettes

Serves 6
quick flaky pastry made with 6 oz
(175 g) plain flour and 4 oz (110 g)
butter (see page 119)
15 mi-cuit prunes, halved lengthways
3 small Cox's apples (unpeeled)
a little ground cinnamon
2 tablespoons runny honey
cream or crème fraîche, to serve

You will also need two 12 x 10 inch
(30 x 25.5 cm) solid baking sheets,
lightly greased, and a 4 inch (10 cm)
plain pastry cutter.

If you can get mi-cuit plums, the lovely squashy half-dried Agen prunes from France, so much the better. If not, then pitted dried Agen prunes will be fine.

Make the pastry as described on page 119 and chill for 30 minutes in the fridge. Then roll out the pastry on a lightly floured surface to ⅛ inch (3 mm), cut out six 4 inch (10 cm) discs and arrange them on the baking sheets. Meanwhile, pre-heat the oven to gas mark 7, 425°F (220°C).

Now cut each apple into quarters, core and then cut each quarter into two. Then arrange five prune halves and four slices of apple in a circle on top of each pastry round, then sprinkle over a little ground cinnamon. Now place the baking sheets in the oven for 10-12 minutes, one tray on the highest shelf, the other on the next one down, until the galettes are golden brown, swapping them over halfway through. Remove from the oven and, while they are still warm, glaze each one by brushing a little of the runny honey over the prunes and apples. Serve warm with cream or crème fraîche.

Poached Pear Galettes

These are exceptionally pretty to look at, and I like to serve them as a sweet ending to a special meal. They're a bit more trouble, but still very easy to make and assemble.

Make the pastry as described on page 119 and chill for 30 minutes in the fridge. Meanwhile, find a lidded saucepan that will fit the pears comfortably, laying them in the pan on their sides. Now mix the wine with the sugar and pour this over the pears, then add the cinnamon stick and ½ vanilla pod. Put the lid on the pan and gently simmer the pears for 45 minutes, until tender when tested with a skewer. Turn them over halfway through the cooking time so the other half sits in the wine and they colour evenly. Towards the end of the cooking time, pre-heat the oven to gas mark 7, 425°F (220°C). Then roll the pastry out to ⅛ inch (3 mm) thick and cut it into six 4 inch (10 cm) circles, then arrange them on the baking sheets.

Now lift the pears from the liquid and halve them by first making a slit in the stalk as you press it on to a flat surface. Then stand each pear upright and cut through the split stalk, halve the pears and remove the cores. Now you need to slice each half into a fan, so take a sharp knife and, starting from the top of the stalk end, about ½ inch (1 cm) in, slice the pear downwards and at a slight angle so you end up with the slices of pear fanning out but still attached to the stalk. Now place each half pear on to a pastry base and fan it out, then place the baking sheets in the oven for 10-12 minutes, one on the top shelf, the other on the next one down, swapping them over halfway through the cooking time.

Meanwhile, you need to reduce the poaching liquid, so first remove the cinnamon stick and vanilla pod, then place the saucepan over a high heat and let it bubble for about 5 minutes. Then, in a cup, mix the arrowroot with a little cold water until you have a smooth paste, then add this to the saucepan, whisking with a balloon whisk all the time. This will thicken the sauce slightly, then remove it from the heat and leave it to cool.

When the tarts are ready, remove them from the oven. Serve hot or cold but, just before serving, pour a little of the sauce over each tart to give them a pretty glaze.

Serves 6
quick flaky pastry made with 6 oz (175 g) plain flour and 4 oz (110 g) butter (see page 119)
3 firm unripe pears, peeled but with the stalks left on
10 fl oz (275 ml) red wine
1 oz (25 g) caster sugar
½ cinnamon stick
½ vanilla pod
1 teaspoon arrowroot

You will also need two 12 x 10 inch (30 x 25.5 cm) solid baking sheets, lightly greased, and a 4 inch (10 cm) plain pastry cutter.

From top: Poached Pear Galette;
Prune and Apple Galette; Apricot Galette
with Amaretto

Wild Mushroom Tartlets with Poached Quails' Eggs

Serves 6
quick flaky pastry made with 4 oz
(110 g) flour and 3 oz (75 g) butter
(see page 119)
18 quails' eggs
1 quantity Foaming Hollandaise
(see page 71)

For the mushroom filling:
10 oz (275 g) small, dark-gilled
mushrooms
¾ oz (20 g) dried porcini mushrooms,
soaked in boiling water and drained
5 shallots, peeled
1 oz (25 g) butter
⅓ whole nutmeg, grated
sea salt and freshly milled black pepper

You will also need six ½ inch (1 cm)
deep fluted quiche tins with a base
diameter of 3 inches (7.5 cm) and a
top diameter of 3½ inches (9 cm),
greased with a little melted butter, a
medium-sized solid baking sheet, and
a 4 inch (10 cm) plain cutter.

This is my version of one of the most brilliant first courses I've ever eaten. It was created by Michel Bourdin, who was head chef at London's prestigious Connaught Hotel. His version has boiled quails' eggs, but I can't bear the fiddle of peeling them, so I poach them, which cuts out a great deal of time and work. I have Michel's approval, as he told me that he originally did them like this. It's still not the swiftest, easiest course, but when you want something really special for a celebration, this is it.

First, place the fresh and soaked mushrooms and shallots in a food processor till finely chopped. Now melt the butter in a medium-sized pan over a high heat, add the mushroom mixture, nutmeg and seasoning, reduce the heat and gently sauté for 20-25 minutes, until all the juices have evaporated. Then remove from the heat and allow to cool.

On a lightly floured surface, roll out the pastry to ⅛ inch (3 mm) thick and cut out six rounds with the cutter, re-rolling the pastry if necessary. Now line each tin with the pastry, pushing it down from the tops so the pastry doesn't shrink during cooking. Trim the pastry around the tops to ¼ inch (5 mm) and prick the bases with a fork, then refrigerate for 30 minutes.

Pre-heat the oven to gas mark 6, 400°F (200°C). Now place the tins on the baking sheet and bake them on the top shelf of the oven for 15 minutes. (All this can be done well in advance. The mushroom mixture should be cooled, then covered and stored in the fridge, and the pastry cases carefully removed from their tins and stored in an airtight container. The Foaming Hollandaise can also be made in advance and kept at room temperature.)

Then, in a medium-sized frying pan half-filled with boiling water from the kettle, you can begin to poach the eggs. Place the pan over a gentle heat and have a bowl of cold water ready. Now, as soon as the pan has fine bubbles all over the base, make a slit in 6 quails' eggs with a small serrated knife, carefully slipping the eggs in to poach. Put a timer on for 1½ minutes, then, after this time and using a draining spoon, remove them, starting with the first one that went in. Transfer them to the bowl of cold water, then repeat the whole process twice until all the eggs are poached.

With everything ready – the mushroom filling, the tartlet cases, hollandaise and the poached eggs – you can now assemble the tartlets.

When you are ready to serve the tartlets, pre-heat the grill to its highest setting. Next, place the tartlet cases on a baking sheet, cover with foil and pop them under the grill 6 inches (15 cm) from the heat to warm through for 5 minutes. Then, while this is happening, re-heat the mushroom mixture in a small saucepan and get it really hot. Then fill the pastry cases with the mushroom mixture and top each one with 3 quails' eggs, using a draining spoon and a wodge of kitchen paper to drain off any water. Next spoon the Foaming Hollandaise over, then pop the whole lot back under the grill again, at least 6 inches (15 cm) from the heat, and watch like a hawk – it should take only 30 seconds for the sauce to warm through and brown slightly. Then switch the grill off and serve on warm plates as quickly as possible.

Caramelised Mincemeat Ravioli

This is a beautiful bite-sized version of mince pies, and I think not as fiddly. If you don't have a pastry wheel you can forgo the frilly edge and use a sharp knife to cut the pastry.

First make the pastry as described on page 119 and chill for 30 minutes. Then remove the rested pastry from the fridge on to a floured surface and shape it into an oblong. Cut the oblong into two, one piece slightly larger than the other, then, on a lightly floured surface, first roll the smaller piece into a rectangle 12 x 10 inches (30 x 25.5 cm), roll it around the rolling pin and transfer it to the baking sheet.

Next brush the surface of the pastry with the beaten egg, then, with the oblong turned lengthways, place 5 level teaspoons of mincemeat along one top edge and carry on with another row until you end up with six rows of mincemeat blobs. Now roll the larger piece of pastry into another oblong approximately 13 x 11 inches (32.5 x 28 cm), transfer this again by wrapping it around the rolling pin, and lay it carefully over the bottom piece of pastry, being careful not to trap too much air. Now gently press the pastry together to seal the little squares, then trim the edges and cut the whole lot into little squares using the pastry wheel. Next, with a pair of small scissors, make 2 little snips in each one to allow the air to escape. Now bake the whole lot in the oven for 15 minutes or until golden brown.

To serve, pre-heat the grill to its highest setting for at least 10 minutes, then sprinkle the ravioli liberally with the sifted icing sugar and place them under the grill, very close to the heat source, for 40-60 seconds. What will happen is the icing sugar will caramelise to a lovely shiny glaze. Then serve dusted with a little more icing sugar as soon as they have cooled enough to eat, or cool and serve cold. Alternatively, re-heat and serve warm later.

Makes 30
quick flaky pastry made with 8 oz (225 g) plain flour and 6 oz (175 g) butter (see page 119)
7 oz (200 g) good-quality mincemeat
1 large egg, beaten
1 oz (25 g) icing sugar, sifted, plus extra for dusting

You will also need a solid baking sheet measuring 16 x 12 inches (40 x 30 cm), lightly greased, and a pastry wheel.

Pre-heat the oven to gas mark 6, 400°F (200°C).

6
Cakes and biscuits for beginners

If you think you can't make a cake, let me tell you now that you most certainly can. Cake-making is not the minefield of possible disaster that many people imagine it to be. Basically, there are only two things you have to remember: number one is to always follow the rules, and number two is to always follow the recipe. Making a cake can never be a throw-it-all-in-and-see-what-happens affair, and people who boast about never following recipes are, I suspect, happy with a good deal of mediocrity. The perfect cake, as I've said, needs close attention to the rules, and once you know what they are, it makes the whole thing blissfully clear and simple.

When making cakes, it's vital that the butter you use is extremely soft

The all-in-one method means that all the ingredients go into the bowl together…

…then are whipped to a smooth, soft consistency using a hand-held whisk

The case for making a cake

A home-made cake has a lot going for it on days when life seems to lack that special edge. So instead of attempting to treat yourself to something bland and boring made in a factory, why not try the real thing? Home baking transports you psychologically to a world of comfort and wellbeing – the quality of life seems utterly assured as your home is filled with the warm, evocative aroma of something quietly and happily baking in the oven.

In my *Book Of Cakes*, published way back in 1977, I wrote: 'A cake is a symbol of love and friendship – if someone actually goes to the trouble of baking a cake specially for family and friends, they can't fail to feel spoiled and cared for.' I haven't changed my mind on that, but perhaps the simplest way to start venturing towards a lifetime of happy cakemaking is to take the rules on board and try to memorise them.

The top five rules of cakemaking

1 It is absolutely crucial to use the correct-sized tin
2 You must have a reliable recipe
3 You need to weigh the ingredients correctly
4 Once the cake is in the oven, don't open the door
5 Make sure your oven is functioning correctly

Tin size

This is where 99 per cent of cakemaking goes wrong. I have, over the years, struggled to encourage manufacturers to standardise tin sizes so that people like me, who write and test recipes, are able to communicate in such a way that as many people as possible can enjoy making cakes. Well, I'm sorry to report that until now I have failed, due, I think, to the unacceptable face of commercialism, which also seeks to undercut the competition.

Let me explain. The most popular everyday cake is probably a sponge cake. Well, it's all quite simple: three eggs and a 6 oz (175 g) flour mix fit an 8 inch (20 cm) tin that's 1½ inches (4 cm) deep; two eggs and a 4 oz (110 g) flour mixture fit a 7 inch (18 cm) tin with the same depth. But out there in the high street you will find 7½, 8¾, 7¾ inches. Why? Because the way manufacturers undercut on price is to make tins fractionally smaller and thus cheaper. There is quite a lot of pile-it-high, sell-it-cheap rubbish out there that claims to be baking equipment, so my advice is to only buy the right-sized tins, which thankfully one manufacturer has guaranteed to make, and though quality is costly in the beginning, it *will* last a lifetime. The cheap versions, which need to be constantly replaced, work out to be a lot more expensive.

Depth of tin

This is also crucial, so a sponge tin has to be at least 1½ inches (4 cm) deep because depth of support at the sides encourages the cakes to rise up and be as light and airy as possible.

Larger cake tins

These seem more easily available. An 8 inch (20 cm) round cake tin is a good average size, but remember that if you use a square tin, the same mixture will fit 7 inches (18 cm); the rule is that square tins should always be 1 inch (2.5 cm) smaller than round ones.

Loaf tins

These change like the wind and vary between manufacturers, but thankfully old-fashioned bread tins, as used in Chapter 4, are always available, so I use these for loaf cake recipes. They come in a 2 lb/900 g (7¼ x 4½ x 3½ inches/ 18.5 x 11.5 x 9 cm) or 1 lb/450 g (6 x 3¾ x 2¾ inches/15 x 9.5 x 7 cm) size.

Weighing ingredients

Provided you have a reliable recipe and the right-sized tin, the next step is to weigh everything carefully. The best scales are the balance kind; they will last a lifetime and never let you down. Weighing ingredients in cakemaking is absolutely vital, so never attempt to make a cake if you don't have any means of weighing the ingredients.

Lining sponge tins

Whether or not you use non-stick tins, it's important to line them with non-stick silicone paper (baking parchment), which gives the cake some protection but also makes it easier to remove from the tin. The way to line a sponge tin is shown in the photograph, above right.

Cooling trays

In most cases, once cakes are cooked it's important to cool them with air circulating around them, so a wire cooling tray is a vital piece of equipment.

Please leave it alone!

One of the perennial problems of beginning to cook is curiosity. You've done it, you've made the cake, but it's now out of your sight sitting behind a closed oven door, and even if it's glass, you can't see over the rim of the tin, so you feel anxious, cut off and all you want to do is just have one little peep. Please don't, because it will be a disaster! Without being too technical, what happens to the cake mixture is that the heat causes the air bubbles within it to push up and expand the mixture, making a light, airy cake, and this only happens if the heat is constant until finally the cake has reached a point where it can't expand any more and the structure is set. What happens if you open the oven door is that you send a rush of cold air in, which diminishes the heat and interrupts the expansion process. So instead of rising to great heights, the cake collapses and sinks into heaviness. So now you know *never* to open the door of the oven until at least three-quarters of the cooking time has elapsed.

It's important that the base of the tin is lined with silicone paper (parchment)

Once the mixture is in the tin, level it off using the back of a spoon

Once cooked, turn the cake on to a wire rack, then peel off the base paper

How do I know if it's cooked?

For years, and when I first started cooking, the rule of thumb here was to stick a skewer in the centre of the cake and, if it came out clean, the centre was cooked. But I have changed my mind on that particular rule, firstly because I never found it reliable, and secondly, if the cake had fruit in it, then obviously if the skewer had passed through a sticky raisin it wouldn't be coming out clean, even if the cake was cooked. Now I feel the best test is to press lightly on the centre surface of the cake with your finger (doesn't matter which one), then, if the cake springs back without leaving an impression, it's cooked; if not, give it another 5 minutes.

Cake ingredients

Because I have attempted to simplify things and make cakemaking easily accessible to absolute beginners, I have only included recipes for cakes that are made by the all-in-one method. This means everything is mixed together in just one mixing, so a few notes on the ingredients might be useful here.

Butter and other fats

This must be very soft indeed (see the picture on page 128) so the flat blade of a knife can make a deep impression all the way through immediately. Therefore, I always leave the butter out of the fridge to stay at room temperature overnight, which works beautifully – but as I said in Chapter 5, you may need to leave a note on the fridge door to remind you. Other fats, such as soft margarine or whipped white vegetable fats, need only be out of the fridge for 30 minutes; they produce excellent results but don't, in my opinion, have the flavour of butter.

Flours and raising agents

In most cases cakes are made with self-raising flour, which already has a raising agent, but all-in-one mixtures need a little extra help, so baking powder is also used. Always sift the flour, lifting the sieve up high to give it lots of air as it falls down into the bowl, as air is an important ingredient.

Eggs

Cakes require large eggs (as do all my recipes), and if you keep them in the fridge, remember to remove them one hour before you start baking as they blend more easily with the other ingredients if they're not too cold.

Ovens

As a cookery writer struggling to give people foolproof recipes, all I can say is if I could wave a magic wand so that we all had the same oven, life would be so simple, but every single oven seems to vary. We have fan ovens, fan-assisted ovens, ovens without fans and then all the Aga-type cookers and so on. A cake is a very good test of an oven – if it browns too much on one side and not on the other, it's not your fault – you need to have your oven checked. If cakes are overcooked or undercooked, the temperature thermostat may be faulty. Remember, it's very simple to have it tested professionally, and it only takes about 5 minutes. Alternatively, what I find really useful is having my own thermometer. You can pop this in the oven when you pre-heat it and it will tell you simply and clearly if your oven temperature is true. If it isn't, then you really must have the oven checked.

Fan ovens

Here you must follow the manufacturer's instructions. Because fan ovens vary from manufacturer to manufacturer, it's impossible for me to give correct timings for all of them. So the answer here is to calculate the cooking time according to your oven instruction manual; ie, in a fan oven the heat temperature will be lower and the cooking time will be slightly reduced, and no pre-heating will be needed.

Conventional ovens

This is my preferred choice, and here it is necessary to pre-heat the oven about 10-20 minutes before the cake goes in.

To line a round, greased cake tin, cut a strip of greaseproof paper slightly longer than the circumference of the tin and 3 inches (7.5 cm) higher. Fold it back about 1 inch (2.5 cm) along its length, then snip it at a slight angle at intervals up to the fold. Now press the paper around the sides – the snipped edge will overlap on the base of the tin for a snug fit. Finally, cut a circle out – using the tin as a template – to fit over the snipped paper over the base

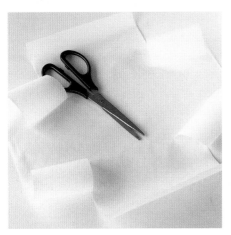

To line a square tin, cut a piece of greaseproof paper to size by first measuring the length and width of the tin and then adding twice its depth. Centre the tin on the sheet of paper, then make four cuts from the paper's edge right up to the corners of the tin. Grease the tin and fit the greaseproof paper inside, folding and overlapping it at the corners. For the base paper, cut a square out, again using the tin as a template, and fit it in the base

A Classic Sponge Cake (with Passion-Fruit Filling)

This sponge cake could also be made in a 7 inch (18 cm) tin (just use two eggs and 4 oz/110 g each of flour, sugar and butter). It can then be filled with jam and cream. And while the soft fruits of summer, when they're available, are perfect for filling sponge cakes, in winter, passion fruit fulfil all the criteria needed, ie, something sharp, fragrant and acidic to contrast with the richness of the cake and cream.

Serves 8
For an 8 inch (20 cm) cake:
6 oz (175 g) self-raising flour
1 rounded teaspoon baking powder
3 large eggs at room temperature
6 oz (175 g) very soft butter
6 oz (175 g) golden caster sugar
½ teaspoon vanilla extract
a little sifted icing sugar, for dusting

For the filling:
6 passion fruit
9 oz (250 g) Mascarpone
7 fl oz (200 ml) fromage frais
1 dessertspoon golden caster sugar
1 teaspoon vanilla extract

You will also need two 8 inch (20 cm) 1½ inch (4 cm) deep sponge tins, lightly greased and the bases lined with silicone paper (parchment).

Pre-heat the oven to gas mark 3, 325°F (170°C).

Take a very large mixing bowl, put the flour and baking powder in a sieve and sift it into the bowl, holding the sieve high to give it a good airing as it goes down. Now all you do is simply add all the other cake ingredients to the bowl and, provided the butter is really soft, just go in with an electric hand whisk and whisk everything together until you have a smooth, well-combined mixture, which will take about 1 minute. If you don't have an electric hand whisk, you can use a wooden spoon, using a little bit more effort. What you will now end up with is a mixture that drops off a spoon when you give it a tap on the side of the bowl. If it seems a little too stiff, add a little water and mix again.

Now divide the mixture between the 2 tins, level it out and place the tins on the centre shelf of the oven. The cakes will take 30-35 minutes to cook, but don't open the oven door until 30 minutes have elapsed. To test whether the cakes are cooked or not, touch the centre of each lightly with a finger: if it leaves no impression and the sponges spring back, they are ready.

Next, remove them from the oven, then wait about 5 minutes before turning them out on to a wire cooling rack. Carefully peel off the base papers, which is easier if you make a fold in the paper first, then pull it gently away without trying to lift it off. Now leave the sponges to get completely cold, then add the filling.

To make this, first slice the passion fruit into halves and, using a teaspoon, scoop all the flesh, juice and seeds into a bowl. Next, in another bowl, combine the Mascarpone, fromage frais, sugar and vanilla extract using a balloon whisk, which is the quickest way to blend them all together. After that, fold in about two-thirds of the passion fruit. Now place the first sponge cake on the plate or cake stand you are going to serve it on, then spread half the filling over it, drizzle the rest of the passion fruit over that, then spread the remaining filling over the passion fruit. Lastly, place the other cake on top, press it gently so that the filling oozes out at the edges, then dust the surface with a little sifted icing sugar.

Banana and Walnut Loaf

This is a lovely, moist cake that keeps well and is perfect for picnics or packed lunches. In the summer it's brilliant served cut in thick slices and spread with clotted cream.

Begin, as soon as the oven has pre-heated, by spreading the nuts out on a baking sheet and toasting them lightly in the oven for 7-8 minutes – use a timer so that you don't forget them. After that, remove them from the oven to a chopping board, let them cool briefly, then chop them fairly roughly. Now, in a bowl, peel and mash 3 of the bananas to a purée with a fork, and peel and chop the other one into ½ inch (1 cm) chunks.

Next you need to take a large mixing bowl and sift the salt, baking powder, cinnamon and both the flours into it, holding the sieve up high to give it a good airing, then adding the bran that's left in the sieve. Now simply add all the remaining ingredients (except the chopped banana and nuts) and, using an electric hand whisk, begin to beat the mixture, first on a slow speed for about half a minute, then increasing the speed to mix everything thoroughly and smoothly. Then lightly fold in the chopped banana and walnuts. You may need to add a drop of milk to give a mixture that drops easily off a spoon when you give it a sharp tap on the side of the bowl.

Next pile the mixture into the tin, level the top with the back of a spoon and sprinkle on the demerara sugar. Bake in the centre of the oven for 1¼-1½ hours, until the cake feels springy in the centre. After that, remove it from the oven and let it cool for about 5 minutes before turning it out on to a wire tray. Then let it get completely cold before serving or transferring it to a cake tin.

Serves 8
4 medium bananas (approximately 12 oz/350 g)
6 oz (175 g) walnut pieces
pinch of salt
1 rounded teaspoon baking powder
1 teaspoon ground cinnamon
4 oz (110 g) plain flour
4 oz (110 g) wholewheat flour
grated zest 1 orange
grated zest 1 lemon
4 oz (110 g) butter at room temperature
6 oz (175 g) soft dark brown sugar
2 large eggs at room temperature

For the topping:
1 tablespoon demerara sugar

You will also need a 2 lb (900 g) loaf tin, lightly buttered.

Pre-heat the oven to gas mark 4, 350°F (180°C).

Austrian Coffee and Walnut Cake with Coffee Cream

This is unashamedly rich and luscious. Firstly, coffee and walnuts have a great affinity; secondly, so do coffee and creaminess; and thirdly, because the cake is soaked in coffee syrup, it's also meltingly moist.

First of all you need to toast all the walnuts, so spread them on a baking sheet and place in the pre-heated oven for 7-8 minutes. After that, reserve 10 halves to use as decoration later and finely chop the rest. Take a very large mixing bowl, put the flour and baking powder in a sieve and sift it into the bowl, holding the sieve high to give it a good airing as it goes down.

Now all you do is simply add all the other ingredients (except the coffee and walnuts) to the bowl and, provided the butter is really soft, just go in with an electric hand whisk and whisk everything together until you have a smooth, well-combined mixture, then fold in the coffee and chopped walnuts. This will take about 1 minute but, if you don't have an electric hand whisk, you can use a wooden spoon and a little bit more effort. What you should end up with is a soft mixture that drops off the spoon easily when you give it a sharp tap; if not, add a spot of water. Divide the mixture between the prepared sandwich tins, spreading the mixture around evenly. Then place the tins on the centre shelf of the oven and bake them for 30 minutes.

While the cakes are cooking you can make up the syrup and the filling and topping. For the syrup, first place the coffee and sugar in a heatproof jug, then measure the boiling water into it and stir briskly until the coffee and sugar have dissolved, which will take about 1 minute. Next, the filling and topping, and all you do here is place all the ingredients, except the reserved walnuts, in a bowl and whisk them together till thoroughly blended. Then cover the bowl with clingfilm and chill till needed.

When the cakes are cooked, ie, feel springy in the centre, remove then from the oven but leave them in their tins and prick them all over with a skewer while they are still hot. Now spoon the syrup as evenly as possible over each one and leave them to soak up the liquid as they cool in their tins. When they are absolutely cold, turn them out very carefully and peel off the base papers – it's a good idea to turn one out on to the plate you're going to serve it on. Then spread half the filling and topping mixture over the first cake, place the other cake carefully on top and spread the other half over. Finally, arrange the reserved walnut halves in a circle all around. It's a good idea to chill the cake if you're not going to serve it immediately.

Serves 8
For the sponge cake:
1½ tablespoons instant coffee mixed with 2 tablespoons boiling water
3 oz (75 g) walnut halves
6 oz (175 g) self-raising flour
1½ teaspoons baking powder
6 oz (175 g) softened butter
6 oz (175 g) golden caster sugar
3 large eggs at room temperature

For the syrup:
1 tablespoon instant espresso coffee powder
2 oz (50 g) demerara sugar
2 fl oz (55 ml) boiling water

For the filling and topping:
1 tablespoon instant espresso coffee powder
1 rounded tablespoon golden caster sugar
10 walnut halves, reserved from the sponge cake
9 oz (250 g) Mascarpone
7 fl oz (200 ml) 8 per cent fat fromage frais

You will also need two 8 inch (20 cm) sandwich tins, 1½ inches (4 cm) deep, lightly greased and the bases lined with silicone paper (parchment).

Pre-heat the oven to gas mark 3, 325°F (170°C).

135

Fresh Coconut Layer Cake

The key word here is 'fresh'. Whilst some cakes are made with desiccated coconut, using fresh coconut puts this into a different league. Fresh coconut is very moist and has a fragrant, slightly sour, sweet flesh that is perfect for this cake.

Serves 8
For the cake:
3 oz (75 g) finely grated fresh coconut
6 oz (175 g) self-raising flour
1 rounded teaspoon baking powder
3 large eggs at room temperature
6 oz (175 g) very soft butter
6 oz (175 g) golden caster sugar
1 teaspoon vanilla extract

For the coconut frosting:
1½ oz (40 g) finely grated fresh coconut
9 oz (250 g) Mascarpone
7 fl oz (200 ml) fromage frais
1 teaspoon vanilla extract
1 dessertspoon golden caster sugar

For the topping and sides:
2 oz (50 g) coarsely grated fresh coconut

You will also need two 8 inch (20 cm) sandwich tins with a depth of 1½ inches (4 cm), lightly greased and the bases lined with silicone paper (parchment).

Pre-heat the oven to gas mark 3, 325°F (170°C).

Before you start this cake, you'll first have to deal with the coconut. Not half as impenetrable as it might seem, as all you do is first push a skewer into the three holes in the top of the coconut and drain out the milk. Then place the coconut in a polythene bag and sit it on a hard surface – a stone floor or an outside paving stone. Then give it a hefty whack with a hammer – it won't be that difficult to break. Now remove the pieces from the bag and, using a cloth to protect your hands, prise the top of a knife between the nut and the shell. You should find that you can force the whole piece out in one go. Now discard the shell and take off the inner skin using a potato peeler. The coconut is now ready to use. The best way to grate coconut flesh is with the grating disc of a food processor, but a hand grater will do just as well.

To make the cake, sieve the flour and baking powder into a large bowl, holding the sieve high to give them a good airing. Now just add all the other ingredients, except the grated coconut, to the bowl and go in with an electric hand whisk and combine everything until you have a smooth mixture, which will take about 1 minute. If you don't have an electric hand whisk, use a wooden spoon, using a little more effort. What you should now have is a mixture that drops off a spoon when you give it a tap on the side of the bowl. If it seems a little stiff, add a drop of water and mix again. Finally, stir in the finely grated coconut and divide the mixture between the tins. Now place them on the centre shelf of the oven for 30-35 minutes. To test whether the cakes are cooked, lightly touch the centre of each with a finger: if it leaves no impression and the sponges spring back, they are ready.

Next, remove them from the oven, then wait about 5 minutes before turning them out on to a wire cooling rack. Carefully peel off the base papers, and when the cakes are absolutely cold, carefully divide each one horizontally into two halves using a very sharp serrated knife.

Now make up the frosting by simply whisking all the ingredients together in a bowl to combine them. Next select the plate or stand you want to serve the cake on – you'll also need a palette knife – then simply place one cake layer on first, followed by a thin layer of frosting (about a fifth), followed by the next layer of cake and frosting, and so on. After that, use the rest of the frosting to coat the sides and top of the cake. Don't worry how it looks: the good thing is that it's all going to be covered with the rest of the grated coconut next. And that's it!

Low-Fat Moist Carrot Cake

I have been making carrot cake for years, and each time it seems to improve with a little tinkering here and there. Last year I attempted a low-fat version rather reluctantly, not believing it was possible. Now I have to admit it's become one of my favourites. It's also one of the quickest, easiest cakes ever.

Serves 12

6 oz (175 g) dark brown soft sugar, sifted
2 large eggs at room temperature
4 fl oz (120 ml) sunflower oil
7 oz (200 g) wholemeal self-raising flour
1½ teaspoons bicarbonate of soda
3 rounded teaspoons mixed spice
grated zest 1 orange
7 oz (200 g) carrots, peeled and coarsely grated
6 oz (175 g) sultanas

For the topping:
9 oz (250 g) Quark (skimmed-milk soft cheese)
¾ oz (20 g) caster sugar
2 teaspoons vanilla extract
1 rounded teaspoon ground cinnamon, plus a little extra for dusting

For the syrup glaze:
juice ½ small orange
1 dessertspoon lemon juice
1½ oz (40 g) dark brown soft sugar

You will also need a non-stick oblong cake tin measuring 6½ x 10 inches (16 x 25.5 cm), top measurement 7 x 10½ inches (18 x 26.5 cm), 1½ inch (4 cm) deep, the base lined with silicone paper (parchment).

Pre-heat the oven to gas mark 3, 325°F (170°C).

Begin by whisking the sugar, eggs and oil together in a bowl using an electric hand whisk for 2-3 minutes. Then sift together the flour, bicarbonate of soda and the mixed spice into the bowl, tipping in all the bits of bran that are left in the sieve. Now stir all this together, then fold in the orange zest, carrots and sultanas. After that pour the mixture into the prepared tin and bake on the centre shelf of the oven for 35-40 minutes, until it is well risen and feels firm and springy to the touch when lightly pressed in the centre.

While the cake is cooking, make the topping by mixing all the ingredients in a bowl until light and fluffy, then cover with clingfilm and chill for 1-2 hours or until needed.

Now you need to make the syrup glaze, and to do this whisk together the fruit juices and sugar in a bowl. Then, when the cake comes out of the oven, stab it all over with a skewer and quickly spoon the syrup over as evenly as possible. Now leave the cake on one side to cool in the tin, during which time the syrup will be absorbed. Then, when the cake is completely cold, remove it from the tin, spread the topping over, cut it into 12 squares and dust with a little more cinnamon.

Spiced Apple Muffin Cake with Pecan Streusel Topping

I have included this because I still get letters from people saying they can't make muffins. My message to them is don't try too hard – undermixing is the golden rule and, once mastered, the American muffin mix makes the lightest cakes in the world. In the summer, you could always substitute the apples for 12 oz (350 g) of fresh apricots, stoned and chopped, or, in the autumn, 12 oz (350 g) of plums, stoned and chopped. In both cases, though, weigh after stoning. This recipe will also make 24 mini or 12 large muffins, cooking them for 20 and 30 minutes respectively.

First of all place the butter in a small saucepan and put it on a gentle heat to melt. Then, as with all muffin mixtures, you need to sift the dry ingredients twice, so place the flour, baking powder, salt, cinnamon, cloves and grated nutmeg in a sieve and sieve them into a bowl. Then, in another large mixing bowl, whisk the eggs, sugar and milk together, pour the melted butter into the egg mixture and give it all another good whisk. Now sift the flour mixture again straight in on top of the egg mixture and fold it in using as *few* folds as possible. Ignore the horrible lumpy mixture you're now faced with and don't be tempted to overmix. I think this is where people go wrong: they can't believe that what looks like a disaster can possibly turn into something *so* light and luscious. Now fold in the chopped apple and then spoon the whole lot into the tin, levelling off the surface.

Next, make the topping, and you can use the same bowl. Just add the flour, sugar and cinnamon and rub the butter in with your fingertips until crumbly. Finally, sprinkle in the nuts and cold water, then press the mixture loosely together. Again, it will be quite lumpy – no problem! Now spoon the topping over the surface of the cake, then bake on the centre shelf of the oven for about 1¼ hours, until it feels springy in the centre. Allow the cake to cool in the tin for 30 minutes before removing the sides, then gently slide a palette knife under the base and transfer the cake to a wire rack to finish cooling. Serve this as fresh as possible, either on its own or warm as a dessert with whipped cream, crème fraîche or vanilla ice cream.

Serves 10-12

12 oz (350 g) Bramley apples (weight after peeling and coring), chopped into ½ inch (1 cm) cubes
4 oz (110 g) butter
10 oz (275 g) plain flour
1 tablespoon plus 1 teaspoon baking powder
½ teaspoon salt
1 heaped teaspoon ground cinnamon
1 teaspoon ground cloves
½ whole nutmeg, grated
2 large eggs at room temperature
3 oz (75 g) golden caster sugar
6 fl oz (175 ml) milk

For the pecan streusel topping:
2 oz (50 g) pecan nuts, roughly chopped
3 oz (75 g) self-raising flour
3 oz (75 g) demerara sugar
1 rounded teaspoon ground cinnamon
1 oz (25 g) soft butter
1 tablespoon cold water

You will also need a 9 inch (23 cm) springform cake tin, lightly greased and the base lined with silicone paper (parchment).

Pre-heat the oven to gas mark 5, 375°F (190°C).

Irish Whiskey Christmas Cakes

Makes four 4 inch (10 cm) square cakes or an 8 inch (20 cm) square cake

For the pre-soaking:

10 fl oz (275 ml) Irish whiskey
1½ teaspoons Angostura bitters
1 lb (450 g) raisins
8 oz (225 g) currants
4 oz (110 g) stoned no-soak prunes
2 oz (50 g) glacé cherries
2 oz (50 g) unblanched almonds
4 oz (110 g) mixed candied peel
½ rounded teaspoon ground cinnamon
½ teaspoon freshly grated nutmeg
½ teaspoon ground cloves
1½ teaspoons vanilla extract
1 tablespoon molasses sugar
grated zest 1 orange
grated zest 1 lemon
½ teaspoon salt

For the cake:

9 oz (250 g) self-raising flour, sifted
9 oz (250 g) demerara sugar
9 oz (250 g) unsalted butter, softened
5 large eggs at room temperature
1 heaped tablespoon apricot jam
1 tablespoon Irish whiskey

For the icing:

1 lb 2 oz (500 g) marzipan (in a block)
1 lb 4 oz (570 g) unrefined golden icing sugar, plus a little extra for rolling
1 large egg white
1 dessertspoon molasses syrup or black treacle
2½ tablespoons Irish whiskey

You will also need an 8 inch (20 cm) square cake tin, greased, the base and sides lined with a double thickness of silicone paper (parchment) to sit 4 inches (10 cm) deep.

If you've never made a Christmas cake before, this one is dead easy, and you won't be disappointed. I now prefer the much thinner layer of marzipan and icing, and the flavour of the Irish whiskey in the icing, as well as the cake, is brilliant. The instructions here are for four small cakes; measurements for the large one are in the caption opposite. If you want to keep the cake for any length of time, let the marzipan dry out (covered with a clean tea cloth) for a week before icing.

One week before you intend to bake the cake, measure out the whiskey, bitters and 3 tablespoons of water into a large saucepan, then roughly chop the prunes, cherries and almonds and finely dice the mixed candied peel. Add these, along with the rest of the pre-soaking ingredients, to the pan, ticking them as you go to make sure nothing gets left out. Now stir and bring the mixture up to simmering point, then, keeping the heat low, simmer very gently, without a lid, for 15 minutes. After that, allow everything to cool completely, then pour the mixture into a large jar with a lid or an airtight plastic container and leave it in the fridge for seven days, giving it a little shake from time to time.

When you're ready to bake the cake, pre-heat the oven to gas mark 1, 275°F (140°C). If you are using a gas oven that was made after 1992, you will need to cook this cake at gas mark 2.

All you need to do is measure out the flour, sugar and butter into a very large bowl, then add the eggs and either whisk or beat with a wooden spoon until everything is evenly blended. Now gradually fold in the fruit mixture until it is evenly distributed. Then spoon the mixture into the prepared tin, levelling the surface with the back of the spoon. Bake in the centre of the oven for 3 hours without opening the door, then cover the cake with a double thickness of greaseproof paper and continue to bake it for a further 30 minutes or until the centre feels springy when lightly touched.

Cool the cake for 45 minutes in the tin, then remove it to a wire rack to finish cooling. When it's completely cold, wrap it in a double layer of greaseproof paper, then foil, and store it in an airtight container.

When you are ready to finish the cake, first take a sharp knife and cut the cake into quarters so you end up with four smaller 4 inch (10 cm) square cakes. Then melt the jam with the whiskey in a small saucepan and stir it a few times until all the lumps have dissolved. Now, using a brush, coat the surface of each cake quite generously with it. Take the marzipan and cut off a quarter of the block, then, on a surface lightly dusted with icing sugar, roll the piece into an 8 inch (20 cm) square. Now, with a sharp knife, cut the square into quarters so you end up with four 4 inch (10 cm) square pieces. Gently take each square and place one on top of each cake, lightly pressing the marzipan down. Next, cut the remaining piece of marzipan in half and roll each half into a strip measuring 6 x 16 inches (15 x 40 cm), then cut each strip in half lengthways so you are left with four strips: one for the sides of each cake. Press each strip lightly around the edges of each cake and pinch to seal at the join with the top piece of marzipan.

For the icing, sieve the icing sugar, then place the egg white and molasses (or black treacle) in a large bowl and, using an electric hand whisk, whisk together thoroughly. Now, with the whisk running, add a tablespoon of icing sugar at a time and keep adding it until the mixture thickens. As it begins to crumble, add a tablespoon of the Irish whiskey to combine the mixture, then carry on adding more icing sugar until it becomes thick. Add another tablespoon of whiskey, then the rest of the icing sugar and whiskey, and keep whisking until everything is blended together.

Now divide the icing into four and, using a palette knife, smooth it over the top and down the sides of each cake, dipping the knife into a small saucepan of simmering water to make it easier to spread. To give the cakes a nice finish, dip the knife in the simmering water once more and make swirls with the knife over the cakes, then leave them to dry overnight. Wrap each cake in greaseproof paper, then in foil, and keep in an airtight container. To decorate the cakes, you'll need four lengths of ribbon, each 4 ft (1.2 m) long and 1½ inches (4 cm) wide. When you're ready to finish the cakes, carefully place a length of ribbon around each one, tying the ends in a bow.

For the 8 inch (20 cm) cake, take the marzipan and cut off a quarter of the block, then roll this piece out to an 8 inch (20 cm) square. Cut the remaining piece in half and roll each half into a strip measuring 3 x 16 inches (7.5 x 40 cm), then use these strips to cover the sides of the cake. To decorate the cake, you will need a length of ribbon 6½ ft (2 m) long and about 1½ inches (4 cm) wide

Irish Tea Bread

It's always hard for me to believe that this simple little fruit loaf can taste so good. When we were testing recipes, this one disappeared the fastest – none of us could resist just one more little bit. It's good all by itself or spread with butter, and it's quite brilliant toasted. The recipe makes two loaves, so you can pop the other one in the freezer and keep it for a rainy day.

Begin this the evening before by placing all the fruits, including the candied peel, in a bowl, then dissolve the sugar in the hot tea, pour this over the fruits, cover the bowl and leave it overnight so the fruits become plump and juicy.

The next day, pre-heat the oven to gas mark 3, 325°F (170°C), then place the nuts on a baking sheet and pop them into the oven for 6-8 minutes (use a timer, as they burn easily). Then, when they're cool, roughly chop them. Next, add the beaten egg mixture to the bowl containing the fruits. Then sift in the flour, add the toasted nuts and give everything a really good mixing. Now divide the mixture between the prepared loaf tins and bake them in the centre of the oven for 1¼-1½ hours, until they feel springy in the centre. Then straight away, loosen them with a palette knife and turn them out on to a wire rack to cool. Then have patience – it won't be long before you can taste some.

Makes 2 small loaves
8 oz (225 g) raisins
8 oz (225 g) currants
8 oz (225 g) sultanas
4 oz (110g) whole candied peel,
cut into ¼ inch (5 mm) pieces
8 oz (225 g) demerara sugar
10 fl oz (275 ml) Lapsang Souchong,
Earl Grey or any other hot tea
4 oz (110 g) pecan nuts
1 large egg at room temperature,
lightly beaten with 2 tablespoons milk
1 lb (450 g) self-raising flour

You will also need two 1 lb (450 g) loaf tins, the bases lined with silicone paper (parchment).

Chocolate Almond Crunchies

Although you can now buy really good-quality biscuits and American cookies, making them at home still has the edge, and as biscuits are so easy, it's a very good place to start if you are a beginner in home baking. I've used 'adult' chocolate in these, but for children, chocolate chips would do fine.

First of all, using a sharp knife, chop the chocolate into small chunks about ¼ inch (5 mm) square. Now put the butter, sugar and syrup in a saucepan, place it on the gentlest heat possible and let it all dissolve, which will take 2-3 minutes. Meanwhile, chop the nuts into small chunks about the same size as the chocolate pieces. When the butter mixture has dissolved, take it off the heat. In a large mixing bowl, sift in the flour and salt and add the porridge oats and half the chocolate and nuts, then give this a quick mix before pouring in the butter mixture. Now, using a wooden spoon, stir and mix everything together, then switch from a spoon to your hands to bring everything together to form a dough. If it seems a bit dry, add a few drops of cold water.

Now take half the dough and divide it into nine lumps the size of a large walnut, then roll them into rounds using the flat of your hand. Place them on a worktop and press gently to flatten them out into rounds approximately 2½ inches (6 cm) in diameter, then scatter half the remaining chocolate and almonds on top of the biscuits, pressing them down lightly. Once you have filled one tray (give them enough room to spread out during baking), bake them on the middle shelf of the oven for 15 minutes whilst you prepare the second tray. When they're all cooked, leave them to cool on the baking sheets for 10 minutes, then transfer them to a wire rack to finish cooling. You could store the biscuits in a sealed container, but I doubt you'll have any left!

Crunchie variations

For *Apricot Pecan Crunchies*, use 2 oz (50 g) of dried apricots and 1½ oz (40 g) of pecans, chopped, instead of the chocolate and almonds.
For *Cherry and Flaked-Almond Crunchies*, use 2 oz (50 g) of dried sour cherries and 1½ oz (40 g) of flaked almonds.
For *Raisin Hazelnut Crunchies*, use 2 oz (50 g) of raisins and 1½ oz (40 g) of hazelnuts.

Makes 18
2 oz (50 g) dark continental chocolate
(75 per cent cocoa)
4 oz (110 g) butter
3 oz (75 g) demerara sugar
1 dessertspoon golden syrup
1½ oz (40 g) whole almonds,
unblanched
4 oz (110 g) self-raising flour
pinch of salt
4 oz (110 g) porridge oats

You will also need two baking sheets measuring 14 x 11 inches (35 x 28 cm), lightly greased with groundnut or another flavourless oil.

Pre-heat the oven to gas mark 3, 325°F (170°C).

From top: Chocolate Almond Crunchie, Apricot Pecan Crunchie, Cherry and Flaked-Almond Crunchie

7

Flour-based sauces and batter

Don't, whatever you do, be
daunted by the subject of
saucemaking. How the enormous
amount of fear that's attached to
the subject was first generated
it's hard to say, but now is the
time to sweep it away, along
with all those packets of strange-
sounding chemicals and
ingredients that masquerade
under the name of sauce. So
stop thinking too thin, too thick
or, worst of all, what about the
lumps; instead, make your mind
up to get to grips with it, learn
how to do it once and for all and
then enjoy a lifetime of making
and enjoying perfect sauces any
time you want to.

Although the entire art of saucemaking is a vast subject, covering many different methods and approaches (see Hollandaise Sauce on page 70 and Traditional English Custard on page 62), here we are concerned with flour-based sauces, which, when you've understood the rules and learned how to master them, will give you a good grounding in the rest of saucemaking.

More power to your elbow

I'm not sure if this old cliché came into being through the subject of saucemaking or not, but it does say something wise, and that is this: when flour, fat and liquid are combined and heated, they always need extremely vigorous whisking. As I said in the chapter on pastry, it's the brain that gives out signals to the hands (or arms in this case) and commands either gentleness or forcefulness, and with sauces it's the latter, so the more vigorously you whisk the better. With all flour-based sauces, once you know this and put it into practice, everything will be within your control – because in the end it's the whisk that controls. Learning in the first place begins with a decision: I will always do what Delia says and whisk like mad!

Lumps are a thing of the past

Flour-based sauces, it has to be admitted, have suffered a bad press. I well remember some years ago Anne Robinson on the BBC's *Points Of View* programme repeatedly showing a TV chef making a horrible lumpy white sauce in close-up. Yes, it was funny, because the chef at the time was saying how smooth and silky it was. Knowing the hazards of television cooking and the heat not always being right when the director says go, I could sympathise. It's a shame in this case that he (the director) didn't think to look at the monitor. But making a sauce at home is nowhere near as hazardous as it is on television, so lumps really are within your control.

In a classic white sauce and all other flour-based sauces, there's only one rule apart from determined whisking, and that is the fat content: it's the flour blended with the fat that ensures lump-free results, so never attempt to blend hot liquid and flour without the presence of fat, as this is what causes lumps.

It is all quite straightforward, a case of once you understand the rules, lumps should never occur. But so what? If you do happen to slip up on the rules or get distracted, then don't forget why sieves were invented.

Now let's first have a look at some of the rules. You need to remember the three ways to make a white sauce.

1 The roux method

Roux is the name given to the mixture of butter and flour that forms the basis of the classic white sauce called béchamel. The butter is melted in the pan, the flour is then stirred in to make a smooth, thick paste, and finally, the liquid is added a little at a time with continual whisking. This is the only way to make a sauce if the liquid is hot, because hot liquid can only be combined with flour if it's first blended with fat, so if you want to make a sauce with hot liquid, ie, fish-poaching liquid, hot vegetable stock or infused milk, remember to use the roux method described here.

2 The all-in-one method

What happens here is that if you are using cold liquid you can simply place all the ingredients, ie, butter, flour and liquid, in a saucepan and whisk continuously and vigorously over the heat until the heat thickens the sauce. By the time the heat penetrates, the butter will have been blended with the flour enough to prevent lumps and the finished sauce will be silky smooth and exactly the same as in the roux method above.

3 The fat-free, no-lump flour method

Yes, it's true. For the first time in history we have an utterly new and quite phenomenal way of making a white sauce, which has changed all the rules somewhat. It's with a flour called *sauce flour*, which has been invented by an extremely clever flour miller who was watching me on television emphasising the absolutely essential presence of fat to avoid lumps. We need not get scientific here, but what he did was work out what it was that made the sauce go lumpy, and then develop a specific type of sauce flour that did not need the presence of fat, and this, thankfully, is now available in some supermarkets. After that he sent me some samples to test, and the happy conclusion is that, sure enough, using the all-in-one method above with cold milk, you can now make a white sauce without any butter at all. Of course, there is some fat in the milk, but there's still a vast difference in the total fat content, which is wonderful news for those on a low-fat diet.

Obviously the richness and flavour of butter are what make a classic creamy white sauce the star it is, but it's good to have the choice of not adding butter on occasions, and I think this is a huge step forward. You can now make a creamy, silky-smooth white sauce with skimmed or semi-skimmed milk and flour with no butter. Amazing.

What's the best saucepan?

A vexed question that has occupied me for years. The absolute truth is that a white sauce is probably the very best test of a saucepan. Why? Because what you want is a saucepan in which the sauce won't catch. If it does you will find that, as you whisk, little bits of scorched sauce will begin to appear. For years I have searched and searched, and at long last I've found what I can only describe as a little gem, left. Since I first started cooking I've always known that heavy-gauge aluminium is the very best conductor of heat in cooking, and now, thankfully, it has at last been declared safe (see page 42).

It provides the perfect pan for making sauces and it's not mega expensive. Not particularly glamorous to look at, but light-years ahead of anything else on performance.

How long should you cook a flour-based sauce?

When you use flour in a sauce, although it will thicken to a smooth creaminess very quickly, it then has to be cooked. This is because the flour can at first taste a little raw. Therefore it's important to remember that all sauces using flour must have 5 minutes' cooking time over the gentlest possible heat, except if you're going to continue to cook the sauce in the oven, as in a lasagne, for example, which means you can cut this initial cooking to 2 or 3 minutes.

Can you make it ahead?

Yes, you certainly can, but a few things to remember first. When the sauce is made, place some clingfilm directly over the surface to prevent a skin from forming, then either keep it warm by placing it over a pan of barely simmering water or, if you want to make it a long way ahead, re-heat it using the same method and don't remove the clingfilm until you are ready to serve. If you find it has thickened a little, this is easy to rectify by adding a little more liquid – milk, stock or cream – to bring it back to the right consistency.

Opposite, clockwise from top right: fatless white sauce, all-in-one white sauce, roux

Classic White Béchamel Sauce

This is the classic way of making a white sauce, using what the French call a roux (see page 147).

Makes about 15 fl oz (425 ml)
15 fl oz (425 ml) milk
a few parsley stalks
1 bay leaf
1 blade of mace or a pinch of
powdered mace (optional)
10 whole black peppercorns
1 slice onion, ¼ inch (5 mm) thick
1½ oz (40 g) butter
¾ oz (20 g) plain flour
salt and freshly milled black pepper

First place the milk in a small saucepan and add the parsley stalks, bay leaf, mace (if using), peppercorns and onion. Then place it over a low heat and let it come very slowly up to simmering point, which will take approximately 5 minutes. Then remove the saucepan from the heat and strain the milk into a jug, discarding the flavourings.

All this can be done ahead of time, but when you want to make the sauce, use the same washed pan and place it over a gentle heat. Begin by melting the butter gently – don't over-heat it or let it brown, as this will affect the colour and flavour of the sauce. As soon as the butter melts, add the flour and, over a medium heat and using a small pointed wooden spoon, stir quite vigorously to make a smooth, glossy paste. Now begin adding the infused milk a little at a time – about 1 fl oz (25 ml) first of all – and stir again vigorously. Then, when this milk is incorporated, add the next amount and continue incorporating each bit of liquid before you add the next. When about half the milk is in, switch to a balloon whisk and start adding large amounts of milk, but always whisking briskly. Your reward will be a smooth, glossy, creamy sauce.

Now turn the heat down to its lowest setting and let the sauce cook for 5 minutes, whisking from time to time. While that's happening, taste and season with salt and freshly milled black pepper. If you wish to keep the sauce warm, all you do is pour it into a warmed jug and cover the surface with clingfilm to stop a skin from forming, then place the jug in a pan of barely simmering water.

All-In-One White Sauce

The golden rule here, as explained earlier, is to use cold milk. So if you want to infuse the milk, pour it into a bowl and let it get completely cold before you begin.

Makes about 15 fl oz (425 ml)
15 fl oz (425 ml) milk – this can be infused (see page 150) but must be cold
¾ oz (20 g) plain flour
1½ oz (40 g) butter
salt and freshly milled black pepper

When you're ready to make the sauce, put the milk in a saucepan, then simply add the flour and butter and bring everything gradually up to simmering point, whisking continuously with a balloon whisk, until the sauce has thickened and becomes smooth and glossy.

Then turn the heat down to its lowest possible setting and let the sauce cook very gently for 5 minutes, stirring from time to time. Meanwhile, taste and add seasoning.

Any Kind of Cheese Sauce

Yes, it's true – any kind of cheese can be used. If you want a mild lactic flavour use a Lancashire, or for something more assertive, how about a sharp Gorgonzola? Or, instead of Cheddar and Parmesan, try Gruyère and Parmesan. Cheese sauce is also very obliging when it comes to odd bits of cheese lurking in the refrigerator, in which case you can use a mixture.

Makes about 1 pint (570 ml)
1 pint (570 ml) milk
1½ oz (40 g) plain flour
1½ oz (40 g) butter
pinch of cayenne pepper
2 oz (50 g) mature Cheddar, grated
1 oz (25 g) Parmesan (Parmigiano Reggiano), finely grated
a little freshly grated nutmeg
salt and freshly milled black pepper

All you do is place the milk, flour, butter and cayenne pepper into a medium saucepan and place it over a gentle heat. Then, using a balloon whisk, begin to whisk while bringing it to a gentle simmer. Whisk continually until you have a smooth, glossy sauce, and simmer very gently for 5 minutes. Then add the cheeses and whisk again, allowing them to melt. Then season with salt, freshly milled black pepper and some freshly grated nutmeg.

Fatless White Sauce

Okay, so you don't get the buttery flavour, but you do get a lovely creamy-smooth, milky white sauce by using sauce flour (see page 147), which is most helpful for those needing to cut the fat content of their diet.

Makes about 10 fl oz (275 ml)
10 fl oz (275 ml) milk – this can be infused (see page 150) but must be cold
¾ oz (20 g) sauce flour
salt and freshly milled black pepper

All you do to make this sauce is place the milk in a small saucepan, then simply add the flour and, over a medium heat, bring everything gradually up to simmering point, whisking vigorously and continuously with a balloon whisk until the sauce has thickened to a smooth, rich creaminess. Then add seasoning and allow it to cook very gently for 5 minutes on the lowest possible heat.

The cheese we used for the sauce in this recipe, as pictured on the following page, was Gorgonzola, but Roquefort, below, is also extremely good.

Begin by heating the oil in the frying pan over a medium heat, then add the onions and let them cook for 3-4 minutes, until lightly tinged brown. Next stir in the rice – there's no need to wash it – and turn the grains over in the pan so they become lightly coated and glistening with oil. Then add the boiling stock, along with the salt, stir once only, then cover with the lid, turn the heat to its very lowest setting and cook for 40-45 minutes. Don't remove the lid and don't stir the rice during cooking, because this is what will break the grains and release their starch, making the rice sticky.

While the rice is cooking, make the sauce, and all you do here is place the milk, butter, flour and cayenne pepper in a saucepan and, using a balloon whisk, whisk on a medium heat, continuing until the sauce becomes thick, smooth and glossy. Then turn the heat to its lowest setting and give it 5 minutes to cook. After that, whisk in the cheese until it has melted, then season with the nutmeg, salt and freshly milled black pepper.

Next, pre-heat the grill to its highest setting, then place a saucepan on the heat, add some boiling water from the kettle, fit a steamer in it and add the cauliflower. Put a lid on and time it for 4 minutes. After that, add the broccoli to join the cauliflower, lid on again, and time it for another 4 minutes.

Now arrange the cooked rice in the baking dish, then top with the cauliflower and broccoli florets. Next pour the sauce over, then, finally, mix the Parmesan with the breadcrumbs and parsley. Sprinkle this all over the top, then place the whole thing under the grill and cook for 2-3 minutes, until the sauce is bubbling and golden brown.

Serves 4
10 oz (275 g) cauliflower florets
10 oz (275 g) broccoli florets
1 tablespoon olive oil
2 medium onions, peeled and sliced into 8 through the root
10 fl oz (275 ml) brown basmati rice
1 pint (570 ml) boiling vegetable stock
1 rounded teaspoon salt

For the blue cheese sauce:
4 oz (110 g) Roquefort or Gorgonzola, cubed
1 pint (570 ml) milk
1½ oz (40 g) butter
1½ oz (40 g) plain flour
pinch of cayenne pepper
a little freshly grated nutmeg
salt and freshly milled black pepper

For the topping:
1 oz (25 g) Parmesan (Parmigiano Reggiano), finely grated
½ oz (10 g) fresh breadcrumbs
1 tablespoon finely chopped fresh parsley

You will also need an ovenproof baking dish with a base measurement of 8 x 6 inches (20 x 15 cm), 2 inches (5 cm) deep, and a 10 inch (25.5 cm) frying pan with a lid.

Roasted Vegetable and Brown Rice Gratin

This, like the previous recipe, is obviously a supper dish for non-meat-eaters, but I have served it to the most dedicated carnivores who, after initial apprehension, have loudly sung its praises.

Serves 4

For the rice:
10 fl oz (275 ml) brown basmati rice
1 tablespoon olive oil
2 medium onions, peeled and finely chopped
1 pint (570 ml) boiling vegetable stock
1 rounded teaspoon salt

For the vegetables:
10 oz (275 g) peeled butternut squash
5 oz (150 g) each celeriac, swede, carrots and parsnip (peeled weight)
2 medium red onions, peeled
1 heaped tablespoon chopped mixed fresh herbs: parsley, thyme and tarragon, for example
1 fat clove garlic, peeled and crushed
2 tablespoons olive oil
salt and freshly milled black pepper

For the cheese sauce:
2 oz (50 g) mature Cheddar, grated
1 oz (25 g) Parmesan (Parmigiano Reggiano), finely grated
1 pint (570 ml) milk
1½ oz (40 g) plain flour
1½ oz (40 g) butter
a little cayenne pepper
a little freshly grated nutmeg
salt and freshly milled black pepper

You will also need a 16 x 12 inch (40 x 30 cm) baking sheet, a 8 x 6 inch (20 x 15 cm) based ovenproof dish and a 10 inch (25.5 cm) lidded frying pan.

Pre-heat the oven to gas mark 8, 450°F (230°C).

For the vegetables, begin by cutting the squash, celeriac, swede, carrots and parsnip into 1 inch (2.5 cm) cubes. Place them and the red onions, each cut into six through the root, in a large bowl, along with the herbs, garlic, a good seasoning of salt and pepper and the olive oil, then toss them around so they get a good coating of oil and herbs. Now arrange them evenly all over the baking sheet, then place this on the highest shelf of the oven to roast for about 30 minutes, or until they are nicely brown at the edges. As soon as they are ready, take them out and reduce the oven temperature to gas mark 6, 400°F (200°C).

For the rice, begin by warming the frying pan over a medium heat, then add the oil and the onions and let them cook for 3-4 minutes, until lightly tinged brown. Next stir in the rice – there's no need to wash it – and turn the grains over in the pan so they become lightly coated and glistening with oil. Then add the boiling stock, along with the salt, stir once only, then cover with the lid, turn the heat to the very lowest setting and cook for 40-45 minutes. Don't remove the lid and don't stir the rice during cooking, because this is what will break the grains and release their starch, which makes the rice sticky.

Meanwhile, make the cheese sauce by placing the milk, flour, butter and a pinch of the cayenne pepper into a medium-sized saucepan, then whisk it all together over a gentle heat until you have a smooth, glossy sauce. Let it cook on the lowest heat for 5 minutes, and after that add half the cheeses. Whisk again and allow them to melt into it, then season the sauce with salt, freshly milled black pepper and freshly grated nutmeg.

When the vegetables and rice are cooked, arrange the rice in the ovenproof dish, then the vegetables on top of that, followed by the sauce, pouring it over and around the vegetables as evenly as possible. Finally, scatter over the remaining cheeses with a sprinkling of cayenne pepper, then return the dish to the oven and give it about 20 minutes or until the sauce is browned and bubbling.

Opposite, top: Roasted Vegetable and Brown Rice Gratin; bottom, Cauliflower and Broccoli Gratin with Blue Cheese

Roast Lamb with Garlic and Rosemary

Serves 6-8
1 leg of lamb weighing about 4 lb
(1.8 kg)
3 large cloves garlic, peeled and thinly
sliced lengthways into about 24 slivers
2 large stems fresh rosemary, cut into
about 24 small sprigs
1 small onion, peeled
salt and freshly milled black pepper

You will also need a solid roasting tin
with a base measuring 11 x 9 inches
(28 x 23 cm) and 2 inches (5 cm) deep.

Pre-heat the oven to gas mark 5,
375°F (190°C).

*I have included this recipe for roast lamb here in the sauce section because
it is served with two sauces: Traditional Gravy on page 163 and the
Rosemary and Onion Sauce below. I find that the Oven-Sautéed Potatoes
Lyonnaises on page 188 make an excellent accompaniment.*

Begin by making about 24 small, deep cuts in the skin of the lamb using a
small, sharp knife. Then push a sliver of garlic, followed by a small sprig of
rosemary, into each cut, and season the meat generously with salt and
freshly milled black pepper. Next, cut the onion in half and place it in
the bottom of the roasting tin, then transfer the lamb to the tin to sit on
top of the onion halves. Cover the tin loosely with foil, then cook in the
oven on a high shelf for 1½ hours. After this, take the foil off and let it
cook for another 30 minutes.

Remove the lamb from the oven, cover loosely with foil again and allow
it to rest for about 20 minutes. Meanwhile, make the gravy (see page 163).

Rosemary and Onion Sauce

Makes about 1 pint (570 ml)
1 rounded tablespoon rosemary leaves
1 large onion, peeled and finely
chopped
1 oz (25 g) butter
1 oz (25 g) plain flour
6 fl oz (175 ml) milk
6 fl oz (175 ml) vegetable stock
2 tablespoons crème fraîche
salt and freshly milled black pepper

*This is good with the roast lamb above, lamb chops, or served with
bangers and mash.*

In a small saucepan, melt the butter and cook the onions over a very gentle
heat for about 5 minutes – it's important not to let them colour, so keep an
eye on them. While that's happening, bruise the rosemary leaves with a pestle
and mortar to release their oil, then chop them very, very finely and add
them to the onion. Then continue to cook as gently as possible for a further
15 minutes, again, without letting the onions colour too much. Next, using
a wooden spoon, stir the flour into the onions and their buttery juices till
smooth, then gradually add the milk, a little at a time, still stirring, followed
by the stock, bit by bit, whilst vigorously whisking with a balloon whisk.

Now taste and season the sauce with salt and pepper and let it barely
simmer on the lowest possible heat for 5 minutes. Next, remove it from the
heat, then liquidise or process half of it, then return it to the saucepan to join
the other half. Then re-heat gently, add the crème fraîche and pour it into
a warmed serving jug.

*Roast Lamb with Garlic and Rosemary
served with Oven-Sautéed Potatoes
Lyonnaises*

English Parsley Sauce

Yes, it's old-fashioned nursery food, but I sometimes think that things like this need a revival. I love it with baked cod cutlets and creamy mashed potatoes, and it's also excellent with gammon. Here, though, I've included my favourite recipe for Salmon Fishcakes specially for the parsley sauce.

Place the milk and the next five ingredients in a small pan, bring everything slowly up to simmering point, then pour the mixture into a bowl and leave aside to get completely cold. When you're ready to make the sauce, strain the milk back into the pan, discard the flavourings, then add the flour and butter and bring everything gradually up to simmering point, whisking continuously with a balloon whisk until the sauce has thickened and is smooth and glossy. Then turn the heat down to its lowest possible setting and let the sauce cook gently for 5 minutes, stirring from time to time. To serve the sauce, add the parsley, cream and lemon juice, taste and season, then serve in a warm jug.

Makes about 15 fl oz (425 ml)
15 fl oz (425 ml) milk
a few parsley stalks
1 bay leaf
1 slice onion, ¼ inch (5 mm) thick
1 blade of mace or a pinch of powdered mace (optional)
10 whole black peppercorns
¾ oz (20 g) plain flour
1½ oz (40 g) butter
4 heaped tablespoons finely chopped fresh parsley
1 tablespoon single cream
1 teaspoon lemon juice
salt and freshly milled black pepper

Salmon Fishcakes

The thing to remember here is that good-quality tinned salmon makes better fishcakes than fresh, so don't be tempted to cook some salmon just for this.

First of all boil the potatoes in salted water for about 25 minutes or until they're absolutely tender when tested with a skewer. (Be careful, though – if they are not tender you will get lumps.) Then drain the potatoes and mash them to a purée with the mayonnaise using an electric hand whisk, then add some seasoning.

Now, in a large mixing bowl, simply combine all the ingredients for the fishcakes together. Mix really thoroughly, then taste and season again if it needs it. After that, allow it to cool thoroughly, then cover the bowl and place it in the fridge, giving it at least 2 hours to chill and become firm.

When you are ready to cook the fishcakes, lightly flour a work surface, then turn the fish mixture on to it and, using your hands, pat and shape it into a long roll, 2-2½ inches (5-6 cm) in diameter. Now cut the roll into 12 round fishcakes, pat each one into a neat, flat shape and then dip them, one by one, first into the beaten egg and then into the matzo meal (or breadcrumbs), making sure they get a nice, even coating all round.

Now, in a large frying pan, heat the oil and butter over a high heat and, when it is really hot, add half the fishcakes to the pan, then turn the heat down to medium and give then 4 minutes' shallow frying on each side. Then drain on crumpled greaseproof paper and keep warm. Repeat with the rest of the fishcakes, adding a little more oil and butter if needed. Serve immediately on hot plates with the parsley sauce, sprigs of parsley and some lemon wedges.

Makes 12 (serves 6)
For the fishcakes:
15 oz (425 g) red salmon
10 oz (275 g) Desirée or King Edward potatoes, peeled and cut into large chunks
2 tablespoons mayonnaise
2 heaped tablespoons chopped fresh parsley
2 heaped tablespoons salted capers or capers in vinegar, drained and chopped
6 pickled gherkins (cornichons), drained and chopped
2 large eggs, hard-boiled and chopped small
1 dessertspoon anchovy paste or 4 anchovies, mashed up
2 tablespoons lemon juice
¼ teaspoon powdered mace
¼ teaspoon cayenne pepper
salt and freshly milled black pepper

For the coating and frying:
a little flour for dusting
1 large egg, beaten
3 oz (75 g) matzo meal or fresh white breadcrumbs
about 2 tablespoons groundnut or other flavourless oil
about ½ oz (10 g) butter

To serve:
1 quantity English Parsley Sauce (see opposite)
a few sprigs fresh parsley
lemon wedges

Salmon Fishcakes with English Parsley Sauce

Moussaka with Roasted Aubergines and Ricotta

Once you've mastered the art of a perfect white sauce you can use it for any number of recipes. This one is a Greek classic, but the little hint of Italy I've added in the shape of Ricotta cheese makes the very best moussaka topping I've tasted. Also, roasting the aubergines is much less tiresome than standing over a frying pan watching them soak up masses of oil.

Serves 6

1 lb (450 g) minced lamb
2 medium-sized aubergines
2 tablespoons olive oil
2 medium onions, peeled and chopped small
2 cloves garlic, peeled and chopped
1 heaped tablespoon chopped fresh mint
1 heaped tablespoon chopped fresh parsley
1 teaspoon ground cinnamon
2 rounded tablespoon tomato purée
3 fl oz (75 ml) red wine
salt and freshly milled black pepper

For the topping:

9 oz (250 g) Ricotta
10 fl oz (275 ml) whole milk
1 oz (25 g) plain flour
1 oz (25 g) butter
¼ whole nutmeg, grated
1 bay leaf
1 large egg
1 tablespoon grated Parmesan (Parmigiano Reggiano)
salt and freshly milled black pepper

You will also need an ovenproof baking dish measuring 10 x 8 inches (25.5 x 20 cm), 2 inches (5 cm) deep, and a 14 x 11 inch (35 x 28 cm) baking sheet.

First of all you need to prepare the aubergines to get rid of their high water content and concentrate their flavour. To do this, remove the stalks and, leaving the skins on, cut them into approximately 1½ inch (4 cm) chunks. Then place them in a colander and sprinkle them with about 1 level dessertspoon of salt. Now put a plate on top of them and weigh it down with something heavy, then put another plate underneath to catch the juices. Leave them like this for 1 hour. Then, shortly before the end of this time, pre-heat the oven to its highest setting. When the hour is up, squeeze out any of the excess juice from the aubergines with your hands and dry them as thoroughly as you can in a clean cloth. Next, spread them out on the baking sheet, drizzle 1 tablespoon of the olive oil over them and toss them around to get a good coating. Now pop the baking sheet in the oven and roast the aubergines for 30 minutes or until they are tinged brown at the edges.

Meanwhile, heat the remaining olive oil in your largest frying pan and fry the onions and garlic gently for about 5 minutes. After that, turn the heat up high, add the minced lamb and brown it for a few minutes, turning it and keeping it on the move. Now cook the whole lot, stirring all the time, for 2-3 minutes. Then reduce the heat and, in a small bowl, mix the mint, parsley, cinnamon, tomato purée and red wine. When they're thoroughly combined, pour them over the meat, season well and cook the whole lot very gently for about 20 minutes, stirring from time to time so it doesn't catch on the base of the pan.

Now remove the aubergines from the oven and reduce the temperature to gas mark 4, 350°F (180°C). It's a good idea to leave the oven door open to cool it down a bit.

Next, make the topping by placing the milk, flour, butter, nutmeg and bay leaf in a saucepan. Using a balloon whisk, whisk over a medium heat until everything comes up to simmering point and the sauce becomes smooth and glossy. Now turn the heat down to its lowest setting and let the sauce cook gently for 5 minutes. Then taste and season, discarding the bay leaf, remove the saucepan from the heat and let it cool a little before whisking in the Ricotta and egg. Give it a good whisk to blend everything thoroughly.

Finally, combine the roasted aubergines with the meat mixture and transfer it all to the baking dish. Then pour the topping over, sprinkle the surface with the Parmesan and bake on the centre shelf of the oven for 50 minutes, by which time the top will be golden brown. Let it stand for 10 minutes to settle, then serve with brown rice and a Greek-style salad of cucumber, tomatoes, olives and crumbled Feta cheese dressed with olive oil and fresh lemon juice.

Gravy training

What is gravy?

Apparently, originally in the 14th century it was a bit of a copy error. The French (who by no means have the last word in cooking) had the word *grane*, and someone at some stage mistakenly copied over the 'n' as a 'v', and for some unknown reason the English kept the 'v' and added a 'y'. Thus, in a 14th-century cookbook we find that oysters, for instance, were stewed 'in their own gravy', meaning with their own juices, plus wine broth, almonds and rice flour, and similar gravies appeared from then on. So the French still, to this day, have only sauce or *jus* (juices), whilst the British have gravy, which is a sauce made from juices and other ingredients. So in all our most prestigious cookbooks, literature, food journals and diaries throughout the centuries, gravy is prominently featured.

British sauce

It is therefore hardly surprising that even our modern generation undoubtedly still has a latent passion for it. True, if you're a food snob, the word does not have such a fashionable ring to it as the French *jus* that dominates restaurant menus, along with perfumed broths, essences and other such pretensions. But it has to be said that gravy is part of our heritage; it comes from a long line of careful cooks who knew how to prepare a perfectly flavoured sauce by utilising precious juices, adding thickening for creamy smoothness and other flavour-enhancing ingredients to provide a beautiful sauce.

Gravy again

Now we can come to the crux of all this, and that is how, since everyone wants to enjoy proper gravy, they are at the same time deeply afraid of attempting to make it. I have written about it and demonstrated it countless times, but still people ask, 'How do you make gravy?'

Witness the horrors that line our supermarket shelves: cubes, packets and granules with long lists of chemicals, producing alien artificial flavour and instant gelatinous gloop – it's no wonder doctors are prescribing more antidepressants with people introducing such gloominess into their lives. But now is the time to move on and, once and for all, with the aid of this book, everyone everywhere who wants to can make proper gravy for ever and ever. It really isn't hard, and there's nothing to be afraid of, so here goes.

Traditional Gravy

First of all remove the meat or poultry from the roasting tin and have a bowl ready, then tilt the tin and you will see quite clearly the fat separating from the darker juices. So now you need to spoon off the fat into the bowl using a tablespoon, but remember, you need to leave 1-1½ tablespoons of fat in the tin. Then, using a wooden spoon, scrape the sides and base of the tin to release any crusty bits, which are very important for flavour. Next, place the tin over direct heat turned fairly low and, when the fat and juices begin to sizzle, add the flour, then quickly dive in with the wooden spoon using brisk circular movements. Speed is of the essence – gentle, faint-hearted stirring is not what's needed here: you should be mixing in the manner of a speeded-up film!

Soon you will have a smooth paste, so now begin to add the hot stock, a little at a time, whisking briskly and blending after each addition. Now turn the heat up to medium and you will find that, as the stock is added and it reaches simmering point, the gravy will have thickened.

Now your own preference comes into play. If the gravy is too thin, let it bubble and reduce a little; if it's too thick, add a little more liquid. Finally, taste and season with salt and freshly milled black pepper, then pour the gravy into a warmed jug ready for the table.

For *pork*, which has pale juices, add onion to the roasting tin. This will caramelise during cooking and give colour to the juices. The onion may also be used with other joints and poultry to give colour.

For *lamb*, add a teaspoon of mustard powder with the flour, a tablespoon of redcurrant jelly to melt into the gravy, and some red wine to add body.

For *duck*, add the grated zest and juice of a small orange, along with a glass of port.

For *beef*, add a wineglass of Sercial Madeira – this enriches the beef flavour magically.

For *instant gravy without a joint*, see the recipe for Roasted-Onion Gravy on page 165.

Makes about 1 pint (570 ml)
the juices left in the roasting tin from cooking meat or poultry
1 rounded tablespoon plain flour
approximately 1 pint (570 ml) hot stock (potato or other vegetable water, for example), but the exact amount will depend on how thick you like your gravy
salt and freshly milled black pepper

You will also need a solid-based, flameproof roasting tin.

Begin by spooning off most of the fat from the roasting tin, leaving a little behind

Now add the flour and briskly mix it in using circular movements

Once you have a smooth paste, add the stock, a little at a time, blending as you go

Increase the heat; you will now see that the gravy will begin to thicken

163

Toad in the Hole with Roasted-Onion Gravy

I can't give this high enough accolades – it's a simply wonderful creation from the humble origins of British cooking. If only you could order it in a restaurant, though. Can I persuade anyone? It is, after all, a sort of fusion food – a fusion of light, crispy, crunchy batter and plump, meaty pork sausages, all moistened with a generous amount of roasted-onion jus. Here's hoping!

Begin by making the batter, and to do this sieve the flour into a large bowl, holding the sieve up high to give the flour a good airing. Now, with the back of a spoon, make a well in the centre, break the egg into it and add some salt and pepper. Now, measure the milk and water in a measuring jug, then, using an electric hand whisk on a slow speed, begin to whisk the egg into the flour – as you whisk, the flour around the edges will slowly be incorporated. Then add the liquid gradually, stopping to scrape the flour into the mixture. Whisk until the batter is smooth. Now the batter is ready for use, and although it's been rumoured that batter left to stand is better, I have never found this, so just make it whenever it's convenient.

Now place the sliced onions in a bowl, add 1 teaspoon of the oil and the sugar and toss the onions around to get the lightest coating, then spread them on the baking tray. Next arrange the sausages in the roasting tin, then place the onions on to a high shelf in the oven, with the sausages on a lower shelf, and set a timer for 10 minutes. When the timer goes off, remove the sausages from the oven but leave the onions in for a further 4-5 minutes – they need to be nicely blackened round the edges. When they are ready, remove them and leave to one side.

Now place the roasting tin containing the sausages over direct heat turned to medium and, if the sausages haven't released much fat, add the tablespoon of oil. When the tin is really hot and the oil is beginning to shimmer – it must be searing hot – quickly pour the batter in all around the sausages. Immediately return the roasting tin to the oven, this time on the highest shelf, and cook the whole thing for 30 minutes.

Now for the gravy. First add the Worcestershire sauce and mustard powder to the stock, then add the onions from the baking tray to a medium-sized pan. Now add the second teaspoon of oil, then, using a wooden spoon, stir in the plain flour. Stir all this together over a medium heat and then switch to a whisk, then gradually add the stock to the pan, whisking all the time, until it's all in. Then bring it up to simmering point and gently simmer for 5 minutes. Taste to check the seasoning, then pour into a warmed serving jug. When the toad is ready, it should be puffed brown and crisp and the centre should look cooked and not too squidgy. Serve it immediately with the gravy, and it's absolutely wonderful with mashed potato.

Serves 2-3

6 good-quality pork sausages – about 14 oz (400 g)
1 tablespoon groundnut or other flavourless oil (if necessary)

For the batter:
3 oz (75 g) plain flour
1 large egg
3 fl oz (75 ml) semi-skimmed milk
2 fl oz (55 ml) water
salt and freshly milled black pepper

For the onion gravy:
8 oz (225 g) onions, peeled and sliced
2 teaspoons groundnut or other flavourless oil
1 teaspoon golden caster sugar
1 dessertspoon Worcestershire sauce
1 teaspoon mustard powder
1 rounded dessertspoon plain flour
15 fl oz (425 ml) vegetable stock made from 1½ teaspoons Marigold Swiss vegetable bouillon powder dissolved in 15 fl oz (425 ml) boiling water
salt and freshly milled black pepper

You will also need a solid flameproof roasting tin with a base of 9 x 6 inches (23 x 15 cm), 2 inches (5 cm) deep, and a baking tray 14 x 10 inches (35 x 25.5 cm).

Pre-heat the oven to gas mark 7, 425°F (220°C).

Canadian Buttermilk Pancakes with Maple Syrup

Canada is where this profoundly unique syrup made from the sap of maple trees is made, and these are the pancakes that a certain Madame Lafond made for me when I was in Quebec; delightfully easy but tasting so light and fluffy. I love the way they puff up, crinkle and get really crisp at the edges. Serve these, as she did, straight from the pan on to warm plates, then absolutely drench them with maple syrup and add a generous dollop of crème fraîche.

Makes about 6
5 oz (150 g) plain flour
½ teaspoon baking powder
pinch of salt
4 fl oz (120 ml) buttermilk
3 fl oz (75 ml) cold water
3 large eggs, beaten
1-2 oz (25-50 g) lard

To serve:
lots of pure maple syrup and crème fraîche

First sieve the flour, baking powder and salt together in a roomy bowl and make a well in the centre. After that, whisk the buttermilk and water together in a jug and gradually whisk this into the bowl, slowly incorporating the flour with each new addition of liquid. Finally, add the eggs a little at a time until you have a smooth batter.

Now place a large, solid frying pan over a medium heat, add 2 teaspoons of the lard and heat it until the fat shimmers. Then, using a tablespoon of batter per pancake, place 2 or 3 spoonfuls into the pan.

They will take about 1 minute to turn golden brown, then turn them over using a spatula and fork, being careful not to splash yourself with the hot fat. Give them another 45 seconds on the other side, by which time they should have puffed up like little soufflés, then briefly rest them on some kitchen paper to absorb any excess fat.

Repeat this with the rest of the batter, adding a little more lard if necessary. They will keep warm in a low oven, but to enjoy them at their best, have everyone seated to eat them as soon as they come out of the pan.

8
Real potatoes

'Cuisine is when things taste like themselves' wrote Curnonsky, a distinguished 19th-century French food writer, and therein lies the whole truth about the art of cooking – how to make something really taste like itself. This is the real challenge that's set before anyone who wants to cook, and never was it more true than in the art of cooking potatoes. So the question is precisely this: how to make a potato really taste like a potato? The answer begins by perhaps rediscovering a healthy respect for what a potato actually is: no longer the humble 'also ran' of the meat-and-two-veg syndrome or something used as a filler to eke out the meat, but now hopefully re-emerging as a solo star on the food stage, loved and valued in its own right.

Potatoes make a comeback

Well, in a way this is true, because in my younger days potatoes were the enemy of the perfect waistline in a less nutritionally enlightened era; it was starch that made you fat, and starchy foods like bread and potatoes had to be avoided. Thankfully, bread and potatoes have now been rescued from this scenario; fat has now emerged as the number one culprit and the major cause of being overweight. This means that large portions of potatoes (without fat) are nutritious, healthy, high in energy-giving carbohydrate and low in calories – only about 70 per 100 g (approximately 4 oz), and, added to that, they are the single most important source of vitamin C in our diet. So potatoes are very 'in' at the moment and it's therefore more important than ever to learn how to make the best of them.

The importance of flavour

Before you even think about how to cook potatoes, as with many other foods, the key to flavour begins in the market place or, more specifically, in the earth. I well remember growing my first crop of new potatoes and discovering that straight from the ground into the cooking pot they were both soggy and tasteless and ended up being a huge disappointment. Why? I had simply grown the wrong variety, one with a high yield but absolutely no flavour.

This problem is a commercial one, too, and high-yield, disease-resistant, good-storage varieties do not always produce good flavour. So for the cook, choosing the right kind of potato is first on the list.

Varieties

Thankfully there are now many more varieties of potato to choose from; we could even be in danger of designer potatoes, like salad leaves, as I have seen both black-fleshed and purple varieties (neither of which have great flavour). But whilst we hear an awful lot about the texture of potatoes – which is measured by two things, waxiness and fluffiness, and the suitability of either of these in certain dishes – we hear very little about flavour. I would therefore like to see potatoes catch up with tomatoes on this, with varieties grown specifically for flavour. But since we are learning how to cook potatoes, here is not the place to study the long lists of various varieties that appear throughout the year, but I would like to point you in the direction of a few varieties which, in my experience, are among the best available at the moment.

New potatoes

Jersey Royal (April to June)

These, of course, have outstanding flavour, more so when they're a little more mature and larger than the tiny marbles that appear in early April. Choose them unwashed with the earth still clinging to them, and they need to be as fresh as possible, so that when you push a piece of skin with your thumb it slides away from the flesh instantly. These are the finest new potatoes of all for steaming and serving hot or cold in a potato salad.

Pentland Javelin (May to July)

These new potatoes also have a firm texture and excellent flavour and, depending on the weather, begin to come into season when the Jerseys finish. I have also grown these and they have excellent flavour.

Salad potatoes

These now appear regularly all year and, as their name suggests, are best eaten cold. Some specialised salad potatoes, though, are more difficult to find: Ratte is an old French variety that has a delicate, nutty, chestnut-like flavour, and Pink Fir Apple a more intense potato flavour with a pink skin and a firm, waxy flesh.

Main-crop potatoes

Desirée

This has always been my all-round reliable favourite because it has the best flavour of all commercially grown potatoes. It has a yellow, creamy, waxy flesh and bright-pink skin. I use it for boiling, jacket potatoes, roast potatoes, chunky chips and oven sautéeing, and I even like Desirée made into mash because of its depth of potato flavour.

King Edward

This is an old favourite and is the best variety if you want floury fluffiness. It's not suitable for boiling, as it tends to break, but it's wonderful for light, fluffy mash and for jacket potatoes where you want a really fluffy inside. This is also my choice for potato gnocchi because it makes them extra light.

Waxy or floury?

The above potatoes all have good flavour, but texture is sometimes a personal choice. I like to ring the changes and so sometimes I want, say, a firm, waxy, full-flavoured jacket potato, so I choose Desirée, and sometimes a more floury one, so it would be King Edward. The same applies to mashed potatoes, and what I would recommend is that you experiment to find out what you personally prefer.

How to cook potatoes

To peel or not to peel?

This is a much-debated question and I have given it a great deal of thought and consideration. My conclusions are these: yes, it's best to leave the skins on, and I never scrape new potatoes, but with main-crop potatoes – and it's a big but – if you're not going to peel them you must then have evenly sized potatoes so they all cook in the same amount of time.

The idea of leaving the skins on is to protect the flesh from the water or steam, which rob the potatoes of flavour. Once you start cutting them into even-sized pieces, that protection is lost. Also, if skins are left on for cooking, I would say that you should then serve the potatoes with their skins, as peeling hot potatoes while holding them in a cloth is okay if it's for one or two people, but for six servings it's quite awkward and hazardous. In Ireland, boiled potatoes are served with skins on and people who don't want to eat them leave them on the side of their plate, and I think this is a good option for steamed or boiled potatoes. I have compared steaming without skins and boiling with and found very little difference in flavour. If you are going to peel the potatoes, then please, please use a potato peeler. All the best of the flavour is near the skin, so you need to pare it off as thinly as possible.

Water – the enemy

I have a beautiful old cookbook called *Henderson's House Keeper Instructions*, and in it potatoes are boiled thus: '…in so small a quantity of water as will be sufficient to keep the saucepan from burning. Keep them close covered and as soon as the skins crack they are enough.'

Need I say more? Remember that having got hold of the perfect-flavoured potatoes, it's water that's going to take away their precious flavour. I have witnessed potatoes being murdered – covered with gallons of water, put on a low heat and left for an hour or even more, like the Victoria Wood joke about British cooking and the lady who put the sprouts on for the Christmas lunch in November! (We've all, I'm sure, experienced it.)

The number one rule here is, first of all, if you are peeling potatoes, don't let them sit around in water for hours before they're needed. If you peel them then try to do so just before you need them.

For cooking, the best way I have found to retain the flavour of the potatoes is not to boil them at all but to steam them. Firstly pour boiling water from the kettle into a pan fitted with a fan steamer (see the photograph, right), then place the potatoes in the steamer, sprinkle with salt (about 1 rounded teaspoon per 1 lb/450 g), and if they're new potatoes tuck in a few sprigs of mint. Then put a tight lid on and let them steam over a lowish heat, which is just needed to keep the water gently boiling until the potatoes are tender. This will take 20-25 minutes, and the best way to test whether the potatoes are tender is to use a thin skewer inserted in the thickest part.

After that, drain off any water beneath the steamer, then place a cloth over the potatoes for 5 minutes, which will absorb some of the excess steam that tends to cling to the potatoes and make them soggy. If you prefer to boil rather than steam, then use as little water as possible, add it boiling from the kettle and put a close lid on. The lid keeps the heat in and they will cook more quickly so spend less time in the water.

Steamed or boiled potatoes – pure and simple

In the recipes that follow I have attempted to give you a good grounding in all the most popular ways of serving potatoes. But don't forget that, cooked with a little care, plain steamed or boiled potatoes can, just on their own, be quite special. And they don't need lashings of butter; a little is a nice addition, but don't drown them with butter as some restaurants still insist on doing. All that does is swamp the delicate natural flavour of the potatoes. Gilding the lily is a sign of insecurity in cooking, and I feel it's so important to renew our confidence in the simplicity of things.

Jacket Potatoes

Could there possibly be anyone in the wide world who doesn't drool at the thought of jacket potatoes with really crisp, crunchy skins and fluffy, floury insides with something lovely melted into them? I'm not speaking of the insipid microwave versions of convenience fame, but the hallowed, reverenced beauty of the real thing. Life is too short, and therefore we need to savour every moment by spoiling ourselves with what is best and not some pale imitation that fails to satisfy. If you ever feel like treating yourself and want something supremely soothing and comforting that costs almost nothing (forget chocolate bars and the like), just bake yourself the biggest potato you can lay your hands on (see the method below), then cut it in half and, as you do, listen carefully to the inviting crackle and crunch of the skin as the knife goes in. Next, with a fork, fluff the floury insides, then add a generous amount of butter and watch it melt and disappear into the clouds of fluffiness. Add rock salt and crushed black pepper, then eat and savour it alone in all its humble, simple glory.

The secret of perfect jacket potatoes like the one described above is not to hurry them – give them up to 2 hours to get the really crunchy skin, learn to use the time when you're out, so they can be ready when you come home, or go and do something else and forget about them till they're ready. Below I have included the master recipe, and this is followed by some ideas for fillings and toppings.

Serves 2
2 large Desirée potatoes, 8-10 oz
(225-275 g) each
a little olive oil
rock salt, crushed
a little butter
salt and freshly milled black pepper

Pre-heat the oven to gas mark 5,
375°F (190°C).

First you need to wash the potatoes and dry them very thoroughly with a cloth, then leave them aside to dry as much as possible. If you're using ready-washed potatoes you need not do this, as the high heat will purify them. Next, prick the skins a few times with a fork, then put a few drops of olive oil over each one and rub it all over the skin. After that, rub in some crushed salt – this will draw out the moisture from the skin and, together with the oil, provide more crunchiness.

Now place the potatoes straight on to the centre shelf of the oven and let them bake for 1¾-2 hours, or until the skins are really very crisp. When you are ready to serve, slit each potato in half lengthways and top with the butter and seasoning. Serve immediately because, after you remove jacket potatoes from the oven, they lose their crispness very quickly, so don't let them hang around.

Soured cream and chive topping

5 fl oz (150 ml) soured cream
approximately ½ oz (10 g) fresh chives
salt and freshly milled black pepper

This simple but great dressing for jacket potatoes was invented in the US, and it's still my number one favourite. All you do is snip the chives with some scissors into a bowl containing the soured cream. Add some seasoning and leave it for about 1 hour before serving, so that the soured cream has time to absorb the flavour of the chives.

In this recipe the potato is scooped out, mixed with soft cheese and topped with leeks and melted cheese.

Stuffed Jacket Potatoes with Leeks, Cheddar and Boursin

To prepare the leek, slice it almost in half lengthways, then fan it out under a running tap to wash away any trapped dirt. Now slice each half into four lengthways, then into ¼ inch (5 mm) slices. After that, put the Boursin into a medium-sized bowl and cut the potatoes in half lengthways. Protecting your hands with a cloth, scoop out the centres of the potatoes into the bowl containing the Boursin, add the milk or cream and season well with salt and freshly milled black pepper. Now quickly mash or whisk everything together, then pile the whole lot back into the potato skins. Now scatter the leeks on top, followed by the grated Cheddar – pressing it down lightly with your hand – then place on the baking sheet and bake in the oven for 20 minutes or until the leeks are golden brown at the edges and the cheese is bubbling.

Serves 2

2 large baked potatoes, 8-10 oz (225-275 g) each (see basic recipe left)
1 leek about 4 inches (10 cm) long, trimmed and cleaned
1½ oz (40 g) mature Cheddar, coarsely grated
1 x 80 g pack *Ail & Fines Herbes* Boursin
1 tablespoon from the top of the milk or single cream
salt and freshly milled black pepper

You will also need a baking sheet measuring 12 x 10 inches (30 x 25.5 cm).

Pre-heat the oven to gas mark 4, 350°F (180°C).

Welsh Rarebit Jacket Potatoes

Serves 2
2 large baked potatoes, 8-10 oz
(225-275 g) each (see page 174)
3 oz (75 g) mature Cheddar, grated
1 tablespoon Red Onion, Tomato and
Chilli Relish (see page 188)
1 heaped teaspoon finely grated onion
1 large egg, lightly beaten
1 tablespoon finely snipped fresh chives

Pre-heat the grill to its highest setting for
10 minutes before the potatoes are ready.

The same topping that goes with toasted bread goes perfectly with jacket potatoes and makes a lovely lunch dish served with a salad. You can make your own relish for this (see page 188), or you could buy it ready-made.

All you do here is combine all the filling ingredients together in a bowl. Then, when the potatoes are ready, cut them in half lengthways and make some criss-cross slits in them, being careful not to cut through the skins and using a cloth to protect your hands. Then divide the topping mixture between the potatoes, place them on the grill pan and grill 2 inches (5 cm) from the heat for 3-4 minutes, until the cheese has puffed up and turned golden brown on top.

Perfect Mashed Potato

This is now my standard all-time mashed potato recipe, adapted and revised from the Winter Collection.

Serves 4
2 lb (900 g) Desirée or King Edward
potatoes
1 dessertspoon salt
2 oz (50 g) butter
4 tablespoons whole milk
2 tablespoons crème fraîche
salt and freshly milled black pepper

Use a potato peeler to pare off the potato skins as thinly as possible, then cut the potatoes into even-sized chunks – not too small; if they are large, quarter them, and if they are small, halve them. Put the potato chunks in a steamer fitted over a large pan of boiling water, sprinkle the salt all over them, put a lid on and steam the potatoes until they are absolutely tender – they should take 20-25 minutes. The way to tell whether they are ready is to pierce them with a skewer in the thickest part: they should not be hard in the centre, and you need to be careful here, because if they are slightly underdone you do get lumps.

When the potatoes are cooked, remove them from the steamer, drain off the water, return them to the saucepan and cover with a clean tea cloth for about 4 minutes to absorb some of the steam, then add the butter, milk and crème fraîche. When you first go in with the whisk, use a slow speed to break the potatoes up, then increase it to high and whip them up to a smooth, creamy, fluffy mass. Taste and, if they need it, season. Note: To make low-fat mashed potatoes, replace the butter, milk and crème fraîche with 5 oz (150 g) of Quark (skimmed-milk soft cheese) and 2-3 tablespoons of semi-skimmed milk.

Perfect mashed potatoes begin with steaming the potato chunks until tender. With the addition of butter, milk and crème fraîche, the result, once whisked, is a smooth, creamy, fluffy mass

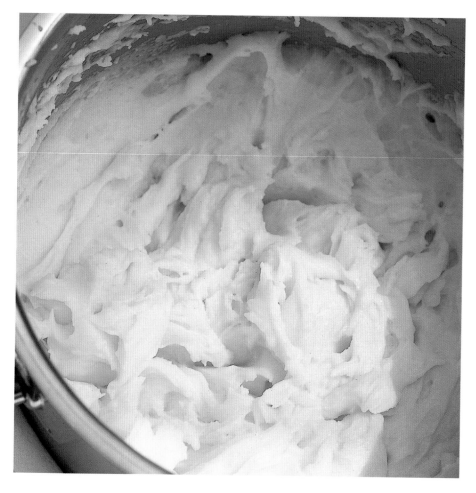

Pork Sausages Braised in Cider with Apples and Juniper

Braised sausages seem to have turned up many times in my books over the years, and because I love them so much, here is yet another version – a lovely, comforting, warm, winter supper dish that needs copious amounts of fluffy mashed potato to spoon the sauce over. Crushing the juniper berries releases their lovely flavour.

Serves 3-4

6 large best-quality pork sausages, weighing about 1 lb (450 g)
15 fl oz (425 ml) strong dry cider
1 tablespoon cider vinegar
1 Bramley apple, cored and sliced into rings (unpeeled)
1 Cox's apple, cored and sliced into rings (unpeeled)
1 dessertspoon juniper berries, crushed slightly either in a pestle and mortar or with the back of a tablespoon
2 dessertspoons olive oil
8 oz (225 g) onions, peeled and sliced into rings
1 large clove garlic, peeled and chopped
8 oz (225 g) lean smoked bacon, roughly chopped
1 tablespoon plain flour
a few sprigs fresh thyme
2 bay leaves
salt and freshly milled black pepper

You will also need a 4 pint (2.25 litre) flameproof casserole dish measuring 8 inches (20 cm) in diameter, 3 inches (7.5 cm) deep, with a tight-fitting lid.

Begin by taking a large, heavy-based frying pan, place it on a medium heat and add 1 dessertspoon of the oil to it. As soon as it's hot, fry the sausages until they are nicely browned on all sides, then, using a draining spoon, transfer them to a plate. Now add the onions, garlic and bacon to the frying pan and cook these until they have also browned at the edges – about 10 minutes.

Meanwhile, place the casserole on to another heat source, again turned to medium, add the other dessertspoon of oil, then, when it's hot, add the apple rings and brown these on both sides, which will take 2-3 minutes. After that, add the sausages, followed by the bacon, onion and garlic, then sprinkle the flour in to soak up the juices, stirring it gently with a wooden spoon. Next add the cider and cider vinegar, a little at a time, stirring after each addition. Then add the thyme, bay leaves and crushed juniper berries, season with salt and pepper, but not too much salt because of the bacon. After that, put the lid on and simmer very gently on the lowest possible heat for 1 hour. Serve with mashed potato.

Pork Sausages Braised in Cider with Apples and Juniper served with Perfect Mashed Potato (see page 176)

Aligot (Mashed Potatoes with Garlic and Cheese)

I first ate this mashed potato with cheese in southwest France, in the Tarn region, and it was, quite simply, the best mashed potato I've ever eaten. Research on my return revealed that it involved a special, lovely cheese called Cantal and, after many experiments, I think I have come up with something comparable, made with farmhouse Lancashire, which has a lovely, fresh, lactic flavour.

Serves 2

1 lb (450 g) Desirée or King Edward potatoes
2 fat cloves garlic, peeled and halved lengthways
1 oz (25 g) butter
8 oz (225 g) Lancashire cheese, grated
salt and freshly milled black pepper

Begin this by placing the garlic in a small saucepan with the butter, then leave it on the gentlest heat possible to melt and infuse for 30 minutes. Meanwhile, thinly pare and discard the skins of the potatoes and cut them into even-sized chunks, or cut any large potatoes into quarters and small ones into halves. Place the potatoes in a steamer, then pour some boiling water straight from the kettle into a saucepan. Fit the steamer over, sprinkle the potatoes with 1 dessertspoon of salt, put a lid on and let them steam for 20-25 minutes, until tender in the centre when tested with a skewer. After this, remove them, transfer to a large bowl (preferably a warm one) and cover with a cloth to absorb some of the steam.

Now, with an electric hand whisk, switch to slow and begin to break up the potatoes, then add the butter and garlic, some black pepper and a handful of the grated cheese. Now switch the speed to high and continue adding the cheese, a handful at a time, while you whisk. There's a lot of cheese, but what will happen is that, as you whisk it in, the potatoes will turn translucent and glossy and, as you lift and whisk, it will form stiff, glossy peaks. When all the cheese is in, serve very quickly. The marinated steak recipe opposite is the perfect accompaniment, but it's also great with sausages.

Note: As the cheese goes in, the mixture becomes stiff and clings to the whisk, but keep going and it will part company with the whisk eventually. Also, if you want to keep it warm, place the bowl over a pan of simmering water, but don't leave it too long.

Having added the butter, garlic and seasoning, throw in a handful of cheese

Increase the speed of the whisk and continue adding the cheese, a handful at a time

As you whisk, the potatoes will turn into a translucent mass, forming glossy peaks

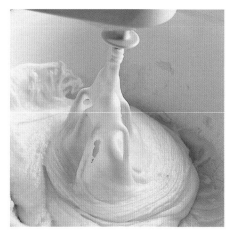

Marinated Rump Steak

This is oh, so simple, but oh, so good. Great if you're organised and can leave the steaks in the marinade the day before you need them, but failing that, a few hours will do. The recipe was created specially to serve with Aligot, but it needs two to eat and two to cook: one to do the steaks and one to whip the potatoes!

Put the steaks in the shallow dish or polythene box, then mix the red wine, Worcestershire sauce and garlic together and pour this over the steaks. Cover with clingfilm or put the lid on, then place in the fridge for a few hours or, preferably, overnight. When you're ready to cook the steaks, drain and dry them carefully with kitchen paper, reserving the marinade.

Now take a medium frying pan, place it on a high heat and heat the oil until it's very hot. Then sear the steaks for 4 minutes on each side and, 2 minutes before the time is up, add the reserved marinade to the pan and let it bubble and reduce by about half. When the steaks are cooked, remove them from the pan to warm serving plates, then, using your sharpest knife, cut them into slices diagonally (see below) and spoon the sauce over. Garnish with the watercress and serve immediately with the Aligot.

Serves 2

2 x 7-8 oz (200-225 g) rump steaks
3 fl oz (75 ml) red wine
3 fl oz (75 ml) Worcestershire sauce
1 large clove garlic, peeled and crushed
1 teaspoon groundnut or other flavourless oil

To garnish:
a few sprigs fresh watercress

You will also need a shallow dish or lidded polythene box large enough to hold the steaks closely and comfortably.

Marinated Rump Steak served with Aligot

Mashed Potato with Three Mustards

This is the perfect accompaniment to gammon steaks, rich beef casseroles or spicy meat casseroles, and, as always, is great with bangers.

Serves 4

2 lb (900 g) Desirée or King Edward potatoes, peeled and steamed as for the Perfect Mashed Potato recipe (see page 176)
1½ tablespoons grain mustard
2 tablespoons French's American mustard
1 tablespoon hot mustard powder
2 rounded tablespoons crème fraîche
2 oz (50 g) butter
3-4 tablespoons from the top of the milk or single cream
salt and freshly milled black pepper

Whilst the potatoes are cooking, mix the crème fraîche with the three mustards in a small bowl. Drain the potatoes and return them to the hot pan, cover with a clean tea cloth for 4 minutes to absorb some of the steam, then add the mustard mixture, butter and some freshly milled black pepper. Then, using an electric hand whisk on a slow speed, break the potatoes up, then increase the speed and whisk them to a light, fluffy mash, adding the milk or single cream. Taste to check the seasoning before serving.

Green Parsley Mash

This is a quite stunning colour and the flavour of the parsley has an amazing affinity with potatoes. This is the perfect mash to serve with fish recipes, but it's also very good with boiled ham or grilled gammon steaks.

Serves 4

2 lb (900 g) Desirée or King Edward potatoes, peeled and steamed as for the Perfect Mashed Potato recipe (see page 176)
2 oz (50 g) fresh parsley
5 fl oz (150 ml) milk
salt and freshly milled black pepper

While the potatoes are cooking, place the parsley, with its stalks, into a small saucepan, add the milk and bring very slowly up to the gentlest simmer possible for 5 minutes or until the parsley is wilted and tender. Then place the whole lot into a liquidiser or processor and blend on a high speed until the parsley is blended into the milk and has turned it a bright green colour – 2-3 minutes – then strain it through a sieve to remove any bits of stalks and return to the pan to keep warm. When the potatoes are tender, drain them and cover with a clean tea cloth and leave for 4 minutes. Then, using an electric hand whisk on a slow speed, start to mash the potatoes, then increase the speed of the whisk and gradually add the parsley milk and a good seasoning of salt and freshly milled black pepper. Whisk until the mash is light and fluffy.

Watercress and Caper Mash

This is another recipe for mashed potato that's great served with fish. I love it with some freshly grilled mackerel or herring, and it's also extremely good with smoked fish.

When the potatoes are tender, drain them and cover with a clean tea cloth and leave for 4 minutes, then add the butter, milk and crème fraîche. Now, using an electric hand whisk, begin to whisk slowly to break them up, then add the watercress, increase the speed of the whisk and continue whisking until the potatoes are smooth and fluffy. Next, stir in the lemon juice and capers and add the seasoning, though you may not need much salt if you are using salted capers.

Serves 4

2 lb (900 g) Desirée or King Edward potatoes, peeled and steamed as for the Perfect Mashed Potato recipe (see page 176)

5 oz (150 g) watercress, stalks removed

1 heaped tablespoon salted capers or capers in vinegar, thoroughly washed and drained

2 oz (50 g) butter

2 tablespoons milk

2 tablespoons crème fraîche

2 tablespoons lemon juice

salt and freshly milled black pepper

Clockwise from top: Aligot, Mashed Potato with Three Mustards, Watercress and Caper Mash, Green Parsley Mash

183

Crunchy Roast Potatoes with Saffron

This is my old favourite recipe for roast potatoes but with a new twist, and that's a flavouring of saffron – not too much, just a hint – and with the added dimension of a deep saffron colour, which makes this look even more irresistible.

Serves 4

2 lb (900 g) Desirée or King Edward potatoes, peeled and cut into approximately 1½ inch (4 cm) pieces
1 teaspoon saffron stamens
1 tablespoon olive oil
salt

You will also need a solid baking tray measuring 16 x 11 inches (40 x 28 cm).

Pre-heat the oven to gas mark 7, 425°F (220°C) and place the baking tray with 2 tablespoons of oil in it to pre-heat as well.

First of all crush the saffron to a powder with a pestle and mortar. Then place the potatoes in a saucepan with sufficient boiling water to almost cover them, add a dessertspoon of salt and half the saffron powder, cover with a lid and simmer gently for 6 minutes. Use a timer, as it's important not to overcook them at this stage.

When the time is up, lift a potato out using the skewer to see if the outer edge is fluffy. You can test this by running the point of a skewer along the surface – if it stays smooth, give them 2 or 3 more minutes. Then drain off the water, place the lid back on the pan and, holding the lid firmly and protecting your hand with a cloth, shake the saucepan vigorously. This is to create a fluffy surface so the finished potatoes will be really crunchy.

Now mix the oil with the rest of the saffron powder, then remove the tray from the oven and place it over a direct medium heat. Next, using a long-handled spoon, carefully but quickly lift the potatoes into the hot fat, tilt the tray and baste them well, then, using a small brush, quickly paint the potatoes with the saffron oil, making sure they are well coated. Now return the tray to the highest shelf of the oven for 40-50 minutes, until the potatoes are golden and crunchy. Sprinkle with a little salt before serving with meat or fish or with the marinated chicken recipe on the next page. Note: Classic plain roast potatoes are cooked in exactly the same way, minus the saffron, and don't forget, it's always important to serve them straight away, before they lose their crunchiness.

Marinated Chicken with Honey and Ginger served with Mango and Sultana Salsa

This is another quick and easy recipe that's helpful for busy people because it needs to be prepared ahead and can then be cooked alongside the Crunchy Roast Potatoes with Saffron on page 184 at the same temperature. So, in theory, you could come home from work and have supper for four ready in about an hour.

Begin this by making two cuts in each chicken breast, about ¼ inch (5 mm) deep, then place the chicken breasts neatly in the ovenproof dish. Now combine all the marinade ingredients in a bowl, whisking them together, then pour this over the chicken breasts, turning them around in the marinade to get them well coated. You now need to cover the dish with clingfilm and leave it in the fridge overnight.

Next, place the sultanas for the salsa with the lime zest and juice in a small bowl so they can plump up overnight. Cover them with clingfilm and store in the fridge.

When you are ready to cook the chicken, pre-heat the oven to gas mark 7, 425°F (220°C). Then remove the clingfilm from the chicken and baste each breast with the marinade. Bake on a high shelf of the oven (or the next one down from the potatoes) for 20-30 minutes.

While the chicken is cooking, remove the skin from the mango using a potato peeler or sharp knife. Then slice all the flesh away from the stone and chop it into small pieces – about ¼ inch (5 mm) dice. Then add it to the sultanas, along with the remaining salsa ingredients, and garnish just before serving with the coriander leaves. Serve the cooked chicken with some of the salsa spooned over and the rest served separately, along with a bowl of the saffron-roasted potatoes.

Serves 4

4 x 6 oz (175 g) bone-in chicken breasts, skin on
salt and freshly milled black pepper

For the marinade:
2 tablespoons runny honey
1 inch (2.5 cm) piece root ginger, peeled and finely grated
1 teaspoon ground ginger
2 cloves garlic, peeled and crushed
zest and juice ½ lime
salt and freshly milled black pepper

For the salsa:
1 medium or ½ large mango
2 oz (50 g) sultanas
zest and juice 1 lime
½ red pepper, deseeded and chopped
½ medium red onion, peeled and finely chopped
1 medium green chilli, deseeded and finely chopped

To garnish:
½ oz (10 g) fresh coriander leaves

You will also need an ovenproof dish measuring 8 x 6 inches (20 x 15 cm) and 1¾ inches (4.5 cm) deep.

Marinated Chicken with Honey and Ginger served with Mango and Sultana Salsa and Crunchy Roast Potatoes with Saffron

186

Potatoes Boulangères with Rosemary

These potatoes are so named because in France they were given to the local baker to place in a bread oven to cook slowly. The nice thing is that you can pop them in your oven and just forget about them until you are ready to serve, and, unlike other potato dishes, they don't mind being kept warm.

Begin by preparing the rosemary, which should be stripped from the stalks then bruised in a pestle and mortar. After that, take two-thirds of the leaves and chop them finely. Now cut the onions in half and then the halves into the thinnest slices possible; the potatoes should be sliced, but not too thinly. All you do is arrange a layer of potatoes, then onions, in the dish, followed by a scattering of rosemary, then season. Continue layering in this way, alternating the potatoes and onions and finishing with a layer of potatoes that slightly overlap. Now mix the stock and milk together and pour it over the potatoes. Season the top layer, then scatter over the whole rosemary leaves. Now put little flecks of the butter all over the potatoes and place the dish on the highest shelf of the oven for 50-60 minutes, until the top is crisp and golden and the underneath is creamy and tender.

Serves 6

2 lb 8 oz (1.15 kg) Desirée or Romano potatoes, peeled
½ oz (10 g) fresh rosemary
2 medium onions, peeled
10 fl oz (275 ml) vegetable stock
5 fl oz (150 ml) milk
1½ oz (40 g) butter
sea salt and freshly milled black pepper

You will also need an ovenproof dish measuring 11 x 8 x 2 inches (28 x 20 x 5 cm), lightly buttered.

Pre-heat the oven to gas mark 4, 350°F (180°C).

187

Oven-Sautéed Potatoes Lyonnaises

Let's face it, though sautéed potatoes are much loved, they are a bother – someone has to stand there and cook, and for four to six people you'll need, at best, four frying pans. The kitchen gets all greasy, too. Until now, that is, because you can, I've discovered, just pop them in the oven and forget about them till they're ready. They're particularly good alongside the Roast Lamb with Garlic and Rosemary on page 156.

Serves 4-6
2 lb (900 g) Desirée potatoes, peeled and, if large, halved
1 dessertspoon salt
3 tablespoons olive oil
1 medium onion, peeled, halved, then cut into ¼ inch (5 mm) slices
rock salt

You will also need a flameproof baking tray measuring 16 x 11 inches (40 x 28 cm).

Pre-heat the oven to gas mark 7, 425°F (220°C).

Place the potatoes in a steamer over boiling water and sprinkle them with the dessertspoon of salt, then put a lid on and let them steam for 10 minutes using a timer. When the time is up, remove the steamer, cover the potatoes with a clean tea cloth and allow them to cool slightly. Meanwhile, place the baking tray plus 2 tablespoons of the oil on to a high shelf of the oven to pre-heat for 10 minutes. Then, when the potatoes are cool enough to handle, slice them into rounds about ⅓ inch (7 mm) thick.

Next, remove the baking tray from the oven and place it over a medium direct heat. Now spoon the potatoes on to the tray and turn and baste them well so they get a good coating of oil, then pop them back in the oven, high shelf again, for 10 minutes. While that's happening, toss the onion slices with the remaining tablespoon of oil in a bowl. When the 10 minutes are up, remove the baking tray from the oven and scatter the onion amongst the potato slices, then return them to the same shelf of the oven for a further 10 minutes. Have a look after this time to make sure they are not becoming too brown, but give them a further 5 minutes if they are not quite brown enough. Then, when they're ready, sprinkle with rock salt and serve immediately.

Red Onion, Tomato and Chilli Relish

This is a recipe I devised especially for the chunky potato chips opposite, which I feel are all the better for some kind of dipping sauce.

Serves 4
1 small red onion, peeled and finely chopped
8 oz (225 g) ripe red tomatoes
½ small red chilli, deseeded and finely chopped
1 clove garlic, peeled and crushed
1 tablespoon dark brown soft sugar
4 fl oz (120 ml) balsamic vinegar
salt and freshly milled black pepper

First you need to skin the tomatoes, so pour boiling water over them and leave for exactly 1 minute before draining them and slipping off the skins (protect your hands with a cloth if they are too hot). Put the onion, chilli, garlic and tomatoes in a food processor and blend until finely chopped, then place the mixture in a saucepan and add the sugar and vinegar. Place the pan over a gentle heat and simmer very gently, without a lid, for 2 hours, by which time the mixture will have reduced to a thick sauce. Towards the end of the cooking time, stir frequently so the sauce doesn't stick to the bottom of the pan. Then taste to check the seasoning and serve hot or cold. Covered in the fridge, the relish will keep for several days.

Oven-Roasted Chunky Chips

These are, believe it or not, low fat – just one dessertspoon of oil between four to six people, so not quite as wicked as it would first seem.

First wash the potatoes very thoroughly, then dry in a clean tea cloth – they need to be as dry as possible; if they're ready-washed, just wipe them with kitchen paper. Leaving the peel on, slice them in half lengthways and then cut them again lengthways into chunky wedges approximately 1 inch (2.5 cm) thick. Dry them again in a cloth, then place them in a large bowl with the oil and a sprinkling of salt. Now toss them around a few times to get them well covered with the oil, then spread them out on the baking tray and place in the oven on a high shelf to roast for about 30 minutes. They should be golden brown and crisp after this time; if not, give them a few more minutes. Finely sprinkle with a little more salt, then serve absolutely immediately.

Serves 4-6
2 lb (900 g) Desirée potatoes
1 dessertspoon olive oil
salt

You will also need a solid baking tray measuring approximately 16 x 11 inches (40 x 28 cm).

Pre-heat the oven to gas mark 8, 450°F (230°C).

For Oven-Roasted Chunky Chips with Garlic and Rosemary (add to the basic recipe above):
2 cloves garlic, peeled and crushed
2 tablespoons bruised and chopped rosemary leaves

Oven-Roasted Chunky Chips served with Red Onion, Tomato and Chilli Relish

189

Gnocchi with Sage, Butter and Parmesan

Once again it's the Italians who are so clever at inventing such simple things out of what seem to be fairly ordinary ingredients but then become something quite outstanding. Thus it is with gnocchi – little dumplings made from potatoes, flour and egg. Not very exciting, you might think, but like real pasta made in the old-fashioned way, gnocchi have a texture and flavour of their own which can absorb and complement other flavours. This recipe is very simple, served with just butter, sage and Parmesan (but is also great with four cheeses, as overleaf). Always make the gnocchi the day you are going to serve them, because they will discolour if left overnight.

Serves 2-3
10 oz (275 g) King Edward potatoes (about 2 medium-sized potatoes)
3½ oz (95 g) plain flour, sifted, plus a little extra for rolling
1 large egg, lightly beaten
salt and freshly milled black pepper

For the sauce:
2 oz (50 g) butter
1 large clove garlic, peeled and crushed
8 fresh sage leaves

To serve:
3-4 tablespoons freshly grated Parmesan (Parmigiano Reggiano)

You will also need a shallow ovenproof serving dish measuring about 10 x 7 inches (25.5 x 18 cm).

First place the potatoes, with their skins on, in a suitably sized saucepan, almost cover with boiling water, add some salt, then put a lid on and simmer for 20-25 minutes, until tender. Then drain well and, holding them in your hand with a tea cloth, quickly pare off the skins using a potato peeler. Then place the potatoes in a large bowl and, using an electric hand whisk on a slow speed, start to break the potatoes up, then increase the speed and gradually whisk until smooth and fluffy. Now let them cool.

Next, add the sifted flour to the potatoes, along with half the beaten egg, season lightly and, using a fork, bring the mixture together. Then, using your hands, knead the mixture lightly to a soft dough – you may need to add a teaspoonful or so more of the egg if it is a little dry. Now transfer the mixture to a lightly floured surface, flour your hands and divide it into quarters. Now roll each quarter into a sausage shape approximately ½ inch (1 cm) in diameter, then cut it, on the diagonal, into 1 inch (2.5 cm) pieces, placing them on a tray or plate as they are cut. Cover with clingfilm and chill for at least 30 minutes, but longer won't matter.

After that, using a fork with the prongs facing upwards, press the fork down on to one side of each gnocchi so that it leaves a row of ridges on each one; at the same time, ease them into crescent shapes. The ridges are there to absorb the sauce effectively. Now cover and chill the gnocchi again until you are ready to cook them.

To cook the gnocchi, firstly bring a large, shallow pan of approximately 6 pints (3.5 litres) of water to a simmer and put the serving dish in a low oven to warm through. Then drop the gnocchi into the water and cook for about 3 minutes; they will start to float to the surface after about 2 minutes, but they need 3 altogether. When they are ready, remove the gnocchi with a draining spoon and transfer them to the warm serving dish. To serve, melt the butter with the garlic over a gentle heat until the garlic turns nut brown in colour – about 1 minute. Next add the sage leaves and allow the butter to froth while the sage leaves turn crisp – about 30 seconds – then spoon the butter mixture over the warm gnocchi. Sprinkle half the Parmesan over and serve the rest separately.

Spinach Gnocchi with Four Cheeses

I dream about eating this recipe on a warm, sunny summer's day outside, but in winter it's still an excellent lunch for two people or as a first course for four. For a variation, instead of using all cheese, halve the amount and add 6 oz (175 g) of crisp, crumbly bacon or pancetta.

Serves 2-3

1 medium King Edward potato –
about 6 oz (175 g)
8 oz (225 g) young leaf spinach
6 oz (175 g) Ricotta
a little freshly grated nutmeg
1 oz (25 g) plain flour, plus a little
extra for rolling
1 large egg
2 oz (50 g) Mascarpone
1 heaped tablespoon freshly
snipped chives
2 oz (50 g) creamy Gorgonzola,
roughly cubed
2 oz (50 g) Fontina, cut into
small cubes
2 oz (50 g) Pecorino Romano,
finely grated
salt and freshly milled black pepper

You will also need a shallow ovenproof
serving dish measuring about 10 x 7
inches (25.5 x 18 cm).

First boil the potato, leaving the skin on, which will take about 25 minutes. Meanwhile, pick over the spinach, remove the stalks, then rinse the leaves. Place them in a large saucepan over a medium heat and cook briefly with a lid on for 1-2 minutes, until wilted and collapsed down. Then drain in a colander and, when cool enough to handle, squeeze all the moisture out and chop finely.

When the potato is cooked, drain and, holding it in a tea cloth, peel off the skin and sieve the potato into a bowl. Next add the spinach, Ricotta, nutmeg and flour to join the potato, then beat the egg and add half, together with some seasoning. Now, gently and lightly using a fork, bring the mixture together. Finish off with your hands and knead the mixture lightly into a soft dough, adding a teaspoonful or more of the beaten egg if it is a little dry. Then transfer the mixture to a floured surface and divide it into four. Roll each quarter into a sausage shape approximately ½ inch (1 cm) in diameter, then cut it on the diagonal into 1 inch (2.5 cm) pieces, placing them on a tray or plate as they are cut. Cover with clingfilm and chill for at least 30 minutes, but longer won't matter.

After that, using a fork with the prongs facing upwards, press the fork down on to each gnocchi, easing it into a crescent shape, so that it leaves a row of ridges on each one. Now cover and chill the gnocchi again until you are ready to cook them.

To cook the gnocchi, have all the cheeses ready. Pre-heat the grill to its highest setting, then bring a large, shallow pan of approximately 6 pints (3.5 litres) of water up to simmering point and put the serving dish near the grill to warm through. Now drop the gnocchi into the water and cook them for 3 minutes; they will start to float to the surface after about 2 minutes, but they need an extra minute. When they are ready, remove them with a draining spoon and transfer them straight to the serving dish. When they are all in, quickly stir in first the Mascarpone and chives, then sprinkle in the Gorgonzola and Fontina, then add some seasoning and cover the whole lot with the grated Pecorino. Now pop it under the grill for 3-4 minutes, until it is golden brown and bubbling. Serve absolutely immediately on hot plates.

Note: The plain gnocchi on page 190 can also be served with four cheeses, as above.

Potato Salad with Roquefort

This potato salad, with creamy, piquant Roquefort and the added crunch of celery and shallots, is good to eat all by itself, but I also like to serve it with cold cuts at a buffet lunch. It's therefore a very good recipe to have around at Christmas.

Place the potatoes in a steamer over boiling water and sprinkle them with a dessertspoon of salt, then put a lid on and let them steam for 20-25 minutes.

Meanwhile, make the dressing. To do this, place the garlic, along with the teaspoon of salt, into a mortar and crush it to a creamy mass, then add the mustard and work that in. Next add the lemon juice, vinegar and, after that, the oil, then whisk everything together thoroughly. Now, in a medium-sized bowl, first combine the crème fraîche and mayonnaise, then gradually whisk in the dressing. When it's thoroughly blended, add the cheese and season with freshly milled black pepper.

When the potatoes are cooked, remove the steamer and place a cloth over them for about 4 minutes to absorb the steam. Then cut any larger potatoes in half, transfer them to a large bowl and, while they are still warm, pour the dressing over them, along with the shallots and celery. Give everything a good gentle mixing, then, just before serving, crumble over the rest of the Roquefort and the spring onions.

Serves 6-8

2 lb (900 g) small new potatoes or salad potatoes
1 oz (25 g) Roquefort, crumbled
4 shallots, peeled and finely chopped
2 celery sticks, trimmed and chopped into ¼ inch (5 mm) pieces
4 spring onions, trimmed and finely chopped
salt

For the dressing:

1½ oz (40 g) Roquefort, crumbled
1 clove garlic, peeled
1 teaspoon salt
1 heaped teaspoon grain mustard
1 tablespoon lemon juice
2 tablespoons balsamic vinegar
2 tablespoons olive oil
5 fl oz (150 ml) half-fat crème fraîche
2 tablespoons mayonnaise
freshly milled black pepper

9

All kinds of rice

If you want to cook perfect rice
– the kind that always stays light
and fluffy, with absolutely every
grain remaining separate – then
I can teach you. But first you
will have to make a promise,
and that is to memorise three
simple little words: *leave it
alone!* If you can do this you
will always be able to cook
long-grain rice perfectly, and
never have to worry about it.

The enemy

The number one enemy of fluffy, separate rice is the wooden spoon or, more specifically, the anxious cook who wields it. It is nervous prodding, poking and constant stirring that ruin rice. So there you are – that's the basic principle for the most common type of rice you'll have to cook, long-grain rice, but, of course, there are other kinds of rice that need different kinds of cooking. So for the beginner it's crucial to know your rice before you attempt to buy or cook it.

Know your rice

The simplest approach to rice cooking is to think in terms of four types of eating categories: first there's the fluffy, separate kind we've talked about; secondly there's the creamy, soupy kind used in risottos; then the clingy, sticky kind used in the Far East; and lastly what I'd call speciality rices, which have a distinctive characteristic of their own and are therefore not really in any of the categories already mentioned.

Brown or white?

Grains of rice, like wheat grains, are sometimes milled, which means the germ and the outer bran layer are removed in the process, revealing the inner grain, which comes in different shades of creamy white to pure white, depending on the variety. If the bran and germ are left intact, the colour of the grain is a rather appealing greeny-brown – hence the name brown rice. Here the flavour is more pronounced, slightly nutty and the texture is less soft, with more bite than white rice.

The advantage is that this rice contains (as you'd expect) more fibre, vitamins and minerals, but it takes longer to cook: 40 minutes as opposed to 15. But it's good to ring the changes, and there are times when I personally prefer brown to white rice for serving with certain dishes – with chilli, for instance, or in a rice salad. On the other hand, if I'm serving curry, I always prefer white rice, but it's good to experiment to find out what your own preferences are.

The long and short of it

What usually determines the 'eating' categories is the shape of the grain (although there is the odd exception, as you will see later).

Long-grain rice is precisely that, and the longer and thinner the grain is, the better the quality. So the grains should be mega-slim, with needle-sharp points at each end: this is the type of rice needed for separate, fluffy grains, and the best quality is called *basmati*. This is more expensive than others, but since cooking is about flavour, it is the one to buy, as it has a far superior taste. Although you will see dozens of varieties of long-grain rice, I believe it's well worth paying that little bit extra for basmati. Whether you are using the brown or the white, it's quite certainly the best.

Medium- and short-grain rice

Here the grains are not long and thin, but rounder and plumper. This group comes in the creamy and sticky eating category described earlier. There are, however, various qualities and national preferences.

Italian risotto rice, sometimes called *arborio* rice, is superb, or for the finest-quality risotto rice of all, look for the names *carnaroli* or *vialone nano*. In creamy, almost soupy risottos the rice is stirred, which releases some of the starch, and it is this that creates the lovely, smooth, creamy mass. The same kind of plump grain is used in Spain, and one of the finest varieties comes from the Valencia region and is called *calasparra*, which is used to make paella, though here the grains are not stirred, so they remain firm and distinct but with a moist, creamy edge.

In Japan there are several varieties of short-grain rice, ranging from the mildly sticky to the very sticky rice used to make sushi (it makes absolute sense that in the countries where chopsticks are used, rice with a stickier, more clinging consistency is far more manageable). This is sometimes called 'glutinous' rice, but it does not, as its name might suggest, contain any gluten and I prefer to describe it as *sticky rice*, which is more accurate.

In Thailand and Southeast Asia the rice grown and preferred is sometimes called *jasmine* or *fragrant rice*, but again I think the title is a little misleading, because it isn't actually any more fragrant than other types of rice. However, the quality is very good, and though it's actually a long-grain rice and when cooked, the grains have a firm texture and a good bite, they have a faint stickiness and tend to adhere to each other. I would say in this case the rice is both fluffy and sticky, and this is how it should be.

Specialist rices

These are rice varieties with their own individual characteristics. The first is *Camargue red rice*. Though other red rices are grown in America, this one, from France, is of superior quality. It is an unmilled short-grain rice with a brownish-red colour, and I would describe its character as earthy and gutsy, with a firm, slightly chewy texture and a nutty flavour. It is excellent in salads and combined with other strong flavours. Because it is a short-grain rice it is very slightly sticky when cooked and not meant to be separate and fluffy.

Black rice, well, it's reddish black, is an Asian rice used for sweet dishes and puddings and turns purple when cooked. It's very fashionable in Australia, where practically every smart restaurant has a special pudding made with cooked black rice dressed with a mixture of palm sugar, coconut milk and lime. If you manage to get some, follow the instructions on the packet, which vary.

Wild rice is not actually a rice grain at all but the seed of a special type of grass grown in the swamps of North America. However, it's called rice, so I've put it on my list because it is cooked and served in exactly the same

Top row, left to right: black rice, Thai fragrant rice, Japanese rice
Centre, left to right: Camargue red rice, brown basmati rice, risotto rice
Bottom row, left to right: wild rice, white basmati rice, pudding rice

way, but needs about 50 minutes. The seeds are very long and most attractive, with a shiny ebony colour, and have a subtle, smoky, nutty flavour. It's good in salads and with gutsy foods with strong flavours. When cooked, the seeds tend to split slightly, but this is quite normal and not some failure in the cooking – though, as with rice grains, it's important not to overcook them.

The 'also rans'

There are, of course, a million and one types of rice, and the list I've given you has what I believe to be the best in quality. The 'also rans', in a way, perpetuate the myth that cooking rice is difficult, and people usually buy them out of fear. Hopefully, *How To Cook* will dispel the myth and we can all enjoy the best quality of flavour when we're cooking rice. Pre-cooked or par-boiled rice is actually cooked before milling: this means the grains are tougher so require more water and a much longer cooking time. This is to help it stay more separate, but in my opinion there is a loss of flavour and I would never choose it. Quick-cook or easy-cook rice has been partially cooked after milling and then dried, so all it has to do is reabsorb water. It is quicker to cook, only 8-10 minutes instead of 12-15, but the loss of character and flavour puts this in the 'sliced white' category, ie, dull and pappy.

Pudding rice

Since I was a small child – a long time ago – we have always had in Britain a variety of short-grain rice called pudding rice; this is the type used the world over in sweet dishes and is best of all, in my opinion, for good Old-Fashioned Rice Pudding (see page 212). It is very sticky when cooked and, simmered in milk, becomes deliciously soft and creamy.

Always measure your rice by volume, using double the amount of water to rice

First cook the onions, then add the rice, turning the grains to coat them in the oil

The next stage is to add the boiling water and salt to the rice in the pan

To wash or not to wash?

I have never washed rice since I discovered that it is possible to wash away some of the nutrients in the process, and in any case modern rice is thoroughly cleaned in the milling. What's more, the water it's cooked in will be boiling, and that, of course, will purify it. I think some of the traditional methods of cooking rice, which require long rinsing and washing, belong to past times, when the rice was not as clean as it is today.

The ten rules for cooking perfect rice

1 Always measure rice by volume and not by weight. Use a measuring jug and measure 2½ fl oz (65 ml) per person (5 fl oz or 150 ml for 2, 10 fl oz or 275ml for 4 and so on).

2 Coating the grains of rice in a little oil before adding the water can help to keep them separate, and adding a little onion (see the recipe that follows) can provide extra flavour. But this is not a necessity – rice can be cooked quite simply in water.

3 The quantity of liquid you will need is roughly double the volume of rice, so 5 fl oz (150ml) needs 10 fl oz (275ml) of water or stock. Always add hot water or stock.

4 Don't forget to add salt, about 1 level teaspoon to every 5 fl oz (150ml) of rice.

5 The very best utensil for cooking fluffy, separate rice is a frying pan with a lid. Over the years I have found that the shallower the rice is spread out during cooking the better. Buying a 10 inch (25.5 cm) pan with a lid would be a good lifetime investment for rice cooking. Failing that, try to find a large saucepan lid that will fit your normal frying pan.

Stir once only – more will break the delicate grains, resulting in sticky rice

Put a lid on, turn the heat to its lowest setting and leave for 15 minutes

Once ready, remove the pan from the heat and cover with a cloth for 5-10 minutes

6 Once the hot liquid has been added, stir once only, cover with the lid and turn the heat down to its lowest setting, Give white rice 15 minutes and brown rice 40.

7 Leave it alone! Once the lid is on, set the timer and go away. If you lift the lid and let the steam out you can slow down the cooking process, and rice should always be cooked as briefly as possible. Even worse, if you stir it you will break the delicate grains and release the starch, and then it will end up sticky.

8 Use a timer – overcooking is what spoils rice. The best way to test if it is cooked is simply to bite a grain. Another way is to tilt the pan and, if liquid collects at the edge, it will need a couple more minutes.

9 When the rice is cooked, remove the lid, turn the heat off and place a clean tea cloth over the pan for 5-10 minutes. This will absorb the steam and help keep the grains dry and separate.

10 Just before serving, use the tip of a skewer or a fork to lightly fluff up the grains.

Perfect Rice

Serves 4
white basmati rice measured up
to the 10 fl oz (275 ml) level in a
measuring jug
1½ teaspoons groundnut or other
flavourless oil
1 small onion, peeled and finely
chopped
1 pint (570 ml) boiling water
1 rounded teaspoon salt

You will also need a frying pan with
a 10 inch (25.5 cm) base and a tight-
fitting lid.

Begin by warming the frying pan over a medium heat, then add the oil and the onions and let them cook for 3-4 minutes, until lightly tinged brown. Next stir in the rice – there's no need to wash it – and turn the grains over in the pan so they become lightly coated and glistening with oil. Then add the boiling water, along with the salt, stir once only, then cover with the lid. Turn the heat to its very lowest setting and let the rice cook gently for exactly 15 minutes. Don't remove the lid and don't stir the rice during cooking, because this is what will break the grains and release their starch, which makes the rice sticky.

After 15 minutes, tilt the pan to check that no liquid is left; if there is, pop it back on the heat for another minute. When there is no water left in the pan, take the pan off the heat, remove the lid and cover with a clean tea cloth for 5-10 minutes before serving, then transfer the rice to a warm serving dish and fluff it lightly with a fork before it goes to the table.

Oven-Baked Risotto Carbonara

I just love pasta with carbonara sauce so much that one day I thought I'd try it with a risotto – same ingredients: pancetta, a strong-flavoured Italian bacon, eggs and sharp Pecorino cheese. The result is outstanding.

First of all, in a large, hot frying pan over a medium heat, fry the pancetta or bacon in its own fat for 4-5 minutes, until it's crisp and golden, then remove it to a plate. Next add the butter to the pan, then the onion, turn the heat down to gentle and let the onion soften in the butter for about 5 minutes. Meanwhile, heat the stock in a small saucepan. Then return the pancetta or bacon to the frying pan and, after that, stir in the rice and move it around until all the grains get a good coating of the buttery juices. Now add the hot stock to the rice, along with some salt and freshly milled black pepper. Let it all come up to a gentle simmer, then transfer the whole lot to the warmed dish, stir it once and then bake, without covering, on the centre shelf of the oven and set a timer for 20 minutes.

When the time is up, gently stir in the Pecorino, folding and turning the rice grains over, then set the timer for a further 15 minutes. Meanwhile, whisk the egg, egg yolks and crème fraîche together, then remove the risotto from the oven and gently stir in this mixture, making sure it is well mixed. Leave the risotto for about 2 minutes, by which time the eggs and crème fraîche will have thickened – but no longer, as it will get too thick. Serve on warm plates with some more Pecorino Romano sprinkled over.
Note: This recipe contains raw eggs.

Serves 2
8 fl oz (225 ml) carnaroli rice
4½ oz (125 g) cubetti (cubed) pancetta or chopped bacon
1 oz (25 g) butter
1 medium onion, peeled and finely chopped
1¼ pints (725 ml) chicken or vegetable stock
3 oz (75 g) finely grated Pecorino Romano, plus some extra for sprinkling
1 large egg
2 large egg yolks
1 heaped tablespoon crème fraîche
salt and freshly milled black pepper

You will also need a round ovenproof dish with a diameter of 9 inches (23 cm), 2 inches (5 cm) deep, placed in the oven when it's pre-heated.

Pre-heat the oven to gas mark 2, 300°F (150°C).

Chinese Stir-Fried Rice

The most important point to remember if you want to fry rice successfully is that it must be cooked but cold. I have used authentic Chinese ingredients here, which are easily obtainable if you live near speciality Chinese suppliers; if not, you can use fresh prawns instead of shrimps and fresh shiitake mushrooms instead of dried.

Serves 4

8 fl oz (225 ml) white basmati rice, cooked as for Perfect Rice (see page 200, but using 16 fl oz/450 ml boiling water), cooled
1 oz (25 g) Chinese dried shrimps
¼ oz (5 g) Chinese dried mushrooms
16 fl oz (450 ml) boiling water
1½ tablespoons groundnut or other flavourless oil
1 small onion, peeled and finely chopped
4 rashers streaky bacon, chopped into ¼ inch (5 mm) pieces
2 oz (50 g) peas, fresh if possible, defrosted if frozen
2 large eggs, lightly beaten
2 spring onions, split lengthways and finely chopped
1 tablespoon Japanese soy sauce

You will also need a wok or frying pan with a 10 inch (25.5 cm) base.

Begin by putting the shrimps and mushrooms in a small bowl, pour over the boiling water and leave them to soak for 30 minutes. Then squeeze the liquid from them, discard the mushroom stalks and slice them finely. Then heat half the oil in the wok or pan and, when it's really hot, quickly fry the onions and bacon for 3 minutes, moving them around in the pan until the bacon is crispy. Then add the shrimps, peas and mushrooms and stir-fry these for about 1 minute. Now add the remaining oil to the pan and, when it's smoking hot, add the rice and stir-fry, this time for about 30 seconds. Now spread the ingredients out in the pan and pour in the beaten eggs. It won't look very good now, but keep on stir-frying, turning the mixture over, and the eggs will soon cook into little shreds that mingle with the other ingredients. Finally, add the spring onions and soy sauce, give it one more good stir and serve.

Chinese Stir-Fried Rice served with Oriental Steamed Fish with Ginger, Soy and Sesame

Oriental Steamed Fish with Ginger, Soy and Sesame

This can be a quick supper dish for the family or it's exotic enough for entertaining: all you need is a fan steamer – bamboo or the old-fashioned kind.

You need to begin this by having a little chopping session. First the ginger, which should be thinly sliced then cut into very fine shreds. The garlic needs to be chopped small, as do the spring onions, making sure you include the green parts as well.

Now place a medium frying pan over a medium heat and, when it's hot, add the sesame seeds and toast them in the dry pan, shaking it from time to time until they're a golden brown colour – this takes only 1-2 minutes. Now transfer the seeds to a bowl.

Next add the oils to the pan and, over a medium heat, gently fry the chopped garlic and ginger – they need to be pale gold but not too brown, so take care not to have the heat too high. After that, add these to the toasted seeds, along with any oil left in the pan, then mix in the lemon juice, soy sauce and chopped spring onions.

Now season the fish, spread three-quarters of the mixture over the surface of each skinned side, roll them up quite firmly into little rolls, then spoon the rest of the mixture on top of each roll. All this can be prepared in advance, as long as the fish is kept covered in the fridge.

Then, when you're ready to cook the fish, line the base of the steamer with the lettuce leaves (or foil if you don't have any). Now place the fish on top, cover with a lid and steam over boiling water for 8-10 minutes. Serve with the Chinese Stir-Fried Rice, left.

Serves 4

1 lb 8 oz (700 g) lemon sole fillets, skinned and cut lengthways down the natural dividing line (ask the fishmonger to do this)
2½ inch (6 cm) piece root ginger, peeled
1 tablespoon Japanese soy sauce
1 rounded tablespoon sesame seeds
1 dessertspoon sesame oil
3 cloves garlic, peeled
2 spring onions
1 dessertspoon groundnut or other flavourless oil
juice 1 lemon
a few outside lettuce leaves, for lining the steamer
salt and freshly milled black pepper

You will also need a fan or bamboo steamer.

Very Red Rice

This was a recipe created for Comic Relief, hence the title, and I always have a good giggle thinking back to the filming of those hilarious cookery demonstrations that were later screened on television. It's also an excellent recipe – good with any barbecue dishes or with the pork chops opposite.

Serves 4

10 fl oz (275 ml) Camargue red rice
1 tablespoon oil
½ oz (10 g) butter
1 small red pepper, deseeded and finely chopped
1 small red onion, peeled and finely chopped
15 fl oz (425 ml) boiling water
1 teaspoon salt

To serve:
2 spring onions, trimmed and finely sliced
a few sprigs watercress

You will also need a 10 inch (25.5 cm) frying pan with a lid.

First heat the oil and butter in the pan over a medium heat. Then turn it up to high and stir-fry the chopped pepper and onion until they are softened and slightly blackened at the edges – 6-7 minutes. After that, turn the heat right down, add the red rice to the pan and stir it around to get a good coating of oil. Now pour in the boiling water and salt and stir again. When it reaches simmering point, put the lid on and let it cook very gently for 40 minutes. After that, don't remove the lid, just turn the heat off and leave it for another 15 minutes to finish off. Garnish the rice with the sliced spring onions and the watercress. Serve with the Oven-Baked Pork Chops in Maple Barbecue Sauce, opposite.

Very Red Rice served with Oven-Baked Pork Chops in Maple Barbecue Sauce

Oven-Baked Pork Chops in Maple Barbecue Sauce

Sorry about the long list of ingredients in this sauce, but it really does take only 5 minutes to make, then cooks into a heavenly, sticky, spicy goo.

First of all mix the olive oil with the lemon juice, then place the pork chops in the roasting tin with the chopped onion tucked amongst them. Season with a little salt and freshly milled black pepper, then brush the chops with the oil and lemon juice. You can, if you like, do this well in advance, just cover with a cloth and leave in a cool place.

Then, when you're ready to cook the pork chops, pre-heat the oven to gas mark 6, 400°F (200°C), then pop them in on a high shelf and cook for 25 minutes exactly. Meanwhile, combine all the sauce ingredients in a jug and, using a small whisk, blend everything thoroughly. Then, when the 25 minutes are up, remove the roasting tin from the oven, pour off any surplus fat from the corner of the tin and pour the sauce all over, giving everything a good coating.

Now back it goes into the oven for about another 25 minutes, and you will need to baste it twice during this time. After that, remove the roasting tin from the oven and place it over direct heat turned to medium. Then pour in the red wine, stir it into the sauce and let it bubble for about 1 minute. Then serve the pork chops on a bed of Very Red Rice with the sauce spooned over and garnish with the sprigs of watercress.

Serves 4

4 large pork chops
1 tablespoon olive oil
1 dessertspoon lemon juice
1 medium onion, peeled and finely chopped
salt and freshly milled black pepper

For the sauce:

2 tablespoons pure maple syrup
3 fl oz (75 ml) red wine
4 tablespoons Japanese soy sauce
2 tablespoons red wine vinegar
1 heaped tablespoon tomato purée
1 heaped teaspoon ground ginger
1 heaped teaspoon mustard powder
2 cloves garlic, peeled and crushed
1½ teaspoons Tabasco sauce

To finish:

2 fl oz (55 ml) red wine
a few sprigs watercress

You will also need a flameproof shallow roasting tin measuring 12 x 8 x 1¾ inches (30 x 20 x 4.5 cm).

Camargue Red Rice Salad with Feta Cheese

This is a lovely salad for outdoor eating on a warm, sunny summer's day.

Serves 4

10 fl oz (275 ml) Camargue red rice
7 oz (200 g) Feta cheese
1 teaspoon salt
1 pint (570 ml) boiling water
2 shallots, peeled and finely chopped
2 oz (50 g) fresh rocket leaves,
finely shredded
3 spring onions, trimmed and finely
chopped, including the green ends
salt and freshly milled black pepper

For the dressing:

1 small clove garlic, crushed
½ level teaspoon salt
1 level teaspoon grain mustard
1 tablespoon balsamic vinegar
2 tablespoons extra virgin olive oil
salt and freshly milled black pepper

You will also need a 10 inch (25.5 cm)
frying pan with a lid.

First put the rice in the frying pan with the teaspoon of salt, then pour in the boiling water, bring it back up to simmering point, then put a lid on and let it cook very gently for 40 minutes. After that, don't remove the lid, just turn the heat off and leave it for another 15 minutes to finish off.

Meanwhile, make the dressing by crushing the garlic and salt in a pestle and mortar, then, when it becomes a purée, add the mustard and work that in, followed by the vinegar and some freshly milled black pepper. Now add the oil and, using a small whisk, whisk everything thoroughly to combine it. Then transfer the warm rice to a serving dish, pour the dressing over and mix thoroughly. Taste to check the seasoning and leave aside until cold. Then add the shallots, the rocket and the spring onions. Finally, just before serving, crumble the Feta cheese all over.

Tiger Prawn Jambalaya

This is one of the easiest and nicest rice dishes, and its origins are in the traditional Cajun cooking of America. It's very easy to adapt it to whatever you have handy – fish, chicken or even pork.

Begin by bringing a pan with 1 pint (570 ml) of water to simmering point. If using raw prawns, drop them into the water for 3 minutes. After that, remove them with a draining spoon, reserving the cooking liquid. (Cooked prawns will not need this pre-cooking.) Now set aside two whole prawns and shell the rest. To do this, just remove the heads by giving them a sharp tug, then simply peel off the rest – which comes away very easily – but leave the tails intact as this makes them look nicer. Now remove the black vein from the back of each prawn, which will come away easily using the point of a sharp knife. Next place the shells in the pan of water and simmer for 30 minutes, without a lid, to make a nice prawn-flavoured stock, then drain and discard the shells. Pour the hot stock into a jug and cover with a plate to keep warm.

Now heat the frying pan over a high heat and brown the pieces of chorizo sausage, without adding any fat, then remove them from the pan to a plate and set aside. Then add a tablespoon of the oil and, when it's hot, fry the onions for 2-3 minutes to brown them a little at the edges, then return the chorizo to the pan and add the garlic, celery, chilli and sliced pepper. Continue to fry for 4-5 minutes, till the celery and pepper are also softened and lightly tinged brown at the edges, adding a little more oil if you need to. Now stir in the rice to get a good coating of oil, then measure out 12 fl oz (340 ml) of the reserved stock and add the Tabasco to it. Next add the chopped tomatoes and bay leaf to the pan, then pour in the stock. Season with salt and freshly milled black pepper, give it all one stir and push the rice down into the liquid. Now turn the heat to low, put a lid on and let it barely simmer for 20 minutes. Then, check the rice is cooked and return the shelled and the two reserved shell-on prawns to the pan, adding a little more stock if necessary. Cover with a lid for 5 more minutes, then serve garnished with the chopped parsley and spring onions.

Serves 2-3

8 raw tiger prawns, shell on, fresh or frozen and thoroughly defrosted, or you could use cooked Mediterranean prawns in their shells
4 oz (110 g) chorizo sausage, peeled and cut into ¾ inch (2 cm) pieces
1-2 tablespoons olive oil
1 medium onion, peeled and cut into ½ inch (1 cm) slices
2 cloves garlic, peeled and crushed
2 sticks celery, trimmed and sliced into ½ inch (1 cm) pieces on the diagonal
1 green chilli, deseeded and finely chopped
1 yellow pepper, deseeded and cut into ½ inch (1 cm) slices
6 fl oz (175 ml) white basmati rice
1 teaspoon Tabasco sauce
3 medium tomatoes, dropped into boiling water for 1 minute, then peeled and chopped
1 bay leaf
1 tablespoon roughly chopped flat-leaf parsley, to garnish
2 spring onions, trimmed and finely sliced, to garnish
salt and freshly milled black pepper

You will also need a 10 inch (25.5 cm) frying pan with a lid.

Spiced Pilau Rice with Nuts

I've always loved the fragrant flavour of spiced pilau rice, and could easily eat it just on its own, adding nuts to give it some crunch. However, it's also an excellent accompaniment to any spiced or curried dish, particularly the chicken recipe that follows.

Serves 4

10 fl oz (275 ml) white basmati rice

1 oz (25 g) unsalted cashew nuts

1 oz (25 g) unsalted shelled
pistachio nuts

1 oz (25 g) pine nuts

2 cardamom pods

¾ teaspoon cumin seeds

½ teaspoon coriander seeds

1½ tablespoons groundnut or other
flavourless oil

1 small onion, peeled and
finely chopped

1 pint (570 ml) boiling water

1 inch (2.5 cm) piece cinnamon stick

1 bay leaf

1 rounded teaspoon salt

You will also need a lidded frying pan
with a 10 inch (25.5 cm) base.

First of all, in the pestle and mortar, crush the cardamom pods and the cumin and coriander seeds. Then, warm the frying pan over a medium heat, add the crushed spices (the pods as well as the seeds of the cardamom), turn the heat up high and toss them around in the heat to dry-roast them and draw out the flavour – this will take about 1 minute. After that, turn the heat back to medium and add the oil, onion and nuts and fry until everything is lightly tinged brown. Next, stir in the rice and turn the grains over in the pan until they are nicely coated and glistening with oil, then pour in the boiling water. Add the cinnamon, bay leaf and a good seasoning of salt, stir once only, then put the lid on, turn the heat down to its lowest setting and let the rice cook for exactly 15 minutes. After this time, take the pan off the heat, remove the lid and cover with a clean tea cloth for 5 minutes. Then empty the rice into a warm serving dish and fluff up lightly with a fork before it goes to the table.

*Marinated Chicken Kebabs with Whole
Spices served with Spiced Pilau Rice
with Nuts*

Marinated Chicken Kebabs with Whole Spices

This is a heavenly combination of textures and fragrant, spicy flavours, and has the added advantage of not being too high in fat. The coriander chutney, pictured below, is a perfect accompaniment, but this dish also goes well with mango chutney if fresh coriander isn't available.

Begin by dry-roasting the cumin and coriander seeds and the cardamom pods over a medium heat for 1 minute, until the seeds begin to jump. Remove from the heat and, once cool, remove the seeds from the cardamom pods and crush them with the cumin and coriander seeds using a pestle and mortar. Next add the ginger, turmeric, garlic and salt and mix everything well.

Now cut each chicken breast into five pieces, place them in a bowl and toss them first in the groundnut or flavourless oil, then in the spice mixture, mixing everything around so they get an even coating. Next add the yoghurt, give everything a good stir and press the chicken down well into the marinade. Cover with clingfilm and refrigerate for a few hours or, preferably, overnight.

To make the chutney, simply whiz everything together in a blender, then pour into a bowl and leave aside for 2-3 hours so the flavours develop.

When you are almost ready to serve, soak the skewers in water for 20 minutes to stop them from burning, then light the barbecue or pre-heat the grill to its highest setting. Next, thread half a bay leaf on to each skewer, then a piece of chicken, a piece of onion and half a chilli. Carry on alternating the chicken, onion and chilli until you have used five pieces of chicken per kebab, then finish with half a bay leaf on each. Make sure you pack everything as tightly as possible, then season, lay the kebabs on the grill rack or barbecue and sprinkle with a little olive oil. If you're grilling, put a heatproof dish lined with foil under the rack and grill the kebabs for 10 minutes on each side, about 4 inches (10 cm) from the heat source, or simply cook over the barbecue.

Now slip the chicken and vegetables from the skewers, using a fork to ease them off, and serve with the Spiced Pilau Rice with Nuts, garnished with lime quarters, and the chutney handed round separately.

Serves 4

4 x 6 oz (175 g) boneless chicken breasts, skin on
4 bay leaves, cut in half
½ red onion, peeled, halved through the root and separated into layers
8 fresh green chillies, halved and deseeded
a little olive oil
salt and freshly milled black pepper

For the marinade:

1 teaspoon whole cumin seeds
1½ teaspoons whole coriander seeds
12 cardamom pods
1 rounded tablespoon peeled and grated root ginger
1 rounded tablespoon turmeric
3 cloves garlic, peeled and crushed
½ teaspoon Maldon sea salt or rock salt
1 tablespoon groundnut or other flavourless oil
10 fl oz (275 ml) natural yoghurt

For the fresh coriander chutney:

1 oz (25 g) fresh coriander leaves
2 tablespoons lime juice
1 fresh green chilli, halved and deseeded
1 clove garlic, peeled
1 tablespoon natural yoghurt
½ teaspoon golden caster sugar
salt and freshly milled black pepper

To garnish:

2 limes, quartered

You will also need four wooden skewers about 10 inches (25.5 cm) long.

Thai Creamed Coconut Chicken

The very good news about this brilliant recipe for busy people is that it's made with ready-cooked chicken. You can, of course, cook the chicken yourself, but either way it's a quick but excellent supper party dish for four people, and extra special served with the Thai Green Rice.

Serves 4
1 cooked chicken weighing about
2 lb 4 oz (1 kg), stripped, or 5 cooked
chicken breasts
14 fl oz (400 ml) coconut milk
1 teaspoon coriander seeds
½ teaspoon cumin seeds
2 cardamom pods, lightly crushed
2 tablespoons groundnut or other
flavourless oil
2 medium onions, peeled
and finely sliced
2 cloves garlic, peeled and crushed
½ oz (10 g) fresh coriander
1 teaspoon turmeric
4 red chillies, deseeded and finely
chopped
1 dessertspoon finely chopped fresh
lemon grass
2 tablespoons lime juice
salt and freshly milled black pepper

To prepare the chicken, remove the skin and cut the flesh into strips about 2½ inches (6 cm) long. Next the spices will need roasting, so heat a large frying pan or wok – without any fat in it – and, when it's really hot, add the coriander, cumin and cardamom pods. Allow the spices to roast briefly – about 45 seconds – shaking the pan from time to time, then tip them into a mortar, removing the seeds from the cardamom pods and discarding the husks, and crush them all fairly finely.

Now add the oil to the frying pan or wok. When it's really hot, fry the onions and garlic over a medium heat for 8-9 minutes, until they're nicely softened. Meanwhile, strip the leaves from the coriander stalks, reserve these, then chop the stalks finely.

When the onions are ready, add the turmeric, chilli, crushed spices and coriander stalks, along with the lemon grass, to the pan. Stir these thoroughly together, then pour in the coconut milk and lime juice. Add some seasoning, then simmer everything gently for about 10 minutes, uncovered, by which time the sauce should have reduced and thickened.

Now add the chicken to the sauce and simmer gently for 10 minutes or so to heat it through completely. Serve the chicken on a bed of Thai Green Rice, garnished with the coriander leaves.

Thai Green Rice

This, thankfully, is a Thai recipe that doesn't require all the speciality ingredients that are sometimes so elusive. The list of ingredients, again, seems rather long, but it is made in moments and has a lovely fragrant flavour.

Serves 4
12 fl oz (340 ml) basmati rice
2 oz (50 g) creamed coconut
8 fl oz (225 ml) boiling water
4 cloves garlic, peeled
3 large or 2 medium-sized fresh green
chillies, deseeded

Begin by dissolving the creamed coconut in the boiling water, then place it in a food processor with the garlic, chillies, ginger and coriander stalks, whizzing until everything is finely chopped.

Leave this aside while you heat the oil over a gentle heat in the frying pan, then add the cinnamon sticks, cloves, peppercorns and cashew nuts to the pan and sauté everything gently for about 1 minute. Next, add the onions and continue to cook over a medium heat until they become softened and pale gold in colour, which will take 8-10 minutes. Next add the rice, then stir once and cook for another 2-3 minutes. After that, add the coconut mixture, give everything a stir, and cook for a further 2-3 minutes. Now add the peas, salt and hot water, bring it all up to a gentle simmer, then cover with the lid. Turn the heat to low and let everything cook very gently for 8 minutes; use a timer here, and don't lift the lid.

Then remove the pan from the heat, take the lid off and cover the pan with a cloth for 10 minutes before serving. Finally, remove the pieces of cinnamon, sprinkle in the lime juice and the finely chopped coriander leaves, then fork the rice gently to separate the grains. Garnish with the reserved whole coriander leaves and serve with the Thai Creamed Coconut Chicken.

1½-inch (4 cm) cube root ginger, peeled
¾ oz (20 g) fresh coriander, leaves removed and finely chopped, the stalks reserved, with a few whole leaves reserved for the garnish
1½ tablespoons groundnut or other flavourless oil
3 x 2 inch (5 cm) pieces cinnamon stick
6 whole cloves
15 black peppercorns
1½ oz (40 g) unsalted cashew nuts, halved
2 medium onions, peeled and finely sliced
4 oz (110 g) fresh peas, or frozen and defrosted
1½ teaspoons salt, or to taste
15 fl oz (425 ml) hot water
2 tablespoons lime juice

You will also need a 9 inch (23 cm) frying pan with a close-fitting lid.

Thai Creamed Coconut Chicken served with Thai Green Rice

Old-Fashioned Rice Pudding

This is the real thing – a mass of creamy rice and a thick brown speckled nutmeg skin. Don't forget to take a sharp knife and scrape off all the bits of caramelised skin that stick to the edges – my grandmother always did that and gave everyone an equal amount.

This is simplicity itself, because all you do is mix the evaporated milk and whole milk together in a jug, then place the rice and sugar in the ovenproof dish, pour in the liquid and give it all a good stir. Grate the whole nutmeg all over the surface (it may seem a lot but it needs it), then, finally, dot the butter on top in little flecks.

Next just carefully pop the dish in the oven on the centre shelf and leave it there for 30 minutes, then slide the shelf out and give everything a good stir. Repeat the stirring after a further 30 minutes, then pop the dish back in the oven to cook for another hour, this time without stirring. At the end of this time the rice grains will have become swollen, with pools of creamy liquid all around them, and, of course, all that lovely skin! This is wonderful served warm with the Plums in Marsala, opposite.

Serves 4-6
4 oz (110 g) pudding rice
14½ oz (410 g) evaporated milk
1 pint (570 ml) whole milk
1½ oz (40 g) golden granulated or caster sugar
1 whole nutmeg
1 oz (25 g) butter

You will also need a round ovenproof dish with a diameter of 9 inches (23 cm), 2 inches (5 cm) deep, lightly buttered.

Pre-heat the oven to gas mark 2, 300°F (150°C).

Plums in Marsala

The mellow but distinctive flavour of Marsala wine, when simmered together with fruit, is something I am particularly fond of. It works well with plums, which, I think, are very good served chilled, along with the warm rice pudding opposite.

First place the plums, vanilla pod and cinnamon sticks in the baking dish, then mix the Marsala with the sugar and pour it over the plums. Now place the dish on the centre shelf of the oven and cook for 40 minutes, uncovered, turning the plums over in the Marsala halfway through the cooking time. Then remove the baking dish from the oven and strain the plums, discarding the vanilla pod and cinnamon sticks, and pour the sauce into a medium-sized saucepan. Bring it up to simmering point, then let it bubble and reduce for 5 minutes. Now mix the arrowroot with a little water in a cup to make a paste, then whisk this into the liquid. Bring the sauce back to simmering point, whisking all the time, until it has thickened slightly and is glossy – about 5 minutes. Then pour it back over the plums and serve them hot or cold.

Serves 6
3 lb (1.35 kg) fresh firm plums
1 pint (570 ml) Marsala
1 vanilla pod
2 cinnamon sticks
3 oz (75 g) golden caster sugar
2 teaspoons arrowroot

You will also need a 10 x 8 inch (25.5 x 20 cm) baking dish, 2 inches (5 cm) deep.

Pre-heat the oven to gas mark 4, 350°F (180°C).

10
Pasta revisited

I think it's about time we gave pasta a radical rethink. In the 1960s only two kinds of pasta were known to most people: spaghetti, which came in tins and was served on toast, and macaroni, which was served either in a cheese sauce or as a pudding. Yet, 40 years later, pasta has exploded into our lives with such force that it's now become almost a standard British staple – we now consume 2 kg per head per year. The trouble is that a lot of this is not, in the strictest sense, real pasta; not in the way it was originally and brilliantly conceived to be. And now many modern pasta makers have, I feel, completely lost the plot.

What is real pasta?

Originally, pasta in Italy was a conception of sheer genius. It began with growing the highest-quality hard wheat, and the name given to this specific type of wheat was durum, from the Latin, meaning hard. After the pasta maker had purchased exactly the right grain, the next important stage was finding the right miller to mill the grain to a certain precise specification – and not to a fine, powdery flour but to something called semolina, which is derived from the italian for 'semi milled' and is quite unlike flour, as semolina is made up of tiny, coarse, corn-coloured granules with sharp edges.

The skill of the pasta maker was to then carefully mix the semolina with cold water. Then, after the mixing came the shaping, and the pasta was forced through special bronze dies, which gave it a specific texture. After that the pasta was dried in open-windowed lofts where either the mountain air or sea breezes – or both, depending on the region – could circulate. This carefully monitored drying process could take up to two days. It was this natural drying process, along with the specifications above, that produced a quality of pasta that had captured within it all the nuttiness and flavour of the wheat grain but also a special texture. The semolina and the effect of the bronze dies produced a roughness at the edges which, in its grand design, would provide, when cooked, the right kind of surface on which the sauce being served with it would adhere and cling and not slide off. So simple, so subtle and so wonderful.

Modern pasta (and clones)

What happened next was that, soon, everybody outside Italy wanted to eat pasta, too, and once this kind of mass production was under way, corners were cut, profit margins came into play, soft flour was added, hot instead of cold water, there were nylon dies, speeded-up hot-air quick-drying, and the whole process underwent a shift from quality to competitive price wars and then it was the 'sliced white' here-we-go-downward-spiral all over again.

But something else has crept into the frame at the same time, and that is the misguided and false conception that fresh pasta is better than dried. Yes, Italians do make and eat a very small amount of *pasta fresca*, but it is a different concept; one that more usually involves a filling, as in ravioli or tortellini. But in this country – and in America – *pasta fresca* has gone crazy. It's now a far cry from the original described above and it's a strange paradox to clone a product that has a natural shelf life of two years, then make it and sell it as fresh, then add something that will give it a longer shelf life and at the same time call the resulting slithery, slimy gloop made with soft flour and eggs pasta.

The other modern misconception is to serve more sauce than pasta. Good pasta should be enjoyed for itself, with a small amount of concentrated sauce used to merely dress it.

The case for good-quality dried pasta

If you want to enjoy cooking and eating pasta at its best, then my advice is to buy good-quality dried pasta. Yes, it does cost more, but we're not talking about great luxury here; we're talking about adding no more than £1 to the cost of a main meal for two people.

There are a few artisanal pasta makers in Italy who still make the real thing, and a supplier is listed on page 698. The only fresh pastas I ever buy are ravioli, stuffed pasta shapes or lasagne sheets, which are, I think, of a far better quality than most of the dried packs. Once you taste quality dried pasta, it will be very hard for you to return to the industrially produced alternatives. It's not just the flavour: the firm, rough texture not only puts it way out in front but actually helps you to achieve that *al dente* 'firm to the teeth' texture that is the mark of well-cooked pasta. Poor quality often ends up sticky and soggy. So when you buy your pasta, make sure it says *pasta di semola di grano duro* – durum wheat semolina pasta.

There are certain dried pastas that contain eggs – *pasta all' uovo* – which add richness, but I now prefer the original semolina and water version and like to keep the richness confined to the sauce.

How to cook perfect pasta

The easiest way to communicate this is to give you a list of what is absolutely essential.

1 Always use a very large cooking pot.
2 Always make absolutely sure you have at least 4 pints (2.25 litres) of water to every 8 oz (225 g) of pasta, with 1 level tablespoon of salt added.
3 Make sure the water is up to a good fierce boil before the pasta goes in.
4 Add the pasta as quickly as possible and stir it around just once to separate it. If you're cooking long pasta, like spaghetti, push it against the base of the pan and, as you feel it give, keep pushing until it all collapses down into the water.
5 You don't need to put a lid on the pan: if it's really boiling briskly it will come back to the boil in seconds, and if you put a lid on it will boil over.
6 Put a timer on and give it 10-12 minutes for top-quality pasta, but because this timing varies according to the shape and quality of the pasta, the only real way to tell is to taste it. So do this after 8 minutes, then 9, and 10, and so on. This only applies when you cook a particular brand for the first time. After that you will always know how long it takes. Sometimes you can give it 1 minute's less boiling and then allow an extra minute's cooking whilst you combine it with the sauce.
7 Have a colander ready in the sink, then, as you are draining the water, swirl it around the colander, which will heat it ready for the hot pasta.

Below, from top: dried spaghetti, penne, macaroni and rigatoni pastas

8 Don't drain it too thoroughly: it's good to have a few drops of moisture still clinging as this prevents the pasta from becoming dry. Place the colander back over the saucepan to catch any drips.

9 Always serve it on deep warmed plates to keep the pasta as hot as possible as it goes to the table.

10 For spaghetti, the very best way to serve it is to use pasta tongs (see the photograph opposite), and always lift it high to quickly separate each portion from the rest.

11 If the pasta is going to be cooked again, in a baked dish like macaroni cheese, for example, give it half the usual cooking time to allow for the time in the oven.

12 *Presto pronto!* In Italian this means soon and quickly. Always work quickly, as pasta won't hang around – if it cools it goes sticky and gluey, so drain it quickly, serve it quickly and eat it quickly.

How to eat spaghetti and other long pastas

This is how I describe this in the *Cookery Course*: 'The big mistake here is trying to wind too much on to the fork at once. Select just two or three strands with your fork and coax them over the rim of the plate. Then, holding the fork at a right angle to the plate, simply wind the fork round and round, so that those few strands extricate themselves from the rest and are twisted round the fork in a little bite-sized bundle. Easier said than done, you're thinking? But remember – practice makes perfect.'

Spaghetti with Olive Oil, Garlic and Chilli

This one is pure pasta eaten and savoured for its own sake with the minimum amount of adornment – just a hint of garlic, chilli and olive oil.

Serves 2

8 oz (225 g) spaghetti or linguine

4 tablespoons Italian extra virgin olive oil

2 fat cloves garlic, peeled and finely chopped

1 fat red chilli, deseeded and finely chopped

freshly milled black pepper

Begin by putting the pasta on to cook. Then, just heat the olive oil in a small frying pan and, when it is hot, add the garlic, chilli and some freshly milled black pepper. Cook these very gently for about 2 minutes, which will be enough time for the flavourings to infuse the oil.

When the pasta is cooked, return it to the saucepan after draining, then pour in the hot oil. Mix well, then serve straight away on warmed pasta plates.

Linguine with Gorgonzola, Pancetta and Wilted Rocket

This is a lovely combination of assertive flavours that harmonise together perfectly.

Serves 2

8 oz (225 g) linguine

4 oz (110 g) Gorgonzola Piccante

4½ oz (125 g) cubetti (cubed) pancetta or chopped bacon

2 oz (50 g) fresh rocket

7 fl oz (200 ml) crème fraîche

1 clove garlic, peeled and crushed

4 oz (110 g) Mozzarella, cut into little cubes

a little freshly grated Parmesan (Parmigiano Reggiano), to serve

salt and freshly milled black pepper

Begin by putting the pasta on to cook and give it 1 minute less cooking time than normal, then place the Gorgonzola Piccante and the crème fraîche in a food processor and whiz it to blend together. Next place a large, solid frying pan over direct heat and, as soon as you think it is really hot, add the cubes of pancetta or chopped bacon and sauté them in their own fat for 3-4 minutes, keeping them on the move to brown all the edges evenly. Then add the garlic to the pan and toss that around for about 1 minute. Next, remove the pan from the heat and add the rocket leaves which, when you have given them a stir, will wilt in the heat of the pan.

When the pasta is ready, drain it immediately and return it to the saucepan. Now add the Gorgonzola mixture, Mozzarella and the contents of the frying pan, then return the pan to a low heat and toss everything together very thoroughly for about 1 minute. Give it a good seasoning of freshly milled black pepper and, if it needs it, a touch of salt, then serve very quickly in hot pasta bowls with some Parmesan sprinkled over.

Classic Fresh Tomato Sauce

It was once said that the greatest wines of Montrachet should be drunk kneeling with the head bowed as a sign of reverence. Well, this is how I feel about this very simple, classic sauce which, made with red, ripe, flavoursome tomatoes and served with pasta, absorbs the very essence of the tomatoes' concentrated flavour. It's still the best pasta sauce of all, and it can be made ahead and re-heated (it even freezes well).

First skin the tomatoes. To do this, pour boiling water over them and leave them for exactly 1 minute or, if the tomatoes are small, 15-30 seconds, before draining and slipping off their skins (protect your hands with a cloth if they are too hot). Now reserve 3 of the tomatoes for later and roughly chop the rest.

Next heat the oil in a medium saucepan, then add the onions and garlic and let them gently cook for 5-6 minutes, until they are softened and pale gold in colour. Now add the chopped tomatoes with about a third of the basil, torn into pieces. Add some salt and freshly milled black pepper, then all you do is let the tomatoes simmer on a very low heat, without a lid, for approximately 1½ hours or until almost all the liquid has evaporated and the tomatoes are reduced to a thick, jam-like consistency, stirring now and then. Roughly chop the reserved fresh tomatoes and stir them in, along with the rest of the torn basil leaves, and serve on pasta with a hint of Parmesan – not too much, though, because it will detract from the wonderful tomato flavour.

Note: When serving this sauce, it is a good idea to give the pasta 1 minute less cooking time than you usually would, then return it to the saucepan after draining and give 1 more minute while you mix in the sauce.

Serves 2 -3 (enough for 12 oz/350 g pasta)
2 lb 8 oz (1.15 kg) fresh, red,
ripe tomatoes
1 tablespoon olive oil
1 medium onion weighing about 4 oz
(110 g), peeled and finely chopped
1 fat clove garlic, peeled and crushed
approximately 12 large leaves
fresh basil
a little Parmesan (Parmigiano
Reggiano), to serve
salt and freshly milled black pepper

To skin the tomatoes, pour boiling water over them and leave for 1 minute

Now drain the water from the pan and slip off the tomatoes' skins

Add the ingredients to the pan and simmer on a low heat for 1½ hours

After this time, the tomatoes will have reduced to a thick, jam-like consistency

Pasta Vialli

This recipe is my adaptation of one I ate in the famous San Lorenzo Italian restaurant in Knightsbridge, which in the 1990s was a favourite with the Chelsea Football Club players. This dish is named after their famous Italian star player and manager at the time, Gianluca Vialli.

Serves 2-3

12 oz (350 g) penne rigate
1 quantity Classic Fresh Tomato Sauce (see page 221)
5 oz (150 g) Mozzarella, chopped into ¾ inch (2 cm) cubes
a little finely grated Parmesan (Parmigiano Reggiano), to serve
a few whole basil leaves, to garnish

Start this by gently re-heating the tomato sauce and putting the pasta on to cook. When you are almost ready to eat, stir the cubes of Mozzarella into the warm sauce and let it simmer gently for 2-3 minutes, by which time the cheese will have softened and begun to melt but still retain its identity. Serve the sauce spooned over the drained pasta, sprinkle with the Parmesan and add a few fresh basil leaves as a garnish.

Penne with Wild Mushrooms and Crème Fraîche

In the Winter Collection, the Oven-Baked Wild Mushroom Risotto was a huge hit, but all the lovely concentrated mushroom flavour works superbly well with pasta, too. Because the pasta will be returned to the pan for 1 minute, don't forget to give it 1 minute less on the initial cooking time.

First pop the porcini in a small bowl, then heat the milk, pour it over the mushrooms and leave them to soak for 30 minutes. Then heat the butter in a medium frying pan over a gentle heat, stir in the shallots and let them cook gently for 5 minutes. Next, strain the porcini into a sieve lined with kitchen paper, reserving the soaking liquid, and squeeze the porcini dry. Then chop them finely and add them to the pan, along with the fresh mushrooms and the balsamic vinegar. Next, season with salt, pepper and nutmeg. Give it all a good stir, then cook gently, uncovered, for 30-40 minutes, until all the liquid has evaporated.

About 15 minutes before the mushrooms are ready, put the pasta on to cook. Then, 2 minutes before the pasta is cooked, mix the crème fraîche with the mushrooms and the mushroom soaking liquid, and warm through in a small saucepan.

Drain the pasta in a colander, return it to the hot pan and quickly mix in the mushroom mixture, then place the pasta back on a gentle heat so it continues to cook for 1 more minute while it absorbs the sauce. Take it to the table in a hot serving bowl and hand the Parmesan round separately.

Serves 4-6

1 lb 2 oz (500 g) penne rigate
1 lb (450 g) mixed fresh mushrooms (flat, chestnut, shiitake or mixed wild mushrooms, for example), finely chopped
½ oz (10 g) dried porcini mushrooms
9 fl oz (250 ml) crème fraîche
3 tablespoons milk
2 oz (50 g) butter
4 large shallots, peeled and finely chopped
2 tablespoons balsamic vinegar
¼ whole nutmeg, grated
lots of freshly grated Parmesan (Parmigiano Reggiano), to serve
salt and freshly milled black pepper

Meatballs with Spaghetti and Fresh Tomato Sauce

The Americans invented meatballs to go with spaghetti, and there are lots of ground rules, but the main criteria for any meatball are that it should have a kind of melt-in-the-mouth lightness and not be heavy and bouncy. These, I think, are just right.

Serves 4 (makes 24 meatballs)
For the meatballs:
8 oz (225 g) minced pork
1 dessertspoon chopped sage leaves
3½ oz (95 g) mortadella or
unsmoked bacon
2 tablespoons freshly grated Parmesan
(Parmigiano Reggiano)
2 tablespoons chopped fresh
parsley leaves
3 oz (75 g) white bread without crusts,
soaked in 2 tablespoons milk
1 large egg
a little nutmeg
salt and freshly milled black pepper

To cook and serve:
1-2 tablespoons groundnut or other
flavourless oil, for frying
1 lb (450 g) spaghetti
1 quantity Classic Fresh Tomato Sauce
(see page 221)
a little Parmesan (Parmigiano Reggiano)
a few fresh basil leaves

To make the meatballs, all you do is place all the ingredients into the bowl of a food processor and blend everything on a low speed until thoroughly blended. If you don't have a processor, chop everything as finely as possible with a sharp knife and blend it with a fork. Now take walnut-sized pieces of the mixture and shape them into rounds – you should end up with 24 meatballs. Then put them in a large dish or on a tray, cover with clingfilm and chill for about 30 minutes to firm up.

Meanwhile, pre-heat the oven to a low setting. Then, when you are ready to cook the meatballs, heat 1 tablespoon of the oil in a large frying pan and, over a fairly high heat, add 12 meatballs at a time and cook them until they are crispy and brown all over, adding a little more oil as necessary. This will take 4-5 minutes per batch, so as they are cooked, remove them to a plate and keep them warm, covered with foil, in the oven.

Meanwhile, cook the pasta and gently warm the tomato sauce. Then drain the pasta, return it to the pan and toss in the tomato sauce, quickly mix well and then pile it on to plates. Top with the meatballs, sprinkle with some freshly grated Parmesan and finish with a few basil leaves.

Gratin of Rigatoni with Roasted Vegetables

This recipe is another good choice for a supper dish with no meat. Oven-roasted vegetables have a magical, toasted, concentrated flavour, and they keep all their dazzling colours intact. For strict vegetarians, exclude the anchovies.

Start off by preparing the courgettes and aubergine an hour ahead of time: chop them into 1½ inch (4 cm) chunks, leaving the skins on, and layer them in a colander with a sprinkling of salt between each layer. Then put a plate on top and weight it down with something heavy, which will draw out any excess moisture from the vegetables. After an hour, squeeze then dry them in a clean tea cloth, then pre-heat the oven to its highest setting.

Now quarter the tomatoes and chop the onion and peppers into 1½ inch (4 cm) chunks. Next, arrange all the vegetables on the baking tray and sprinkle with the olive oil and chopped garlic. Give everything a good mix to coat all the pieces with the oil, then spread them out as much as possible. Season with salt and freshly milled black pepper, then roast on a high shelf in the oven for 30-40 minutes, until browned and charred at the edges. Meanwhile, put a large pan of water on to boil for the pasta.

About 5 minutes before the vegetables are ready, cook the rigatoni in the boiling water for exactly 6 minutes – no longer. Drain the pasta in a colander, transfer it to a large mixing bowl and combine it with the roasted vegetables, olives, anchovies, capers and the sauce. At this point turn the heat down to gas mark 6, 400°F (200°C), leaving the door open to let it cool down a bit quicker. Now layer the mixture into the gratin dish, a third at a time, sprinkling the Mozzarella over each layer and finishing with Mozzarella. Finally, sprinkle the mixture with the heaped tablespoon of Parmesan. Bake in the oven for another 6 minutes, and serve very hot with just a leafy salad and a sharp dressing to accompany it.

If you want to make this ahead of time, it will need 35-40 minutes in the oven at gas mark 6, 400°F (200°C) to heat it through from cold.

Serves 4

6 oz (175 g) rigatoni
1 heaped tablespoon grated Parmesan (Parmigiano Reggiano), for the topping
1 pint (570 ml) cheese sauce (as on page 152, omitting the Cheddar and using 2 oz (50 g) of Parmesan

For the roasted vegetables:

2 medium courgettes
1 small aubergine
1 lb (450 g) tomatoes, skinned
1 medium onion, peeled
1 small red pepper, deseeded
1 small yellow pepper, deseeded
3 tablespoons extra virgin olive oil
2 cloves garlic, peeled and chopped
2 oz (50 g) pitted black olives, chopped
4 anchovy fillets, drained and chopped
1 heaped tablespoon salted capers or capers in vinegar, rinsed and drained
2 oz (50 g) Mozzarella, grated
salt and freshly milled black pepper

You will also need an ovenproof baking dish measuring 10 x 8 x 2 inches (25.5 x 20 x 5 cm), and a baking tray measuring 16 x 11 inches (40 x 28 cm).

Spinach and Ricotta Lasagne with Pine Nuts

This recipe is an absolute hit with everyone who eats it – even my husband, who professes not to like spinach! The combination of the four cheeses is its secret, and it is always on my top-10 list if I'm entertaining people who don't eat meat.

Serves 4-6
For the sauce:
1½ pints (850 ml) milk
2 oz (50 g) butter
2 oz (50 g) plain flour
1 bay leaf
2½ oz (60 g) Parmesan (Parmigiano Reggiano), freshly grated
salt and freshly milled black pepper

For the lasagne:
12 fresh lasagne sheets (weighing about 9 oz/250 g)
1 lb 5 oz (600 g) young leaf spinach
8 oz (225 g) Ricotta
2 oz (50 g) pine nuts
knob of butter
¼ whole nutmeg, grated
7 oz (200 g) Gorgonzola Piccante, crumbled
7 oz (200 g) Mozzarella, coarsely grated
salt and freshly milled black pepper

You will also need an ovenproof dish measuring about 9 x 9 inches (23 x 23 cm), 2½ inches (6 cm) deep, well buttered.

Pre-heat the oven to gas mark 4, 350°F (180°C).

Begin this by making the sauce, which can be done using the all-in-one method. This means placing the milk, butter, flour and bay leaf together in a saucepan, giving it a good seasoning, then, over a medium heat, whisking the whole lot together continually until it comes to simmering point and has thickened. Now turn the heat down to its lowest possible setting and allow the sauce to cook gently for 5 minutes. After that, stir in 2 oz (50 g) of the Parmesan, then remove it from the heat, discard the bay leaf and place some clingfilm over the surface to prevent a skin from forming.

Now you need to deal with the spinach. First of all remove and discard the stalks, then wash the leaves really thoroughly in two or three changes of cold water and shake them dry. Next, take your largest saucepan, pop the knob of butter in it, then pile the spinach leaves in on top, sprinkling them with a little salt as you go. Now place the pan over a medium heat, put a lid on and cook the spinach for about 2 minutes, turning the leaves over halfway through. After that, the leaves will have collapsed down and become tender.

Next drain the spinach in a colander and, when it's cool enough to handle, squeeze it in your hands to get rid of every last drop of liquid. Then place it on a chopping board and chop it finely. Now put it into a bowl, add the Ricotta, then approximately 5 fl oz (150 ml) of the sauce. Give it a good seasoning of salt and pepper and add the grated nutmeg. Then mix everything together really thoroughly and, finally, fold in the crumbled Gorgonzola.

Now you need to place a small frying pan over a medium heat, add the pine nuts and dry-fry them for about 1 minute, tossing them around to get them nicely toasted but being careful that they don't burn. Then remove the pan from the heat and assemble the lasagne. To do this, spread a quarter of the sauce into the bottom of the dish and, on top of that, a third of the spinach mixture, followed by a scattering of toasted pine nuts. Now place sheets of pasta on top of this – you may need to tear some of them in half with your hands to make them fit. Now repeat the whole process, this time adding a third of the grated Mozzarella along with the pine nuts, then the lasagne sheets. Repeat again, finishing with a layer of pasta, the rest of the sauce and the remaining Parmesan and Mozzarella. When you are ready to cook the lasagne, place it on the middle shelf of the pre-heated oven and bake for 50-60 minutes, until the top is golden and bubbling. Then remove it from the oven and let it settle for about 10 minutes before serving.

Sicilian Pasta with Roasted Tomatoes and Aubergines

Aubergines, tomatoes and Mozzarella are the classic ingredients of any Sicilian sauce for pasta, and roasting the tomatoes and aubergines to get them slightly charred adds an extra flavour dimension.

Serves 2

8 oz (225 g) spaghetti

12 large tomatoes (roughly 2 lb/900 g)

1 large aubergine, cut into 1 inch (2.5 cm) cubes

2 large cloves garlic, peeled and finely chopped

about 4 tablespoons olive oil

12 large basil leaves, torn in half, plus a few extra for garnish

5 oz (150 g) Mozzarella, cut into ½ inch (1 cm) cubes

salt and freshly milled black pepper

You will also need two baking trays measuring 14 x 10 inches (35 x 25.5 cm).

Pre-heat the oven to gas mark 6, 400°F (200°C).

First of all place the aubergine cubes in a colander, sprinkle them with salt and leave them to stand for half an hour, weighed down with something heavy to squeeze out the excess juices.

Meanwhile, skin the tomatoes by pouring boiling water over them and leaving them for 1 minute, then drain off the water and, as soon as they are cool enough to handle, slip off the skins. Cut each tomato in half and place the halves on one of the baking trays (cut-side uppermost), then season with salt and freshly milled black pepper. Sprinkle over the chopped garlic, distributing it evenly between the tomatoes, and follow this with a few drops of olive oil in each one. Top each tomato half with half a basil leaf, turning each piece of leaf over to give it a good coating of oil. Now place the baking tray on the middle shelf of the oven and roast the tomatoes for 50-60 minutes or until the edges are slightly blackened.

Meanwhile, drain the aubergines and squeeze out as much excess juice as possible, then dry them thoroughly with a clean cloth and place them in the other baking tray. Then drizzle 1 tablespoon of the olive oil all over them and place them on the top shelf of the oven, above the tomatoes, giving them half an hour.

Towards the end of the cooking time, cook the pasta. When the tomatoes and aubergines are ready, scrape them, along with all their lovely cooking juices, into a saucepan and place it over a low heat, then add the cubed Mozzarella and stir gently. Now drain the pasta, pile it into a warm bowl, spoon the tomato and aubergine mixture over the top and scatter over a few basil leaves.

Souffléd Macaroni Cheese

I've made many a macaroni cheese in my time, but this, I promise you, is the best ever.

Begin by having all your ingredients weighed out and the cheeses grated. Fill a large saucepan with 4 pints (2.25 litres) of water containing a dessertspoon of salt and put it on the heat to bring it up to the boil. Then, in a small saucepan, melt the butter over a gentle heat, add the onions and let them soften, without browning and uncovered, for 5 minutes. Then add the flour to the pan, stir it in to make a smooth paste, then gradually add the milk, a little at a time, stirring vigorously with a wooden spoon. Then switch to a balloon whisk and keep whisking so you have a smooth sauce. Then add some salt and freshly milled black pepper, as well as the nutmeg, and leave the sauce to cook gently for 5 minutes. After that, turn off the heat and whisk in the Mascarpone and egg yolks, followed by the Gruyère and half the Parmesan.

Next place the baking dish in the oven to heat through, then drop the macaroni into the boiling water and, as soon as the water returns to a simmer, give it 4-6 minutes, until *al dente* (it's going to get a second cooking in the oven). When it has about 1 minute's cooking time left, whisk the egg whites to soft peaks. Drain the pasta in a colander, give it a quick shake to get rid of the water, then tip it back into the pan and stir in the cheese sauce, turning the pasta over in it so it is evenly coated. Then lightly fold in the egg whites, using a cutting and folding movement so as to retain as much air as possible.

Remove the warm dish from the oven, pour the pasta mixture into it, give it a gentle shake to even the top, then scatter the reserved Parmesan over and return the dish to the oven on a high shelf for 12 minutes or until the top is puffy and lightly browned. Serve it, as they say in Italy, *presto pronto*. Note: To make this for four people, just double the ingredients and use a 10 x 8 x 2 inch (25.5 x 20 x 5 cm) dish, increasing the cooking time by 3-5 minutes.

Serves 2 generously
6 oz (175 g) macaroni
1 oz (25 g) butter
1 medium onion (about 4 oz/110 g), peeled and finely chopped
1 oz (25 g) plain flour
10 fl oz (275 ml) milk
¼ whole nutmeg, freshly grated
3 oz (75 g) Mascarpone
2 large egg yolks, lightly beaten
2 oz (50 g) Gruyère, finely grated
2 oz (50 g) Parmesan (Parmigiano Reggiano), finely grated
2 large egg whites
salt and freshly milled black pepper

You will also need a shallow ovenproof baking dish with a base measurement of 8 x 6 inches (20 x 15 cm), 2 inches (5 cm) deep, lightly buttered.

Pre-heat the oven to gas mark 6, 400°F (200°C).

Baked Cannelloni

I have discovered that the best way to make this excellent supper dish is to buy sheets of fresh lasagne that don't need pre-cooking, which are now widely available. The filling, conveniently, is the meatball mixture on page 224.

Serves 4
For the filling:
8 fresh lasagne sheets (weighing about 6 oz/175 g)
1 quantity meatball mixture (see page 224)
5 oz (150 g) Mozzarella, diced
1½ oz (40 g) finely grated Parmesan (Parmigiano Reggiano), plus a little extra to serve

For the béchamel sauce:
1 pint (570 ml) milk
2 oz (50 g) butter
1¼ oz (35 g) plain flour
1 bay leaf
good grating of whole nutmeg
2½ fl oz (65 ml) double cream
salt and freshly milled black pepper

You will also need a baking dish with a base measurement of 7 x 9 inches (18 x 23 cm), 2 inches (5 cm) deep, buttered.

Make the sauce first by placing the milk, butter, flour, bay leaf, nutmeg and seasonings into a medium-sized saucepan over a medium heat, then, whisking all the time, slowly bring it up to simmering point until the sauce has thickened. Then turn the heat down to its lowest setting and let the sauce simmer for about 5 minutes, then remove the bay leaf, stir in the cream, taste to check the seasoning, cover and leave aside.

Now pre-heat the oven to gas mark 4, 350°F (180°C), then cut the lasagne sheets in half so that you have 16 pieces. Next divide the meatball mixture in half and then each half into eight, then lightly roll each of these into a sausage shape about 3 inches (7.5 cm) long. Place each one on to a piece of lasagne and roll it up, starting from one of the shorter edges. As you do this, arrange them in the baking dish with the join underneath – what you should have is two rows neatly fitting together lengthways in the dish. Now pour the sauce over and scatter the Mozzarella cubes here and there. Finally, scatter the Parmesan over the top and place the dish on the centre shelf of the oven to bake for 40 minutes, by which time it should be golden brown and bubbling. Then remove it from the oven and let it settle for about 10 minutes before serving. Finally, sprinkle a little extra Parmesan over.

11

The serious cook's store cupboard

(or capers in the larder)

Why the curious sub-title, you're thinking. Nostalgia, really, because it dates back to the late-1970s, when I was a very coy, shy TV cook hardly daring to look up at the camera. I was trying to expound the virtues of capers as a useful cooking ingredient, and what I said was, 'I always have capers in my larder.' To which I received a very humorous letter from a gentleman curious to know just what kinds of capers I got up to in my larder!

What do I mean when I use the word serious? I suppose what I'm trying to say is that some people like to flirt with the subject of cooking – dip in and out, try a recipe here and there – but everyone knows the difference between a flirtation and a serious relationship: at some point flirtation stops and some kind of commitment begins. Cooking is absolutely like that. If I really, truly want to know how to cook well, then I certainly can, but somewhere along the line a decision has to be made – yes, I am now going to get serious, not just flirt with the idea, but really make a commitment to doing it properly so I can get the best out of eating and cooking for the rest of my life.

What does getting serious mean?

If you want to know how to cook then you need to begin by making life as easy as possible, and this means giving a little time and investment to, first, getting the right utensils and cooking equipment (something that is emphasised all through *How To Cook*). Secondly, you need to have a well-stocked store cupboard.

Because I'm at the receiving end of a great deal of letters and comments, there is a familiar old carp that surfaces regularly amongst people who only flirt with cooking. 'Why do I have to go out and buy all those expensive ingredients just for one recipe?' Or, 'Can't I use curry paste in your recipe instead of all that tedious roasting and grinding?' First, if your kitchen cupboard is well stocked you won't often have to make special shopping trips and spend more money. Secondly, most storecupboard ingredients come in bottles or jars and have a long shelf life, so they cost very little over a period of time. And thirdly, dry-roasting and grinding spices in a pestle and mortar can all be done and dusted in 4 minutes at the outside. What that will then give you is twice or three times the depth of flavour.

Flavour is the most important word in cooking

If you're going to bother to cook, you need to get the very best flavour from all the ingredients you use. This doesn't mean that convenience ingredients don't have their place – obviously they do because there are always going to be days when we're simply not able to do much cooking. But on the days when we can, it's wonderful to have a stock of spices and flavouring ingredients within reach – a pinch of this, a splash of that – as and when we need them.

What about the cost?

For some reason, spending money on recipe ingredients and kitchen equipment is sometimes difficult and countless people just muddle along and make do. But think of it this way: if you want to learn to drive you have to pay for lessons, then you can enjoy a lifetime of driving, which will improve your quality of life. Same with cooking: a little investment at the beginning and you'll have years of pleasure in cooking and eating really well.

The well-stocked store cupboard

In the photograph on the previous page, you'll see what every serious cook should have on stand-by. You can use the list that follows in this chapter to have an annual check, which I always try to do in January. It's then that I throw out all stale ingredients and do one shop to replace them. I have learnt the hard way: I've been caught out so often in the past – just about to make a cake that needs mixed spice, for instance, only to find to my horror that mine is a year out of date and very un-spicy.

What you don't need

Certainly not all those foodie designer ingredients that you receive as gifts or buy in an unguarded moment. Be ruthless – you're never going to use that obscure fruit liqueur that Auntie brought back from Yalta, the pickled greengages that date back to the 1980s, or the gaudy-coloured fruit vinegar that looks like bath essence. They're like clothes you never wear, just taking up valuable space. So pack them off to the church bazaar and make room for something really useful.

The basics

What follows is what I think is a good basic list – not everything you're ever going to need, but what you should always have available.

Salt

The very best kind of salt for all cooking is, in my opinion, English sea salt from Maldon, in Essex. It's not a powdery pouring salt that contains chemicals to stop it getting damp and make it pour freely, but an absolutely pure salt that tastes of the sea. If you do a side-by-side tasting you'll find it is less sharp but somehow saltier (so you need to use less).

Maldon salt consists of very pretty, small white crystalline flakes that crush very easily between your fingers for cooking with. For the table, use it either in a good-quality salt mill or a small salt cellar. Crushed sea salt gives jacket potatoes a really crispy crust, and it's wonderful coarsely crushed over chips (or anything fried). I once discovered by accident, sitting at a restaurant table, that a fat, chunky chip wrapped in a rocket leaf, then dipped first in mayonnaise, then in sea salt, is a quite wickedly brilliant combination!

Peppercorns

You might be amused to know that when I first started writing a column for London's *Evening Standard* in 1972 I used to be unmercifully teased about my constant references to 'freshly milled black pepper'. Was that the precursor to the cranberries or liquid glucose of later years? No, I don't recall anyone actually selling out, but I quite definitely had a campaign going. I said I would always refer to pepper as freshly milled and black until I saw no more of the white, musty, dusty stuff that people sprinkle on their food. I'm still campaigning strongly because, even now, unbelievably, it continues to turn up occasionally in restaurants.

Black pepper

Black peppercorns are whole immature berries that are harvested while still green and dried in the sun till they turn black. The berries contain a white inner kernel – the hottest part of the berry, which is quite fiery when used on its own – and a black outer husk, which has all the aromatic fragrance that enhances the flavour of food. Thus if you use the whole berries you get a little bit of fire and a lot of aromatic fragrance.

White pepper

Here the berries are allowed to mature before harvesting, the husks are discarded and the white kernels dried to become white peppercorns. The dried berries, stored whole, will keep their aroma for a long time, but once they have been powdered to dust in a factory, hung about on the shelf and stagnated in a pepper pot, there is no surprise that the result is a million miles from the fragrance you can keep locked up in your pepper mill.

Sichuan pepper

Despite its name, this is not actually from the same family as black, white and green peppercorns, but comes from a type of ash tree. It's used in Oriental cooking and is an ingredient of Chinese five-spice powder.

Cayenne pepper

This is an absolute must in the kitchen. It's hot and fiery and needs to be used with extreme caution, but it is brilliant for that little sprinkling of piquancy. It's made from one of the hottest types of chilli, which is dried, then crushed to a powder including the seeds. I'm forever using a pinch here and there, and I love it sprinkled on smoked fish or prawn cocktail. Although spices, once ground, do not have a long shelf life, cayenne does seem to go on longer than most but still needs replacing fairly regularly.

Mustard

Yes, it's true – if you think about it, mustard is the one and only home-grown English spice, and for my money it's the best. I admit this is a personal thing: I like the ferocious kick of English mustard that makes its presence felt even when only very little is used. Although it comes in powdered form, it does have a good shelf life and can be made up as and when you require.

How to make mustard

The oils in mustard are what give it its pungency, but these are not developed in the whole seed or the dry milled powder. What is needed to release their flavour is the chemical reaction brought on by the addition of cold water (not hot, which causes a different reaction), just enough to make a thickish paste. Always make up your mustard in advance, as it needs a good 10-15 minutes for the flavour to develop fully. Mustard is also a good emulsifier: it can help to stabilise something like mayonnaise, and can provide a slight thickening to vinaigrette or Cumberland sauce.

Made-up mustards

There are three of these I would recommend, but first it should be noted that once they are exposed to the air, they deteriorate rapidly and lose much of their kick. This means the lid must be replaced firmly and quickly each time the mustard is used.

Dijon mustard

From Burgundy, in France, this is not as fiery as English mustard, tempered by the mixture of unripe grape juice (verjuice) or diluted wine vinegar. It is extremely good but it's very difficult to keep it fragranced once opened.

Wholegrain mustard

This is a mixture of mustard seeds, spices and wine vinegar, milder than straight made-up mustard but very good for the store cupboard as it not only adds flavour to dressings and sauces but also a lovely seedy texture. It keeps better than Dijon, but still replace the lid quickly to prevent the air from affecting it.

American mustard

You can't really have a barbecue without some of this famous mustard, which comes in squeezy bottles and is a mixture of mustard, turmeric, paprika and other spices. No decent frankfurter or sausage in a hot dog should ever be without it drizzled back and forth over the surface.

Mustard mayhem…

Like olive oils and wine vinegars, mustard suffers greatly from the designer effect, with every flavour, colour and texture under the sun creeping into the mustard jar. My advice is, don't bother. Even if you like the flavour of dill mustard or similar, once opened it will deteriorate very quickly. So don't make the mistakes I've made: one spoonful of some exotic mustard today and the whole lot thrown out several weeks later. If you want dill or tarragon or anything else in your mustard, it's best to add it yourself.

Bottled sauces

Worcestershire sauce

The very best-loved of English bottled sauces. I know an American foodie who has crates of the stuff sent over, because the American version never tastes as good. It's such a clever sauce because if you were asked (and didn't know) what the main ingredient was, you would never guess. It's

Clockwise from top: English mustard powder, Dijon mustard and wholegrain mustard

anchovies, but only the finest anchovies from the Basque region of Spain, blended with shallots, onions and garlic and matured for three years. Worcestershire sauce is a flavour provider and enhancer, a real stalwart for jazzing up stocks, gravies and sauces, and for enlivening disappointing ready-meals. Even outside the kitchen it has another pride of place, and that's at every glitzy bar from Teesside to Thailand – because no Bloody Mary anywhere in the world could not include it.

Soy sauce

In this country we were quite slow switching on to soy sauce, but now – wow! – soy sauce has landed. It is an ancient and crucially important ingredient in the Far East, used not just for seasoning but also for dipping, marinating, tenderising and at the same time purifying. What we need to concern ourselves with for the purposes of cooking is the enormous range in quality, and for cooks who care about quality the best soy sauce is made in Japan, where it is naturally fermented from wheat, soya beans, salt and water (the only ingredients that should appear on the label). Short-cut unnaturally fermented soy sauces are not in the same league, so if you stick to Japanese you'll be sure you're using the best.

Fish sauce (nam pla)

An even later arrival in this country, and in the beginning only available in specialist oriental food shops. Now it is much more widely distributed, and in supermarkets at last. You could almost say this is an Eastern version of Worcestershire sauce, not so much in flavour but in the way it gives the same kind of lift to other ingredients. As its name suggests, it is a fermentation of small, whole fish (sometimes shrimps) and is quite salty, so a little goes a long way. It's an essential ingredient in Vietnamese and Thai cooking, and because of the growing popularity of these cuisines (which I personally love), it has become a staple storecupboard ingredient.

Tabasco sauce

Hot liquid chillies in a bottle. Perfect if you want to perk something up with just a dash of heat, and also useful when you've added fresh chillies to a recipe and they haven't quite provided the heat you wanted – a few drops will supplement it beautifully. There are lots of chilli sauces around, but I find Tabasco has the best chilli flavour.

Organic tomato ketchup

This is simply in a different league to other tomato ketchups. It is totally true to the tomatoes it's made from, as their flavour has not been eclipsed by sugar or artificial sweetness. It's useful in cooking where you want to add true tomato flavour, and it's also great with fish and chips.

Redcurrant jelly

Redcurrant jelly is an invaluable ingredient for sauces, gravies or just to serve with lamb or game, but do make sure it's a good-quality one with a high fruit content, such as Tiptree: cheaper versions are far too sweet, which obliterates the real flavour of the redcurrants.

Cranberry jelly

I always keep cranberry jelly in my cupboard, too – it's good as an instant accompaniment to chicken or game, or can be used in sauces.

Mayonnaise

Home-made is preferable, but, it has to be said, not always practical, so a good-quality bottled mayonnaise should always be on hand. I find I don't use it often enough to buy it in large jars, so, because it stores better unopened, I find a couple of smaller jars are a better bet than having a third of a large jar lurking in the fridge waiting to be used.

Pure vanilla extract

As you'd expect, this is extracted from pure vanilla pods and not made synthetically (extract is the key word; essence is not the same thing). It's very useful for sauces, custards and a million and one sweet dishes or wherever a touch of vanilla flavour is required.

Greek or other types of honey

Personal preference reigns here. I love Greek mountain honey, which stretches as you lift it on the spoon – it never seems too sweet, but full of fragrance with caramel overtones. That said, whichever honey you prefer, it's a storecupboard must. For a quick snack, spread with good butter on freshly baked bread or spoon over thick Greek yoghurt. For recipes see pages 430 and 454.

Maple syrup

Once you get into the habit of pouring maple syrup over porridge or Greek yoghurt and using it in place of sugar to sweeten all kinds of things, you're sure to get addicted. And because Buttermilk Pancakes (page 166) are so quick and easy to make, having some maple syrup to hand means you're never short of an almost-instant dessert. Note: once opened it needs to be stored in the refrigerator and used within 3 months.

Gravy browning

Although, if I'm roasting meat (particularly beef), I often put an onion in to caramelise and colour the gravy, at other times it's useful to be able to add a spot of rich colour if a gravy looks too pale. Gravy browning is just dark caramelised sugar, so a couple of drops won't affect the flavour but will enrich the colour.

Tinned and bottled ingredients

Anchovies

Probably one of the most significant ingredients of all. Not only are they supremely good and highly prized in their own right, they are also very effective in enhancing the flavour of other ingredients. From my studies of 18th-century cooking in England I know that a barrel of anchovies was indispensable in many kitchens to enliven all sorts of recipes. 'But I don't like anchovies,' some of you are thinking. True, they are strong and gutsy – an acquired taste, you could say – but they do grow on you. So keep

trying a little here and a little there until you acquire it, and don't forget that most people who say they don't like anchovies do like Worcestershire sauce, in which anchovies are the main ingredient.

Anchovy essence

This is also a great flavour enhancer and is the British equivalent of the fish sauce of the Far East. As such, it can be used in oriental recipes when fish sauce is not available.

Storecupboard tomatoes

We are very fortunate to have instant tomatoes any time we want them – perhaps they are the most widely used storecupboard ingredient of all. First there's the tinned – chopped or whole – and sometimes in the winter months their flavour in cooking is superior to fresh, provided, of course, they're Italian, as these are way and above the best. Tomato purée and sun-dried tomato paste are also very useful, as are sun-dried tomatoes preserved in oil. But one new ingredient I've grown to love is mi-cuit tomatoes, which are half dried. The tomato flavour is concentrated but they are still quite squidgy and not as chewy as those that are totally dried.

Capers

These little Mediterranean berries – sometimes tiny, sometimes fat and squashy – are another acquired taste, but do persevere. Capers add a lively piquancy to all kinds of dishes, especially sauces and fish. Nobody likes their first alcoholic drink, but we've all experienced how soon *that* catches on, and it's the same with capers. You can buy them either preserved in salt (which I prefer) or in vinegar. Either way you need to place them in a sieve and rinse them under cold water first. Capers in vinegar will keep well once opened, provided the vinegar covers them completely. If it doesn't you'll need to do some topping up.

Cornichons

What we used to get were midget gherkins bottled in malt vinegar that seared your throat, but now, thankfully, we get the real thing, crunchy and fragrant. They are another must in the store cupboard, not just for eating with pâtés or served with drinks but as an important ingredient in tartare sauce (see page 272) and fish recipes.

Horseradish and wasabi

Horseradish is not just a good ingredient for accompanying roast beef or smoked fish, but also for adding flavour to sauces. It can be difficult to find a good creamed horseradish – what happens to the tear-inducing prickle of freshly grated horseradish once it's creamed and bottled is a mystery – but Colman's, English Provender and Wiltshire Tracklements are the best. Now we can also buy Japanese wasabi. Ground from a cousin of our horseradish and called wasabi root in Japan, it is mixed with cold water just like mustard. Although its main use is as a condiment for sushi (delicious), it is also brilliant mixed into creamed horseradish to give it back its kick. Just use a ¼ teaspoon of wasabi powder to 2 tablespoons of creamed horseradish.

Opposite page, left to right: salted capers, caper berries and capers preserved in vinegar. Above: anchovy fillets

Olives

A must in every store cupboard, and although you can buy loose olives at deli counters (and it's good to buy small amounts to find which varieties you like), always have them tucked away in the larder in jars or tins as well. That means you can be spontaneous whenever you want to use olives in cooking. I like to have two kinds available: Greek calamata olives, which are quite large, and the tiny purple-brown Provençal ones, which are good for garnishes. Try to buy good-quality olives, and avoid the pitted ones, which are not the best. An olive pitter, *left*, will make removing the stones fairly easy.

Stem ginger in syrup

I always have a jar of this handy – it's lovely in cakes, it does wonders for rhubarb (see page 398), and can be used chopped as a garnish and sprinkled with its syrup over ice cream. It keeps for ages, so it doesn't matter if you're not using it often. My favourite ginger cake is made with this (see page 260).

Coconut milk

This is taken from fresh-grated coconut that has been soaked in water and squeezed to extract a creamy substance. It's great for instant use, as one of the wonderful things about Thai cooking is it can be spontaneous and quick, provided you have all the necessary ingredients in the cupboard.

Creamed coconut

This comes in block form and can be used to enrich curries and sauces. All you do here is grate it, then, using a whisk, blend it with boiling water to a creamy liquid.

Dried coconut powder

A great storecupboard stand-by, this is particularly good in Thai fishcakes (see the recipe on page 276).

Kaffir lime leaves

Fresh, these are very hard to track down, but now they come freeze-dried rather like bay leaves, but with that unmistakable oriental-Thai flavour. Use dried, pounded in a pestle and mortar or soaked in a little hot water, and they're almost as good as new. Fresh leaves can be kept in the freezer.

Shrimp paste

Another Thai ingredient, this is made from fermented salted shrimps that are pounded into a concentrated paste, but it must be cooked and not used in its raw state. Once opened, you need to store it in the fridge with a tight lid on and place it in a polythene bag, as it has quite a strong aroma. But that said, it helps to give a wonderfully authentic flavour to Thai recipes.

Dried shrimps

These have lots of concentrated shrimp flavour, unlike tired and tasteless frozen prawns, which have no value at all. They are available in oriental shops, but have only a short shelf life – about 4 weeks – so buy them in small quantities and, again, keep them refrigerated. They need to be soaked in hot water for 15 minutes before using.

Below, from left: dried shrimps, rice noodles, Thai fish sauce and shrimp paste. Bottom: dried kaffir lime leaves

Dried mushrooms

Without doubt one of the best ingredients to hit British food shops in the last few years. However much we value them and are grateful for them, cultivated mushrooms will never have the flavour of mushrooms grown in the wild. But now that we can buy dried wild mushrooms, we can all enjoy that special flavour without having to search in country meadows, woods or Wimbledon Common at the break of dawn. Both the French and the Italians produce excellent dried mushrooms, and their native varieties, which include ceps and morels in France and porcini in Italy, are best of all. This means you can always add a touch of luxurious concentrated mushroom flavour whenever you are cooking with mushrooms.

Marigold Swiss vegetable bouillon powder

This is without doubt an ingredient that has revolutionised modern cooking. Before Marigold you had to either make your own stock or resort to the dreaded chemically flavoured cube. Fresh stock can now be bought in supermarkets, but it's expensive and not instantly available. Marigold is made with vegetables and has only pure vegetable flavour, meaning you can have instant stock any time. If there were good-ingredient awards, this would win first prize.

Gelatine

I always try to keep a stock of both powdered and leaf gelatine, and I use both regularly. The powdered variety is added and used in several different ways, which is explained fully in each recipe. Leaf gelatine is always used in the same way, and instructions and photographs are on page 408.

Unrefined sugars

These are made from pure unrefined sugar cane, and are pictured, *right.* This means the colour and flavour that is naturally present in sugar cane has not been refined out to make the sugar pure white. The most recent addition to this range is unrefined icing sugar. I love its flavour and pale-caramel colour when made into icing, and so would now not use white.

Golden syrup

A very British favourite, something that should always be available for sauces, puddings, butterscotch, sticky toffee sauce, treacle puddings or spread thickly on home-made bread with a generous amount of butter.

Molasses

This is the dark-ebony syrup that's left over after sugar has been refined – in unrefined sugars the molasses is included in different degrees. It's very concentrated, so only a little is needed. When I first started cooking you could buy dark (as opposed to golden) syrup. Now it's no longer available, but a little molasses added to golden syrup gives the same effect. One important point, though: now that molasses is widely available, always use it in place of black treacle in recipes – more expensive, but lots more rich, luscious flavour.

Unrefined sugars, clockwise from top right: molasses, golden granulated, dark muscovado (on spoon), light brown soft, golden icing sugar, dark brown soft, demerara, light muscovado and golden caster sugar

Alcohol for cooking

A most important section this one, because a touch of alcohol in any shape or form makes a significant difference to a wide variety of cooking: a splash of wine in a sauce or to deglaze a pan, or as a component in cakes, puddings and casseroles. The list is endless.

Beer and stout

These are good in slowly braised casseroles, particularly with beef or venison when they are subject to long, slow cooking. All the bitterness is cooked away, leaving a rich, mellow, dark sauce.

Strong dry cider

This is always available in my kitchen. It keeps longer than wine and can be used in any recipe that requires wine (making it less expensive). In some cases it is even better than wine, particularly with pork and apples (see page 308). If you have fried some pork sausages, remove them from the pan and keep warm, then deglaze by adding 5 fl oz (150 ml) of cider and a teaspoon of cider vinegar to the pan, let it bubble and reduce, scraping the base of the pan, until it becomes syrupy, then pour over the sausages before serving.

Wine

Using wine in your cooking can transform something quite ordinary into something extremely special, and now that you can buy quarter bottles with screw-tops you can always have some handy. If you have fried some pork chops or a steak, use white for the former, red for the latter, to deglaze the pan (see above) and provide a concentrated sauce to spoon over.

Fortified wines

These are absolute stars, both for drinking and in the kitchen, and over the 40 years I have been cooking I have used them in recipes time and time again. Basically, the ones I use most are dry manzanilla sherry, dry sercial Madeira, Marsala and, lastly, port, which seems to crop up around Christmas time a lot. They all keep well if sealed properly after use.

Spirits

When I first started writing recipes I was always terribly aware of the cost, and when a certain dish called for spirits I would always add the phrase 'available in miniatures'. Now I don't, because I have realised it is actually cheaper to buy the large bottle, the contents of which can be kept almost indefinitely. Here I would choose brandy, whisky, Calvados and rum as the four spirits most likely to be included in recipes.

Shaosing brown rice wine

This always adds that wonderfully authentic flavour and aroma to Chinese cooking. Dry sherry can be used instead, but it's worth hunting around oriental food shops for the real thing if you can.

Armagnac

This is the first cousin of Cognac but with its own special, distinctive flavour. It has a great affinity with prunes, so I have used it both in the brownies and the cake recipe on pages 465 and 466 respectively.

Spices

Always a tricky subject, because it is spices that come under the hammer most often from people who 'don't want to spend a fortune on one recipe'. I would suggest, however, that although the initial expense may seem large, if you think about it teaspoon by teaspoon in recipes over the course of a year, they represent a fraction of the overall cost. Having said that, though, what price is it worth for my very ordinary kitchen to be transformed by the alluring aromas of far-away exotic places? Once the spices are roasted and ground, I can close my eyes and be transported instantly to a Turkish bazaar, a Moroccan market, India, the Caribbean, Africa and the Far East – all are encapsulated in even the humblest collection of spices.

The case for whole spices

For cooks at home, there's no doubt that, for the most part, buying spices whole is best. First, and most importantly, spices, once ground, quickly lose much of their original pungency, whilst whole spices keep their exotic flavour and fragrance locked in for far longer. Then, when the spices are dry-roasted and subjected to heat, all those sublime flavours and aromas can be drawn out in a matter of moments.

Ready-ground spices

Without in any way detracting from what I've just said about whole spices, there are one or two exceptions: it is difficult, for example, to grind cloves or cinnamon, paprika is already ground from dried sweet peppers, cayenne from chilli peppers, and for baking it is easier to use a ready-made mixed spice mix. There is also a case for ground ginger in the kitchen, as it has different uses from fresh ginger. But I would repeat, these spices do not have a long shelf life, so replace them frequently. The best way to buy them is in refill packs, which are less expensive than the jars.

The *How To Cook* spice collection

Obviously whole books have been written about spices, but I will confine myself here to what I believe to be the essential list for every cook. It is hard to communicate in words their individual fragrances and flavours, but here is a little information about each one.

Allspice

This looks like a smooth peppercorn but larger, and it is so called because it is supposed to resemble in flavour a mixture of cloves, nutmeg and cinnamon. However, it is not really like any one of them but has a unique flavour of its own. It is sometimes called Jamaican pepper or pimento, and is used in marinades and pickles – you'll see the whole berries used in jars of commercial pickled herrings, and you can catch some of its flavour in the recipe for Tunisian Aubergine Salad on page 358.

Cardamom

This is an Eastern spice that comes encased in its own sun-dried pods, which are pale green or grey. Inside there is a treasure of tiny black, highly aromatic seeds. This is an important spice in curries, but it also turns up in sweet dishes – I once tasted a cardamom cake in which the flavour of the cardamom had permeated and mingled with the sweetness beautifully. I almost always throw in the pods as well to get every bit of flavour.

Cinnamon (whole and ground)

This is a popular spice that comes from the inner bark of a tree belonging to the laurel family. When whole, its design is exquisite: reddish-brown, brittle-layered curls that are hollow inside. Ground, it is used in home-baked puddings and desserts, and whole in fruit compotes, mulled wines and curries. In Greek cooking a little cinnamon finds its way into savoury dishes, such as the moussaka recipe on pages 160-1. There is something evocative in the smell of home baking when cinnamon is involved, as it reminds me of small bakery shops from when I was a child.

Coriander (whole, never ground)

The leaves of coriander (like fresh limes) became the subject of Delia hype in the early 1990s. I'm unrepentant because attention was drawn to two very important ingredients. But here we are concerned not with the leaves but with the tiny beige-brown seeds, a magical spice that is said to have the flavour of roasted orange peel. Since I have been using the leaves I have come to discern the connection between the two, even though they're at the same time different. Coriander seeds are important in curries, Middle Eastern and Greek dishes.

Cloves

Cloves are like little dark-wooden nails, and can be used almost as such pressed into onions (for bread sauce) or oranges (mulled wine) or studded all over a piece of sugar-and-mustard-glazed gammon. They do have a very pungent aroma and flavour – people who were subjected to oil of cloves as a cure for toothache can't stand them, so strong was their impact – but used subtly cloves are one of my favourite spices and I still love them in apple pies and crumbles.

Cumin (whole)

These are tiny elongated brown-grey seeds, essential to curries, but also widely used in Mexican, Middle Eastern and Moroccan cooking. Roasted and ground, they have a warm, earthy flavour that is intensely fragrant. The combination of cumin and allspice in the Tunisian Aubergine Salad recipe on page 358 is a fine example of the role of spices in cooking.

Fenugreek (whole)

These are tiny, pale-coloured seeds to which I was introduced when a friend gave me a recipe for Sri Lankan curry (*Summer Collection*), a country where they are used widely, as indeed they are in Indian cooking. I have also used them in my Egg and Lentil Curry on page 18. Their

Opposite page, clockwise from top: cumin seeds, cardamom pods, juniper berries, coriander seeds, star anise, nutmeg and (centre) Sichuan peppercorns

flavour is strong, so little is needed, and they are usually used as part of a blend with other spices.

Juniper

A beautifully fragrant spice that is used to make gin, so think of gin and you've got juniper. The berries are purple-black, slightly wrinkled and grow wild in hill country. They ripen in autumn, so perhaps that is why juniper is often served with game and pork, wild boar and other autumnal recipes. It is quite pungent and a little goes a long way. When you place them in a mortar and begin to crush them, their deep fragrance and the anticipation of their flavour cannot fail to please.

Nutmeg and mace (whole)

Nutmeg is one of my favourite spices, one that we in this country have included in recipes throughout our history – think of a speckled brown custard tart, or the shiny nutmeg skin on a rice pudding (see page 212). It's curious how the French have ignored nutmeg, but the Italians and Spanish adore it as much as we do, using it in cheese dishes, pasta sauces and fillings, creamy béchamel and spinach. But a warning: you must never even think of buying nutmeg ready-ground, as it quickly loses all its charm. Instead always have some whole nutmeg and a grater, and grate it as and when you need it. Mace, as you can see in the photograph on page 233, is the outer casing of the nutmeg, resembling a thick meshed cage, which is dried and becomes brittle. It is sold in pieces (blades) and can be used in infusions, such as flavouring milk for a white sauce (see page 150). Ground mace has also been included in British recipes for potted meats, shrimps and fish pâtés. It is impossible to grind it at home, so this one has to be bought ready-ground and the date carefully watched.

Paprika (ground)

This is a spice that's ground from dried sweet red peppers – both mild and hot – and comes labelled as such. In this case hot does not really mean chilli-hot, but more piquant, so have no fear. It is made in Hungary and used extensively in Hungarian and Austrian dishes (in wonderful pepper-scented stews such as goulash or chicken paprika). The Spanish also produce paprika and it turns up in many of their recipes – the famous chorizo sausage is made with it. Recently Spain has been producing smoked paprika from dried smoked peppers, and this has added a whole new dimension to this particular spice. Once again, remember the rule: buy in small quantities and replace frequently.

Saffron

This is made from the dried stamens of a variety of purple crocus. It is therefore expensive, but the good news is you need only very little – the flavour is powerful and so is the colour (see Crunchy Roast Potatoes with Saffron on page 184). You can buy it ready-ground, but I find it best to buy the stamens whole and then pound them to a powder with a pestle and mortar. It can then be mixed with a little water before adding to a recipe, or the powder can be added directly. If, like me, you worry that your paella (see page 328) doesn't look quite as colourful as the one you had in Spain, fear not: you don't need more saffron – in Spain they sometimes cheat and add food colouring!

Star anise

Open a jar of star anise and you're immediately transported to the heart of Chinatown, where the shops seem to be permeated with its exotic aroma. The star shape is the pod and the tiny seeds nestle inside each star petal. It is usually used whole, like cardamom pods, and always looks very pretty. Its flavour faintly resembles aniseed but with warm, spicy overtones.

Turmeric

This is a root that belongs to the ginger family and in some oriental shops can be bought fresh, but the powdered version has been dried and pounded. It has a very fragrant aroma and a brilliant yellow-ochre colour, which is what makes Indian pilau rice that lovely pale yellow. It is also a major ingredient in our own beloved piccalilli. I always use a little in every curry mixture, as much for its fragrance as for its colour. Because it comes ready-ground, it doesn't have a long shelf life, so keep an eye on the date stamp.

Storecupboard extras

Obviously you'll need flour, pasta, rice and all the staples covered so far, but here is a list of other useful storecupboard ingredients that – as you begin to cook more and more – you might want to include. This, however, will depend very much on your own tastes and what you cook most often. Because the shelf life of these products is sometimes short, you might like to buy as and when you need them, as a two-year-old half-bag of almonds is only fit for the bird table, as I know to my cost.

Dried fruits: sour cherries, apricots, prunes and vine fruits – currants, raisins, sultanas and so on.

Nuts: unsalted pistachios (these actually keep well in the freezer), unblanched almonds, roasted unsalted peanuts, walnuts, pecans, brazils and pine nuts.

Coarse semolina for gnocchi (page 452).

Sweet oat biscuits and Grape-Nuts for cheesecake bases (page 454).

Chocolate and cocoa powder: unlike the items above, these should *always* be included, and notes on these are on pages 458 and 459.

The extended store cupboard

What I have included in this chapter is by no means an exhaustive list: there are literally hundreds of fascinating and useful storecupboard ingredients that I have not included but that you may want to use. What I have done is try to include what I use most of and what I feel is a good start for beginners.

Pad Thai Noodles with Shrimps

There's a long story attached to this recipe. I first ate it in a small street café in Ko Samui, an island off Thailand. It was so supremely good that my husband videoed it in close-up so that I could recreate the whole thing at home. I did, and here it is – every bit as good, I'm glad to say.

Serves 2 as a main course
4 oz (110 g) rice noodles (medium width, about ⅛ inch/3 mm thick)
2 tablespoons dried shrimps
6 oz (175 g) raw headless tiger prawns (if frozen, thoroughly defrosted)
3 tablespoons groundnut or other flavourless oil
2 cloves garlic, peeled and crushed
2 medium red chillies, deseeded and finely chopped
½ medium red onion, thinly sliced into half-moon shapes
2 tablespoons Thai fish sauce
juice 1 large lime (about 2 tablespoons)
2 large eggs, lightly beaten

For the garnish:
2 heaped tablespoons fresh coriander leaves
2 oz (50 g) natural roasted unsalted peanuts, roughly chopped or crushed in a pestle and mortar
2 spring onions, chopped, including the green parts

You will also need a deep frying pan with a diameter of 10 inches (25.5 cm), or a wok.

The way to tackle this is by having all the ingredients on the list prepared and assembled in front of you. First of all place the dried shrimps in a jug, cover with some boiling water and soak for 10 minutes, then do the same with the noodles, placing them in a bowl and making sure they're totally submerged in boiling water. After this time, drain the noodles in a colander and rinse them in cold water, then drain the shrimps. Now, to prepare the prawns, peel off and discard the shells, then you need to devein them. To do this, make a slit all along their backs using a small, sharp knife and remove any brownish-black thread, using the tip of the knife to lift it out. Now chop each prawn into 3.

When you're ready to start cooking, heat the oil in the frying pan or wok over a high heat until it is really hot. Then, first add the garlic, chilli and red onion and fry for 1-1½ minutes, or until the onion is tender, then, keeping the heat high, add the soaked dried shrimps and the prawns and fry for a further 2 minutes, or until the prawns have turned pink and are cooked. After that add the fish sauce and the lime juice, then stir this around for just a few seconds before adding the noodles. Now toss them around for 1-2 minutes, or until the noodles are heated through. Next add the beaten egg by pouring it slowly and evenly all over. Let it begin to set for about 1 minute, then stir briefly once more until the egg is cooked into little shreds. Then mix in half the garnish and give one final stir before serving absolutely immediately in hot bowls with the rest of the garnish handed round to be sprinkled over.

Anchoïade with Toasted Goats' Cheese Croutons

It's true that, because of overkill, everybody is tired of sun-dried tomatoes, but now we can buy semi-dried tomatoes, called mi-cuit or sun blush, which are more squashy and succulent, with lots of concentrated tomato flavour.

This is literally made in moments: all you do is place all the ingredients in a food processor, then briefly process until the mixture is chopped roughly. Store it in a bowl covered with clingfilm at room temperature till needed.

For the croutons, cut the baguettine into 12 slices on the diagonal (about ½ inch/1 cm thick), then spread very thinly with the goats' cheese and season with salt and pepper. Place on the baking tray and bake on the centre shelf of the oven for 20 minutes, until crisp and golden.

To serve, spread the anchoïade generously on to the baked croutons, garnish with the basil leaves and olives, and serve with something like a well-chilled Provençal rosé.

Instead of the croutons you could use the goats' cheese, onion and potato bread (see page 84), toasted under the grill, as pictured below.

Serves 4
2 oz (50 g) anchovy fillets, drained
2 mi-cuit tomatoes
1 ripe tomato, skinned
1 heaped dessertspoon tomato purée
2 shallots, peeled
8 black olives, pitted
2 cloves garlic, peeled
1 teaspoon fresh oregano
1 tablespoon roughly chopped fresh basil
1 teaspoon white wine vinegar
freshly milled black pepper

For the croutons (makes 12):
1 oz (25 g) soft goats' cheese
1 baguettine (small baguette)
salt and freshly milled black pepper

To garnish:
basil leaves
black olives (preferably small Provençal ones)

You will also need a baking tray measuring 10 x 14 inches (25.5 x 35 cm).

Pre-heat the oven to gas mark 4, 350°F (180°C).

Linguine with Sardines, Chilli and Capers

Good old tinned sardines are now becoming fashionable again and are an ideal storecupboard ingredient, great for serving on toast sprinkled with a little balsamic and lots of seasoning. This is also the perfect storecupboard meal for two, made in moments and great for students or anyone on a tight budget. I love the shape of linguine, but any pasta can be used.

Serves 2

8 oz (225 g) dried linguine
1 x 120 g tin sardines in olive oil, well drained and flaked into bite-sized pieces
1 tablespoon sardine oil, reserved from the tin
1 red chilli, deseeded and finely chopped
1 tablespoon salted capers, rinsed and drained
1 clove garlic, peeled and chopped
1 x 200 g tin Italian chopped tomatoes, well drained, or 4 ripe, medium-sized tomatoes, skinned and diced
a few fresh basil leaves, roughly torn, to garnish
salt and freshly milled black pepper

First of all you need to cook the pasta. Always use a large cooking pot and make sure you have at least 4 pints (2.25 litres) of water for every 8 oz (225 g) of pasta and 1 level tablespoon of salt. Bring the water up to a good fierce boil before the pasta goes in and cook it for 8-12 minutes without a lid, until *al dente*.

Meanwhile, heat the tablespoon of sardine oil in a small frying pan, fry the garlic and chilli for about 4 minutes, until softened, then add the tomatoes, sardines and capers and gently heat them through, stirring occasionally. Taste and season with salt and freshly milled black pepper.

When the pasta is ready, drain it into a colander, then quickly return it to the saucepan. Add the sauce, toss it around thoroughly for 30 seconds or so, then serve in hot pasta bowls with the torn basil sprinkled over.

Mexican Guacamole

The first time I ever used Tabasco (hot chilli sauce) was when I made my first guacamole. This spicy Mexican purée, made with fresh avocados, chillies and ripe tomatoes, is still a great favourite. Serve it as a first course with good crusty bread or as a dip with raw vegetable strips. Don't make guacamole more than 3 hours ahead, though, or it will discolour.

First it's important to have ripe avocados. All you do is halve them, remove the stones, then cut them into quarters, remove the flesh from the skin and place it in the bowl of a food processor. Now, using a teaspoon, scrape away any green part of the avocado flesh that has adhered to the skin and add this, as this will help to give lots of green colour. Now skin the tomatoes by pouring boiling water over them, then leave them for exactly 1 minute before draining and slipping off their skins (protect your hands with a cloth). Then halve them and pop them in to join the avocado, followed by the garlic, onion and chillies, and then add the lime juice, a few drops of Tabasco and some salt and pepper. Now whiz it all to a smooth purée, pile it into a serving bowl and cover with clingfilm. Chill till you need it and serve it sprinkled with the fresh coriander leaves.

Serves 4
2 ripe avocados
2 large, red, ripe tomatoes
2 small cloves garlic, peeled and sliced
½ red onion, cut into quarters
2 small red chillies, halved and deseeded
juice 2 limes
a few drops Tabasco
2 tablespoons fresh coriander leaves, to garnish
salt and freshly milled black pepper

Marinated Pork with Jerk Seasoning and Grilled Pineapple Salsa

In the Caribbean, jerk seasoning comes either wet or dry. The latter is made with dried herbs, which I don't usually have available, so this is the wet version – great for a barbecue or just plain-grilled.

Serves 6
6 large British pork chops
1 large red chilli, deseeded
½ small red onion
½ tablespoon chopped fresh
flat-leaf parsley
1 clove garlic, peeled
¾ inch (2 cm) piece fresh root ginger,
peeled and sliced
½ teaspoon Maldon sea salt
½ teaspoon allspice berries, ground
¼ fresh nutmeg, grated
⅛ teaspoon ground cinnamon
⅛ teaspoon ground cloves
juice 1 lime
1 tablespoon Japanese soy sauce
1 tablespoon groundnut or other
flavourless oil
1 tablespoon molasses sugar
10 fl oz (275 ml) dry white wine
salt and freshly milled black pepper

For the pineapple salsa:
1 medium pineapple
1 tablespoon groundnut or other
flavourless oil
1 tablespoon runny honey
1 small red onion, peeled and very
finely chopped
½ medium red chilli, deseeded
and diced
juice 1 lime
2 tablespoons chopped fresh
coriander leaves
salt and freshly milled black pepper

You will also need a baking tray
measuring 11 x 16 inches (28 x 40 cm).

Start this way ahead of time: trim the fat off the chops and season them with salt and pepper, then place all the other ingredients, except the wine, in a food processor and mix to a thick paste. Next spread half the paste over the base of a shallow dish, place the pork chops on top, then spread the rest of the paste over the surface of each chop. Now cover the dish with clingfilm and leave for a few hours so the flavours can develop.

Meanwhile, make the salsa, and to do this you need to first pre-heat the grill to its highest setting, then mix the oil and honey with a good seasoning of salt and black pepper. Then, using a sharp knife, cut the top and bottom off the pineapple and, standing it upright on a chopping board, remove the skin using a large serrated knife, then dig out the 'eyes' using the tip of a potato peeler. Now cut the pineapple in half lengthways, then lay each half, cut-side down, on the surface and slice each into 6 long wedges. After that, trim off the inner core. (See the photographs on page 419.) Next brush each wedge with the honey mixture and place them on the baking tray, then pop them under the grill about 1½ inches (4 cm) from the heat and grill for 10-15 minutes, until they become nicely charred; you'll need to turn them halfway through the cooking time. After that, remove them from the grill and allow them to cool slightly before chopping roughly into ½ inch (1 cm) pieces and mixing them with the remaining salsa ingredients. Then set aside till needed.

When you're ready to cook the chops, pre-heat the grill to its highest setting for at least 10 minutes. Place the chops on the same baking tray, making sure their surface is completely covered with the marinade (reserve the marinade left in the dish), then grill them 3 inches (7.5 cm) from the heat for about 15 minutes. After that, turn them over, spread the surface with the rest of the marinade and grill for another 15 minutes, until the chops are cooked and the surface is nice and crisp. Remove the pork to a serving dish, then scrape any crusty bits and remaining marinade from the baking tray into a small saucepan. Add the dry white wine, let it bubble and reduce by about a third, and pour it over the pork before seasoning. Serve with the salsa.

Beef Curry Dopiaza

The word dopiaza means double onion, and because I really love thick, spicy onions, it's what I always order in Indian restaurants. My recipe is not authentic, but I feel it is as good as any I've had.

Serves 4

2 lb (900 g) chuck steak, chopped into
1 inch (2.5 cm) pieces
1 rounded teaspoon cumin seeds
1 rounded teaspoon coriander seeds
3 cardamom pods (whole)
1 teaspoon fennel seeds
1 teaspoon whole fenugreek
(alternatively, use powder)
3 tablespoons groundnut or other
flavourless oil
1 lb (450 g) onions, peeled and
sliced into half-moon shapes about
½ inch (1 cm) thick
3 cloves garlic, peeled and crushed
3 green chillies, deseeded and
finely chopped
1 tablespoon ground turmeric
1 tablespoon freshly grated peeled
root ginger
2 medium tomatoes, skinned
and chopped
3 oz (75 g) creamed coconut
10 fl oz (275 ml) boiling water
5 fl oz (150 ml) natural yoghurt
salt and freshly milled black pepper

To serve:
juice 1 lime
1 tablespoon chopped fresh
coriander leaves

You will also need a lidded flameproof
casserole with a capacity of 4 pints
(2.25 litres).

First of all you need to roast the whole spices, and to do this place them in a small frying pan or saucepan over a medium heat and stir and toss them around for 1-2 minutes, or until they begin to look toasted and start to jump in the pan. Now transfer them to a pestle and mortar and crush them to a powder.

Next place 2 tablespoons of the oil in the casserole over a high heat and, when it is really hot, brown the pieces of meat a few at a time. Remove them to a plate, then add the rest of the oil and, when that's really hot, too, fry the onions till well browned – about 10 minutes – then add the garlic and chilli and cook for a further 2 minutes.

Next return the meat to the pan, add the crushed spices, fenugreek powder (if you were unable to buy it whole), turmeric, ginger and tomatoes and stir everything around. Next grate the creamed coconut into a bowl and combine it with the boiling water using a whisk, then, when it has dissolved, pour it into the casserole, followed by the yoghurt and some seasoning. Now bring the mixture up to a slow simmer, put the lid on the casserole and simmer very gently for 2 hours. Just before serving, add the lime juice and sprinkle over the chopped fresh coriander. Serve with spiced basmati rice and Coriander Chutney (see page 209).

*Beef Curry Dopiaza served with
Basmati Rice, Coriander Chutney
and Mango Chutney*

Lambs' Kidneys with Two Mustards

This is a lovely light recipe for summer, when lambs' kidneys are at their plump best. I like to keep the mustard flavour quite subtle, but if you like it more pronounced, just add a little more mustard.

Serves 2-3

1 lb (450 g) lambs' kidneys
1 heaped teaspoon mustard powder
2 heaped teaspoons hot wholegrain mustard
½ oz (10 g) butter
1 dessertspoon groundnut or other flavourless oil
1 small onion, peeled, halved and thinly sliced into half-moons
4 oz (110 g) small open-cup mushrooms, cut into ¼ inch (5 mm) slices
3 fl oz (75 ml) dry white wine
7 fl oz (200 ml) crème fraîche
salt and freshly milled black pepper

You will also need a frying pan with a diameter of 10 inches (25.5 cm).

First prepare the kidneys: cut them in half horizontally and snip out the white cores with scissors – if you don't the kidneys will be tough – then peel off and discard the skins. Next place the frying pan over a high heat and heat the butter and oil together. When it's hot and foaming, add the kidneys and cook for 3 minutes, turning them over halfway through. Next remove them to a plate, then add the onion to the pan and, keeping the heat high, cook for 3-4 minutes, until softened and brown at the edges. Now add the mushrooms and cook for another 1-2 minutes, until the juices just start to run out, then add the white wine and let it bubble and reduce to half its original volume. Finally, add the crème fraîche and mustards. Now give everything a good seasoning, stir well and carry on reducing the liquid for 2-3 minutes. Finally, return the kidneys and their juices to the sauce and heat through for about 1 minute. Serve right away with plain basmati rice.

This is quite an exotic recipe, a wonderful combination of flavours that develop and permeate the pork as it cooks very slowly. The surprising thing is the casserole takes only 6 minutes or so to prepare from start to finish. Serve it with Thai fragrant rice.

All you need to do is arrange the pork in a single layer in the base of a lidded flameproof casserole with a capacity of 4 pints (2.25 litres), then simply mix all the other ingredients (except the cinnamon and star anise) together, give them a good whisk and pour over the pork. Now tuck in the cinnamon sticks and star anise, place the casserole on the hob and bring everything up to a very gentle simmer. Put the lid on and simmer over the gentlest-possible heat for 45 minutes. At that point turn the pieces of pork over, replace the lid and simmer for 45 minutes more.

For the stir-fry, first prepare the vegetables: the cauliflower should be separated out and cut into tiny florets, and the same with the broccoli. Wash and trim the leeks, then halve and thinly slice them, while the spring onions should be sliced into matchsticks, as should the ginger. Finally, cut each head of pak choi into 6 wedges through the root.

When you're ready to cook, heat the oil over a high heat in a wok. Add the ginger and garlic and fry for 10 seconds, then add the cauliflower and broccoli and stir-fry for 1 minute. Next add the leeks and stir-fry for another minute. Add the spring onions and pak choi, toss everything together, then add the liquid and sugar. Reduce the heat to medium, put a lid on and cook for 4 minutes, stirring occasionally. Serve the pork and stir-fried greens with the spring onions and chilli sprinkled over each portion, remembering to remove the cinnamon sticks and star anise first. Note: if you like, spinach leaves can be used instead of pak choi.

Serves 4-6
2 lb (900 g) shoulder of British pork, chopped into 1 inch (2.5 cm) cubes
4 fl oz (120 ml) Japanese soy sauce
1 rounded tablespoon freshly grated peeled root ginger
1 dessertspoon molasses sugar
1 small onion, peeled and finely chopped
2 cloves garlic, peeled and crushed
2 medium red chillies, deseeded and finely chopped
4 fl oz (120 ml) Shaosing brown rice wine or dry sherry
2 x 3 inch (7.5 cm) cinnamon sticks
2 whole star anise

For the stir-fried green vegetables:
4 oz (110 g) cauliflower
6 oz (175 g) broccoli
2 medium leeks
4 spring onions
2 inch (5 cm) piece root ginger, peeled
10 oz (275 g) pak choi
2 tablespoons groundnut or other flavourless oil
2 cloves garlic, peeled and thinly sliced
3 tablespoons Japanese soy sauce
3 fl oz (75 ml) Shaosing brown rice wine or dry sherry
3 fl oz (75 ml) water
1 dessertspoon golden caster sugar

To garnish:
2 spring onions, cut into fine shreds 1 inch (2.5 cm) long
½ medium red chilli, deseeded and cut into fine shreds

Preserved Ginger Cake with Lemon Icing

In all my years of cooking, this is, quite simply, my favourite cake. It's simple but absolute heaven. The spiciness of the ginger within the moist cake, coupled with the sharpness of the lemon icing, is such that it never fails to please all who eat it.

Makes 15 squares
5 pieces preserved stem ginger in syrup, chopped
2 tablespoons ginger syrup (from jar of stem ginger in syrup)
1 heaped teaspoon ground ginger
1 heaped teaspoon grated fresh root ginger
6 oz (175 g) butter, at room temperature, plus a little extra for greasing
6 oz (175 g) golden caster sugar
3 large eggs, at room temperature
1 tablespoon molasses syrup
8 oz (225 g) self-raising flour
1 tablespoon ground almonds
2 tablespoons milk

For the topping:
juice 1 lemon
8 oz (225 g) unrefined golden icing sugar
2 extra pieces preserved stem ginger in syrup

You will also need a non-stick cake tin measuring 6 x 10 inches (15 x 25.5 cm), 1 inch (2.5 cm) deep, and some silicone paper (parchment) measuring 10 x 14 inches (25.5 x 35 cm).

Pre-heat the oven to gas mark 3, 325°F (170°C).

First prepare the cake tin by greasing it lightly and lining it with the silicone paper: press it into the tin, folding the corners in to make it fit neatly (see page 131) – the paper should come up 1 inch (2.5 cm) above the edge.

To make the cake, take a large mixing bowl and cream the butter and sugar together until light and fluffy. Next break the eggs into a jug and beat them with a fork until fluffy, then gradually beat them into the mixture, a little at a time, until all the egg is incorporated. Next fold in the ginger syrup and molasses; the best way to add the molasses is to lightly grease a tablespoon, then take a tablespoon of molasses and just push it off the spoon with a rubber spatula into the mixture. Now sift the flour and ground ginger on to a plate, then gradually fold these in, about a tablespoon at a time. Next fold in the almonds, followed by the milk, and lastly the grated root ginger and pieces of stem ginger. Now spread the cake mixture evenly in the cake tin, then bake on the middle shelf of the oven for 45-50 minutes, or until the cake is risen, springy and firm to touch in the centre. Leave the cake to cool in the tin for 10 minutes, then turn it out on to a wire rack and make sure it is absolutely cold before you attempt to ice it.

For the icing, sift the icing sugar into a bowl and mix with enough of the lemon juice to make the consistency of thick cream – you might not need all the lemon juice. Now spread the icing over the top of the cake, and don't worry if it dribbles down the sides in places, as this looks quite attractive. Cut the remaining ginger into 15 chunks and place these in lines across the cake so that when you cut it you will have 15 squares, each with a piece of ginger in the centre. It's absolute heaven. If you'd like one or two of these cakes tucked away for a rainy day, they freeze beautifully – simply defrost and put the icing on half an hour before serving.

12

Fish without fear

Why is it that people are afraid to cook fish? Is it fear of the unknown, the unfamiliar, or are there now just too many varieties to choose from, making it difficult for a beginner to know where to start? Given that so many people love eating fish but so few want to cook it, I feel my task here is to reassure those of you who are afraid and try to provide a sort of simple introduction to the whole subject of fish cooking, which will hopefully persuade you to try.

It has to be said that fish is in the premier league as far as the 21st-century diet is concerned. Perhaps the singularly most important reason for this is speed – because for people who lead busy, pressured lives it's one of the few ingredients that can provide a main-course supper dish that's not only elegant, stylish and bang up-to-the-minute, but at the same time takes as little as 10 and rarely more than 30 minutes to prepare from start to finish.

But there's more. Nutritionally fish is not only rich in first-class protein, which is an essential part of our daily diet, but at the same time it happens to be, conveniently, low in fat (for the most part). Then, by some extra miracle of nature, the group known as oily fish (a bad description, because they actually contain a very small amount of fat) contains substances known as omega-3 fatty acids that are beneficial in preventing clogged arteries, which cause heart diseases and certain skin conditions. We should therefore all be eating and, more importantly, enjoying more fish. So here goes – I am going to have a big crack at persuading you. Let's first examine what the pitfalls might be.

The fear factor

Here, familiarity is the key – getting to know about fish and understanding it will automatically make you much more comfortable, so read on.

I don't know how to handle it

There's a bit of hand-me-down mythology here. Who says it necessarily needs handling? This is merely a kickback from the days when cooks had to deal with freshly landed fish that needed scaling, gutting, filleting and so on. With modern fishmongers, fish counters and chill cabinets, all this work is done for you. If you want to, you can now buy fish skinned, boned and ready to cook, which probably means less handling than trimming the average steak. Sometimes, as with jointing a chicken, some handling is needed, but only for those who choose it. Anyway, here all the handling you will ever need to know about will be explained to remove all the fear.

What about the bones?

Well, firstly, as explained above, there don't have to be any at all. However, if you really enjoy eating a wide variety of fish that is not always filleted, there's no bones about it (excuse the pun), provided you know how to handle and deal with them. This includes a few basic lessons, not just on preparation for cooking but also on how to actually eat the fish once it arrives on the plate (see the next point).

And the skin?

I used to be absolutely terrified of skinning a piece of fish because I simply didn't know how to do it, then I was taught and I've never looked back.

So, if I can teach you how to do it (see page 267), you, too, will no longer have any fears. But let me say that as a fish lover, I feel that leaving the skin on is sometimes preferable because it can give extra flavour to the dish (in which case it can simply be left on the side of the plate). However, it's now become fashionable in restaurants to sear the de-scaled skin of certain fish at very high temperatures so that it becomes so crisp that it resembles crackling, and this is, I have to say, quite delicious!

What about the smell?

There really shouldn't be any. If you have a reliable fishmonger and you buy fresh fish, it should not smell unpleasant; in fact the opposite is true – the smell of fresh fish sizzling in the pan can be quite appetising. As with all cooking, however, kitchens need to be well ventilated, with a window open or an extractor fan on. Kippers are perhaps the exception to this no-smell rule, but keep the window wide open as you cook them, or, if you get the chance, try cooking them outside on the barbecue: no smells to linger, and char-grilled they taste absolutely wonderful.

Where have all the fishmongers gone?

It has to be said that if you want to cook and enjoy eating fish, then your source is vital. Sadly, high-street food suppliers are victims of parking restrictions and I imagine we can put much of the blame for the demise of our fishmongers on those horrid yellow lines, making the free-parking offer of the supermarkets much more practical. However, there are still good fishmongers who need our support. What happens in supermarkets is that some fish counters, together with the pre-packed fish they sell, are of superb quality, others not so, but because this does vary enormously from store to store, the best guide is your nose. If, as you walk towards the fish counter, you can smell fish, don't approach it.

How much do I need?

I would say 7-8 oz (200-225 g) per person for boned white fish; on the bone (whole trout, plaice, mackerel and so on), 10-12 oz (275-350 g) each; and richer fish, such as salmon or tuna, 6-8 oz (175-225 g) would be right.

What kind of fish?

For a beginner I feel the best way forward is to get to know just a few varieties of fish and what to expect from them, so what I've tried to do here is firstly put them into groups to give you an initial guide.

Firm and flaky

This is essentially the cod family, which includes cod, haddock, hake and whiting. If you want a fairly firm, flaky flesh that is moist and succulent with a delicate flavour, this is what you'll get from this group.

Firm and meaty

This group, as these words imply, has more bite to it, and because it's more robust in texture, it can stand up to more vigorous cooking. Turbot and halibut are in this league, as are monkfish tails, and all have a fine flavour.

Delicate

This includes most of the group we call flat fish, and their texture varies. Skate, *left*, has sweet white flesh and an excellent texture; Dover sole has a fairly firm flesh with a fine flavour; lemon sole has a more delicate flesh and not such a good flavour; plaice is one of my own favourites, as it has a very fragile flesh and a lovely fragrant flavour of the sea, but only in the right season (June to November).

Lots of gutsy flavour

The oily fish group are for those who like real flavour, and herring, mackerel, sardines, sprats and whitebait all belong to this family – juicy and succulent, with tons of flavour. Here you are going to have to negotiate with bones, but it's worth it for the taste alone.

The king of fish

The salmon is definitely crowned king. Caught wild, it leaves the sea to enter the rivers, and it has just about everything: firm yet delicate flesh, and all the flavour of the sea. Farmed, it can be excellent or very poor. Thankfully it's easy to tell (*see left*) – too many white fat layers mean poor quality. The reason for this, believe it or not, is lack of exercise. The wild salmon negotiates strong currents, giving it a kind of 'aerobic' existence, and good farmed salmon comes from lochs and areas where strong currents exist.

Trout

Salmon trout – or sea trout, as it's sometimes called – looks like a small salmon, but though it has the appearance of salmon, it's less fatty and the flesh is more delicate. Trout proper is its small freshwater cousin that lives in lakes, rivers and streams. Wild it's called brown trout, is exceptionally special and only available if you know someone who goes fishing, but farmed it's called rainbow trout and is not so flavoursome.

Smoked fish

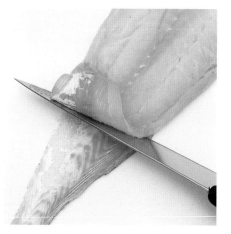

All the fish just mentioned can be smoked, and the flavour of the smoke and fish is an inspired combination. Finnan haddock is smoked on the bone, but is also sold as fillets, as is cod and whiting. Arbroath smokies are small young haddock or whiting that are smoked to a dark-bronze colour, which actually cooks them, so they only need re-heating. Smoked mackerel and kippers are similarly smoked, so no cooking is needed here, either; the grill or barbecue is enough to re-heat them.

There's nothing to be afraid of

Now you are embarking on a journey of learning how to cook fish, but although I have said everything can be prepared for you, I am including instructions on how to bone and skin fish – just in case you want to learn, or perhaps find yourself the lucky recipient of some freshly caught fish.

How to skin a fillet of fish

All you need is a flat surface and a sharp knife. First of all angle the knife at the thinner or tail end of the fillet, or, if it's all the same thickness, just start at one end. Cut a little bit of the flesh away from the skin – enough to get the knife angled in. Now, using your fingertips, hang on to the skin, clasping it as firmly as possible, then push the knife with your other hand, keeping the blade at an angle, *opposite, bottom left*. Push at the skin, not the flesh, remembering the skin is tough and the knife won't go through it. What's happening is the knife blade, as it slides between the skin and the flesh, is cutting the skin away. If you're not experienced, don't worry if you're left with a few patches of skin, you can just gently cut these away. Practice is all you need and you'll soon be able to feel when the angle of the knife is right.

How to bone a whole fish

This method applies to herring, mackerel and trout. First ask the fishmonger to scale and trim the fish, and if he will bone it for you, so much the better; if not, it really is dead simple. All you do is cut along the belly of the fish with scissors, snipping off the head, fins and, if you need to, the tail, then place it flesh-side down on a flat surface. Now, using a rolling pin, give the fish a few sharp taps to flatten it out. Next press very firmly with your thumbs or the handle of a wooden spoon, *top right*, all along the back bone of the fish, which will loosen it. Now turn the fish skin-side down and, using a sharp knife and starting at the head end, gently ease the back bone away, *centre*: as it comes away, almost all the little bones will come away with it. Any that don't can be removed afterwards, and tweezers are helpful here. Finally, cut away the dark belly flaps using scissors, *bottom*.

How to cook fish

Set out over the next few pages are simple guidelines for various methods of cooking fish. Then, when you have tried the recipes, which each describe in detail how to cook the fish, you will have a fairly broad knowledge and, I hope, feel comfortable with fish cookery for the rest of your life. The timings that follow are guidelines, so just remember that thicker pieces of fish will need the longer times, thinner pieces the shorter.

Poaching

Poached smoked haddock, topped with a couple of fresh, lightly poached eggs and served with some brown bread and butter, is one of the quickest and best comfort meals I know. Poaching is fast, easy and no-fuss, and if you want to serve a sauce with the fish, then using the poaching liquid introduces the flavour of the fish itself. Thus the liquid from white fish poached in a mixture of half milk and half water can be used for a parsley sauce, and the cooking liquid from smoked fish fillets poached in the same way can be used to make a basic white sauce to which chopped hard-boiled eggs and chives can be added. Either sauce can be finished off beautifully with a tablespoon of cream or crème fraîche.

Rolled fish fillets, for example plaice or sole, can be poached in white wine or cider, which again will make a lovely sauce. Trout can be poached in a pan of water to which a glass of dry white wine or cider has been added, along with a few sprigs of fresh herbs, a couple of bay leaves, slices of lemon, thin onion slices and a few black peppercorns. Don't bother with fish kettles, which take up far too much storage space, as large, whole fish are better oven-baked in foil.

Poaching guidelines

Rolled fillets of sole and plaice will take 4-5 minutes, and the cooking liquid – dry white wine or cider – can be used to make a sauce. White or smoked fish fillets and fish steaks weighing 6-7 oz (175-200 g) will take 6-8 minutes, depending on their thickness. Whole trout weighing 10-12 oz (275-350 g) each will take 8-10 minutes – less for small fish. Use enough liquid to half-cover the fish and make sure the pan has a well-fitting lid.

Steaming

Steaming, like poaching, is great for calorie counters, as no fat is needed, so if you're cutting the fat in your diet, steaming fish is definitely for you. You can use either a traditional fan or bamboo steamer. I think steaming – as oriental cooks have discovered – is particularly good for rolled fillets of plaice, sole or trout, as they retain their shape perfectly and remain beautifully moist. Add about 2 inches (5 cm) of boiling water to the saucepan, then fit the steamer over, making sure it doesn't come into contact with the water, and cover with a tight-fitting lid.

Steaming guidelines

Whole Dover sole, lemon sole or plaice weighing 10-12 oz (275-350 g) will take 7-8 minutes; rolled fillets of the above, 7-8 minutes; trout fillets, rolled, will take 7-8 minutes; white or smoked fish, steaks and fillets weighing 6-7 oz (175-200 g), 8-10 minutes.

Shallow-frying

I have evocative memories of my grandmother shallow-frying skate wings, her favourite fish, which she first dipped in seasoned flour – they were golden and crisp at the edges and there were always special Victorian bone-handled fish knives and forks on the table. I think shallow-fried fish makes a simple but very tempting supper dish, but you need to follow a few basic rules to get it absolutely right. First the fish must be dried thoroughly with kitchen paper, and because the flesh of white fish is so delicate, there needs to be some kind of coating – seasoned flour, white or wholemeal, beaten egg and breadcrumbs.

The second rule is you must have the fat hot enough – olive oil or a mixture of groundnut or other flavourless oil and butter are my favourites. There should be enough to cover the pan and give a depth of about ⅛ inch (3 mm), and the most vital point is that it must be really hot. Watch the oil as it's heating and you will see a shimmering haze that will cue you as to when to add the fish. If in doubt, add a small cube of bread, which should sizzle quite fiercely; if it doesn't the oil is not hot enough. The idea is to seal the fish in the hot fat on both sides – it is only when the fat isn't hot enough that fried fish tastes oily. Always drain shallow-fried fish on crumpled greaseproof or absorbent kitchen paper before serving.

Shallow-frying guidelines

Whole Dover sole, lemon sole or plaice weighing 10-12 oz (275-350 g) each, 4-6 minutes each side; fillets of the above, 2-3 minutes each side; fish steaks and fillets weighing 6-7 oz (175-200 g), 5-6 minutes each side; skate wings, 4-5 minutes each side; whole herring or mackerel weighing 8-10 oz (225-275 g), 5-6 minutes each side; kippers weighing 9-10 oz (250-275 g), 4 minutes each side; sprats, 2-3 minutes each side.

Down with deep-frying

I have, I'm afraid, eliminated deep-frying from my own cooking repertoire. I think times have changed and we've all moved on from not only the bother of it but the 'write your name in it' layer of grease it leaves on the kitchen walls. Yes, there are deep-frying machines, but they're a bother to clean and take up too much space. I now prefer to use a high temperature oven-roasting for chips (see page 189), and fish I feel can be very successfully shallow-fried. Meanwhile, I can still enjoy deep-fried fish and chips from my local chippy and other deep-fried foods in restaurants and let *them* have the bother of cleaning the ceiling and walls.

Oven-baking

This and foil cookery (on the following page) are trouble-free ways of cooking certain fish because, as long as you put on a timer, you can pop the dish in the oven and forget all about it. Having said that, though, there are one or two things to be wary of. White fish, steaks and fillets on their own could end up being dry, so these are best brushed liberally with melted butter and protected with a buttered piece of foil lightly placed on top. However, if you use a topping to add moisture, the foil is not needed. Whole fish oven-bake beautifully if brushed liberally with butter or oil, and if a stuffing is added to the body cavity this will help keep the fish moist.

Oven-baking guidelines

Pre-heat the oven to gas mark 6, 400°F (200°C). For white fish or smoked fish fillets and steaks, brushed with butter and wrapped in buttered foil and weighing 6-7 oz (175-200 g), allow 15-20 minutes; whole mackerel, trout or herring weighing 10-12 oz (275-350 g) each, 25-30 minutes; tilapia weighing 12-14 oz (350-400 g), 15 minutes.

Oven-roasting

This is, in all the years I have been cooking, a breakthrough for me, as it cuts out a lot of shallow-frying and grilling. What happens is the oven is pre-heated to its highest setting (about gas mark 8, 450°F, 230°C), the fish then gets a real blast of heat, which cooks it quickly and retains all its moist juices. I hate standing watching grills or, equally, getting greasy from deep-frying; oven-roasting cuts down time and effort, and also, used instead of frying, cuts down the fat, which is always a good thing.

Foil-wrapped fish

You can, if you wish, foil-wrap fish and then cook it in a steamer, under the grill, on the barbecue or in the oven. The advantage is that all the flavours and juices are retained inside a sealed parcel. It's best to follow individual recipes for timings, but I have found that foil-wrapping is the best way to cook either a whole or large piece of salmon or a salmon trout. If, in the summer, you want to serve the fish cold, you can leave it inside its parcel until you're ready to serve it, which will keep it moist and juicy.

To cook salmon, I like the slow method, which very gently cooks the fish to absolute perfection. If you want to cook a whole salmon for a party, the fish can be cut in half, wrapped in two foil parcels, then, after baking and cooling, the two halves can be put back together once the skin has been removed and the join hidden by a band of cucumber slices. The oven temperature for this is gas mark ½ (S or E on some models), 250°F (120°C). Add 2-3 bay leaves to the body cavity and some sprigs of fresh tarragon, season with salt and pepper and tuck in 1-2 oz (25-50 g) of butter. Then wrap the whole thing in a double sheet of foil, loosely but sealing it tightly, place on a baking tray and bake in the pre-heated oven for the following cooking times. For a 1 lb 8 oz (700 g) salmon, 1 hour 10 minutes; 2 lb (900 g), 1 hour 30 minutes; 3 lb (1.35 kg), 2 hours; 4 lb (1.8 kg), 2 hours 30 minutes; 5 lb (2.25 kg), 3 hours.

Whole salmon trout or sea trout can be prepared as above and cooked with the same timings according to the weight. Salmon steaks weighing up to 8 oz (225 g) each need to be baked at a higher temperature than this: gas mark 4, 350°F (180°C). Wrap them – either individually or 4-6 at a time – in well-buttered foil, but first season them, adding torn bay leaves, sprigs of tarragon and 1 tablespoon of white wine per steak. Seal the edges of the foil securely and bake on a high shelf of the oven for 20 minutes. Salmon fillets weighing 5-6 oz (150-175 g) each will take 15-20 minutes.

Grilling and barbecuing

This is something of a minefield to give timings for, because domestic grills vary so much, as do shelf distances from the source of the heat, so bear this in mind when following these guidelines, especially with barbecues, where accurate degrees of heat cannot be measured. First remember to always line your grill pan with buttered foil, as this makes it easier to wash and prevents any fishy flavours from lingering in the pan. White fish needs to be brushed generously with melted butter and basted with more melted butter whilst cooking to prevent any dryness.

When using a barbecue have some melted butter handy to brush on the fish, and it's best to use one of the special fish grills, as this keeps the fish neatly intact without it breaking or sticking. Trout, mackerel and other small, whole fish all respond well to this cooking method, and you can add herbs and seasoning. For domestic grills always pre-heat them to their highest setting a good 10 minutes in advance.

Approximate grilling times

Whole Dover sole, lemon sole or plaice weighing 10-12 oz (275-350 g), 4-6 minutes each side; fillets of sole or plaice, 2-3 minutes each side; fish fillets and steaks weighing 6-8 oz (175-225 g), allow 5-6 minutes each side, flesh-side first, and have extra butter ready for basting during cooking; whole mackerel weighing 8-10 oz (225-275 g), make 3 diagonal scores on each side, and if you wish tuck in a slice of lemon or lime, brush with melted butter and grill for 6-7 minutes each side. Whole herring weighing 6-8 oz (175-225 g), score and butter as above and allow 4-5 minutes' grilling time each side; kippers weighing 9-10 oz (250-275 g), place a knob of butter on the flesh side and allow 4-5 minutes each side.

Microwaving

This is a tricky subject, and one that causes a great dilemma for the cookery writer. As microwave ovens are not standard and the power levels vary, it's difficult to give any kind of standard guidelines. The best course if you want to cook fish in the microwave is to follow the instructions in the individual manufacturer's handbook. But the danger with cooking fish in this way is that a few seconds more than it actually needs will render it overcooked and sometimes dry. For this reason I think cooking fish in a microwave is not at all easy for beginners and, because conventional cooking is quick and easy anyway, I would begin with this.

Fried Skate Wings with Very Quick Home-made Tartare Sauce

Serves 2

1 lb (450 g) skate wings (2 small, or 1 large and cut in half)
1 heaped tablespoon seasoned flour
2 tablespoons light olive oil

For the tartare sauce:

1 large egg
½ teaspoon Maldon sea salt
1 small clove garlic, peeled
½ teaspoon mustard powder
6 fl oz (175 ml) light olive oil
1 dessertspoon lemon juice
1 tablespoon fresh flat-leaf parsley leaves
1 heaped tablespoon salted capers, rinsed and drained
4 cornichons (baby gherkins)
freshly milled black pepper

To serve:

a few sprigs fresh flat-leaf parsley
1 lemon, sliced into wedges

You will also need a frying pan with a diameter of 10 inches (25.5 cm).

People are scared of this, one of the finest and most delicious fish of all. But don't be: the flesh slides away from those ribby, gelatinous bones with simplicity and ease (see the photograph on page 266), so do give it a try. I love it just plain with lemon squeezed over or with tartare sauce. This sauce has a mayonnaise base, which in this case is made by the quick method: that is, using a whole egg and a food processor or blender. This sauce will keep in a clean screw-top jar in the refrigerator for up to a week. It can also be served with any plain-grilled fish or with fishcakes.

Begin by making the tartare sauce. Break the egg into the bowl of the processor, add the salt, garlic and mustard powder, then switch the motor on and, through the feeder tube, add the oil in a thin, steady trickle, pouring it as slowly as you can (which even then takes only about 2 minutes). When the oil is in and the sauce has thickened, add some pepper and all the other ingredients. Now switch on the pulse button and pulse until the ingredients are chopped – as coarsely or as finely as you want. Lastly, taste to check the seasoning, then transfer to a serving bowl.

When you are ready to cook the skate wings, take the frying pan and put it over a gentle heat to warm up while you wipe the fish with kitchen paper and coat them with a light dusting of the seasoned flour. Now turn the heat up to high, add the oil to the pan and, as soon as it's really hot, add the skate wings. Reduce the heat to medium and fry them for 4-5 minutes on each side, depending on their size and thickness. To test if they are cooked, slide the tip of a sharp knife in and push to see if the flesh parts from the bone easily and looks creamy-white. When the fish is ready, remove it to warm serving plates, garnish with the parsley and serve with the tartare sauce and lemon wedges to squeeze over.

Note: for a change to the tartare sauce, replace lemon juice and parsley with lime juice and fresh coriander.

To make tartare sauce, simply place the egg, salt, garlic and mustard powder in the food processor, then add the oil in a thin, steady stream through the feeder tube. Once the sauce has thickened, add the remaining ingredients and pulse to the desired consistency, then season and transfer to a serving bowl

Roasted Fish with a Parmesan Crust

This works superbly well with plaice fillets, but sole would be excellent, or thicker fish fillets such as cod or haddock, in which case allow 5 minutes extra cooking time. I don't feel it needs a sauce, but a green salad with a lemony dressing would be a good accompaniment.

Serves 2

1 lb (450 g) plaice fillets (4 fillets)

3 oz (75 g) freshly grated Parmesan (Parmigiano Reggiano)

4 oz (110 g) white bread, slightly stale, cut into cubes

a handful of fresh curly parsley leaves

2 oz (50 g) melted butter, plus a little extra for brushing

salt and freshly milled black pepper

To garnish:

1 lemon, cut into quarters

a little fresh curly parsley

You will also need a baking tray measuring 11 x 16 inches (28 x 40 cm) and some kitchen foil.

Pre-heat the oven to gas mark 8, 450°F (230°C).

First of all prepare the baking tray by lining it with foil and brushing the foil generously with melted butter. Now wipe the fish with kitchen paper, then lay the fillets on the foil and season them with salt and black pepper. Next place the cubes of bread and parsley leaves in a food processor and switch on the motor to whiz it all to fine crumbs, then add the Parmesan, melted butter, ½ a teaspoon of salt and some pepper and pulse again to mix them in. Now spread the crumb mixture over the fish fillets, drizzle over a little more melted butter and then place the baking tray on a high shelf in the oven for 7-8 minutes, or until the crumbs have turned a golden brown. Serve with the lemon quarters to squeeze over and a sprig of parsley as a garnish.

Fried Herrings with Oatmeal and a Beetroot Relish

Why is it that fresh sardines are so highly thought of and yet herrings are largely ignored? Firstly they're very closely related, so their taste is similar; secondly, herrings don't have to be imported and therefore are fresh, plump and bright, and, being larger, they have more lovely, juicy flesh. Any leftover beetroot relish can be kept in the fridge for a couple of days.

Begin by making the beetroot relish, and to do this simply mix all the ingredients together and sprinkle with the chopped parsley.

Now wipe the herrings with kitchen paper, then place them, flesh-side up, on a plate and season well. Dip both sides into the seasoned flour, then dip the flesh-side only into first the beaten egg, then the oatmeal, pressing it down firmly into their flesh. Now heat the lard or oil in the frying pan over a high heat until it's shimmering hot, then fry the herrings flesh-side (oatmeal-side) down for 2-3 minutes, or until they look golden and crusty when you lift a little with a spatula. Now flip them over using a spatula and fork and let them cook for another 1-2 minutes, then transfer them to crumpled greaseproof or kitchen paper to drain before serving with the relish and some waxy potatoes. Garnish with the parsley and lime wedges.

Serves 2

2 medium-sized herrings weighing 10-12 oz (275-350 g) each when whole, boned (see page 267)
3 oz (75 g) pinhead oatmeal (coarse oatmeal)
2 heaped tablespoons seasoned plain flour
1 large egg, beaten
2 tablespoons lard or flavourless oil
salt and freshly milled black pepper

For the beetroot relish:
6 oz (175 g) cooked beetroot, chopped into ¼ inch (5 mm) dice
2 shallots, peeled and finely chopped
4 cornichons (baby gherkins), finely chopped
1 heaped tablespoon salted capers, rinsed and drained
1 dessertspoon red wine vinegar
1 dessertspoon good-quality mayonnaise
a little chopped fresh parsley, to serve
salt and freshly milled black pepper

To garnish:
a few sprigs fresh flat-leaf parsley
a few lime wedges

You will also need a frying pan with a diameter of 10 inches (25.5 cm).

Thai Fishcakes with Sesame and Lime Dipping Sauce

The ingredients list for these noble little Thai-inspired fishcakes looks very long but the good thing is they can be made and cooked with incredible speed. Serve them as a first or main course, or they're also good as canapés to serve with drinks, in which case make them smaller.

Serves 4 as a main course, 8 as a starter
1 lb (450 g) any white fish fillets, skinned and cut into chunks
1 stem lemon grass, roughly chopped
1 fat clove garlic, peeled
½ inch (1 cm) piece fresh root ginger, peeled and roughly chopped
3 tablespoons fresh coriander leaves, plus a few sprigs to garnish
2 kaffir lime leaves, roughly chopped (if unavailable leave them out)
zest 1 lime (the juice goes in the sauce)
1 medium red chilli, deseeded
½ small red pepper (use only ¼ if it's a large one), deseeded and roughly chopped
3 oz (75 g) dried coconut powder
2 tablespoons lightly seasoned plain flour
2-3 tablespoons groundnut or other flavourless oil, for frying
salt and freshly milled black pepper

For the dipping sauce:
1 teaspoon sesame seeds
1 tablespoon sesame oil
1 tablespoon lime juice
1 dessertspoon Thai fish sauce
1 tablespoon Japanese soy sauce
1 medium red chilli, deseeded and very finely chopped

You will also need a frying pan with a diameter of 10 inches (25.5 cm).

To make the fishcakes you first of all need to put the lemon grass, garlic, ginger, coriander leaves, kaffir lime leaves, lime zest, chilli and red pepper into a food processor, then turn the motor on and blend everything fairly finely. After that add the cubes of fish, process again briefly until the fish is blended in, then finally pour in the coconut powder through the feeder tube. Switch on the motor again but be careful at this stage not to overprocess – all you need to do is briefly blend it all for 2-3 seconds.

Then tip the mixture into a bowl, add some seasoning and shape the fishcakes into 24 fairly small, thin, flattish, round shapes about 2 inches (5 cm) in diameter. If you like you can make them ahead to this stage, but spread them out in a single layer, cover with clingfilm and keep them in the refrigerator till needed.

Meanwhile, make the dipping sauce. To do this, first of all begin by toasting the sesame seeds. Using a small, solid frying pan, pre-heat it over a medium heat, then add the sesame seeds and toast them, moving them around in the pan to brown them evenly. As soon as they begin to splutter and pop and turn golden, they're ready – this will take 1-2 minutes. Then remove them from the frying pan to a serving bowl and simply stir in the rest of the ingredients.

When you're ready to cook the fishcakes, first coat them in the seasoned flour, then heat 2 tablespoons of the oil in the frying pan over a high heat and, when it's really hot, turn the heat down to medium and fry the fishcakes briefly for about 30 seconds on each side to a pale golden colour. You will need to cook them in several batches, adding a little more oil if necessary. As they cook, transfer to a warm plate and keep warm. Serve with the dipping sauce, garnished with the remaining coriander.

Luxury Smoked-Fish Pie

I first introduced this in the 'Cookery Course', but this time round I've made it less of a family supper dish and into something more suitable for entertaining. Serve it with some sprigs of watercress for garnish, and I always think fish pie is lovely with fresh shelled peas.

Serves 6

8 oz (225 g) undyed smoked haddock fillet
2 Manx boneless kipper fillets
8 oz (225 g) Arbroath smokies
8 oz (225 g) smoked salmon or smoked salmon trimmings
15 fl oz (425 ml) whole milk
1 bay leaf
6 black peppercorns
a few stalks fresh parsley
2 oz (50 g) butter
2 oz (50 g) plain flour
5 fl oz (150 ml) single cream
3 tablespoons chopped fresh parsley
2 large eggs, hard-boiled and chopped
1 heaped tablespoon salted capers, rinsed and drained
4 cornichons (baby gherkins), chopped
1 tablespoon lemon juice
a few sprigs fresh watercress, to garnish
salt and freshly milled black pepper

For the topping:

2 lb (900 g) Desirée potatoes
2 oz (50 g) butter
2 tablespoons crème fraîche
1 oz (25 g) Gruyère, finely grated
1 tablespoon finely grated Parmesan (Parmigiano Reggiano)
salt and freshly milled black pepper

You will also need an ovenproof baking dish measuring 9 inches (23 cm) square and 2 inches (5 cm) deep, buttered.

Pre-heat the oven to gas mark 6, 400°F (200°C).

First of all arrange the haddock in a baking tin, pour over the milk and add the bay leaf, peppercorns and parsley stalks, then bake, uncovered, on a high shelf of the oven for 10 minutes. Meanwhile, remove the skin from the kipper fillets and skin and bone the Arbroath smokies – the flesh will come off very easily (see page 267). Then chop them into 2 inch (5 cm) pieces, along with the smoked salmon, if the slices are whole, then place all the prepared fish in a mixing bowl. Next, when the haddock is cooked, strain off the liquid and reserve it, discarding the bay leaf, parsley stalks and peppercorns. Then, when the haddock is cool enough to handle, remove the skin and flake the flesh into largish pieces, adding it to the bowl to join the rest of the fish.

Next make the sauce, and do this by melting the butter in the saucepan, stir in the flour and gradually add the fish liquid bit by bit, stirring continuously. When all the liquid is in, finish the sauce by gradually adding the single cream, then some seasoning, and simmer for 3-4 minutes, then stir in the chopped parsley. Now add the hard-boiled eggs, capers and cornichons to the fish, followed by the lemon juice and, finally, the sauce. Mix it all together gently and carefully so as not to break up the fish too much, then taste and check the seasoning and pour the mixture into the baking dish.

Now, to make the topping, peel and quarter the potatoes, put in a steamer fitted over a large saucepan of boiling water, sprinkle with a dessertspoon of salt, put a lid on and steam until they are absolutely tender – about 25 minutes. Then remove the potatoes from the steamer, drain off the water, return them to the saucepan and cover with a clean tea cloth to absorb some of the steam for about 5 minutes. Now add the butter and crème fraîche and, on the lowest speed, use an electric hand whisk to break the potatoes up, then increase the speed to high and whip them up to a smooth, creamy, fluffy mass. Taste, season well, then spread the potatoes all over the fish, making a ridged pattern with a palette knife. Now finally sprinkle over the grated cheeses and bake on a high shelf in the oven for 30-40 minutes, or until the top is nicely tinged brown. Serve each portion garnished with the watercress.

Roasted Butterflied Tiger Prawns in Garlic Butter

This is an amazingly good first course for garlic lovers and needs lots of really crusty baguette to mop up all the delicious juices. It is also delightfully simple and can be prepared well in advance.

Serves 4

20 raw, shell-on large tiger prawns
(about 1lb 8 oz/700 g), thoroughly
defrosted if frozen
4 cloves garlic, peeled and crushed
3 oz (75 g) butter, softened
1 heaped tablespoon chopped
fresh parsley
grated zest and juice ½ lemon
salt and freshly milled black pepper

To serve:

1 dessertspoon chopped fresh parsley
1 lemon, quartered

You will also need 4 individual gratin
dishes with a base diameter of 5 inches
(13 cm), buttered, or a baking tray
measuring 11 x 16 inches (28 x 40 cm),
also buttered.

To butterfly the prawns, first of all pull off the heads and legs with your fingers, then simply peel away the shells, which come away very easily, but leave the tails still attached, as this makes them look prettier. Now turn each prawn on its back and, with the point of a sharp knife, make a cut down the centre of each prawn, *below left*, but do not cut through. Ease open with your thumb like a book and remove the brownish-black thread, *below centre*, scraping it away with the point of the knife – it should also come away easily. Next rinse the prawns and pat them dry with kitchen paper, then place them in the buttered gratin dishes or on the baking tray.

Next make the garlic butter, and all this involves is taking a large fork and combining the rest of the ingredients together in a small bowl. Now spread equal quantities of the garlic butter over the prawns. You can now cover the whole lot with clingfilm and chill in the fridge till needed.

To cook the prawns, pre-heat the oven to gas mark 8, 450°F (230°C), remove the clingfilm if you've made them in advance, and then place the dishes on the highest shelf of the oven and let them cook for 6-7 minutes (they will need only 5 minutes if you've used a baking tray). Serve sprinkled with the parsley and garnish with the lemon quarters.

Because British domestic grills are so variable in their efficiency I think a ridged grill pan (see page 296) is a very good investment. It's particularly good for thick tuna steaks and gives those lovely charred stripes that look so attractive.

First of all brush the grill pan with a little of the olive oil, then place it over a very high heat and let it pre-heat till very hot – about 10 minutes. Meanwhile, wipe the fish steaks with kitchen paper, then place them on a plate, brush them with the remaining olive oil and season both sides with salt and pepper. When the grill pan is ready, place the tuna steaks on it and give them about 2 minutes on each side.

Meanwhile, make the vinaigrette by placing all the ingredients in a small saucepan and whisk them together over a gentle heat – no actual cooking is needed here, all this needs is to be warm.

When the tuna steaks are ready, remove them to warm serving plates, pour the vinaigrette all over and serve with steamed new potatoes.

Char-Grilled Tuna with Warm Coriander and Caper Vinaigrette

Serves 2
2 tuna steaks weighing about 8 oz (225 g) each
1 tablespoon extra virgin olive oil
salt and freshly milled black pepper

For the vinaigrette:
1 heaped tablespoon roughly chopped fresh coriander leaves
1 heaped tablespoon salted capers, rinsed and drained
grated zest and juice 1 lime
1 tablespoon white wine vinegar
1 clove garlic, peeled and finely chopped
1 shallot, peeled and finely chopped
1 heaped teaspoon wholegrain mustard
2 tablespoons extra virgin olive oil
salt and freshly milled black pepper

You will also need a ridged grill pan.

Oven-Roasted Fish with Potatoes and Salsa Verde

This recipe is delightfully different and makes a complete meal for two to three people with perhaps a simple green salad with a lemony dressing as an accompaniment. Chunks of skinless cod fillet are good in this, but any firm, thick white fish could be used – chunks of monkfish tail would be particularly good for a special occasion.

Serves 2-3

1 lb (450 g) cod fillet, skinned
(see page 267)
1 lb 4 oz (570 g) Desirée or King
Edward potatoes
1 tablespoon olive oil
1 heaped tablespoon finely grated
Parmesan (Parmigiano Reggiano)
salt and freshly milled black pepper

For the salsa verde:
1 clove garlic, peeled
1 teaspoon Maldon sea salt
2 anchovy fillets, drained and chopped
1 teaspoon wholegrain mustard
1 tablespoon salted capers, rinsed,
drained and roughly chopped
1 heaped tablespoon finely chopped
fresh basil
1 heaped tablespoon finely chopped
fresh parsley
2 tablespoons olive oil
1½ tablespoons lemon juice
freshly milled black pepper

You will also need an ovenproof baking
dish measuring 7½ inches (19 cm)
square and 2 inches (5 cm) deep,
lightly buttered.

To begin this recipe you need to set to work preparing the salsa verde ingredients and have them lined up ready. Now crush the garlic with the salt using a pestle and mortar and, when it becomes a purée, simply add all the prepared ingredients and whisk well to blend them thoroughly.

Now turn the oven on at gas mark 6, 400°F (200°C). Next prepare the potatoes: put the kettle on, then peel and chop them into ¼ inch (5 mm) slices. Place them in a shallow saucepan, then add salt and just enough boiling water to barely cover them. Simmer, with a lid, for 7-8 minutes – they need to be almost cooked but not quite – then drain off the water and cover them with a cloth for 2-3 minutes to absorb the steam.

Now arrange half the potatoes over the base of the baking dish and season well, wipe the fish with kitchen paper, cut it into 1½ inch (4 cm) chunks and arrange it over the potatoes, seasoning again. Next spoon the salsa verde all over and arrange the rest of the potato slices over, overlapping them slightly. Then brush them lightly with the olive oil, season once more and sprinkle the cheese over. Now bake the whole lot on a high shelf of the oven for about 30 minutes, by which time the fish will be cooked and the potatoes golden brown.

Tiger Prawn Risotto with Lobster Sauce

Sounds rather grand, doesn't it? But it's not, because this in some ways is a cheat's recipe, as it's baked in the oven, which means no tiresome stirring, and the sauce is a ready-made lobster bisque – or you could use French fish soup – laced with dry sherry, then bubbled with Gruyère cheese under the grill.

First of all place the baking dish in the oven to pre-heat. Meanwhile, in the frying pan, melt the butter and, over a medium heat, sauté the onion for 7-8 minutes, until soft. Now stir the rice into the buttery juices so it gets a good coating, then pour in the lobster bisque (or soup) and sherry and season. Give it a good stir and bring it up to simmering point, then pour the whole lot into the baking dish and return it to the oven, uncovered, for 35 minutes.

Towards the end of the cooking time, pre-heat the grill to its highest setting. Take the risotto from the oven, taste to check the seasoning, then add the prawns. Next, scatter the cheese over the top and drizzle the cream over. Now place the dish under the grill for 2-3 minutes, until the cheese is brown and bubbling, then serve immediately, garnished with the watercress and the extra cheese sprinkled over.

Serves 2

6 oz (175 g) cooked peeled tiger prawns, defrosted if frozen
6 oz (175 g) risotto (arborio) rice
1 x 780 g jar lobster bisque or French fish soup
1½ oz (40 g) butter
1 medium onion, peeled and finely chopped
3 fl oz (75 ml) dry sherry
2 oz (50 g) Gruyère, finely grated, plus a little extra to serve
2 tablespoons whipping cream
a few sprigs fresh watercress, to garnish
salt and freshly milled black pepper

You will also need an ovenproof baking dish measuring 9 inches (23 cm) square and 2 inches (5 cm) deep, and a large frying pan.

Pre-heat the oven to gas mark 2, 300°F (150°C).

Roasted Salmon Fillets with a Crusted Pecorino and Pesto Topping

This recipe, invented by my good friend Lin Cooper, started life under the grill, but now, in my attempt to more or less eliminate the grill, I'm happy to say that it cooks very happily and easily in a high oven. One word of warning, though: it works much better with fresh pesto sauce from supermarkets than it does with the bottled kind.

Serves 2

2 x 5-6 oz (150-175 g) salmon fillets, about ¾ inch (2 cm) thick, skinned (see page 267)
1 rounded tablespoon finely grated Pecorino cheese
2 tablespoons fresh pesto sauce
squeeze lemon juice
2 tablespoons fresh breadcrumbs
salt and freshly milled black pepper

You will also need a baking tray measuring 10 x 14 inches (25.5 x 35 cm), covered in foil and lightly oiled.

Pre-heat the oven to gas mark 8, 450°F (230°C).

Begin by trimming the fillets if needed, and run your hand over the surface of the fish to check that there aren't any stray bones lurking. Now place the fish on the prepared baking tray and give each one a good squeeze of lemon juice and a seasoning of salt and pepper.

Next, give the pesto a good stir and measure 2 tablespoons into a small bowl, mix a third of the breadcrumbs with it to form a paste and spread this over both fish fillets. Then, mix half the cheese with the remaining breadcrumbs and scatter this over the pesto, then finish off with the remaining cheese.

Now place the baking tray on the middle shelf of the oven and cook for 10 minutes, by which time the top should be golden brown and crispy and the salmon just cooked and moist. Serve with steamed new potatoes.

13
How to cook meat

'Oh dear, oh dear, oh dear' was the oft-heard lament of Tony Hancock, a truly great comedian whom some of you may not be old enough to remember. No matter – those words for me are always so applicable when things go badly wrong, as, it has to be said, they did for the meat industry. Hopefully we are now recovering, lessons have been learnt and the quality of meat in this country is the best in the world, as it always has been.

I am personally a great lover of both fish and vegetarian food, but I am also a dedicated meat-eater.

I've always been a meat person. Pure and simple. I come from a long line of meat people. I well remember how my grandparents ate meat every day of their lives and at the same time enjoyed perfect health. And how my mother recovering from an operation and with a low blood count was prescribed lots and lots of red meat by her doctor.

There's absolutely no doubt in my mind that good meat is good for you. Everyone who lives, breathes and exists needs protein, and meat provides what is called first-class protein all by itself. Eating just 8 oz (225 g) in any one day gives an adult all they need without having to think about it.

In Britain, because the country's made up of a large presence of hill country where vegetables don't grow but there's lots of lush, green grazing, we're lucky to have what I believe to be the best meat in the world, and, from the earliest times throughout the centuries, all our cookery books contain lashings of meat recipes. William Cobbett, that great 19th-century chronicler of the English countryside, gave this advice to a young man looking for a wife: 'Never mind if she can embroider continents into a piece of cloth, watch carefully how she deals with a lamb chop!'

Thus the purpose of this chapter is to encourage you to enjoy eating and cooking good meat. We don't have to eat meat every day, and a healthy, interesting diet should be varied and include fish or vegetarian meals, but when we do cook meat what we need to know is how to get the very best out of it.

Roasting

Originally what the term roasting described was meat being placed near a fire, usually on a spit, with air circulating around it. Then, as the spit was turned, all sides of the meat were exposed to the fire and the whole was gradually and evenly cooked.

Nowadays we're not technically roasting in the true sense of the word any more. Thankfully, we don't have to fan flames and rake coals to get the required heat; all we have to do is simply switch on a domestic oven to absolutely any heat we require, which makes oven-roasting simple, efficient and very, very easy.

The only thing we need to learn from our hard-working ancestors is to take care. If we want the best results possible, it's well worth reading and absorbing some of the following notes. Then, once they're understood fully, and so long as the right kind of care is taken, roasting meat will always be successful and enjoyable.

What about the fat?

If you never learn any other lesson about meat cooking, please learn this one. If you want to enjoy meat at its most succulent and best you need to understand that fat is absolutely necessary. It doesn't have to be eaten (my husband never eats the fat), but it does need to be there. The fat in the meat contains a lot of the flavour and provides natural basting juices both from without and within. So don't choose meat that is too lean – let the fat do its wondrous work of enhancing flavour and succulence during cooking.

Ten guidelines when roasting meat

1) The cut

If you want to serve the roast meat of old England for a special occasion, it's best to get as large a joint as possible. The perfect roast includes a lovely crusty outside and lots of tender, succulent, juicy meat within. And while you're dreaming about that, consider how lovely it will be eaten cold or made into other dishes. A large joint, if you have some left over for other meals, can be quite economical, too.

The loin or the thick end of a leg of pork, the wing rib (three ribs) of beef or a leg of lamb will serve a large family, and these joints are all excellent for simple roasting at a high temperature. But what you also need to remember is that there are other cuts that are more suitable for lower-temperature roasting, which can be bought in smaller joints. If you try to cook a joint that's meant for slow-roasting at a high temperature, it will end up tough and dry.

2) Bone in or out?

When you cook meat on the bone, the bone inside provides an excellent conductor of heat – this means that the meat will be cooked more evenly with less loss of juices. I always prefer to cook meat on the bone as it definitely has more flavour and I think the meat cooked nearest the bone is the best part. However, the bones can be removed and the joint rolled neatly, making it much easier to carve, so it's just a matter of personal taste in the end.

3) Heat

For simple roasting of a prime joint, it is important to pre-heat the oven to a very high temperature. This gives the meat a very quick and efficient blast of heat so that the edges seize up and the precious juices inside are less likely to escape.

4) Added ingredients for roasting

I find that when roasting a joint of beef or pork, if you tuck a small halved onion underneath it at the edges, it caramelises during the roasting and provides both flavour and colour to the juices for the gravy. When cooking lamb, if you insert little slivers of garlic and rosemary leaves into the flesh, this imparts a lovely flavour and fragrance whilst roasting. You can insert garlic slivers and rosemary into a pork joint, too, if you want to give it a slightly different flavour.

Another tip: if you want to give an extra-crisp finish to the surface fat of a joint, lightly coat it with some flour, and for beef use some dry mustard along with the flour. Unless you're slow-roasting you won't need to add any fat to a joint specifically meant for roasting, as there will be sufficient natural fat within the joint itself.

5) Basting

Wise old cooks knew that to keep a joint really succulent while it was roasting it was important to baste it two or three times using a long-handled spoon. Use an oven glove to slide the roasting tin halfway out of the oven (or, if it's easier, take it out completely – but close the oven door to keep the heat in), then tilt the pan and thoroughly baste the joint with the fat and juices. The exception to this is pork, firstly because it has enough fat within it to provide a kind of internal basting and, secondly, if you spoon fat over the skin, you won't get good crackling.

6) When is it cooked?

If your oven is checked regularly and not faulty, the cooking times given in this chapter should serve you well. But the only way to really know if the meat is cooked to your liking is to first insert a flat skewer into the thickest part of the meat, then remove it and press the surface hard with the flat of the skewer and watch the colour of the juices that run out. If you like your meat rare (as in beef), the juices will still be faintly red; for medium the juices will still be faintly pink, and if you like it cooked all the way through, then the juices should run completely clear and not pink.

Remember, though, that meat continues to cook a little while it's relaxing, so if you like your beef rare, you'll need to take this into account.

7) All those precious juices

The reason roasting meat needs care and attention is that if it's badly cooked, it ends up dry. Careful cooking means doing all you can to keep those precious juices intact. The number-one rule is not to overcook; number two is to baste (see point 5); and number three is to always allow time for the meat to relax before you start to carve it.

What happens to meat during the cooking process is that it shrinks slightly, and juices, as they heat up, begin to bubble up to the surface. Some do escape (but not entirely, if you're making gravy). If you then carve the meat straight from the oven, all those surface juices will be lost, but if you allow the meat to relax for 30 minutes before carving, the surface juices will have time to gradually seep back down into the meat. There will still be a little coming out as you carve, so it's good to have a carving board with a little channel around the edge – then even these juices can be incorporated into the gravy.

8) Gravy

I never put meat on a roasting rack as I think the part that sits directly in the roasting tin provides lots of crusty sediment that improves the gravy. Gravy made with the meat juices ensures that every last drop of flavour and juice enhances the meat itself (see page 163).

9) Carving

A lot of people imagine that they can't carve very well, but the truth is probably that the knife they are using simply isn't sharp enough. What you really need to do is buy a good-quality carving knife and a sharpening steel and simply practise. I was taught by a butcher, who said knives should be sharpened little and often. I have also found the following advice good for anyone who wants to learn: hold the steel horizontally in front of you and the knife vertically, *right*, then slide the blade of the knife down, allowing the tip to touch the steel, first on one side of the steel and then on the other. If you really can't face it, there are knife sharpeners available.

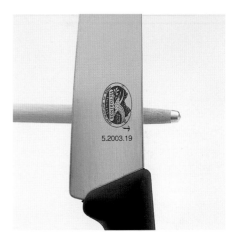

10) Serving suggestions

Most of the traditional accompaniments to roast meat are already well known: horseradish or mustard with beef, savoury stuffing and apple sauce with pork, and mint sauce and redcurrant jelly with lamb.

How to roast beef

Choose sirloin or wing rib (three ribs) on the bone weighing about 6 lb (2.7 kg). Pre-heat the oven to gas mark 8, 450°F (230°C), season with salt and pepper and rub the fat with a dusting of flour and dry mustard. Roast at this temperature for 20 minutes, then reduce the temperature to gas mark 5, 375°F (190°C) and continue to roast – basting at least three times – for 15 minutes per lb (450 g) for rare, plus 15 minutes more for medium, and another 30 minutes for well done. Rest for 20-30 minutes before carving.

How to roast pork with crackling

Use a 5 lb (2.25 kg) loin of pork, on the bone but chined (this means the bone is loosened), and pre-heat the oven to gas mark 8, 450°F (230°C). Make sure the surface skin is really dry, then rub in Maldon sea salt and roast for 25 minutes, then lower the temperature to gas mark 5, 375°F (190°C) and allow 35 minutes per lb (450 g). Don't baste the pork, or the crackling won't be crisp. Relax for 20-30 minutes before carving.

How to roast lamb

For instructions on roasting lamb, turn to page 312.

Braising and pot-roasting

There's something about meat slowly braising in the oven in a casserole, filling the kitchen with sublime aromas and invoking pangs of hunger and anticipation of what's to come. I call it 'feel-good food' – comforting and soothing. It can rarely be done properly in busy restaurants that are short of oven space, so if you want to really spoil your friends as well as your family, choose something from this section for entertaining.

Fast food is all very well and has its place in busy lives, but slow cooking has in a way become a luxury, simply because of its rarity. 'But I don't have time for it,' you might be thinking. But I'm saying, yes, you do – just read on.

Ten guidelines when braising and pot-roasting

1) Dispelling the myth

The myth is that slow cooking is a lot of bother and takes too much time. The truth is that it doesn't in fact take any more time than other cooking; the only time taken up is whilst it sits happily all by itself in the oven, leaving the cook blissfully free to get on with other things.

2) Think slow

The principle to grasp here is that slow cooking really should be just that – too much bubble and boil always impairs the flavour and texture of the meat. What you want to aim for is this: the barest shimmer of movement with the occasional bubble just breaking the surface. Using a heavy flameproof casserole, you need to bring the mixture up to a gentle simmer, then put a close-fitting lid on and place it on the lowest shelf of a pre-heated oven at gas mark 1, 275°F (140°C). This gives just the right amount of heat and thus allows the very best flavours of the ingredients to be drawn out and married together.

3) Choosing the right cut

Without getting too technical, I think it's worth noting that in most cases forequarter meat (which comes from the front half of the animal) is best for slow cooking because this is the bit that works harder, stretching and pulling the rest along all the time (examples for beef include brisket joint, and braising and stewing beef). Muscle and tissue begin to build up as the animal matures, and this, together with a marbling of fat in-between the meat fibres, seems happily to be tailor-made for slow cooking.

What happens when the meat is subjected to a gentle heat over a long period of time is that this is all slowly rendered down and does a splendid job of permeating the meat fibres, keeping them succulent and at the same time adding body, substance and, most important of all, flavour. So for this reason, cuts such as rump, sirloin or fillet steaks should never be cooked slowly, as they do not contain the magic ingredients above!

4) What kind of cooking pot?

Old-fashioned cooks used earthenware cooking pots and sometimes, in order to seal them tightly, put a paste of flour and water on before the lid to give a perfect seal. Nowadays we have attractive flameproof casseroles so we can cook in them on top of the stove, in the oven and even bring them to the table. This would be my choice, because I think it's important to bring the ingredients up to simmering point on the hob before they go into a slow oven. If you prefer an earthenware cooking pot, then you must pre-heat it and make sure the ingredients are well up to simmering point before they're poured quickly into the pot and then put in the oven. Without this precaution the ingredients won't come up to simmering point for a very long time in a slow oven.

I have found that an approximately 4 pint (2.25 litre) capacity flameproof casserole is a good all-round family size and that a 6 pint (3.5 litre) casserole is a very useful size for entertaining. The modern way to seal the lid tightly is to use a double sheet of foil placed under the lid.

5) Browning meat

This is where care is really needed – and just a little patience. If the meat is seared around the edges, two things happen. Firstly, the crusty, rather charred surface provides flavour and colour and, secondly, as the edges of the meat seize up, this helps keep the juices in. What you need to remember is to only brown a few pieces of meat at a time. It's tempting to shove the whole lot in and cut corners, but if you crowd the pan, too much steam will be created and you will never, ever brown the meat.

Use a good, solid frying pan, get it really hot before adding oil or fat, then, as soon as the oil is smoking hot, add about six cubes (or one steak) at a time, browning them well on all sides and removing them before adding the next batch.

6) Adding liquid

Liquid has a very important role in slow meat cookery, because not only does it provide moisture but, as it mingles with the meat juices, it's what provides the finished sauce. Now, fortunately, we can all buy ready-prepared lamb and beef stock in supermarkets, which will help to enhance the flavour of both the meat and sauce. Another liquid that suits meat cookery very well is beer: both pale ale and stout are transformed into rich, fragrant sauces when subjected to long, slow cooking.

Wine – both red and white – is superb for sauces, and for a very special occasion Madeira wine makes one of the greatest sauces of all. If you want to add a touch of luxury that's really economical, the best thing to use is cider, either dry or medium – every kitchen should have some handy.

Fresh tomatoes, skinned and chopped, or tinned chopped tomatoes will also respond well to slow cooking and provide body to the sauce.

7) How much meat?

This depends largely on appetite. I found it very difficult when I did a book of recipes for one to balance portions that would suit a hungry student and a not-so-hungry pensioner. However, I think 6-8 oz (175-225 g) per person is a good guide. If a recipe says 'serves 4-6', it gives you the chance to size up the appetites and make your own judgement.

8) Skimming

Although meat can be trimmed of excess fat, the presence of some fat in braising cuts of meat is vital for flavour and succulence. In some cases, say with neck of lamb or oxtail, the excess fat will escape and bubble up to the surface, so if you're intending to serve this straight from the oven, tilt the casserole slightly and spoon off the fat, which will clearly separate from the juice. Any that you can't actually skim off with a spoon can be soaked up by lightly placing folded wodges of absorbent kitchen paper on the surface.

Finally, as most slow-cooked recipes taste better re-heated the next day, leaving the dish overnight means that the fat will completely solidify and can then be lifted off very easily before re-heating.

9) Thickening

If you're making a casserole, the easiest way to thicken the sauce is to add some flour to the ready-browned meat, onions and so on, stir it in to soak up all the excess juice, then gradually add all the liquid, a little at a time, stirring and mixing well after each addition. With pot-roasting it's best to add the thickening later. This can be done by straining the liquid into a saucepan, then reducing it slightly by fast-boiling, which concentrates the flavour, and adding a mixture of butter and flour or olive oil and flour (1½ tablespoons of flour to 1 oz/25 g of butter or 1 tablespoon of olive oil to thicken about 15 fl oz/425 ml of liquid). Arrowroot is another thickening agent that gives a fine glaze and a smooth-textured sauce, and it's very easy to use – just blend with a little cold water before adding to the liquid.

10) Freezing and re-heating

Casseroles and braised dishes often improve in flavour if they're made a day ahead, cooled, refrigerated and re-heated, in which case pre-heat the oven to gas mark 4, 350°F (180°C) and give it 35-45 minutes altogether. It's very important that the casserole reaches a gentle simmer. Casseroles and braised dishes also freeze very well in foil containers, but make sure they're thoroughly defrosted before re-heating. Discard the cardboard lids, cover with a double sheet of foil and re-heat as above.

Grilling, frying and baking

In contrast to cuts of meat for braising, the meat that comes from the hind quarter of the animal is, for the most part, more tender, and for this reason has the advantage of being more suitable for fast cooking. If you're looking for a meal in a hurry, the quick-cooking grilling or frying cuts are the ones to go for. Some of these can also be used for oven-baking with other ingredients or with a sauce.

Ten guidelines when grilling, frying and baking

1) Choosing the right cuts for grilling or frying

Beef steaks, pork steaks, pork escalopes (good for frying), lamb cutlets and chops are ideal – and if you're in a real hurry there's something called 'flash-fry' steaks, which cook in 1 minute flat. Most of these can now be bought ready trimmed and cut into strips for the fastest of all cooking – stir-frying.

2) The healthy option

If you want – or have been told – to cut the fat in your diet, grilling is for you, as it enables you to enjoy lean meat with the minimum of fat. If you place the meat on a grill rack with a tray underneath, you'll find a percentage of fat within the meat will run out during the cooking. The secret here is not to overcook, otherwise the meat will be dry.

3) Grilling meat

What grilling should achieve is a lovely seared, faintly charred outside edge with the rest of the meat very tender and juicy within – this is the closest thing to cooking on an open fire, as, when the meat is placed on a rack, the air circulates and this gives the grilled meat its unique flavour.

If you're using a domestic grill, what you need to do is pre-heat it to its highest setting at least 10 minutes before you want to start cooking, and remember to try and position the meat 2-3 inches (5-7.5 cm) from the heat, turning the meat over halfway through to grill the other side. Timings vary because the thickness of meat differs, so you need to use a skewer or the blade of a small knife inserted in the thickest part to test if the juices are the right colour. Approximate timings are as follows.

For a steak 1 inch (2.5 cm) thick (ie sirloin or rump), 1½-2 minutes on each side for rare; medium, 3 minutes on each side; and well done, about 4 minutes on each side.

For a fillet steak 1½ inches (4 cm) thick, give it 5 minutes on each side for medium; 1 minute less each side for rare; and 1 minute more for well done.

Pork chops will need approximately 10 minutes on each side, and pork steaks slightly less. Lamb chops would need about 10 minutes each side, and cutlets about 5 minutes each side.

Never season meat before grilling, frying or browning, as salt draws out the precious juices you're trying to keep in (but do remember to season before serving).

A ridged grill pan, *left*, is a very efficient way of grilling meat, as well as other foods – just smear the pan with very little oil, pre-heat it for about 10 minutes and use the timings just listed.

4) Frying meat

Whether you choose to grill or fry meat is, to a certain extent, personal choice. Grilling, as we've already discussed, gives special flavour to meat, but you do lose some of the juices. Frying, on the other hand, means that all the escaped juices are there in the frying pan and can be spooned over the meat or used with reduced wine to make a sauce.

5) Hot as you dare

It's very important when you're frying meat to have the heat as high as possible, so the frying pan has to be one with a thick, solid base to conduct the heat properly. What you need to do is place the pan over direct heat turned to high and let the pan become very hot before you add the smallest amount of oil or fat, just to cover the pan surface. Then, as soon as the fat itself is smoking hot, holding the piece of meat in both hands, drop it directly down so that the whole of the surface hits the heat at the same moment. What this does is sear the meat, sealing the edges and encouraging the juices to stay inside.

For steaks (rump and sirloin), give them 1 minute's searing each side, then turn the heat down to medium and cook them for no more time at all if you like them really rare ('blue'), otherwise, for medium-rare give them 2-3 more minutes on each side; medium, 3-4 more minutes on each side; and well done, 4-5 more minutes on each side.

For fillet steak 1½ inches (4 cm) thick, after the initial searing you'll need another 6 minutes' cooking time, turning it over halfway through; give it 2 minutes less for rare and 2 minutes more for well done. Once again, all these timings are approximate because the thickness of the meat will vary.

6) Adding fats and oils

If you're cutting down on fat, then grill without fat or oil; however, if that is not your priority, it is better to brush very lean meat such as pork steaks with a little melted butter, and fillet steaks with a little oil before grilling. If you're frying steaks, then use a little oil or a small piece of beef dripping, which will withstand the very high temperatures.

If you're frying pork, the best thing to use is a little butter and oil mixed together so that you get the flavour of the butter, and the oil stops it from burning.

7) Marinating

This really does enhance the flavour of meat for grilling. If you marinate cubed lamb (from leg steaks), use the juice of a lemon and 6 tablespoons of oil to 1 lb 8 oz (700 g) of meat, adding a dessertspoon of chopped oregano and some slivers of onion. Leave them in the marinade overnight, turning a couple of times, then thread the cubes of meat and slivers of onion on to flat skewers. You can make delicious kebabs and grill them for 15-20 minutes, basting with some of the marinade as you cook them. You can also do exactly the same with cubed pork, only this time using a dessertspoon of crushed rosemary leaves and giving them 5 more minutes' grilling time.

8) Glazing

One interesting way of grilling meat is to add a glaze to it before it goes under the grill. The best and probably the simplest one I've come across is to spread a thin layer of English mustard over the meat and then dip it in demerara sugar. Once this coating hits the heat, it gives a lovely shiny barbecue-flavoured crust. I like it best with lamb cutlets, but you could always use it with pork ribs. Either way, give them 5 minutes' grilling on each side.

9) Stir-frying

If you cook with gas, then a classic rounded wok is perfect for a stir-fry, but if you're using electricity you need to have a wok with a special flat base. If you don't have a wok, don't worry – you can still stir-fry with a large, roomy frying pan. Either way, remember that speed is what it's all about. Heat the wok or pan until it's very hot indeed, then add oil and, as it sizzles, add the meat and constantly stir it around so that it comes into constant contact with the heat on all sides (the meat should be half-cooked before the vegetables are added).

10) Oven-baking

There is a method of cooking meat that comes somewhere in-between fast- and slow-cooking, and that is oven-baking. One of the best things about it is that it leaves you free to do other things.

You can oven-bake pork or lamb chops in a shallow tin by seasoning them and tucking chopped onion in around them and baking them at gas mark 6, 400°F (200°C) for 30-40 minutes, depending on the size and thickness of the chops. After that, you can deglaze the roasting tin with wine, cider or stock to make a gravy with the juices.

Shepherd's Pie with Cheese-Crusted Leeks

This recipe can be made either with fresh minced lamb (shepherd's pie), fresh minced beef (cottage pie) or minced leftover beef or lamb from a cooked joint (in which case cut the initial cooking time to 15 minutes). In the following recipe we're using fresh minced lamb, and what puts this dish in the five-star category is the delicious crust of cheese and leeks.

Serves 4
1 lb (450 g) minced lamb
1 tablespoon olive oil
2 medium onions, peeled
and chopped
3 oz (75 g) carrot, peeled and chopped
very small
3 oz (75 g) swede, peeled and chopped
very small
½ teaspoon ground cinnamon
1 teaspoon chopped fresh thyme
1 tablespoon chopped fresh parsley
1 tablespoon plain flour
10 fl oz (275 ml) fresh lamb stock
1 tablespoon tomato purée
salt and freshly milled black pepper

For the topping:
2 oz (50 g) mature Cheddar,
coarsely grated
2 medium leeks, cleaned and cut
into ½ inch (1 cm) slices
2 lb (900 g) Desirée or King Edward
potatoes
2 oz (50 g) butter
salt and freshly milled black pepper

You will also need a large lidded frying pan or saucepan, and a 7½ inch (19 cm) square baking dish, 2 inches (5 cm) deep, well buttered.

Begin by taking the frying pan or saucepan and, over a medium flame, gently heat the olive oil. Now fry the onions in the hot oil until they are tinged brown at the edges – about 5 minutes. Add the chopped carrot and swede and cook for 5 minutes or so, then remove the vegetables and put them to one side. Now turn the heat up and brown the meat in batches, tossing it around to get it all nicely browned. You may find a wooden fork helpful here, as it helps to break up the mince. After that, give the meat a good seasoning of salt and pepper, then add the cooked vegetables, cinnamon, thyme and parsley. Next stir in the flour, which will soak up the juice, then gradually add the stock to the meat mixture until it is all incorporated. Finally, stir in the tomato purée. Now turn the heat right down, put the lid on the pan and let it cook gently for about 30 minutes.

While the meat is cooking you can make the topping. Peel the potatoes, cut them into even-sized pieces and place in a steamer fitted over a large pan of boiling water, sprinkle with some salt, put a lid on and steam until they're completely tender – about 25 minutes. While this is happening, pre-heat the oven to gas mark 6, 400°F (200°C).

When the potatoes are done, drain off the water, return them to the saucepan, cover with a clean tea cloth to absorb the steam and leave them for about 5 minutes. Next add the butter and mash them to a purée – the best way to do this is with an electric hand whisk. Don't be tempted to add any milk here, because the mashed potato on top of the pie needs to be firm. Taste and add more salt and pepper if necessary. When the meat is ready, spoon it into the baking dish and level it out with the back of the spoon. After that, spread the mashed potato evenly all over. Now sprinkle the leeks on top of the potato, scatter the cheese over the leeks and bake the whole thing on a high shelf of the oven for about 25 minutes, or until the top is crusty and golden.

Entrecôte
Hongroise

As I've said before, I prefer to cook steak in a frying pan because, as some of the precious juices are bound to escape, they can be incorporated into the sauce to give extra body and flavour.

Serves 2

2 entrecôte or sirloin steaks weighing about 8 oz (225 g) each, removed from the fridge about 1 hour before you need them
1 tablespoon light olive oil
3 shallots, peeled and finely chopped
1 small red pepper, deseeded and finely diced
6 fl oz (175 ml) red wine
1 tablespoon half-fat crème fraîche
¼ teaspoon paprika
a few sprigs fresh watercress, to garnish
salt and freshly milled black pepper

You will also need a solid frying pan with a diameter of 10 inches (25.5 cm).

First of all heat half the oil in the frying pan over a high heat, then fry the chopped shallots and pepper until they're softened and tinged dark brown at the edges – about 6 minutes – and remove them to a plate. Now add the remaining oil to the pan and, keeping the heat high – the pan should be as hot as you dare – season the steaks with coarsely milled black pepper, but no salt yet, as this encourages the juices to come out. Now add the steaks to the hot pan and press them gently with a spoon so that the underneath is seared and becomes crusty. Cook the steaks for about 3 minutes each side for medium, 2 for rare and 4 for well done. Then, about 2 minutes before the end of the cooking time, return the shallots and peppers to the pan, pour the wine around the steaks and, still keeping the heat high, boil until reduced and syrupy. Then add the crème fraîche and stir it into the sauce, then season with salt and sprinkle in the paprika. Serve the steaks on hot plates with the sauce spooned over and garnish with watercress. They're lovely served with jacket potatoes and a salad.

Entrecôte Marchand de Vin

This classic French recipe has the simplest-possible sauce for a fried steak. The red wine bubbles down and deglazes the pan so that all the lovely flavours of the steak are incorporated into the sauce.

First of all heat half the oil in the frying pan over a high heat, then fry the chopped onion until it's softened and tinged dark brown at the edges – about 6 minutes – and remove to a plate. Now add the remaining oil to the pan and, keeping the heat high – the pan should be as hot as you dare – season the steaks with coarsely milled black pepper, but no salt, as this encourages the juices to come out. Now add the steaks to the hot pan and press them gently with a spoon so that the underneath is seared and becomes crusty. Cook the steaks for about 3 minutes each side for medium, 2 for rare and 4 for well done. Then, about 2 minutes before the end of the cooking time, return the onion to the pan, pour the wine around the steaks and, keeping the heat high, boil until reduced and syrupy. Serve the steaks on hot plates with the sauce spooned over. Chunky Chips (page 189) and a green salad would be very good with this.

Serves 2

2 entrecôte or sirloin steaks weighing about 8 oz (225 g) each, removed from the fridge about 1 hour before you need them
1 tablespoon light olive oil
1 small onion, peeled and finely chopped
6 fl oz (175 ml) red wine
freshly milled black pepper

You will also need a solid frying pan with a diameter of 10 inches (25.5 cm).

Individual Steak, Mushroom and Kidney Pies

Steak and kidney is one of the most wonderful combinations of flavours I know, provided ox kidney and no other is used. If it's cut really small, most people who think they don't like kidney will enjoy the rich, luscious flavour without even noticing it's there.

Serves 6

2 lb (900 g) chuck steak or blade, cut into 1 inch (2.5 cm) cubes
8 oz (225 g) dark-gilled mushrooms, quartered
8 oz (225 g) ox kidney, trimmed and cut into very small cubes
2 tablespoons beef dripping
8 oz (225 g) onions, peeled and thickly sliced
2 tablespoons plain flour
2 tablespoons Worcestershire sauce
½ teaspoon finely chopped fresh thyme
1 pint (570 ml) beef stock
salt and freshly milled black pepper

For the pastry:

12 oz (350 g) plain flour, plus a little extra for rolling
pinch of salt
3 oz (75 g) lard, at room temperature
3 oz (75 g) butter, at room temperature
about 1½ tablespoons cold water
a little beaten egg, to glaze

You will also need 6 x 15 fl oz (425 ml) pie dishes or ovenproof soup bowls with top diameters of 5 inches (13 cm) or an ovenproof pie dish with a diameter of 9 inches (23 cm), and a lidded flameproof casserole with a capacity of 6 pints (3.5 litres).

Pre-heat the oven to gas mark 1, 275°F (140°C).

I think the flavour of steak and kidney is improved enormously if you take a bit of time and trouble over initially browning the meat. What you need to do is melt 1 tablespoon of the beef dripping in a large, solid frying pan. When the fat is really hot, pat the cubes of meat with kitchen paper and add them a few at a time, but don't crowd the pan; if you put too much in at once, this creates a steamy atmosphere and the meat won't brown, so brown the pieces on all sides in batches, adding them to the casserole as you go.

Once the meat is browned, add the rest of the dripping to the frying pan and do exactly the same with the kidney. When these have joined the meat, keep the heat high and brown the onions in the frying pan, turning and moving them until they are nicely browned at the edges – 6-7 minutes. Then, using a draining spoon, transfer the onions to the casserole, place it over a direct heat for 2 minutes before seasoning, then add the flour and stir with a wooden spoon until it's been absorbed into the meat juices. It doesn't look very nice at this stage, but that's not a problem. All you do next is add the Worcestershire sauce, thyme and mushrooms, followed by the stock and seasoning. Stir well, bring everything up to a gentle simmer, put the lid on the casserole and place in the pre-heated oven, on the centre shelf, and leave it there for about 2 hours, or until the meat is tender.

Meanwhile, make the pastry. First of all sift the flour with the pinch of salt into a large bowl, holding the sieve up high to give it a good airing. Then add the lard and butter and, using only your fingertips, lightly and gently rub the fat into the flour, again lifting the mixture up high all the time to give it a good airing. When everything is crumbly, sprinkle in the cold water. Start to mix the pastry with a knife and then finish off with your hands, adding more drops of water till you have a smooth dough that leaves the bowl clean. Then pop the pastry in a polythene bag and let it rest in the refrigerator for 30 minutes.

Once the meat is ready, transfer the cooked meat and its gravy to the dishes (or dish) and allow it to cool.

When you are ready to make the pies, pre-heat the oven to gas mark 7, 425°F (220°C), then roll out the pastry on a floured surface. Take a small saucer (about 5½ inches/14 cm in diameter) and cut out 6 rounds – you may have to re-roll the pastry to get all 6. Then, using the trimmings, roll out a strip about 3 x 14 inches (7.5 x 35 cm) and cut it into 6 to make borders for the pies. First dampen the edges of each dish with water and place a strip of pastry around the rim of each one, pressing down well. Next dampen the pastry strips, then place one pastry round on top of each dish and seal carefully. Now use the blunt side of a knife to knock up the edges, then flute them using your thumb to push out and your forefinger to pull in again (see the photos). For the large pie, cut out a 10 inch (25.5 cm) circle of pastry, using the trimmings to make strips for the border.

Now make a hole in the centre of each pastry lid to let the steam out during baking, and brush the surface with the beaten egg. Place on a large baking sheet, then cook in the oven on the centre shelf for 25-30 minutes for the small pies, or 35-40 minutes for the large one, by which time the pastry should be golden brown and crusty.

Note: the pies can be filled and topped the day before, covered and chilled, then just brushed with egg and popped in the oven when you need them – by the time the pastry is cooked the steak and kidney will be bubbling hot.

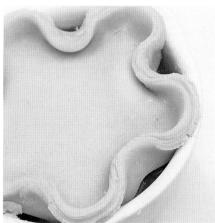

Latin American Beef Stew with Marinated Red-Onion Salad

This is very colourful and has lots of great flavours and textures – ideal for entertaining because all the vegetables are already in it, so all it needs is some plain rice.

Serves 4-6
2 lb (900 g) braising steak, cut into
1 inch (2.5 cm) cubes
1 rounded tablespoon cumin seeds
1 rounded tablespoon coriander seeds
2 tablespoons olive oil
2 medium red onions, peeled and
roughly chopped
3 medium red chillies, deseeded and
finely chopped
6 cloves garlic, peeled and crushed
1 heaped tablespoon plain flour
1 x 220 g tin chopped tomatoes
16 fl oz (450 ml) brown ale
5 fl oz (150 ml) red wine
12 oz (350 g) butternut squash,
peeled, deseeded and cut into 1 inch
(2.5 cm) cubes
8 oz (225 g) fresh sweetcorn (about
2 cobs), or frozen and thoroughly
defrosted
1 red pepper, deseeded and roughly
chopped into 1½ inch (4 cm) pieces
salt and freshly milled black pepper

For the red-onion salad:
1 medium red onion, peeled and
thinly sliced into half-moon shapes
grated zest 1 lime and juice 2 limes
3 tablespoons chopped fresh
coriander leaves

You will also need a lidded flameproof
casserole with capacity of 6 pints
(3.5 litres).

Pre-heat the oven to gas mark 2,
300°F (150°C).

First of all you need to roast the spices, and to do this place them in a small frying pan or saucepan over a medium heat and stir and toss them around for 1-2 minutes, or until they begin to look toasted and start to jump in the pan. Now transfer them to a pestle and mortar and crush them to a powder.

Next pat the cubed meat with kitchen paper, then place the casserole over a high heat. Add 1 tablespoon of the oil and, as soon as it's really hot, brown the meat about 6 cubes at a time, till it's well browned and crusty. As the cubes cook, remove them to a plate and brown the rest in batches. Then heat the other tablespoon of oil and fry the onions, chilli and garlic until they're nicely tinged brown at the edges. Now add the flour and stir this in to soak up the juices. Next add the spices and return the meat to the casserole, then add the tomatoes, ale and wine, season and stir well, then bring it up to simmering point, put the lid on the casserole and place in the centre of the oven for 2 hours.

After that add the squash, sweetcorn and red pepper, stir again and return the casserole to the oven for a further 40-45 minutes. Meanwhile, to make the salad, mix the red onion with the lime zest, juice and coriander in a small bowl and set aside to marinate for at least 15 minutes before serving, then hand it round separately as a garnish.

Mini Boeufs
en Croûte

If you want luxury, think fillet steak, and if you want to turn a 6 oz (175 g) fillet into a man-sized portion, encase it with a wild-mushroom stuffing in the very thinnest-possible layer of puff pastry. What you'll then have is a delectable combination of juicy steak, concentrated mushrooms and a very crisp crust. Good news, too, if you're entertaining: these can be prepared several hours ahead and just popped in the oven when you're ready for them.

Serves 4

4 x 6 oz (175 g) fillet steaks, cut from the middle of the fillet so they're nice and thick
9 oz (250 g) bought puff pastry
1 teaspoon beef dripping
a little brandy
1 large egg, beaten
6 fl oz (175 ml) red wine
salt and freshly milled black pepper

For the filling:
½ oz (10 g) dried porcini mushrooms
1 large onion, peeled
8 oz (225 g) dark-gilled open-cap mushrooms
1 oz (25 g) butter
freshly grated nutmeg
salt and freshly milled black pepper

You will also need a solid baking sheet, well buttered, and a solid frying pan.

Begin by making the filling well ahead, as it needs to be chilled before you use it. Start off by soaking the porcini in boiling water for 20 minutes, and while that's happening the onion and open-cap mushrooms will need to be chopped as finely as possible. If you have a food processor you can do this in moments; if not, use a very sharp knife and chop them minutely small. When the porcini have had 20 minutes, squeeze out all the excess liquid, then chop them small as well. Now, in a medium saucepan, melt the butter and stir in the onions and mushrooms to get a good buttery coating, then season well with salt, pepper and a few gratings of fresh nutmeg.

What you need to do now is turn the heat to its lowest setting and cook, uncovered, allowing the juices from the mushrooms to evaporate slowly. This will take about 35 minutes altogether – stir it from time to time and what you should end up with is a lovely concentrated mixture with no liquid left. Spoon the mixture into a bowl, cool and chill in the fridge.

A few hours before you want to serve the steaks, heat the beef dripping in the frying pan until it's smoking hot, or, as the chef who taught me to cook said, 'Hot as you dare!' Now place the steaks 2 at a time in the pan and give them 30 seconds on each side – what you're trying to achieve here is a dark, seared surface without cooking the steaks – then remove them to a plate. Turn the heat off under the pan, but don't wash it, because you're going to need it again later.

While the steaks are cooling, cut the pastry into 4 pieces and roll each one out thinly to about a 7½ inch (19 cm) square; trim the edges to get a neat square and reserve the trimmings. As soon as the steaks are cold, brush them with a little brandy, season with salt and pepper, then lightly brush the surface of each pastry square with the beaten egg. Reserve 1 tablespoon of the mushroom mixture for the sauce, then place about an eighth of the remaining mixture in the middle of each square of pastry, then top with a steak. Now place the same amount of mushroom mixture on top of each steak, then bring 2 opposite corners of pastry up to overlap in the centre, tucking in the sides as if you were wrapping a parcel, brush the pastry all over with more beaten egg and bring the 2 remaining corners up to overlap each other. Be careful to seal the pastry only gently, because if you wrap it too tightly it tends to burst open in the oven. If you like you can use the reserved trimmings to make leaves for decoration.

Then, using a fish slice, gently lift the parcels on to the baking sheet, cover with a clean tea cloth and chill for at least 30 minutes, or until you're ready to cook them. When you are, pre-heat the oven to gas mark 7, 425°F (220°C), pop them in the oven on a high shelf and cook for 25 minutes, which will give you medium-rare steaks. If you want them well done, give them 5 minutes more; if you want them rare, give them 5 minutes less.

While they're cooking, pour the wine and reserved mushroom mixture into the frying pan. Let it all bubble and reduce by about a third – this will deglaze the pan and you can then spoon a little of the reduction around each portion before it goes to the table. One word of warning: you must have your guests seated and ready before this is served, because if the steaks wait around, they go on cooking inside the pastry.

Fast-Roast Pork with Rosemary and Caramelised Apples

It's hard to believe that you can serve a roast for six people in about 40 minutes flat from start to finish, but you can, and here it is. It's also outstandingly good, dead simple, can be prepared in advance and, once tried, I'm sure you'll want to make it again and again.

Serves 6

2 thick British pork tenderloins (weighing 12 oz/350 g each after trimming)
1 rounded tablespoon fresh rosemary leaves
3 Granny Smith apples, skins left on, cored and cut into 6 wedges each
2 cloves garlic, peeled and cut into thin slices
1½ oz (40 g) butter
1½ tablespoons cider vinegar
1 small onion, peeled and finely chopped
1 tablespoon demerara sugar
8 fl oz (225 ml) strong dry cider
2 heaped tablespoons half-fat crème fraîche
salt and freshly milled black pepper

You will also need a flameproof baking tray measuring 11 x 16 inches (28 x 40 cm), lightly buttered.

Pre-heat the oven to gas mark 8, 450°F (230°C).

First of all, using a small, sharp knife, make little slits all over the pork and push the slivers of garlic into them, turning the fillet over so the garlic is in on both sides. Next place the rosemary leaves in a mortar and bruise them with a pestle to release their fragrant oil, then chop them very finely.

Now melt the butter and combine it with the cider vinegar, then brush the meat with some of this mixture, sprinkle with half the rosemary and season with salt and pepper. Scatter the onions over the buttered baking tray and place the pork on top. All this can be prepared in advance, then covered with clingfilm.

When you want to cook the roast, prepare the apples by tossing them with the remaining cider vinegar and butter mixture, then arrange them all around the pork on the baking tray and sprinkle with the sugar and the rest of the rosemary. Place the baking tray in the oven on a high shelf and roast for 25-30 minutes (this will depend on the thickness of the pork), until the pork is cooked and there are no pink juices.

After that remove the baking tray from the oven and transfer the pork and apples to a hot serving dish, cover with foil and keep warm. Meanwhile, pour a little of the cider on to the tray, over the heat, to loosen the onions and juices from it, then pour into a saucepan over a medium heat, add the rest of the cider and let it bubble and reduce by about a third – this will take about 5 minutes. Then whisk in the crème fraîche, let it bubble a bit more and add some seasoning.

After the pork has rested for about 10 minutes, transfer it to a board and carve it into thick slices, then return them to the serving plate to rejoin the apples. Pour the sauce over and serve as soon as possible. Roast potatoes and braised red cabbage are particularly good with this.

Spanish Braised Pork with Potatoes and Olives

This is a brand new version of a recipe originally published in the 'Cookery Course' – the pork slowly braises in tomatoes and red wine, absorbing the flavour of the olives. Because I now cook potatoes in with it, all it needs is a green vegetable or a salad for a complete meal. I started off stoning the olives, but I now prefer them whole, as they look far nicer.

Serves 4-6

2 lb (900 g) shoulder of British pork, trimmed and cut into bite-sized pieces
1 lb (450 g) salad potatoes, halved if large
1½ oz (40 g) black olives
1½ oz (40 g) green olives
1 lb (450 g) ripe red tomatoes
2 tablespoons olive oil
2 medium onions, peeled and sliced into half-moon shapes
1 large red pepper, deseeded and sliced into 1¼ inch (3 cm) strips
2 cloves garlic, peeled and chopped
1 heaped teaspoon chopped fresh thyme, plus a few small sprigs
10 fl oz (275 ml) red wine
2 bay leaves
salt and freshly milled black pepper

You will also need a lidded flameproof casserole with a capacity of 6 pints (3.5 litres).

Pre-heat the oven to gas mark 1, 275°F (140°C).

First skin the tomatoes: pour boiling water over them and leave them for exactly 1 minute before draining and slipping off their skins, then roughly chop them. Now heat 1 tablespoon of the oil in the casserole over a high heat, pat the cubes of pork with kitchen paper and brown them on all sides, about 6 pieces at a time, removing them to a plate as they're browned. Then, keeping the heat high, add the rest of the oil, then the onions and pepper, and brown them a little at the edges – about 6 minutes.

Now add the garlic, stir that around for about 1 minute, then return the browned meat to the casserole and add all the thyme, tomatoes, red wine, olives and bay leaves. Bring everything up to a gentle simmer, seasoning well, then put the lid on and transfer the casserole to the middle shelf of the oven for 1¼ hours. After that add the potatoes, cover the pan again and cook for a further 45 minutes, or until the potatoes are tender.

Pork Chops with a Confit of Prunes, Apples and Shallots

This is a great recipe. The confit goes equally well with crispy roast duck, and is brilliant served with a rough pork-based pâté.

You can make the confit at any time – the day before, even. All you do is cut the apple into quarters, remove the core, then cut the quarters into ½ inch (1 cm) slices, leaving the skin on. Then just place all the ingredients together in a medium-sized saucepan, bring everything up to a gentle simmer, then let it cook as gently as possible, without a lid, for 45 minutes to an hour – you'll need to stir it from time to time – until all the liquid has reduced to a lovely sticky glaze.

When you're ready to cook the pork chops, dip them lightly in the seasoned flour, shaking off any surplus. Now heat the oil in the frying pan and, when it's really hot, add the butter. As soon as it foams, add the chops and brown them on both sides, keeping the heat fairly high. Then lower the heat and continue to cook the chops gently for about 25 minutes in total, turning them once. While they are cooking, warm the confit, either in a saucepan or in a dish covered with foil in a low oven, while you warm the plates; the confit shouldn't be hot – just warm. After that, increase the heat under the frying pan, then pour in the cider for the glaze and let it bubble briskly and reduce to half its original volume, which should take about 5 minutes. Serve the chops on the warmed plates, with the cider glaze spooned over and some confit on the side.

Serves 4
4 thick British pork chops
1 heaped tablespoon seasoned flour
1 tablespoon groundnut or other flavourless oil
½ oz (10 g) butter

For the confit:
5 oz (150 g) pitted pruneaux d'Agen
1 good-sized Granny Smith apple
4 shallots, peeled and cut into 6 wedges through the root
10 fl oz (275 ml) strong dry cider
2 fl oz (55 ml) cider vinegar
1 tablespoon dark brown soft sugar
2 good pinches powdered cloves
⅛ teaspoon powdered mace

For the cider glaze:
8 fl oz (225 ml) strong dry cider

You will also need a solid frying pan with a diameter of 10 inches (25.5 cm).

311

Roast Leg of Lamb with Shrewsbury Sauce

This is one of my favourite ways of cooking lamb, particularly in winter – plainly roasted with lots of basting to keep it juicy and succulent, then incorporating all the meat juices and crusty bits into what is truly one of the best sauces ever created. It's sweet and sharp at the same time and complements the lamb perfectly.

Serves 6-8

5 lb (2.25 kg) leg of lamb
1 small onion, peeled and sliced
a few sprigs fresh rosemary, to garnish
salt and freshly milled black pepper

For the Shrewsbury sauce:

2 tablespoons plain flour
1 heaped teaspoon mustard powder
1 pint (570 ml) beaujolais or other light red wine
5 rounded tablespoons good-quality redcurrant jelly, such as Tiptree
3 tablespoons Worcestershire sauce
juice 1 lemon
salt and freshly milled black pepper

You will also need a solid-based, flameproof roasting tin.

Pre-heat the oven to gas mark 5, 375°F (190°C).

First of all place the meat in the roasting tin, tucking the slices of onion beneath it. Season the surface with salt and freshly milled black pepper, then place it, uncovered, in the pre-heated oven on the middle shelf. Roast for 30 minutes per lb (450 g) – for a 5lb (2.25 kg) leg this will be 2½ hours. Make sure that you baste the lamb at least 3 times while it is cooking, as this will help keep it juicy and succulent. If you like to serve your lamb quite pink, give it 30 minutes less cooking time. To tell if the lamb is cooked to your liking, insert a skewer into the centre, remove it, then press the flat of the skewer against the meat: as the juice runs out, you will see to what degree the meat is cooked – the pinker the juice, the rarer the meat. When it is cooked as you like it, remove it to a carving board and keep it in a warm place to rest for 30 minutes.

Now, to make the sauce, spoon off any surplus fat from the roasting tin, tipping it to one side and allowing the fat to separate from the juices; you need to leave about 2 tablespoons of fat behind. Now place the tin over a direct heat turned to low and stir in the flour and mustard powder until you have a smooth paste that has soaked up all the fat and juices. Next add the wine, a little at a time, mixing with a wooden spoon after each addition. Halfway through, switch from the spoon to a whisk and continue to whisk until all the wine has been incorporated. Now simply add the redcurrant jelly, Worcestershire sauce, lemon juice and seasoning, then whisk again until the jelly has dissolved.

Now turn the heat to its lowest setting and let the sauce gently bubble and reduce for about 15 minutes, then pour it into a warm serving jug. Carve the lamb, garnish with the rosemary, pour a little of the sauce over and hand the rest round separately.

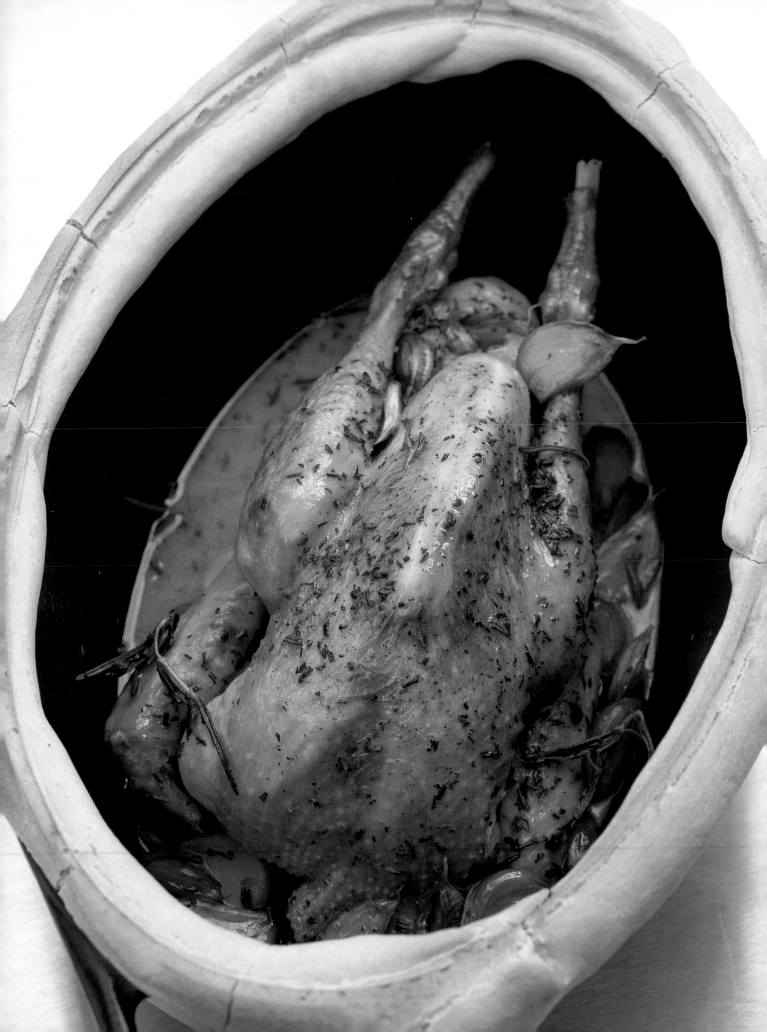

14

Chicken and other birds

If you sometimes feel depressed or let down, if you're suffering from the pressures of life, or simply having a plain old grey day, my advice is to roast a chicken. I'm not precisely sure why, but there is, and always has been, some magical 'cure-all' involved in the whole process. Sometimes you need to turn your back on the complications of life, give yourself some space and become homespun and happy for just a couple of hours. It really does act as a kind of therapy.

For starters, just imagine the smell of it: even when you wander past some fast-food rotisserie it hits you with that evocative come-hither aroma – and multiply that 10 times over when you have one roasting in your own kitchen. And what about the sound of it? All those juices sizzling and spluttering; and finally the vision of it – plump, bronzed and shining as it emerges from the oven! It doesn't have to be complicated, either. A simple roast chicken can be served just as it is, with chunky chips or crusty bread and a salad. And really good roast chicken is just as much of a treat when it's cold. But then it *can* be all kinds of other things, too: very smart and special, stuffed with herbs, served with sauces... Can there be anyone on earth who doesn't long to eat roast chicken? (Except vegetarians, of course!) There's one proviso, and that is that the chicken has to be a really good one to start with, one traditionally and naturally reared for the table to provide the best eating quality.

First catch your chicken

Seventy-five years ago chickens were slowly reared and fattened for the table. They were fine birds: strong and plump, with lots of succulent, juicy flesh and luscious, concentrated chicken flavour. A whole family could dine on a roast chicken and still have some left over. Roast chicken was very special – not an everyday thing, but something to be anticipated, savoured and looked forward to. The sad thing is there are young (and not-so-young) people who have never actually tasted the real thing. The reason? Progress. Now I'm not against progress – far from it – but it can sometimes run away with us, forcing us to rein in a bit and try to get back on track.

What's gone wrong?

Mass production means masses of cheap chickens. We have created new breeds of fast-growing chickens that can be reared very intensively, which means limited living space in a computer-controlled environment and feed containing antibiotics and growth promoters. The average life span of one of these hens is less than 50 days. At the end of this short, uncomfortable life the chicken is then plunged into scalding-hot water, after which a mechanical process removes its feathers. During this process it is absorbing water – up to 7.4 per cent of its own body weight – and then it's likely to be frozen, water and all. The result is coarse-grained, watery, limp chicken that has no flavour at all.

How can we put it right?

For the most part we can't, because a large section of the community wants cheap chicken and doesn't care about flavour. OK, everyone is free to choose, but ironically, up until now, that has not been the case. People who really do care about flavour have been very limited in their choice, and tracking down a real, naturally reared old-fashioned chicken has not been easy. This has to change, and I am reminded of how often I've been told, when attempting to improve the quality of ingredients, that there's no demand for it. But here I am campaigning again and, hopefully, creating a demand that will ultimately provide us all with a real choice.

What is a proper old-fashioned chicken?

1) The first thing we need to be concerned with is breeding. The bird has to be slow-growing, or rather it has to grow naturally, as nature intended. It must have a reasonable life span – not less than 81 days.

2) It needs (to use a modern phrase) to have its own space and not live in overcrowded conditions.

3) It has to be truly free range. There is, in this country, a bit of a free-range fantasy that has been put about. If you buy a chicken that is labelled 'free range', what that can mean is 'sort-of free range'. We have a kind of cockeyed labelling law that includes three types of 'free-range' chickens. Without going into details, my advice is to forget the words 'free range' on their own, which don't indicate the best-flavoured chicken, and look for the words Traditional Free Range or, in some cases, Free Range Total Freedom.

The best type of chicken is truly free to *range*, to have 24-hour access to the outdoors, to breath fresh air, to have access to a large meadow, field or orchard to peck and scratch about, and to have a truly natural existence; to be protected from foxes and other vermin by an electric security fence, to have shelter from the weather when needed, to have a place to roost and a plentiful supply of grain and fresh water.

4) The next question to ask is has it been dry-plucked? Real chicken does not get dunked into hot water. For the flavour to be at its best, dry-plucking is the optimum process.

5) A little age adds a lot of flavour! This old adage was never more true. If you hang a chicken with its guts intact in a controlled temperature it will, like cheese, mature naturally, which will concentrate the flavour.

I repeat, I'm all for progress, but I've never wanted good food to be only for the privileged few who are in the know. What I've observed is that the very best food producers in the world today are those who use traditional skills and methods alongside the latest technology.

Where can you buy real chicken?

I have found that, after a lot of campaigning, free-range is now much more widely available and is the best-flavoured. The label may also state either 'raised in the open air' or 'raised in total freedom'. Whether you want a small (what I would call an everyday) chicken weighing about 3 lb (1.35 kg) and suitable for very fast roasting (see page 324), or a chicken for casseroling, or chicken joints, they are all available free-range. But the crowned king of free-range chickens is Old Fashioned Original Chicken. The method of producing this chicken, which fulfils all the criteria just mentioned, has been pioneered by Paul and Derek Kelly of Danbury in Essex, and is now being adopted by other suppliers around the country. See page 698 for further details.

How to roast a chicken

I want to give two options here: one is for a traditional Sunday home-roast chicken and the other a fast-roast chicken that can be adapted in various ways with different sauces and flavours. But first a few points to remember.

Does it need to be trussed?

No. The original idea of trussing was merely to make the bird look neater, but I find it's easier to cook if it hangs loose. So cut away and discard any trussing strings if they are present.

Which way up should I roast it?

On its back is my favoured way, sitting it directly in the roasting tin. Why? Because I have found that the more robust meat of the chicken is sitting next to the direct heat this way, and this, in the end, provides lovely crispy bits to a) serve and eat, and b) be scraped up into the sauce or gravy, giving it an extra dimension. Some cooks say you should begin by roasting a chicken upside down, then on its side, then on its back, but I don't think the breast part, which is the most delicate, should be in direct contact with the heat of the roasting tin. Also, turning very hot, slithery chicken over on its side, breast and so on during cooking is not a good idea. I tend not to use a rack for chicken for the reason outlined above, but I do use one for duck (see page 323).

Will it be dry?

No, I promise it won't, as long as you are careful, follow the guidelines given and don't overcook it. With the slower, traditional roasting, fat, streaky bacon placed on the breast provides protection as well as a gradual slow-basting of the breast, and the pork in the stuffing provides the same internally, so all this – and the chicken's natural juices – keeps it moist. Don't forget that the better the quality of chicken, the moister and easier it will be to cook. In the case of fast-roast chicken, because the bird is in the oven for a much shorter time, less evaporation occurs and the chicken stays beautifully moist.

When is it cooked?

Obviously if you stick to the timings for slow-roasting given on page 330 you shouldn't go far wrong, but there are two tests: one is to insert a thin skewer into the thickest part of the leg, remove it and press it flat against the flesh to see if the juices run clear; the second one is to give the leg a tug – if it has some give in it and is not too resistant, that indicates the chicken is cooked. If you are in real doubt, cut a bit of the leg away and look at the area of meat where the thigh joins the body – there should be no visible pink juices.

Fast- or slow-roasting?

I have, after a number of experiments, come up with a method of roasting a smaller chicken at the highest temperature in the oven, and I have to say it's absolutely ace. With a bigger bird, slow-roasting is recommended: here you have a more melting, tender, finished texture, whereas with fast-roasting the flesh is firmer but still tender, as the chicken is younger. What's good is to have a choice – the slower method for leisurely family meals at weekends and the fast for the midweek, after-work scenario.

Why does it need to rest before carving?

When a chicken is cooked, the heat in the oven causes all the internal juices to bubble up to the surface just under the skin – sometimes you can see the skin almost flapping with the amount of juice inside it. Because of this you should always allow the bird to rest for at least 15 minutes before carving it, so that all these wonderful juices travel back from whence they came and keep everything lovely and moist. The fibres of the chicken will also relax, and this will make carving easier.

How do I carve a chicken?

Very easily, provided you have a sharp knife (see page 291) and follow the instructions given below.

To carve a chicken, insert the knife between the leg and body and remove the thigh and drumstick in one piece

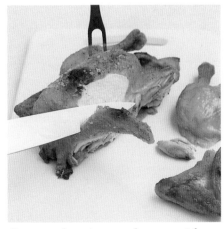

Remove the wing on the same side, then slice the breast. Repeat this on the other side of the bird

Finally, divide the drumstick and thigh, cutting through the joint so you have two leg portions

Jointing chicken

1) *Using a very sharp knife, begin by cutting through the parson's nose, then stand the chicken in a vertical position*

2) *Now insert the knife into the cut you've just made and cut straight down the back of the chicken*

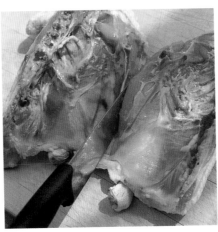

3) *Place the chicken skin-side down, open it out flat like a book and cut right through the breastbone*

4) *Now turn the chicken halves over, stretch out the leg and cut through the line dividing the leg from the breast*

5) *For six portions, turn the legs over, find the thin white line at the centre of the joint and cut through it*

6) *If you need eight portions, simply cut the breast portion in half*

Chicken Cacciatora

This is my version of the famous Italian classic – best made in the autumn when there's a glut of red, ripe, full-flavoured tomatoes, but it's still good in winter, as there are now some well-flavoured varieties available. Either way, the tomatoes need to be very red and ripe.

First of all heat the oil in the casserole over a high heat and season the chicken joints with salt and pepper. Then, when the oil gets really hot and begins to shimmer, fry the chicken – in 2 batches – to brown it well on all sides: remove the first batch to a plate while you tackle the second; each joint needs to be a lovely golden-brown colour all over. When the second batch is ready, remove it to join the rest. Now add the onions to the casserole, turn the heat down to medium and cook for 8-10 minutes, or until they are softened and nicely browned at the edges.

Meanwhile, skin the tomatoes. To do this, pour boiling water over them and leave them for exactly 1 minute before draining and slipping off their skins (protect your hands with a cloth if they are too hot), then chop them quite small.

When the onions are browned, add the garlic to the casserole, let this cook for about 1 minute, then add the tomatoes, tomato purée, rosemary, bay leaf, white wine and white wine vinegar. Now add some seasoning and bring it up to the boil, then let it bubble and reduce (without covering) to about half its original volume, which will take about 20 minutes. Now add the chicken pieces, stir them around a bit, then put the lid on and allow to simmer gently for 40 minutes, until the chicken joints are cooked through. This is good served with green tagliatelle, noodles, rice or a simple vegetable.

Serves 4

1 x 3 lb (1.35 kg) Traditional Free Range chicken, jointed into 8 pieces (see opposite page)
1 tablespoon olive oil
2 largish onions, peeled and thickly sliced
1 lb 8 oz (700 g) ripe red tomatoes
2 large cloves garlic, peeled and crushed
1 tablespoon tomato purée
1 tablespoon fresh rosemary leaves, bruised and finely chopped
1 bay leaf
10 fl oz (275 ml) dry white wine
1 tablespoon white wine vinegar
salt and freshly milled black pepper

You will also need a lidded flameproof casserole with a capacity of 6 pints (3.5 litres).

Other birds

These are simply those birds, besides chicken, that are specifically bred for the table – what used to be known as domestic poultry. In this chapter I have included guinea fowl, quail and farmed duck.

Guinea fowl

Guinea fowl is unusual in that it is neither totally wild nor truly domesticated. It has been reared for the table in this country since Elizabethan times. Its flavour is somewhere between pheasant and chicken and, though it isn't as plump as chicken (one will really only serve two people), it does have an extra-gamey flavour. You can use it for any chicken recipe, but if you want to make something like coq au vin, where the bird needs to be jointed, ask the butcher to do it, as it's quite difficult.

Quail

These are completely domesticated game birds, bred in this country for the table. Don't be taken in by their tiny appearance, which is, in fact, quite deceptive – they are surprisingly plump and the flesh is delicious. Serve two quail per person and, apart from the very special recipe for Roast Quail Wrapped in Pancetta and Vine Leaves with Grape Confit on page 332, another good way to serve them is to place a sage leaf on the breast of each bird, wrap each one in bacon, them place them on a bed of previously softened onions and mushrooms, along with 5 fl oz (150 ml) of dry white wine, cider or Madeira. Then braise them in a medium oven – gas mark 4, 350°F (180°C) – and give them 40-45 minutes.

Duck

Ducks – or, if they are under two months old, ducklings – come in a variety of sizes, anything from 2 lb (900 g), to 7 lb (3.2 kg) at Easter and Christmas. Everyone associates Aylesbury with ducks, which is where production in this country used to be centred, but now most commercial ducks come from Lincolnshire and Norfolk and are very distant descendants of the original Aylesbury breed. The majority come oven-ready, weighing 4-5 lb (1.8-2.25 kg), and will feed four people.

Barbary ducks, a French breed, are fairly widely available in this country. They are usually three months old and can be anything from 3 to 7 lb (1.35 to 3.2 kg), depending on whether they're male or female (the males are much bigger). They are less fatty than other birds and quite meaty.

In my opinion the very best type of duck available at the moment is a relatively new breed developed in England called Gressingham, and it's a cross between Pekin and the wild mallard. The result is a bird with a rich, gamey flavour and, although sometimes smaller (3 lb-5 lb 8oz/ 1.35-2.45 kg), it has a lighter frame and therefore has as much meat on it as a conventional bird twice its weight.

Roast duck at last!

In over 40 years of cooking and writing recipes, duck has posed some problems. It is a magnificent bird – rich and succulent, with bags of flavour; it has masses of fat, which is not a problem, because it all comes out in the cooking; but what the cook has to aim for is that elusive, really crunchy, almost crackling-like skin, with moist, tender flesh beneath. I used to belong to what I call the semi-Chinese school, which meant vastly overcooking it to get it really crisp but losing much of the succulent flesh in the process. I've also tried the complicated Chinese method of boiling it first, then drying and roasting it. Both methods were never quite right. Now, after all these years, I've cracked it – fast-roasting is the answer (see the recipe on page 326): perfect roast duck every time without a worry.

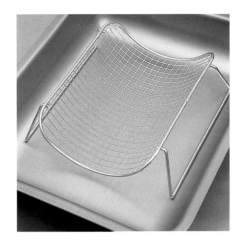

Because so much fat comes out of the duck as it's cooking, it needs to sit either on a roasting rack, *right*, or on some crumpled kitchen foil to allow the fat to drain away from the bird, making the skin really crisp.

Carving

It has to be said that this is another 'at last', after years of cutting a roast duck into rather inelegant quarters. I have now discovered the correct way to carve the whole thing into eight perfect portions to serve four people. This is thanks to my friend and poultry specialist Bill Curran, and below we have photographed his ingenious method.

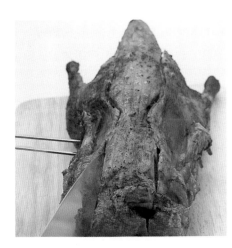

Turn the bird on to its breast and cut down through the meat along the full length of the back bone on either side, then turn the duck on to its back

Next, cut the meat away from the carcass, keeping the knife close to the bone. When you reach the base of the bird, carefully cut through the leg joint

Cut each half of the duck between the leg and the breast, then cut the leg into two pieces at the joint. Finally, divide the breast into two

Fast-Roast Chicken with Lemon and Tarragon

Here it is, as promised earlier: a revolution in the best way to roast a small chicken. The flavourings can vary in any way you like – crushed chopped rosemary leaves, sage leaves or thyme can be used, or a mixture of herbs, and you could replace the garlic with a couple of finely chopped shallots. It's a great recipe for adapting to whatever you have handy.

Serves 4

1 x 3 lb (1.35 kg) Traditional Free Range chicken
½ small lemon, thinly sliced and the slices halved, plus the juice of the remaining lemon
2½ tablespoons chopped fresh tarragon leaves
2 cloves garlic, peeled and crushed
½ oz (10 g) softened butter
1 dessertspoon olive oil
10 fl oz (275 ml) dry white wine
salt and freshly milled black pepper

You will also need a solid-based, flameproof roasting tin measuring 9 x 11 inches (23 x 28 cm), 2 inches (5 cm) deep.

Pre-heat the oven to gas mark 8, 450°F (230°C).

Begin by taking the chicken from the fridge about an hour before you intend to cook it (obviously if it's a hot day give it about 30 minutes only), and remove the string that holds the legs of the bird together so that the joints are loose – this will take the chill off the bird and help it to cook in the shorter time.

Now make a garlic and herb butter by placing the garlic, 2 tablespoons of the chopped tarragon leaves and the butter in a bowl and combine them with a fork, adding some salt and pepper. Then place the herb butter inside the body cavity of the bird, along with the halved lemon slices. Smear a little of the olive oil over the base of the roasting tin, place the chicken in it, then smear the rest of the olive oil all over the skin of the bird. Lastly, season well with salt and black pepper and then pop the roasting tin into the lower third of the oven. Now let it roast for 45 minutes without opening the oven door. When this time is up, remove the bird from the oven. Next put a wooden spoon into the body cavity and, using a spatula to hold the breast end, tip the chicken and let all the buttery juices and slices of lemon pour out into the roasting tin, then transfer the bird on to a carving board, cover with foil and let it rest for 20 minutes.

Meanwhile, using a tablespoon, skim off the excess fat from the juices in the roasting tin, then place the tin over direct heat, add the wine and lemon juice and let the whole lot bubble and reduce to about half its original volume. Now add the remaining tarragon, then taste and check the seasoning. Carve the chicken on to warm plates and add any juices to the sauce. Spoon the sauce over the chicken and serve.

Crisp Roast Duck with Confit of Sour Cherries

This is it – the best method of roasting duck I've found to date – and of all the lovely sauces, this one – made with dried sour cherries – is the loveliest. It's important to remember, however, that the duck should be as dry as possible, so buy it 24 hours in advance, remove and discard the wrapping and giblets, dry it in a clean tea cloth and leave it uncovered on a plate in the fridge till needed.

Serves 4
1 x 4 lb (1.8 kg) Gressingham duck
(weight with giblets)
fresh watercress, to garnish
sea salt and freshly milled black pepper

For the confit of sour cherries:
3 oz (75 g) dried sour cherries
7 fl oz (200 ml) dry red wine (cabernet sauvignon, for example)
1 oz (25 g) golden granulated sugar
1 tablespoon good-quality red wine vinegar

You will also need a roasting rack or some kitchen foil, and a roasting tin measuring 9 x 11 inches (23 x 28 cm), 2 inches (5 cm) deep.

Pre-heat the oven to gas mark 8, 450°F (230°C).

You need to start this recipe the day before you want to serve it by first soaking the cherries for the confit in the red wine overnight.

The next day, prepare the duck by wiping it again. Now, using a small skewer, prick the fatty bits of the duck's skin, particularly between the legs and the breast. Now either place the duck on the roasting rack in the tin or make a rack yourself by crumpling the kitchen foil and placing it in the bottom of the roasting tin. Season with coarse sea salt and freshly milled black pepper, using quite a lot of salt, as this encourages crunchiness. Now place the tin on the centre shelf of the pre-heated oven and roast the duck for 1 hour and 50 minutes. During the cooking time, using an oven glove to protect your hands, remove the tin from the oven and drain the fat from the corner of the tin – do this about 3 times (the fat is brilliant for roast potatoes, so don't throw it away).

Meanwhile, to make the confit, place the soaked cherries and wine in a saucepan, along with the sugar and wine vinegar. Bring the mixture up to a gentle simmer, give it all a good stir and let it barely simmer, without a lid, for 50 minutes to 1 hour, stirring from time to time. What will happen is that the wine will slowly reduce so there's only about 3 tablespoons of free liquid left.

When the cooking time is up, allow the duck to rest for 20 minutes or so, then carve (see the photographs on page 323) and serve garnished with the fresh watercress, with the sour-cherry confit poured over each portion.

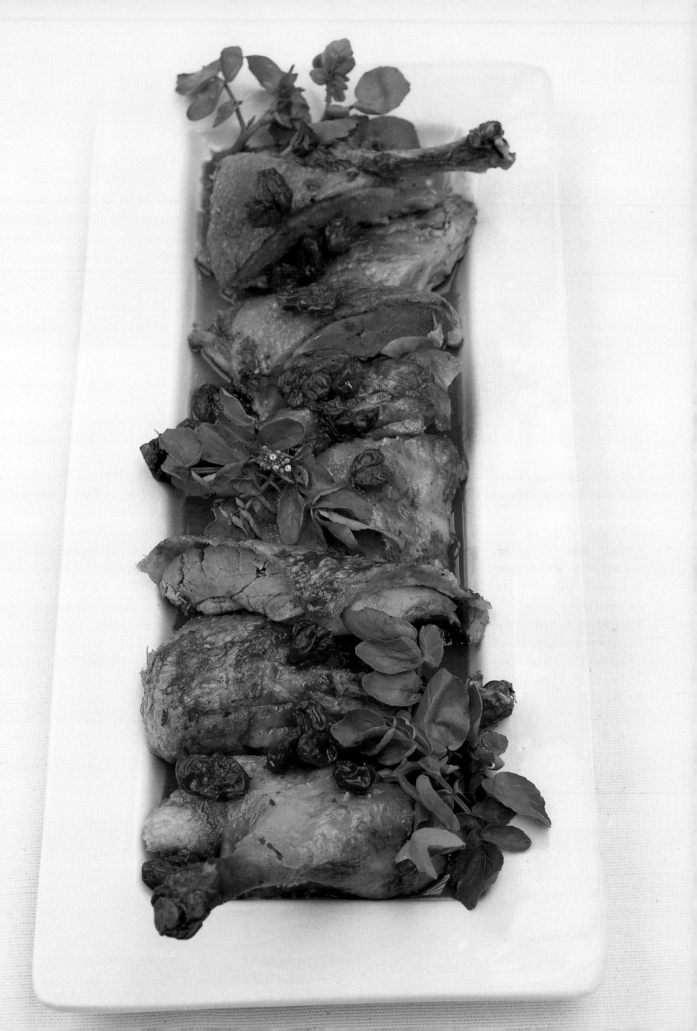

Paella

I've had lots of hits and misses with this Spanish classic, adding ridiculous, overwhelming amounts of saffron to try getting it as yellow as it is in Spain. Then I found out the Spanish sometimes use colouring! So here at last is the Delia paella – easy, no fuss, and the good thing is it serves six people as a complete meal needing no accompaniment.

Serves 6

12 oz (350 g) Calasparra paella rice
2 tablespoons olive oil
1 x 3 lb (1.35 kg) Traditional Free Range chicken, jointed into 8 pieces (see page 320)
1 large onion, peeled and roughly chopped
1 red pepper, deseeded and roughly chopped into chunks
4 oz (110 g) chorizo sausage in a piece, skin removed and cut into ½ inch (1 cm) dice
2 cloves garlic, peeled and crushed
1 heaped teaspoon paprika
¼ teaspoon cayenne pepper
½ teaspoon saffron strands (½ x 0.4 g sachet)
8 oz (225 g) ripe red tomatoes, skinned and roughly diced
2 pints (1.2 litres) boiling water
12 raw tiger prawns, shell-on, defrosted if frozen, 4 with heads, 8 without
2 oz (50 g) fresh or frozen shelled peas
1 lemon, cut into wedges, to garnish
salt and freshly milled black pepper

You will also need a shallow paella pan with a base diameter of 10 inches (25.5 cm), a top diameter of 13 inches (32.5 cm) and a capacity of 7 pints (4 litres).

Once you have peeled, chopped, prepared and assembled everything, heat the oil in the pan over a fairly high heat. Now season the chicken joints, adding 4 of them to the hot oil to sauté on all sides until golden brown, then remove them to a plate and do the same with the other 4 joints. Next add the onion, pepper and chorizo and fry these over a medium heat for 6-8 minutes, or until they're nicely tinged brown at the edges. Now add the garlic, paprika, cayenne and saffron and cook for another minute, then return the chicken to the pan, followed by the tomatoes, plenty of seasoning and the boiling water. Next bring everything up to a gentle simmer, turn the heat down and cook, uncovered, for 10 minutes.

After that, remove the chicken pieces and set them aside, then pour the rice into the centre of the pan. Bring everything back up to the boil, give a final stir and simmer, still uncovered, for about 10 minutes. During that time, shake the pan occasionally and move it around on the hob a little if the hob plate is not as big as the base of the pan. Next return the chicken, along with the prawns and peas, to the pan and continue to simmer for 15-20 minutes, or until the rice is cooked, adding a little more hot liquid if you think it's necessary. Now shake the pan again, making sure the rice is completely immersed. Turn the prawns over halfway through the cooking time – they will turn pink when cooked. The rice at the edges of the pan will take longest to cook, so to test that the paella is ready, take a little of the rice from the edges and check it's cooked through, then remove the pan from the heat and cover with a clean tea cloth for 5 minutes to absorb some of the steam. The paella is now ready – just garnish with the lemon wedges and don't forget to have hot plates ready to serve it on.

Stir-Fried Chicken with Lime and Coconut

It's hard to credit that a recipe as simple and as quick as this could taste so good, but I can assure you it's an absolute winner.

First of all chop the chicken into bite-sized pieces and place them in a bowl with the lime juice and zest. Stir well and leave them to marinate for an hour.

When you're ready to cook the chicken, heat the oil in the pan or wok over a high heat, add the chicken pieces and stir-fry for 3-4 minutes, until they're golden. Then add the chilli, stir-fry for 1 more minute, and add the coconut milk, fish sauce and half the coriander and spring onions. Cook for another 1-2 minutes, then serve with Thai fragrant rice and the remaining coriander and spring onions sprinkled over.

Serves 2

2 Traditional Free Range boneless, skinless chicken breasts
grated zest and juice 1 large lime
5 fl oz (150 ml) tinned coconut milk
1 dessertspoon olive oil
1 green chilli, deseeded and finely chopped
1 dessertspoon Thai fish sauce
4 heaped tablespoons fresh coriander leaves
4 spring onions, cut into 1 inch (2.5 cm) shreds, including the green parts

You will also need a frying pan with a diameter of 10 inches (25.5 cm), or a wok.

Traditional Roast Chicken with Apple, Sage and Onion Stuffing, Cranberry and Sage Sauce and Chicken-Giblet Gravy

This is what I described at the beginning of this chapter – a family roast chicken, moist and succulent for Sunday lunch, with lots of crispy bacon, real chicken-flavoured gravy, some very savoury stuffing and a sauce. All it needs is some vegetables with piles of crunchy roast potatoes, and some family and friends to share the feast.

Apple, sage and onion stuffing

If you have a food processor, making stuffing is a doddle: all you do is switch the motor on, add the pieces of bread and process to crumbs, then add the parsley, sage, apple and onion quarters and process till everything is finely chopped. Next trim any sinewy bits from the chicken livers, rinse under cold water, pat them dry, then add them, together with the sausage meat, mace and seasonings. Give a few pulses in the processor until it is all thoroughly blended, remove the stuffing from the processor with a spatula, then place in a polythene bag and store in the fridge until it is required. If you're doing this by hand, just finely chop all the ingredients, combine in a bowl and refrigerate as above.

Traditional roast chicken

Pre-heat the oven to gas mark 5, 375°F (190°C).

First of all the chicken needs to be stuffed, and to do this you begin at the neck end, where you'll find a flap of loose skin: gently loosen this away from the breast and you'll be able to make a triangular pocket. Pack about two-thirds of the stuffing inside, as far as you can go, and make a neat round shape on the outside, then tuck the neck flap under the bird's back and secure it with a small skewer or cocktail stick. Take the remaining stuffing and place it in the body cavity (the fat in the pork will melt and help to keep the bird moist inside). Now place the chicken in the roasting tin and smear the butter over the chicken using your hands and making sure you don't leave any part of the surface unbuttered.

Season the chicken all over with salt and black pepper, then arrange 7 slices of the bacon, slightly overlapping, in a row along the breast. Cut the last rasher in half and place one piece on each leg. I like to leave the rind on the bacon for extra flavour, but you can remove it if you prefer.

Place the chicken in the oven on the centre shelf and cook for 20 minutes per lb (450 g), plus 10-20 minutes extra – this will be 1 hour and 50 minutes to 2 hours for a 5 lb (2.25 kg) bird, or 2 hours 10 minutes to 2 hours 20 minutes for a 6 lb (2.7 kg) bird. The chicken is cooked if the juices run clear when the thickest part of the leg is pierced with a skewer. It is important to baste the chicken at least 3 times during the cooking – spooning over the juices mingling with the bacon fat and butter helps to keep the flesh succulent.

During the last basting (about half an hour before the chicken is cooked), remove the now-crisp bacon slices and keep them warm. If they

Serves 6-8
For the roast chicken:
1 x 5-6 lb (2.25-2.7 kg) Traditional Free Range chicken
2 oz (50 g) butter, at room temperature
8 rashers traditionally cured smoked streaky bacon
salt and freshly milled black pepper

For the apple, sage and onion stuffing:
1 dessert apple, cored and quartered
1 heaped tablespoon fresh sage leaves
1 small onion, peeled and quartered
4 oz (110 g) fresh white bread, crusts removed
1 tablespoon fresh parsley leaves
reserved chicken livers from the giblets
8 oz (225 g) minced pork or good-quality pork sausage meat (I often use skinned sausages)
¼ teaspoon powdered mace
salt and freshly milled black pepper

You will also need a flameproof roasting tin measuring 10 x 14 inches (25.5 x 35 cm), 2 inches (5 cm) deep.

are not crisp, just leave them around the chicken to finish off. For the final 15 minutes of cooking, hike the heat up to gas mark 7, 425°F (220°C), which will give the skin that final golden crispiness.

When the chicken is cooked it is important to leave it in the warm kitchen (near the oven), covered in foil, for 30 minutes, which will allow it to relax. This is because when the chicken is cooking all the juices bubble up to the surface (if you look inside the oven you will actually see this happening just under the skin), and what relaxing does is allow time for all these precious juices to seep back into the flesh. It also makes it much easier to carve. When you serve the chicken, make sure everyone gets some crispy bacon and stuffing. Serve with the Chicken-Giblet Gravy and Cranberry and Sage Sauce.

For the chicken-giblet gravy

Simply place the giblets, water, carrot, onion, herbs, peppercorns and salt in a medium-sized saucepan and simmer very gently with the lid almost on for 2 hours. Then strain the stock into a jug and cool and chill in the fridge. Any fat on the surface is easily removed when cold. To make the gravy, after removing the chicken from the roasting tin, tilt the tin and remove most of the fat, which you will see separates quite clearly from the juices – you need to leave about 2 tablespoons of fat behind. Now place the roasting tin over direct heat turned to fairly low, and when the juices begin to sizzle, sprinkle in the plain flour, stirring vigorously till you get a smooth paste, then add the giblet stock, little by little, exchanging the wooden spoon for a whisk. Whisk thoroughly until all the stock is incorporated, bring the whole lot up to simmering point, then taste and season with salt and freshly milled black pepper.

For the cranberry and sage sauce

All you do here is combine everything in a small saucepan and whisk over a gentle heat until the cranberry jelly has melted. Then pour the sauce into a serving jug and leave till needed (it doesn't need re-heating – it's served at room temperature). Although I love to serve this sauce in summer, in winter my favourite accompaniment is Traditional Bread Sauce from my Christmas book.

For the chicken-giblet gravy:
8 oz (225 g) frozen chicken giblets (reserving the livers for the stuffing), thoroughly defrosted
1½ pints (850 ml) water
1 medium carrot, roughly chopped
½ onion
a few fresh parsley stalks
sprig fresh thyme
1 bay leaf
½ teaspoon black peppercorns
2 rounded tablespoons plain flour
salt and freshly milled black pepper

For the cranberry and sage sauce:
6 tablespoons cranberry jelly
2 dessertspoons chopped fresh sage
3 tablespoons balsamic vinegar
salt and freshly milled black pepper

Roast Quail Wrapped in Pancetta and Vine Leaves with Grape Confit

I am a self-confessed quail convert, having shunned them for years as being undersized and fiddly. I was wrong. They are plump and meaty and, because they are self-contained, they are one of the easiest birds to cook and serve. Vine leaves, which impart a lovely flavour, are available in some stores and specialised food shops, but if you can't find them, you can use foil loosely crumpled around each quail instead.

Serves 4
8 quail
3 oz (75 g) sliced pancetta, preferably smoked
16 fresh vine leaves or 1 x 227 g pack preserved vine leaves in brine
a little olive oil
salt and freshly milled black pepper

For the grape confit:
6 oz (175 g) red or black seedless grapes, halved
1 teaspoon golden granulated sugar
3 tablespoons red wine
1 tablespoon red wine vinegar

You will also need a baking tray measuring 10 x 14 inches (25.5 x 35 cm), and some string.

Pre-heat the oven to gas mark 7, 425°F (220°C).

First of all make the grape confit by dissolving the sugar in the wine and wine vinegar, then add the grapes and let them simmer very gently, without a lid, for 40 minutes, or until the liquid has reduced to a syrup.

If you are using fresh vine leaves, blanch them by dipping them in boiling water for a few seconds until they go limp, then pat them dry and remove the stalks. If you have preserved vine leaves, rinse them under the tap and pat them dry. Now wipe the quail with kitchen paper and remove any trussing string, then rub them with olive oil and season.

Next, cover the breasts with the pancetta, dividing it equally between them. Now sit each quail on a vine leaf, with the legs pointing towards the stalk end, and wrap the leaf up each side, then put another leaf over the breast and tuck it in underneath the quail. Now tie each quail with a piece of string to keep the leaves in place, then lay them on the baking tray and cook on a high shelf of the oven for 15 minutes. After that, take them out, untie the string and, holding the quail in a cloth, unpeel the top leaf (leaving the second leaf and pancetta intact). Now return the quail to the oven to brown and crisp, which will take another 15 minutes. When you've removed them from the oven, let them rest for about 10 minutes before serving with the grape confit.

Guinea Fowl Baked with Thirty Cloves of Garlic

Before you cry off this one, remember that garlic, simmered gently for 1¼ hours, mellows deliciously, losing much of its pungency. I have to admit it's probably not the thing to eat before a first date, but otherwise it's utterly sublime. In this recipe, an inedible huff paste is used to make a perfect seal for the lid of the casserole, ensuring that all the juices and fragrances remain intact. It's made in moments, but if you want to you could use foil instead – bearing in mind it will not be quite as effective.

First of all dry the guinea fowl as much as possible with kitchen paper and season it well. Next, melt the butter and oil in the casserole, then, keeping the heat fairly high, brown the guinea fowl carefully on all sides. This will seem a bit awkward, but all you do is protect your hands with a cloth and hold the guinea fowl by its legs, turning it into different positions until it is a good golden colour all over; this will take 10-15 minutes in all. After that, remove the guinea fowl from the casserole, add the cloves of garlic and rosemary sprigs, toss these around, then replace the guinea fowl and sprinkle the chopped rosemary all over. Next, pour the wine all around it and let it gently come up to simmering point.

Meanwhile, place the flour in a bowl and add the water – it should be enough to make a soft but not sticky dough – then divide the dough into 4 and roll each piece into a cylinder about 9 inches (23 cm) long on a lightly floured surface. Now position these all around the rim of the casserole – it doesn't matter what they look like. Place the casserole lid carefully on top, pressing down gently and making sure there are no gaps. Alternatively, simply place a double sheet of foil over the casserole before putting the lid on. Now place the casserole in the oven and cook for 1 hour exactly, then remove the lid and let the guinea fowl continue to cook for another 10 minutes, to re-crisp the skin. Next remove the guinea fowl from the casserole and allow it to rest for 10 minutes before carving.

Serve the carved guinea fowl with the garlic cloves alongside and the cooking juices poured around it. The idea is to squash the garlic cloves with a knife to release all the creamy pulp and, as you eat, dip the pieces of guinea fowl into it. Creamy mashed potatoes would be a wonderful accompaniment here.

Serves 4
1 x 4 lb (1.8 kg) guinea fowl
30 cloves garlic, unpeeled (3-4 heads)
½ oz (10 g) butter
1 dessertspoon olive oil
6 small sprigs fresh rosemary
1 heaped tablespoon rosemary leaves, bruised and chopped
10 fl oz (275 ml) white wine
salt and freshly milled black pepper

For the huff paste:
8 oz (225 g) plain flour, plus a little extra for dusting
5 fl oz (150 ml) cold water

You will also need a lidded flameproof casserole large enough to hold the guinea fowl comfortably – about 8 pints (4.5 litres).

Pre-heat the oven to gas mark 6, 400°F (200°C).

Grilled Lemon Chicken Kebabs with Gremolata

This is what we all need – something easy to prepare, really fast to cook that also tastes exceptionally good. Serve with rice or salad or both, or, instead of the rice, warm crusty bread to dip into the juices.

Serves 2

2 Traditional Free Range boneless chicken breasts, skin-on
juice 1 lemon, plus 1 teaspoon grated lemon zest
3 thick slices lemon, cut into quarters
2 fl oz (55 ml) olive oil
1 clove garlic, peeled and crushed
1 dessertspoon chopped fresh oregano
1 teaspoon white wine vinegar
2 bay leaves, torn in half
salt and freshly milled black pepper

For the gremolata:

1 clove garlic, peeled and finely chopped
1 heaped teaspoon grated lemon zest
1 tablespoon chopped fresh parsley

You will also need 2 wooden skewers, 10 inches (25.5 cm) long, soaked in water for at least 30 minutes before you start cooking.

Begin by chopping each piece of chicken into 5 chunky pieces, leaving the skin on, and place them in a bowl, along with the lemon juice and zest, oil, garlic, oregano, white wine vinegar and plenty of seasoning. Cover and leave to marinate overnight or for a few hours – or for as much time as you have.

To cook the chicken, pre-heat the grill to its highest setting at least 10 minutes ahead, then first thread half a bay leaf on to the first skewer, followed by a quarter-slice of lemon, then a piece of chicken. Carry on alternating the lemon and chicken until you have used 5 pieces of chicken, finishing off with a lemon quarter and another bay-leaf half at the end and making sure you pack everything together as tightly as possible. Repeat with the second skewer, then place them both on a grill rack, and underneath the rack place a heatproof dish to catch the juices. The kebabs should be 4 inches (10 cm) from the grill, and as they cook you need to baste them with the marinade juices. They will need 10 minutes on each side to cook through and become nice and dark and toasted at the edges.

While they're under the grill, mix the gremolata ingredients together and have it ready. When the chicken is done, transfer it to a serving plate and keep warm. Now put the rest of the marinade, plus the basting juices, in a saucepan and boil to reduce to a syrupy consistency, which will take about 2 minutes. Pour this over the chicken and sprinkle the gremolata all over as it goes to the table.

15

A vegetable calendar

I will never forget Victoria Wood at the Albert Hall in 1996 doing one of her splendid monologues in which she described how an aunt of hers always put the sprouts on for the Christmas lunch in November! It was the older people in the audience who laughed the loudest because, of course, we all remembered the waterlogged, rather grey, overcooked vegetables of our schooldays.

Without going into the historical reasons for this poor culinary image British cooks are heir to, let's just say that things have thankfully changed. Though we are still very much a meat-loving nation, we have of late developed a much more healthy reverence and respect for vegetables, which have now become absolute stars in their own right and not some 'also-ran' to help the meat go down.

How to cook perfect vegetables

The answer to this question lies in just one word: carefully. Vegetables need care and attention if we're going to get the best out of them. 'Catch the moment' is a good phrase, because there is a moment when they are cooked to perfection and then, beyond that, they begin to deteriorate.

Whereas I suspect the problem of overcooking was related to a fear of the vegetables not being quite done enough, we now seem to be facing the absolute opposite problem – an equal fear of overcooking that results in almost raw, inedible vegetables that you'd be hard pushed to get your fork into. So whilst it can be argued that overcooked vegetables should be banned for ever, I would like to see the opposite extreme banned, too. I have nothing against good, honest, raw vegetables, but if they're meant to be cooked, they must be.

Catching the moment?

I am always being asked what my favourite piece of cooking equipment is, and the answer is unequivocal: a small, flat skewer – I keep a whole bunch of them hanging near where I cook. It's the only way I can tell if, say, a cauliflower floret, a potato or a Brussels sprout is cooked. As the skewer slides into the thickest part of the vegetable you can feel if it's tender by the amount of give. A very small, sharp paring knife will do the same job, but a skewer is better. If you practise the skewer test every time you cook vegetables you'll soon get the feel of 'catching the moment'.

Is water the enemy?

I would say yes, mostly, but not always. On the whole, the more water you have, the more it dilutes the flavour of the vegetable. If you're boiling, the water should barely cover the vegetables, because a brief encounter is what we're really looking for. Always use boiling water from the kettle so that you don't use too much – you can see instantly when it barely covers the vegetables and doesn't need more. So always be very sparing with water, except for boiling cabbage, where, after many years of experimenting, I have concluded that it needs plenty of boiling water to cover so that its brief encounter with the fast-boiling water cooks and tenderises it as quickly as possible. All vegetable cooking water contains nutrients, so use it as stock whenever possible. In the vegetable cooking methods that follow, I will indicate the amounts of water needed.

Is steaming better?

Sometimes quite definitely, other times not. As we have prepared *How To Cook*, my team and I have conducted side-by-side tests so that when steaming is better, it will be indicated. In some cases, steam rather than water helps to preserve more flavour, but in other cases, steaming does not tenderise sufficiently and because it takes longer it can affect flavour. I would urge you to invest in a fan steamer – a wonderful piece of equipment that can be slipped into any-sized saucepan, meaning you always have the choice of being able to steam.

Oven-roasting

When grilled vegetables became fashionable in other parts of the world, the vagaries of the British domestic grill were never going to be able to cope without a great deal of hassle. Since my first experience with high-temperature oven-roasting of vegetables in the *Summer Collection*, I am now thrilled and delighted to have discovered this method of cooking vegetables. I now almost never grill or sauté, which demands time, standing around watching, waiting and turning, whereas oven-roasting, besides leaving you in peace, has the huge advantage of requiring less fat. I do, however, sometimes use a ridged grill pan, which gives plenty of vision and no bending backaches from peering under a conventional grill.

Which is the best method?

There isn't one. All vegetables respond differently to different ways of cooking, so what I will do is indicate which method I think is best for each vegetable.

Eating vegetables in season

Once upon a time nature provided us with a perfectly varied diet, leaving us blissfully free of a large amount of decision-making. This in turn gave an added dimension to everyday eating in that we could enjoy anticipating what each month in each year would bring and really look forward to it.

Now modern technology and progress have provided something else. Fast jets. This means that at any given time in the calendar, produce from around the world can be dispatched within hours and absolutely everything is always available all year round. What this means is that, along with the good fortune of being able to eat almost anything we feel like when we like, we have also lost something, and that is an appreciation of what individual items taste like when they are harvested in their natural environment, in their best season. Thus we have pallid sprouts in July and woolly strawberries at Christmas. There's also the added problem of travel time and distribution, which often means fruits and vegetables are picked immature and unripened, with a resulting loss of flavour and quality.

I am not against progress and I do appreciate fresh shelled peas from Kenya – they don't have the tender melt-in-the-mouth flavour of home-grown in June, but they're better than frozen. I also love having fresh Israeli basil in the winter months when mine has died off. However, if we want to know how to cook we first need to know how to buy home-grown vegetables in season that have the finest quality and flavour: tight little button sprouts after the first November frost has sharpened their flavour; the finest young green stalks of asparagus in early May; the very red, sweet, sun-ripened tomatoes of early autumn; and the quite unmatched flavour and melting texture of British runner beans. For this reason I will indicate the best season for each vegetable and hopefully encourage you to reintroduce this natural rhythm of nature into your day-to-day eating.

Asparagus

Mid-April to the end of June, depending on the weather
I have now almost completely given up making things with asparagus, because apart from the very thin sprue, which I like to chop and put in Eggs en Cocotte (page 37), I think asparagus is best eaten as it is, hot with foaming melted butter or hollandaise sauce poured over, or warm or cold with a good vinaigrette (see page 375).

To cook asparagus, take each stalk in both hands and bend and snap off the woody end, then trim the ends with a knife to make them neater. Lay the asparagus stalks on an opened fan steamer (or an ordinary steamer will do) – they can be piled one on top of the other – then place them in a frying pan or saucepan, pour in about 1 inch (2.5 cm) of boiling water from the kettle, then season with salt, put a lid on and steam for 5-6 minutes, or until they feel tender when tested with a skewer.

Serve the asparagus on hot plates with some sauce poured over the tips. Pick them up with your hands and eat down to the tough ends, dipping in the sauce after each bite. Also, don't forget to have finger bowls and napkins at the ready. 1 lb 4 oz (570 g) of asparagus will serve 4 as a starter.

Aubergines

At their best July to September
Chefs and cooks seems to have an endless debate about aubergines – to salt and drain or not to salt and drain. I'm for the former. I do take the point that the modern aubergine has evolved to a state where it does not contain bitter juices, but the juices are there nonetheless and I find salting and draining gets rid of excess moisture and concentrates the flavour – there's nothing worse than a watery aubergine.

Aubergines also have a capacity to absorb other flavours, so are great mixed with tomatoes and spices, cheese or pulses. They also absorb oil at an incredible rate, so frying is not recommended. I find the best way to cook them is either by oven-roasting (page 358) or char-grilling (page 380).

Beetroot

Available all year round

A truly magnificent vegetable, but sadly its reputation in this country has been ruined by one thing alone – malt vinegar, a lethal culinary weapon that kills off the flavour of anything it comes into contact with (apart from its affinity with pickled onions and its ability to counteract the fattiness of fish and chips). So poor old beetroot is often despised as a consequence of formerly being confined to the pickle jar. Yet cooked as a vegetable or in a salad it has a superb earthy flavour and a wonderful rich, vibrant colour.

To cook beetroot: there are two methods here; one is long and slow in the oven, which is suitable for larger, older beetroot; and the other is for the first small bunches of fresh beetroot that appear in June.

To cook 1 lb (450 g) of winter-stored beetroot in the oven – try to use even-sized beetroot if you can – begin by pre-heating the oven to gas mark 3, 325°F (170°C). Now prepare the beetroot by leaving the trailing root intact but trimming the green stalk so only 1 inch (2.5 cm) is left. Wash well under cold running water, but leave the peel on. Now place the beetroot in a parcel of double foil, sealing well. Place the parcel on a baking sheet and bake on the middle shelf of the pre-heated oven for 3 hours. To test if it's cooked, you should be able to ease the skin away with your thumbs.

For boiled beetroot, take one bunch of small summer beetroot, prepare as above and place it in a medium saucepan, then add salt and enough boiling water to barely cover. Simmer, covered, for 20-30 minutes, until the skin eases away when pushed away with your thumbs.

Peel and serve hot as a vegetable or cold with vinaigrette in a salad.

Broad beans

Best late-June and July

In the *Cookery Course* I gave a recipe for very young broad beans in their pods; in fact the beans are hardly formed and the finger-thick pods are delicious. If you grow them or know someone who does, it's worth giving it a try. However, the beans themselves later on have much to offer. If they're young and tender just steam them for about 3 minutes; if they're a bit older, boiling is best as it softens and tenderises the skin – add salt, barely cover with boiling water and give them 3-4 minutes.

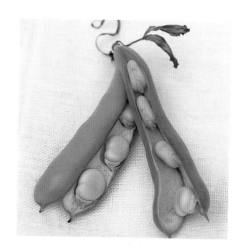

Older broad beans, when quite large, can be blanched in boiling water for 1 minute, then drained and, when cool enough, the skins slipped off. As you do this they will split in two, then you can finish cooking them in steam till tender – 2-3 minutes. Broad beans have a wonderful affinity with boiled ham and gammon steaks, and partnered with pancetta (Italian cured bacon) they make a brilliant salad (see page 377). 1 lb (450 g) of broad beans in the pod will serve 2.

Broccoli (calabrese)

English season, June to November

This is a vegetable that, because it's imported all year round, turns up far too often on restaurant menus. However, it's good to enjoy it in season. Prepare it by cutting it into even-sized florets measuring about 2 inches (5 cm) each, then steam them till tender – 4-5 minutes. Serve with a squeeze of lemon juice, a little butter or a sprinkle of grated cheese to just melt into the flower heads. You can also roast broccoli tossed in a little oil and seasoning – just place in a pre-heated oven at gas mark 6, 400°F (200°C) for 25 minutes.

Alternatively, to stir-fry for 2 people, separate 8 oz (225 g) of florets into 1 inch (2.5 cm) pieces and slice the stalk bits into tiny diagonal slices. Stir-fry in 1 dessertspoon of very hot oil for 1 minute, then add 1 teaspoon of grated ginger and a crushed clove of garlic, stir-fry for another minute, then add 1 tablespoon of soy sauce and 1 tablespoon of dry sherry. Cover with a lid and continue to cook until tender – about 2 more minutes.

Broccoli (sprouting)

February to March

After the lean winter months, the first fresh green vegetable to herald spring is sprouting broccoli, with its purple or white flowery heads. It has a lovely, sweet, very green kind of flavour and tender stalks. I like to eat the leaves, stalks and heads when it's very young. Steam them, sprinkled with salt, for 3-4 minutes. You will need 4 oz (110 g) per person.

Brussels sprouts

Best from November to February

Mini cabbages that grow on thick stalks is how I would describe Brussels. In Norfolk, on my way to football matches on Saturdays, I can buy them still attached to their two-foot-high stalks, which means I can 'pick' them fresh as I need them through the week.

People either love or hate Brussels sprouts, and I am devoted to them – with provisos. I never buy them till November, because I think that frost sharpens their flavour; sprouts at the end of summer are never as good. Also, they're difficult to cook if too large, so small, tight buttons about 1 inch (2.5 cm) in size are best. The larger, more opened, walnut-sized sprouts are more difficult to cook but can be used in purées or soups.

To cook Brussels sprouts, there's no need to make incisions in the stalks. All you need to do for 1 lb (450 g) of sprouts is take off the outer leaves if they look a bit weary (if not leave them on), sprinkle with salt and steam them for 5-8 minutes, depending on their size, but watch carefully and remember undercooking is just as bad as overcooking, so use a skewer to test when they're tender. Another way to serve them is to have a frying

pan with ½ a teaspoon of butter and ½ a teaspoon of oil very hot, then, after giving them about one minute's less steaming, toss them around in the hot pan to finish cooking and to turn them fairly brown at the edges. This last method can be varied by adding a couple of rashers of chopped streaky bacon, cooked first till crisp, or at Christmas it's nice to add 4 oz (110 g) of chopped, peeled, cooked chestnuts and brown these, too. 1 lb (450 g) of Brussels sprouts will serve 2-3 people.

Cabbage
Varieties available all year
A cabbage is honest goodness with no pretensions. It is a supremely beautiful vegetable, an absolute work of art visually, and with its tight, audibly squeaky leaves bursting with goodness and vitality, why is it not acknowledged and revered? The overcooking of former years has made it a much-maligned vegetable in the western world. Chefs and restaurants continue to largely ignore seasons and prefer to offer endless dull green string beans and the ever in-season calabrese broccoli.

When were you last offered a bowl of fragrant, buttered green cabbage in a restaurant? Isn't it time for a rethink? Fresh cabbage lightly cooked is full of goodness, packed with vitamins, minerals and flavour and it's not expensive. So I hope I can encourage you to start eating more of it.

Types of cabbage
Spring greens or cabbage greens
Not really spring greens any more, as they are now available all year round, but they seem to have a luscious edge in spring that is lacking in the winter months. Look for small, tender leaves that look perky, sound squeaky and are not too floppy and tired.
Winter cabbages
These are the larger, fatter, rounded varieties. Savoy, *right*, has crinkly leaves and a superb flavour; January King has flowery leaves with a purple tinge; round cabbage has green outer leaves but gets whiter towards the centre and is good for coleslaw.
Pointed cabbage
This is a lovely variety – tight, green and leafy. Best in April, May and June, as it's home-grown, but still good imported from Spain at other times of the year.

Buying cabbage
Cabbage should always be eaten as fresh as possible – it loses nutrients if stored for too long. An unwrapped fresh cabbage should look bright and crisp, with its outer leaves intact (often if it's had its outer leaves removed, it was because they were limp, which is not a good sign). The heart should feel firm and the leaves should squeak as you pull them apart.

To prepare cabbage: with a leafy variety such as spring greens it's best to discard any tired, floppy outside leaves, then separate the other leaves down to the central bud and place them one by one on a flat board. Then, using a sharp paring knife, cut out the stalks, running the point of the knife down each side. When the stalks have been removed, pile the leaves on top of each other and, using a larger knife, shred the cabbage into strips, then do the same with the centre bud to shred that, too. For a more compact variety, such as Savoy, once the outer leaves have been discarded, halve and then quarter the cabbage lengthways, then cut out the hard core from each quarter and discard. Finally, slice thinly across each quarter to shred it.

To cook cabbage: I have tried every method under the sun and I am now convinced that boiled cabbage needs plenty of water. The secret is to shred it quite finely and cook it briefly in rapidly boiling water. What I do is pack it down quite tightly into a saucepan, sprinkle with salt, then place the pan over a high heat, pour boiling water from the kettle in, which re-boils instantly, and time it for 3-5 minutes.

The one way to tell if it's cooked is to bite a piece, as you would pasta. Then tip it into a colander and squeeze as much excess water out as you can, using a saucer to press the cabbage down. Then turn the saucer on its side and use chopping movements, which pushes any excess water out. Serve it straight away in a hot bowl, tossing it with a minute amount of butter, and season it with salt and pepper. One medium-sized cabbage will serve 4 people.

Carrots

June to November, or April and May from Spain
Summer bunched carrots (home-grown) are my favourites – sweet and delicate, great for simply munching raw or grated into salads. The first of these to appear in spring come from Spain and have a particularly good flavour.

To cook summer carrots, there's absolutely no need to peel here – just rinse them under a cold running tap and cut off the stalks only, just a fraction above the end. This leaves the inside of the carrot intact and, I feel, preserves the flavour. Place them in a steamer, sprinkle with a little salt and steam for about 7 minutes, or until tender when pierced with a skewer but still retaining some firmness and bite. Serve plain, or I like them tossed in butter mixed with some chopped fresh tarragon leaves.

To cook winter carrots: these are available from storage all year round. My favourite way to cook them plainly is to scrape off the skins and cut them into 2 inch (5 cm) chunks, then place them in a saucepan with salt and enough boiling water to barely cover them. Give them about 20 minutes, or until tender but with a little firm bite in the centre, then drain and place them in a food processor and, using the pulse movement, 'chop' the carrots quite small, but don't overdo it or you'll have a purée.

Quickly return them to the saucepan using a spatula to scrape them back in quickly, add a knob of butter and some freshly milled black pepper, then place them over a gentle heat and stir them around for a couple of minutes to get the heat back in. 1 lb (450 g) of carrots will serve 4.

Cauliflower and cape broccoli

December to March

Home-grown cauliflowers are available all year, but in the winter months we grow something called cape broccoli, which has dark-purple curds instead of the creamy-white. This has a more distinctive flavour and is good, I think, to ring the changes. They're both cooked in the same way, so remove the tough outer leaves, keeping the younger tender ones, which not only can be cooked and eaten, but their presence in the cooking imparts extra flavour.

To cook a cauliflower, first of all separate it into largish florets by turning the cauliflower upside down, then just insert a small sharp knife and cut through to separate the heads into about 3 inch (7.5 cm) florets. Then place them, along with the leaves, in a steamer, sitting them up vertically (ie stalk-side at the base, flower heads up). Now pop a bay leaf in, which has a fragrant affinity with cauliflower. I also add some salt, and I like to use another very English flavouring, nutmeg, which I grate lightly over the surface of the florets. Now pour in boiling water from the kettle and steam for 6-7 minutes, or until tender when tested with a skewer. Serve with a little butter or grated cheese, or in our modern variation of cauliflower cheese on page 357. One medium cauliflower will serve 4 people.

Celeriac

Best through the winter months

Celeriac, at first sight, is probably the ugliest, most uninteresting-looking vegetable there is, but there is a hidden agenda here, for underneath the spiney roots and ugly skin is a soft, velvety flesh that, when mashed, has the creaminess of potato with the added subtle flavour of celery. But that's not all: celeriac is excellent roasted in the oven and also raw in a salad, cut into tiny julienne matchstick strips and served with a creamy dressing.

To prepare celeriac, first of all have no fear in paring off the skin really thickly. What you need to do is peel off enough to leave behind only the creamy-white flesh, with no brown bits left behind. Because the root channels are interwoven into the base of the bulb you will need to cut all this away, so it's always useful to remember only three-quarters of what you buy can be used. Cut the rest into chunks and, as you do so, pop them in some cold salted water to prevent discolouring. Now you can either dry them well and roast (see page 356) or boil them and combine them with equal quantities of boiled potatoes and mash.

Celery

Available almost all year round

Celery is as English as the Stilton cheese it's often partnered and perhaps enjoyed best of all with: fresh, crunchy and crisp in the autumn with a good cheese board, some fresh-shelled walnuts and a glass of vintage port.

Originally, the older varieties of so-called 'dirty' celery from the flat black-earthed Fenlands of East Anglia had a short season – from October to January. If you're lucky enough to eat some there is much washing to do, but the flavour is exceptional, particularly after a light frost, when it's sweetest of all. However, a really severe frost can wipe the whole crop out, so growing it can be a hazardous occupation and in the past during hard winters there was sometimes none available. English Fenland growers have overcome this by not only developing new varieties that can be grown in summer, but have also overcome the severities of a British winter by growing English varieties in the warm climate of Spain. This means extremely good celery is available practically all year round, with a gap from about April to June. If you can get 'dirty' celery in November it is worth all the tedious washing, but it's also good to have English varieties available all year.

To prepare celery, first of all remove the tough, large outer stalks, and as these are usually distinctively stringy, take a sharp paring knife and pare off the strings, *above left*. Now trim off the outer skin around the root and cut the head vertically so that some of the sweet, edible root is still intact, then cut into 6-8 layered vertical strips, *left*.

Courgettes

Best home-grown from mid-June to October

Courgettes are baby marrows, and don't I know it! I used to grow them, but if I wasn't vigilant about picking them every day in season they seemed to turn into marrows overnight – and marrow for supper night after night is *not* a good idea! Now I would rather buy them small and tender. Courgettes are a delicate vegetable, with not a great deal of their own flavour, and like aubergines they have a high water content that can render them watery and dull. I like them chunkily cut and roasted in the oven, as in Oven-Roasted Ratatouille in the *Summer Collection*, or marinated in a vinaigrette with herbs (see page 361), which allows them to absorb some real flavour.

Fennel

Home-grown, May to September

Sometimes called Florence fennel, or its charming Italian name is *finocchio*. Fennel is like a fat, bulbous celery, with the same crunchy texture but with a marked aniseed flavour. Fennel can be thinly sliced and eaten raw in salads or shaved very finely with a mandolin and dressed with vinaigrette. It's also very good cooked and served as a vegetable.

To prepare fennel, first trim off the green shoot at the top; if the fronds aren't too droopy you can use them as a garnish. Then cut it diagonally into a pointed shape. Next slice off the root part at the other end and remove any outer toughened or brown layers. Slice the bulb in half and then again into quarters. Now you can take a little of the stalky core out, but not all, because you want the layers, including the inner green part, to stay intact.

To cook fennel, cut it into quarters, steam it for 10 minutes, or until tender, then have a frying pan with 1 teaspoon each of oil and butter really hot and sauté the fennel till it's golden brown at the edges. Finally, sprinkle with a tablespoon of freshly grated Parmesan whilst it's still in the pan and let it rest for a few seconds, then serve with a little more grated Parmesan sprinkled over and the chopped feathery fronds if there are any. Serves 2.

Leeks

Best home-grown from September to May

Leeks are a very fine vegetable indeed. Though they are related to onions, they have a far more subtle and somehow nobler taste, I think. Leeks lend themselves to other flavours superbly, too: great with potatoes, in a soup or with cheese (see Leek and Goats' Cheese Tart, page 108), in salads with vinaigrette, and they also respond beautifully to quick stir-frying. Watch the season, though, as home-grown leeks get a bit woolly and tired in the late spring and summer and the imported ones never seem quite as good. Remember, too, that the smaller and thinner the leeks are the sweeter their flavour is, so avoid the very fat, heavy ones.

To prepare leeks, buy a little more than you need, because there's going to be quite a bit of trimming. First take off the tough outer leaves and trim off most of the very green part. Now, using a sharp knife, place the leek on a flat surface and make an incision vertically about halfway down (because of the intricate layers, there can be dust and grit trapped in-between, usually in the upper part). Now turn on the cold tap and fan out the layers of leek to rinse them through and rid them of any hidden dirt, *right*.

Buttered Leeks

This is my favourite way of cooking leeks – very gently, in their own juices and served as a vegetable, particularly at the end of winter when there's not an awful lot else available.

When the leeks are trimmed and washed, cut them all the way through vertically, then chop them into 1 inch (2.5 cm) pieces. Now place a small frying pan over a medium heat, add the butter and let it melt – it needs to lightly coat the surface of the pan. Now add the leeks and some seasoning, stir them around, then turn the heat down to low and let them cook gently for about 5 minutes without a lid, stirring them 2 or 3 times. There will be quite a lot of juice that collects in the pan, so use a draining spoon to serve.

Serves 2

1 lb (450 g) leeks, trimmed – you need 12 oz (350 g) trimmed weight
½ teaspoon butter
salt and freshly milled black pepper

Mushrooms

Mushrooming is a word that's used to describe something that's grown overnight, and I have to say that's precisely the word I would use to describe the mushroom market. Whereas once we could buy only buttons or caps, we are now presented with an amazing variety of sizes, shapes and colours. Let's not be too dazzled by looks, though, because some of them appear more interesting than they actually taste.

Because season and availability fluctuate, here we need to concern ourselves mostly with how to get the best out of whatever is available. My own firm favourite cultivated mushrooms are the flat, open, dark-gilled variety and the smaller pink-gilled open caps. (I have never thought the pale, insipid button mushrooms were even worth bothering with.) There are now chestnut mushrooms and the large version called portabella, too. I also like shiitake (particularly in an omelette), a saffron-yellow variety called pied de mouton, and now we can buy the best-flavoured wild mushrooms of all, Italian dried porcini (known as ceps in France) and another French variety called morels. I now find getting the finest mushroom flavour in cooking is never a problem.

To prepare mushrooms, don't wash them is the first rule – they already have a lot of moisture and washing them means they absorb even more, which can make them soggy. Take a damp piece of kitchen paper and wipe each mushroom clean, or use a special mushroom brush, which brushes away any dirt. Don't peel them, either, because the peel has lots of flavour. I always use the mushroom stalks, except with shiitake, as they are a bit chewy in this case and so need to be trimmed down almost to the cup. If the mushrooms are small, leave them whole, if not, cut through the stalk, then into halves or quarters.

Sautéed Mushrooms

Serves 2
8 oz (225 g) mushrooms, prepared as described
1 teaspoon olive oil or butter
salt and freshly milled black pepper

First imagine a plump, round, fat, juicy mushroom, then think of a shrivelled dried mushroom – the difference is moisture, and because the dried one has masses more flavour, having lost the moisture, I feel that the thing to aim for when cooking mushrooms is to get as much of the moisture out as possible so as to concentrate the flavour. No need to use very much oil or butter, as mushrooms tend to soak this up at an alarming rate. Always remember, too, that as the moisture evaporates they lose half their original volume.

Heat the olive oil or butter in a frying pan and, when it's hot, throw in the mushrooms and toss them around by shaking the pan. Season with salt and pepper, then turn the heat down to very low and just let the mushrooms cook gently, uncovered, so that all the juice evaporates and the flavour of the mushrooms becomes more concentrated. Leave them like that for 30 minutes, stirring them around once or twice.

Once the mushrooms have lost much of their moisture content they can then be used in an omelette or simply as they are. You could also add a peeled and chopped clove of garlic 5 minutes before the end and finish off with a sprinkling of chopped fresh flat-leaf parsley.

Onions and shallots

Available all year

Where would cooks be without onions? One of the principal flavour-makers in the kitchen, stews, soups, casseroles, quick salads and sauces are all enhanced by this most humble but wonderful of vegetables, together with its tiny, milder cousin the shallot, which also plays an important role.

Over the years I've been given countless methods of how not to cry when preparing them. One enterprising person even sent me a battery-operated fan to fan away the fumes, but I can honestly say that nothing really works. For chopping, however, food processors have made things a lot easier, and now there aren't as many tears as there used to be.

How to prepare onions

Slicing: if you want to slice them, cut off the root end, then peel away the skin. Slice in whole round slices and separate into rings, or else cut the onion in half first and then slice into half-moon shapes.

Chopping: rough chopping is as above, making about 3 cuts vertically across each onion and then 3 horizontally.

Chopping small (without a processor): this time leave the root intact, then peel away the skin from the top end. Now cut the onion in half and place each half on a flat surface, round-side up. Next, make cuts vertically from the root end but leaving the root intact to hold it together, *top right*. Then make horizontal cuts across the vertical cuts whilst you hold on to the root end firmly, *right*. The last cut will be the little root bit, and this can be discarded.

Oven-Fried Onions

Well, they're actually roasted, but you get the same effect without having to stand over them. They are particularly lovely served with sausages and mash or for steak and onions.

Serves 2
8 oz (225 g) onions, peeled
1 teaspoon groundnut or other flavourless oil
1 teaspoon golden caster sugar

Pre-heat the oven to gas mark 7, 425°F (220°C).

First of all you need to cut the onions into ¼ inch (5 mm) slices, then place them in a bowl, add the oil and sugar and toss the onions around to get the lightest coating. Then spread them out on a baking tray and place on a high shelf of the oven for 14-15 minutes – they need to be nicely blackened round the edges.

Shallots

These are like little baby onions, sometimes bright purple-pink and sometimes creamy-white. Cooked slowly as a confit they make a lovely accompaniment to beef. In a medium pan, simmer 12 oz (350 g) of peeled whole shallots with 7 fl oz (200 ml) of red wine, 1 fl oz (25 ml) of red wine vinegar and seasoning. Keep the heat very low and cook, without a lid, for about 1 hour and 10 minutes, turning the shallots over halfway through. After this time, add half a teaspoon of sugar to give a lovely sticky glaze, and cook for another 5 minutes. Serves 4.

They are lovely pickled (see the Christmas book), or simmered whole in casseroles and braised dishes, and I love them chopped very finely in salads (see pages 377 and 383).

Parsnips

Best November to February
What an absolute star a parsnip is – full of soft, juicy flesh and fragrant, sweet flavour. They are lovely plain, steamed, mashed and roasted, and one of my favourite parsnip recipes is in the Christmas book, where they are baked in the oven with Parmesan.

I like them best after the frosts have arrived, which really does intensify their flavour. Because parsnips are stored, they tend to go a bit woody towards the end of the winter, so enjoy them at their best between November and February. If you can, buy small, young parsnips that don't need peeling and coring; the older, larger, late-winter parsnips need the peel taken off and the cores cut out. Then cut them into even-sized pieces and steam for 10-15 minutes, and serve with plenty of salt and freshly milled black pepper and a little butter. For roasting, prepare them in the same way, toss in a little oil and season. Place on a pre-heated roasting tray and roast in the oven pre-heated to gas mark 7, 425°F (220°C) for 30-40 minutes, depending on the size of the parsnips. 1 lb (450 g) of parsnips will serve 4 people.

Peas

Home-grown, best in June and July
One very sad but thought-provoking incident happened to me a few years ago. I was buying fresh peas in the pod in a supermarket, and the sixth-former doing a Saturday job on the checkout asked me if I could tell her what they were. Perhaps the positive side of that comment was a kind of affirmation that I really needed to do *How To Cook*.

Fresh-shelled peas are one of the most delightful vegetables of all – young and tender, they melt in the mouth when cooked and taste wonderful raw. Sure, it takes a bit of time to shell them, but sitting by an open window or in the garden on a bright summer's day shelling peas can be wonderful therapy. When they first arrive they're incredibly sweet and tender, but later on they get bigger and have quite a different character and flavour. I like both equally. Imported Kenyan peas are not quite as good as the summer home-grown peas, but I think we are very fortunate to have them available all year round, and ready-shelled, too.

To cook young, fresh shelled peas, first remember to buy 8 oz (225 g) in the pod per person. After shelling, pop them in a steamer with some salt and give them 1 minute before you bite one; they shouldn't take any longer than 2 minutes in all. If they are a bit older, they may need 3-4 minutes.

This is a good recipe for slightly older peas, which, in my opinion, sometimes have more texture and flavour than the younger ones. However, if the peas you are using are very young, give them far less cooking time – 8 minutes at the most.

First trim the spring onions: you need only the white bulbs (the rest can be chopped and saved for something such as a stir-fry). Pull off any thick, stalky bits from the rocket and tear the larger leaves in half. Now all you do is put all the ingredients in a large saucepan, cover with a lid, bring them up to simmering point and simmer gently for 8-15 minutes, depending on the age of the peas.

Peppers

Best season, summer and autumn

Once an exotic import from the Mediterranean, now an everyday, ever-available staple but best home-grown in the summer and autumn. Peppers actually come in all kinds of colours, but red, green and yellow are the most widely available. When peppers are grown they begin green, and then, if left on the stalks to mature, this mellowing results in red peppers, with a sweeter flesh (which is better if they are to be eaten raw or only lightly cooked). But the green ones do have a special character of their own – a sharper, more robust flavour, which stands up to long, slow cooking. For this reason I am very much against any snobbish dismissal of green peppers as being somehow inferior. In fact certain cuisines, such as Cajun and Creole, seem to only ever include green peppers in their recipes. Yellow peppers are more like red in flavour, and their golden-yellow colour can look very pretty in certain dishes.

To prepare peppers, firstly slice the top off the pepper, including the stalk, then, with the tip of a small knife, scrape out the seeds and core. Now slice the pepper into quarters, and again, using the tip of the knife, slice away any very white, pithy bits. Then slice or chop according to

Braised Peas, Rocket and Spring Onions

Serves 6
3 lb (1.35 kg) peas (unshelled weight), freshly shelled
2½ oz (60 g) fresh rocket
12 bulbous spring onions
1½ oz (40g) butter
3 tablespoons water
pinch golden caster sugar
1 rounded teaspoon Maldon sea salt

the recipe. If the recipe calls for finely chopped pepper, you can use the round lid bit around the stalk and chop that, too.

To cook peppers: to peel or not to peel is the vexed question. I say don't bother. After discovering the recipe for Piedmont-Roasted Peppers – which are lovely in the autumn when the peppers are in season and the tomatoes are ripe and red – and publishing it in the *Summer Collection*, I decided they were the very best cooked peppers I'd ever tasted, so I stopped going to the bother of peeling them. So all the recipes I have done since then use the peppers as they are, skins and all. They can be sautéed, stir-fried in strips till blackened at the edges and tender, or oven-roasted, sprinkled firstly with olive oil and seasoning, then placed in the oven at gas mark 8, 450°F (230°C) for 30-40 minutes.

Chilli peppers
Available all year

Forgive the pun, but the whole subject of chillies is a hotbed of confusion: there are so many varieties, and availability fluctuates from one variety to another. The only real guide is individual taste. I would avoid the fat, round, scorching Scotch bonnet pepper unless you are a real hot-chilli lover. What I tend to do is buy the larger, fatter kind, which are usually not so fiercely hot, and if I want really hot then the tiny Bird Eye chillies used in Asian cooking are the ones to go for, because they are always reliably hot. The other point to remember is that green is usually marginally hotter than red. There is a safety net, though: if you find you're using fresh chillies and they haven't given you quite enough heat, all you do is add a few drops of Tabasco (see page 238) to top up the fire.

How to prepare chillies: very carefully. Why? Because the membrane and the seeds inside are the hottest part and can burn delicate skin. American cookbooks often advise using rubber gloves, but washing your hands with soap and water after handling should be OK. What happens is if your hands touch the delicate skin on your face or, worse, eyes, it can burn the skin. So slice the tops off, cut them in half lengthways, hold down the tip of each chilli half with your finger and, using a sharp knife, scrape away all the membrane and seeds and discard them. After that, either slice the chilli or chop it finely, then carefully wash your hands.

Winter pumpkin and squash
Winter pumpkin: home-grown, October to November; imported, September to November. Squash: all year

The bright-orange lantern pumpkins available around Halloween do not have a great deal of flavour, so in my opinion are not worth serving as a vegetable. However, the smooth, silky texture makes wonderful soup, and gives the best texture in Pumpkin Pie (see pages 112-3) or in pumpkin and sweetcorn soup (page 365).

Butternut squash is available all year, because when our season finishes we import it from Africa, and its buttery, nutty texture is one of my own favourites. It is shaped like a bottle and has both a nutty flavour and a good firm texture excellent for roasting and braising (see the recipes on pages 356 and 304 respectively).

To prepare pumpkin or squash, you need a good, sharp, heavy knife, and first you cut the vegetable in half and then into quarters. After that scoop out the fibrous bits and all the seeds with a spoon or knife, then, this time using a small but very sharp knife, peel away the tough skin. Finally, cut the pumpkin flesh into cubes or slices.

Runner beans

August to mid-September

This vegetable is, for me, the crown prince of all British vegetables. Although runner beans are imported all year round, they're never quite the same as our own end-of-summer crop, which provides a feast for almost two months. If you're growing your own the beans must be harvested young because the whole lot is eaten, pod and all. Runner beans have in the recent past been a misunderstood vegetable, rarely seen in restaurants, even in peak season. The problem is that people, chefs included, rarely know how to prepare and cook them. If they're simply chopped into little diamond shapes, the skins take longer to cook than the insides and they end up being either grey and overcooked or undercooked and tough.

Old-fashioned cooks like me use something called a bean slicer, *right*. The runner beans are simply fed through a channel, and a wheel with blades is turned by hand so that the runner beans are sliced very finely. This means only the briefest cooking time is needed and the beans taste deliciously fresh and green. So good are they that you don't ever need a specific recipe, maybe just a smidgen of butter and some salt and black pepper. In fact I could happily eat a whole plateful and nothing else.

To prepare and cook runner beans, first take a sharp paring knife and strip away the stringy bit on the join at either side of each bean. Then feed them through a bean slicer, which should be fixed to the edge of a table, and have a plate underneath it to catch the slices. If you don't have a bean slicer, slice the beans in exactly the same way using a paring knife. 1 lb 8 oz (700 g) of runner beans will serve 4 people.

Spinach

Home-grown, best from May to October

Very green and very good for you, spinach is packed with vitamin C. What you need to be most aware of is that spinach contains a great deal of water, so what looks like a huge amount won't be when it's cooked.

To prepare spinach: fresh spinach can be rather dusty or muddy. The best way to deal with this is to pick out and discard any damaged or brown leaves and remove any tough stalks, fill the sink with cold water, then plunge the spinach in the water and swirl the leaves around. Do this in two or three changes of water, then let it all drain in a colander, shaking it well over the sink. Young spinach leaves can be wiped and used raw in a delicious salad.

To cook spinach: absolutely no water ever. For 1 lb (450 g) of spinach leaves, melt ½ oz (10 g) of butter in a large, thick-based saucepan, then, keeping the heat at medium, pack the spinach leaves in. Add some salt, put on a tight-fitting lid and let it cook for about 30 seconds, then take the lid off and you'll find the spinach has collapsed down into the butter. Give it a stir so that the top leaves get pushed down to the base of the pan, replace the lid and give it another 30 seconds or so, shaking the pan a couple of times – I find the whole operation takes less than 2 minutes. Next drain the spinach in a colander, pressing it well with a saucer to get rid of any excess water. You can now return it to the pan and add seasoning: spinach is enhanced beautifully with a little cream or crème fraîche. It also, like cauliflower, has an affinity with nutmeg, so season with salt and freshly milled black pepper and a few gratings of whole nutmeg. Spinach as a vegetable goes beautifully with smoked haddock (see the recipe on page 396). If you're serving spinach as a vegetable you will need 8 oz (225 g) per person.

Swede

Home-grown, best in winter

I love the unique flavour of swedes, which seems to epitomise all the goodness of home cooking. They have long been of service to cooks because their presence in stews and casseroles not only ekes out the meat to make it go further, but also adds a presence that offers something of its own flavour, whilst at the same time absorbing some of the meat flavours as well. Swede is also good served solo as a vegetable.

To prepare swede, all you need here is use a potato peeler to peel it in precisely the same way as a potato, slicing off the root end first with a knife. Then just cut the swede into suitably sized chunks.

To cook swede, cut it into 1 inch (2.5 cm) dice and steam for about 10 minutes, or until tender, then whiz to a purée in a food processor or mash with a fork, adding a knob of butter, salt and lots of freshly milled black pepper. This method also works very well using half swede and half carrot, but in this case I like it chopped small rather than puréed.

For roast swede cut the chunks larger – 1½ inches (4 cm) – place the cubes in a bowl, adding (for 1 lb/450 g) 1 dessertspoon of olive oil and some seasoning. Toss the swede around to get all the pieces coated in the oil, then place them on a baking tray and roast in a pre-heated oven set to gas mark 7, 425°F (220°C) for 30-35 minutes, until the swede is nicely toasted brown at the edges. This amount will serve 4 people.

Sweetcorn

Home-grown from July to October

Aesthetically one of the most beautiful vegetables, I think – such a visual work of art. Outside, the pale-green casings cover firm, silky-white threads, and all this to protect the plump, pale-golden kernels, full of juicy sweetness.

To prepare sweetcorn you'll need to remove the kernels, so first of all remove the green part and all the silky threads. Then stand the cob upright on a flat board and, using a very sharp paring knife, carefully scrape off all the kernels, keeping the knife deep in the husk so you get the whole kernel.

To cook sweetcorn: for corn on the cob, one way is to steam the cobs for about 15 minutes, or until the kernels feel tender when tested with a small skewer. Then dress with a little melted butter, season well with plenty of salt and freshly milled black pepper and eat straight from the cob. If you stick a small fork into each end, you can pick the whole thing up, or you can chop the cob into smaller sections that can be lifted with your hands. Don't forget the napkins and finger bowls.

By far the best and most delicious way to cook and eat corn on the cob is to strip the casing and silky threads off as described above, toss the cobs in a little olive oil, season well with salt and black pepper and roast on an open barbecue. Watch them carefully, turning them all the time, until they're toasted golden brown – 5-10 minutes. You will need one medium head of corn per person.

Warning: never try to cut corn husks before cooking, as it's virtually impossible. After cooking, a very sharp knife will cut them into chunks you can bite straight into. Finally, sweetcorn kernels stripped from the cob and oven-roasted can be served as a vegetable or used to make the Pumpkin Soup with Toasted Sweetcorn on page 365.

Turnips

Baby turnips, best in June and July; winter turnips, all year

In early June I love seeing the first young bunches of carrots, and the same goes for turnips – so pretty, about the size of golf balls, with deep-purple tinges to their creamy-white flesh and topped with frilly leaves. In winter they're less tender and can be steamed and mashed to a purée with an equal amount of steamed potatoes, with the addition of a little cream and butter. I love them sliced wafer-thin in Cornish pasties and roasted as a vegetable (they can be used in the recipe on the following page). Turnips are prepared in exactly the same way as swede (see left).

To cook baby turnips, dice 1 lb (450 g) of peeled turnips into ¾ inch (2 cm) cubes. Steam them for 3 minutes, sprinkled with a little salt, then sauté in melted butter, tossing them around for about 10 minutes, until tender. This quantity of turnips will serve 4 people.

Oven-Roasted Winter Vegetables

This is always going to be an easy option if you're entertaining, as all the vegetables get cooked without any attention. One thing I have found invaluable, too, is being able to prepare them well ahead, which gives you that organised feeling. This is a particularly lovely combination of vegetables, but you can vary it with whatever is available.

All you do is cut the vegetables into large, chunky pieces (no smaller than 1½ inches/4 cm) – leaving the celeriac until last, as it may discolour if left for too long – place in a large bowl, then add the herbs, garlic, olive oil and lots of seasoning and just use your hands to mix them. The prepared vegetables can now be kept in a sealed plastic bag in the fridge for 2-3 days.

When you're ready to cook the vegetables, spread them out on the baking tray and cook in the pre-heated oven on a high shelf for 30-40 minutes, until they're tender and turning brown at the edges.

Serves 6

Vegetable quantities are prepared weights

12 shallots, peeled

12 oz (350 g) peeled and deseeded butternut squash

12 oz (350 g) peeled sweet potato

12 oz (350 g) peeled swede

12 oz (350 g) peeled celeriac

1 tablespoon freshly chopped mixed herbs (rosemary and thyme, for example)

2 large cloves garlic, peeled and crushed

3 tablespoons olive oil

salt and freshly milled black pepper

You will also need a baking tray measuring 11 x 16 inches (28 x 40 cm).

Pre-heat the oven to gas mark 7, 425°F (220°C).

356

Cauliflower with Two Cheeses and Crème Fraîche

No need to make a white sauce for this one – the beauty of half-fat crème fraîche is that you can simmer it into a creamy sauce in moments. This could be an accompanying vegetable for four, it could make a main course for two served with rice, or I like it with penne pasta – England meets Italy, sort of thing!

First of all place the cauliflower florets and a few of the inner leaves in a steamer with the pieces of bay leaf tucked amongst it. Pour in some boiling water from the kettle, add some freshly grated nutmeg and salt, then cover and steam the cauliflower till tender – about 12 minutes. After this time, test the thickest parts with a skewer to see if they are tender, then remove it to the baking dish and cover with a cloth to keep warm.

Now pour 3 fl oz (75 ml) of the steaming water into a saucepan, add the crème fraîche and simmer, whisking well, until it has thickened very slightly, then add the cheeses. Heat this gently for about 1 minute, whisking, until the cheeses have melted, then season the sauce to taste. Now pour the sauce over the cauliflower and scatter the spring onions and remaining Parmesan over, then sprinkle with the cayenne. Finally, place the dish under the hot grill until the cauliflower has browned and the sauce is bubbling.

Serves 4 as a vegetable or 2 for supper
1 medium cauliflower, separated into florets
1½ oz (40 g) Parmesan (Parmigiano Reggiano), finely grated, plus 1 heaped tablespoon extra to finish
1½ oz (40 g) Gruyère, finely grated
2 heaped tablespoons half-fat crème fraîche
2 bay leaves, torn in half
a little freshly grated nutmeg
2 spring onions, very finely chopped, including the green parts
pinch cayenne pepper
salt and freshly milled black pepper

You will also need an ovenproof baking dish measuring 7½ inches (19 cm) square and 2 inches (5 cm) deep.

Pre-heat the grill to its highest setting.

Tunisian Aubergine Salad with Coriander and Yoghurt

This is my adaptation of an Elizabeth David recipe. I never actually made it from her book, but one of my favourite restaurants, Chez Bruce, in Wandsworth, London, regularly serves it as a first course. It's so wonderful I never have anything else if it's on the menu.

Serves 4 as a starter

1 lb 8 oz (700 g) aubergine, chopped into ½ inch (1 cm) cubes
2 rounded tablespoons chopped fresh coriander
1 lb 8 oz (700 g) ripe red tomatoes
about 3 tablespoons olive oil
1 heaped teaspoon cumin seeds
1 teaspoon allspice berries
1 large onion, weighing about 10 oz (275 g), peeled and finely chopped
1 large red chilli, deseeded and finely chopped
4 cloves garlic, peeled and finely chopped
2 rounded tablespoons chopped fresh mint
salt and freshly milled black pepper

To serve:

1 tablespoon olive oil
8 pitta breads, warmed
4 tablespoons Greek yoghurt
1 rounded tablespoon chopped fresh coriander
1 rounded tablespoon chopped fresh mint

You will also need 2 baking trays, one measuring 11 x 16 inches (28 x 40 cm), the other measuring 10 x 14 inches (25.5 x 35 cm).

You'll need to start this recipe the day before you want to serve it. First salt and drain the aubergines: place them in a large colander and, as you add them, sprinkle with 1 tablespoon of salt, then cover with a plate and weigh it down with a few scale weights or a similar heavy object. Now place the colander on a plate and leave the aubergine to drain for 1 hour. When it has been draining for 30 minutes, pre-heat the oven to gas mark 8, 450°F (230°C).

Meanwhile, skin the tomatoes. To do this, pour boiling water over them and leave for exactly 1 minute before draining them and slipping off their skins, protecting your hands with a cloth if they are too hot. Cut them in half and place them cut-side up on the smaller baking tray, which should be lightly oiled, and brush the tomatoes with a little olive oil as well. Set to one side.

Now you need to dry-roast the cumin seeds and allspice berries, and to do this place them in a small frying pan or saucepan over a medium heat and stir and toss them around for 1-2 minutes, or until they begin to look toasted and start to jump in the pan. Now transfer them to a pestle and mortar and crush them to a powder.

When the aubergines are ready, squeeze them to get rid of any excess juices, dry them in a clean tea cloth, then place them in a bowl, add 1 tablespoon of the oil and toss them around so they get a good coating. After that, spread them out on the larger baking tray and place both baking trays in the oven, with the aubergines on the top shelf and the tomatoes on the next one down. Give them about 25 minutes, by which time the aubergines should be tinged golden brown at the edges and the tomatoes soft. Remove the vegetables from the oven and, when the tomatoes are cool enough, chop them into quite small pieces.

Meanwhile, heat 2 more tablespoons of the oil in a large frying pan over a medium to high heat and fry the onions until soft and pale gold – about 5 minutes – then add the chilli and garlic and fry for 1 more minute. Next add the chopped tomatoes, aubergines and crushed spices, stir well, add the herbs and season with salt and freshly milled black pepper. Bring everything up to a gentle simmer, then remove the pan from the heat and pile everything into a serving dish. Leave for 24 hours, or longer if possible, covered in the fridge. Serve the salad at room temperature, drizzled with the olive oil. Serve with the warm pitta breads, about a tablespoon of Greek yoghurt with each serving and the fresh herbs scattered over.

Quick-Braised Celery

Serves 4-6
1 head celery, trimmed, de-stringed
and cut into 3 inch (7.5 cm) pieces
1 oz (25 g) butter
1 medium onion, peeled and
thinly sliced
3 oz (75 g) carrot, peeled and
thinly sliced
8 fl oz (225 ml) made up Marigold
Swiss Bouillon stock
1 tablespoon chopped fresh parsley
salt and freshly milled black pepper

You will also need a frying pan with a
diameter of 10 inches (25.5 cm).

Celery has such a lot going for it as a raw ingredient in salads, and because of that we rather forget how good it is cooked and served as a vegetable. This method is delightfully quick and easy, and tastes just wonderful.

First of all melt the butter in the frying pan and begin to cook the onions for 3-4 minutes over a medium to high heat, until lightly golden, then add the carrots and cook for a further 2 minutes. Now add the celery and continue to fry for 5 minutes more, or until everything is slightly browned at the edges. Season with salt and black pepper, then pour in the hot stock and place a lid on the pan. Turn the heat down and simmer gently for 20 minutes, until the vegetables are almost tender, then take the lid off and increase the heat to medium and continue to simmer till the liquid has reduced and become slightly syrupy – about 5 minutes. Serve the celery with the juices poured over and sprinkled with the parsley.

Oven-Roasted Carrots with Garlic and Coriander

This is a recipe for the large, chunky carrots of winter, which lack the sweet, delicate flavour of new carrots in summer. In the oven they turn slightly blackened and caramelised at the edges, which, together with the coriander seeds, gives an added flavour dimension.

Serves 4
1 lb (450 g) winter carrots, wiped
if dusty
2 cloves garlic, peeled and crushed
1 dessertspoon coriander seeds
½ teaspoon black peppercorns
½ teaspoon Maldon sea salt
1 dessertspoon olive oil

You will also need a baking tray
measuring 10 x 14 inches (25.5 x
35 cm).

Pre-heat the oven to gas mark 8,
450°F (230°C).

Begin by cutting the carrots into 1½ inch (4 cm) chunks, but no smaller. Next, dry-roast the coriander seeds and peppercorns in a small frying pan or saucepan over a medium heat, stirring and tossing them around for 1-2 minutes, or until they begin to look toasted and start to jump in the pan. Now empty them into a pestle and mortar and crush them coarsely, then put the carrot chunks and crushed spices in a bowl.

Next, put the garlic cloves and salt in the mortar, crush to a purée, then whisk in the oil. Now toss this mixture around with the carrots and spices, then spread it out on the baking tray. Pop it into the oven on a high shelf and roast until the carrots are tender when tested with a skewer – 30-40 minutes.

Note: the carrots can be prepared well in advance and kept in a polythene bag in the fridge.

If you grow courgettes then this recipe is superb for serving the ones that – if you don't keep a sharp eye on them – become baby marrows overnight. If you don't, then this is still a superb way to serve courgettes as a salad with cold cuts.

To prepare the courgettes, trim off the stalky ends and, if they are small, simply slice them in half lengthways; if they are larger, cut them in 4 lengthways. Then place them in the steamer, pour in some boiling water, sprinkle the courgettes with a little salt and let them cook, covered, for 10-14 minutes, depending on their size – they need to be firm but tender.

Meanwhile, prepare the dressing by pounding the garlic with the salt in a pestle and mortar until it becomes a creamy paste. Now work in the mustard, then the vinegar and a generous amount of black pepper. Next add the oil and give everything a good whisk, then add the herbs. When the courgettes are ready, remove them to a shallow serving dish, then pour the dressing over them. Allow them to get cold, then cover with clingfilm and leave in a cool place or the fridge for several hours, turning them over in the marinade once or twice. These still taste good after 3 days, so you can make them in advance if you prefer.

Serves 4
1 lb (450 g) courgettes
Maldon sea salt

For the herb vinaigrette:
1 teaspoon snipped fresh chives
1 teaspoon finely chopped
fresh tarragon
1 teaspoon finely chopped fresh parsley
1 teaspoon fresh rosemary leaves,
bruised and finely chopped
1 clove garlic, peeled
1 teaspoon Maldon sea salt
1 rounded teaspoon wholegrain
mustard
2 tablespoons white wine vinegar
4 tablespoons olive oil
freshly milled black pepper

You will also need a steamer.

Below, left to right: Quick-Braised Celery, Oven-Roasted Carrots with Garlic and Coriander, Marinated Courgettes with a Herb Vinaigrette

Cabbage with Bacon, Apples and Cider

The flavours of this recipe combine beautifully, and I think it's an exceptionally good accompaniment to sausages and mash.

Serves 4-6

1 lb (450 g) green cabbage, cut into 4 sections and core and stalk removed
4½ oz (125 g) cubetti (cubed) pancetta or chopped bacon
1 Granny Smith apple, cored and chopped small
2 tablespoons strong dry cider
2 tablespoons cider vinegar
1 dessertspoon olive oil
1 small onion, peeled and finely chopped
2 cloves garlic, peeled and crushed
1 bay leaf
1 sprig fresh thyme
salt and freshly milled black pepper

You will also need a frying pan with a diameter of 10 inches (25.5 cm).

First of all shred the cabbage into ¼ inch (5 mm) pieces, then place the frying pan over direct heat and dry-fry the pancetta or bacon until crispy and golden – about 5 minutes – and remove it to a plate. Now add the oil to the pan and, when it's hot, fry the onions over a medium heat for 5 minutes: they also need to be turning golden brown at the edges. Now turn the heat up to its highest setting and add the cabbage, stirring continuously for about 3 minutes, keeping it on the move and tossing it around. Return the pancetta or bacon to the pan and add the apple, garlic, bay leaf and thyme, seasoning well with salt and black pepper. Toss the mixture around for a few seconds, then add the cider and cider vinegar and continue to cook, with the heat still high, for 1-2 minutes. Finally, remove the bay leaf and thyme, taste and season and serve as soon as possible.

Slow-Cooked Root Vegetable Soup

Something happens to vegetables when they're cooked very slowly for a long time: their flavour becomes mellow but at the same time more intense, and your kitchen is filled with aromas of goodness. This soup is also completely fat-free.

There's not much to do here once everything is peeled and chopped. All you do is place everything in the casserole and bring it up to a gentle simmer, then put the lid on, place it in the lowest part of the oven and leave it there for 3 hours, by which time the vegetables will be meltingly tender. Next remove the bay leaves and process or liquidise the soup in several batches to a purée, then gently re-heat, and serve the soup in bowls with a teaspoon of Greek yoghurt swirled into each and garnished with the fresh chives.

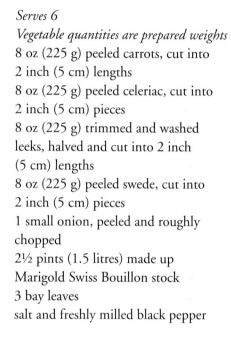

Serves 6
Vegetable quantities are prepared weights
8 oz (225 g) peeled carrots, cut into
2 inch (5 cm) lengths
8 oz (225 g) peeled celeriac, cut into
2 inch (5 cm) pieces
8 oz (225 g) trimmed and washed
leeks, halved and cut into 2 inch
(5 cm) lengths
8 oz (225 g) peeled swede, cut into
2 inch (5 cm) pieces
1 small onion, peeled and roughly
chopped
2½ pints (1.5 litres) made up
Marigold Swiss Bouillon stock
3 bay leaves
salt and freshly milled black pepper

To serve:
6 teaspoons fat-free Greek yoghurt
a few fresh chives, snipped

You will also need a lidded flameproof casserole with a capacity of 6 pints (3.5 litres).

Pre-heat the oven to gas mark 1, 275°F (140°C).

Bubble and Squeak Rösti

Bubble and squeak is a classic leftover recipe for greens, but making it rösti-style and adding some mature Cheddar add a new dimension. These little individual rösti are brilliant served with sausages or leftover cold turkey and ham and a selection of pickles.

Serves 4 (makes 8 rösti)
1 lb (450 g) Desirée or Romano potatoes (this should be 3 evenly sized potatoes weighing about 5 oz/150 g each)
3 oz (75 g) spring greens or green cabbage (trimmed weight)
2 oz (50 g) mature Cheddar, coarsely grated
1 tablespoon plain flour
1 oz (25 g) butter
1 dessertspoon olive oil
salt and freshly milled black pepper

You will also need a baking tray measuring 10 x 14 inches (25.5 x 35 cm).

First scrub the potatoes, then place them in a medium saucepan with a little salt. Pour boiling water over to just cover them, then simmer gently with a lid on for 8 minutes. Drain the potatoes, then, while they are cooling, remove any stalks from the spring greens or cabbage and finely shred the leaves into ¼ inch (5 mm) slices. This is easy if you form them into a roll and then slice them. Drop the spring greens or cabbage into boiling water for 2 minutes only, then drain and dry well.

When the potatoes have cooled, peel them, then, using the coarse side of a grater, grate them into a bowl. Season with salt and freshly milled black pepper, then add the grated cheese and greens or cabbage and, using 2 forks, lightly toss together.

To assemble the rösti, shape the mixture into rounds 3 inches (7.5 cm) wide and ½ inch (1 cm) thick. Press them firmly together to form little cakes and dust lightly with the flour. If you want to make them ahead, place them on a plate and cover with clingfilm – they will happily sit in the fridge for up to 6 hours.

To cook the rösti, pre-heat the oven to gas mark 7, 425°F (220°C), placing the baking tray on the top shelf of the oven. Melt the butter and add the oil, then brush the rösti on both sides with the mixture. When the oven is up to heat, place the rösti on the baking tray and return it to the top shelf of the oven for 15 minutes, then turn the rösti over and cook them for a further 10 minutes. Once cooked, it's all right to keep them warm for up to 30 minutes.

Pumpkin Soup with Toasted Sweetcorn

This is a very fine combination: the soft, velvety texture of the pumpkin makes the soup deliciously creamy and the toasted sweetcorn provides contrasting flavour and some crunch.

Begin by melting the butter in the saucepan, then add the onion and soften it for about 8 minutes. After that add the chopped pumpkin (or butternut squash), along with half the sweetcorn, then give everything a good stir and season with salt and pepper. Put the lid on and, keeping the heat low, allow the vegetables to sweat gently and release their juices – this should take about 10 minutes. Next, pour in the milk and stock and simmer gently for about 20 minutes. Put the lid on for this but leave a little gap (so it's not quite on) because, with the presence of the milk, it could boil over. Keep a close eye on it anyway.

While that's happening, pre-heat the grill to its highest setting for 10 minutes. Mix the rest of the sweetcorn with the melted butter, spread it out on a baking tray, season with salt and pepper and pop it under the hot grill about 3 inches (7.5 cm) from the heat – it will take about 8 minutes to become nicely toasted and golden, but remember to move the sweetcorn around on the baking tray halfway through.

When the soup is ready, pour it into a food processor or blender and blend it to a purée, leaving a little bit of texture – it doesn't need to be absolutely smooth. You will probably need to do this in 2 batches. Serve the soup in warm bowls with the toasted sweetcorn sprinkled over.

Serves 6

1 lb 8 oz (700 g) pumpkin or butternut squash, peeled, deseeded and chopped into 1 inch (2.5 cm) dice
1 lb 4 oz (570 g) sweetcorn (off the cob weight, from 5-6 cobs)
1 oz (25 g) butter
1 medium onion, peeled and finely chopped
10 fl oz (275 ml) whole milk
1¼ pints (725 ml) made up Marigold Swiss Bouillon stock
1 teaspoon melted butter, for the sweetcorn
salt and freshly milled black pepper

You will also need a lidded saucepan with a capacity of 3 pints (1.75 litres).

16

Salads and dressings for beginners

The title of this chapter is meant, hopefully, to reassure those who find themselves rather confused about precisely what a well-dressed salad should actually be, something that has somehow eclipsed the simple joy of dressing and eating a salad.

Forty years ago olive oil was, in this country, medicinal and came from chemists, and because we are a beer-brewing country rather than a winemaking one, our vinegar was distilled from malt. Boots' olive oil and malt vinegar were, as you can imagine, not the desired components of a good salad dressing, and in the lean post-war years salads in ordinary households were served with a dressing of bottled salad cream, a modern commercial version of an 18th-century recipe for English salad sauce made with cream and egg yolks.

We have now, thankfully, moved on from there, but, in my opinion, we have perhaps gone too far. Yes, it's wonderful to have a choice of olive oils and a selection of wine vinegars, but supermarkets now have wall-to-wall oils and sometimes half as many vinegars. It seems that every country in the world can produce oils and vinegars, and not just from the humble olive or the grape but from everything under the sun – witness pumpkin seed oil, grapefruit oil, seaweed vinegar, rose petal vinegar! Even tourist and gift shops sell designer oils and vinegars, which are often made from some unlikely ingredients. They are utterly superfluous to most people's everyday needs and end up lurking unused and abandoned in the back of a cupboard. Even worse, I get letters asking me what to do with them!

Because I feel that, were I a beginner today, I wouldn't actually know where to start learning, I thought it might be helpful to concentrate on basic everyday salads and dressings. Oils do not have a very long shelf life, so if we want to enjoy them at their best, having half a dozen varieties on the go is not helpful unless you are doing an awful lot of cooking on a daily basis. So let's start with what, in my opinion, is the best type of olive oil for a salad dressing, and tackle the most pertinent question first.

What is extra virgin olive oil?

Before we can understand 'extra virgin' we first have to clarify the word 'virgin'. What it describes, quite simply, is oil pressed from the fruit of the olive tree under conditions that cause no deterioration of the finished oil – the olives are not damaged, bruised or subjected to adverse temperatures or too much air, and they must not have undergone any additional treatment such as heat or blending (other than with other virgin olive oil). The supreme quality is measured by acidity or, more precisely, the lack of it – too much acidity gives a harsher flavour, which can, with skill, be refined out. What is simply termed olive oil is often a blend of lesser-quality refined oils with some virgin added to give the right balance of flavour.

Extra virgin olive oil could, in fact, have another name – perfect virgin olive oil, because this is precisely what it is: virgin olive oil with no flaws whatsoever. By law the acidity of extra virgin olive oil is never more than 1 per cent, and what does this mean? Flavour. First there is an aromatic fragrance, then a sweetness not marred by acidity, and then an abundant taste of fruit, verdant and luscious, not tasting like olives exactly but like some other mysterious, unique fruit. Like very fine wine, extra virgin olive oil is both rich and flavoursome.

Which country produces the best olive oil?

Difficult to answer, this. The olives of each country have their own character and flavour, which will even vary from region to region: a Tuscan olive oil, for instance, is different to a Ligurian olive oil. If I were being a purist I would suggest that Provençal dishes should be made with oils made in Provence, and Italian, Greek or Spanish dishes made with the oil produced in that country. But unless you do masses of cooking it's best to find an olive oil you're happy with, and my recommendation is to have an extra virgin oil for special occasions, along with an everyday blended oil.

What about other oils?

What you need to be careful of is having endless bottles of oils that you hardly use, because, as I've said, the shelf life of any oil is never very long. However, I would include the following in my store cupboard – along with olive oil – as a good selection for both cooking and making dressings.

Groundnut oil

An excellent all-rounder with the advantage of having no marked flavour yet at the same time being quite luscious. It is perfect for making mayonnaise, with just a little olive oil added for flavour, and it's an extremely useful oil for cooking – oriental dishes in particular, because with these the flavour of olive oil is alien and too strong. Warning: because groundnut oil is made from peanuts, people who suffer from any nut allergy should avoid it (and warn anyone cooking for them as well).

Grapeseed oil

This is an alternative mildly flavoured oil. It's more expensive than groundnut oil, but if you are at all worried about the nut-allergy problem, grapeseed oil will do the same work both in dressings and in cooking.

Sesame oil

An excellent oil, and rich in nutty sesame flavour. It's great in oriental dishes and dressings, but needs to be used very sparingly, as the flavour can be overwhelming.

Walnut oil

This is a great addition to the repertoire of oils. It has all the flavour of crushed walnuts and is therefore particularly good in salads that contain walnuts. However, it does become rancid quite quickly, so monitor its shelf life once it's opened.

Flavoured oils

These are definitely not for me. Apart from the fact that they take up valuable storage space, it seems logical that if you want to incorporate other flavours in your oils, they are best added fresh. So add your own garlic, chilli, lemon or herbs and so on as and when you want to.

How to store oils

This has to be in the coolest-possible place, though not in the fridge, as oil solidifies when it gets too cold. Light is not good for oils, either, so a cool, dark corner would be the best place to store them. Most oils have date stamps, so watch these, and although it is more expensive to buy in smaller quantities, it is still cheaper than throwing out stale oil that never got used.

Vinegars for salads

Personally I would want to have about half a dozen vinegars available. They keep better and for longer than oils, so it's good to have a varied selection suitable for different kinds of salads, confits and sometimes cooked dishes. You will find dozens of designer varieties available but, as always, I say keep it simple and buy the best quality you can afford – some cheaper vinegars are too acidic and lacking in flavour.

Wine vinegar

Originally the French word *vinaigre*, from which we get our word vinegar, meant sour wine, but now it embraces all similar liquids where alcohol is turned into acetic acid. As you might expect, wine vinegar comes either red or white, and the best quality is that made by the Orléans method, which, because of its long, slow fermentation in oak casks, has depth of flavour without the overpowering acidity.

Balsamic vinegar

After struggling in the past to find good-quality wine vinegar, when *aceto balsamico* (as it's called in Italy) appeared, it was like discovering heaven. It is not a wine vinegar but a grape vinegar, made from fresh-pressed grape juice, aged in barrels of oak, ash, cherry wood, mulberry and juniper – all contributing to its unique flavour. Each year new grape juice is added and skilfully blended over a period of 8 to 12 years to produce the dark, sweet-sour amber liquid that makes one of the best salad dressings of all.

Sherry vinegar

A very special vinegar made, if I may say, from a very special drink. I love Spanish sherry, both to drink and to cook with, and the vinegar from the sherry grape must has its own delightfully rich, sweet, nutty flavour. Though quite different from *balsamico*, it is equally good sprinkled over salads and cooked vegetables just by itself.

Cider vinegar

As you'd expect, a vinegar distilled from cider, milder and less acidic than wine vinegar. It has a lovely fragrant apple flavour and is good for salad dressings, particularly if the salad contains fruit.

Rice vinegar

It's marvellous how vinegar turns up around the world distilled from whatever grows locally, so it's not surprising that in the Far East vinegar is made from rice. The Japanese have the best quality, and I always have some handy for making oriental salads and dipping sauces.

Lemons and limes

There are times when vinegar can be dispensed with and the acidic content of a salad dressing can be provided by lemon or lime juice. In fact I would say that if you want to cut the fat in your diet for any reason, lemon and lime juice alone squeezed over salad ingredients give a lovely zest and piquancy of their own. Lime is especially good for oriental dressings, while the combination of lemons and olive oil gives the classic flavours of the Mediterranean to a bowl of very simple salad leaves.

Other ingredients

Mustard, both plain and wholegrain, has an emulsifying effect that thickens the dressing. Garlic, if you like it, adds flavour, and Maldon sea salt and freshly milled black pepper are two absolute essentials.

What makes the perfect dressing?

For once there are no rules. Food snobs sometimes like to make them, but the truth is it's about personal taste: some like more vinegar, some less, some like to add sugar, others (me) never do. So when you begin to make salad dressings, it's you who should taste and you who should decide just how much of this or that you want.

Equipment

Do invest in a pestle and mortar, a simple time-honoured item that will serve you for a lifetime. With a pestle and mortar you can pound and crush the ingredients needed for making most salad dressings. Blenders will do the job and are occasionally preferable for large quantities, but you don't always want to be bothered with them for small amounts. Once you have blended your dressing, a small loop whisk, *right*, will combine it quickly and efficiently; alternatively you can keep a small screw-top jar handy and use it to shake and amalgamate the ingredients together.

Salad ingredients

Herein lies the subject for a book by itself, because most ingredients can be made into salads – meat, fish, vegetables, rice and so on. Here I will confine myself to specific salad vegetables, starting with a very pertinent point.

Lettuce or leaves?

For me it would be lettuce all the way; a salad needs bite, crunchiness and some substance. Yes, there are leaves that make good salads, but there are now too many kinds of designer leaves grown, bought and used merely for their looks. That's OK up to a point – we can all appreciate a pretty garnish of colourful leaves – but delicate leaves that get soggy when they're washed, before being packed in plastic bags, and just disintegrate once they meet with a dressing are, in my opinion, to be avoided (except for garnishing).

What kind of lettuce?

Again, it's what you personally like, but my own recommendations would be as follows.

Round lettuce

Sometimes called Butterhead, it may not look very promising, but usually has a cluster of crisp, sweet leaves nestling in the centre that partner most dressings very well.

Cos lettuce

If fresh, this is reliably crisp and crunchy, with a good flavour, and can take strong, thick, creamy dressings such as Caesar.

Crispheart lettuce

As good as its name, this is a lettuce with good flavour and lots of crunch.

Escarole lettuce and Quattro Stagioni (Four Seasons)

A colourful pair, the former has pale-green leaves and the latter pinkish-red edges. They are not crisp, but their flavour is good as long as you give them lighter dressings.

Frisée

This comes with very crunchy, curly leaves, but because it is related to the chicory family, it has a slightly bitter taste, which is fine if matched with highly flavoured dressings.

Rocket

I make no secret of the fact that this is one of my favourite salad leaves. Why? It's traditionally English and has been used in salads since Elizabethan times. It has a lovely concentrated buttery flavour and goes with any dressing. Not, I think, good as a salad leaf just on its own, because it's not crisp, and a lot of it seems somehow to be too concentrated and 'in your face'. However, added fifty-fifty to crisp lettuce, it makes, I think, one of the nicest green salads of all.

Lamb's lettuce

This leaf comes in delicate little sprigs with clusters of leaves, and is good both for garnishing and mixing with other lettuce types. Because it does not keep well, it needs to be used fairly quickly.

Watercress

Popular with everyone, watercress is a bit like rocket, with its own distinctive, fresh, peppery flavour. I think it's too strong to be used on its own, but it's wonderful combined with lettuce, used as a garnish and for giving its own unmatched flavour to soups and sauces.

Not recommended

Given that everything is largely a matter of personal taste, I would nevertheless explain why I would not recommend certain lettuces and leaves. Iceberg is crunchy but that's all: it tastes of absolutely nothing. As for Little Gem, I have a feeling this was originally grown for its long shelf life. For housebound people, a Little Gem is better than no lettuce at all, but for those who have a choice I would give it a miss; it's rather tough and stalky, with an earthy flavour. Lollo Rosso, Lollo Biondo, Oak Leaf and others are good to look at but pretty dull to eat.

How to prepare salad leaves

All lettuces and salad leaves should be eaten as fresh as possible, but first of all I've found the best way to store lettuces is to remove the root, but otherwise leave them whole and enclose them in a polythene bag in the lowest part of the fridge. I believe washing should be avoided if possible, as once the leaves are wet it's difficult to dry them again and you simply can't get dressing on to wet salad leaves. What I prefer to do is take a damp piece of kitchen paper and wipe each leaf – this way the lettuce leaves remain dry and can more easily be coated with dressing. Now, I realise many people will not agree with me here and will want to wash the leaves: in that case plunge the separated leaves briefly into cold water and place them in a salad basket, then either hang them up after a good shaking or else swing the basket round and round out-of-doors. Finish off by drying the leaves carefully with kitchen paper.

Never use a knife when you prepare lettuce, because cutting tends to brown the edges of the leaves. Breaking up the leaves too soon can cause them to go limp quickly, so always leave them whole, if possible, until you're ready to serve the salad (and even then use your hands to tear them rather than a knife).

Other salad ingredients

Avocados

A ripe, buttery-textured avocado, served with a really good vinaigrette, is simplicity itself. The way to tell if an avocado is ripe is to hold it in the palm of your hand and give it some gentle pressure; if ripe, you'll feel it 'give' slightly.

Salad or spring onions

Indispensable in the kitchen, and especially in salads. You won't find the best kind in the supermarket, but if you are near a farm shop, tiny, thin, very young spring onions are delicious served whole with just the root trimmed.

Cucumber

A home-grown cucumber in the late-English summer is a luxury for its fragrant, cool, pronounced cucumber flavour – if you can get hold of one. In any case, English home-grown cucumbers do have the best flavour and it's difficult to find a well-flavoured imported cucumber in the winter. For the best results, and if you have time, salting, as you would an aubergine, does draw out some of the excess water content and helps concentrate the flavour.

What about the seeds? No problem. These are part and parcel of the cucumber, so I never bother to remove them. Then there's the question of whether to peel or not to peel. I say not, because I like the colour, texture and flavour of the peel, but if the cucumber has a very tough skin, use a potato peeler so only the outer skin is pared off. It's also possible to just pare off strips of skin, a kind of halfway house. The exception is small, ridged cucumbers, which sometimes have quite knobbly skins and are usually best peeled.

Chicory heads

Tight little buds of crunchy leaves, sometimes with pale-green edges, sometimes pink-edged. They have a slightly bitter taste that calls for a flavourful dressing.

Fennel

This is brilliant cooked, but sliced very thinly it's also lovely raw in a salad.

Beetroot

This can be added to salads cooked (see page 341), or else raw and thinly shredded into julienne strips.

How to make a vinaigrette dressing

It has to be said that this is always going to be a matter of personal taste according to how much acidity you like and what your preferences are as to flavourings and so on. I seem to suffer from some kind of mental handicap with dressings, which roughly means that other people's salad dressings always seem to taste better than my own – my husband's particularly. Here I have set out my favourite version of vinaigrette, but it's adaptable: you can use red or white wine vinegar, a different mustard or no mustard; if you like it sharper, use a higher ratio of vinegar, and if you want it less sharp use a higher ratio of oil. The following combination is my own personal favourite.

Begin by placing the salt in the mortar and crush it quite coarsely, then add the garlic and, as you begin to crush it and it comes into contact with the salt, it will quickly break down into a purée. Next add the mustard powder and really work it in, giving it about 20 seconds of circular movements to get it thoroughly blended. After that, add some freshly milled black pepper.

Now add the vinegars and work these in in the same way, then add the oil, switch to a small whisk (see the photograph on page 371) and give everything a really good, thorough whisking. Whisk again before dressing the salad.

Note: vinaigrette dressing is best made and used as fresh as possible, because once the oil is exposed to the air it loses some of its fragrance. If you want to prepare things ahead, proceed up to the vinegar stage and leave adding the oil till the last minute.

Serves 4-6; halve the ingredients for 2-3
1 rounded teaspoon Maldon sea salt
1 clove garlic, peeled
1 rounded teaspoon mustard powder
1 dessertspoon balsamic vinegar
1 dessertspoon sherry vinegar
5 tablespoons extra virgin olive oil
freshly milled black pepper

You will also need a pestle and mortar.

American Chef's Salad

A chef's salad is so named because it is supposed to be an innovative way of using whatever you happen to have handy to create a main-course salad. Ham, salami, chicken, turkey or any cold meat could be used for this one; similarly any kind of cheese or salad vegetable. This happens to be one of my favourite combinations, but once you get the gist of it I'm sure you'll have lots of other ideas.

Serves 6-8 as a main course

6 oz (175 g) lean streaky bacon
8 oz (225 g) French garlic sausage in one piece
4 oz (110 g) small open-cup mushrooms
3 oz (75 g) Roquefort or other cheese
2 ripe avocados
1 round lettuce, outer leaves removed
1 Cos lettuce, outer leaves removed
2 oz (50 g) watercress, stalks removed
2 oz (50 g) rocket, stalks removed
4 spring onions, finely chopped

For the dressing:

5 fl oz (150 ml) soured cream
1 small clove garlic, peeled and crushed
2 tablespoons good-quality mayonnaise
1 heaped teaspoon wholegrain mustard
2 tablespoons extra virgin olive oil
1 tablespoon white wine vinegar
1 tablespoon lemon juice
salt and freshly milled black pepper

Before you start, pre-heat the grill to its highest setting and let it heat up for at least 10 minutes. Meanwhile, combine all the dressing ingredients in a jug or bowl and whisk them together well, tasting to check the seasoning.

Now place the bacon on some foil on the grill pan, and grill until it's very crispy – about 7 minutes – then remove it to drain on some kitchen paper and crumble it into small pieces. Next slice the garlic sausage, first into ¼ inch (5 mm) slices, then cut the slices into ¼ inch (5 mm) strips. After that, wipe the mushrooms and slice them fairly thinly (but not paper-thin). Next crumble the cheese and peel and slice the avocados.

To serve the salad, tear up the lettuce leaves and place them in a large bowl with the watercress and rocket. Scatter in the bacon, sausage, mushrooms, cheese and avocado and mix well. Just before serving, add half the dressing and mix together. Add the remaining dressing and toss again so that everything gets a good coating. Finally, sprinkle over the spring onions and serve immediately. This needs lots of good rustic bread on the table.

Broad-Bean Salad with Pancetta and Sherry Vinegar

The fresh broad bean season seems to be so short, I always feel the need to feast as much as possible when I can, hence this salad. It's good as a first course or to serve alongside other salads in a cold buffet. Remember, when buying broad beans in the shell you'll need 1 lb (450 g) in weight to get 4 oz (110 g) once shelled.

Begin this by pre-heating the grill to its highest setting for 10 minutes or so, then place the pancetta (or bacon) on a piece of foil and grill it 3 inches (7.5 cm) from the heat for about 4 minutes; it's important to get it really crisp. Then, as soon as it's cool enough to handle, crumble it into tiny pieces. Now place the shelled beans in a medium saucepan, add a level teaspoon of salt and pour in enough boiling water to barely cover them. When they come back to the boil, put a lid on, turn the heat down and simmer them gently for about 5 minutes. It's very important not to overcook them, so a timer would be useful here.

While they're cooking, make the dressing by first crushing the garlic and salt with a pestle and mortar until it becomes a creamy paste, then work in the mustard powder and follow this with the vinegar and a generous amount of coarsely milled black pepper. Next add the oil and give everything a good whisk. When the beans are cooked, drain them in a colander, then place them in a serving bowl, toss them in the dressing and give it all a good stir. Now sprinkle in the pancetta, herbs and chopped shallots, taste to check the seasoning, give everything one more good mix, then cover the bowl with a cloth and leave aside for a couple of hours so the beans can absorb all the flavours.

Serves 4 generously
4 lb (1.8 kg) young broad beans, shelled
4 oz (110 g) sliced smoked pancetta or smoked streaky bacon
1 tablespoon chopped mixed fresh herbs (parsley, chives, basil and thyme, for example)
2 shallots, peeled and finely chopped
salt and freshly milled black pepper

For the dressing:
2 tablespoons sherry vinegar
1 large clove garlic, peeled
2 teaspoons Maldon sea salt
2 teaspoons mustard powder
5 tablespoons extra virgin olive oil
freshly milled black pepper

White Bean and Tuna Fish Salad with Lemon Pepper Dressing

This is my version of an old Italian favourite, and I think the addition of a sharp lemon dressing and some buttery rocket leaves gives a lovely edge.

*Serves 4 as a main course or
6 as a starter*
9 oz (250 g) cannellini beans
2 x 200 g tins tuna fish in oil
1 oz (25 g) rocket, stalks removed
2 oz (50 g) red onion, peeled and
sliced into thin rounds
salt and freshly milled black pepper

For the dressing:
grated zest 1 lemon
3 tablespoons lemon juice
1 rounded teaspoon black peppercorns
2 cloves garlic, peeled
1 tablespoon Maldon sea salt
1 heaped teaspoon mustard powder
3 tablespoons extra virgin olive oil
3 tablespoons tuna oil, reserved from
the tins of tuna

Begin this the night before you are going to make the salad by placing the beans in a bowl and covering them with cold water to soak. Next day, drain the beans, then put them in a large saucepan, cover with fresh water and bring them up to simmering point. Boil for 10 minutes, then cover and simmer gently for 1¼-1½ hours, or until tender.

Meanwhile, empty the tuna fish into a sieve fitted over a bowl and allow it to drain. Then, to make the dressing, first crush the garlic and salt using a pestle and mortar till the garlic is pulverised, then work the mustard powder into this. Now push the mixture to one side, add the peppercorns and crush these fairly coarsely. Next add the grated lemon zest, along with the lemon juice, olive oil and tuna oil (the rest of the tuna oil can be discarded). Whisk everything together very thoroughly, then, when the beans are cooked, drain them, rinse out the saucepan and return the beans to it. Now pour the dressing over while the beans are still warm, give everything a good stir and season generously.

To serve the salad, arrange three-quarters of the rocket leaves over the base of a serving dish, spoon the beans on top and add the tuna fish in chunks. Then add the rest of the rocket leaves, pushing some of the leaves and chunks of tuna right in amongst the beans. Finally, arrange the onion slices on top and serve straight away, allowing people to help themselves. Warm, crusty ciabatta bread would be an excellent accompaniment.
Note: if you forget to soak the beans overnight, you can rinse the beans with cold water and place them in a saucepan, cover with plenty of water, bring up the boil for 10 minutes, then turn off the heat and leave them to soak for 2 hours. Next, bring them up to the boil and boil gently for 1½-2 hours, or until the beans are tender.

Char-Grilled Aubergine and Roasted-Tomato Salad with Feta Cheese

Serves 4

2 medium aubergines
8 small, ripe plum tomatoes
7 oz (200 g) Feta cheese, cut into thin slices
8 tablespoons extra virgin olive oil
1 heaped tablespoon torn fresh basil leaves
2 tablespoons balsamic vinegar
4 oz (110 g) assorted salad leaves
7 fl oz (200 ml) half-fat crème fraîche
a little paprika
salt and freshly milled black pepper

You will also need a baking tray measuring 10 x 14 inches (25.5 x 35 cm), and a ridged grill pan.

Pre-heat the oven to gas mark 6, 400°F (200°C).

I am indebted to Chris Payne, who very generously gave me this splendid recipe. If you don't possess a ridged grill pan, you could grill the aubergine slices till nicely browned and tender. Either way, this is a truly delicious combination of textures and flavours.

First of all skin the tomatoes by covering them with boiling water for 1 minute, then drain them and slip off their skins. Cut them in half and place them on the baking tray, cut-side up, then season well, drizzle 1 tablespoon of the olive oil over and place them on the top shelf of the oven to roast for 50-60 minutes. After this time, leave them aside to cool.

While they're cooling, cut the aubergines across into ½ inch (1 cm) slices, lay the slices on a board and lightly sprinkle them with salt on both sides. Leave them for 20 minutes to draw out some of the excess moisture, then blot them dry with kitchen paper. Next, brush them on both sides using 1 tablespoon of the olive oil and season with freshly milled black pepper. Brush the grill pan lightly with olive oil and place it over a high heat, then, when it is very hot, cook the aubergines in batches for about 2½ minutes on each side (this should take about 20 minutes in all).

Now pour the remaining 6 tablespoons of olive oil into a large bowl, add the basil and balsamic vinegar, then toss the cooked aubergines in this marinade and leave them in a cool place until you are ready to serve.

Divide the salad leaves between 4 plates and arrange the tomatoes and aubergines alternately all around. Then place equal quantities of the Feta slices in the middle of each salad and drizzle with the remaining marinade. Finally, put 1 tablespoon of crème fraîche on top of each salad and sprinkle a little paprika over.

Spiced Carnaroli Rice Salad

This is a lovely spicy salad with Moroccan overtones – perfect for a buffet lunch, party or serving with cold cuts and spicy chutneys.

Serves 4

10 fl oz (275 ml) carnaroli rice
¾ teaspoon cumin seeds
½ teaspoon coriander seeds
2 cardamom pods
1 dessertspoon groundnut or other flavourless oil, plus 1 teaspoon
1 oz (25 g) pine nuts
1½ oz (40 g) currants
1½ oz (40 g) ready-to-eat dried apricots, chopped into ¼ inch (5 mm) pieces
1 inch (2.5 cm) piece cinnamon stick
1 bay leaf
1 pint (570 ml) boiling water
1 large red onion
3 spring onions, trimmed and finely chopped
Maldon sea salt

For the dressing:

2 tablespoons groundnut or other flavourless oil
4 tablespoons lemon juice

You will also need a lidded frying pan with a diameter of 8 inches (20 cm).

First roast and crush the spices. To do this you need to place the cumin and coriander seeds and cardamom pods in the frying pan over a medium heat and stir and toss them around for 1-2 minutes, or until they begin to look toasted and start to jump in the pan. Now transfer them to a pestle and mortar and crush them to a powder.

After that, add the dessertspoon of oil to the frying pan set over a medium heat. When the oil is hot, sauté the nuts, currants and apricots until the nuts are golden brown. Next stir in the rice and roasted spices, cinnamon stick and bay leaf and turn the grains over in the pan till they're nicely coated and glistening with oil. Now pour in the boiling water, add some salt, stir once only, then put the lid on, turn the heat down to its lowest setting and let the rice cook for exactly 15 minutes. Don't remove the lid, and remember what was said on page 200 – absolutely no stirring.

While the rice is cooking, pre-heat the grill to its highest setting. Peel and slice the red onion into ¼ inch (5 mm) rounds, then brush one side with half the teaspoon of oil, place them on a grilling rack directly under the grill and cook till the edges have blackened – 4-5 minutes – then turn them over. Brush the other side with the rest of the oil and grill them as before. After that, remove them and let them cool.

When the rice is cooked, take the pan off the heat, remove the lid and cover with a clean tea cloth for 5 minutes to absorb the steam. Now empty the rice into a warm serving dish and add about two-thirds of the spring onions. Whisk the oil and lemon juice together and pour this over the rice before fluffing it up with a fork, then garnish the salad with the grilled onions and remaining spring onions before serving.

Salade Niçoise

Nothing has changed much here over the long years I've been cooking and writing recipes – this is still one of the best combinations of salad ingredients ever invented. Slick restaurants often attempt to do trendy versions with salmon, char-grilled tuna and the like, but the original reigns supreme. In Provence lettuce was sometimes used, sometimes not, but I now like to abandon the lettuce in favour of a few rocket leaves.

To make the vinaigrette dressing, start off with a pestle and mortar. First of all crush the flakes of sea salt to a powder, then add the peeled clove of garlic and pound them together, which will immediately bring out the garlic's juices and turn it into a smooth paste. Next add the mustard powder, work that in, then add the vinegar and some freshly milled black pepper and mix thoroughly until the salt dissolves. Finally, add the olive oil. Now stir the herbs into the vinaigrette – it will look rather thick but will spread itself out beautifully once you toss it into the salad. Just before you dress the salad, pour everything into a screw-top jar and shake vigorously so it's thoroughly blended.

For the salad, begin by preparing the tomatoes. Place them in a bowl, pour boiling water over them, then, after 1 minute, drain and slip off their skins, protecting your hands with a cloth if you need to. Now cut each tomato in half and hold each half in the palm of your hand (cut-side up), then turn your hand over and squeeze gently until the seeds come out; it's best to do this over a plate or bowl to catch the seeds. Now cut each tomato into quarters. Then, in a large salad bowl, arrange the tomatoes, rocket leaves, cucumber, potatoes, beans and chopped shallots in layers, sprinkling a little of the dressing in as you go. Next arrange chunks of tuna and egg quarters on top, then arrange the anchovies in a criss-cross pattern, followed by a scattering of olives, the chopped parsley and a final sprinkling of dressing. Now you need to serve the salad fairly promptly, and needless to say it needs lots of warm, crusty baguette with Normandy butter to go with it.

Serves 4-6 as a light lunch
12 oz (350 g) red ripe tomatoes
4 oz (110 g) rocket, stalks removed
½ small young cucumber, cut into smallish chunks
1 lb (450 g) new potatoes, cooked and sliced
4 oz (110 g) French beans, cooked
4 shallots, peeled and finely chopped
2 x 200 g tins tuna fish in oil, well drained
2 large hard-boiled eggs, peeled and quartered
2 oz (50 g) anchovy fillets
2 oz (50 g) black olives
1 tablespoon chopped fresh parsley

For the vinaigrette dressing:
1 teaspoon Maldon sea salt
1 clove garlic, peeled
1 rounded teaspoon mustard powder
1 tablespoon wine or balsamic vinegar
6 tablespoons extra virgin olive oil
2 tablespoons finely chopped fresh herbs (chives, tarragon, parsley, basil, chervil or mint, for example); if using fresh oregano and thyme, use just ½ teaspoon each in the mix
freshly milled black pepper

Thai Grilled-Beef Salad with Grapes

This recipe was given to me by chef Norbert Kostner at the Mandarin Oriental Hotel in Bangkok when I visited the cookery school there. It's lovely served as a first course or included in a cold-buffet menu.

Serves 4

1 lb (450 g) rump steak in 1 piece,
1 inch (2.5 cm) thick
6 oz (175 g) red or black seedless
grapes, halved
2-3 medium red chillies, halved
and deseeded, or 3-4 Bird Eye
chillies, whole
2 cloves garlic, peeled
1 inch (2.5 cm) piece fresh root
ginger, peeled
6 sprigs fresh coriander, plus 3
tablespoons chopped fresh coriander
1 sprig fresh mint, plus 3 tablespoons
chopped fresh mint
3 tablespoons Thai fish sauce
grated zest 1 lime, plus 3 tablespoons
lime juice (juice of about 2 limes)
2 teaspoons palm sugar or light
brown soft sugar
3-4 stems lemon grass, very finely sliced
6 kaffir lime leaves, rolled into a
cigar shape and very finely shredded
(optional)
4 oz (110 g) rocket, stalks removed

To garnish:
1 teaspoon toasted sesame seeds
1 teaspoon chopped fresh chives

Pre-heat the grill to its highest setting.

First you need to grill the beef in advance, and for medium-rare give it 2-3 minutes on each side. Be careful not to overcook the steak: it needs to be quite pink, as the lime juice in the dressing 'cooks' the beef a bit further. If you'd prefer to use a ridged grill pan, pre-heat it for 10 minutes, then cook the steak for 1½-2 minutes on each side. Once the beef is grilled, allow it to rest for 10 minutes before slicing it into thin strips.

Meanwhile, to make the dressing, blend the chillies, garlic, ginger and sprigs of coriander and mint in a processor until finely chopped, then add the fish sauce, lime juice and sugar and whiz again to blend everything. Pour the dressing over the beef strips, then sprinkle the lemon grass, lime leaves (if using), lime zest and remaining herbs over. Add the rocket and grapes and toss everything together, then scatter the garnish over.

American Blue-Cheese Dressing

I love American salad dressings, and especially this one. The blue cheese can be Roquefort, if you want to splash out, or Gorgonzola, which crumbles particularly well. The only stipulation is that the cheese has to be gutsy; a subtle, faint-hearted one will get lost amongst all the other strong flavours.

Start off by crushing the garlic clove (or cloves), together with the salt, to a creamy mass in a pestle and mortar, then add the mustard and work that in. Next add the lemon juice, vinegar and, after that, the oil. Mix everything together thoroughly, then, in a bowl, combine the soured cream and mayonnaise and gradually whisk into the dressing ingredients. When all is thoroughly blended, add the chopped spring onions and the crumbled blue cheese and season with freshly milled pepper. The dressing is now ready to use, and I think a few crunchy croutons are a nice addition here.

To make these, toss ¼ inch (5 mm) cubes of bread – approximately 4 oz (110 g) in all – in a bowl with a dessertspoon of olive oil, spread them out on a baking sheet and bake in an oven pre-heated to gas mark 5, 375°F (190°C) for 10 minutes.

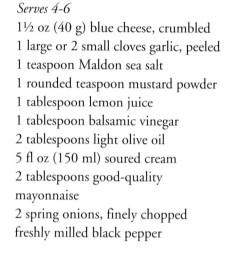

Serves 4-6
1½ oz (40 g) blue cheese, crumbled
1 large or 2 small cloves garlic, peeled
1 teaspoon Maldon sea salt
1 rounded teaspoon mustard powder
1 tablespoon lemon juice
1 tablespoon balsamic vinegar
2 tablespoons light olive oil
5 fl oz (150 ml) soured cream
2 tablespoons good-quality mayonnaise
2 spring onions, finely chopped
freshly milled black pepper

Marinated Kipper Fillets and Potato Salad with Coriander Seeds and Cracked Pepper

Serves 4 as a main course or 8 as a starter
6 kipper fillets
2 teaspoons coriander seeds
2 teaspoons black peppercorns
6 shallots, peeled and cut into
thin rings
2 bay leaves, each snipped into
3-4 pieces
1 lemon, thinly sliced and cut in half
juice 2 lemons
1 dessertspoon dark brown soft sugar
2 rounded teaspoons wholegrain
mustard
5 fl oz (150 ml) extra virgin olive oil

To serve:
1 lb 8 oz (700 g) new potatoes,
scrubbed but skins left on
a few sprigs fresh flat-leaf parsley
Maldon sea salt

You will also need a shallow dish with
a capacity of 1½ pints (850 ml).

This is a salad that can mostly be made way, way ahead – up to a week, believe it or not. Then all you do is steam some potatoes to go with it, or alternatively you can serve the kipper fillets as they are, and instead of the potatoes have a pile of buttered wholemeal bread on the table.

To get the best fragrance from the coriander seeds and peppercorns, pop them in a small frying pan and place them over a medium heat to dry-roast for 2-3 minutes. Move them around the pan until they start to jump, then put them in a pestle and mortar and crush them fairly coarsely.

Next, prepare the kipper fillets by turning them skin-side up on a flat surface, then, with a sharp knife, lift the skin away at the tail end. Now discard the knife and simply pull the skin from the flesh. If it clings at any point, just use the knife again and ease it away. Now snip each one in 4 lengthways, then cut them into 1½ inch (4 cm) pieces and lay the strips in the dish – this will probably have to be in 2 layers to fit them in – sprinkling the pepper and coriander mixture all over each layer. Next, scatter the shallot rings, bay leaves and lemon slices all over, tucking them in-between the kipper fillets here and there.

Now, in a bowl, whisk together the lemon juice, sugar, mustard and oil, and when they're very thoroughly mixed, pour the mixture over the kippers. Cover with clingfilm and put a plate on top with some kind of weight on it to keep the kippers submerged, then place in the fridge and let them marinate for a minimum of 24 hours or up to a week.

When you want to serve the salad it's important to remove the kippers from the fridge at least an hour beforehand. Now steam the potatoes, generously sprinkled with salt, for 20-30 minutes (depending on their size), and, when they're cooked, place a cloth over them to absorb the steam for 5 minutes. Chop them roughly, divide them between the plates, spoon some of the kipper marinade over, then arrange the kippers and everything else on top. Finish off with a few sprigs of flat-leaf parsley.

17

What's new in the dairy

'You may drive out Nature with a pitchfork, but she will ever hurry back to triumph in stealth over your foolish contempt.'

Never were these words, from Horace's *Epistles*, more true than in the dairy. In my long career of food writing, I have seen fashions, fads and so-called health scares arrive with the force of a destructive tidal wave one moment, then recede and disappear without trace the next, leaving everyone reeling in confusion.

My conclusion is that nutritionists a) often disagree with each other, and b) change their minds anyway as more and more facts come to light.

Meanwhile nature, thankfully, remains steadfast and does – if you wait long enough – still have the last word. Perhaps dairy foods more than any other have suffered being in the nutritional firing line in the past, but thankfully they have now been reinstated, as everyone's now discovered that the so-called-healthy hydrogenated-fat alternatives were not so healthy after all, and added to that, nature's very own dairy products have a unique and magical property called flavour that no man-made alternative has ever been able to match.

The fat problem

Yes, it's true that since we have evolved a more sedentary way of living we have had to cut the fat content in our diets. We now no longer serve our vegetables swimming with butter, perhaps we spread a little less of it on our bread and, of course, we now all love and applaud olive oil. But believe me, the home kitchen is not where our excess of eating fat has come from – we cannot blame dairy foods or the fat content of a good square meal. If we want to know why we consume more fat, we have to look, I'm afraid, at how our consumption of processed and snack foods and chocolate bars has grown. These have hidden amounts of fat that we don't take into account. What we eat per head in this country in chocolate bars alone adds up to 10 fl oz (275 ml) of double cream per person per week. Not that chocolate bars and other snacks foods are bad in themselves, but we desperately need to find the balance that so often gets overlooked in the heat of the health debate.

There is a crazy kind of imbalance, largely due to ignorance, that people seem hardly aware of – we eat fattening snacks and then have only skimmed milk because we are 'cutting down', or a Danish pastry with a high fat content accompanied by an artificial sweetener in our coffee. Someone who never eats snack foods but pours double cream on their apple pie at the weekend is, I'm quite positive, consuming far less fat. So, let's get dairy foods out of the firing line and enjoy them not in excess but in the perfect balance of a normal healthy diet.

A dairy explosion

When I first started writing about cooking, dairy foods were simply whole milk, single cream and double cream. Soured cream was not that widely available – perhaps just sometimes in specialised food shops; yoghurt was only available in health shops; and you only ever ate clotted cream if you went to the West Country. Now if you approach the dairy section in any large supermarket you can see a veritable explosion has taken place: miles and miles of yoghurts of every type and flavour, and an enormous range of different kinds of dairy products that, for me personally and for cooks everywhere, have been such a delight to discover and introduce into a whole range of cooking and recipes. But, with all this enormous choice available, it can be confusing, so here, before we move into the recipes, I want to give each dairy product an explanation.

Whole milk

The reason whole milk is so good for growing children is that it has many nutrients needed for good health. It has a natural fat content of 3.5 per cent, contains protein and carbohydrates, and is a good source of calcium, an important mineral for growing children's bones and teeth. In addition to all that, it's packed with vitamins and minerals. It's for these reasons that anyone living on a budget should choose milk first and foremost – in fact milk is the cheapest nourishment on offer.

In cooking, whole milk should be used to make white sauces and milk puddings, and substituting half the amount of stock needed with milk when making vegetable soups gives a lovely creamy texture and flavour.

Semi-skimmed milk

This has all the virtues of whole milk, except that some of the fat has been removed, leaving between 1.5 and 1.8 per cent. Because of this, it is actually better in tea and coffee, and, I think, works better in batters for pancakes or Yorkshire puddings. For anyone wishing to cut some of the fat content in their diet, semi-skimmed milk is an excellent choice, as it still retains some creaminess.

Skimmed milk

This is the one for people who are following a low-fat diet, as only a trace (0.3 per cent) remains. Even so, skimmed milk is still highly nutritious and is an excellent source of calcium, and contains everything whole and semi-skimmed milk has but without the fat. It can be used in all recipes requiring milk, but obviously won't give the same degree of creaminess.

Breakfast milk

This is also sometimes known as Channel Island milk, which comes from Guernsey and Jersey cows. It is the richest, creamiest milk of all and has the highest fat content at around 5 per cent. Really you could describe this as luxury milk and, as the name suggests, it's best of all for pouring on cereals or porridge. Needless to say, though, it is also wonderful for making creamy sauces and milk puddings.

Pasteurised milk

This is simply milk that has undergone heat treatment: a mere 5 seconds at 72°C purifies it but, at the same time, leaves all the important vitamins, minerals and proteins virtually unchanged.

Homogenised milk

When you leave pasteurised or other milk to stand, the small amount of cream present settles at the top. What homogenisation does, through a special treatment, is distribute the cream (milk-fat globules) evenly throughout the milk so this separation does not occur.

Buttermilk

This used to be a by-product of butter-making, hence its name, but now we have specially cultured buttermilk, which is made by adding a culture to skimmed milk. It has the same acidic flavour as the original and is perfect for making extra-light scones, soda bread and American-style pancakes.

Double cream

When cows' milk reaches the dairy, it contains a liquid substance called butterfat, and this, when it's skimmed off the surface of the milk, is cream, or what we know as double cream. It is extremely rich, with a minimum fat content of 48 per cent. Because of this it can stand being boiled in cooking without separating, and can be whipped to a fluffy, spreadable consistency.

When whipping double cream, though, you have to be extra careful, as overwhipping can give a grainy, slightly separated appearance (and if you really overwhip it, you'll end up with butter). One of the ways to prevent this happening is to add a couple of tablespoons of milk per pint (570 ml) of cream and, if you are using an electric hand whisk, make sure that you turn the speed right down when it looks thick enough. Double cream is also rich and luscious served just as it is, chilled as a thick pouring cream.

Whipping cream

This is a lighter version of double cream, with at least 35 per cent fat, and it whips beautifully without being quite so rich. Whipping cream is also good as a pouring cream, again, if you want something that's not too rich. If you're not Scottish (Scots don't approve), try pouring whipping cream over hot porridge, along with some unrefined brown sugar to melt and marble into little pools. I also think whipping cream is good for swirling on top of desserts, giving you that 'not-quite-so-high-in-calories' satisfaction.

Single cream

This is a much thinner cream, good for pouring and for cooking with when you need more creaminess than milk. Because it has only a minimum of 18 per cent fat, it's not suitable for boiling, as it will curdle.

Extra-thick double or single cream

These are as described for double or single cream, but have been treated to give them a consistency that is suitable for spooning on to pies and desserts without having to bother with whisking them first.

Soured cream

This is a lovely product, made with fresh single cream that is soured by adding a natural culture similar to that used in yoghurt. It is unique as a dairy product, and, in my opinion, is the very best topping for jacket potatoes (mixed with snipped fresh chives). If you are lucky enough to get some caviar, soured cream and chives make wonderful accompaniments.

Crème fraîche

For me, crème fraîche is the number one top of the pops cook's ingredient in the cream family. Because, by law, milk for cream has to be pasteurised, this has undoubtedly affected the flavour and made it blander than it was in former times. The French (more particularly the Normans, as Normandy is the world's richest dairy area), not content with this diminished flavour, created a special way of adding a culture to their cream and allowed it to mature and develop the faintly acidic flavour that was lost in pasteurisation.

The best crème fraîche comes from a strictly controlled area of Normandy and has all the rich, luscious flavour that the area is famous for. If you open a pot and closely look at it, you can see the wonderful creamy-yellow colour of the real thing, *right*. The reason it is specially loved by cooks is it has a longer shelf life than double cream, so you can take a spoonful here and there, replace the lid and use it again. Now we can also buy half-fat crème fraîche, which is less rich but still contains all the creamy flavour of the full-fat version. Finally, the other supreme virtue of crème fraîche is that when you use it in cooking, it never curdles and separates – you can bubble and boil it and never be afraid.

Clotted cream

Wait for it – this is the big one! Perhaps you'd rather not know, but it has at least 55 per cent butterfat. Clotted cream has a unique and special dairy colour, like pale buttercups, and is thick, rich and utterly irresistible. It is a speciality of the rich pastureland of the West Country, and is made by heating the cream to evaporate some of the liquids, so, in a sense, you could call it concentrated cream. It is heaven spread on scones with home-made preserves, and extra special on tart fruit pies. It's not for every day, but everyone should treat themselves to some just once in a while.

Yoghurt

The staple snack of the 1980s and 1990s has proved to be yoghurt, and producers never seem to tire of yet more variations and flavours. In the kitchen, yoghurt is a useful dairy ingredient and can be used in many ways. But what exactly is yoghurt? Very briefly, it's milk – whole, semi-skimmed, skimmed or dried – first pasteurised by heat treatment, then cooled to 41°C or 45°C and inoculated with a specially prepared culture. Then the whole thing is incubated at a warm temperature until the acidity reaches a certain level and setting takes place. The yoghurt is then cooled and chilled, ready to be eaten or stored. Apart from preserving the milk, the process adds acidity to the flavour, which is pleasant to eat as it is but is also incredibly good for adding character and flavour to all kinds of dishes. Wholemilk yoghurt contains 3.4 per cent fat; low-fat yoghurt contains 1-2 per cent fat; and diet, virtually fat-free yoghurt contains 0.2 per cent fat or less.

Organic wholemilk yoghurt

This is a yoghurt made with organic whole milk produced on dairy farms that meet Soil Association requirements, who control the animal feeds and pastureland. It is a completely natural product and contains only 3-4 per cent fat. This is suitable for vegetarians.

Genuine Greek yoghurt

This is another of my absolute favourite dairy ingredients. It's a special yoghurt made from cows' or sheep's milk, which is boiled in open vats so that its liquid content is reduced. The result is a much thicker consistency, giving a more concentrated yoghurt with a fat content of 8-10 per cent. I have a special fondness for it and I love serving it well chilled with lots of lovely Greek mountain honey poured over and pistachios sprinkled on top – in fact I think this is one of the simplest and nicest desserts. Greek yoghurt is also a very useful ingredient in cooking, since it can replace some of the cream when you wish to lighten dairy desserts. Now you can buy low-fat Greek yoghurt, with 9 per cent fat, and an amazing 0 per cent, too. Don't buy Greek-*style* yoghurt, though, as it simply isn't the same. Look for the genuine Greek version, which is very widely available.

Cottage cheese

This is a very popular cheese because of its low fat content, and is a firm friend of the waist watcher. It is made from skimmed milk that is first heat-treated, then a starter culture is added that forms the curds and whey. These are then washed several times in chilled water to remove the whey, and the curds are then drained and, finally, given a very light dressing of cultured cream. The result is a mild, faintly acidic cheese with just a hint of creaminess but not a great deal of character and flavour. Cottage cheese should always be eaten as fresh as possible, and is best served sprinkled with snipped fresh chives and seasoned with coarse salt and black pepper.

Cream cheese

This has a soft, smooth, buttery texture and varies enormously according to its fat content. Standard cream cheese has 45 per cent fat, but there are many variations, such as the light and extra-light versions, which can be used in recipes to replace full-fat cream and curd cheese if a lower fat content and fewer calories are required.

Curd cheese

This is similar to cream cheese but with a lower fat content and, like cottage cheese, has had a lactic starter added. This gives it a light acidity and a light flavour, colour and texture. It is sometimes called medium-fat soft cheese. I like it best of all for cheesecakes because it gives them a lighter flavour and texture, as you will discover on page 454.

Quark

This is a soft white cheese made from skimmed milk, so it is low in fat and ideal for slimmers. Use instead of butter in scrambled eggs or mashed potatoes (see pages 34 and 176), or in place of full-fat curd cheese.

Ricotta

This, strictly speaking, is not really a cheese but a sort of by-product of cheesemaking. It is made from the drained whey and then cooked; in Italian, the word ricotta means re-cooked. It has a mild, fresh lactic flavour and contains only 14 per cent fat. It is actually delicious just by itself served with summer fruits, and I have eaten it freshly made in Apulia, Italy, sprinkled with coarse salt, pepper and olive oil, with really good bread.

Mascarpone

In my opinion, Mascarpone is the richest and most aristocratic of the new wave of dairy products. Thick, yellow and creamy, with a very high fat content (40 per cent) but a distinctive, rich dairy flavour, it forms the main part of the famous tiramisu. There again, it is lovely served alone with soft fruits or in a cheesecake. Because of its high fat content, it can be lightened by mixing it with an equal quantity of fromage frais and used as a filling for sponge cakes or as a topping for desserts. Add a small amount of sugar to sweeten the mixture and what you get is the flavour of Mascarpone given a lighter texture, and, if you are watching your waistline, far less guilt! I can also recommend Mascarpone spread on sweet biscuits (digestives or sweet oat biscuits) with fresh strawberry jam. Mascarpone is also brilliant for adding to sauces.

Fromage frais

Fromage frais is a fresh curd cheese introduced to this country from France and made from pasteurised cows' milk. Basically, it has very little fat, but cream is added to make 4 per cent (or 8 per cent) fromage frais. The 4 per cent is fine eaten on its own with honey or fruit purée, or used as a topping – especially for anyone on a low-fat diet. The 8 per cent is the best one for cooking. Either of these can be used in savoury sauces or as a topping for jacket potatoes with a few snipped chives. Alternatively, there is a diet virtually fat-free version (0.1 per cent), which is ideal in dips. For a cool, light, low-fat dessert, see the recipe on page 408.

Smoked Haddock with Crème Fraîche, Chive and Butter Sauce

This is a great recipe, a) because it's the most wonderful combination of flavours, and b) because it takes only 12 minutes from start to finish. Serve it with spinach cooked in its own juices with a little butter, then drain well and you'll have a sublime meal in no time at all.

Serves 2

12-14 oz (350-400 g) smoked
haddock or smoked cod, skinned,
or same weight golden haddock
cutlets, skinned
2 rounded tablespoons crème fraîche
1 heaped tablespoon snipped
fresh chives
½ oz (10 g) butter, diced
5 fl oz (150 ml) whole milk
freshly milled black pepper

You will also need a frying pan with a
diameter of 10 inches (25.5 cm).

First place the fish in the frying pan and add a little freshly milled black pepper but no salt. Then pour in the milk (it won't cover the fish, but that doesn't matter), bring it up to simmering point and simmer gently, uncovered, for 8-12 minutes if you're using pieces of smoked haddock or cod, or 8 minutes for golden haddock cutlets. You will be able to see quite clearly when they are cooked, as the whole thing will become pale and opaque.

Now carefully remove the fish to a plate using a fish slice, increase the heat and add the crème fraîche to the pan. Continue to simmer, uncovered, for 2-3 minutes, until the sauce reduces and thickens slightly, then whisk in the butter and return the fish to the sauce briefly. Scatter in the chives, let it bubble for about 30 seconds and it's ready to serve.

Entrecôte Steak with Crème Fraîche and Cracked Pepper Sauce

This is a special supper dish for two people celebrating a birthday or anniversary or for those who just want a treat. It needs a good bottle of red wine, and jacket potatoes with a leafy salad would be good accompaniments. I usually make this with a tub of fresh beef stock from the supermarket.

First of all you need to reduce the stock to half its original volume, so put it in a small saucepan and boil rapidly for about 10 minutes, then taste and add some salt if it needs it. Now measure the Cognac into a jug.

When the steaks are at room temperature, season them well with salt, then place the frying pan over a high heat and, when it's really hot, add the butter and oil, which should start to foam immediately. Now drop the steaks into the hot pan and, keeping the heat high, give them 3 minutes on one side for medium or 2 minutes for rare. Use a timer and try to leave them alone – no prodding! Now turn them over and give them another 2 minutes on the other side for medium or 1 minute for rare. After that pour in the Cognac, let it splutter and reduce, and follow it first with the reduced stock and finally the crème fraîche and crushed pepper. Give it all a good stir, then let everything bubble, reduce and amalgamate for about 1 more minute, then serve the steaks on warmed plates with the sauce spooned over.

Serves 2

2 x 8 oz (225 g) entrecôte or sirloin steaks, at least 1 inch (2.5 cm) thick, removed from the fridge about 1 hour before you need them
2 rounded tablespoons crème fraîche
2 teaspoons black peppercorns, coarsely crushed
10 fl oz (275 ml) fresh beef stock
2 tablespoons Cognac
1 teaspoon butter
1 teaspoon oil
Maldon sea salt

You will also need a solid frying pan with a diameter of 10 inches (25.5 cm).

Gooseberry Yoghurt Fool

I now find that lusciously thick genuine Greek yoghurt makes the best fruit fool of all, as it allows the full flavour of the fruit to dominate. If you're serving this to someone who doesn't like yoghurt, don't worry – they won't know.

Serves 6

2 lb (900 g) gooseberries, topped and tailed with scissors
10 oz (275 g) Greek yoghurt
5 oz (150 g) golden caster sugar

You will also need a shallow 9 inch (23 cm) square or round ovenproof baking dish and 6 serving glasses, each with a capacity of 6 fl oz (175 ml).

Pre-heat the oven to gas mark 4, 350°F (180°C).

For the fullest flavour, I think gooseberries are best cooked in the oven. So first place them in the baking dish, sprinkle in the sugar and bake them on the centre shelf of the oven, uncovered, for 20-30 minutes, or until tender when tested with a skewer. After that tip them into a sieve set over a bowl to drain off the excess juice. Now reserve about a quarter of the cooked gooseberries for later, then place the rest in the bowl of a food processor, add 4 tablespoons of the reserved juice and whiz to a thick purée.

After that, leave the purée to get quite cold, then empty the yoghurt into a bowl, give it a stir, then fold in half the purée. Now spoon this mixture into the serving glasses, spoon the rest of the purée on top and, finally, add the reserved gooseberries. Cover the glasses with clingfilm and chill till you're ready to serve, then serve with some Pecan Shortbreads (see page 406) cut into smaller rounds.

Rhubarb Yoghurt Fool

For a delicious variation on the recipe above, trim and wash 1 lb 4 oz (570 g) of rhubarb and cut it into 1 inch (2.5 cm) chunks. Place in a baking dish, sprinkle with 3 oz (75 g) of golden caster sugar and add 1 teaspoon of chopped fresh root ginger, then cook in the oven, at the same temperature, for 30-40 minutes, until tender. Now drain the rhubarb as above, then purée all the rhubarb, along with 2 tablespoons of the reserved juice. When cool, fold half the purée into 7 fl oz (200 ml) of Greek yoghurt in a bowl, then divide it between 4 serving glasses and spoon the remaining purée on top. Finally, cut 2 pieces of stem ginger into matchstick lengths and use them to garnish the fool. Cover and refrigerate until needed. This amount will serve 4 people.

Toffee-Fudge Bananas with Toasted Nuts

The world record for making this recipe is not 5 minutes, but just 3 – it's quite simply the fastest dessert recipe I've ever come across. It's also amazingly good, and if it is conceivable that anybody on this earth does not love delectably thick Greek yoghurt, then you can make it just as well with whipped cream.

Right, on your marks, get ready… Pop the brazil nuts, spread out on some foil, under the grill about 4 inches (10 cm) from the heat and put a timer on for 3 minutes (if you don't have a timer keep an eye on them, because they will burn if you forget them), then keep them to one side for later.

Now peel and slice the bananas into thin rounds and place them in a large bowl, then add the yoghurt and mix well. Next divide the mixture between the serving glasses and simply sprinkle the sugar equally over the 4 portions of banana. Now cover with clingfilm and leave in the fridge for about 3 hours – after this time the sugar will have transformed itself into lovely pools of fudge sauce. Now all you need to do is chop the toasted nuts, sprinkle them on top, serve and wait for the compliments.

Serves 4
2 large, ripe bananas
2 oz (50 g) brazil nuts
1 lb 2 oz (500 g) Greek yoghurt
5 oz (150 g) molasses sugar

You will also need 4 individual serving glasses, each with a capacity of 7 fl oz (200 ml).

Pre-heat the grill to its highest setting.

Classic Crème Caramel

Over the years I've experimented with what should be the best crème caramel, using double cream, crème fraîche and half and half of these in the mixture. Now I prefer to use just single cream, which gives the whole thing a sort of wobbly lightness. So this, I now think, is the ultimate.

Serves 4-6
For the caramel:
6 oz (175 g) white caster sugar
2 tablespoons tap-hot water

For the custard:
5 fl oz (150 ml) whole milk
10 fl oz (275 ml) single cream
4 large eggs
1 teaspoon pure vanilla extract

To serve:
about 10 fl oz (275 ml) pouring cream

You will also need a soufflé dish with a capacity of 1½ pints (850 ml), 5 inches (13 cm) in diameter, 3 inches (7.5 cm) deep, and a deep roasting tin.

Pre-heat the oven to gas mark 2, 300°F (150°C).

Begin by making the caramel (see the pictures on page 469). To do this put the sugar in a saucepan and place it over a medium heat. Leave it like that, keeping an eye on it, until the sugar begins to melt and just turn liquid around the edges, which will take 4-6 minutes. Now give the pan a good shake and leave it again to melt until about a quarter of the sugar has melted. Now, using a wooden spoon, give it a gentle stir and continue to cook and stir until the sugar has transformed from crystals to liquid and is the colour of dark runny honey – the whole thing should take 10-15 minutes. Then take the pan off the heat and add the water, being a bit cautious here, as it sometimes splutters at this stage. Now you may need to return the pan to a low heat to re-melt the caramel, stirring until any lumps have dissolved again. Then quickly pour two-thirds of the caramel into the soufflé dish, tipping it round the base and sides to coat.

Now make the custard. To do this, pour the milk and cream into the saucepan containing the rest of the caramel, then place this over a gentle heat and this time use a whisk to thoroughly combine everything. Don't panic if you get a great clag of caramel clinging to your whisk or there's some stuck around the edges of the pan – remember that the saucepan is over the heat and the heat *will* melt it. Eventually is the word, so be patient. When it's all melted, remove the pan from the heat. Next break the eggs into a large bowl or jug and whisk them, then pour the hot milk that's now blended with the remaining caramel into this mixture, whisking it in as you pour. Next add the vanilla extract and, after that, pour the whole lot through a sieve into the caramel-lined dish. If you have any unmelted caramel left on the base of the pan, fill the pan with hot water and a drop of washing-up liquid and place it over the heat again to clean it off.

Now place the soufflé dish in the roasting tin and pour in enough tap-hot water to come two-thirds of the way up the dish. Place the whole thing on the centre shelf of the pre-heated oven and leave it there for 1¼ hours, until the custard is set in the centre, which means it should feel firm and springy to the touch. Then remove it from the roasting tin and, when it's completely cold, cover with clingfilm and chill thoroughly for several hours in the fridge before turning out.

When you're ready to serve, loosen it around the sides with a palette knife, put quite a deep serving plate on top and then turn it upside down and give it a hefty shake. What you will then have is a delicious, light, set caramel custard surrounded by a pool of golden caramel sauce. Serve it cut in slices with some pouring cream to mingle with the caramel.

These are the lightest little scones you'll ever come across, but what is raspberry butter, you're wondering. The answer is that, traditionally, country people used to use up surplus summer fruits by making fruit cheeses. Damsons, for instance, can be cooked long and slow until they are concentrated into a thick, cheese-like consistency. Fruit butters are similar, but not quite so thick. This version, made with raspberries, has all the concentrated flavour and aroma of the fruit, perfect for piling on to scones with generous amounts of clotted cream.

Makes about 10 scones
2-3 tablespoons buttermilk, plus a little extra for brushing
8 oz (225 g) self-raising flour, plus a little extra for dusting
pinch of salt
3 oz (75 g) butter, at room temperature
1½ oz (40 g) golden caster sugar
1 large egg, beaten

For the raspberry butter:
1 lb (450 g) raspberries
6 oz (175 g) golden granulated sugar

To serve:
clotted cream

You will also need a lightly greased baking tray dusted with flour, and a 2 inch (5 cm) pastry cutter.

Pre-heat the oven to gas mark 7, 425°F (220°C).

To make the raspberry butter, purée the raspberries in a food processor, then pass them through a fine nylon sieve, pressing with a wooden spoon so that as much juice as possible gets through – you should get about 15 fl oz (425 ml). Now place the purée in a medium saucepan with the sugar and heat very gently until the sugar has dissolved. Then turn up the heat so the mixture boils rapidly for 8-10 minutes, but keep stirring from time to time so it doesn't catch on the base. When it's ready, the mixture should have reduced by one third and a wooden spoon drawn across the base of the pan should leave a trail for 1-2 seconds only, but be careful not to overcook it, or you will get glue. Then pour it into a serving dish and leave to one side to cool and set for at least an hour.

For the scones, begin by sifting the flour and salt into a bowl, rub the butter lightly into the mixture until it looks like breadcrumbs, then add the sugar. Now, in a jug, beat the egg and 2 tablespoons of the buttermilk together and start to add this to the rest, mixing the dough with a palette knife. When it begins to come together, finish off with your hands – it should be soft but not sticky (if the dough seems too dry, add a little more buttermilk, a teaspoon at a time).

When you have formed the dough into a ball, tip it on to a lightly floured surface and roll it into a circle at least 1 inch (2.5 cm) thick – be very careful not to roll it any thinner; the secret of well-risen scones is to start off with a thickness of no less than an inch. Cut out the scones by placing the cutter on the dough and giving it a sharp tap – don't twist it, just lift it up and push the dough out. Carry on until you are left with the trimmings, then bring these back together to roll out again until you can cut out the last scone.

Place the scones on the baking tray, brush them lightly with the buttermilk and dust with a little flour. Now bake on the top shelf of the oven for 10-12 minutes, or until they are well risen and golden brown, then remove them to a wire rack to cool. Serve the scones thickly spread with raspberry butter and lots of clotted cream.
Note: don't forget that scones don't keep well, so in the unlikely event of there being any left, pop them in the freezer. The raspberry butter, however, can be kept in the refrigerator for a couple of weeks.

Eton Mess

This recipe, inspired by the strawberry and cream dessert traditionally served at Eton College on the 4th of June, is great for nervous meringue makers – because the meringues are broken up it simply doesn't matter if they weep, crack or collapse. So you can practise making them over and over with this dish until you get them perfect and, at the same time, enjoy this amazingly good summer dessert. Don't forget, though, to make the meringues the day before you want to serve the pudding.

Serves 6

6 oz (175 g) golden caster sugar
3 large egg whites
1 lb (450 g) fresh strawberries, hulled
1 rounded tablespoon unrefined icing sugar
1 pint (570 ml) double cream

You will also need a baking tray measuring 11 x 16 inches (28 x 40 cm), lined with non-stick silicone paper (parchment).

Pre-heat the oven to gas mark 2, 300°F (150°C).

First have the caster sugar measured out ready, then place the egg whites in a scrupulously clean bowl and whisk until they form soft peaks that slightly tip over when you lift the whisk. Next, add the sugar, about a tablespoon at a time, and continue to whisk until each tablespoon of sugar has been thoroughly whisked in. Now simply take rounded dessertspoonfuls of the mixture and place them in rows on the lined baking tray. Place the baking tray in the oven on the centre shelf, turn the heat down to gas mark 1, 275°F (140°C) and leave the meringues there for 1 hour. After that, turn the oven off and leave the meringues in the oven to dry out overnight, or until the oven is completely cold.

When you're ready to make the pudding, chop half the strawberries and place them in a blender together with the icing sugar. Whiz the whole lot to a purée, then pass it through a nylon sieve to remove the seeds. Now chop the rest of the strawberries and whip up the double cream to the floppy stage.

All the above can be done in advance, but when you are ready to serve, break up the meringues into roughly 1 inch (2.5 cm) pieces, place them in a large mixing bowl, add the chopped strawberries, then fold the cream in and around them. After that, gently fold in all but about 2 tablespoons of the purée to give a marbled effect. Finally, pile the whole lot into a serving dish, spoon the rest of the purée over the surface and serve as soon as possible.

Pecan Shortbreads with Raspberries and Raspberry Purée

If you like classic crème pâtissière (French pastry cream) but have no time to make it, a combination of ready-made custard and crème fraîche makes a lovely alternative. If you use it to sandwich together crisp, wafer-thin pecan shortbreads, raspberries and raspberry purée, you have a real winner for summer entertaining.

To begin, toast the pecans by spreading them out on a baking tray and popping them in the oven for 8 minutes. Then, once cool, place them in a processor and grind them down until they look rather like ground almonds.

Now, in a mixing bowl, cream the butter and icing sugar together until light and fluffy, then gradually work in the sifted flours, followed by the ground pecans, bringing the mixture together into a stiff ball. Place the dough in a polythene bag and leave in the fridge to rest for 30 minutes. After that, roll it out to a thickness of ¼ inch (5 mm), then stamp out 16 rounds by placing the cutter on the pastry and giving it a sharp tap, then simply lift the cutter and the piece will drop out. Now arrange the biscuits on the baking trays and lightly prick each one with a fork. Bake for 10-12 minutes, leave on the baking trays for about 10 minutes, then remove to a wire rack to cool completely.

While the shortbreads are cooling, place the raspberries for the purée in a bowl, sprinkle them with the sugar and leave for 30 minutes. After that, purée them in a processor and pass through a nylon sieve to remove the seeds, then place in a serving bowl, cover and chill till needed.

For the raspberry filling, whisk the crème fraîche in a mixing bowl with an electric hand whisk until it becomes really stiff, then add the custard and vanilla extract and whisk again, also until thick. Cover and chill till needed. Just before serving, spread equal quantities of the cream mixture over 8 of the biscuits, then arrange the raspberries on top, not forgetting to reserve 24. Spoon some purée over, then sandwich with the remaining shortbreads. Place 3 raspberries on top of each one, and lightly dust with the icing sugar.

Note: don't be tempted to prepare these too far in advance, because once the filling goes in the shortbreads begin to lose their crunchiness.

Serves 8
For the pecan shortbreads:
4 oz (110 g) pecans
5 oz (150 g) softened butter
2½ oz (60 g) unrefined golden icing sugar
5 oz (150 g) plain flour, sifted
2½ oz (60 g) rice flour or ground rice, sifted

For the raspberry purée:
8 oz (225 g) fresh raspberries
2 tablespoons golden caster sugar

For the raspberry filling:
1 lb (450 g) fresh raspberries, reserving 24 for the garnish
7 fl oz (200 ml) crème fraîche
5 fl oz (150 ml) fresh custard
2 drops vanilla extract

To garnish:
24 whole fresh raspberries, reserved from the filling
unrefined golden icing sugar, to dust

You will also need 2 baking trays measuring 11 x 16 inches (28 x 40 cm), lightly greased, and a 3½ inch (9 cm) round pastry cutter.

Pre-heat the oven to gas mark 4, 350°F (180°C).

Fromage Frais Creams with Red Fruit Compote

In the 'Winter Collection' I made these with Mascarpone, but this low-fat alternative is, I feel, every bit as good as the rich version and the perfect accompaniment to any fruit compote. I like this best made with leaf gelatine, but I've also included instructions for powdered gelatine.

Serves 6

1 lb 12 oz (800 g) 8 per cent fat fromage frais

7 g leaf gelatine

5 fl oz (150 ml) semi-skimmed milk

3 oz (75 g) golden caster sugar

1 vanilla pod, split lengthways

For the compote:

8 oz (225 g) fresh plums

8 oz (225 g) fresh cherries

8 oz (225 g) fresh blueberries

8 oz (225 g) fresh strawberries

8 oz (225 g) fresh raspberries

2 oz (50 g) golden caster sugar

You will also need 6 x 6 fl oz (175 ml) mini pudding basins, lightly oiled with a flavourless oil, and an ovenproof baking dish measuring 9 inches (23 cm) square and 2 inches (5 cm) deep.

Pre-heat the oven to gas mark 4, 350°F (180°C).

If you are using leaf gelatine, simply place the sheets in a bowl and cover with cold water, *below left*, then leave them to soak for about 5 minutes, till softened, *below centre*. Meanwhile, place the milk in a saucepan with the sugar and vanilla pod and heat gently for 5 minutes, or until the sugar has dissolved. Then take the pan off the heat and all you do now is squeeze the leaf gelatine in your hands to remove any excess water, then add it to the hot milk, *below right*. Give it all a thorough whisking and leave to cool.

Next, in a large mixing bowl, whisk the fromage frais until smooth, then add the cooled gelatine and milk mixture, removing the vanilla pod, and whisk again really well. Now divide the mixture between the pudding basins, filling them to within ½ inch (1 cm) of the rims. Finally, cover with clingfilm and chill in the fridge for at least 3 hours.

To make the compote, begin by preparing the plums: cut them round their natural line into halves, remove the stones, then cut each half into 4 and place in the ovenproof dish, along with the whole cherries and blueberries. Now sprinkle in the sugar, then place the dish on the centre shelf of the oven without covering and leave it there for 15 minutes. Next stir in the strawberries, halved if large, and return the dish to the oven for 10-15 minutes, or until the fruits are tender and the juices have run out of them. Finally, remove them from the oven and stir the raspberries into the hot juices, then allow it to cool, cover with clingfilm and chill.

To serve the creams, gently ease each one away from the edge of the basin using your little finger, then invert them on to serving dishes and serve with the compote spooned all around.

If you'd prefer to use powdered gelatine instead of leaf, place 3 tablespoons of the milk in a small bowl, then sprinkle the contents of an 11 g sachet over the milk and leave it to stand for 5 minutes. Meanwhile, heat the rest of the milk in a small saucepan, along with the vanilla pod and sugar, until the sugar has dissolved, then remove it from the heat and whisk in the soaked-gelatine mixture. Allow to cool, then just whisk into the fromage frais and continue as for the main recipe.

Coffee Cappuccino Creams with Cream and Sweet Coffee Sauce

If you are a coffee fan, this is the *coffee dessert – the best ever! It is based on an old-fashioned recipe for honeycomb mould, which sometimes separates into layers, but sadly it often doesn't. Therefore, I have now given up on layers because, anyway, it tastes absolutely divine. You can make this and serve it in Irish coffee glasses or plain glasses. The contrast of the unsweetened coffee cream mingling with the sweetened sauce and a generous amount of pouring or whipping cream is just gorgeous.*

Serves 6

6 heaped teaspoons instant espresso coffee powder
5 fl oz (150 ml) water
1 x 11 g sachet gelatine powder
10 fl oz (275 ml) whole milk
3 large eggs, separated
1 rounded teaspoon cornflour
7 fl oz (200 ml) crème fraîche

For the sauce:

3 heaped teaspoons instant espresso coffee powder
6 oz (175 g) golden granulated sugar
8 fl oz (225 ml) water

To serve:

5 fl oz (150 ml) double cream

You will also need 6 x 7 fl oz (200 ml) serving glasses.

Begin by soaking the gelatine: pour the water into a small bowl, sprinkle in the gelatine and let it soak for 5 minutes. Meanwhile, pour the milk into a medium saucepan and place it over a gentle heat. Then, in a bowl, whisk the egg yolks and cornflour together and, when the milk is very hot and just about to simmer, pour it over the egg-yolk mixture, whisking as you do. Now return the whole lot to the same saucepan, adding the soaked gelatine and coffee powder, then return the pan to the heat and continue to whisk until the custard is thickened and the gelatine and coffee are completely dissolved. Remove the pan from the heat and pour the custard into a large mixing bowl, leave it to cool, then whisk in the crème fraîche.

In another bowl, and using a clean whisk, whisk the egg whites to the soft-peak stage. Now fold 2 tablespoons of the egg whites into the coffee custard to loosen the mixture, then gently fold in the rest. Pour the mixture into the glasses and leave, covered with clingfilm, in a cool place for about 2 hours, then chill in the fridge until needed.

To make the coffee sauce, gently heat the sugar and water together and whisk till all the sugar granules have completely dissolved, then simmer gently for 15 minutes without a lid, until it becomes syrupy. Next, dissolve the coffee in 1 dessertspoon of warm water, stir this into the syrup and transfer it to a serving jug to cool. Meanwhile, whip up the cream to the floppy stage and, when you're ready, serve the coffee creams topped with whipped cream and the coffee syrup poured over.
Note: this recipe contains raw eggs.

18

Fruits for cooking

I think a sub-title for this chapter could be 'How to preserve our heritage'. There is, unfortunately, a price to pay for progress, and while fruits from around the world jetting into our supermarkets daily bring a permanent abundance of choice, it's sad that our own fruit growers are being forced into decline.

I am not against progress; I enjoy having such a wide choice. I feel privileged that I can shop around the world just a few miles from where I live and I love being able to bite into a crunchy fresh apple in June that hasn't gone woolly with storage. It also has to be said that some fruits need the sunshine that's so often elusive in this country. But at the same time I hope that British fruit growers won't ever give up, and we need to encourage them by buying British wherever possible: Kentish cherries, Bramley apples, old-fashioned oval-shaped damsons, Scottish raspberries and countless others. It's important that with all the dazzling choice before us we look at labels and countries of origin and give our fruit growers all the support we can.

On the pages that follow I have tried to give a kind of first-time overall view of various fruits and how to prepare and cook them. This is not, by any means, a comprehensive list, but a look at fruits that are most likely to be used in any day-to-day cooking repertoire.

Apples

It's on the subject of the apple, more than any other fruit, that chefs and cooks often part company. As one of the latter, and being born and bred in England, I am quite definitely a Bramley lover. Chefs, even English ones, are usually educated in French ways, and as the French never had Bramley apples they're not included in classic cuisine. But the Bramley is a star: it has an acidic yet fragrant apple flavour and it cooks to a fluffiness not required in French dishes but very much part of English cooking through the ages – as English as apple pie. That said, there are recipes that require firmer apples to keep their shape, and Cox's and Granny Smiths are both excellent for this purpose.

There are many other varieties of home-grown apples, but in cooking I tend to mostly use these three. They are always widely available and their best season is from the end of August through to March. As the seasons go I tend to cook with apples in the winter months and use other fruits that are more plentiful during the summer. When I first started cooking, seasons were so important and truly dictated the rhythm of cooking through the year, and as I've said elsewhere, I still find this variation makes cooking more interesting.

When it comes to preparing apples for cooking, unless you're going at the speed of lightning, you will need a bowl of lightly salted water, as this will prevent them from browning. First of all you need a small, sharp knife and a potato peeler. Cut each apple in half, then cut one half into quarters using the knife, taking out the core and pips. Now, using the peeler, pare off the skin (if the recipe requires it), then, depending on the recipe, slice or chop the apples and add them to the bowl of water as they are prepared. Use them as quickly as possible, draining in a colander and drying them with a tea cloth first.

Apricots

Here's a fruit that cannot be grown without warm sunshine, so we have to rely on Mediterranean countries for supplies. Picked straight from the tree, an apricot can be delightful to eat raw, warm from the sun, but once they arrive here I feel they need light cooking to bring out the best apricot flavour. The season is short – June to August – but dried apricots are now available all year round and can nearly always be used in apricot recipes.

When it comes to preparing apricots, there's no need to peel them – all you do is cut the apricot around the natural line into two halves, then, holding the half containing the stone in one hand, give a little twist and squeeze as you remove the stone with the other hand. To cook apricots, you can use them in place of plums in the recipe on page 427.

Bananas

A little bit of heaven is a ripe, fragrant, soft-fleshed banana mashed with a fork with just a little brown sugar and piled on to thick slices of buttered crusty wholemeal bread (home-made, see Chapter 4). That and a cup of freshly brewed tea can give anyone renewed strength in the middle of a working day.

When choosing bananas, remember that to be ripe enough to eat the skins must be all yellow with no green bits near the stalk. Also, the riper they are the better they taste – sweeter and more fragrant. A really ripe and ready-to-eat banana will have little brown freckles on its yellow skin, but be warned: ripe and ready means just that, so eat it soon or it might be a little too ripe tomorrow! Remember, too, that bananas come from hot countries and hate the cold, so never, ever put them in the fridge, as the shock of it turns them black. Bananas also tend to discolour if they are exposed to the air, so if you are preparing them for a recipe they should be tossed in lemon juice if they have to wait around. However, when they're submerged and cut off from the air they stay creamy white with no problem. The recipe for Toffee-Fudge Bananas with Toasted Nuts on page 399 is one of the simplest and easiest desserts I know.

Cherries

I remember baskets of Kentish cherries, ripe and red, or 'whites', which were actually pale and creamy with a rosy blush. These have the finest flavour of all cherries and there are still Kentish growers. Because English cherries are in short supply, however, I am grateful to other European countries and the US for sending us a plentiful stock throughout the summer. They are expensive, because cherries are laborious to hand pick, but because the season is relatively short I always make the most of it and seem to eat them practically every day.

What we buy mostly are dessert cherries, but sour cherries, called morello, are brilliant for cooking, with a wonderful, quite unique, concentrated cherry flavour. Because there's a very short supply we only seem to be able to buy the dried here, but bottled ones can be good and morello cherry jam is superb both spread on bread and scones and in a sauce to serve with duck. I have lately discovered that dessert cherries cooked with wine and wine vinegar also make a superb sauce for duck or gammon, so I would serve this in the summer, and then in the winter months make it with dried sour cherries.

Figs

Like apricots, fresh figs ideally need to be eaten picked from the tree, warm from the Mediterranean sunshine, fully ripened and bursting with soft, luscious flesh. If their sweetness is then combined with some thinly sliced Parma or Serrano ham, you would have a feast indeed. Although they are imported throughout most of the year, the best of the European crop (from Turkey and Greece) are at their most luscious in autumn. They should be dark purple, feel soft to the touch when you buy them and their skins should have a soft bloom, which needs to be wiped off with damp kitchen paper. Eat them just as they are, or as a topping for sweet galettes (see pages 122 and 123), or arranged in overlapping slices, brushed with honey and baked for 10-12 minutes at gas mark 7, 425°F (220°C). Another very unusual way to serve them is as a starter; see the recipe for Roasted Figs with Gorgonzola and Honey-Vinegar Sauce on page 430.

Lemons

Imagine a world without lemons or a kitchen that didn't always have a lemon tucked away. Can there be a more widely used fruit or absolutely essential ingredient in cooking in the Western world?

Lemons, which are available all year round, contain lots of sharp, acidic juice, but also a fragrant oil that's found in the zest (the coloured outer layer of the skin). In a drink such as a dry Martini or gin and tonic, this pared-off outer skin releases its fragrant oil to give a subtle lemon hint. In cooking, lemon zest is every bit as treasured as the juice, and our heritage of rich fruit Christmas cakes, puddings and mincemeat all contain not only lemon juice and zest but candied lemon peel, giving extra fragrance and flavour. It's always best to use lemons as fresh as possible, but I find extra lemons keep better if they're stored in a polythene bag in the salad drawer of the fridge.

Squeezing

It is said that rolling the lemon with the palm of your hand on a flat surface using a bit of pressure will ensure you get more juice. When my mother made pancakes on Pancake Day she would put plates to warm in the oven and pop the lemon in, too, as this, she said, produced more juice. Either way, I think a wooden lemon squeezer inserted into a half lemon and squeezed and twisted is a wonderfully easy way to extract the juice.

Zesting

If you want finely zested lemon, a grater will do the job, but you need to take care not to include the bitter pith just beneath the zest. Best of all is a lemon zester, which removes only the outer zest and the fragrant oils. A great lemon recipe is the grilled lemon chicken kebabs on page 334.

Limes

Whilst lemon trees grow and thrive in the Mediterranean, they can't survive the hot, steamy humidity of Asian countries – so enter limes, yet another supreme gift of nature. Limes, like lemons, are filled with fragrant acidic juice and the zest contains the same high-flavoured oils. Though limes are a small green lookalike lemon, their flavour is distinctly different. I love limes and always have them in my kitchen. If you want a low-fat salad dressing, look no further – just squeeze lime juice all over and it's remarkable how it offers both its own flavour and at the same time manages to enhance other flavours in the salad. The same applies to the juice, which really enhances the flavour of mango, pawpaw and pineapple.

Mangoes

When you're standing before a ripe, plump mango and you can feel its soft ripeness and smell its quite overwhelming fragrance, that is a time to rejoice. Fast jets now mean everybody can enjoy this most luscious and succulent of fruits, with its dazzling orange-yellow flesh. The fruit itself is fragrant, with a custard flavour. That said, a mango is always rather awkward to prepare, but first you need to check that it's ripe. Colour is not an indication: the skins are variously green, red, yellow-orange or even vaguely purple. As with an avocado you need to hold the fruit in your hand and feel a 'give' of softness when you exert a little pressure. Smell, too, can help you – the riper it is the heavier the perfume.

I love to eat mango on its own with a squeeze of lime, which seems to bring out the flavour of the fruit. Mango salsa on page 186 goes beautifully with chicken, and you'll find Thai Fish Curry with Mango on page 425 quite exquisite.

How to prepare a mango

The best way to start is to place the mango on a flat surface (I often use a dinner plate to catch the juice). Remember there is a large flat stone in the centre, so take a sharp knife, hold the mango in a vertical position, then slice it lengthways either side of the stone, *top right*. Now hold each slice, flesh-side up, and this time, using a small knife, cut a criss-cross pattern into the flesh right down to the skin but being careful not to cut through the skin, *right*. Now you can turn the whole thing inside out and simply cut away the cubes of mango into a bowl, then tip in any juices that are left on the plate.

Slicing the mango

Mangoes can be sliced, but only if they're just ripe and not too soft. This time you need a potato peeler to finely peel off the skin, then hold the mango in one hand and, with a small knife, cut out a slice, *left*, taking the knife down to the stone either side of it, then remove the slice and carry on cutting slices all the way round.

Too ripe

If the mango is too soft and fibrous to chop or slice, cut the cheeks off the mango (as shown on the previous page), then scoop out the flesh and make a purée in the processor with a little lime juice. Lovely as a sauce for something sweet or savoury, or add half its quantity of Greek yoghurt to make a fragrant mango fool.

Oranges

Oranges feature every bit as regularly as lemons in recipes: the famous French classic bigarade (orange and port) sauce served with duck, for instance, and my own favourite classic English sauce, Cumberland, which features orange and lemon, where the juices and finely shredded zest are combined with port and redcurrant jelly. Then there is also, of course, that great British invention, marmalade, which no other country's preserve has ever been able to match. Made with the bitter oranges of Seville that arrive at Christmas, no marmalade made with any other citrus fruit has that tangy intensity of flavour, where the sharpness of the oranges wins hands down over the sugar, totally eliminating that over-sweetness that so often masks the true flavour of the fruit in preserves.

Buying oranges is such a hit and miss affair, and a dry, sour or extra-pithy orange is really not pleasant. So, for eating straight there's only one type of orange that never fails to please, and that's the Spanish navels that arrive in November but disappear at the end of February. They are distinctive in that they have a so-called 'navel', and inside there's a sort of baby fruit attached. I'm not saying other varieties of orange are not good, but with navels you're never disappointed. The good news here is that other countries are now growing them, too, so watch out for navelinas in spring and early summer, and the late-summer version from Argentina.

Peaches and nectarines

Oh to be either in Spain or Italy when the peaches are ripe and fragrant and just about to fall from the trees. The peach, beloved of artists, is a beauteous thing, with its deep-crimson rosy bloom and voluptuous bright-yellow flesh oozing with juice. When we're lucky enough to eat them just like that – ready, ripe and warm from the sun – we need have no thought of recipes. But in this country, where peaches can't be grown on a large scale, we have to suffer tired imports picked too early, so that once the hard flesh becomes soft enough it has often turned woolly, dry and tasteless. Both nectarines and peaches come with white flesh, but the yellow, in my opinion, has more flavour.

However, unripened peaches and their first cousin, nectarines, can be somewhat rescued in cooking, so poaching them in Marsala (*Summer Collection*) is a good idea.

Pineapple

When I first started cooking I was slightly scared of pineapples, not knowing quite how to come at them or where to start with my knife. When I was a child, pineapple came tinned in neat rings packed in syrup. My favourite teacher, Elizabeth David (though only through books), came to my aid and, as always, explained it perfectly, which gave me immense satisfaction as I proudly took the pineapple to the table sprinkled with a little sugar and Kirsch.

First you need to buy a ripe pineapple: look for proud, lively green tufts that don't look too aged or tired. Give one a tug if you can: if it's ripe it should pull off easily. The other thing to look for is the little thorny bits that stick out – they should be brown. The colour of the pineapple itself is not always a guide: some from Central America are very green and others from the Ivory Coast are golden amber. Feel the pineapple at the base: it should give and feel soft if it's ripe, and don't forget to smell its strong pineapple perfume, probably telling you more than anything if it's ready to eat.

I have now created my own way of dealing with a pineapple. Needless to say, the tough, elusive-looking object needs a really sharp knife. First slice off the leafy top and about ½ inch (1 cm) of the fruit with it – you need to get this as straight as possible. Put it to one side, then cut off the opposite end, which can be discarded. Now stand it upright and slice off the skin vertically in slices, *top right*, going all the way round. What you will now have is a whole peeled pineapple, and what you need to do next is use the tip of a potato peeler to dig out the 'eyes', *centre right*, which are similar to those of a potato. Now slice the pineapple vertically in half, then into quarters. The central core can be a bit tough, so slice this off along the centre of each quarter, *bottom right*, then cut the quarters into slices about ⅓ inch (7 mm) thick. Arrange these in overlapping circles, then sprinkle with a light dusting of sugar and a little Kirsch (rum is also very good) and pop the leafy top in the centre.

Plums, greengages and damsons

Whilst peaches and nectarines may make us think we are disadvantaged living further north, plums and damsons more than adequately make up for it. I have a small Victoria plum tree in my garden in Suffolk, and I love eating them straight from the tree in late summer, giving them a faint

squeeze to see which ones are fully ripe, then eating just a few each day for breakfast and lunch until they're all gone. There are several other varieties of home-grown plums, all suitable for cooking or eating raw when fully ripe. Greengages, because of their colour, are deceptive – they can look unripe and forbidding but taste very sweet. I like to cook both greengages and plums in a compote of Marsala wine (see page 213).

Damsons are my favourite member of the plum family. The true damson is small and oval, almost almond-shaped, with dark indigo-purple skin covered in a soft bloom and bright-green sharp-sour flesh that, when cooked with sugar, produces darker, reddish-purple juice. The secret of the damson's utter charm is that because it's a sharp fruit its flavour is not killed by sugar, so damson jam remains perfectly tart and not over-sweet. One of my all-time favourite recipes is for damson chutney: in 30 years I've never been without a little hoard of it stashed away in my cupboard under the stairs. It does wonders for bangers or makes a very sophisticated accompaniment to cold cuts, and I particularly love serving sausages with jacket potatoes and dipping the potato skins in a luscious pile of damson chutney.

Rhubarb

Although it came here originally from Russia, rhubarb is, for me, an extremely English fruit, arriving at a very important time in the calendar – early spring, when there's absolutely no other interesting fruit in season. It really is a curious, wonderfully different fruit – no other comes to us as an elongated stalk. Watching it grow almost secretly under its umbrella of wide green leaves in the garden is fascinating.

As early as March we can buy the tender, pink stalks of forced rhubarb, which have a delicate, youthful flavour. Then in May we begin to see that the rhubarb is a deeper, rosier red. Later on, in June and July, it will be dark crimson, more acid and less sweet, so a little more sugar is needed at this time. Use it in our crumble recipe on page 432, in one-crust pies, or in the Old-Fashioned Rhubarb Trifle on page 428.

When it comes to preparing and cooking rhubarb, first trim off the leaves and cut the stalks into 1 inch (2.5 cm) chunks. I never, ever simmer or boil rhubarb because it tends to mash up, so to keep the pieces intact, it's best to bake it in the oven using 3 oz (75 g) of sugar to each 1 lb 8 oz (700 g) of fruit, pre-heating the oven to gas mark 4, 350°F (180°C). Place it in a shallow dish and give it 30-40 minutes, uncovered. This amount will serve 4 people.

Soft fruits

Blackberries

There is still something very satisfying about blackberrying, although I usually find someone has been there first, plucking off the best ones at the lowest levels! Don't be thwarted – take a walking stick and summon down the upper branches; take some gloves, too, or your hands will be very scratched, and a basket if you're really up for it, or a polythene box if you're not quite so determined!

Either way, wild brambles or blackberries have a character and flavour that the cultivated ones have never captured. It's tricky, though, because if we have a wet summer they will be plump, fleshy and juicy; if we have a dry summer they will be very small and seedy. So, given the vagaries of wild blackberries, the cultivated kind are better than none. Blackberries are absolutely brilliant mixed with apples in a one-crust pie, or why not try them instead of apple in the crumble recipe on page 432?

Blackcurrants

Of all the little sparkly jewels that appear in the height of summer (their season being from June to August), blackcurrants are the richest, with a strong flavour and sharpness that can stand up to sugar. If you like their gutsy, in-your-face flavour there's a French company that makes a range of jams without sugar, using only concentrated fruit juices – its blackcurrant jam packed with fruit is the best I've ever tasted. Good bread, creamy butter and superlative jam makes, for my money, one of the simplest yet most luxurious snacks ever invented.

Blackcurrants make an excellent purée – for six people just take 8 oz (225 g) of currants and 3 oz (75 g) of caster sugar. First remove the stalks from the currants, then sprinkle them with the sugar in a bowl. Leave to stand for 30 minutes, then you can either sieve them directly back into the bowl or, to make the sieving easier, process them first, then sieve into the bowl. Taste to check that you have added enough sugar, then pour into a jug and chill until you're ready to serve.

Blueberries

When I was small my Welsh grandmother used to make tarts with a fruit called bilberry – little berries that grew wild, with purple flesh that yielded dark, deep-red juice. The blueberry is apparently its cousin, and grows wild in North America and Canada, but these are dark indigo-blue

outside and inside the flesh is green. The cultivated blueberries we buy here are larger, plump and juicy and very handsome to look at, and they are best and cheapest in the summer.

In America, blueberries are served with buttermilk pancakes for breakfast, in pies and in blueberry muffins (*Summer Collection*). I have used them in the recipe for Fromage Frais Creams with Red Fruit Compote on page 408 – a lovely summery combination.

Raspberries

A truly exquisite soft fruit that needs hardly any adornment. I like them served on a plate spread out in a single layer with a minute sprinkling of sugar, and I eat them just like that as often as I can during the season, which runs from July to October. Treat them more or less like strawberries – no water if possible, and covered if you're forced to keep them in the fridge.

Raspberries, like strawberries, also lend themselves to countless recipe ideas. Damaged, over-soft fruits make marvellous tarts, and if you sieve them and add icing sugar to taste you have a wonderful sauce for pouring over ice cream or strawberries.

Redcurrants and whitecurrants

Redcurrant jelly is an absolute must-have as a storecupboard ingredient (see page 238), but I also like the combination of redcurrants mixed with strawberries and raspberries in equal quantities for one of the simplest of desserts. Hand round caster sugar and cream and summer is in every spoonful. Whitecurrants can be used as well for added contrast of colour, and this combination makes a lovely filling for the meringue recipe given on page 60.

To prepare currants, all you need to do for a hasty separation of currants from stalks is take a bunch in one hand, hold the stalk firmly, then slide the stalk in-between the prongs of a fork held in the other hand. Now pull from top to bottom, sliding all the currants off in one swift movement.

Strawberries

I think it's true to say that English strawberries are the best in the world, particularly in June and July, although the season now extends from May to October. Our red, ripe strawberries are in quite a different league to the imported varieties that continue to turn up in the winter months.

If you want to really enjoy a feast of strawberries, my advice is to drive off somewhere either to pick your own or buy direct from the grower. Always let your nose be your guide: the plastic boxes have air holes, so make sure the strawberries have a strong, ripe scent, which indicates a good flavour.

Strawberry know-how

To get the most pleasure out of strawberries it's best to know how to treat them before you eat them. This means a bit of TLC, because their sheer beauty can be lost by bad handling.

1) Try to pick your own.

2) Eat them the same day or store in a cool place with the hulls intact.

3) Fridges and strawberries don't like each other. Low temperatures rob them of fragrance and flavour and somehow transfer the flavour to other ingredients in the fridge (uncovered milk or cream can quickly absorb strawberry flavours).

4) Please don't wash them. They tend to absorb water, which makes them mushy, so this also means it's not a good idea to buy them after heavy rain. Just wipe them with damp kitchen paper.

5) Leave the hulls in as long as possible and only remove them an hour or so before eating.

6) If you're forced to put them in the fridge, try sugared strawberries, which involves slicing them in half, sprinkling with caster sugar and storing them in a tightly lidded polythene box. During the storage the juices will mingle with the sugar and form a lovely strawberry-flavoured syrup. Remove from the fridge about an hour before serving.

Exotics

These are not often used in cooking as such but they do make a very splendid fruit salad (see the following page), so I will briefly explain how to deal with them.

Kiwi fruit

You can use a potato peeler here to pare off the skin and slice it, or if you want to eat one whole, slice the top off and scoop the flesh out with a teaspoon, as if you were eating a boiled egg.

Lychees

To prepare this fragrant, juicy little fruit, peel off the papery skin, slice the fruit round the middle, separate it into halves and discard the stone.

Passion fruit

When you buy passion fruit, look for a crinkled skin, which is a sign of ripeness, then just slice the fruit in half and scoop out the edible seeds and all the lovely juicy flesh that surrounds them.

Pawpaw (or papaya)

When ripe a pawpaw should, like an avocado, have some 'give' when you hold it in your hand and exert a little pressure. To prepare it, slice it in half vertically, scoop out the seeds, pare off the skin and slice or chop.

Clockwise from top left: passion fruit, pawpaw, kiwi fruit and lychees

Tropical Fruit Salad in Planter's Punch

Planter's punch, a popular drink throughout the Caribbean, is a delicious combination of rum, orange, lime and pineapple juice, with just a trace of cinnamon and nutmeg. The syrup for this fruit salad is based on exactly the same combination, which makes it very special indeed.

Serves 8

2 bananas, peeled and chopped into
1 inch (2.5 cm) chunks
8 oz (225 g) seedless black
grapes, halved
1 pawpaw, peeled and chopped into
1 inch (2.5 cm) chunks (see page 423)
1 large mango, peeled and chopped
into 1 inch (2.5 cm) chunks (see
page 417)
1 small pineapple, peeled and chopped
into 1 inch (2.5 cm) chunks (see
page 419)
2 oranges, peeled and cut into
segments
8 oz (225 g) lychees, peeled, stoned
and halved (see page 423)
2 kiwi fruit, peeled, halved and
cut into ½ inch (1 cm) slices (see
page 423)
4 passion fruit, halved
1 whole nutmeg

For the syrup:

4 oz (110 g) golden granulated sugar
2 small cinnamon sticks
10 fl oz (275 ml) water
pared zest and juice 2 limes
4 fl oz (120 ml) freshly squeezed
orange juice
4 fl oz (120 ml) pineapple juice
5 fl oz (150 ml) dark rum

Begin by making up the syrup: put the sugar, cinnamon and water in a small saucepan, then add the lime zest. Now, over a gentle flame, heat slowly until all the sugar has dissolved – it will take about 10 minutes. Stir it with a wooden spoon: you should have no sugar crystals left clinging to the spoon when you turn it over. After that, remove it from the heat and allow it to cool.

Add the prepared fruit to a large serving bowl, scooping the seeds from the halved passion fruit using a teaspoon, then strain in the cold syrup, along with the fruit juices, lime juice and rum. Stir well before covering with clingfilm and chilling in the fridge. As you serve the fruit salad, sprinkle a little freshly grated nutmeg over each serving.

Thai Fish Curry with Mango

You won't believe how utterly simple and easy this is, and yet it tastes exotic and wonderful and, what's more, it can all be prepared well in advance and the fish added about 10 minutes before you want to eat it. You can also make this using 1 lb 8 oz (700 g) of raw, peeled tiger prawns, added in place of the fish.

Begin by emptying the coconut milk into the pan or wok and stir while you bring it up to the boil, then reduce the heat to medium and cook until the fat separates from the solids. This will take 20 minutes or so, and you will have about 1 pint (570 ml) left. Now make the curry paste, and all you do is put everything in a food processor or blender and whiz until you have a rather coarse, rough-looking paste and everything is perfectly blended.

Now, over a medium heat, add the curry paste and fish to the pan and, once it has reached simmering point, give it 4 minutes. Finally, add the mango and cook for a further 2 minutes. Serve the curry with the coriander sprinkled over and Thai fragrant rice as an accompaniment. To prepare the curry in advance, make everything up, keeping the paste covered in the fridge, then, 10 minutes before you want to serve, bring the coconut milk back up to the boil, then add the paste, fish and mango as above.

Serves 4 generously
2 lb (900 g) firm fish fillet (Greenland halibut, cod or haddock, for example), skinned and chopped into 1½ inch (4 cm) chunks
1 large mango, peeled and cut into ¾ inch (2 cm) pieces (see page 417)
2 x 400 ml tins coconut milk

For the curry paste:
2 medium red chillies, halved and deseeded
grated zest and juice 1 lime
2 stems lemon grass, roughly chopped
1 inch (2.5 cm) piece fresh root ginger, peeled and sliced
4 cloves garlic, peeled
1 small onion, peeled and quartered
1 teaspoon shrimp paste
3 tablespoons Thai fish sauce

To garnish:
3 tablespoons chopped fresh coriander leaves

You will also need a deep frying pan with a diameter of 10 inches (25.5 cm), or a wok.

Plum and Cinnamon Oat Slices

This is really an all-fruit recipe – it's exceptionally good with plums, but I love it with fresh or dried no-soak apricots, or apples, raspberries and blueberries; in fact you can add whatever is in season. It's wonderful served either warm as a dessert with cream, or cold with ice cream, instead of cake with tea. It's also a great recipe for children to make, as it's so easy.

Start by cutting all the plums in half, around and through their natural line, give a little twist to separate the halves and remove the stones, then cut them into thin slices. Now place them in a bowl and toss them around with the cinnamon. Next mix the flour and porridge oats together with the salt in a mixing bowl, then melt the butter and sugar in a small saucepan over a fairly gentle heat, stirring from time to time until the butter has melted. Now mix the melted butter and sugar with the oat mixture, starting with a wooden spoon but finishing off with your hands so you end up with a lump of dough. Now halve the dough and press one half of the mixture into the baking tin, pressing it firmly all over the base with your hands like a wall-to-wall carpet. Next scatter the plums evenly over the surface, then top with the remaining oat mixture, again pressing down firmly.

Now place the tin on the centre shelf of the oven and bake for 25-30 minutes, or a bit longer if you like the top really crispy. Then remove the tin from the oven and allow to cool for about 10 minutes before marking into 15 squares – to do this make 2 cuts lengthways, then 4 cuts widthways, and don't worry if they're not all even. Unless you want to serve these warm, leave to cool completely in the tin.

Note: if you want to serve this as a dessert, it can be made in a round 9 inch (23 cm) springform tin, in which case it can be cut into 8-10 wedges and served warm from the oven.

Makes 15
1 lb (450 g) fresh plums
1 rounded teaspoon ground cinnamon
10 oz (275 g) organic plain wholemeal flour
5 oz (150 g) organic porridge oats
1 teaspoon salt
8 oz (225 g) butter
4 oz (110 g) light brown soft sugar

You will also need a non-stick baking tin measuring 10 x 6 inches (25.5 x 15 cm) and 1 inch (2.5 cm) deep, lightly greased.

Pre-heat the oven to gas mark 6, 400°F (200°C).

Opposite, top: Apricot and Cinnamon Oat Slice; bottom: Plum and Cinnamon Oat Slice

Old-Fashioned Rhubarb Trifle

*Old-fashioned because when I was a child – a very long time ago –
I used to love jelly trifles, and my mother would always make one
for my birthday. This is a much more adult version, and the sharp,
fragrant acidity of the rhubarb makes it a very light and refreshing
dessert for spring and early summer.*

Serves 6
1 lb 8 oz (700 g) fresh rhubarb
4 oz (110 g) golden caster sugar
grated zest and juice 1 orange
2 oz (50 g) pecans
6 trifle sponges
3 tablespoons marmalade
4 fl oz (120 ml) sercial Madeira
about 10 fl oz (275 ml) freshly
squeezed orange juice
1 x 11 g sachet gelatine powder
12 oz (350 g) fresh custard
7 oz (200 g) Greek yoghurt

To serve:
a little pouring cream (optional)

You will also need an ovenproof baking
dish measuring 7½ inches (19 cm)
square and 2 inches (5 cm) deep,
and 6 individual serving bowls or
1 large trifle bowl with a capacity of
3½ pints (2 litres).

Pre-heat the oven to gas mark 4,
350°F (180°C).

To prepare the rhubarb, cut it into 1 inch (2.5 cm) chunks and add these
to the baking dish. Then sprinkle in the caster sugar, together with the
zest and juice of the orange. Now pop the whole lot in the oven without
covering and let it cook for 30-40 minutes, until the rhubarb is tender but
still retains its shape. At the same time, place the pecans in the oven and
put a timer on for 7 minutes to toast them lightly, then you can either
leave them whole or chop them roughly.

While the rhubarb is cooking, slice the trifle sponges in half
lengthways, spread each half with the marmalade, then re-form them and
cut each one into 3 little sandwiches. Now arrange them either in the
individual serving bowls or the large trifle bowl. Then make a few stabs in
the sponges and sprinkle the Madeira carefully over them, then leave it all
aside so it can soak in.

When the rhubarb is cooked and has become completely cold, taste it
– if it is a bit sharp, add a little more sugar. Take a draining spoon and
carefully remove the chunks of rhubarb, placing them in and amongst the
sponges. Now pour all the juices from the dish into a measuring jug and
make this up to 18 fl oz (510 ml) with the orange juice.

Next, pour 8 fl oz (225 ml) of this into a small saucepan, scatter the
gelatine over, whisk it and leave it to soak for 5 minutes. Then place the
pan over a gentle heat and whisk everything until all the gelatine has
completely dissolved – about 2 minutes – then return this to the remaining
juice in the jug and give it all another good whisk. Now pour it over the
sponges and rhubarb. When it is completely cold, cover it with clingfilm
and leave in the fridge till completely set. The last thing you need to do is
whisk the custard and Greek yoghurt together in a mixing bowl, then
spoon this mixture over the set jelly.

Now cover with clingfilm again and chill until you're ready to serve.
Don't forget to sprinkle the toasted pecan nuts over just before serving,
and, although it doesn't strictly need it, a little chilled pouring cream is
a nice addition.

Roasted Figs with Gorgonzola and Honey-Vinegar Sauce

This may sound like an unlikely combination but it's simply brilliant – a first course that's fast, unusual and absolutely no trouble to prepare.

Serves 4 as a starter
12 ripe figs
6 oz (175 g) Gorgonzola Piccante, chopped into ¼ inch (5 mm) dice
salt and freshly milled black pepper

For the sauce:
2 tablespoons Greek honey
2 tablespoons red wine vinegar

You will also need a baking tray measuring 10 x 14 inches (25.5 x 35 cm), oiled.

Pre-heat the grill to its highest setting.

All you do is wipe and halve the figs, then place them, cut-side up, on the baking tray. Season with salt and freshly milled black pepper, then pop them under the grill for 5-6 minutes, until they're soft and just bubbling slightly. When the figs are ready, remove the baking tray from the grill and divide the cheese equally between them, gently pressing it down to squash it in a bit. Then pop them back under the grill for about 2 minutes, until the cheese is bubbling and faintly golden brown.

Meanwhile, make the sauce by combining the honey and vinegar together, then serve the figs with the sauce poured over.

Spiced Oranges in Port

This is a great Christmas recipe because you can make it ahead, it keeps well and can be used to accompany cold cuts of poultry, game or pork and it is especially good served with cooked ham, hot or cold.

First you need to dry-roast the coriander seeds and cardamom pods, and to do this place them in a small frying pan or saucepan over a medium heat and stir and toss them around for 1-2 minutes, or until they begin to look toasted and start to jump in the pan, then lightly crush them in a pestle and mortar. Now arrange the orange wedges in the base of the casserole, skin-side down, then sprinkle the spices on top (the pods of the cardamom seeds can go in as well). Next add the rest of the ingredients, then, over a gentle heat, slowly bring everything up to simmering point. Put the lid on and pop the casserole in the oven on a low shelf and leave it there for 3 hours, by which time the orange skins will be meltingly tender. When the oranges have cooled, store them in a jar or a lidded polythene box in the fridge for a couple of days to allow the flavours to develop.

Serves 6-8
2 navel oranges, each cut into
16 wedges, skin left on
6 fl oz (175 ml) tawny port
1 teaspoon coriander seeds
6 cardamom pods
4 whole cloves
1 inch (2.5 cm) piece fresh root ginger, peeled and cut into thin slices
½ cinnamon stick
4 oz (110 g) light brown soft sugar
4 fl oz (120 ml) water

You will also need a lidded flameproof casserole with a diameter of 8 inches (20 cm) and a capacity of 4 pints (2.25 litres).

Pre-heat the oven to gas mark 1, 275°F (140°C).

Apple and Almond Crumble

This is another movable feast because absolutely any fruit can be used. I love it with peaches or apricots in summer, in spring it's good with rhubarb, and in autumn I use half blackberries and half apples. Whatever fruit you use, though, the great thing about the topping is that it bakes to a lovely short, crumbly crispness that is almost crunchy.

Serves 6-8

1 lb 8 oz (700 g) Bramley apples
8 oz (225 g) Cox's apples
1 oz (25 g) light brown soft sugar
1 teaspoon ground cinnamon
¼ teaspoon ground cloves

For the crumble:

4 oz (110 g) whole almonds, skin on
3 oz (75 g) chilled butter, cut into small dice
6 oz (175 g) self-raising flour, sifted
2 teaspoons ground cinnamon
4 oz (110 g) demerara sugar

To serve:

custard or pouring cream

You will also need either an oval ovenproof baking dish measuring 7½ x 11 inches (19 x 28 cm) and 1¾ inches (4.5 cm) deep, or a round ovenproof baking dish with a diameter of 9½ inches (24 cm) and 1¾ inches (4.5 cm) deep.

Pre-heat the oven to gas mark 6, 400°F (200°C).

Begin by preparing the apples. I always find the best way to do this is to cut them first in quarters, then pare off the peel with a potato peeler and slice out the cores. Now cut them into thickish slices and toss them in a bowl with the sugar, cinnamon and ground cloves, then place them in the baking dish and put to one side.

Next make the crumble, which couldn't be simpler, as it is all made in a processor. All you do is place the butter, sifted flour, cinnamon and sugar in the processor and give it a whiz till it resembles crumbs. Next add the almonds and process again, not too fast, until they are fairly finely chopped and there are still a few chunky bits. If you don't have a processor, in a large bowl, rub the butter into the sifted flour until it resembles crumbs, then stir in the cinnamon, sugar and almonds, which should be fairly finely chopped by hand. Now simply sprinkle the crumble mixture all over the apples, spreading it right up to the edges of the dish, and, using the flat of your hands, press it down quite firmly all over; the more tightly it is packed together the crisper it will be. Then finish off by lightly running a fork all over the surface.

Now bake the crumble on the centre shelf of the oven for 35-40 minutes, by which time the apples will be soft and the topping golden brown and crisp. Leave it to rest for 10-15 minutes before serving, then serve it warm with custard or pouring cream.

Key Lime Pie

This is a very famous recipe from Florida, where a certain special variety of limes called Key limes are used. Their season is short and there aren't enough grown to export; however, the pie tastes just as good with other varieties of lime in this authentic American recipe.

Serves 8-10
For the base:
3½ oz (95 g) butter
6 oz (175 g) digestive biscuits
2 oz (50 g) Grape-Nuts

For the filling:
1 tablespoon grated lime zest
(zest 3 limes)
5 fl oz (150 ml) lime juice
(juice 4-5 large limes)
3 large egg yolks
14 oz (400 g) condensed milk

To finish:
a little crème fraîche
lime slices

You will also need a loose-based flan tin with a diameter of 9 inches (23 cm), 1 inch (2.5 cm) deep, and a solid baking sheet.

Pre-heat the oven to gas mark 4, 350°F (180°C).

Traditional Key lime pie has always had a crumb crust, and I have discovered recently that the addition of Grape-Nuts breakfast cereal gives the whole thing extra crunch. So begin by placing the butter in a pan over the lowest heat to melt, then crush the digestive biscuits. The easiest way to do this is to lay them out flat in a polythene bag and crush them with a rolling pin, rolling over using a lot of pressure. Now empty the contents of the bag into a bowl and mix in the Grape-Nuts, then add the melted butter and mix well. Next place the butter-crumb mixture in the flan tin and, using your hands, press it down evenly and firmly all over the base and up the sides of the tin. Then place it on the baking sheet and bake on the centre shelf of the oven for 10-12 minutes, or until crisp and golden brown.

While that's happening, place the egg yolks and lime zest in a bowl and, using an electric hand mixer, whisk them for about 2 minutes, or until the egg has thickened, then add the condensed milk and whisk for another 4 minutes. Finally, add the lime juice and give it another quick whisk, then pour the whole lot on to the baked crust and return it to the oven for another 20 minutes, or until it feels just set when you lightly press the centre with your little finger. Now remove it from the oven and, when it's completely cold, cover it with clingfilm and chill until needed. Serve cut in slices with crème fraîche and a twist of lime for decoration.

19

Cheese in the kitchen

Cheese with 'L' plates is how I want to introduce this chapter, because for a beginner, getting to grips with cheese as a universal subject can be a little fearsome. That said, though, cheese for me will always be one of nature's supreme culinary gifts, for the same magic ingredient the world over originally preserved the excess milk yields of four species (cows, goats, sheep and, to a small degree, buffalo) and transformed them into such a vast eclectic miscellany of textures and flavours, national and regional.

All of these are governed by varying climatic conditions, the types of grazing or feeding, with mountain air, sea breezes, highlands and marshlands all playing their part – and not forgetting the wealth of human skill and creativity that goes not just into the making of the cheese but into its careful ripening and maturing.

In a very short space of time – just 40 years – we have all moved into a vast new world of cheese. I can remember when there was only a handful of British cheeses to choose from, but now we're witnessing something akin to a cheese revolution. There are now not only countless excellent British regional cheesemakers, but a good number of exceptional Irish cheeses available, too. All this has taken place alongside a multiplicity of imported varieties. So to say we're spoilt for choice would be something of an understatement!

Cheese – the ultimate fast feast

What else can provide, all by itself, an instant but interesting, complete nourishing meal without any cooking? One 15th-century writer reverently described it as being part of the Trinity of the Table, along with good bread and fine wine. Another revered combination, equally sublime but perhaps more British, would be the partnership of good, sharp cheese with real ale, crusty home-baked bread and home-made chutney (or the Irish version, with Guinness or Murphy's and home-baked soda bread).

Without bread, cheese has a wonderful affinity with crackers, oatcakes or digestive biscuits, the last adding a touch of sweetness to a sharp, assertive cheese. Or, as my Yorkshire grandparents taught me, the combination of the same with some rich, dark, brandied fruitcake makes a lovely sharp and sweet contrast – great at Christmas with a glass of port.

The milder, lactic cheeses, such as Cotherstone or Lancashire, are great with crisp, sharp apples, while blue cheeses seem to have an affinity with crunchy celery and fresh-shelled walnuts. In Italy, Pecorino Romano is often served with ripe, fragrant pears, and in Spain they serve thin slices of their famous Manchego with a sweet paste made of quince.

Cheese for eating (the five families)

For a beginner, the easiest way to get a knowledge of cheese is to place them into five groups, or families.

1) Squidgy and creamy

These are called soft-paste cheeses and are distinctive in that they have floury, unwashed rinds. The most famous of these are Camembert, Brie and Coulommiers, all from Normandy. Now there is strong competition from Ireland in their version and another beautiful cheese called Cooleeney. Other popular squidgy-creamy cheeses are Brie de Meaux, Reblochon, Emlett (sheep) and Tymsboro (goat).

2) Medium-soft

These are slightly firmer than the previous group, but still have a soft texture, and they undergo a washing process that keeps the rind moist and helps to encourage fermentation. Pont l'Evêque is from Normandy, whilst Taleggio is from Italy. Other cheeses I would include in this group include Livarot, also from Normandy, and Durrus and Milleens, both of which are from Ireland.

3) Hard and not so hard

This family includes pressed, uncooked cheeses, where the curds are drained and bandaged in a cheese cloth, placed in moulds and then kept under pressure for up to 24 hours. The hardest of these are Pecorino Romano, Grana Padano and the world-famous Parmesan (Parmigiano Reggiano). Pecorino is a sheep's cheese very much like Parmesan, but has a coarser, sharper flavour.

Then comes the less-hard group, including Cheddar, Leicester, Double Gloucester and Cheshire, as well as the hard but crumbly varieties, such as Lancashire, Cotherstone and Feta.

Finally, there are the cheeses with holes, which have undergone a sort of cooking process before being put into moulds and pressed as above. During the maturing period fermentation occurs internally, and this creates the little air pockets, or holes, that distinguish this type of cheese, of which the most famous are Gruyère and Emmental.

4) The blues

What happens here is the cheese is injected with a harmless penicillin mould while the cheese is being made. This lies quite dormant during the maturation process, but then later on needles are inserted to allow air in, activating the mould, which then spreads itself in tiny bluish-green veins throughout the cheese during the rest of the maturing period. Three countries claim to have the finest blue cheese: from France, Roquefort, from Italy, Gorgonzola, and from England, Stilton, all great cheeses indeed, although I would say that Cashel Blue from Ireland is another great blue.

Other examples are Shropshire Blue, Bleu de Bresse and Dolcelatte (a milder Gorgonzola).

5) Goats' cheese

These can be like any of the groups above, from a soft, spreadable young cheese with a mild flavour, to a well-matured, strong, zesty, very goaty-flavoured one. For eating I like the strong-flavoured French Crottins de Chavignol, the English Chabis, or Mine Gabhar, which is Irish. The log-shaped Chèvre, dusted in ashes, is a medium-matured softer goats' cheese. For a fresh farmhouse goats' cheese with a milder flavour that also grills very well, Perroche is superb. But because the quantity of goats' cheese made on farms fluctuates with the seasons, it is often in short supply. There are farm-made soft-rind goats' cheeses labelled Welsh or Somerset, which are fine for cooking.

Fresh soft curd cheeses

This is the unfermented fresh cheese collection – all are made from skimmed, semi-skimmed, whole milk or cream. Because these are not strictly in the same cheese class as those just mentioned, information about these is in the dairy chapter (pages 394 and 395), where I think they sit more happily.

How to serve a good cheese board

Keep it simple is my philosophy on this one, and what I would do is choose one cheese from each of the following groups: one soft, squidgy cheese (Camembert, for example), one hard cheese (unpasteurised Cheddar), one blue cheese (Cashel Blue), one medium-soft (Taleggio) and one goats' cheese (Crottin). A cheese board sample is photographed left. Simply pick any five cheeses, using the lists to guide you as to what you would prefer.

Pasteurised or unpasteurised?

Pasteurised is a word that causes much debate both within the world of cheesemaking and amongst consumers and cheese lovers everywhere. In cheesemaking the skill is directed towards the flavour and aroma of the finished cheese. This is derived from the animal that has given its milk and the plant oils it has digested. We have all experienced that particular taste and smell, which we are at a loss to describe other than it's like tasting the farm or the countryside. Every good cheese, like every fine wine, has its own unique and special earthiness, which is linked to its equally unique and special environment.

Thus if raw, untreated milk is used to make the cheese, all that's described above is left intact and unimpaired. What pasteurisation (heat-treating the milk) does is destroy any harmful microorganisms, which may be a good thing when the traditional care and skill of the cheesemaker has not been adhered to, but the bad thing is it can destroy much of the flavour-enriching microorganisms at the same time. So it is argued that pasteurised cheese can never have the distinctive and unique flavour that will satisfy a true cheese lover. I would say that in my own experience I have found this to be absolutely true, and I would always go that extra mile for an unpasteurised Camembert or Cheddar. However, there is a new generation of skilful and clever cheesemakers who are making excellent cheeses with pasteurised milk, so in the end, let your palate be your guide.

Cheese for cooking

Some cheeses are best simply for eating as they are; others are good to eat and also respond extremely well in cooking; others are best kept just for cooking, and below I have put cooking cheeses into three categories.

Strong and assertive

Stilton	Strong unpasteurised Cheddar
Gorgonzola	Parmesan (Parmigiano Reggiano)
Pecorino	Crottin
Roquefort	

Cheesy but subtle

Gruyère	Medium Cheddar
Feta	Lancashire
Fontina	Brie
Medium goats' cheese	

Subtle and creamy

Mozzarella	Taleggio
Ricotta	Mild goats' cheese

Good melting cheeses

This group melts in a flash, so is excellent for cooking, and includes Fontina, Gruyère, Mozzarella and smoked Mozzarella (Scamorza).

How to store cheese

This is a question there is no absolute definitive answer to. I have heard of suitable cool places: a spare bedroom (no heating on), garages, garden sheds and car boots, but it all depends on the weather. I was once storing and ripening a Camembert in my garage, and the weather turned warm when I was away and my mother was looking after the house. I got a call that said something like, 'I think there's something dead in your garage.'

Storing cheese in the fridge at too low a temperature means the flavour can be impaired, but if the weather is hot, sweaty cheese is hardly preferable.

The real answer to this question is to buy your cheese from a reliable supplier (see page 698). You will then receive it in good condition so it's ready to eat, so the very best thing to do is eat it a.s.a.p., otherwise store the cheese, wrapped carefully – with no cracks or bits showing – in either waxed paper or greaseproof or parchment paper, sealed with adhesive tape or an elastic band. If the weather is cool, any of the places mentioned above is suitable, if not then place it in the lowest part of the refrigerator. Clingfilm is not recommended, but I do keep my Parmesan in a polythene bag tied at the top in a cheese box in the fridge, and it keeps very well.

Welsh Rabbit with Sage and Onions

Rarebit or rabbit? I like the latter, which (so the story goes) is what the hunter had for his supper when the rabbits had escaped his gun.

*Serves 4 for lunch or as a starter or
2 as a main course*

4 large, thick slices from a good-
quality white sandwich loaf
1 dessertspoon chopped fresh sage
1 rounded dessertspoon grated onion
8 oz (225 g) mature Cheddar, grated
1 rounded teaspoon mustard powder
4 tablespoons brown ale
1 large egg, beaten
1 teaspoon Worcestershire sauce
a pinch cayenne pepper

You will also need a grill pan or baking
tray lined with foil.

Pre-heat the grill to its highest setting.

Begin by mixing all the ingredients together, apart from the bread and cayenne pepper. Now place the bread under the grill and toast it on both sides till crisp and golden, then remove it to a toast rack for 3 minutes to get really crisp. After that, divide the cheese mixture into 4, spread it over the toast – right to the edges so they don't get burnt – then sprinkle each one with a light dusting of cayenne pepper. Then back they go under the grill, 3 inches (7.5 cm) from the heat, until the cheese is golden brown and bubbling, which will take 4-5 minutes. Serve it just as it is or with some salad leaves and a sharp dressing.

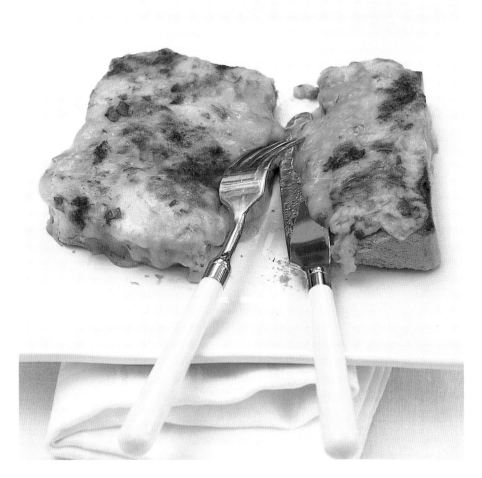

Crumpet Pizza

Well, a crumpet pizza does make sense if you think about it – soft, squidgy bread that gets lightly toasted for just a bit of crunch, then all those wonderful holes so that the cheese and other ingredients can melt right down into it. And because crumpets are quite small, the fillings get piled up very high and it all becomes rather lovely.

All you do is lightly toast the crumpets on each side (they can be quite close to the heat at this stage) – they need to be lightly golden, which takes about 1 minute on each side. Then remove them to a baking sheet and all you do is pile up the Gorgonzola and Mozzarella on each crumpet, then sprinkle with the chopped walnuts and, finally, place the sage leaves – first dipped in the olive oil – on top. Now back they go under the hot grill, but this time 5 inches (13 cm) from the heat source, for 5 minutes, by which time the cheeses will have melted, the walnuts toasted and the sage become crisp. Then you can serve them absolutely immediately.

You can get really creative and make up loads more ideas of your own. Obviously the whole thing can be very easily adapted to whatever happens to be available.

Serves 4 as a snack or 2 as a main course
4 crumpets
6 oz (175 g) Gorgonzola, cubed
2 oz (50 g) Mozzarella, cubed
2 oz (50 g) chopped walnuts
12 medium-sized fresh sage leaves
1 tablespoon olive oil

Pre-heat the grill to its highest setting.

Mexican Enchiladas with Cheese

What are enchiladas? Well, they're Mexican wheat-flour pancakes that can be spread with some spicy salsa and stuffed with almost anything you have handy – in this case cheese – and then baked. An excellent light lunch dish served with a salad.

Serves 4 for lunch or as a starter or 2 as a main course
For the salsa:
1 x 400 g tin chopped tomatoes
1 medium green chilli (the fat, squat variety that isn't too fiery)
1 medium red onion, peeled and finely chopped
2 heaped tablespoons chopped fresh coriander leaves, plus a little extra to garnish
juice 1 lime
salt and freshly milled black pepper

For the enchiladas:
4 large flour tortillas
4 oz (110 g) Wensleydale, grated
5 oz (150 g) Mozzarella, grated (a block of Mozzarella is best for this)
7 fl oz (200 ml) half-fat crème fraîche

You will also need an ovenproof baking dish measuring 9 inches (23 cm) square and 2 inches (5 cm) deep, lightly oiled, and a frying pan.

Pre-heat the oven to gas mark 4, 350°F (180°C).

Begin by making the salsa: first tip the tomatoes into a sieve over a bowl to let the excess liquid drain away. Next remove the stalk from the chilli, cut it in half, remove and discard the seeds, chop the flesh very finely and place it in a bowl. Then add half the chopped onion, the drained tomatoes, chopped coriander leaves and lime juice, and season well with salt and pepper. Now give everything a thorough mixing.

Meanwhile, mix the two cheeses together in a bowl. Next put the frying pan over a high flame to pre-heat and, when it's hot, dry-fry each of the tortillas for 6 seconds on each side. Place one tortilla on a flat surface and spread a tablespoon of salsa over it, but not quite to the edges, sprinkle over a heaped tablespoon of the cheese mixture, then follow this with a tablespoon of the crème fraîche. Then roll the tortilla up and place it in the baking dish with the sealed-side down. Repeat this with the others, then spread the remaining crème fraîche on top of the tortillas in the dish and sprinkle the rest of the salsa over the top, followed by the remaining cheeses and red onion. Now place the dish on a high shelf of the oven for 25-30 minutes, garnish with the extra coriander and serve absolutely immediately – if you keep them waiting they can become a bit soggy.

Toasted Goats' Cheese with Blackened Sherry-Vinegar Onions

Toasted goats' cheese became very fashionable in the 1990s, and not surprisingly, as it's still a supremely good way to enjoy good goats' cheese just on the point of melting. The blackened onions make a great accompaniment – lots of lovely gutsy flavour.

Serves 4

2 x 100 g soft-rind goats' cheeses, such as Welsh or Somerset (or 4 Crottins)
3 fl oz (75 ml) sherry vinegar
1 lb (450 g) large, mild Spanish onions (about 3)
1 oz (25 g) molasses sugar
2 tablespoons extra virgin olive oil
1 small curly lettuce
2 oz (50 g) rocket, stalks removed
salt and freshly milled black pepper

For the vinaigrette:

1 clove garlic, peeled
1 rounded teaspoon Maldon sea salt
1 rounded teaspoon mustard powder
1 dessertspoon balsamic vinegar
1 dessertspoon sherry vinegar
5 tablespoons extra virgin olive oil
freshly milled black pepper

You will also need a baking tray measuring 10 x 14 inches (25.5 x 35 cm) for the onions, and a smaller, solid baking tray, lightly oiled, for the goats' cheese.

Pre-heat the oven to gas mark 8, 450°F (230°C).

Begin this by roasting the onions: first you need to mix the sugar and vinegar together in a large bowl and give it a good whisk, then leave it to one side for 10 minutes or so for the sugar to dissolve. Meanwhile, peel the onions, then, leaving the root intact, cut each one into 8 sections through the root, so in half first and then each half into 4. Then add the onions and oil to the vinegar and sugar mixture and toss them around so they get a good coating. After that, spread them out on the baking tray, pouring the rest of the dressing over and season well. Now place them on a high shelf in the oven and cook for 15 minutes; after that turn them over and give them another 15 minutes. Towards the end of the cooking time, check them and remove and set aside any that are in danger of over-blackening. Continue to cook the rest till they are all fairly dark, then remove them from the oven and set aside – they're not meant to be served hot.

When you are ready to serve the salad, pre-heat the grill to its highest setting for at least 10 minutes. Then make the vinaigrette dressing by first crushing the garlic and salt to a creamy paste in a pestle and mortar, then work in the mustard. Now switch to a whisk and add the vinegars and oil, then season with freshly milled black pepper. Next slice each goats' cheese in half so you have 4 rounds, season these with freshly milled black pepper. Now place them on the oiled baking tray and grill them 3 inches (7.5 cm) from the heat for 5-7 minutes, until they are brown on top and soft (if you use the smaller crottins these take only 3-4 minutes).

While they're grilling, arrange some lettuce leaves on each serving plate and divide and scatter the rocket between them. Then, when the cheese is ready, place one in the middle of each plate, scatter the onion all round and, finally, drizzle the vinaigrette dressing over each salad. Needless to say, lots of crusty bread should be available.

Pasta with Four Cheeses

I know you can see only three cheeses in the smaller picture below, but there is a hidden one, because Torta Gorgonzola is in fact made from layers of two cheeses, Gorgonzola and Mascarpone, as you can see from the main picture. Add to that Ricotta and some Pecorino and you have a five-star recipe – including the best-quality pasta, of course!

You need to start this by measuring out the cheeses on a plate to have them at the ready, then cook the pasta in plenty of boiling salted water for 1 minute less than the full cooking time (if you're using Martelli or other good-quality pasta this would be 11 minutes) – but you need to know your pasta, so see Chapter 10. As soon as it's ready, drain the pasta in a colander and immediately return it to the saucepan so that it still has quite a bit of moisture clinging to it. Now quickly add the chives, Ricotta, Torta Gorgonzola and Pecorino, and stir till the cheese begins to melt. Serve it in hot bowls with the extra Pecorino on the table to sprinkle over.

Note: if you can't find Torta Gorgonzola, there is a very similar layered cheese called Torta di Dolcelatte, which you could use instead.

Serves 2

8 oz (225 g) dried pasta (penne, for example)
2 oz (50 g) Ricotta
3 oz (75 g) Torta Gorgonzola, diced
1 oz (25 g) Pecorino Romano, finely grated, plus a little extra to serve
2 tablespoons snipped fresh chives
Maldon sea salt

Cauliflower Soup with Roquefort

This is a truly sublime soup, as the cauliflower and Roquefort seem to meld together so well, but I have also tried it with mature Cheddar, and I'm sure it would be good with any cheese you happen to have handy. More good news – it takes little more than 40 minutes to make.

The stock for this is very simply made with all the cauliflower trimmings. All you do is trim the cauliflower into small florets and then take the stalk bits, including the green stems, and place these trimmings in a medium-sized saucepan. Then add the water, bay leaves and some salt, bring it up to the boil and simmer for 20 minutes with a lid.

Meanwhile, take another large saucepan with a well-fitting lid, melt the butter in it over a gentle heat, then add the onion, celery, leek and potato, cover and let the vegetables gently sweat for 15 minutes. Keep the heat very low, then, when the stock is ready, strain it into the pan to join the vegetables, adding the bay leaves as well but throwing out the rest. Now add the cauliflower florets, bring it all back up to simmering point and simmer very gently for 20-25 minutes, until the cauliflower is completely tender, this time without a lid.

After that, remove the bay leaves, then place the contents of the saucepan in a food processor or liquidiser and process until the soup is smooth and creamy. Next return it to the saucepan, stir in the crème fraîche and cheese and keep stirring until the cheese has melted and the soup is hot but not boiling. Check the seasoning, then serve in hot bowls, garnished with the chives.

Serves 4-6

1 medium, good-sized cauliflower (about 1 lb 4 oz/570 g)
2 oz (50 g) Roquefort, crumbled into small pieces
2½ pints (1.5 litres) water
2 bay leaves
1 oz (25 g) butter
1 medium onion, peeled and chopped
2 sticks celery, chopped
1 large leek, trimmed, washed and chopped
4 oz (110 g) potato, peeled and chopped into dice
2 tablespoons half-fat crème fraîche
salt and freshly milled black pepper

To serve:
1 tablespoon snipped fresh chives

Caramelised Balsamic and Red-Onion Tarts with Goats' Cheese

The long, slow cooking of red onions and balsamic vinegar gives a lovely sweet, concentrated, caramel consistency. These are then spooned into crispy cheese-pastry cases and topped with goats' cheese and thyme. Serve as a special first course with some balsamic-dressed salad leaves.

Makes 8

For the pastry:
3 oz (75 g) butter, at room temperature
6 oz (175 g) plain flour, plus a little extra for rolling
2 oz (50 g) mature Cheddar, grated
½ teaspoon mustard powder
a pinch cayenne pepper
a little cold water
1 large egg, beaten, for brushing

For the filling:
6 tablespoons balsamic vinegar
2 lb (900 g) red onions, peeled and very finely sliced
2 x 100 g soft-rind goats' cheeses, such as Welsh or Somerset, top and bottom rinds removed and discarded, each sliced into 4 rounds
1 oz (25 g) butter
1 dessertspoon chopped fresh thyme
8 sprigs fresh thyme
a little olive oil
cayenne pepper, for sprinkling
salt and freshly milled black pepper

You will also need 8 mini flan tins, each with a base diameter of 4¼ inches (11 cm), ¾ inches (2 cm) deep, greased, and a 6 inch (15 cm) plate to cut around.

Pre-heat the oven to gas mark 4, 350°F (180°C).

First make the pastry by rubbing the butter lightly into the flour, then add the cheese, mustard and cayenne, plus just enough cold water to make a smooth dough – 1-2 tablespoons. Then place the dough in a polythene bag to rest in the refrigerator for 20 minutes. After that, roll it out as thinly as possible and use the plate as a guide to cut out 8 rounds. Line the greased flan tins with the pastry and lightly prick the bases with a fork, then place on a baking sheet and cook on the centre shelf of the oven for 15-20 minutes, or until the pastry is cooked through but not coloured. Then allow the pastry cases to cool on a wire rack and store them in an airtight container until they are needed.

To make the filling, melt the butter in a heavy-based medium-sized saucepan, stir in the onions, balsamic vinegar and chopped thyme, season and let everything cook very gently without a lid, stirring often, for about 30 minutes, until the mixture has reduced down, taken on a lovely glazed appearance and all the excess liquid has evaporated. Then let the mixture cool until you are ready to make the tarts.

To bake the tarts, brush a little beaten egg over each pastry case and pop them back in the oven – same temperature as before – for 5 minutes: this helps to provide a seal for the pastry and stops it from becoming soggy. Now spoon the onion mixture into the cases and top each one with a slice of goats' cheese and a sprig of thyme that has first been dipped in the olive oil. Finally, sprinkle with a little cayenne pepper and bake for 20 minutes.

Cheese and Herb Fritters with Sweet-Pepper Marmalade

If you want to serve a meal without meat or fish, this is just the thing. It's also a great recipe for using up odd bits of cheese, which can be varied as long as the total amount ends up being 12 oz (350 g) for four people or 6 oz (175 g) for two. The sweet-pepper marmalade is an amazingly good accompaniment and keeps well, so can be made in advance.

Begin this by sifting the 2 oz (50 g) of flour and cayenne pepper into a large bowl and season with salt and black pepper, then make a well in the centre and break the eggs into it. Now gradually whisk in the eggs, incorporating any bits of flour from the edge of the bowl as you do so. Next whisk in the milk until you have a smooth batter, then gently stir in the grated cheeses and herbs. Now cover the bowl and leave it to stand in a cool place for about an hour, as this allows all the flavours to develop.

While that's happening you can make the sweet-pepper marmalade. First heat the oil in a saucepan over a medium heat and, when it's hot, add the onion and peppers. Cook them, tossing them around from time to time, until golden and tinged brown – about 10 minutes – then add the garlic and cook for another minute. Now add the sugar, cider vinegar and cider, stir and bring everything back up to simmering point. Then season with salt and freshly milled black pepper, turn the heat down to its lowest setting and simmer gently, uncovered, for 1¼ hours, or until the liquid has almost evaporated and you have a thick, marmalade consistency.

When you're ready to cook the fritters, take 1 tablespoon of the mixture at a time and make 12 rounds, flatten them gently to about 2½ inches (6 cm) in diameter, then lightly dust each one with the seasoned flour. Next, heat the oil over a highish heat in the frying pan and, when it's shimmering hot, cook half the fritters over a medium heat for 45-60 seconds each side, or until golden brown and crispy. Then carefully lift them out of the pan to drain on crumpled greaseproof or kitchen paper. Keep the first batch warm while you cook the second, then serve with the sweet-pepper marmalade. A green salad would make a good accompaniment.

Serves 4
4 oz (110 g) Feta, finely grated
4 oz (110 g) Gruyère, finely grated
4 oz (110 g) mature Cheddar, finely grated
3 heaped tablespoons chopped mixed herbs (basil, thyme, oregano and parsley, for example)
2 oz (50 g) plain flour, plus 1 slightly rounded dessertspoon seasoned flour
2 good pinches cayenne pepper
2 large eggs
2 tablespoons milk
3 tablespoons olive oil
salt and freshly milled black pepper

For the sweet-pepper marmalade:
2 large red peppers, deseeded, thinly sliced into lengths, then cut into 1 inch (2.5 cm) pieces
1 tablespoon olive oil
1 medium onion, peeled and finely chopped
2 cloves garlic, peeled and crushed
2 tablespoons dark brown soft sugar
3 tablespoons cider vinegar
8 fl oz (225 ml) medium cider
salt and freshly milled black pepper

You will also need a frying pan with a diameter of 10 inches (25.5 cm).

Semolina Gnocchi with Gorgonzola

In Chapter 8 we made potato gnocchi, but this is another quite different version, made with semolina instead of potato. They are equally charming, with crisp, baked edges, and are light and fluffy on the inside. Remember, though, that the mixture needs to be prepared the day before you want to serve the gnocchi.

Serves 3-4
5 oz (150 g) coarse semolina
2 oz (50 g) Gorgonzola Piccante, chopped into small dice
10 fl oz (275 ml) milk
10 fl oz (275 ml) water
freshly grated nutmeg
2½ oz (60 g) Parmesan (Parmigiano Reggiano), finely grated
2 large eggs
2 oz (50 g) Ricotta
salt and freshly milled black pepper

You will also need a non-stick baking tin measuring 6 x 10 inches (15 x 25.5 cm), 1 inch (2.5 cm) deep, lined with silicone paper (parchment), a 2 inch (5 cm) pastry cutter and an ovenproof baking dish measuring 7½ inches (19 cm) square and 2 inches (5 cm) deep, lightly buttered.

First of all you'll need a large saucepan, and into that put the milk and water, along with a good grating of nutmeg, 1 teaspoon of salt and some freshly milled black pepper. Then sprinkle in the semolina and, over a medium heat and stirring constantly with a wooden spoon, bring it all up to the boil. Let the mixture simmer gently for about 4 minutes, still stirring, until it is thick enough to stand the spoon up in, then remove the pan from the heat and beat in 2 oz (50 g) of the Parmesan and the eggs. Now adjust the seasoning, then pour the mixture into the prepared tin and spread it out evenly with a spatula. When it's absolutely cold, cover the tin with clingfilm and leave it in the fridge overnight to firm up.

When you are ready to cook the gnocchi, pre-heat the oven to gas mark 6, 400°F (200°C). Turn the cheese and semolina mixture out on to a board and peel away the silicone paper, then cut the mixture into 2 inch (5 cm) rounds with the pastry cutter, reshape the trimmings and cut out more rounds until the mixture is all used up. I quite like rounds, but if you prefer you can cut out squares or triangles – it makes no difference. Place them slightly overlapping in the baking dish, then dot with the Ricotta and sprinkle over the Gorgonzola, followed by the rest of the Parmesan. Bake on a high shelf of the oven for 30 minutes, until the gnocchi are golden brown and the cheese is bubbling.

Begin by adding the semolina to the milk and water mixture in the pan

Bring to the boil, then simmer till you can stand the spoon upright in the mixture

Next beat in the grated Parmesan and eggs, then taste to check the seasoning

Spread the mixture out in the tin and, once cold, cover and refrigerate overnight

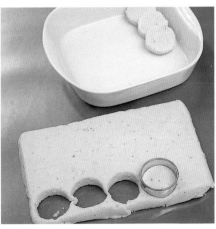

Turn the mixture out, peel the base paper away and stamp the gnocchi out

Lay them in the dish, add the remaining cheeses and bake until golden brown

Curd Cheesecake with Greek Yoghurt, Honey and Pistachios

Well, the title says it all, and you can imagine what a brilliant combination of flavours and textures this is. It's quite simply one of the best cheesecakes ever, and perfect for parties, as it's quite large. It's also extremely good topped with summer fruits, in which case add 2 oz (50 g) of caster sugar to the curd cheese and top with 1 lb (450 g) of any mixture of soft fruit, then dust with icing sugar before serving. Don't forget that cheesecakes are best left in the warmth of the oven to get cold, as this stops them from cracking, so you need to think ahead.

First of all make the cheesecake base: first melt the butter in a saucepan over a very low heat, then spread the biscuits out flat in a polythene bag and crush them firmly with a rolling pin. Next tip the crumbs into a bowl, along with the chopped pistachios. Now add the Grape-Nuts and melted butter and mix everything together, then spread the mixture over the base of the tin, pressing it down very firmly, and pop it on the baking sheet and into the oven for 20 minutes.

Now, in another bowl, combine the curd cheese, eggs and vanilla and beat with an electric hand whisk until the mixture is smooth and velvety. Then pour this into the tin, on top of the crumbs, smooth the top and place it back on the baking sheet on the centre shelf of the oven for 30 minutes, then turn the oven off and let the cheesecake get quite cold in the oven. After that it should be covered and chilled for at least 2 hours, or preferably overnight.

To serve, unmould the cheesecake, spread the surface with the yoghurt first, then drizzle with the honey and scatter the pistachios over. Serve with extra honey at the table to spoon over.

Serves 10-12

1 lb 8 oz (700 g) curd cheese
2 oz (50 g) shelled unsalted pistachios, roughly chopped
3 oz (75 g) butter
6 oz (175 g) sweet oat biscuits
1 oz (25 g) Grape-Nuts cereal
3 large eggs, beaten
2 teaspoons vanilla extract

To finish:

7 oz (200 g) Greek yoghurt
3 tablespoons Greek honey, plus a little extra to serve
about 1 oz (25 g) shelled unsalted pistachios, roughly chopped

You will also need a springform tin with a diameter of 9 inches (23 cm), and a solid baking sheet.

Pre-heat the oven to gas mark 2, 300°F (150°C).

20
Proper chocolate

Evocations of the chocolate of
my childhood have flooded my
mind while pondering this
introduction. Even when I was
very small I much preferred the
dark, sophisticated adult-tasting
chocolate to the over-sweet
milky version. I had a favourite
brand – no longer available,
unfortunately – called Nestlé
Superfine, which was always
given to me on birthdays.

Sometimes it was a straight chocolate bar; sometimes it contained clusters of dark, highly roasted almonds. Either way it was always an enormous treat, not only to be anticipated but to be savoured right down to the very last square. Those were the days of sweet rationing in the early years after the war, and I sometimes think it's sad that the specialness of chocolate has faded. Now it's available everywhere from kiosks, tobacconists and vending machines and so has become just an ordinary everyday item. Worse than that, the mass marketing of chocolate has brought an inevitable downgrading in quality, and the nation's increasing addiction to sugar and sugar substitutes has meant that chocolate is not always eaten for itself but as a backdrop, more to satisfy a craving for sweetness, so much so that if you're addicted to sweet substances like diet cola and so on the true glory of chocolate will probably escape you. What, then, is the true glory?

To discover it we need to consider how much *actual* chocolate is in a chocolate bar. It is a moot point. Close examination of the packaging will reveal that it can be as high as 75 or as low as 20 per cent. For chocolate lovers – and particularly for the cook – these variations need explaining.

What is chocolate?

Chocolate comes from the cocoa bean, the fruit of the cacao tree, which grows in Africa, South America and the West Indies, and the beans vary in quality and flavour. After roasting and crushing, the beans become a thick paste called chocolate mass, and this is composed of cocoa solids and cocoa butter, which is chocolate's natural oil. Cocoa solids, once they are crushed again and sieved, become cocoa powder. For chocolate, however, cocoa butter is essential, as this is what gives it its melting qualities, and the higher the proportion, the better the chocolate. We need not concern ourselves here with the complexities of how the beans are transformed into the silky-textured ingredient known as chocolate; what we do need to know is how much actual cocoa the chocolate contains. My advice is not to worry about technical words such as cocoa mass, cocoa butter or cocoa solids, but to look fairly and squarely at the word cocoa on the packet. How much does it have? Manufacturers usually use the words 'cocoa solids', and we need 75 per cent if we want an intensely chocolatey flavour, and if we are cooking with it and adding it to other ingredients (which will dilute it somewhat), it's essential to get the highest-possible cocoa-solid content.

What is *not* chocolate?

If only 20 per cent of the essential component, cocoa solids, is present in a chocolate bar, this means 80 per cent of it comprises something else. This can be vegetable fat or butterfat, emulsifiers, milk solids, flavourings and, worst of all, sugar – so much of it that the small quantity of cocoa solid is killed. The reason for this is that mass marketing is always about price. Real chocolate costs more money, so the higher the cocoa content, the higher the price. But here we are concerned with how to cook, and with chocolate that means getting the best you can afford.

How to buy chocolate

Thankfully people are rediscovering real chocolate and, for eating, it is even possible for the connoisseur to buy chocolate made from single-estate cocoa plantations, each with their own distinctive characteristics. These will be clearly marked 75 per cent cocoa solids and you will find just three ingredients listed: cocoa, sugar and cocoa butter. For cooking it's now easy to buy 75 per cent cocoa-solid chocolate, which will contain an emulsifier called lecithin and, sometimes, a flavouring such as vanilla.

Milk and white chocolates

With milk chocolate, the chocolate's intense flavour is purposely diluted to produce a creamier taste. This is achieved by adding whole milk solids, sometimes in equal quantity to the cocoa solids. White chocolate is not actually chocolate at all. Made from milk solids, sugar and fat, with a little cocoa butter added, it has a bland, over-sweet taste. Neither is ideal for cooking as such, but both are useful for coating or topping (see page 470).

Listen to the snap

We had great fun, while filming the television series, demonstrating how to tell good chocolate from not-so-good. The secret is in the snap. When you break off a piece of good-quality chocolate it makes a sharp, quite definite 'snap'. With a lesser chocolate it is just a dull break – if you hear anything at all. We found the sensitive microphone picked up the snap superbly, so that none of us could be in any doubt ever again.

Cooking with chocolate

I have learnt how to deal with chocolate the hard way, as I have, more often than I care to remember, ended up with a claggy lump fit only for the bin. The outcome of these disasters is that I now know the solution to the problem of melting chocolate: that is to follow the instructions below to the letter and never rush it! I know it's a bore, but believe me, you have to wait.

How to melt chocolate

Here you'll need a large heatproof bowl to sit over a saucepan containing a couple of inches of barely simmering water, making sure the base of the bowl doesn't touch the water. Break up the chocolate, add the pieces to the bowl and, keeping the heat at its lowest, leave them to melt – it will take 5-10 minutes to become smooth and glossy (though the time will vary depending on the amount of chocolate – individual timings are given in each recipe). Then remove the pan from the heat, give the chocolate a good stir and it's ready.

A Very Chocolatey Mousse

This was the chocolate recipe of the 1960s, but it has now, sadly, been eclipsed by other eras and their equally fashionable recipes. So time for a revival, I think, because it's certainly one of the simplest but nicest chocolate desserts of all.

Serves 6
7 oz (200 g) dark chocolate (75 per cent cocoa solids), broken into pieces
4 fl oz (120 ml) warm water
3 large eggs, separated
1½ oz (40 g) golden caster sugar

To serve:
a little whipped cream (optional)

You will also need 6 ramekins, each with a capacity of 5 fl oz (150 ml), or 6 individual serving glasses.

First of all place the broken-up chocolate and warm water in a large heatproof bowl, which should be sitting over a saucepan of barely simmering water, making sure the bowl doesn't touch the water. Then, keeping the heat at its lowest, allow the chocolate to melt slowly – it should take about 6 minutes. Now remove it from the heat and give it a good stir until it's smooth and glossy, then let the chocolate cool for 2-3 minutes before stirring in the egg yolks. Then give it another good mix with a wooden spoon.

Next, in a clean bowl, whisk the egg whites to the soft-peak stage, then whisk in the sugar, about a third at a time, then whisk again until the whites are glossy. Now, using a metal spoon, fold a tablespoon of the egg whites into the chocolate mixture to loosen it, then carefully fold in the rest. You need to have patience here – it needs gentle folding and cutting movements so that you retain all the precious air, which makes the mousse light. Next divide the mousse between the ramekins or glasses and chill for at least 2 hours, covered with clingfilm. I think it's also good to serve the mousse with a blob of softly whipped cream on top.
Note: this recipe contains raw eggs.

Chocolate-Crunch Torte with Pistachios and Sour Cherries

This is the easiest chocolate recipe ever invented – I first made a more basic version on children's television. Since then it's got much more sophisticated, but the joy of its simplicity and the fact that no cooking is required make it a real winner for busy people.

Begin this the day before by soaking the dried cherries and raisins in the rum overnight. When you are ready to make the torte, place the broken-up chocolate and butter in a large heatproof bowl, which should be sitting over a saucepan of barely simmering water, making sure the bowl doesn't touch the water. Then, keeping the heat at its lowest, allow the chocolate to melt – it should take about 6 minutes to become smooth and glossy. Now remove the bowl from the pan, give the chocolate a good stir and let it cool for 2-3 minutes. Next, fold in the whipped cream, followed by the soaked fruits in rum, the pistachios and chopped biscuits, and give it all a good mix. Finally, spoon it into the cake tin as evenly as possible, cover with clingfilm and chill for a minimum of 4 hours. To serve, dust the surface with a little cocoa powder, cut the torte into wedges, then serve with crème fraîche, whipped cream or pouring cream.

Serves 12

8 oz (225 g) dark chocolate (75 per cent cocoa solids), broken into pieces
4 oz (110 g) unsalted pistachio nuts, roughly chopped
2 oz (50 g) dried sour cherries
2 oz (50 g) raisins
3 tablespoons rum
2 oz (50 g) butter
5 fl oz (150 ml) double cream, lightly whipped
8 oz (225 g) sweet oat biscuits, roughly chopped

To serve:
a little cocoa powder, to dust
crème fraîche, whipped cream or pouring cream

You will also need a loose-based cake tin with a diameter of 8 inches (20 cm), 1½ inches (4 cm) deep, lightly greased with a flavourless oil.

Melting Chocolate Puddings

This, I suspect, could be the *chocolate recipe for the 21st century – very light, very chocolatey individual baked puddings that have a melted fudge-chocolate sauce inside that oozes out as you put your spoon in. My thanks to Galton Blackiston and everyone at Morston Hall in Norfolk for giving me their recipe.*

Serves 8

7 oz (200 g) dark chocolate (75 per cent cocoa solids), broken into pieces

7 oz (200 g) butter, diced

2 tablespoons brandy

4 oz (110 g) golden caster sugar

4 large eggs, plus 4 large egg yolks

1½ teaspoons vanilla extract

2½ oz (60 g) plain flour

To serve:

a little pouring or whipped cream

You will also need 8 mini pudding basins, each with a capacity of 6 fl oz (175 ml), generously brushed with melted butter.

First of all place the broken-up chocolate, along with the butter and brandy, in a large heatproof bowl, which should be sitting over a saucepan of barely simmering water, making sure the bowl doesn't touch the water. Then, keeping the heat at its lowest, allow the chocolate and butter to melt slowly; it should take 6-7 minutes. Then remove it from the heat and give it a good stir until it's smooth and glossy.

While the chocolate is melting, place the sugar, whole eggs, yolks and vanilla extract in a large mixing bowl, place it on a tea towel to steady it, then whisk on a high speed with an electric hand whisk until the mixture has doubled in volume – this will take between 5 and 10 minutes, depending on the power of your whisk. What you need to end up with is a thick, mousse-like mixture that, when you stop the motor and lift the whisk, leaves a trail like a piece of ribbon (*see below left*).

Now you need to pour the melted-chocolate mixture around the edge of the bowl (it's easier to fold it in from the edges) and then sift the flour over the mixture. Using a large metal spoon, carefully but thoroughly fold everything together. Patience is needed here; don't be tempted to hurry it, as careful folding and cutting movements are needed, and this will take 3-4 minutes.

Now divide the mixture between the pudding basins (it should come to just below the top of each one) and line them up on a baking tray. If you like, the puddings can now be covered with clingfilm and kept in the fridge or freezer until you need them.

When you're ready to bake the puddings, pre-heat the oven to gas mark 6, 400°F (200°C). Remove the clingfilm and bake on the centre shelf of the oven for 14 minutes if they have been chilled first, but only 12 if not; after that time the puddings should have risen and feel fairly firm to the touch, although the insides will still be melting. Leave to stand for 1 minute before sliding a palette knife around each pudding and turning out on to individual serving plates. If you're cooking these puddings from frozen, give them about 15 minutes' cooking time and allow them to stand for 2 minutes before turning out. Serve absolutely immediately, with some chilled cream to pour over.

As the puddings cool, the melted chocolate inside continues to set, so they can, if you like, be served cold instead as a fudgey-centred chocolate cake with whipped cream.

Note: this recipe contains partially cooked eggs.

Cheat's Chocolate Trifle

This one's either for people who don't like to cook or for devoted cooks who nonetheless need something really speedy. First you need to zip round the supermarket to collect the ingredients, then, after the cherries have soaked, this is all made in moments.

Serves 8

3 double-chocolate-chip American-style muffins
7 oz (200 g) dark chocolate
(75 per cent cocoa solids)
1 x 680 g jar pitted morello cherries, drained and soaked overnight in
3 fl oz (75 ml) dark rum
2 tablespoons morello cherry jam or conserve
9 oz (250 g) Mascarpone
14 oz (400 g) fresh custard
10 fl oz (275 ml) whipping cream

You will also need a trifle bowl or serving dish with a capacity of 4 pints (2.25 litres).

You need to start this recipe the day before you want to serve it, and all you do at this stage is soak the drained cherries overnight in the rum. The next day, begin by slicing the muffins horizontally in half, then spread each slice with some jam and weld the slices back together to their original muffin shape. Now cut each one vertically into 4 pieces approximately ¾ inch (2 cm) wide, and lay these all around the base of the trifle bowl or serving dish. Now take a skewer and stab them to make holes, then strain off the rum the cherries have been soaking in and sprinkle it all over the muffins, scattering the cherries on top.

Now, reserving 2 oz (50 g) of the chocolate for decoration, break the rest up into squares. Place the broken-up chocolate in a large heatproof bowl, which should be sitting over a saucepan of barely simmering water, making sure the bowl doesn't touch the water. Then, keeping the heat at its lowest, allow the chocolate to melt slowly – it should take about 5 minutes to become smooth and glossy. Remove the bowl from the pan and give it a good stir, then let the chocolate cool for 2-3 minutes.

While that's happening, put the Mascarpone in a bowl and beat to soften it, then add the custard and whisk them together. Next whisk in the cooled melted chocolate, then pour the whole lot over the soaked muffins and cherries. Now whip the cream to the floppy stage, then carefully spoon this over the trifle, spreading it out with a palette knife. Lastly chop the rest of the chocolate (using a piece of foil to protect it from the heat of your fingers as you steady it), shredding it very finely. Sprinkle the shreds over the surface of the trifle, cover with clingfilm and chill until needed.

Chocolate and Prune Brownies

I never much cared for the flavour of orange and chocolate or raspberries and chocolate, but prunes and chocolate are, for me, a heavenly partnership. Plus, if, for a special occasion, you soak the prunes in Armagnac, so much the better. Brownies can be served warm as a dessert or just eaten cold as they are.

Begin this the night before you are going to make the brownies by soaking the chopped prunes in the Armagnac. The next day, begin by pre-heating the oven to gas mark 4, 350°F (180°C), then chop the almonds roughly, place them on a baking sheet and toast them in the oven for 8 minutes. Please use a timer here, or you'll be throwing burnt nuts away all day.

While the almonds are toasting, put the chocolate and butter together in a heatproof bowl fitted over a saucepan of barely simmering water, making sure the bowl doesn't touch the water. Allow the chocolate to melt – 4-5 minutes – remove it from the heat, then beat till smooth. Next, stir in the other ingredients, including the prunes and Armagnac, until well blended. Now spread the mixture into the prepared tin and bake on the centre shelf for 30 minutes, or until slightly springy in the centre, then leave it to cool for 10 minutes before cutting into squares and transferring to a wire rack.

Makes 15

2 oz (50 g) dark chocolate (75 per cent cocoa solids), broken into pieces
2 oz (50 g) pitted pruneaux d'Agen, chopped and soaked overnight in
2 fl oz (55 ml) Armagnac
2 oz (50 g) skin-on almonds
4 oz (110 g) butter
2 large eggs, beaten
8 oz (225 g) demerara sugar
2 oz (50 g) plain flour
1 teaspoon baking powder
¼ teaspoon salt

You will also need a non-stick baking tin measuring 10 x 6 inches (25.5 x 15 cm) and 1 inch (2.5 cm) deep, lightly greased and lined with silicone paper (parchment).

Chocolate, Prune and Armagnac Cake

This is the very lightest chocolate cake of all, the reason being that no flour is used – it's simply made with eggs and cocoa powder. It's very fragile, almost soufflé-like, but once you've tried it you'll never want any other kind. Don't forget to start this a couple of days ahead if possible by heating the prunes with the Armagnac and leaving them to soak up all the delicious flavour.

Start off by first placing the egg whites in a large, clean, grease-free bowl. Put the yolks in another bowl, along with the sugar, and whisk them until they just begin to turn pale and thicken – be careful not to thicken them too much; they need approximately 3 minutes' whisking. After that, gently fold in the sifted cocoa powder.

Next, with a spanking-clean whisk, beat the egg whites until stiff but not too dry. Now, using a metal spoon, fold a heaped tablespoon of the egg white into the chocolate mixture to loosen it up a little, then carefully and gently fold in the rest of the egg white, slowly and patiently trying not to lose any air. Now divide the mixture equally between the prepared sandwich tins and bake near the centre of the oven for 15 minutes. They won't appear to be cooked exactly, just set and slightly puffy and springy in the centre, so when they're taken out of the oven they will shrink (but that's normal, so don't panic). Leave the cakes to cool in their tins, then slide a palette knife around the edges, gently invert them on to a board and carefully strip off the base papers.

To make the filling for the cake, first of all set aside 10-12 of the largest prunes, then place the rest, plus any remaining soaking liquid, in a processor, along with the crème fraîche, and whiz to a purée. After that, transfer the purée straight from the processor on to one half of the cake, placed carefully on to a plate first, then spread the purée out and place the other half of the cake on top.

Now all you need is the chocolate covering. For this place the broken-up pieces of chocolate in a large heatproof bowl, which should be sitting over a saucepan of barely simmering water, making sure the bowl doesn't touch the water. Then, keeping the heat at its lowest, allow the chocolate to melt slowly – it should take about 5 minutes to become smooth and glossy. Then remove it from the heat and give it a good stir, then let the chocolate cool for 2-3 minutes.

Now take each one of the reserved prunes and dip it into the melted chocolate so that half of each one gets covered. As you do this place them on a sheet of parchment paper to set. Next, stir the crème fraîche into the chocolate, then use this mixture to cover the surface of the cake. Spread it over carefully with a palette knife, making ridges with the knife as you go. Now decorate the cake with the chocolate prunes. Cover the whole thing with an upturned, suitably sized bowl or polythene cake container, and keep it in the fridge until about an hour before you need it.

Serves 8

For the cakes:
6 large eggs, separated
5 oz (150 g) golden caster sugar
2 oz (50 g) cocoa powder, sifted

For the filling:
14 oz (400 g) pitted pruneaux d'Agen, soaked overnight (or longer if possible) in 4 fl oz (120 ml) Armagnac (see the introduction)
1 tablespoon crème fraîche

To finish:
5 oz (150 g) dark chocolate (75 per cent cocoa solids), broken into pieces
1 tablespoon crème fraîche

You will also need 2 x 8 inch (20 cm) loose-based sandwich tins, 1½ inches (4 cm) deep, the bases and sides well oiled and the bases lined with silicone paper (parchment).

Pre-heat the oven to gas mark 4, 350°F (180°C).

Chocolate
Crème Brûlées

What chocolate mousse had been to the 1960s, crème brûlée was to the 1990s, suddenly appearing on almost every restaurant menu. It's truly a great British classic that easily lends itself to variations like this one – a smooth, velvety chocolate custard topped with a very crunchy caramel. Because of the vagaries of domestic grills, I've done a cheat's version of the caramel topping, or there's an alternative using a cook's blowtorch.

Serves 6

5 oz (150 g) dark chocolate (75 per cent cocoa solids), broken into pieces
1 pint (570 ml) whipping cream
6 large egg yolks
2 oz (50 g) golden caster sugar
1 rounded teaspoon cornflour

For the caramel:
6 oz (175 g) white granulated sugar

You will also need 6 ramekins, each with a base diameter of 2½ inches (6 cm), a top diameter of 3 inches (7.5 cm), and 2 inches (5 cm) deep.

Start the crème brûlées the day before you want to serve them. Place the broken-up chocolate, along with 5 fl oz (150 ml) of the cream, in a large heatproof bowl sitting over a saucepan of barely simmering water, making sure the bowl doesn't touch the water. Then, keeping the heat at its lowest, allow the chocolate to melt slowly – it should take 5-6 minutes. Remove it from the heat and give it a good stir until it's smooth and glossy, then remove the bowl from the pan and let the mixture cool for 2-3 minutes.

After that, whisk the egg yolks, caster sugar and cornflour together in a separate bowl for about 2 minutes, or until they are thick and creamy.

Now, in a separate pan, heat the remaining cream just up to simmering point and pour it over the egg-yolk mixture, whisking as you pour. Return the whole lot to the pan and continue to stir over a gentle heat until it thickens – this will take 2-3 minutes. Next, whisk the melted chocolate and cream together until completely smooth, add a little of the custard mixture to it and continue to whisk it in. After that, add the remaining custard, whisking until everything is really smooth. Then divide the custard between the ramekins, making sure you leave a ½ inch (1 cm) space at the top for the caramel. Now leave them to cool, cover the pots with clingfilm and chill overnight in the fridge.

A few hours before serving the brûlées, make the caramel. To do this, put the granulated sugar in a small saucepan, place it over a medium heat and leave it like that, keeping an eye on it. When the sugar begins to melt around the edges, *opposite, top*, and just starts to turn liquid – which will take 4-6 minutes – give the pan a good shake and leave it again to melt until it's about a quarter melted. Now, using a wooden spoon, give it a gentle stir, *opposite, centre*, and then continue to cook until the sugar has transformed from crystals to liquid and is the right colour – amber or like dark runny honey, *opposite, bottom*. Keep stirring gently until you're sure all the sugar has dissolved. The whole thing should take 10-15 minutes.

Now remove the pan from the heat, remove the clingfilm and pour the caramel over the custards, covering the surface of each one. Tilt the ramekins gently from side to side to get an even, thin covering of caramel, then leave them for a few minutes for the caramel to harden, and cover them loosely with foil (don't use clingfilm, or the moisture from the brûlées will soften the caramel). Return them to the fridge until needed.

These also freeze well, but do this before the caramel is added. In this case, put the caramel on them after removing the custards from the freezer, but as the caramel will set almost immediately, tilt the ramekins from side to side as soon as you've poured the caramel over each one to distribute it evenly. Allow them to soften in the fridge for 2 hours before serving.

Note: you can use a blowtorch to get a much thinner layer of caramel if you prefer. Simply sprinkle 1 rounded teaspoon of golden caster sugar over each ramekin of chocolate custard and, using a water spray, first mist the surface lightly – this will help the sugar to caramelise quickly without burning. Now, using sweeping movements, pass the flame of the blowtorch across each brûlée until the sugar melts and caramelises.

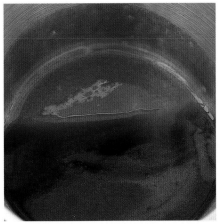

Miniature
Choc Ices

This is an unashamedly fun recipe, great for special parties and at Christmas, or to serve instead of chocolates or mints at the end of a meal. But although it's fun, the choc ices are seriously good to eat, particularly if you buy the best-quality ice cream. I have used three different chocolate toppings here, but to make it simpler, you can use just one.

Makes 25-30

1 x 500 ml tub good-quality vanilla ice cream
5 oz (150 g) dark chocolate (75 per cent cocoa solids), broken into pieces
5 oz (150 g) good-quality white chocolate, broken into pieces
5 oz (150 g) good-quality milk chocolate, broken into pieces
2 heaped tablespoons shelled unsalted pistachio nuts, roughly chopped
2 heaped tablespoons toasted chopped hazelnuts

You will also need 2 baking trays, a shallow polythene box measuring 8 x 5 x 2½ inches (20 x 13 x 6 cm), with a lid, and a 1 inch (2.5 cm) melon scoop, silicone paper and about 30 cocktail sticks.

You need to begin this recipe the night before, so as soon as you get the ice cream home, transfer it to the polythene box and spread it out in an even layer, then put the lid on and pop it in the freezer overnight. At the same time, line the baking trays with silicone paper, place these one on top of the other and put them in the freezer as well.

When you're ready to start making the choc ices, begin by putting a small saucepan of water on to boil. Remove the ice cream and one baking tray from the freezer, then dip the melon scoop in boiling water before making each ice. Just draw the scoop all along the frozen ice cream to form little rounds, and quickly transfer each one to the frozen tray. You do need to work at high speed here, so no distractions if possible, but if you find the ice cream is getting too soft to work with, just whack everything back in the freezer and continue later. (With no interruptions you should be able to do them all in one session.) Next insert a cocktail stick into the centre of each ice, then put them all back in the freezer for a minimum of 2 hours, because the ice-cream balls need to get really hard again.

After the 2 hours, melt the chocolates separately. For this, first place the broken-up pieces of dark chocolate in a large heatproof bowl sitting over a saucepan of barely simmering water, making sure the bowl doesn't touch the water. Then, keeping the heat at its lowest, allow the chocolate to melt slowly – it will take about 5 minutes to become smooth and glossy. Then remove the chocolate from the heat, give it a good stir and let it cool while you repeat this process with the 2 other chocolates (the white and milk chocolates will take 3-4 minutes to melt). Next it's very important to allow each chocolate to cool completely to room temperature before coating the ices, or the ice cream will melt. So start off by coating a third of the ice-cream balls with the white chocolate: lift each ice cream up off the tray using the cocktail stick and, holding it over a plate, spoon the chocolate over to coat the ice cream completely. Now scatter with a few chopped pistachios (but not over the bowl of chocolate!), then return to the baking tray; you'll find the chocolate will harden around the ice cream immediately. Next, coat a third in milk chocolate, then the rest in the plain chocolate, and scatter these with the toasted hazelnuts. Pop them back in the freezer as soon as you can and serve straight from the freezer.

Other nuts can be used, or finely chop up 4 pieces of crystallised stem ginger and mix with one of the chocolates before coating the ice creams. Note: if you want to make these a long time ahead, cover with freezer foil.

Chocolate Mini Muffins with Toasted Hazelnuts

These were invented specifically for children to make for the 1997 Comic Relief campaign with red cherries on top. This is a more adult version, but children can still make them using chocolate drops for melting and cherries instead of nuts.

Makes 24

2 oz (50 g) dark chocolate (75 per cent cocoa solids), roughly chopped
5 oz (150 g) plain flour
2 tablespoons cocoa powder
1 dessertspoon baking powder
¼ teaspoon salt
1 large egg, lightly beaten
1½ oz (40 g) golden caster sugar
4 fl oz (120 ml) milk
2 oz (50 g) butter, melted and cooled slightly

For the topping:

2 oz (50 g) hazelnuts, roughly chopped
3 oz (75 g) dark chocolate (75 per cent cocoa solids), broken into pieces

You will also need 2 x 12-hole mini-muffin tins, well greased or lined with mini-muffin paper cases.

Pre-heat the oven to gas mark 6, 400°F (200°C).

You need to begin this recipe by toasting the hazelnuts for the topping. To do this, place the chopped nuts on a baking sheet and toast them in the pre-heated oven for 5 minutes; it's important to use a timer here.

Next, for the muffins, start off by sifting the flour, cocoa powder, baking powder and salt into a large bowl. Then, in a separate bowl, mix together the egg, sugar, milk and melted butter. Now return the dry ingredients to the sieve and sift them straight on to the egg mixture (this double sifting is essential because there won't be much mixing going on). What you need to do now is take a large spoon and fold the dry ingredients into the wet ones – quickly, in about 15 seconds. Don't be tempted to beat or stir, and don't be alarmed by the rather unattractive, uneven appearance of the mixture: this, in fact, is what will ensure that the muffins stay light. Now fold the chopped chocolate into the mixture – again with a minimum of stirring; just a quick folding in.

Divide the mixture between the muffin cups, about 1 heaped teaspoon in each, and bake on a high shelf of the pre-heated oven for 10 minutes, until well risen. Then remove the muffins from the oven and cool in the tins for 5 minutes before transferring them to a cooling tray.

While they're cooling, make the topping. To do this, place the broken-up chocolate in a small heatproof bowl, which should be sitting over a saucepan of barely simmering water, making sure the bowl doesn't touch the water. Then, keeping the heat at its lowest, allow the chocolate to melt slowly – it should take about 3 minutes to melt and become smooth and glossy. Then remove it from the heat and give it a good stir, then let the chocolate cool for 2-3 minutes.

Then, when the muffins are cool enough to handle, spoon a little melted chocolate on to each one, then place it back on the cooling tray and scatter the hazelnuts over the top of each muffin.

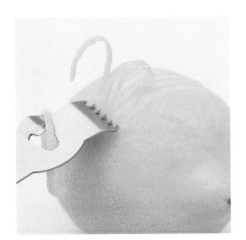

21
Equipment for serious cooks

If you want to be a good cook and enjoy pleasurable, trouble-free cooking, then you're simply going to have to think about investing in the right kind of tools for the job. It's amazing that, when it comes to cooking equipment, there is so often a kind of make-do, 'I'll get around to it one day' mentality.

What so often lurks behind the doors of the very smartest designer kitchen cupboards is a whole battery of blunt or bent, cheap impulse purchases that, instead of serving you, will in the end just make life more difficult. So, if you are going to attempt to cook well, why not make it as easy as possible and begin by carefully selecting, bit by bit, the right kind of quality equipment that will serve you a lifetime?

How to survive the commercial jungle

My aim here is to try and steer you through the commercial jungle out there and help you focus on what's really useful. You have two problems to overcome: one is the dazzle of design and good looks – buying an item because it's aesthetically pleasing and not for how it performs; the other is being beguiled by price – why pay a lot when you can get away with paying less?

Both these attitudes need to be addressed. Number one is easier to come to terms with – it's a decision. I simply want only quality and performance, not dazzling design. Number two is more tricky. There are hordes of manufacturers out there trying to undercut each other on price, which means that any time A undercuts B, the quality suffers. It gets cheaper and flimsier and nastier.

Think carefully about price

Well, it's obvious if you think about it: twenty-four buckled cake tins bought over a period of years are actually going to cost you far more than one solid cake tin that lasts. How many scratched and peeling non-stick frying pans have you got through so far? If you're concerned about cost, then quality will actually be cheaper in the long run.

Where do I begin?

Right here. After a lifetime of cooking and experiencing all the pitfalls, I have compiled the following, hopefully comprehensive, beginners' guide to what is useful, helpful and performs well – and also what is superfluous to everyday requirements.

Knives and cutting edges

Ever since the Stone Age we have used cutting implements for our food, and number one on the list of equipment for any kitchen must always be knives. But what kind? Good news here, because you *don't* need a long list of hugely expensive and heavy chef's knives, as you probably won't be doing much skinning, filleting or boning. But you do need *good* knives. The best for home cooking are light to hold, with flexible blades. (The flexibility makes sharpening easier.) Here is what I would call my ideal set in order to make every task a simple one, though it is possible to start with just one or two.

Serrated palette knife: This is a beautifully versatile knife. It cuts bread and cakes, spreads icing and cream, loosens sticky edges around tins and slides under and lifts biscuits from baking trays. It is also useful to have a smaller one for spreading over and sliding round smaller dishes, such as ramekins.

Cook's knives: A 7 inch (18 cm) long cook's knife is essential for chopping herbs and slicing and chopping up meat and vegetables. I would also choose two smaller cook's knives with serrated edges and in different sizes, plus a rounded-end serrated knife, which is excellent for slicing tomatoes swiftly and easily.

Kitchen scissors: Got to have them – they have so many uses, from snipping chives to cutting air vents in pies. My great-grandmother's were called bacon scissors, but sadly, it's hard to find any bacon with rind nowadays!

Potato peeler: So often, most of the flavour and nutrients in vegetables are near the skin and with a good peeler, you really are removing only the peel.

Curved paring knife: I like my curved paring knife for paring and peeling thicker skins when a potato peeler won't do the job.

From top to bottom:
Serrated palette knife
7 inch (18 cm) cook's knife
Sharpening steel
Kitchen scissors
Small serrated knife
Potato peeler
Curved paring knife
Smaller palette knife
Rounded-end serrated knife

Taking care of knives

It's important to keep your knives sharp, and practice makes perfect when using a sharpening steel *(see photograph on page 477)*. Hold the steel horizontally in front of you and the knife vertically, then slide the blade of the knife down, allowing the tip to touch the steel, first on one side of the steel and then on the other. Start slowly and then speed up. Sharpen little and often is the best advice I was given by a butcher.

If possible, store your knives in a wooden block or on a magnetic rack, so they're not crashing around in drawers against other instruments, which can damage the blades.

Never chop on a laminated, marble or any other hard surface, as this can blunt blades. Instead, use wooden or polypropylene chopping boards, as these have a certain amount of give that will ensure that the blades don't get damaged.

Clockwise, from left: four-sided grater, Microplane® Grater, nutmeg grater, zester

Graters and zesters

Four-sided grater: A handy tool for grating small amounts of cheese or vegetables. Each side grates to a different fineness. I tend to use two of the sides: the coarse grater for, say, Cheddar, and the slightly finer side for Parmesan. The very prickly-looking side tends to grate too finely and gets very clogged up.

Microplane®Grater: This flat version is relatively new, and super-efficient at grating fresh ginger. There are three kinds: very fine, coarse and coarser again. Be careful when grating citrus zests, though, as I find it can remove some of the bitter pith as well.

Nutmeg grater: Worth mentioning here because nutmeg is a spice that quickly loses its edge if bought ready-ground. The small one pictured here incorporates a little box to hold one or two nutmegs, which makes it very handy and time-saving.

Zester: When you want only the outer zest of a lemon (or lime or orange) and none of the bitter pith, a zester does the job perfectly. The outer zest of the fruit contains all the fragrance and oils that give maximum flavour.

Grinding, crushing and squeezing

If flavour is the prime concern of the cook, then 'whole' is a very important word. Ingredients that come ready-ground lose much of their fragrance, character and flavour, so the ideal here is always to buy an ingredient whole and grind it yourself.

Pestle and mortar: (*see right*) The best investment you can make for grinding and crushing is a heavy, unglazed porcelain bowl (the mortar) with a rounded tool (the pestle) that pounds anything and everything. It will last a lifetime and serve you in countless ways: with it you can bruise rosemary leaves to release their fragrant oils, crush whole roasted spices, pound the leaves of basil and other herbs, and reduce a clove of garlic and some flakes of salt into a creamy mass in seconds – and there is absolutely no better way to combine ingredients for a salad dressing (see page 375).

Salt and pepper mills: The virtues of whole peppercorns and flakes of sea salt have already been described, but clearly they need mills to grind them. Not an easy one this, as about 80 per cent of what's on offer either doesn't work ever, or works for a while, then packs up on you. Avoid gadgets and hideous novelties that don't do the job. Stick with it, though; there isn't really any alternative but to go to a quality kitchen supplier and get ones that will last. I have had mine since I first started cooking and they are still serving me well.

Citrus reamer: (*see right*) Such a simple but fine invention. Push it into a lemon half (or other citrus fruit), twist it and out flows the juice.

Lemon squeezer: (*see right*) If you don't want to spend time fishing out pips, then a classic lemon squeezer will catch them for you.

Sieving, sifting and straining

Sieves: (*see left*) If you have been faithfully following my advice on sauces, it could be said you'll never have to sieve out any lumps – and I would put money on that! However, you *will* need to sift flour and icing sugar, extract the pips from soft fruit and use a sieve for puréeing small quantities. I have two sizes of metal sieve and one nylon – the latter is best for soft fruit as the metal can sometimes discolour it. I also keep a tiny sieve, like a tea strainer, in my spoon drawer – perfect for sprinkling a small amount of cocoa or icing sugar.

Dredgers: (*see left*) I think two of these would be ideal: one for sprinkling flour lightly and evenly all over pastry when you are rolling it out; the other one for icing sugar – great at Christmas when you are baking batches of mince pies that call for a hefty dredging.

Colander: (*see left*) Can't live without this one. Straining liquid from a pan with the lid slightly off is not a good idea – either too much water is left behind or some of your, say, spaghetti escapes along with it. A colander guarantees no hassle and if you want to squeeze the juice out of spinach, chop cooked cabbage, soak and drain aubergines or strain anything at all, it will do the job perfectly.

Spoons, forks and whisks

Spoons: (*see left*) A selection of wooden spoons in varying sizes would be ideal, plus a large and a small one with a pointed end, which is useful when you need to get into the corners of pans. A long-handled, large-bowled metal spoon is useful for basting without burning your arm, and a shorter-handled version is what's needed for folding mixtures quickly and efficiently. Two draining spoons (a long-handled and a short-handled one) are indispensable for skimming and separating – or even lifting baked beans on to toast without too much juice.

Forks: (*see left*) I love wooden forks for scrambling eggs or fluffing rice, and a large metal fork has one-hundred-and-one uses, such as beating eggs for an omelette instead of whisking.

Whisks: (*see left*) A balloon whisk is for spontaneous whisking when you don't want to drag out the electric version. The Wonder Whisk does the same for very small quantities – it will bring a salad dressing together in a trice, for instance.

Spatulas, slices and tongs

Spatulas: (*see left*) There are now dozens of versions of the famous Rubber Maid® spatula, but it is still an absolute whiz, as it can miraculously clean up every last bit of mixture from any shape of bowl.

Slices: (*see left*) Every kitchen needs a good flexible fish slice, but beware, though – there are lots of good-lookers around that don't do the job. Flexibility is the key here – if it's too heavy or rigid it will be awkward and difficult to use, so try to find one with lots of bendy give in it. You'll also need a good triangular cake slice, similarly flexible, which will double up for lifting out wedges of pie or prising biscuits off baking trays.

Kitchen tongs: Not least for turning sausages effectively and efficiently. There are lots of awkward duds around but I've discovered some professional chef's catering tongs that are the best ever.

Weighing and measuring

I fervently believe that, for the most part, cooks should always weigh everything. If you are someone who has cooked every day, all day, for a lifetime and have a fairly modest repertoire, then perhaps your instincts and judgements are so well developed you don't need to use scales. If so, lucky you. For the rest of us, living in the fast lane, trying to juggle our commitments, careers and families, this is absolutely not so. What scales do is remove the fear and the worry when you don't have time to think what day it is, let alone what 4 oz (110 g) of pasta actually looks like. Weighing leaves you be, leaves you free and yet guarantees perfection every time. There are, of course, occasions when it's impossible to be precise. How sharp is a lemon? How much juice does one lemon have compared with another? Weighing or measuring does not prevent you from tasting and adding more of this or that – it just ensures all will be pretty well in the end without you having to worry about it.

Scales: (*see right*) Let's look at the cowboys first. I, and all the people who work with me, are of one mind about electronic scales: totally unreliable and an absolute no-no. They run out of battery power when you least expect it (such as in the middle of making a cake); if you want to weigh ½ oz (10 g) it's tricky because digital figures don't cope very well with small amounts; and last, but by no means least, they have a limited life, so it's soon time to bin them and start all over again. The other type that gets points for great design but doesn't do the job is scales with a spring mechanism and a needle that points to the correct weight – except the needle often wobbles and wavers and fails. These also have a short life.

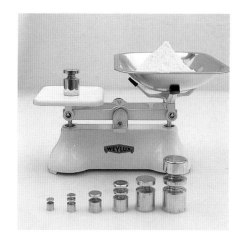

All I have to say is, if you want to cook well, there is only one truly accurate way to weigh ingredients and that is to invest in old-fashioned, time-honoured balance scales. It's a small investment for years of worry-free accuracy. With balance scales, everything is instant: you put on the required weight, add the ingredients and can see immediately when the balance of the two has been achieved. You can, as I do, have one set of metric weights and one of imperial. (Anyone over 50 is still likely to think in imperial measures, so if a recipe is all metric you can then proceed without worry.)

Measuring jug: (*see right*) A glass measuring jug (Pyrex is best) shows you in seconds what 3 fl oz (75 ml) looks like, and this is an essential – teacups or half-teacups are not the answer. It is also vital when cooking rice, as this is always measured by volume rather than by weight.

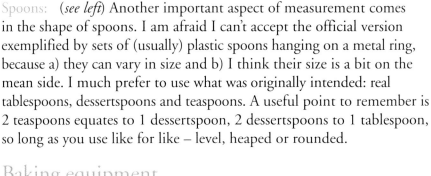

Spoons: (*see left*) Another important aspect of measurement comes in the shape of spoons. I am afraid I can't accept the official version exemplified by sets of (usually) plastic spoons hanging on a metal ring, because a) they can vary in size and b) I think their size is a bit on the mean side. I much prefer to use what was originally intended: real tablespoons, dessertspoons and teaspoons. A useful point to remember is 2 teaspoons equates to 1 dessertspoon, 2 dessertspoons to 1 tablespoon, so long as you use like for like – level, heaped or rounded.

Baking equipment

It could be said that home baking is on the decline. With a million-and-one chocolate bars and a prolific amount of factory-baked goods on offer, why should we *want* to do any home baking? My own theory is that the instinct to be creative – to bake something now and again – is still part of our nature. And while home baking may not be as popular as it was, there are still enough of us who long for that home-baked quality that can never come out of a factory. So, I would like to encourage you to give yourself, as well as family and friends, a home-baked treat now and then.

This list of equipment will stand you in good stead for a lifetime, but don't buy anything – cake tins, baking trays, whatever – unless it looks solid enough to last. They will be more expensive than the flimsy versions but, believe me, it is cheaper to buy something only once. My mother still has the cake tins she used when I was a child! It is obviously not necessary to go out and buy the whole lot at once; perhaps each time you want to give home baking a try you could add to your collection.

Rolling pin: This needs to be wooden, plain and straight, without handles, which get in the way when you want to roll out large sheets of pastry.

Brushes: (*see left*) The flatter brushes, which look like miniature decorator's brushes, are the best for large surfaces, while the rounder shape is okay for brushing round rims of pastry. Don't ever put pastry brushes in the dishwasher – they collect nasty bits of grit. Just wash them in warm, running water and a little washing-up liquid and rinse them thoroughly.

Cutters: (*see left*) Fluted or plain or both, these come in tins where all the different sizes fit inside one another, from 3½ inches (9 cm) to 1 inch (2.5 cm). They're essential for making tartlets, biscuits and scones.

Cake tins: (*see photograph on page 474*) Indispensable for making sponge cakes, for me, is a very solid set: a 7 inch (18 cm) tin makes a 2-egg 4 oz (110 g) mixture, double-layer sponge cake, and the 8 inch (20 cm) one is for a 3-egg 6 oz (175 g) mixture. Springform tins are equipped with a metal clip to release the sides, which is excellent for cheesecakes or anything that needs careful unmoulding. For springform and deep cake tins, I would choose the same measurements as the sponge tins (not least because most of my cake recipes fit these sizes).

Loaf tins: (*see photograph on page 474*) Here I always stick to the old-fashioned bread tin shapes. These still have the capacity to hold 1 lb/450 g (6 x 3¾ x 2¾ inches/15 x 9.5 x 7 cm) or 2 lbs/900 g (7¼ x 4½ x 3½ inches/18.5 x 11.5 x 9 cm) of mixture, which, again, all my recipes fit.

Quiche, tart and pie tin: Solid is still the name of the game, and it's good to have at least two sizes of loose-bottomed quiche or tart tin: a 7½ inch (19 cm) one for a small quiche or tart and a 9 inch (23 cm) or 10 inch (25.5 cm) one for family-sized recipes. I also like to have a sloping-sided, deep-rimmed pie tin (*see photograph on page 474*) – one with a 7 inch (18 cm) base and a 9 inch (23 cm) top measurement is the size here.

Baking trays and tins: (*see right*) Sturdy baking trays and tins are, again, a lifetime's investment. Pre-heated in the oven, a baking tray will ensure the pastry base of a pie or quiche will be crisp – just one of its many uses. I use three sizes: 8 x 12 inch (20 x 30 cm), 10 x 14 inch (25.5 x 35 cm) and 11 x 16 inch (28 x 40 cm). Roasting tins come in a host of different sizes, but the key, when roasting meat in them, is that they mustn't be too deep – otherwise the meat will just steam.

Cooling racks: (*see photograph on page 474*) Simple, but so important in baking. Without a rack, cakes and biscuits left to cool on a flat surface become soggy, as steam gets trapped underneath. I think you'll find it useful to have two.

Lattice cutter: This one took the nation by storm when I did my Christmas series, and it is truly innovative. Wheel it across a piece of rolled-out dough and, hey presto, you have a perfect pastry lattice to put on the top of a pie.

Saucepans, frying pans and casseroles

Saucepans: (*see photograph on following page*) These are probably going to be the most important purchase a cook will make. There is so much rubbish out there and millions of pounds spent to beguile you into buying them, so here you really do need some help. What you want is something solid and reliable, and I have spent years searching out what I've now finally come to believe is the best.

There is no doubt that heavy-gauge aluminium is the very best conductor of heat. I have demonstrated in earlier chapters its importance in making omelettes and cooking sauces: no sticking, no catching, no scorching. I would banish the traditional non-stick brigade entirely, having suffered so many peeling, scratched and useless non-stick non-starters. Manufacturers needn't talk to me about being careful – you know, never having the heat high and using plastic spoons and forks etc. I am a cook and if I want to sear a steak, I want the pan to be blasting hot and I don't want to then turn my steak over with some flimsy plastic fork that the heat will melt. Fortunately, about ten years ago, I discovered a range of pans produced in Germany, made from heavy-gauge aluminium but with a non-stick surface called titanium, which is forty times harder than stainless steel.

So, at last, high heat, no problem; metal utensils, no problem. Expensive, but one purchase is for life, so cheaper than a long line of dismal failures. All the pans, including the frying pans, have lids, and even the handles can withstand an oven temperature of up to gas mark 10, 500°F (260°C), which means the frying pan can then double up as a shallow casserole or a roasting tray.

Cast-iron ridged griddle: Since it's now fashionable to char-grill so many things, this is a useful addition, and especially good for Bruschetta (see page 91) giving the bread that lovely charred flavour.

Casseroles: I have found that an approximately 4 pint (2.25 litre) capacity flameproof casserole is a good, all-round family size and that a 6 pint (3.5 litre) casserole is a very useful size for entertaining.

Taking care of pans

Sorry, but there is one bit of bad news here. The chemicals in the dishwashing process tend not to be good for saucepans. So, just get into the habit of soaking them in cold water to get rid of any residue, then they will be easy to wash in warm, soapy water – and it will give you much more room in the dishwasher for other items.

Steamers

I do like to steam lots of things so I've got three types of steamer (*see left*). There's the classic double-pan one that stands over a saucepan and will hold a large pudding; a fan steamer that is brilliant for vegetables, even asparagus, which I always trim and lay out horizontally; and finally, a Chinese bamboo steamer I use for fish.

Miscellaneous

Oven thermometer: This is useful for gauging when the temperature is correct, particularly as ovens can vary. It's also crucial for those with an Aga or similar oven, as it can tell you what the temperature is on each shelf in the top and bottom oven.

Sugar thermometer: (*see photograph opposite*) Handy for making sweets and toffee, and an essential item for our Chocolate Fudge on page 696.

Tape measure: If a recipe stipulates the base measurement of a tin or dish, I can never be sure by guessing it, so I always have a tape measure handy.

Kitchen timer: Memories are fallible and a timer can save a lot of hard work from going out of the window.

Pasta tongs: (*see photograph opposite*) These really do lift spaghetti out of the pan very efficiently and quickly without losing any.

Garlic press: (*see photograph opposite*) This one's for speed. It does save time, especially the easy-cleaning version that doesn't clog up.

Clockwise, from top left: double-pan steamer, Chinese bamboo steamer and fan steamer

Apple corer: (*see right*) A simple little tool that makes very quick work of removing the entire core, pips and all.

Melon baller: (*see right*) Useful, not just for melon, but for scraping the centre out of an apple (see Lucy's Tarte Tatin on page 496).

Ice-cream scoop: (*see right*) Gives you a beautifully rounded blob of ice cream in half a second.

Bean slicer: Runner beans are my absolute favourite vegetable and when they're sliced thinly with a slicer (see page 353), they can be cooked until tender in a matter of moments.

Skewers: (*see right*) Last but definitely not least, the only way I can tell how my meat or fish is cooking, or whether my vegetables are tender. This is an item I don't think I could ever cook without.

What I think you don't need

Because space is always at a premium in any kitchen and everyone has some item of equipment that lurks unused, taking up precious space, now might be a good time to talk about what *not* to put on that wedding list.

Potato ricer: Because the potatoes get cold, and anyway, an electric hand whisk makes a better job of mashed potatoes.

Asparagus steamer: Why give it houseroom when an ordinary steamer does the job perfectly?

Fish kettle: Cooking fish slowly in kitchen foil (see Baked Whole Salmon with Sauce Verte on page 686) produces moister flesh than poaching *and* the flavour isn't all going into the water.

Canelle knife: Because a good potato peeler does the same job.

Piping bags: Simply because life is too short.

Ceramic baking beans: Thankfully, I have pioneered a way to pre-bake a crisp pastry case without them (see page 107).

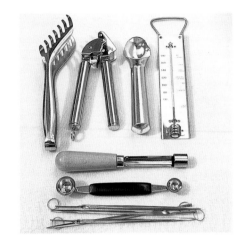

Top row, left to right: pasta tongs, garlic press, ice-cream scoop, sugar thermometer
Bottom row, top to bottom: apple corer, melon baller, skewers

Pepper-Crusted Fillet of Beef with Roasted Balsamic Onions and Thyme

This is one of the easiest ways I know to serve four people something special very quickly and very easily. If you have a first course and a pud, there is enough for six. It goes really well with Potatoes Boulangères with Rosemary (see page 187).

Serves 4-6

1 lb 12 oz (800 g) middle-cut fillet of British beef
1 rounded dessertspoon black peppercorns (or a tablespoon, if you like it really hot)
2 fl oz (55 ml) balsamic vinegar
1 lb (450 g) medium red onions
2 tablespoons chopped fresh thyme
1 tablespoon olive oil, plus a little extra to smear
1 tablespoon molasses sugar
salt

For the sauce:
1 heaped teaspoon plain flour
½ pint (275 ml) red wine
1 tablespoon Worcestershire sauce
1 tablespoon balsamic vinegar

You will also need a large baking tray.

If you can, start this off a couple of hours in advance (or longer, if that suits). All you do is first smear the beef with a little olive oil, then crush the peppercorns coarsely with a pestle and mortar. Tip them into a fine sieve, which will sift out the really hot inner bits and leave you with the fragrant outer bits, and press these all over the surface of the beef.

When you're ready to cook the beef, pre-heat the oven to gas mark 8, 450°F (230°C). Then, to prepare the onions, you first need to mix the sugar and balsamic vinegar together in a large bowl, give the mixture a good whisk, and then leave it to one side for about 10 minutes to allow the sugar to dissolve.

Meanwhile, peel the onions, then, leaving the root intact, cut each one into eight sections through the root, so, in half first, then each half into four. Then add the onions and the tablespoon of oil to the sugar-and-vinegar mixture and toss them around so they get a good coating. After that, spread the onions out on the baking tray, leaving space for the beef in the centre. Then pour the rest of the dressing over them, sprinkle over the thyme leaves and season well with salt.

Now place the beef in the centre of the baking tray, then into the oven on the highest shelf, and cook for 15 minutes; after that, turn the onions over and return the tray to the oven, giving it another 15 minutes, if you like your beef rare. For medium, remove the onions after the 30 minutes, keep them warm, and give the beef another 10 minutes with the oven switched off. If you like it well-done, leave it for another 15-20 minutes. Either way, keep everything warm while you make the sauce.

To do this, put a quarter of the onions into a small saucepan over a medium heat, then stir in the flour to just coat the onions and gradually whisk in the red wine, Worcestershire sauce and balsamic vinegar. Let it just come up to simmering point, then turn the heat down and simmer gently until the sauce has reduced by about a quarter.

To serve, carve the beef, pouring any escaped meat juices into the sauce, and serve garnished with the onions, the sauce poured over.

Braised Beef Goulash with Smoked Pimentón

I've always loved goulash and would definitely list it among my top casserole recipes, but now, since the advent of the spicy, deep-flavoured pimentón (smoked paprika) from southern Spain, goulash has an even greater appeal. I love this served with whole-grain brown rice cooked with onion, and some buttered green cabbage or spicy red cabbage.

Serves 6

2 lb 8 oz (1.15 kg) British chuck steak (braising steak), trimmed and cut into 1½ inch (4 cm) cubes
1 tablespoon each hot and sweet pimentón, plus a little extra to sprinkle
2 tablespoons olive oil
3 large onions, peeled and chopped
2 garlic cloves, crushed
2 tablespoons plain flour
3 bay leaves
1 x 400 g tin Italian chopped tomatoes
1 x 230 g tin chopped tomatoes
2 medium red peppers
salt and freshly milled black pepper

To serve:

8 fl oz (225 ml) soured cream

You will also need a lidded, flameproof casserole with a capacity of 6 pints (3.5 litres).

Pre-heat the oven to gas mark 1, 275°F (140°C).

Begin by heating the oil in the casserole over a highish heat until it is sizzling hot. Then brown the cubes of beef on all sides, cooking a few at a time. They need to be a good, deep nutty brown colour. As they brown, transfer them to a plate, using a draining spoon.

Now, with the heat turned down to medium, stir in the onions and cook them for about 5 minutes, or until they begin to brown and caramelise at the edges. Then stir in the garlic and return the meat to the casserole. Next, sprinkle in the flour and pimentón and give everything a stir to soak up the juices. Now, add the bay leaves and the contents of both tins of tomatoes, and season well with salt and freshly milled black pepper. Let it all come slowly up to simmering point. Then cover the casserole with a tight-fitting lid and transfer it to the middle shelf of the oven to cook very slowly for exactly 2 hours.

Meanwhile, prepare the peppers by halving them, removing the seeds and pith and cutting the flesh into strips roughly measuring 1 x 2 inches (2 x 5 cm). Then, when the 2 hours are up, stir the chopped peppers into the goulash, replace the lid and cook for a further 30 minutes.

Just before serving, take the casserole out of the oven, let it stand for 5 minutes, then stir in the soured cream to give a lovely marbled, creamy effect. Finally, sprinkle over a little more pimentón, and serve straight from the casserole.

Note: If you prefer a milder goulash, use 2 teaspoons of sweet pimentón.

Easy Omelette Arnold Bennett

This is an adaptation of a famous omelette created by a chef at The Savoy Hotel for an author who wrote an entire novel while staying there. It's a truly wonderful creation – a flat but very fluffy open-faced omelette made with smoked Finnan haddock.

To begin with, measure the crème fraîche into a medium saucepan and bring it up to a gentle simmer. Add some freshly milled black pepper, but don't add salt yet because the haddock can be quite salty. Then pop in the prepared fish and let it poach gently, uncovered, for about 5 minutes.

Meanwhile, make up the sauce: separate one of the eggs, breaking the yolk into a small bowl and reserving the white in another bowl. Add the cornflour to the yolk and whisk well.

When the fish is cooked, use a draining spoon to lift it out into a sieve placed over the saucepan, to allow all the liquid to drain back. Press lightly to extract every last drop, then place the sieve containing the fish on a plate. At this point, pre-heat the grill to its highest setting.

Now bring the liquid in the pan back up to simmering point, then pour it on to the egg yolk, whisking all the time. Then return the whole mixture to the saucepan and gently bring it back to just below simmering point, or until it has thickened – no more than 1 or 2 minutes. After that, remove it from the heat and stir in the fish, tasting to see if it needs any salt. Next, whisk up the egg white to the soft-peak stage and carefully fold it in.

Now for the omelette. First beat the 4 remaining eggs with some seasoning. Next, melt the butter and oil in the frying pan until foaming, swirling them round to coat the sides and base. When it's very hot, add the eggs, let them settle for about 2 minutes, then begin to draw the edges into the centre, tilting the pan to let the liquid egg run into the gaps.

When you feel the eggs are half set, turn the heat down and spoon the haddock mixture evenly over the surface of the eggs, using a palette knife to spread it. Now sprinkle the Gruyère over the top and place the pan under the grill, positioning it roughly 5 inches (13 cm) from the heat source. The omelette will now take 2-3 minutes to become puffy, golden brown and bubbling. Remove it, garnish with chives, and let it relax for 5 minutes before cutting it into wedges and serving it on warmed plates.

Serves 2 as a supper dish or 3 as a light lunch with salad

8 oz (225 g) smoked haddock, skin and bones removed, cut into ½ inch (1 cm) chunks
2 rounded tablespoons crème fraîche
5 large eggs
½ teaspoon cornflour
½ oz (10 g) butter
1 teaspoon olive oil
2 oz (50 g) Gruyère, grated
freshly snipped chives, to garnish
salt and freshly milled black pepper

You will also need an omelette pan (or frying pan) with a diameter of 8 inches (20 cm).

Very Sticky Prune and Date Cake

Cakemaking is really easy, but only when the two major rules are followed: always weigh everything and always use the right-sized cake tin. For a newcomer investing in some balance scales, this cake alone will justify your investment! It's one of the easiest ever, but with a flavour that is really special – dark and caramelised, with lots of luscious fruit, and it keeps really well in an airtight tin.

Begin by placing all the fruit in a largish saucepan (it needs to be large because the mixture splutters a lot), then add the butter, condensed milk and water and bring everything up to the boil, stirring frequently with a wooden spoon to prevent the mixture sticking. Now turn the heat down to low and simmer for exactly 3 minutes, stirring now and then. Don't worry about the appalling look of what will be a very sloppy mixture – this is quite normal. After that, transfer the mixture to a large mixing bowl and let it cool down for about 30 minutes.

While it's cooling, weigh out the flours and sift them into a bowl with the bicarbonate of soda and a pinch of salt. (When sieving wholemeal flour you frequently find small quantities of bran left in the sieve – these can be tipped on to the already-sifted flour.) Pre-heat the oven to gas mark 3, 325°F (170°C).

When the fruit mixture has cooled, stir in the flour using a large metal spoon, then add the tablespoon of chunky marmalade. Now spoon the mixture into the prepared tin and, because this cake does get rather brown on top if not protected, you should cover it with a double square of silicone paper (parchment) with a hole the size of a 50p piece in the centre. Then pop it on to the centre shelf of the oven and bake for 2-2¼ hours.

After removing the cake from the oven, let it cool in the tin for 10 minutes before turning out on to a wire rack. Then, when the cake is completely cold, gently heat the sieved marmalade in a small saucepan with the tablespoon of water and brush the glaze all over the top of the cake to make it lovely and shiny.

Serves 16

6 oz (175 g) ready-to-eat dried prunes, roughly chopped
8 oz (225 g) pitted dates, roughly chopped
4 oz (110 g) raisins
4 oz (110 g) currants
10 oz (275 g) butter, plus a little extra for greasing
1 x 397 g tin condensed milk
10 fl oz (275 ml) water
5 oz (150 g) plain flour
5 oz (150 g) wholemeal flour
¾ teaspoon bicarbonate of soda
1 heaped tablespoon chunky marmalade
2 tablespoons sieved marmalade, to glaze
1 tablespoon water
salt

You will also need an 8 inch (20 cm) square cake tin, greased, the base and sides lined with silicone paper (parchment), plus extra to cover the cake during baking.

Traditional Lemon Meringue Pie

Everyone on my cookery team agrees that this famous English classic needs a revival. It is supremely light, squashy and fragrant with lemons. How did we ever forget about it?

Serves 6
For the pastry:
4 oz (110 g) plain flour, plus
a little extra for dusting
1 oz (25 g) softened butter, cut
into smallish lumps
1 oz (25 g) softened lard, cut
into smallish lumps
1 tablespoon cold water
salt

For the filling:
grated zest and juice 2 large lemons
10 fl oz (275 ml) water
3 tablespoons cornflour
2 oz (50 g) golden caster sugar
3 large egg yolks
1½ oz (40 g) butter

For the meringue:
3 large egg whites
6 oz (175 g) golden caster sugar

You will also need a 1½ inch (4 cm) deep, sloping-sided, non-stick pie tin with a ½ inch (1 cm) rim, a base diameter of 7 inches (18 cm) and a top diameter of 9½ inches (24 cm); and a baking tray measuring 11 x 16 inches (28 x 40 cm).

Start by making the pastry: first sift the flour and a pinch of salt into a large bowl, holding the sieve up high to give the flour a good airing. Then add the butter and lard and, using only your fingertips, lightly rub the fat into the flour, again lifting the mixture up high. When everything is crumbly, sprinkle in the water. Start to mix the pastry with a flat-bladed knife and then finish off with your hands, adding a few more drops of water until you have a smooth dough that will leave the bowl clean. Then pop the pastry into a plastic food bag and let it rest in the fridge for 30 minutes. Pre-heat the oven to gas mark 5, 375°F (190°C) and pop in the baking tray to pre-heat at the same time.

Next, transfer the pastry to a flat, lightly floured surface and roll it out to a circle about ½ inch (1 cm) larger all round than the rim of the tin. Cut a ½ inch (1 cm) strip from the edge of the pastry, dampen the rim of the tin with water and fix the strip round it, pressing down well. Dampen the strip before lining the tin with the pastry circle, making sure you don't trap any air underneath it. Then prick the base all over with a fork. Place the tin on the baking tray and bake on a high shelf in the pre-heated oven for 20-25 minutes, or until cooked through. After that, remove the pastry case from the oven, and immediately lower the heat to gas mark 2, 300°F (150°C) for the meringue.

Meanwhile, make the filling. Measure the water into a jug, and spoon the cornflour and sugar into a bowl. Add enough of the water to mix the cornflour to a smooth paste, then pour the rest of the water, along with the grated lemon zest, into a small saucepan. Bring this up to the boil, then pour it gradually on to the cornflour, mixing all the time until it's smooth.

Now return the mixture to the saucepan and bring it back to the boil, still mixing. Next, simmer very gently for about a minute, stirring all the time to prevent it from catching. Then remove the pan from the heat and beat in the egg yolks, lemon juice and, finally, the butter. Now pour the lemon mixture into the pastry case.

Finally, for the meringue, use a large, grease-free bowl and in it, whisk the egg whites until they form stiff peaks. Now beat in a quarter of the sugar at a time until it is all incorporated, then spoon the meringue on top, taking it to the very edge of the pastry rim with a palette knife, so it seals the edge completely. (With your knife you can also make a few decorative swirls.) Bake in the oven on the centre shelf for 45 minutes, by which time the meringue will have turned pale beige, and be crisp on the outside and squashy within. Serve warm or cold, but if warm, leave it to settle for about 20 minutes. Chilled pouring cream is a nice accompaniment.

Buttermilk Scones with Cheshire Cheese and Chives

Makes 6
3 oz (75 g) Cheshire cheese, grated
2½-3 tablespoons buttermilk
1 rounded tablespoon freshly
snipped chives
6 oz (175 g) self-raising flour, plus
a little extra for dusting
½ teaspoon mustard powder
cayenne pepper
1 oz (25 g) butter, plus a little
extra for greasing
1 large egg
½ teaspoon salt

For the tops:
a little milk for brushing
1 oz (25 g) Cheshire cheese, grated
cayenne pepper

You will also need a 2¼ inch
(5.5 cm) fluted cutter, and a baking
tray measuring 10 x 14 inches
(25.5 x 35 cm), well greased.

Pre-heat the oven to gas mark 7,
425°F (220°C).

I'm convinced cheese scones were invented to use up the last remnants of some wonderful cheese – in this case, Cheshire – but you could use any type of cheese you happen to have. When you're down to the last bit, that is the time to make these meltingly light, squidgy scones. Serve them for tea on Sunday, warm from the oven and spread with butter.

Start by sifting the flour into a bowl, holding the sieve up quite high to give the flour an airing, then add the mustard, salt and one really good pinch of cayenne pepper. Mix them in thoroughly, then rub the butter in, using your fingertips, until it's all crumbly. Now mix in the 3 oz (75 g) grated cheese, along with the chives.

Next, beat the egg with 2½ tablespoons of buttermilk and gradually add it to the dry ingredients, mixing first with a knife, then with your hands to make a soft dough – if it seems a little dry, add another ½ tablespoon of buttermilk, or enough to make a soft, smooth dough that will leave the bowl clean. It's important not to overwork the dough or the scones will be heavy.

Now transfer the dough to a flat, lightly floured surface and roll it out as evenly as possible to around 1 inch (2.5 cm) thick – be very careful not to roll it out too thinly. The secret of well-risen scones is to start off with a thickness no less than an inch (2.5 cm). Then, using a fluted cutter, cut out six scones. You may need to re-roll the dough to cut out all six.

Now place the scones on the baking tray, brush the tops with milk, then sprinkle the rest of the grated cheese on top of each one, along with a faint sprinkling of cayenne pepper. Bake them on a high shelf for 15-20 minutes until the scones are risen and golden brown. Then cool a little on a wire rack, but serve warm.

Scottish Semolina Shortbread

This is a very buttery, crumbly shortbread – the real thing, and something that can't be bought, however much you pay for it. Using fine semolina gives it a lovely crunchy texture.

First of all, beat the butter in a bowl with a wooden spoon to soften it, then beat in the sugar, followed by the sifted flour and semolina. Work the ingredients together with the spoon, pressing them to the side of the bowl, then finish off with your hands until you have a smooth mixture that doesn't leave any bits in the bowl.

Next, transfer the dough to a flat, lightly floured surface and roll it out gently to a round (giving it quarter turns as you roll) about the same diameter as the tin, then transfer the round to the tin. Now lightly press in the mixture evenly, right up to the fluted edges. (To make sure it is even, you can give it a final roll with a small glass tumbler.) Finally, prick it all over with a fork – or it will rise up in the centre while it's baking.

Bake the shortbread for 55-60 minutes on the centre shelf of the oven – it should have turned pale gold and feel firm in the centre. Then remove it from the oven and, using a palette knife, mark out the surface into 12 wedges. Leave it to cool in the tin, then, when it's cold, cut it into wedges. Dredge with the remaining golden caster sugar and store in an airtight plastic box or tin until you are ready to serve them.

Note: If you're going to make and serve home-made ice cream, it's nice to serve small, thin shortbread biscuits to go with it. All you do is follow the recipe above, using half the mixture. Roll out the dough thinly, to a thickness of about ⅛ inch (3 mm) and cut it out into approximately 24 shapes using 2 inch (5 cm) cutter. Bake them (at the same temperature) for 15-20 minutes, or until pale gold. Then cool them on a wire rack and, if you want, drizzle some lemon icing (3 oz/75 g icing sugar, 1 tablespoon lemon juice) over them. If you don't want icing, just sprinkle with sugar and, either way, store them in an airtight plastic box or tin.

Makes 12 wedges

3 oz (75 g) fine semolina (or polenta)
6 oz (175 g) butter, at room temperature
3 oz (75 g) golden caster sugar, plus a little extra for dredging
6 oz (175 g) plain flour, sifted, plus a little extra for dusting

You will also need an 8 inch (20 cm) loose-based, fluted flan tin, 1¼ inches (3 cm) deep.

Pre-heat the oven to gas mark 2, 300°F (150°C).

Remove the shortbread from the oven, but don't cut it straight away – mark the surface into 12 wedges with a palette knife and leave to cool in the tin, right, before storing in an airtight plastic box, far right.

Lucy's Tarte Tatin

Lucy Crabb, who was the Executive Chef at our restaurant at Norwich City Football Club, made the very best Tarte Tatin (Caramelised Apple Flan) I've ever tasted. She insisted on French apples for this great classic from the Loire Valley, but if you want to use English apples, such as Cox's, it will still be wonderful.

Serves 6

For the pastry:

4 oz (110 g) plain flour, plus a little extra for dusting

1 oz (25 g) unsalted butter, at room temperature, cut into smallish lumps

1 oz (25 g) lard, at room temperature, cut into smallish lumps

2-3 tablespoons cold water

For the filling:

8 large Golden Delicious apples

3 oz (75 g) softened unsalted butter

6 oz (175 g) golden caster sugar

You will also need a non-stick, heavy-based frying pan that is ovenproof (including the handle), with a base diameter of 9½ inches (24 cm), 1½ inches (4 cm) deep.

First of all, you need to make the pastry, so it has time to rest. Begin by sifting the flour into a large mixing bowl from a height, then cut the fats into the flour with a knife, before rubbing the mixture lightly with your fingertips, lifting everything up and letting it fall back into the bowl to give it a good airing. When the mixture reaches the crumb stage, sprinkle in enough water to bring it together to a smooth dough that leaves the sides of the bowl absolutely clean, with no crumbs left. Give it a light knead to bring it fully together, then place the pastry in a plastic food bag and chill it in the fridge for 30 minutes.

To make the filling, peel the apples and then cut them in half vertically and remove the core. (Lucy did this with a melon baller, which worked brilliantly and kept the centre very neat.) Next, spread the softened butter evenly over the base of the pan and sprinkle the sugar over the top. Then, place the apples in concentric circles, cut side up. When you get to the centre, you may have to cut them into quarters to fill any gaps. Now you need to place the pan over a low heat so the butter and sugar melt very slowly together, which will take 8-10 minutes in all. When they have melted, increase the heat slightly, as you now want the sugar to caramelise. Gently shake the pan from time to time, so the apples don't stick and burn on the bottom. (Lucy always said that this is not a dessert you can walk away from, as the minute you do, the sugar will burn.) Meanwhile, pre-heat the oven to gas mark 7, 425°F (220°C). It will take about 20-25 minutes for the sugar to reach a rich amber colour and, by that time, the apples should be soft but still retain their shape. When that has happened, remove the pan from the heat.

Now remove the pastry from the fridge, transfer it to a flat, lightly floured surface and roll it out to an 11½ inch (29 cm) round. Fit it over the top of the pan, allowing some to tuck down at the edge, which doesn't have to be too neat. Prick the pastry base all over with a fork so the steam is released when it's cooking and the pastry doesn't go soggy. Next, place the pan on the centre shelf of the oven and bake the tart for 20-25 minutes, or until the pastry is crisp and golden brown.

Remove it from the oven using really thick oven gloves and allow it to cool for about 5 minutes. Now the whole thing gets interesting. Take a plate or tray larger than the pan and place it over the top. Then, using an oven glove to hold the handle, invert the pan on to the plate, giving it a little shake before you do. Serve the tart warm, with lashings of crème fraîche. I have to say, any left over is still wonderful served cold.

Easter Simnel Cake

This is a new and very easy angle on a traditional recipe. Simnel cake was not originally baked at Easter but on Mothering Sunday, as a kind of mid-Lent treat. Somehow or other, it got postponed until the great feast of Easter itself – which, in my book, is precisely where it deserves to be, since it makes the perfect family treat for a bank-holiday weekend. This version is baked with chunks of marzipan interspersed in the cake mixture, which melt deliciously into the fruit.

Serves 12

4 oz (110 g) whole, unblanched almonds
1 lb (450 g) golden marzipan in a block
8 oz (225 g) plain flour
3 teaspoons baking powder
1 rounded teaspoon mixed spice
14½ oz (410 g) mincemeat
12 oz (350 g) mixed dried fruit
2 oz (50 g) whole candied peel, chopped
grated zest 1 orange
grated zest 1 lemon
5 oz (150 g) light soft brown sugar
5 oz (150 g) well softened butter, plus a little extra for greasing
2 tablespoons milk
3 large eggs

To decorate:

a little icing sugar, for dusting
9 oz (250 g) ready-to-roll icing
1 dessertspoon redcurrant jelly
marzipan reserved from the cake
1 large egg yolk, beaten

You will also need a deep, 8 inch (20 cm) round cake tin, the base and sides lined with a double layer of buttered silicone paper (parchment), plus extra to cover the cake during baking.

Pre-heat the oven to gas mark 6, 400°F (200°C).

You need to begin by toasting the almonds to give them some extra crunch and flavour. So, spread them out on a baking tray and pop them into the pre-heated oven for 8-10 minutes. Don't guess the time; please use a timer – they need to be lightly toasted to a golden brown colour and you could end up with an expensive mistake if you try to guess! Now remove the almonds and reduce the oven temperature to gas mark 2, 300°F (150°C). Then, when the almonds are cool, chop them roughly. Next, unwrap the marzipan, cut the block into two halves, re-wrap one of them for use later and chop the remaining half into ½ inch (1 cm) cubes. Toss them in a tablespoon of the flour from the cake.

Now for the cake itself. Take your largest mixing bowl, sift in the flour, baking powder and spice, then simply place all the ingredients, except the squares of marzipan and the decorating ingredients, into the bowl. Then take an electric hand whisk (preferably) or, failing that, a wooden spoon, and give everything a really good mixing – which will take 2-3 minutes – to get it all perfectly and evenly distributed. Finally, gently fold in the squares of marzipan and any remaining flour from tossing them.

Now, using a rubber spatula, spoon the mixture into the prepared tin and level the surface. Place a suitably sized square of double-layered silicone paper (parchment) with a hole the size of a 50p piece in the centre, over the top. Place the cake on the centre shelf of the oven and bake for 2¾-3¼ hours. Have a look at it after 2¾ hours – the cake is cooked when the centre feels springy when lightly pressed. When it is baked, leave it in the tin for 30 minutes before turning it out on to a wire rack to cool.

For the decoration, first dust a work surface with icing sugar and roll out the icing to the same size as the top of the cake. (You can use the base of the tin as a guide here.) Then brush the top of the cake with the redcurrant jelly and fit the icing on top, pressing it securely all round and using a rolling pin to level it as much as possible, and trim off any overhanging pieces.

Next, roll out the reserved marzipan to a rectangle about 9 x 6 inches (23 x 15 cm) and cut it into 12 long strips about ½ inch (1 cm) wide. Assembling the lattice goes as follows: first lay half the strips across the cake, leaving about a ¾ inch (2 cm) gap between each strip. Then begin to thread the rest of the strips, one at a time, under and over the first ones, at right angles. Finally, use some scissors to snip away the overhanging marzipan and press firmly all round to make the edges as neat as possible.

Now pre-heat the grill for at least 10 minutes and, when it's really hot, brush the marzipan strips with the egg yolk and place the cake under the grill, about 4 inches (10 cm) from the heat source. Give it about 30 seconds, watching it like a hawk, until it turns a toasted brown colour. It is now ready to serve or be stored.

22
Gadgets that work

There's something very human about us all being seduced into buying gadgets, and I have to admit, I have had my fair share. But something a lifetime of cooking has taught me is to distinguish between what, in the end, just gathers dust at the back of a cupboard, and what, by contrast, can do a job of work for you and really save you time. My mother always says if you haven't worn something for a whole year you're never going to, so give it to the charity shop. The same applies to gadgets.

Kitchen casualties

While I know what suits one person won't suit another, my own casualties of time – things that take up precious space but are not really needed – are as follows. A slow cooker, because I can cook slowly on top of a stove or in a smaller oven. A pasta machine, because a) I prefer dried pasta and b) I have no time in my life to make my own. A sandwich toaster, which I used once then never took out of its box again (and, in any case, sandwiches can be grilled – see Croque Monsieur on page 92).

Then there's a pressure cooker. No good if you have animals because its high-pitched noise frightens the wits out of them. A deep fat fryer: I really don't need this huge, bulky object, and I also think that deep-frying in general at home is not needed – I find I can shallow-fry things just as easily without large quantities of messy oil. A salad spinner (remember those?): literally a waste of space, and anyway, a clean tea cloth or a wodge of kitchen paper dries salad leaves much more efficiently. Although I once had an ice-cream maker with a pre-freezing bowl, it never worked for me: either the bowl just took up too much room in the freezer, or, if I didn't keep it in the freezer, I never had time to re-freeze it.

I'm sure there are lots more kitchen casualties that many of you have accumulated, but now let's move on to what, over the years, has really served me well.

Electric hand whisk

I was brought up with something called a rotary whisk, which had a little handle you had to turn furiously to power the blades. Alternatively, there was the smarter and altogether purer way to whisk, which involved a copper bowl and a balloon whisk. Either way, being confronted with a mixing bowl and a mixture needing six minutes of what Victoria Wood's dinner ladies would call 'a bit of wellie' is not my idea of having fun in the kitchen.

But, to be poised by any kind of bowl, electric whisk in hand, to flick a switch and then dream or listen to music while it obeys your every desire – creating volume, whipping to silky smoothness or simply combining things instantly – makes for a much easier and more pleasant life all round.

Hand-held is best. Yes, I know you can buy a grander version, one that is free-standing, has its own bowl and lots of attachments that mean you can walk away while it does its work – so why don't I have one?

(i) Space: free-standing mixers are big, cumbersome things that take up unbelievable kitchen space.

(ii) Air: once the mixture is in the bowl and the whisk head is lowered, it all gets a bit enclosed and not enough air (a most important ingredient) is allowed to circulate.

(iii) Feel: in all my years of cooking I have always liked to get the feel of what I am mixing; under- or over-beating can be avoided as, with experience, you begin to feel when a mixture is right.

The blissful thing about an electric hand whisk is that you can tuck it into a cupboard or drawer, out of sight, and bring it out only when needed. You can use it in a bowl or a saucepan. It is convenient and quick, and afterwards, all you do is pop the beaters in a dishwasher or wash them up by hand. The best one to look for is the most powerful, so look at the wattage. We have found 250W to be powerful enough.

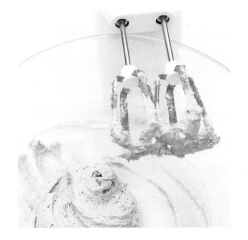

How you can best use an electric hand whisk. Obviously, top of the list is whisking egg whites: a powerful electric whisk and a large bowl (to give you lots of air) will give the best volume in the shortest time.

Mashing potatoes: I have tried ricers, which are very fiddly, and the potato gets cold while you fiddle. Mashers definitely need too much elbow grease, and in a food processor, the mixture just goes gloopy. But the fluffy, creamy mash produced by an electric hand whisk is a joy.

Proper home-made mayonnaise: what a chore this used to be, but it can be made in 7-10 minutes from start to finish using an electric hand whisk.

Cakes: I'm not sure I would actually make a cake that often if I didn't own an electric hand whisk – imagine creaming butter and sugar to that whipped, light, fluffy stage without one. Yes, a wooden spoon can do the job, but oh, the agony and the aching arm – all the more so as you beat the eggs in bit by bit.

Zabaglione

The Italians have invented a beautiful dessert, which is called zabaglione in Italy and sabayon in France. This involves whipping not the whites but the yolks to a voluminous, foamy mass along with some alcohol – in this case, Marsala wine from Sicily.

Serves 6
8 large egg yolks
4 dessertspoons golden caster sugar
75 ml (3 fl oz) Marsala

You will also need an electric hand whisk and six serving glasses.

You need to start this by putting a large saucepan, filled with a couple of inches of water, on a lowish heat to bring it up to a gentle simmer. Then place the egg yolks and sugar in a heatproof mixing bowl large enough to sit over the saucepan without touching the water. Start to whisk them (not on the heat yet) with the electric hand whisk until the mixture is pale and creamy – this will probably take about 4 minutes. Now gradually whisk in the Marsala bit by bit, about a dessertspoon at a time.

Next, transfer the bowl to the saucepan – keeping the heat very low and making sure the bowl doesn't touch the water. Continue whisking until the mixture thickens and becomes foamy. This can sometimes be rather slow (it usually takes 10-15 minutes), but don't be tempted to turn the heat up because, if the mixture becomes too hot, it will curdle. You could do a crossword (one-handed!), listen to the radio or have a natter with someone to pass the time!

When it does thicken, the whisk should leave a clear trail when it is lifted out of the mixture. If you have someone to help, ask them to warm the glasses by dipping them in a bowl of hot water and drying them off just before serving the zabaglione in them.

Note: This recipe contains partially cooked eggs.

Place the yolks and sugar in a bowl and whisk until pale and creamy.

Gradually add the Marsala, then whisk over the heat for 10-15 minutes, until thick.

Once the mixture has thickened, the whisk should leave a clear trail when lifted out.

Food processor

Although this is not an absolutely essential piece of equipment, because you can certainly chop, grate, slice, knead and mix everything by hand, it does do all these things very quickly and efficiently and saves you masses of time and energy. After years of using one myself, I am convinced every serious cook should have a food processor – it's a really great piece of equipment.

There are dozens of different designs and sizes, but I would say that if you invest in the largest, with the most powerful motor, you will have the best of everything. Quality never comes cheap, and beware of what looks like a bargain but may have a short life and not do the job really well. A warning: the blade in a food processor will wear out in time, so if your machine begins to show signs of not performing as it should, it probably needs a sharp new one, which can be ordered from a kitchen shop or direct from the manufacturer. Some top-of-the-range models have either an additional small bowl and blade for reduced quantities, or a blender attachment for making small amounts of, say, hollandaise or pesto.

Know your food processor. When you buy a food processor and begin to use it, you will soon get the feel of how it performs. One of the most common misuses is to overdo it. This was more of a problem before the pulse button was invented, when something chopped could become something liquidised, over-processed nuts became an oily, claggy mess, and puréed meat made hamburgers or rissoles very bouncy! With the pulse button you can see what is happening after each burst, which is important, but care must still be taken not to over-process.

What does a food processor do? First on the list is chopping, particularly large quantities. It can chop a pound of onions in seconds, as well as other vegetables, fruits and nuts. I love my food processor best when I feed it cubes of bread, which it instantly turns into breadcrumbs. (Some of you will be too young to remember the tedious job of grating bread into breadcrumbs by hand.) Also, if you want to make a stuffing, the onions, breadcrumbs and herbs can all be whizzed together – a brilliant time-saver. It can also evenly chop meat much more efficiently than the old-fashioned mincers that squeezed the meat through blades.

Slicing: Yes, it's good at this too. With a special attachment, you can deal with cucumbers, apples, cabbages, potatoes – in fact, whatever needs to be sliced – evenly and precisely. You can even choose thick or thin slices.

Mixing and puréeing: There are a million-and-one things you can mix in a food processor: whole-egg mayonnaise, for instance, can be mixed in moments. It can then be made into chunky tartare sauce, with capers, cornichons (baby gherkins) and parsley chopped in at the end. Taste it and you will never want the shop-bought version ever again. If you are nervous about making pastry, or if the fat from the fridge is too hard to rub in by hand, the food processor will make it extremely well, provided, at the end, you add the water a little at a time to get a good consistency. Sometimes, when you are serving vegetables, it's nice to ring the changes and whip them into a purée – with a little crème fraîche and some butter, it will make a lovely velvety-smooth parsnip purée. I also like to add steamed swede and carrots together to the bowl of the food processor while they are still hot, and whiz them, not to a purée, but to the coarsely chopped stage.

Grating: Grating large quantities – not just of breadcrumbs – can be arduous by hand. A good food processor will have various grating discs so you can grate cheese and vegetables. It makes light work of something really hard, such as fresh coconut (as in the Green Coconut Sambal that accompanies the Spiced Lamb Curry on page 554), and if you need a large amount of freshly grated Parmesan, it is all speedily and easily done.

What doesn't a food processor do? Number one on this list is mashed potatoes. It seems logical that it should, I know, but absolutely not. Something happens to them in the food processor that makes them gloopy and glue-like – not nice at all. Although you *can* use it to make cakes (such as sponge cakes), I feel the space inside the bowl is too confined and doesn't let the air in, so I wouldn't choose to make a cake in mine. The same applies to whisking: there is a whisk attachment that allows you to whisk egg whites but, again, I feel I'm not going to get as much air in, so I always use an electric hand whisk. As for herbs, I feel a good, sharp knife makes a better job of chopping herbs on their own (though herbs added to other mixtures are fine). A food processor can overdo the job and make them rather wet and soggy. Lastly, it's good for puréeing soups if you want a coarser texture, but it can only be done in small quantities or the soup spills over.

Checklist before you buy a food processor: Have you got room to spare? Having it plugged in and ready to go is vital – if it's stashed away in a cupboard you won't want to be bothered. Invest in the best. You could begin with a smaller, cheaper model, but I think a good-sized, powerfully motored, top-of-the-range one will serve you best in the long run. Check the level of the blades as they sit in the bowl – they need to be as low down as possible. The higher they are, the less effective the machine, because a small quantity of ingredients will just sit in the bottom with the blades merrily whizzing about above and the two never meeting!

Belarussian Carrot Salad

A few years ago I was privileged to be invited to a very special family meal in Minsk prepared by Sasha Shevchuck and her mother, Irina. Irina gave me her recipe for this simple, but oh-so-good carrot salad, which is perfect for winter when other salad ingredients are not at their best.

Serves 4-6 as a side dish
1 lb (450 g) carrots, peeled
1 dessertspoon coriander seeds
2 tablespoons groundnut or other flavourless oil
1 small onion, peeled and sliced
2 cloves garlic, finely chopped
cayenne pepper

For the marinade:
2 tablespoons cider vinegar
1 teaspoon salt

You will also need a food processor.

First of all, grate the carrot using the fine grater blade on your food processor. After that, transfer it to a bowl, pour over the marinade ingredients and mix to make sure everything is well coated. Then, cover and leave aside for at least 3 hours or, preferably, overnight in the fridge. If the carrots are very fresh, they develop too much juice, which should then be poured away.

Next, you need to dry-roast the coriander seeds. To do this, place them in a small frying pan over a medium heat and stir and toss them around for 1-2 minutes or until they begin to look toasted and start to jump in the pan. Now transfer them to a pestle and mortar and crush them lightly.

After that, heat the oil in the same frying pan. Add the onion and fry until golden. Allow to cool a little, then drain the oil through a sieve on to the carrots and discard the onion, which was there just to give some flavour. Now add the coriander seeds to the carrots, along with the garlic and a pinch of cayenne pepper, and give everything a good stir before serving. Covered, the salad will keep for a couple of days in the fridge.

Return to the blender

When food processors were born, we witnessed a kind of kitchen revolution: it was claimed that this piece of highly efficient equipment would do absolutely everything – and make blenders redundant. We have already looked at the functions of the food processor and applauded its virtues, but what did not stand the test of time was its ability to blend soups. Even though some had blender attachments, these were too small for the serious soupmaker. In a processor, soupmaking is still a messy business and you never quite achieve a uniform smoothness. Early in the food processor years, blenders disappeared from kitchen shops altogether. Thankfully, they are now back in, in large numbers and every price range.

What will a blender do? It will make very light work of blending soups to a good, smooth, uniform texture – and it can happily cope with as much as 1¾ pints (1 litre) of liquid at a time. This, for me, is its prime function. What else can blenders do? Well, food processors are not always good at blending small quantities, so if you want a small amount of mayonnaise, hollandaise, breadcrumbs, pesto or anything else that needs brief blending, you may find a blender does a better job.

What it *doesn't* do is grate or chop; it pulverises. So herbs, for instance, just get mashed to a pulp, which is okay for pesto but not other recipes. (In this respect, *liquidiser* is probably a more accurate term than blender because it pulverises ingredients almost to a liquid.)

Full-blown blender or hand-held version? With the hand-held blender you have to do a little more work. In the goblet of a full-blown blender, ingredients are pulverised in seconds at the press of a button, though some may find the bother of washing the goblet a chore (even if they are dishwasher-proof nowadays). With a hand-held version, you have to manipulate it into the corners of bowls and pans to make sure the blades are reaching all the parts they need to. Which you use is a matter of personal choice. Indeed, if you don't really enjoy cooking (particularly making and eating home-made soup), you may not need a blender at all. But I feel a serious cook will always appreciate having both a blender *and* a food processor because, together, they provide a useful service in so many different areas of cooking. However, it is worth pointing out that a mini-chopper will deal very well with herbs and small quantities of other ingredients.

Slow-Cooked Celery and Celeriac Soup

Because the vegetables are very slowly cooked, this soup has lots of lovely flavour, and it's quite satisfying and filling, particularly with some Celeriac and Lancashire Cheese Bread (see opposite).

Serves 6
1 lb (450 g) celery stalks (weight after trimming), leaves reserved
1 lb (450 g) celeriac (weight after peeling)
1 medium onion, peeled
2½ pints (1.5 litres) hot stock made with Marigold Swiss vegetable bouillon powder
3 bay leaves
salt and freshly milled black pepper

To garnish:
6 rounded teaspoons natural yoghurt (or crème fraîche)
2 teaspoons celery salt
a few celery leaves

You will also need a blender, and a lidded, flameproof casserole with a capacity of 6 pints (3.5 litres).

Pre-heat the oven to gas mark 1, 275°F (140°C).

Just a word first about preparing the vegetables. You need to use a potato peeler to pare off any really stringy bits from the outside stalks of the celery. The nice thing is that the outside stalks are fine for soups – so if you're using a whole head of celery, once you've weighed out the amount you need, you can keep the tender inside stalks for munching on. Peeling the celeriac will mean you lose quite a bit of the outside, as it's always very fibrous. Once that's done, weigh it and cut it into large chunks. The celery should also be cut into large chunks, and the same with the onion.

All you do now is pop the whole lot into the casserole, then add the stock and bay leaves, along with some salt and freshly milled black pepper. Bring it all up to simmering point on the hob, then put the lid on and transfer it to the oven to simmer very gently and slowly for 3 hours. After that, remove the bay leaves, allow the soup to cool a little, then blend it in batches until smooth. (A large bowl to put each batch in is helpful here.)

Then, return the soup to the casserole and bring it back to a gentle simmer, tasting to check the seasoning before serving. Serve in hot bowls with the yoghurt (or crème fraîche) spooned on top and the celery salt sprinkled over, garnished with a few celery leaves.

Celeriac and Lancashire Cheese Bread

This is yet another version of one of my most favourite and blissfully easy breads (see Goats' Cheese, Onion and Potato Bread with Thyme, on page 84), which is crunchy and crusty on the outside and soft and squidgy within.

All you do is sift the flour into a large mixing bowl, add the spring onions, two-thirds of the crumbled cheese, the cayenne pepper and the salt. Then, using the coarse side of a grater, grate in the celeriac as well.

Now give everything a really good mix. Beat the egg and milk together and, using a palette knife to mix, gradually add it all to the mixture until you have a loose, rough dough.

Now transfer it to the baking tray and, still keeping the rough texture, shape it into a round with your hands. Next, lightly press the rest of the cheese over the surface, sprinkle with a little flour and bake the bread on the middle shelf of the oven for 45-50 minutes, or until golden brown.

Cool on a wire rack and eat as fresh as possible. This is lovely served still warm, and if you have any left over, it's really good toasted.

Serves 6

6 oz (175 g) celeriac (weight after peeling)
4 oz (110 g) Lancashire cheese, roughly crumbled into ½ inch (1 cm) pieces
6 oz (175 g) self-raising flour, plus a little extra for the top of the loaf
4 spring onions, finely chopped, including the green parts
⅛ teaspoon cayenne pepper
1 large egg
2 tablespoons milk
1 teaspoon salt

You will also need a small baking tray, very well greased.

Pre-heat the oven to gas mark 5, 375°F (190°C).

Carrot and Artichoke Soup

This is one of my most favourite soups ever. Firstly, it has an extremely rich, beautiful colour – almost saffron-like, I would say. And secondly, the combination is so unique, people can never quite guess what it is. Jerusalem artichokes don't look user-friendly, but once you've cut off and discarded all the knobbly bits, the flavour is quite outstanding.

Serves 6-8
1 lb (450 g) carrots
1 lb 8 oz (700 g) Jerusalem artichokes
(weight before peeling)
3 celery stalks
3 oz (75 g) butter
1 medium onion, peeled and
roughly chopped
2½ pints (1.5 litres) hot stock made
with Marigold Swiss vegetable
bouillon powder
salt and freshly milled black pepper

To garnish:
6-8 teaspoons crème fraîche
6-8 leaves fresh flat-leaf parsley

You will also need a blender, and a large saucepan with a capacity of about 6 pints (3.5 litres).

Start by peeling and de-knobbling the artichokes and, as you peel them, cut them into rough chunks and place them in a bowl of cold, salted water to prevent them from discolouring. Then scrape the carrots and slice them into largish chunks. Next, use a potato peeler to pare off any stringy bits from the celery and then roughly chop it.

Now melt the butter in the saucepan and soften the onion and celery in it for 5 minutes, keeping the heat fairly low. Then drain the artichokes and add them to the pan, along with the carrots. Add some salt and, keeping the heat very low, put a lid on and let the vegetables sweat for 10 minutes to release their juices.

After that, pour in the stock, stir well, put the lid back on and simmer very gently for a further 20 minutes, or until the vegetables are soft. Now allow the soup to cool a little, then blend it in batches. (A large bowl to put each batch in is helpful here.) Taste to check the seasoning and re-heat the soup very gently until it just comes to simmering point. Serve it in hot bowls, garnishing each one with a swirl of crème fraîche and a few leaves of parsley.

Jerusalem artichokes, far left; Carrot and Artichoke Soup, garnished with crème fraîche and flat-leaf parsley, left.

Ajo Blanco – Chilled Almond Soup

My friend Neville, who has a house in Andalusia surrounded by almond trees, gave me this supremely wonderful recipe for Chilled Almond Soup, generously laced with garlic, that is made by the locals who live there. You can make it up to five days ahead – as Neville says, it goes on improving in flavour.

First you need to blanch the almonds. To do this, place them in a bowl, pour in enough boiling water to cover and leave them aside for 3-4 minutes. Then drain them in a colander and simply squeeze the nuts out of their skins into the bowl.

After that, put the almonds in the blender and pour in the olive oil. (The oil should just cover the almonds – if it doesn't, add a little more.) Then, add the peeled garlic, vinegar and salt and liquidize until everything is smooth. Now, with the motor still running, slowly add the cold water. Pour the soup into a large bowl and if it seems too thick, add a little more water. Then cover the bowl with clingfilm and keep it well chilled until you're ready to serve.

Just before serving, stir in the ice cubes and ladle the soup into the chilled bowls. Garnish with the grapes and apple slices.

Serves 4

7 oz (200 g) unblanched almonds (preferably Spanish almonds – never ready-blanched for this recipe)
7 fl oz (200 ml) Spanish olive oil
3 cloves garlic, peeled
1 dessertspoon sherry vinegar
about 12 fl oz (340 ml) cold water
2 teaspoons salt, or more, to taste

To serve:
8 ice cubes
4 oz (110 g) black grapes, deseeded and halved
1 dessert apple, peeled, cored and thinly sliced

You will also need a blender and four chilled soup bowls.

Breadmaker

I went to great pains to explain the principles of breadmaking in Chapter 4, and I do still feel that it can be a very pleasurable, sometimes therapeutic experience. I also feel it is a very important part of learning how to cook. Having said that, the advent of the automatic breadmaking machine has added a very special experience to day-to-day living. It's quite simply an outstanding invention, almost miraculous, when you think that a freshly baked, crusty, full-flavoured loaf can be delivered to you warm from baking after just a simple assembly of ingredients and the push of a button. Even with your pressured, busy life, your house can be filled with that unique aroma of yeasty earthiness and goodness. That simple pleasure alone can raise your life experience to another level. (If you have any doubts, just think of all that tacky, spongy stuff that comes out of factories in the name of bread.)

Your breadmaker will not only deliver you a finished loaf, you can, alternatively, just use it to do all the hard work of mixing and kneading and let it deliver just the dough, which you can then make into pizzas, or shape into rolls or plaits, and so, enjoy the fun bits of breadmaking.

Breadmaker rules: There are, of course, rules that must be obeyed: Breadmakers are not flexible – they do what they do. Because of this, *they* rule, not you, so you can't be casual about it and not follow the manual precisely. In fact, once you get to know the ropes, you will begin to use it on automatic pilot, without even thinking about it. To familiarise yourself with the process, it's best to start with the manufacturer's own recipes, then move on to others (including mine). The most important rule of all is to add the ingredients in the correct order according to the manual – that one is not negotiable.

What's going on in there? Of course, it's like putting a cake in the oven: the suspense is killing you and you're dying to know what's going on. Well, it's okay during the mixing to lift the lid and have a peek – in fact, it's better if you *do* after about 10 minutes, as it might need a bit more flour if the mixture is too soft, or a bit more water if it's too stiff. After that, when the dough is rising and baking, peeping is strictly not allowed, as it can drastically affect the temperature and spoil everything.

Flour and yeast: The good thing about a breadmaker is producing bread with no additives and from the best-quality flours. (I've also discovered that Carrs Flour Mills, the clever people who invented sauce flour to prevent lumps in sauces, have developed a range of high-quality mixes specifically designed to be used in breadmakers, which come complete with their own sachet of yeast.) There is also a special powdered yeast suitable for use in machines.

Any snags? Yes, if you don't follow the rules! Also, bread doesn't like extremes of temperature, which can kill the yeast, so ingredients need to be at room temperature before you start. They must all be weighed accurately, too, so if you're not the weighing type, don't buy a breadmaker. Lastly, if you're going to leave the machine on a timer, when you place the ingredients in, make sure the yeast is not in contact with the liquid.

To sum up, I think breadmakers are great – the natural flavour of wheat in freshly baked bread with a crisp, crunchy crust is one of life's simplest and best pleasures. Add to that some creamy Normandy butter and home-made preserves (see page 566) and, believe me, eating doesn't come much better.

Pitta Bread

Home-made pitta bread is such a treat, and with a breadmaker to make the initial dough, it's not a lot of bother. I love the way they puff up and become hollow.

Makes 12

1 lb 2 oz (500 g) strong white bread flour, plus 2 tablespoons for dusting
2 teaspoons easy-blend yeast
1 oz (25 g) butter, at room temperature, plus a little extra for greasing
11 fl oz (310 ml) water
1½ teaspoons salt

You will also need a breadmaker, and a baking tray measuring 11 x 16 inches (28 x 40 cm), lightly greased.

To make the dough, tip all the ingredients into the breadmaker in the order stated in your manual. Then set the machine to the dough only setting (as the pittas are going to be baked in the oven). Now simply press start and let the machine do all the work.

When you are ready to bake the pittas, pre-heat the oven to gas mark 7, 425°F (220°C). Then transfer the dough from the breadmaker to a flat, lightly floured surface, divide it into 12 equal portions and roll out three of them to oval shapes measuring roughly 4 x 8 inches (10 x 20 cm), covering the remaining dough with a clean tea cloth. Dust the tops lightly with flour and place them on the baking tray. Now pop them into the oven, on a high shelf, and bake them for 8-10 minutes, or until they have become golden and puffy.

Meanwhile, prepare the next three portions and when the first ones are ready, remove them from the oven and wrap them in another tea cloth. (If they're allowed to cool without this, they get too crisp, and a pitta should be soft, not crunchy.) Now just carry on cooking and wrapping the rest of the pittas. It's nice to serve them fresh from the oven with Tunisian Aubergine Salad (page 358) or Hummus (page 542), or, if you're making them in advance, warm them through briefly in the oven before serving.

Filled Focaccia with Ham and Melted Fontina

I suppose I would describe this as a kind of hot, home-made sandwich. Lovely to serve straight from the oven for lunch. We've used ham, cheese and sage here, but any kind of filling at all would be fine, including vegetables such as mushrooms or preserved artichokes, or salami – the permutations are endless.

Serves 4
For the dough:
9 oz (250 g) strong white bread flour, plus a little extra for dusting
1 teaspoon easy-blend yeast
5 fl oz (150 ml) water
1 dessertspoon olive oil, plus a little extra for greasing
1 teaspoon salt

For the filling:
6 oz (175 g) sliced Parma ham
12 oz (350 g) Fontina (or Gruyère)
3 tablespoons chopped fresh sage leaves
freshly milled black pepper

For the top:
15 small sprigs fresh rosemary
2 tablespoons olive oil
1 teaspoon sea salt

You will also need a breadmaker, and a baking tray measuring 11 x 16 inches (28 x 40 cm), well greased (or a pizza baking stone).

Pop the ingredients for the dough into the breadmaker in the order your manual instructs. Set it to the dough only setting (as the focaccia is going to be baked in the oven) and press the start button.

Meanwhile, towards the end of the time, prepare the filling ingredients, separating the slices of ham and cutting the cheese into thin slices. When the dough is ready, remove it from the machine, turn it out on to a flat, lightly floured surface, divide it into two and then roll out one half to form a rough, rounded rectangle about 11 x 8 inches (28 x 20 cm).

Then place it on the baking tray (or pizza stone) and arrange the slices of ham on top, making sure they go right up to the edge. Follow this with the cheese, right up to the edge again, then scatter over the sage. Now give it a good seasoning of freshly milled black pepper. Then roll out the remaining dough, lay it on top of the first, pinching the edges together all the way round to completely enclose the filling. Now cover it with a clean tea cloth and leave it to puff up again for about 30 minutes. Meanwhile, pre-heat the oven to gas mark 6, 400°F (200°C).

When the dough is ready, make 15 little dimples in it with your finger and press in the sprigs of rosemary. Finally, drizzle over the olive oil and sprinkle with the salt. Bake for 20-25 minutes, or until the dough is crisp and golden. Serve the focaccia, cut into squares or wedges, straight from the oven.

Poppy and Sesame Seed Rolls

This is a very rich dough – so good, in fact, you can eat these buttery-flavoured rolls on their own, without any extra butter.

First of all, put the breadmaker to work by placing all the ingredients for the dough into it in the order your manual instructs. (If it seems like a lot of butter, don't worry, it will all work perfectly well.) Now set it to the dough only setting (as the rolls are going to be baked in the oven), press the start button and let the machine do all the work.

When the dough is ready, turn it out on to a flat, lightly floured work surface and knead and shape it into roughly an 8 inch (20 cm) square.

Now brush the top of the dough with the beaten egg. Next, combine the poppy and sesame seeds in a small bowl and sprinkle them evenly over the top of the dough. After that, take a large, sharp knife and cut the dough into 16 squares, roughly measuring 2 inches (5 cm). Don't worry about getting perfect shapes – they can be quite haphazard.

Now transfer them to the baking tray, leaving a space between each one, as they will prove and rise before baking. Leave them for about 30 minutes. Meanwhile, pre-heat the oven to gas mark 5, 375°F (190°C).

After that bake the rolls on the centre shelf of the oven for 25-30 minutes, or until they're crisp and golden brown. If you're making them in advance, warm them through briefly in the oven before serving.

Makes 16
For the dough:
1 lb 2 oz (500 g) strong white bread flour, plus a little extra for dusting
2 teaspoons easy-blend yeast
1 teaspoon golden caster sugar
4 oz (110 g) butter, at room temperature, plus a little extra for greasing
11 fl oz (310 ml) water
1½ teaspoons salt

For the topping:
1 tablespoon poppy seeds
1 tablespoon sesame seeds
1 large egg, beaten

You will also need a breadmaker, and a baking tray measuring 11 x 16 inches (28 x 40 cm), well greased.

Blowtorch

Way back in the 1960s, when Elizabeth David first had her own kitchen shop, I remember being there when a customer was buying a salamander – a heavy, round iron weight on the end of a steel rod. The idea behind it was that if you heated it until it was red hot and then placed it over the sugar surface of a crème brûlée, it would instantly caramelise it (the point being to bypass the British domestic grill, with all its vagaries and unreliability). Mrs David suggested to the said lady (and me, as well, because I couldn't resist buying one, too) that we should practise with ramekins filled with tinned rice pudding first, so as not to waste gallons of cream and eggs. It turned out to be sound advice, as I got through several tins of rice pudding without a single success.

Thus, the art of acquiring that thin, glass-like coating of caramel eluded me. British grills, after all those years, are *still* universally unreliable: until recently, it seemed the only answer was to make up a caramel and pour it on top of the set custard (see pages 468-9). Then along came the answer and, when the chef's blowtorch first hit the kitchen shops, it was a must-have for all who wanted to cook.

However, the early consignments were not quite the ticket – too faint-hearted by half – so you would spend absolutely ages just getting one ramekin caramelised. Next stop, DIY stores – why not get the genuine article and really give your brûlée a blast? But that was not the answer either, because the heat was too fierce, and I was envisaging hundreds of firefighters up and down the country taking me to task for recommending their use!

But, at last, a great step for mankind: there is now a blowtorch that does the job perfectly. It is self-igniting and makes short shrift of changing sugar into caramel (see Alain's Passion Fruit Brûlée, opposite, and Summer-Fruit Brûlée on page 524). It does a few other jobs as well, such as helping unmould a jelly, skinning tomatoes and giving a smoky, charred taste to aubergines. It is now a standard item in *How To Cook*.

Alain's Passion Fruit Brûlée

My thanks to Alain Benech, our very French chef at the football club, whom I persuaded to part with his delicious recipe for you all to make. Whenever it goes on the menu, it's very popular and always sells out.

Begin by cutting the passion fruit in half and, using a teaspoon, scoop the fruit and seeds out into a large, deep mixing bowl. Then add the egg yolks and 3 oz (75 g) of the sugar to the bowl and, using an electric hand whisk on a high speed, whiz all the ingredients together for about 5 minutes, or until the mixture is frothy and pale in colour. Meanwhile, heat the cream and milk in a saucepan over a medium heat, whisking now and then, until hot but do not boil.

Now, with the whisk on a slow speed, add the hot cream into the mixture, keeping the whisk running as you do so. Then strain the custard through a sieve into a large jug, discarding the passion fruit seeds.

Next, you need to put the ramekins into the roasting tin and fill them with the mixture. Now fill the tin with boiling water from the kettle to about halfway up the sides of the ramekins and place it on the centre shelf of the oven. Let the puddings cook gently for 40 minutes. They are ready when the custard is set but still wobbles when you move them gently. At this point, remove them from the oven and allow them to cool, then cover them with clingfilm and chill them in the fridge for about 2 hours, or, preferably, overnight.

After that, sprinkle each ramekin evenly with some of the remaining 2 oz (50 g) of sugar, dividing it equally. Then very lightly spray the surface with water, using the spray bottle. (This helps melt the sugar, speeding up the caramelising process.) Now use the blowtorch to melt and caramelise the sugar. To do this, hold it over each ramekin, aiming the tip of the flame at the sugar – it will immediately begin to bubble and melt, and soon turn to a golden caramel. As soon as the sugar has reached a dark brown colour, move on to the next one and continue until they've all got a lovely glazed brown surface. It will take about 10 minutes in all. After that, allow to cool before serving.

Serves 8
6 large passion fruit (about 9 fl oz/ 250 ml pulp)
14 fl oz (400 ml) double cream
2 fl oz (55 ml) milk
7 large egg yolks
5 oz (150 g) golden caster sugar

You will also need eight 1½ inch (4 cm) deep ramekins with a base diameter of 3 inches (7.5 cm) (or eight similar-sized heatproof glass bowls); a large roasting tin; a plastic spray bottle; and a chef's blowtorch.

Pre-heat the oven to gas mark 2, 300°F (150°C).

Summer-Fruit Brûlée

Here is another brûlée recipe. If you have invested in a chef's blowtorch, you'll be able to get lots of that lovely, thin, caramelised crust.

Serves 6

1 lb 8 oz (700 g) soft fruits
(including one or more of the following:
raspberries, redcurrants, loganberries,
blackberries and blackcurrants)
4 oz (110 g) golden caster sugar
10 fl oz (275 ml) whipping cream
10½ oz (295 g) Greek yoghurt
6 oz (175 g) demerara sugar

You will also need a serving dish with
a base measurement of 10 x 6½ inches
(25.5 x 16 cm), 2 inches (5 cm) deep,
a plastic spray bottle and a chef's
blowtorch.

First pick over the fruit and place it in a large saucepan (or flameproof casserole). Sprinkle it with the caster sugar and then put the pan (or casserole) over a gentle heat for 3-5 minutes, or until the sugar melts and the juices begin to run, but try not to over-stir, or the fruit will break down to a mush. After that, transfer the fruit to the serving dish with a slotted spoon and allow it to get quite cold. Now whip the cream until thick, fold it into the yoghurt and spread this mixture all over the fruit, taking it right up to the edges of the dish to seal the fruit underneath. Then cover with clingfilm and chill in the fridge for at least 2 hours.

About 2 hours before you want to serve the brûlée, spread the surface thickly and evenly with the demerara sugar, then spray it very lightly with water, using the spray bottle. (This helps melt the sugar and speeds up the caramelising process.) Now use the blowtorch to caramelise the sugar on top. To do this, hold it over the dish, aiming the tip of the flame at the sugar – it will immediately begin to bubble and melt and soon turn to a golden caramel. As soon as that area has reached a dark brown colour, move the blowtorch and continue to caramelise the sugar all over the top. Because the surface is large, it will take about 10 minutes.

Now leave the brûlée to cool, then pop it back in the fridge, uncovered, where the sugar will form a crusty, crunchy surface – wonderful!

Two luxury items

These last two gadgets – an ice-cream maker and an espresso coffee machine (see page 532) – are expensive, unashamed luxuries that are by no means essential. But, if you're anticipating a wedding or having a special birthday, you might like to consider putting them on your list, or treating yourself at some stage in your life when, after years of hard work in the kitchen, you think you deserve them.

Ice-cream maker

It can't be denied that there are now some very good commercially made ice creams available. But that said, it's very satisfying to make your own, to use the purest and best ingredients and to spoil your family and friends with the results.

Making ice cream before the days of refrigeration was honestly a trial, what with hand-cranked churns, packs of ice and so on. Even with modern freezers it's something of a palaver: timing it, hoicking it out, mixing it, then repeating the whole performance over again – not to mention the risks of over- or under-freezing. Yet again, cooks have been truly blessed: there are now fully automatic ice-cream makers with their own in-built freezing and churning unit. So, real home-made ice creams can be made from start to finish in just 30 minutes. What's more, if you like a soft consistency (as I sometimes do) you can serve them straight away without even putting them in the freezer.

How does it work? Basically, all you need to do is switch the machine on about 10 minutes before you want to use it (or as instructed in your manual) – rather like pre-heating the oven in reverse. (It takes time for the machine to reach the right freezing temperature.) While that's happening, you make up your mixture and just pour it into the container. Then, when you switch on, the motorised paddles automatically churn the ice cream as it freezes, breaking down the ice crystals and producing a velvety-smooth texture and just the right consistency. Because you're in charge of the ingredients, you are also assured of the best possible flavour. Finally, it's as convenient to clean as it is to operate: the removable components are dishwasher-proof or very easy to rinse by hand. Couldn't be simpler.

Any drawbacks? Home-made ice cream is best eaten within a week of being made, but since you can make it as and when you need it in just a few minutes, I don't see this as a problem. Ideally, the machine should be kept out and not transferred in and out of cupboards – it doesn't like being shifted about because it unsettles the intricacies of the freezing unit. So, the only real drawback is one of space. If you have the room and are happy to keep it out on the counter top, you'll get enormous pleasure out of making and eating real ice cream, knowing it doesn't contain additives, emulsifiers, flavourings, stabilisers or preservatives. It also allows you to experiment with so many different recipes – if there's a glut of raspberries, you can make raspberry ice cream, if it's the Seville orange season you can make a sorbet… there's a whole world of ice creams, sorbets and parfaits out there just waiting for you to try them.

Note: If you don't have an ice-cream maker, you can still make ice cream. After you have made up your mixture, transfer it to a lidded plastic box and put it in the coldest part of the freezer for two hours, or until the contents become firm at the edges. At this stage, empty out the box into a mixing bowl and whisk the ice cream with an electric hand whisk to break down the ice crystals. Return the box to the freezer and freeze for another two hours, then repeat the whisking process. Refreeze the ice cream (if making a sorbet that contains a generous quantity of alcohol, as on page 529, freeze overnight) until 30-45 minutes before you want to serve it, at which time you should transfer it to the fridge to soften.

Zabaglione Ice Cream with Biscotti

Once you've mastered the art of Zabaglione on page 504, you've got the perfect base for a brilliant ice cream, and if you fold in some crushed biscotti (hard-baked, brittle biscuits) it all gets very Italian and lovely. It's quite nice to serve some whole biscotti to go with it.

Serves 4
For the zabaglione:
4 large egg yolks
2 oz (50 g) golden caster sugar
2½ fl oz (65 ml) Marsala

For the ice cream:
10 fl oz (275 ml) double cream
3 oz (75 g) almond biscotti, crushed to crumbs, plus extra biscuits to serve

You will also need an ice-cream maker (pre-frozen according to the manufacturer's instructions), and a lidded plastic box measuring 7 x 5½ x 2½ inches (18 x 14 x 6 cm).
(If you don't have an ice-cream maker, instructions for making ice cream without one are on page 527.)

Begin by whipping the cream to the 'floppy' stage and then transfer to the fridge to chill. Now make the Zabaglione, as described on page 504. Next, remove the bowl from the heat, cover and allow the mixture to cool completely, which will take about 30 minutes.

When the mixture is absolutely cold, gently stir, and fold in the double cream. Then pour the mixture into the ice-cream maker and freeze-churn for 20-30 minutes until the ice cream is soft-set.

Now transfer the mixture to a bowl and stir in the biscotti crumbs. Serve straight away, or freeze in the plastic box for 1-2 hours until firm, transferring to the fridge 30 minutes before serving to allow the ice cream to soften and become easy to scoop.

Note: This recipe contains partially cooked eggs.

Spike's Apple Sorbet

Spike is the nickname of our friend Galton Blackiston, who is the owner and chef of the Michelin-starred country-house hotel Morston Hall in Norfolk. He's a fanatical Norwich City supporter, so we always end our meals there with lots of football tales until the early hours. He has generously allowed me to adapt his brilliant apple sorbet recipe.

First of all, chop the apples into ½ inch (1 cm) cubes and place them in a food processor, along with the lime juice, membrillo (or jam), sugar and Calvados, and process everything to a fine purée. Now set a large, fine nylon sieve over an equally large bowl and pour the puréed mixture through it, pushing it with the back of a spoon to get as much apple pulp through as possible. All that should be left in the sieve are the tiny flecks of apple peel, which can be discarded.

Now you need to be fairly swift or the apple will discolour. Pour the mixture into the ice-cream maker and freeze-churn. This may take a little longer than usual, due to the generous quantity of alcohol. Either serve straight away or spoon it into the plastic box and freeze for later. From the freezer, it will need 20 minutes in the fridge to soften before serving.

Serves 6
8 Granny Smith apples, washed and cored (no need to peel)
juice 4 limes
4 oz (110 g) membrillo (quince paste) or apricot jam
4 oz (110 g) golden caster sugar
4 fl oz (120 ml) Calvados

You will also need an ice-cream maker (pre-frozen according to the manufacturer's instructions), and a lidded plastic box with a base measurement of 8 x 5 x 2 inches (20 x 13 x 5 cm).
(If you don't have an ice-cream maker, instructions for making ice cream without one are on page 527.)

Preserved Ginger Ice Cream

This is one of the creamiest ice creams I know, and it provides a perfectly luscious backdrop to the strong, assertive flavours of stem ginger. Serve in some crisp Molasses Brandy Snap Baskets (see opposite), with a little of the ginger syrup poured over – a great combination.

Serves 4-6
4 pieces preserved stem ginger, chopped into ¼ inch (5 mm) cubes
2 tablespoons stem ginger syrup
10 fl oz (275 ml) double cream
10 fl oz (275 ml) single cream
4 large egg yolks
1 oz (25 g) golden caster sugar
2 slightly rounded teaspoons cornflour
3-4 drops pure vanilla extract

To garnish:
2 pieces preserved stem ginger, chopped
a little extra stem ginger syrup

You will also need an ice-cream maker (pre-frozen according to the manufacturer's instructions), and a lidded plastic box measuring 7 x 5½ x 2½ inches (18 x 14 x 6 cm). (If you don't have an ice-cream maker, instructions for making ice cream without one are on page 527.)

First of all, whip the double cream until it reaches the 'floppy' stage but isn't too thick, then pop it into the fridge to chill.

Now make a custard – first pour the single cream into a saucepan, then carefully heat it to just below boiling point. Meanwhile, beat together the egg yolks, sugar and cornflour in a bowl until absolutely smooth.

Next, pour the hot cream on to this mixture, whisking as you pour. Now return the custard to the pan and continue to whisk it over a medium heat until it has thickened and come up to boiling point again. (Ignore any curdled appearance, which may come about if you don't keep whisking and have the heat too high. The cornflour will stabilise it, so don't worry – it will regain its smoothness when cooled and whisked.)

Now rinse the bowl and pour the custard into it. Then place it in another, larger bowl of cold water, with a few ice cubes, stirring it now and then until absolutely cold. Next, fold into the custard the chilled, whipped cream, ginger syrup and vanilla extract. Now pour the whole lot into the ice-cream maker and freeze-churn for 20-30 minutes until the ice cream is soft-set. Quickly fold in the chopped stem ginger, then spoon it into the plastic box and freeze until firm, which will take 1-2 hours.

Transfer the ice cream to the fridge 45 minutes before serving to allow it to soften and become easy to scoop. Garnish with the stem ginger and serve with a little of the syrup poured over.

Serve the Preserved Ginger Ice Cream in the Molasses Brandy Snap Baskets, with a little stem ginger syrup poured over.

Molasses Brandy Snap Baskets

I think these are really fun to make, and the crunchy caramel flavour is the perfect partner to any ice cream – particularly Preserved Ginger Ice Cream (see opposite).

Measuring golden syrup is a sticky business, and for this recipe the easiest way to deal with it is to first weigh out the sugar and then weigh the golden syrup on top, so it sticks to the sugar and not the scale pan. Next, put the whole lot into a medium-sized, heavy-based saucepan, together with the butter, and heat gently for about 5 minutes, or until all the sugar has dissolved, there are no granules left and the mixture is completely smooth. (The way to test this is by looking at some on the back of a spoon.) Then remove the pan from the heat and beat in the flour and ginger, followed by the brandy.

Now place 2 tablespoons of the mixture on to the lined baking tray, allowing space for them to spread as they cook to make two circles roughly 7 inches (18 cm) in diameter. Bake on the middle shelf for 7 minutes, keeping a close eye on them for the last 2 minutes' cooking time.

When they're ready, remove the tray from the oven and allow the brandy-snap circles to cool for a couple of minutes before lifting one from the tray and moulding it over the upturned, greased jam jar, pressing the edges out to get a frilly basket shape. If they get too cool to mould, don't worry about it – just pop them back in the oven for a minute and then try again. If you're unsure of yourself, have several goes at it – but it *is* easier than it sounds!

As soon as the first basket is ready – it only takes about a minute – place it on a cooling rack and quickly mould the second one. Then repeat the whole process in twos until they're all complete. The brandy snap baskets can be made several hours in advance and stored in an airtight tin.

To serve, place them on a plate and fill with a large scoop of ice cream. If it's the Preserved Ginger Ice Cream, pour a little ginger syrup over and decorate with a few pieces of chopped preserved ginger.

Makes 6
1 teaspoon brandy
2 oz (50 g) molasses sugar
1½ oz (40 g) golden syrup
2 oz (50 g) butter, plus a little extra for greasing
1½ oz (40 g) plain flour, sifted
¾ teaspoon ground ginger

You will also need a baking tray measuring 11 x 16 inches (28 x 40 cm), lined with silicone paper (parchment), and a jam jar with a base diameter of about 2 inches (5 cm), well-buttered.

Pre-heat the oven to gas mark 4, 350°F (180°C).

Mould the brandy-snap circles over an upturned, greased jam jar, pressing the edges to get a frilly shape.

531

Espresso coffee machine

Obviously, this is neither essential nor part of a *batterie de cuisine* for cooks, except that, if you're slaving away in the kitchen, you deserve a really good cup of coffee now and then. The machine I have offers unashamed luxury. You can choose espresso, regular black or cappuccino, and the coffee comes in neat little capsules with lots of blends to choose from. When you have made the coffee, you just throw the capsules out, which means no messy washing-up, no coffee grounds, no plungers that get stuck halfway. (In contrast, cleaning the plunger-type coffee-makers is a nightmare.)

Initially, this machine did seem quite expensive, particularly as the coffee has to be delivered. But, when I remember all the cold leftover coffee we used to throw away, I'm sure there is far less waste. The machine is easy to clean and has a transparent water chamber at the back that enables you to see quite clearly when it needs topping up. Because we live in a hard-water area, ours needed to be serviced after about a year and the company efficiently sent a special container to ship it back for servicing – so full marks for after-sales service. It is expensive, but when something really serves you well and gives so much pleasure to you and all those you serve coffee to, then, over a period of time, it's cheap at the price.

Vanilla Bean Ice Cream with Espresso

This is my long-standing, classic vanilla ice cream recipe, which I think is much improved of late, having incorporated a whole vanilla pod, with its speckly seeds, and crème fraîche, with its slightly acidic but very dairy flavour. However, it's also excellent if you replace the crème fraîche with double cream. I also love it made with untreated Jersey cream, which I get from my local farmers' market.

First of all, you need to make the custard, so begin by splitting the vanilla pod lengthways and, using the end of a teaspoon, scoop out the seeds into a mixing bowl. Next, pour the single cream into a saucepan, add the pod and then carefully heat the cream up to just below boiling point. While that's happening, place the vanilla seeds, egg yolks, custard powder and sugar in a mixing bowl and whisk until absolutely smooth.

Next, pour the hot cream on to this mixture, discarding the pod, and whisking as you pour. Now return the custard to the pan and continue to whisk it over a medium heat until it has thickened and come up to boiling point again. (Ignore any curdled appearance, which may come about if you don't keep whisking and have the heat too high. The custard powder will stabilise it if you pour it into a bowl and whisk, and it will become quite smooth.)

When the custard is ready, place the bowl in another, larger bowl of cold water, with a few ice cubes, stirring it now and then until it's absolutely cold. Then fold the crème fraîche into the custard, pour the whole lot into the ice-cream maker and freeze-churn until the mixture is soft-set. If you prefer it set a little firmer, or you want to eat it later, freeze it in the plastic box for 1-2 hours until firm – but whenever you come to remove it from the freezer, transfer it to the fridge for 30 minutes to soften before serving. Then scoop it into heatproof glasses or serving bowls and pour some hot espresso over each one just before serving.

Note: Little thin Shortbread Biscuits (see page 495) are good with this ice cream.

Serves 6
1 vanilla pod
12 fl oz (340 ml) hot espresso coffee
10 fl oz (275 ml) single cream
4 large egg yolks
2 slightly rounded teaspoons custard powder
2 oz (50 g) golden caster sugar
10 fl oz (275 ml) crème fraîche

You will also need an ice-cream maker (pre-frozen according to the manufacturer's instructions); a lidded plastic box measuring 7 x 5½ x 2½ inches (18 x 14 x 6 cm); and six heatproof glasses (or serving bowls).
(If you don't have an ice-cream maker, instructions for making ice cream without one are on page 527.)

23

How to cook pulses

Pulses have somehow managed to re-invent themselves. Whereas once they were discounted and ridiculed as being food fit only for the poor, now they've become chic, occupying premier position on the shelves of the very smartest food shops, and firmly re-established as a vital part of new-age cooking and eating.

The kind of dismissive comments we used to hear about pulses included describing the poorest of meals as a 'beanfeast', and someone having nothing at all as 'not having a bean'. The reason for this is that what we call first-class protein – meat, fish, eggs, cheese and so on – is usually expensive, while pulses are cheap. Nonetheless, they are highly nutritious and therefore, the next best thing. In fact, if you combine them with grains (as in the Creole dish of rice and red beans), what you get is something nutritionally equal to first-class protein. Our most popular snack in Britain, beans on toast, fulfils all the criteria of a highly nutritious meal. I think this reincarnation of pulses is for the most part due to the rise of vegetarianism, and along the way, meat-eaters, too, have come to appreciate pulses, with or without meat.

What are pulses?

It is the generic term for a whole family of fresh, dried or canned vegetables – beans, peas and lentils – a gift of nature, providing an abundance of produce through the summer to last the winter months. After harvesting, the fresh vegetables are dried and stored, and to cook them (with the exception of lentils and split peas), they have to be pre-soaked and reconstituted.

What's good about them? First of all, apart from their nutritional value, what I like about them is that they're always sitting in my cupboard offering me plenty of choice and variety. No time to shop for vegetables? Just cook some pulses. Secondly, pulses collectively have one very great virtue – an enormous capacity to absorb other flavours. They may have little to offer plain-boiled but, magically, when you marry them with other, stronger flavours, they are transformed. A chilli con carne, for instance, needs very little meat because the red kidney beans absorb the beefy flavour, making a small amount go a very long way.

What's not good? With the exception of lentils and split peas, pulses have to be pre-soaked and need quite long cooking, so you have to think ahead. You can be spontaneous with a bag of frozen peas, but, with pulses, you do need to plan. It's not a big deal, though: it just means popping them into cold water before you go to bed at night or, alternatively, quick-soaking them (see opposite). The only other thing you have to consider is how old they are. A year on your shelf is their maximum – after that, throw them out because they will never soften during the cooking.

What about tinned pulses? Yes, you *can* be spontaneous with tinned pulses, but, with a couple of exceptions, I'm against them, because they're simply inferior – often over-sweet and slimy. At a pinch, they can be used in short-cut, no-cooking dishes, but for food lovers, they do need to be freshly cooked. The two exceptions to this are tinned marrowfat peas and flageolets, which I think respond best to the canning process.

What about soaking? All pulses need to be washed under cold, running water and any broken ones or alien bits discarded. Then, with the exception of lentils and split peas, they need soaking. If it is convenient, soak them overnight in 4 pints (2.25 litres) of cold water per 8 oz (225 g). If you need them today and haven't the time for this, simply bring them up to the boil (using the same quantity of water), boil for 10 minutes and leave them to soak for two hours.

If you are soaking pulses overnight, some, such as kidney beans, still need 10 minutes' fast-boiling to purify them before cooking. This is because they sometimes contain toxins in their outer skins, which are destroyed by the fast-boiling.

Cooking pulses

Being tough and hard, pulses need long, slow cooking (and this long, slow marrying with other flavours is what they're particularly good at), but the key is *careful* cooking – over-cooking results in their skins splitting and the pulses disintegrating. It used to be said that salt should not be added during cooking, as it encourages liquid out of and not into dried things, but I believe this was the legacy of pulses being kept for too long (before we had date-stamping). Now I always add salt during the cooking as it really does give a better flavour. It may, in some cases, mean a little longer cooking, but it's worth it – salt never seems to be absorbed properly when added at the end. Lastly, don't forget pulses are great in salads and salsas – again, they absorb the flavours of the other ingredients and the dressings.

Varieties of pulses

With so many varieties from all round the world, it's not possible to include them all here, so what I've aimed to do is introduce you to those pulses most widely available in this country. Anyway, in most recipes you can ring the changes and experiment with other varieties that will need roughly the same treatment and cooking times. For instance, try using black beans in a chilli instead of red, or red beans in a soup in place of white.

Adzuki beans: These look like little, shiny red pills, with a white line running down one side. I have used them successfully in salads, but when I visited Japan, I was fascinated to discover they are used in sweet dishes, where they seem to have a texture and flavour similar to chestnuts. I was so impressed I brought back a recipe – Sesame Blancmange with Sweetened Compote of Adzuki Beans – that you'll find on page 557.

Black beans: Very good-lookers, these are shiny, ebony-black, kidney-shaped beans. They make a luscious, dark, velvety soup, but can be used in any kidney-bean recipe – I love spicy Black Bean Chilli (in the *Winter Collection*) with Avocado Salsa stirred in at the end.

Black-eyed beans: These are pale and creamy in colour, kidney-shaped with little black 'eyes'. I have made them into Mashed Black-Eyed Beancakes (also in the *Winter Collection*), popular in the Caribbean. They are also very much part of traditional cooking in the Deep South of America.

Top row, left to right: butter beans, black beans, chickpeas

Second row: marrowfat peas, green split peas, green lentils

Third row: yellow split peas, borlotti beans, kidney beans

Fourth row: Puy lentils, haricot beans, pinto beans

Fifth row: cannellini beans, red split lentils, judion beans

Sixth row: adzuki beans, flageolet beans, black-eyed beans

Borlotti beans: These are definitely the aristocrats of the bean world, both in looks and in flavour. They are grown in Italy and I would describe their appearance as pale pinky-beige, with dark red, marbled veins. They are not quite so widely available as some of the other varieties, but you can find the name of an Italian stockist on page 698. I have used them in Tuscan Bean and Pasta Soup with Rosemary on page 548.

Butter beans: Just coming back into their own, having suffered from being boiled dry and tasteless in the frugal canteen-cookery of my schooldays. However, put them into a slowly cooked, Old-Fashioned Shin of Beef Stew (see page 552) and they become something else altogether: fat, plump, mealy and full of meaty flavour. I also discovered them served in a salad in Paris, with lots of chopped shallots and flat-leaf parsley, in a wonderful garlicky vinaigrette. The best butter beans, if you can find them, are the Spanish judion beans.

Cannellini beans: The upper-class version of the humble haricot (see below). These are so pretty – rather elongated and like pale, creamy, translucent porcelain. Lovers of Italian cooking will instantly recognise them in Tonno e Fagioli, the white bean and tuna fish salad (see page 378). They have a great affinity with pork, bacon and Italian sausages, and the ability to soak up all their richness.

Chickpeas: These are definitely from the top drawer of the pulse family, with a firm texture that doesn't disintegrate, and a lovely nutty flavour. One of my all-time best soup recipes – Chickpea, Chilli and Coriander (in the *Winter Collection*) – is made with chickpeas, I have included them in a Moroccan Baked Chicken dish (also in the *Winter Collection*), and here I have used them in a Spiced Chickpea Cakes recipe (see page 550). Finally, I simply had to include Hummus in this chapter (see page 542), as home-made, it knocks the socks off anything out of a supermarket.

Flageolet beans: Beautiful to look at, these small, pastel green beans are actually under-developed cannellini beans, harvested while still young. They have their own distinctive yet delicate flavour and a smooth, silky texture. They are a wonderful match for lamb – either braised along with it, as in Lamb with Flageolets (in the *Winter Collection*), or cooked separately with onion, garlic and herbs, to serve alongside roast lamb.

Haricot beans: Fine in a can of baked beans, they are small and squat and the poorer cousin to the cannellini. I would stick with serving them on crisp, buttered toast and not choose them for cooking.

Lentils: The easiest of all the pulses, because they don't need pre-soaking. The tiny, French, greeny-black Puy lentils have far and away the best flavour and I always keep some in my store cupboard for when there's no time to shop for vegetables. They are excellent cooked with an onion first sweated in olive oil with rosemary or thyme, and simmered in red wine. I love them equally in salads, and there's a recipe for Lentil Salsa on page 592. Then there are the green-brown lentils (with a hint of terracotta), which, although they don't have the depth of flavour of the Puy, are still excellent and can be used in exactly the same way. They're particularly good in soups or made into little cakes with vegetables, as in my recipe for Chilladas (in *The Illustrated Cookery Course*). The best recipe ever for these is the Lentil Sauce on page 543. Split orange lentils are really only good for soups, having very little intrinsic flavour, as their outer skins have been removed; I would therefore always recommend using whole lentils.

Dried peas: Can't tell you how much I love these. I love peas at all stages of their development: from the young and tender, to be eaten raw or lightly cooked, to older peas, braised with lettuce and onion, to our friends here – dried whole peas, and split peas, yellow and green. Let us salute here our famous mushy peas, the essential accompaniment to fish and chips in the north of England. In this chapter, I have revived another great northern dish, Pease Pudding, a thick, luscious combination of marrowfat peas and onions simmered alongside a Smoked Collar of Bacon (see page 544). Split peas of both varieties make extremely good soup, as they are still as flavoursome as whole dried peas, with the added advantage of not needing any soaking.

Pinto beans: Very pretty, cream-coloured beans with red veins, a staple food in Mexico – so I've used them here in a Mexican Chicken Chilli dish (see page 551). They can, in fact, be used in virtually any dish that calls for beans and, when borlottis are hard to find, I always use pintos instead.

Red kidney beans: A suitable grand finale to this list, they are a great favourite everywhere – but please, *not* out of tins, because they will be but pale shadows of the freshly cooked ones. They are the star turn in chilli con carne. What a shame that sublime combination of meat, chillies and red kidney beans has become so bastardised in restaurants the world over. Home-made, it provides me with one of my best pleasures in cooking – lifting the lid and catching a whiff of the simmering beans, with their own quite distinctive, seductive aroma.

Others: There are many more variations from around the world you might like to try. (The soaking/cooking methods are the same for most pulses.) Among these are Soy beans (best, I think, for soy sauce and not for cooking), Ful medames (small brown beans used in Middle Eastern cooking), and Brown beans (a larger version popular in Scandinavian cooking). Then there are Dried broad beans, dark brown and similar – though, in my opinion, not as good as – butter beans. And finally, Dhals: a whole array of various forms of lentils in their whole or split guises.

Braised Lamb Shanks with Cannellini Beans

This is delightfully simple as everything goes into one pot, no accompaniments are needed, and it provides a complete menu for two people. It is also very good with flageolet or borlotti beans to ring the changes.

Serves 2

2 lamb shanks (each weighing about
1 lb/450 g)
4 oz (110 g) dried cannellini beans,
pre-soaked and drained (see page 536)
4 medium-sized, ripe tomatoes
1 large stick celery
2 tablespoons olive oil
2 cloves garlic, chopped
1 large onion, peeled and cut into
eighths through the root
1 large carrot, peeled and chopped
into 2 inch (5 cm) chunks
15 fl oz (425 ml) red wine
1 fresh bay leaf
2 tablespoons fresh rosemary bruised
in a mortar, then chopped, plus 4
sprigs, to garnish
salt and freshly milled black pepper

You will also need a lidded, flameproof casserole with a capacity of 4 pints (2.25 litres).

Begin by skinning the tomatoes. Place them in a heatproof bowl and pour boiling water on to them. Leave them for exactly a minute, then remove them and slip off their skins (protecting your hands with a tea cloth if they are hot). Then chop them fairly roughly. Next, using a potato peeler, remove the worst of the stringy bits from the celery and cut it into 2 inch (5 cm) chunks. Now pre-heat the oven to gas mark 1, 275°F (140°C).

After that, you need to heat the oil in the casserole over a highish heat. Then, season the lamb shanks with salt and freshly milled black pepper and, when the oil is really hot, brown them on all sides, holding them at the bone end while protecting your hand again with the tea cloth, and turning them round in the hot oil.

When they're nicely browned, remove them to a plate and, keeping the heat high, add the celery, onion and carrots and brown them as well, turning and tossing them around for about 6 minutes. Now stir in the garlic, cook for one minute, then add the drained beans and give everything another good stir.

Next, add the tomatoes, wine, bay leaf, chopped rosemary and some seasoning. Then, finally, place the lamb shanks on top and when everything is beginning to simmer, cover with the lid and transfer the casserole to the oven to braise very slowly for 3 hours. Serve garnished with the sprigs of rosemary.

Hummus bi Tahina

Couldn't have a chapter on pulses without this famous favourite. Yes, I do know it's sold absolutely everywhere but let me tell you, this home-made version is way above anything you will have bought. It is also an essential accompaniment to our gorgeous Pitta Bread on page 518.

Serves 6

4 oz (110 g) dried chickpeas, pre-soaked (see page 536), then drained and the water discarded
5 fl oz (150 ml) tahina paste
juice 2 lemons
2 fat cloves garlic
4 tablespoons olive oil, plus a little extra for drizzling
cayenne pepper
black olives and Greek-style pickled chillis, to serve
salt

You will also need a blender.

To begin with, put the chickpeas in a medium-sized saucepan, cover them with fresh water and bring them to the boil, along with a pinch of salt. Then reduce the heat to low, cover and simmer gently for 1½-2 hours, or until they are tender.

Then, drain them, reserving the cooking liquid, and put them into a blender, together with the lemon juice, garlic, olive oil and 5 fl oz (150 ml) of the liquid. Switch on and blend, adding the tahina paste to the mixture as the blades revolve, stopping the blender every now and then to push the mixture down into the goblet. The consistency should be something like mayonnaise so, if you think it's too thick, add a little more of the cooking liquid. Then season to taste with cayenne pepper and salt.

Now place the hummus in a serving bowl and drizzle with olive oil. Serve with olives, pickled chillis and warm pitta breads.

Shaun Hill's Sautéed Scallops with Lentil Sauce

Everyone I know in the world of cooking and catering agrees unanimously that this is the best lentil recipe ever invented. Shaun Hill, one of Britain's most outstandingly gifted chefs, served this in his restaurant, The Merchant House, in Ludlow, and he has generously allowed me to adapt it and use it here.

To cook the lentils for the sauce, place them in a saucepan with the stock and a pinch of salt and simmer gently with a lid on for 40-45 minutes, until they're really soft and beginning to break up. Then drain them, reserving the cooking liquid.

Now heat half the oil in the medium-sized frying pan over a medium heat, add the onion, garlic and ginger and fry until pale golden – about 8 minutes. Meanwhile, skin the tomatoes. To do this, place them in a heatproof bowl and pour boiling water on to them. Leave them for exactly a minute, then remove them, slip off their skins (protecting your hands with a cloth if they're hot) and finely chop them.

Next, remove the pan from the heat, add the cardamom seeds, stir for a few seconds, then add the tomatoes, two-thirds of the cooked lentils and all the cooking liquid. After that, whiz the whole lot to a purée in a food processor, then add the remaining lentils. All this can be done in advance.

When you are ready to finish the dish, re-heat the lentil purée, whisk in the butter, crème fraîche and lemon juice, and taste and season with salt and freshly milled black pepper. Finally, add the coriander and keep the lentil mixture warm while you cook the scallops.

To do this, heat the large frying pan over a high heat without adding any fat. Dry the scallops and corals with kitchen paper. When the pan is searing hot, lightly brush them on both sides with the remaining oil and season with salt and freshly milled black pepper.

Now add them to the pan and let them cook without moving for about one minute, until the underside is dark brown and caramelised, then use a small palette knife to flip them over. Continue to cook for 30 seconds on the other side, but no more. What you are aiming for is a golden, caramelised outside, with a soft and barely cooked inside. It's important to have your frying pan really hot to get the dish right – if the scallops boil or steam, they will lose the concentrated flavour needed to balance the sauce.

To serve, arrange the scallops on warmed serving plates or in clean scallop shells, then spoon over the lentil sauce and garnish with the sprigs of coriander.

Serves 6 as a starter

18 plump, fresh scallops, cleaned, with the corals attached
2 oz (50 g) green lentils (no need to soak), rinsed
10 fl oz (275 ml) hot stock made with Marigold Swiss vegetable bouillon powder
2 dessertspoons groundnut or other flavourless oil
½ medium onion, peeled and chopped
1 fat clove garlic, crushed
1 inch (2.5 cm) fresh root ginger, peeled and finely grated
2 large, ripe tomatoes
1 dessertspoon cardamom pods, seeds removed and husks discarded
2 oz (50 g) unsalted butter
1 tablespoon crème fraîche
juice ½ lemon
¾ oz (20 g) fresh coriander, chopped, plus 6 sprigs, to garnish
salt and freshly milled black pepper

You will also need one medium-sized and one large, heavy-based frying pan.

543

Smoked Collar of Bacon with Pease Pudding and Creamy Onion Mustard Sauce

Serves 6

1 smoked bacon collar joint (weighing about 3 lb/1.35 kg), all packaging and string removed
1 small onion, peeled and studded with a few cloves
2 fresh bay leaves
1 small carrot, peeled
6 black peppercorns

For the pease pudding:

6 oz (175 g) dried marrowfat peas, pre-soaked and drained (see page 536)
1 small onion, peeled and quartered
1 fresh bay leaf
1 sprig fresh thyme
1 oz (25 g) butter
1 large egg, beaten
whole nutmeg
salt and freshly milled black pepper

For the sauce:

1 large onion, peeled and finely chopped
1 rounded teaspoon mustard powder
1 rounded teaspoon wholegrain mustard
1½ oz (40 g) butter
1 oz (25 g) plain flour
6 fl oz (175 ml) milk
salt and freshly milled black pepper

You will also need a lidded, flameproof casserole with a capacity of 6 pints (3.5 litres), a 16 inch (40 cm) square piece of muslin, and some kitchen foil and string.

Let me explain the appeal of this delightfully unfashionable, totally forgotten delicacy. First, collar of bacon has more flavour than the leaner, middle-cut gammon. Secondly, I'm sure many people have forgotten – or never actually tasted – dried marrowfat peas with their mealy texture and concentrated flavour. Then, when we add an onion and mustard sauce, the combination of the whole is utterly sublime. What you can do after boiling the bacon is reserve and freeze the stock to make the recipe called The London Particular – Green Split Pea Soup (see page 546).

Start off by cooking the pease pudding. To do this, place the peas in a pan, pour in just enough fresh water to cover, then add the onion, bay leaf and thyme (but no salt). Bring it up to a gentle simmer, put the lid on and cook for about an hour, or until the skins split and the peas are tender – they will be having some more cooking so they don't need to be absolutely smashed.

Next, drain off the cooking water, discarding the thyme and bay leaf, then put the peas and the onion into a bowl and mash them with a large fork, along with the butter, beaten egg, a seasoning of salt and freshly milled black pepper and a few gratings of nutmeg. Now transfer the mixture to sit in the centre of the square of muslin, gather the edges into the centre, then, leaving a bit of room for it to expand, tie with string.

What you need to do next is place the bacon in the casserole along with the small onion studded with cloves, the bay leaves, carrot and peppercorns, then tie the pease pudding to the handle of the pan so it sits alongside the bacon. Cover with cold water and bring the whole lot up to a gentle simmer. Put the lid on and let it cook very gently for 1¼ hours.

When the bacon is cooked, transfer it to a dish, cover with kitchen foil and let it rest. Leave the pudding in the casserole but ladle out 6 fl oz (175 ml) of the cooking water into a measuring jug. If you want to make The London Particular, reserve and freeze the rest of the stock. Next, make up the sauce: in a smallish saucepan, melt 1 oz (25 g) of the butter and add the onion, and when you've stirred it so it's nice and buttery, let it cook on the lowest possible heat for about 20 minutes. It's important not to let it colour, so give it a stir from time to time.

Now, using a wooden spoon, stir in the flour and the mustard powder until smooth, then, add the milk a little at a time, followed by the stock, switching to a balloon whisk, and whisking well after each addition. Now season the sauce with salt and freshly milled black pepper to taste, and let it barely simmer for 5 minutes. After that, stir in the grain mustard and the rest of the butter, then pour the sauce into a warmed serving jug.

Carve the bacon joint into slices to serve with the pease pudding, and have some extra mustard on the table. I serve this with mashed potatoes and boiled, buttered Savoy cabbage, but smaller steamed potatoes, such as Anya or Charlotte, would also be good.

The London Particular – Green Split Pea Soup

This soup, made with the bacon stock from the Smoked Collar of Bacon (see page 544), is so named because of the thick 'peasouper' London fogs that were so prevalent during the first half of the last century.

Serves 6

12 oz (350 g) green split peas
(no need to soak), rinsed
3½ pints (2 litres) stock from the
Smoked Collar of Bacon (see page
544), with added water if needed
1 large celery stalk, destringed
and chopped
4 oz (110 g) butter
6 oz (175 g) smoked streaky bacon,
rind removed, diced
1 medium onion, peeled and
roughly chopped
1 large carrot, peeled and sliced
salt and freshly milled black pepper

To garnish:

2 oz (50 g) crustless white bread cut
into ⅓ inch (8 mm) cubes for croutons
2 oz (50 g) crisp bacon, reserved from
the soup

You will also need a very large
saucepan.

First strain off 3½ pints (2 litres) of the stock into the saucepan and bring it just up to simmering point, then add the split peas, stir well, cover, and simmer very gently for about 30 minutes.

Meanwhile, heat 1 oz (25 g) of the butter in a medium-sized saucepan and add 4 oz (110 g) of the bacon, along with the prepared vegetables. Then cook them over a medium heat until softened and nicely golden – this will take about 15 minutes.

After that, the bacon and softened vegetables can be transferred to join the stock and split peas. Then put the lid back on and simmer very gently for a further 40-50 minutes.

In the meantime, heat a large frying pan (without any fat in it) and fry the remaining bacon until it is really crisp, then transfer it to a plate, using a draining spoon. Next, add 2 oz (50 g) of the butter to the pan, and as soon as it begins to foam, add the cubes of bread and fry these, tossing them around for about 5 minutes, until they are also nice and crisp. Then remove them to join the bacon, using a draining spoon.

When the soup is ready, either process or blend it, then return it to the saucepan. Taste to check the seasoning, adding a little more of any reserved stock if it seems a little too thick. Just before serving, melt the remaining butter into it, then ladle into hot soup bowls and sprinkle each one with the croutons and crispy bacon bits.

Although I am not a vegetarian, I really love this alternative version to meat, with its diverse combination of dried pulses and fresh vegetables. It's also extremely popular with veggie customers in our restaurant at the football club.

First put the drained beans into a saucepan with the split peas and lentils. Add the boiling water and some salt, cover and simmer gently for 50-60 minutes, or until the pulses have absorbed the water and are soft. Then remove them from the heat and mash them just a little with a large fork.

Now pre-heat the oven to gas mark 5, 375°F (190°C), and put the potatoes on to steam. Next, roughly chop all the vegetables, pile the whole lot into a food processor and process until chopped small. Next, melt the butter in a large frying pan over a medium heat, add the vegetables and cook gently for 10-15 minutes, stirring now and then until they're softened and tinged gold at the edges.

Meanwhile, skin the tomatoes. Place them in a heatproof bowl and pour boiling water on to them. After exactly a minute (or 15-30 seconds, if they are small), remove them (protecting your hands with a cloth if the tomatoes are hot), slip off their skins and slice them.

After that, add the vegetables to the pulses mixture, along with the herbs, spices, and salt and freshly milled black pepper to taste. Then spoon the mixture into the baking dish and arrange the tomatoes in overlapping slices on the top.

As soon as the potatoes are cooked, place them in a bowl, add the butter, milk and goats' cheese, whisk to a smooth purée, season with salt and freshly milled black pepper and spread the potato over the rest of the ingredients in the dish. Finally, sprinkle over the Pecorino and bake the pie on the top shelf of the oven for 20-25 minutes, or until the top is lightly browned. If you want to prepare this in advance, it will need about 40 minutes in the oven.

Serves 4

4 oz (110 g) dried black-eyed beans, pre-soaked and drained (see page 536)
3 oz (75 g) green split peas (no need to soak), rinsed
3 oz (75 g) green lentils (no need to soak), rinsed
1¼ pint (725 ml) boiling water
2 oz (50 g) peeled carrots
2 oz (50 g) peeled swede
2 oz (50 g) peeled celeriac
1 large onion, peeled
1 small green pepper, deseeded
2 oz (50 g) butter, plus a little extra for greasing
1 heaped tablespoon chopped mixed fresh herbs, such as sage, rosemary, thyme and parsley
¼ teaspoon ground mace
¼ teaspoon cayenne pepper
salt and freshly milled black pepper

For the topping:

4 oz (110 g) soft goats' cheese
1 lb 8 oz (700 g) potatoes, peeled
8 oz (225 g) tomatoes
2 oz (50 g) butter
2 tablespoons milk
1 oz (25 g) Pecorino cheese, grated
salt and freshly milled black pepper

You will also need a steamer; and a round baking dish with a diameter of 9 inches (23 cm), 2 inches (5 cm) deep, buttered.

Tuscan Bean and Pasta Soup with Rosemary

This is Tuscany in a bowl, with all those lovely Italian flavours in a big, hefty soup – perfect for the winter months with a light main course to follow. Alternatively, it is a complete lunch, with just some cheese and a salad to follow.

Serves 4

8 oz (225 g) dried borlotti beans, pre-soaked and drained (see page 536), soaking liquid reserved

4 oz (110 g) short-cut macaroni

1 heaped tablespoon fresh rosemary, bruised in a mortar, then very finely chopped

2 tablespoons olive oil

1 large onion, peeled and finely chopped

2 cloves garlic, crushed

2½ tablespoons tomato purée

Parmesan (Parmigiano Reggiano), grated or shaved, to serve

salt and freshly milled black pepper

You will also need a blender.

First heat the oil in a large saucepan, add the onion and let it cook gently for about 10 minutes without colouring. Then add the garlic and cook for another minute. Now add the tomato purée and rosemary, stir for a minute and then pour in the beans, together with 3 pints (1.75 litres) of the reserved water (topping up the liquid, if necessary) and some salt. Now bring everything up to simmering point and simmer very gently, partially covered, for about an hour, or until the beans are tender.

After this time, taste and season with salt and freshly milled black pepper, then pour half the soup into the blender and liquidise until it's absolutely smooth. Now return the puréed half to the pan to join the rest of the beans, bring back to a gentle simmer, then add the macaroni and simmer for a further 10-12 minutes, stirring from time to time, until the pasta is cooked. Serve in hot soup bowls with lots of the Parmesan.

Spiced Chickpea Cakes with Red Onion and Coriander Salad

Serves 6 as a starter or 4 as a main course

8 oz (225 g) chickpeas, pre-soaked (see page 536)
1 heaped teaspoon each coriander and cumin seeds, dry-roasted (see page 554)
1 teaspoon ground turmeric
2 oz (50 g) butter
1 small green pepper, deseeded
2 small red chillies, deseeded
1 small onion, peeled and finely chopped
3 fat garlic cloves, finely chopped
½ oz (10 g) fresh coriander, plus a few sprigs to garnish
1 lb 2 oz (500 g) Greek yoghurt
grated zest ½ lemon
1 dessertspoon lemon juice
1 large egg, beaten
3 tablespoons wholemeal flour or chickpea flour (gram flour)
2 tablespoons groundnut or other flavourless oil
salt and freshly milled black pepper

For the salad:
1 medium red onion, peeled and thinly sliced into half-moon shapes
3 tablespoons fresh coriander leaves
1 teaspoon grated lemon zest
juice 1 lemon

At Norwich City Football Club, we're always trying out new ideas for vegetarians. This one's a real winner and can hold its own against any meat or fish recipe. If you're serving it as a main course, it's nice with some nutty brown rice.

Drain the chickpeas, then cover them with fresh water and add a pinch of salt. Bring to a simmer and cook for 30 minutes. Then drain in a sieve.

Meanwhile, prepare the salad. All you do is mix the onion with the lemon zest, juice and coriander in a small bowl and then set it aside for at least 30 minutes.

Next, transfer the roasted coriander and cumin seeds to a pestle and mortar and crush them to a powder. Now finely chop the pepper and the chilli and gently fry them, along with the onion and garlic, in the butter in a saucepan for 5 minutes, until they have softened and begun to turn brown. Then stir in all the spices and continue to cook for 30 seconds.

Next, process the chickpeas, along with the coriander, until everything is evenly chopped, but not to a purée – the chickpeas should still have some of their texture. Then transfer them to a bowl and stir in the onion mixture, 3 tablespoons of the Greek yoghurt, and the lemon zest and juice. Now give it all a really good mix, taste, and add plenty of seasoning.

As soon as the mixture is cool enough to handle, form it into 12 cakes about 2 inches (5 cm) in diameter and ½ inch (1 cm) thick for a starter, or eight larger cakes if you are serving them for a main course.

Now coat each cake with the beaten egg and dust with flour. Next, heat the oil in a large frying pan over a high heat and when it's really hot, fry them in two batches to a golden brown colour for about a minute on each side. Drain them well on kitchen paper and serve as soon as possible with the red-onion salad and 2 tablespoons of yoghurt per person. Garnish each one with a sprig of coriander.

Mexican Chicken Chilli with Yellow Tomato Salsa

I have to admit they probably won't have heard of this in Mexico, but I've so named it because it's a dish based on a couple of Mexican themes: firstly, there are the delightful pinto beans, and secondly, the cheese is melted into the sauce. Anyway, Mexican or not, it's a great recipe.

Start by stripping the coriander leaves into a small bowl, then cover it with clingfilm and pop it into the fridge. Now chop the coriander stalks very finely. Next, heat the oil in the casserole and, over a gentle heat, cook the onions, garlic, chillies and coriander stalks for about 10 minutes, stirring once or twice until softened.

Meanwhile, grind the roasted cumin seeds to a powder in a pestle and mortar, then add them, along with the drained beans, to the casserole and stir. Now sprinkle in the flour and give it another good stir. Next, gradually add the stock, followed by the Tabasco sauce and a little salt, bring everything to a simmer and cook, covered, on the lowest heat possible for 1¼-1½ hours, until the beans are tender.

In the meantime, make the salsa. Simply combine half the reserved coriander leaves and the rest of the salsa ingredients and add seasoning. Mix well, then cover and leave aside to allow the flavours to develop.

When the chilli has had its initial cooking time, deseed the pepper and cut it into ½ inch (1 cm) pieces. Then stir the chicken and pepper into the casserole, season well with salt and freshly milled black pepper, cover, and simmer for a further 30 minutes.

In the meantime, mix the Mozzarella with the cream, then, when the 30 minutes are up, add it to the casserole. Simmer gently, uncovered, for a further 20-25 minutes, stirring now and again, by which time the cheese should have melted and formed a smooth sauce. Finally, stir in the lime juice and the remaining coriander leaves. Serve with a little rice and a green vegetable, such as runner beans, and hand the salsa round separately.

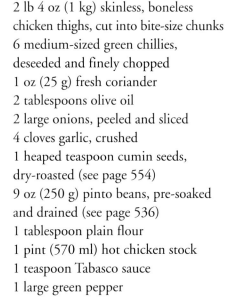

Serves 6

2 lb 4 oz (1 kg) skinless, boneless chicken thighs, cut into bite-size chunks
6 medium-sized green chillies, deseeded and finely chopped
1 oz (25 g) fresh coriander
2 tablespoons olive oil
2 large onions, peeled and sliced
4 cloves garlic, crushed
1 heaped teaspoon cumin seeds, dry-roasted (see page 554)
9 oz (250 g) pinto beans, pre-soaked and drained (see page 536)
1 tablespoon plain flour
1 pint (570 ml) hot chicken stock
1 teaspoon Tabasco sauce
1 large green pepper
8 oz (225 g) Mozzarella, grated
2½ fl oz (65 ml) double cream
juice ½ lime
salt and freshly milled black pepper

For the salsa:

9 oz (250 g) yellow (or red) tomatoes, skinned (see page 543), deseeded and finely chopped
½ small red onion, peeled and very finely chopped
half the reserved coriander leaves, roughly chopped
juice ½ lime
few drops Tabasco sauce
salt and freshly milled black pepper

You will also need a lidded, flameproof casserole with a capacity of 6 pints (3.5 litres).

Old-Fashioned Shin of Beef Stew with Butter Beans and Crusted Onion Dumplings

The good old-fashioned family stew – meat and vegetables simmering gently and slowly together, and in this slowness, releasing precious juices that mingle to provide intense yet mellow flavours and the tenderest of textures. Let's not be duped into thinking we don't have the time. This stew actually takes very little time – you'll be amazed. The time it does take is not yours. Tucked away in the oven, it will leave you free to go out for a couple of hours if you want to, ready to greet you with evocative, comforting aromas when you come home. I have included some dumplings in this recipe (because I like them!), but even without them it is perfectly good.

Serves 6

3 lb (1.35 kg) shin of British beef or stewing beef, in 2 inch (5 cm) chunks
12 oz (350 g) butter beans (or judion beans), pre-soaked and drained (see page 536)
2 oz (50 g) plain flour
8 oz (225 g) each celery, carrots, swede
6 small onions (12 oz/350 g)
4 sprigs fresh thyme
3 bay leaves
1½ pints (850 ml) premium dry cider
1 tablespoon Worcestershire sauce
salt and freshly milled black pepper

For the dumplings:

1 small onion, peeled and finely chopped
a teaspoon groundnut or other flavourless oil
8 oz (225 g) self-raising flour, plus a little extra for dusting
1 heaped teaspoon mustard powder
4 oz (110 g) suet
1 tablespoon freshly snipped chives
3 tablespoons cold water
salt and freshly milled black pepper

You will also need a lidded, flameproof casserole with a capacity of 8 pints (4.5 litres).

Pre-heat the oven to gas mark 1, 275°F (140°C).

Start off by placing the flour in a large bowl and seasoning it with 1½ teaspoons of salt and some freshly milled black pepper. Now dip each chunk of meat into it to get a good coating, then transfer them to a plate. Next, prepare the vegetables. Use a potato peeler to pare the worst of the stringy bits from the celery, then cut it into 2 inch (5 cm) chunks. Peel the carrots and swede and cut them into similar size chunks. Lastly, peel the onions but leave them whole. Now toss them all in the remaining flour and transfer them, along with the meat and the beans, to the casserole, layering the ingredients alternately and sprinkle in any flour still in the bowl. Add the thyme and bay leaves, season with salt and freshly milled black pepper, then pour in the cider, plus the Worcestershire sauce. Put the casserole on the hob and bring it up to a gentle simmer before covering with the lid, placing a sheet of kitchen foil under it to ensure a tight seal. After that, place it on the middle shelf of the oven to cook for 4½ hours.

After this time, remove the casserole from the oven, set it aside, turn the temperature up to gas mark 6, 400°F (200°C) and make the dumplings. Fry the onion in the oil until brown and caramelised, then allow to cool. After that, sift the flour, mustard powder and a little salt together, then add the suet, chives and onion, and season with freshly milled black pepper and a bit more salt. Now sprinkle the water over all the ingredients and then, using first a knife and then your hands, bring it all together to form a soft dough, adding a little more water if you need to.

Next, transfer the dough to a flat, lightly floured surface, divide it into 12 portions and roll each one into a little round, using the palms of your hands. Add them to the casserole so that a part of each one can be seen just above the surface of the stew. Return the casserole to the top shelf of the oven and cook, without the lid, for a further 25-30 minutes, until the dumplings are golden brown and crusty.

Spiced Lamb Curry with Chickpeas, Green Coconut Sambal and Tomato-and-Red-Onion Pickle

There is, I have to admit, some work involved in this one, but I absolutely promise the depth and flavour of fresh coconut make it really worth that bit of extra time. If you're serving this to guests, the good thing is that all the work can be done in advance, so all you have to do is cook some plain basmati rice to accompany it (see page 200).

Serves 6

2 lb (900 g) neck of British lamb, trimmed and cut into 1 inch (2.5 cm) cubes
1 rounded teaspoon cumin seeds
1 rounded teaspoon coriander seeds
6 cardamom pods, crushed
1 rounded teaspoon ground fenugreek
1 rounded teaspoon ground turmeric
8 oz (225 g) dried chickpeas, pre-soaked (see page 536), drained and soaking liquid reserved
3 medium onions, peeled
1 fat clove garlic
4 bird eye chillies, deseeded
4 tablespoons groundnut or other flavourless oil
1 inch (2.5 cm) fresh root ginger, peeled and grated
milk from 1 fresh coconut
grated flesh ½ fresh coconut (weighing about 3 oz/75 g)
3 oz (75 g) creamed coconut, grated
salt and freshly milled black pepper

You will also need a lidded, flameproof casserole with a capacity of 6 pints (3.5 litres).

First chop the onions, garlic and bird eye chillies quite small in a food processor, then heat 2 tablespoons of the oil in the casserole and cook them gently for 5 minutes to soften. Now heat the remaining oil in a large frying pan and when it's nice and hot, quickly brown the cubes of meat. (You will have to do this in about three batches.) Next, sprinkle the ginger and the spices over the onion mixture in the casserole and stir to soak up the juice, then cook gently for 2 minutes. Now pre-heat the oven to gas mark 2, 300°F (150°C).

To prepare the coconut, first push a thick skewer into the three holes in the top, then drain out the milk and reserve it for the recipe. Next, place the coconut in a plastic bag and sit it on a hard surface – a stone floor or an outside paving stone. Then give it a hefty whack with a hammer – it won't be that difficult to break. Now remove the pieces from the bag and, using a cloth to protect your hands, prise the tip of a kitchen knife between the nut and the shell. You should find you can force the whole piece out in one go. After that, discard the shell and take off the inner skin using a potato peeler. Once you have rinsed it, the coconut will now be ready to use.

The best way to grate coconut flesh is with the fine grating disc of a food processor, but a hand grater will do the job, too. Grate it, reserving half for the sambal.

Next, pour the coconut milk into a measuring jug and make it up to 1½ pints (850 ml) with the chickpea-soaking liquid. Slowly pour this into the casserole, stirring all the time. Next, stir in the grated fresh and creamed coconut and then transfer the browned meat to the casserole, along with the chickpeas. Finally, season with salt and freshly milled black pepper, then bring everything up to simmering point, cover and cook in the centre of the oven for 2 hours.

To make the sambal, first dry-roast the cumin seeds. To do this, place the seeds in a small frying pan over a medium heat and stir and toss them around for 1-2 minutes, or until they begin to look toasted, smell fragrant and start to jump in the pan. Now use a pestle and mortar and crush them to a powder.

Next, grate the shallots using the fine grater blade of the food processor, then remove them to a bowl. Process the remaining ingredients, this time with the chopper blade, until they are all finely chopped. Add this mixture, along with the cumin and the reserved grated coconut, to the shallots.

Next, make the tomato-and-red-onion pickle. All you do is mix the tomatoes with the onion, coriander, lime juice and chilli powder in a small bowl and set the mixture aside to marinate for at least 15 minutes.

Serve the sambal as an accompaniment to the curry, along with the tomato-and-red-onion pickle and some plain basmati rice that has been cooked with a cinnamon stick and bay leaf.

For the sambal:
grated flesh ½ fresh coconut, reserved from the curry
3 shallots, peeled
½ oz (10 g) fresh coriander leaves
1 tablespoon fresh mint leaves
1 medium-sized green chilli, deseeded
½ inch (1 cm) fresh root ginger, peeled
½ teaspoon cumin seeds

For the pickle:
3 medium-sized ripe but firm tomatoes, skinned (see page 543), deseeded and thinly sliced
1 medium red onion, peeled and sliced into thin half moons
1 dessertspoon chopped fresh coriander leaves
juice 1 large lime
a few pinches chilli powder

Clockwise, from left: Spiced Lamb Curry with Chickpeas, basmati rice, Green Coconut Sambal, and Tomato-and-Red-Onion Pickle

Braised Sausages with Borlotti Beans, Rosemary and Sage

You can use any beans in this recipe, but borlotti are the best of all. The smokiness of the pancetta is also important, but if you can't get it, use smoked bacon.

Serves 2-3
1 lb (450 g) good, meaty pork sausages
8 oz (225 g) dried borlotti beans, pre-soaked and drained (see page 536), soaking liquid reserved
1 heaped teaspoon chopped fresh rosemary, plus 2-3 sprigs to garnish
1 heaped teaspoon chopped fresh sage, plus 2-3 leaves to garnish
1 tablespoon olive oil
4 oz (110 g) sliced smoked pancetta (or smoked bacon), chopped
1 large red onion, peeled and chopped
2 cloves garlic
10 fl oz (275 ml) dry white wine
salt and freshly milled black pepper

You will also need a lidded, flameproof casserole with a capacity of 4 pints (2.25 litres).

Pre-heat the oven to gas mark 1, 275°F (140°C).

First of all, heat the oil in the casserole over a medium heat and carefully brown the sausages, turning them occasionally so they are a nice golden brown colour on all sides – this will take 8-10 minutes.

After that, remove them to a plate, then add the pancetta to the frying pan, turn up the heat and toss it around for about 5 minutes, or until it's golden brown at the edges. Now, using a draining spoon, transfer it to join the sausages, then turn the heat down again to medium and soften the onion for 10 minutes in the juices left in the pan, stirring it around from time to time. Then add the garlic and cook for another minute.

Next, add the drained beans to the casserole, along with the herbs, then the sausages and pancetta, tucking them in among the beans, and finally, add the wine and 10 fl oz (275 ml) of the reserved water. Season with salt and freshly milled black pepper and bring everything up to simmering point on the hob. Now put a lid on the casserole and transfer it to the centre shelf of the oven to cook slowly for 3 hours. Serve garnished with the sprigs of rosemary and sage.

I don't think this needs any other vegetable but a green salad, and some Italian cheese would be nice to follow.

This dish is delightfully cool and intriguing. It's quite interesting to ask whoever you're serving it to to guess what it's flavoured with! I think it's a great dessert to serve if your main course has a Japanese theme.

The compote can be prepared well in advance. All you do is place the beans and their soaking liquid in a medium-sized saucepan over a medium to high heat and bring to the boil. Boil for 10 minutes, turn the heat down, cover with a lid and let them simmer for 30 minutes, topping up with a little more water if necessary. Then drain, reserving the cooking liquid, and make this up to 16 fl oz (450 ml), using cold water.

Next, return the liquid and the beans to the pan, add half the sugar, stir to dissolve it and continue to simmer for 10 minutes, this time without a lid. Then add the remaining sugar and salt and simmer until you have a nice syrupy consistency, which will take 15-20 minutes.

Meanwhile, pre-heat a large, heavy-based frying pan over a medium heat. Add the sesame seeds, stirring and keeping them on the move for 1-2 minutes, until they start to pop. Watch them like a hawk – be careful not to let them brown too much or burn. Remove them from the pan to a plate and leave to cool.

Next, transfer the compote to a bowl and, in the rinsed saucepan, bring the milk up to the boil, add the sesame seeds and leave them to infuse until the milk is completely cold.

To make the blancmange, put the water and sugar into a small saucepan over a medium heat, stir to dissolve the sugar, boil for a minute, then remove the pan from the heat and sprinkle in the gelatine, stirring until it has completely dissolved.

Now strain the sesame seeds and milk through a fine sieve into a large jug. (It does need to be very fine, as you don't want to push them through. If your sieve is not a fine one, line it with muslin or gauze.) When you've strained the milk through, you'll need to use the bowl of a ladle to press the sesame seeds to extract all the milk.

Now add the gelatine-and-sugar mixture to the milk, whisking to combine it all thoroughly, then pour into the pudding basins. Cover with clingfilm and chill in the fridge until set.

To serve, briefly dip the bottom of the basins into hot water, then invert them on to serving dishes and spoon the compote around them, reserving a few adzuki beans for decoration.

Serves 4
For the blancmange:
4 oz (110 g) sesame seeds
1 pint (570 ml) whole milk
5 fl oz (150 ml) water
1½ oz (40 g) golden caster sugar
1 x 11 g sachet powdered gelatine

For the compote:
4 oz (110 g) adzuki beans, pre-soaked (see page 536) in 1 pint (570 ml) water, soaking liquid reserved
3 oz (75 g) golden caster sugar
½ teaspoon salt

You will also need four mini pudding basins with a capacity of 6 fl oz (175 ml), or a pudding basin with a top diameter of 6 inches (15 cm), a bottom diameter of 3 inches (7.5 cm) and a capacity of 1¼ pints (725 ml).

24

First steps in preserving

Why would anyone want to make preserves in these modern times? After all, in the shops, there's a wealth of real jams with high fruit content, and chutneys and pickles from around the world. It was okay when our ancestors grew too much for their immediate needs and had to put things by to liven up the dreariness of winter. But our problem now is too much choice, too much food every single month of the year. My answer, as I embark on teaching you how to preserve fruit and vegetables, is that for all the choice available, not a lot of it measures up to home-made.

I hate over-sweet chutney and factory-made piccalilli (I've not found a good commercial one yet), and no manufacturer has ever been able to make Seville Orange Marmalade with all the chunkiness, depth and tangy flavour of the home-made (see page 564). Yes, there are a few exceptions and I confess to being a keen fan of farmers' markets, where you can buy some fabulous preserves. In fact, I have an excellent recipe for runner-bean chutney in my *Summer Collection*, but now that my local farm shop (Alder Carr in Needham Market) sells one every bit as good, I never bother to make it.

Nevertheless, these are exceptions and there's a great deal of creative satisfaction in seeing a row of shiny jars filled with good things stored away ready to enliven all kinds of meals. I particularly love it at Christmas, with all those cold cuts crying out for what has become a ritual in our house – chunky sautéed potatoes and an array of lovely pickles and chutneys. I'm a romantic and confess to wanting to keep alive our country's great tradition of preserving, so I am anxious for you to learn the basic techniques, which are not difficult once you understand them. If you've been strawberry-picking and have an over-abundance, or (as I did once, honestly) climbed a tree and hand-picked a basket of damsons, then a mouthful of summer in the depths of winter in some strawberry preserve spread over hot, buttered crumpets, or a bowl of Spiced Damson Chutney (see page 569) to dip your jacket potato skins into will give that pleasurable edge to everyday life.

Equipment

Preserving pan: Not strictly necessary unless you want to make really large quantities – actually, for beginners, it's better to make small quantities just to get the feel of preserving. Having said that, I do have one – when I make Spiced Damson Chutney, I like to make a lot because, not only am I crazy about it, I always want to give some to friends. There's no point in buying a really big pan. Buy the smaller size, because modern domestic hobs are simply not powerful enough to bring a huge pan of marmalade, or similar, to what used to be called a rolling boil. Stick to a heavy-gauge aluminium pan – it is the best conductor of heat and is not as expensive as stainless steel (but don't leave acid fruit in the pan after it cooks). The capacity of the pan in the photograph on page 563 is 15¾ pints (9 litres).

Funnel: (*see left*) A simple little thing, but so important when you are trying to fill the jars. It prevents sticky blobs spilling over the edges and down the sides.

Jars: (*see left*) Ideally, you should invest in some proper preserving jars because they have their own tight-sealing lids that make life much simpler. Look after them and they will serve you year after year and easily justify the initial cost. You can, of course, use commercial jars, but one thing to remember is that the lids for pickles and chutneys must be plastic-coated, as the vinegar can corrode metal. Either way, lids are essential. Cellophane covers won't work for pickles and chutneys. Also, it is important to remember to fill the jars as full as possible, not leaving any gaps.

Waxed discs: Preserves should always be sealed while still hot, and the seal is provided by waxed discs – little circles of paper covered with a thin layer of wax – placed over the surface of chutneys or jams, waxed side down. They are widely available in kitchen shops and stationers, or by mail order.

Muslin: You can now buy ready-made squares of muslin in various sizes, and these are what are needed to wrap the pickling spices that are suspended in a pan of chutney or the orange pips that are needed in marmalade. Ordinary gauze, available at chemists, does just as good a job.

Labels: Personally, I don't bother with the rather badly designed fancy brigade. I just buy stationers' self-adhesive, plain white labels. Labelling and dating is important – you might like to know you still have some preserve left from a vintage year!

Sterilised jars: Vital – because preserves that are going to be kept for long periods need to start off in spanking clean, sterilised jars – but perfectly simple. Just wash the jars and lids in warm, soapy water, rinse well (again in warm water), then dry them thoroughly with a clean tea cloth, place them on a baking tray and pop them in a medium oven, gas mark 4, 350°F (180°C) for a minimum of 5 minutes. Add their contents while they are still hot.

How to make jams, marmalade and preserves

Home-made jams are made from just two ingredients, fruit and sugar, unlike some of their cousins on the supermarket shelves. In fact, I am a passionate studier of labels and have rarely come across any commercially made jam or marmalade that contains only fruit and sugar. So, both in terms of quality and economy, it makes sense to make them at home and add that touch of luxury to everyday eating.

Jam is essentially preserved fruit. The fruit, if it's in good condition (and slightly under-ripe) contains in its cell walls a natural setting agent called pectin. This, together with the natural acid from the fruit, is released when the fruit is boiled with sugar. As it boils, the sugar concentrates and all three – sugar, acid and pectin – combine to form a mass that eventually reaches 'setting point'.

The fruit should be dry, since the water content of damp fruit will dilute the pectin and the acid and render them less active. Any dusty fruit should only be wiped with damp kitchen paper, and anyway, the boiling will effectively purify the fruit. Slightly under-ripe fruit actually contains more pectin and fruit acid than over-ripe fruit (which should therefore be avoided). With those fruits that contain less acid than others, this deficiency is made up by adding lemon juice.

The proportion of sugar to fruit varies according to the type of fruit used. I believe really sharp fruits, such as damsons or loganberries, make the best jams because they are not overpowered by the sweetness of the sugar, and the fruit flavour is predominant. This is also why I think Seville oranges make the best marmalade, tasting of oranges rather than sugar. Of course, other fruits also make good jams – providing the fruit content is high and there's not too much sugar.

Ten steps to jam-making

1 Sugar has a hardening effect, so tough-skinned fruits should always be simmered *before* the sugar is added to the pan.

2 Conversely, soft-skinned fruits, such as strawberries, which tend to disintegrate when cooked, should be soaked in sugar *first,* to harden them and help keep the fruit whole in the finished jam.

3 The sugar should be completely dissolved before the jam reaches the boil, otherwise it will be difficult to set and the finished jam will be sugary. To test if the sugar has dissolved, dip a wooden spoon in, turn it over and if no sugar crystals are visible in the liquid that coats the back of the spoon, it has indeed dissolved. (To be quite sure, stir well and repeat this test a couple of times.) To speed up the dissolving process, you can warm the sugar in a bowl in the oven before adding it.

4 Don't try to make too large a quantity of jam in one go. It will take far too long to come to the boil, and then will not boil rapidly enough to produce a good set.

5 How to test for a set: at the same time as you begin cooking the fruit, place three or four saucers in the freezing compartment of the fridge. When you have boiled the jam for the given time, remove the pan from the heat and place a teaspoonful of the jam on to one of the chilled saucers. Let it cool back in the fridge, then push it with your finger: if a crinkly skin has formed on the jam, then it has set. If it hasn't, continue to boil for another 5 minutes, then do another test.

6 Don't worry about any scum that rises to the surface while the jam is boiling – if you keep skimming it off, you'll finish up with no jam at all! Instead, wait until you have a set, then remove the jam from the heat and stir in a small lump of butter, which will disperse the scum.

7 Once the jam has set, leave it to settle for 15 minutes or so – particularly with jam containing whole fruit, such as strawberry or damson, or chunky marmalade – to prevent the fruit from rising to the top when it's poured into the jar. Then pour into clean, dry, hot jars, filling them as near to the top as possible. Straightaway, place a waxed disc over the surface, then seal with a lid. Wipe the jars with a warm, damp cloth.

8 Don't put the labels on until the jam is cold – otherwise the heat will prevent them sticking properly and they'll fall off for sure.

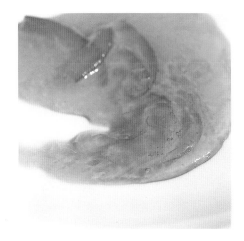

To test for a set, place a teaspoonful of the preserve on to a chilled saucer, cool in the freezer, then test by pushing with your finger to see if a wrinkly skin forms. If so, the preserve is set.

9   Store in a cool, dry and preferably dark place. Too much light is not good for storage, while a damp or steamy atmosphere can cause mould to develop on the surface of the jam.

10 If things go wrong: if the jam hasn't set after cooling and potting, tip it all back into the pan and boil again, adding the juice of a small lemon; if mould develops on the surface of jam in a jar, remove it with a spoon, along with about half an inch (1 cm) of the jam underneath – rest assured, the remainder of the jam will not be affected – and place a waxed disc dipped in brandy on top.

How to make chutneys and pickles

I have always thought of chutneys and pickles as an essentially English thing, but of course, like so many of our seemingly traditional foods, they actually have their origins in our long history as a trading nation. The word 'chutney' is Hindustani, and what we are familiar with now is the result of our earlier efforts to reproduce in this country the exotic recipes brought back by our traders in India in the 18th century. They were a great hit at the time and have since become virtually an indigenous part of our cuisine – in a way that the food of no European country ever has.

I'm a total devotee. I just love the idea of putting food by for later. Actually, I love all the things we eat with pickles and chutney, too: cold cuts, pork pies, Scotch eggs, ploughman's lunch and, of course, curries! Over the years I have been cooking, I have acquired a long list of recipes, and those in this chapter are a few of my established favourites, as well as some of my latest discoveries. But first, a few notes to help you get started.

What is chutney? What are pickles? Chutney is a combination of chopped fruits or vegetables (or both) that has been simmered with vinegar, sugar and spices until reduced to a thick purée, which is then potted and sealed, and should last for ages. Pickles, on the other hand, are not minced or chopped, but fruits and vegetables preserved whole or in chunks.

How do I know when the chutney is ready? There's a very simple test (*see photograph, right*). When the chutney appears thick enough, make a channel with a wooden spoon across its surface. If it leaves a channel imprinted for a few seconds without being filled by spare vinegar, it is ready.

The cardinal rule: Unless a recipe says otherwise, never eat chutneys or pickles until they have matured and mellowed – you need to store them for at least three months before eating. Freshly made, they taste harsh and vinegary – I'll never forget a letter I received when I first started publishing recipes: 'I've just made your chutney and it's disgusting!' I now know to warn you to be patient. Both pickles and chutneys need to be stored in a cool, dry, dark place – a cupboard under the stairs would be ideal, or else in a box in the garage or under a bed in the spare room.

To test if the chutney is thick enough, make a channel across the surface, if it leaves an impression for a few seconds without being filled by spare vinegar, it is ready.

Traditional Seville Orange Marmalade

You can find some very good shop-bought marmalade now, but it's still never ever like home-made. The intensely sharp, bitter Seville oranges here hold their own, conquering the sweetness of the sugar; that fresh, intensely orange fragrance and flavour are unmatched in any preserve anywhere in the world.

Makes six 1 lb (350 ml capacity) jars
2 lb (900 g) Seville oranges
4 pints (2.25 litres) water
1 lemon
4 lb (1.8 kg) golden granulated sugar, warmed
½ teaspoon butter

You will also need a preserving pan or a large, heavy-based saucepan; a 9 inch (23 cm) square of muslin (or gauze); some string; a funnel; and six 1 lb (350 ml capacity) jars, sterilised (see page 561).

Simmer the marmalade gently for two hours, uncovered, to allow the liquid to reduce and the orange peel to become completely soft.

Begin by measuring the water into the pan, then cut the oranges and lemon in half and squeeze the juice out of them. Now add the juice to the water, and place the pips and any bits of pith that cling to the squeezer on the square of muslin (or gauze), laid over a small bowl. Now cut the orange peel into quarters with a sharp knife, and then cut each quarter into thinnish shreds. As you cut, add the shreds to the water; any pips or spare pith you come across should go on the muslin (or gauze). The pith contains a lot of pectin, so don't discard any and don't worry about any pith and skin that clings to the shreds – it all gets dissolved in the boiling.

Now tie up the pips and pith loosely in the muslin (or gauze) to form a little bag, and tie this on to the handle of the pan with string, so that the bag is suspended in the water. Then bring the liquid up to simmering point and simmer gently, uncovered, for 2 hours, or until the peel is completely soft – test a piece carefully by pressing it between your finger and thumb. At this point, pop three or four saucers into the freezer compartment of the fridge to chill.

Next, remove the bag and leave it to cool on a saucer. Then pour the sugar into the pan and stir it now and then over a low heat, until you can see all the crystals have melted when you test the liquid on the back of a spoon – check this carefully, as it's important. Now increase the heat to very high and squeeze the bag over the pan to extract all the sticky, jelly-like substance that contains the pectin. You can do this by pressing the bag between two saucers or by using your hands. As you squeeze, you'll see it ooze out. Stir or whisk it into the rest.

As soon as the mixture reaches a fast boil, start timing. After 15 minutes, remove the pan from the heat, spoon a little of the marmalade on to one of the chilled saucers and pop it back in the freezer compartment for a few seconds. You can tell if it is set by pushing the mixture with your finger: if the surface wrinkles, it is; if not, continue to boil the marmalade and give it the same test at about 10-minute intervals until it does set.

After that, remove the pan from the heat. (If there's a lot of scum, most of it can be dispersed by stirring in the half teaspoon of butter, and the rest can be spooned off.) Leave the marmalade to settle for 20 minutes.

Pour it into the hot, sterilised jars with the aid of the funnel, filling them as full as possible, cover straight away with waxed discs and seal while still hot. Label when cold and store in a dry, cool, dark place. Then hurry up and make some toast to try some!

Dark Apricot
and Almond
Conserve

Most fruit conserves are made in summer, so it's good to be able to make this one in the depths of winter when it's too cold to go out. Serve it on some warm scones (see page 403) or toasted crumpets.

Makes three 1 lb (350 ml capacity) jars
1 lb (450 g) dried apricots
2 oz (50 g) whole unblanched almonds
1 pint (570 ml) water
1 lb (450 g) dark soft brown sugar
juice 4 lemons

You will also need a preserving pan or a 6 pint (3.5 litre) heavy-based saucepan; a funnel; and three 1 lb (350 ml capacity) jars, sterilised (see page 561).

You need to begin this the night before because the apricots need to be soaked, so put them in a bowl and pour the water over them.

The next day, pop three or four saucers into the freezer compartment of the fridge (for testing the setting point later on). Then, place the apricots, along with their soaking water, in the pan and simmer them very gently for about 30 minutes or until they're really tender when tested with a small skewer. Now add the sugar and, keeping the heat very low, allow it to melt and all the granules of sugar to completely dissolve – if not, the conserve will be grainy in texture. To test this, dip in a wooden spoon, and as the liquid runs off the back of it, you will be able to see clearly if there are any granules left. When the sugar has dissolved, turn the heat up to high. Next, add the lemon juice and almonds and boil rapidly for 15 minutes, stirring from time to time to prevent the conserve catching on the base of the pan.

When the time is up, remove the pan from the heat and place a teaspoonful of the conserve on one of the chilled saucers. Allow it to cool for about 30 seconds by putting it back in the fridge, then push it with your little finger: if a crinkly skin has formed, then the conserve has set. If not, boil it again for another 5 minutes and do another test, repeating three or four times if necessary, then remove the pan finally from the heat. Let it stand for 15 minutes to allow the conserve to settle. After that, pour it through the funnel into the hot, sterilised jars, filling them as full as possible, and seal straight away with waxed discs and tight-fitting lids. Wait till the conserve is cold before putting on the labels and then store it in a cool, dry, dark place.

Lemon Curd

Lots of lovely recipes call for lemon curd and, once again, it's something that is never quite the same when shop-bought.

Begin by lightly whisking the eggs in a medium-sized saucepan, then add the rest of the ingredients and place the saucepan over a medium heat. Now whisk continuously using a balloon whisk until the mixture thickens – about 7-8 minutes. Next, lower the heat to its minimum setting and let the curd gently simmer for a further minute, continuing to whisk. After that, remove it from the heat.

Now pour the lemon curd into the hot, sterilised jars, filling them as full as possible, cover straight away with waxed discs, seal while it is still hot and label when it is cold. It will keep for several weeks, but it must be stored in a cool place.

Makes three 1 lb (350 ml capacity) jars
grated zest and juice 4 large
juicy lemons
4 large eggs
12 oz (350 g) golden caster sugar
8 oz (225 g) unsalted butter, at room
temperature, cut into small lumps
1 dessertspoon cornflour

You will also need three 1lb (350 ml capacity) jars, sterilised (see page 561).

Spiced Cranberry and Claret Jelly

Even if it's not Christmas, it's such a treat to always have some home-made cranberry jelly on standby in your cupboard to serve with game or roast chicken or pâté – it livens up so many things and gives you a taste of luscious cranberries all year round.

Makes about one 17½ fl oz (500 ml) preserving jar
3 lb 8 oz (1.6 kg) cranberries
1 cinnamon stick
a few juniper berries
2 cloves
18 fl oz (510 ml) good claret
18 fl oz (510 ml) water
golden granulated sugar

You will also need a nylon sieve with a top diameter of 9½ inches (24 cm) (or 2 smaller sieves); some muslin (or gauze); and a 17½ fl oz (500 ml) preserving jar, sterilised (see page 561).

First of all, place the cranberries, cinnamon stick, juniper berries, cloves and water in your largest saucepan and simmer them over a gentle heat for 25-30 minutes, or until the cranberries have burst and become tender and mushy. Then empty the entire contents of the pan into the sieve, lined with the muslin (or gauze) and placed over an equally large bowl or jug, and leave it to drip for a minimum of 8 hours or, preferably, overnight. Do not be tempted to press the cranberries; the juice may become cloudy, but it's important to leave it alone to drip away.

The next day, chill three or four saucers in the freezer compartment of the fridge. Now measure the juice and, for every 1 pint (570 ml), weigh out 10 oz (275 g) of sugar. Pour the juice back into the rinsed pan, add the sugar and stir over a gentle heat until all the sugar has completely dissolved. Then add the claret, bring the mixture up to a fast, rolling boil and boil hard for about 10 minutes. (I always use a timer.)

After 10 minutes, test for a set. Remove the pan from the heat while you do so. Put a teaspoonful of jelly on to one of the chilled saucers, pop it back into the fridge for a few seconds, then push a finger gently through it. If the surface of the jelly wrinkles, setting point has been reached. If not, continue to boil and re-test at 5-minute intervals. Once the jelly has set, leave it to settle for 15 minutes or so, then pour it into the hot, sterilised jar, filling it as full as possible, cover straight away with a waxed disc, then seal tightly and label when cold. Store in a cool, dry, dark place.

Note: It is never practical to state the exact yield in a jelly recipe because it all depends on the ripeness of the fruit and the time allowed for dripping.

Spiced Damson Chutney

There are chutneys and chutneys, but this one is simply the best of all. It is something I couldn't live without, having it permanently on my shelf. I love it with cold cuts, with cheese, but best of all, sausages and jacket potatoes – dipping crisp, crunchy potato skins into this dark, spicy, deeply flavoursome preserve is one of life's great pleasures.

You've got two options here. One is to halve the damsons, slitting them down the natural line of the fruit and twisting out the stones – very tedious. The other is to stew them gently with ½ pint (275 ml) of the vinegar and then, wearing rubber gloves, remove the stones as they separate themselves from the flesh – also tedious but, either way, it will only take about 25 minutes and I promise you it is well, well worth it. Place them in a preserving pan, then core the apples but leave the peel on, and finely chop them in a processor. Then process the onions, adding both these to the pan.

After that, crush the garlic and add that, followed by the ginger, raisins, sugar and the (remaining) vinegar. Then sprinkle in the salt and stir everything thoroughly. Now wrap the cinnamon, allspice and cloves in the muslin (or gauze) and tie the top loosely with the string to form a little bag, which should then be tied on to the handle of the pan and suspended among the rest of the ingredients.

Now bring everything to the boil, then lower the heat and let the chutney simmer very gently for 2-3 hours, stirring it occasionally and rather more often towards the end to prevent it sticking to the bottom. When almost all the vinegar has disappeared and the chutney has thickened to a soft consistency, do the channel test – if it is ready, when you draw a channel with a wooden spoon across its surface, it will leave an imprint for a few seconds without filling up with vinegar. While it is still warm, pour it into the hot, sterilised jars, filling them as full as possible. Cover each with a waxed disc and seal tightly with a vinegar-proof lid. Label when cold and store the chutney in a cool, airy cupboard, leaving it to mellow for at least 3 months before eating.

Makes six 1 lb (350 ml capacity) jars
3 lb (1.35 kg) damsons
2 heaped teaspoons ground ginger
2 small cinnamon sticks
1 oz (25 g) allspice berries
1 dessertspoon cloves
2 pints (1.2 litres) malt vinegar
1 lb (450 g) cooking apples (no need to peel)
3 largish onions, peeled
3 cloves garlic
1 lb (450 g) seedless raisins
1 lb (450 g) dark soft brown sugar
1 lb (450 g) demerara sugar
2 tablespoons sea salt

You will also need a preserving pan, or a very large, heavy-based saucepan; a 12 inch (30 cm) square piece of muslin (or gauze); some string; and six 1 lb (350 ml capacity) jars, sterilised (see page 561).

Spiced Pickled Agen Prunes in Armagnac

It's great to have a jar of these pickles in the cupboard to serve with cold meats or pâtés, but I think they also make a wonderful accompaniment to Crisp Roast Duck (see page 326).

Makes five 1lb (350 ml capacity) jars
2 lb (900 g) Agen prunes, pitted
6 cloves
2 blades mace
6 allspice berries
5 small sticks cinnamon
5 tablespoons Armagnac
1 tablespoon Lapsang Souchong tea
1 pint (570 ml) good-quality red wine vinegar
8 oz (225 g) light muscovado sugar

You will also need five 1lb (350 ml capacity) jars, sterilised (see page 561).

You need to begin this the night before. Measure 2 pints (1.2 litres) of boiling water into a measuring jug, then stir in the tea and allow it to steep for 3 minutes. Meanwhile, put the prunes into a large, non-metallic bowl. Now strain the tea and allow it to cool completely before pouring it over the prunes. Then cover the bowl with a clean tea cloth and leave them to soak overnight.

Next day, put the vinegar, along with the sugar and spices, into a medium-sized saucepan, bring everything slowly up to the boil, and allow to simmer for 15 minutes. Meanwhile, drain off the tea and pack the prunes into the hot, sterilised jars, filling them as full as possible. Now transfer the liquid from the pan to the jug and carefully pour it over the prunes, swivelling the jars to make sure they are completely covered. Finally, spoon a tablespoon of Armagnac into each jar, then cover straight away with a waxed disc and seal tightly with a vinegar-proof lid. When the pickles are cold, label the jars and store in a cool, dry, dark place for at least 3 months – the prunes will go on getting better as they mature.

Clockwise, from top: Piccalilli, Spiced Pickled Agen Prunes in Armagnac, and Smoky Tomato Chutney

Smoky Tomato Chutney

Pimentón – smoked paprika – gives a smoky flavour to this dark, luscious, red tomato chutney. Great to serve with hamburgers and sausages, and lovely with sharp Cheddar cheese. If you prefer a milder chutney just use the sweet pimentón.

Makes four 1 lb (350 ml capacity) jars
4 oz (110 g) sun-blush (or mi-cuit) tomatoes
2 lb 8 oz (1.15 kg) red, ripe tomatoes
1 tablespoon hot pimentón
1 tablespoon sweet pimentón
1 dessertspoon coriander seeds
1 dessertspoon mustard seeds
2 fat cloves garlic, peeled
2 large onions, peeled and quartered
4 oz (110 g) light muscovado sugar
½ pint (275 ml) good-quality red wine vinegar
1 heaped teaspoon salt

You will also need a preserving pan or large heavy-based saucepan; a funnel; and four 1 lb (350 ml capacity) jars, sterilised (see page 561).

First of all, drain the sun-blush tomatoes of excess oil and pat dry with kitchen paper. (If using mi-cuit tomatoes, there will be no need to drain them.) Then heat a small, heavy-based frying pan and dry-roast the coriander and mustard seeds over a medium heat, turning them over and stirring them round for 2 minutes to draw out their flavour. Then crush them together with a pestle and mortar – not very much; they just need to be broken up.

Now, making the chutney is going to be a lot easier if you have a food processor. In the past, an old-fashioned mincer was used for chutneys, and a processor is even faster, but if you have neither, then you just need to chop everything uniformly small.

Add the sun-blush (or mi-cuit) tomatoes to the food processor and chop till roughly ¼ inch (5 mm) in size. Then add the fresh tomatoes and process briefly until they are the same size. Now pour the whole lot into the pan. Next, add the garlic and onions to the processor and process these to about the same size. Then transfer them to join the tomatoes and add the crushed spices, pimentón, sugar, vinegar and salt.

Bring everything up to simmering point, stirring all the time, then, when you have a gentle simmer, reduce the heat to low and let it cook very gently, uncovered, for 3-3½ hours. It doesn't need a great deal of attention – just come back now and then to give it a stir to prevent it sticking.

The chutney is ready when all the liquid has been absorbed and the mixture has thickened to a nice soft consistency. The way to test for the right moment is by using a wooden spoon to make a trail all the way across the top of the chutney – if the trail fills with the vinegary juices, it's not ready; when the spoon leaves a trail that does not fill with juice, it is.

You need to watch the chutney carefully at the end because undercooking will make it too sloppy and overcooking will make it dry. When it is ready, allow it to cool a little and pour it through the funnel into the hot, sterilised jars, filling them as full as possible. Cover each one straight away with a waxed disc and seal with a vinegar-proof lid while it's still hot, but don't put a label on until it's cold. Store the chutney in a cool, dry, dark place for 8 weeks to mellow before using.

Piccalilli

Good piccalilli is something you can't buy factory-made – it's never really successful. So, why not make your own? It's lovely with sharp English cheeses, with cold cuts and, perhaps best of all, with a fresh, crusty pork pie.

First place the cauliflower florets, onions and 2 pints (1.2 litres) vinegar in a large saucepan, then add the nutmeg and allspice and bring to the boil. Cover and simmer for 8 minutes. Remove the lid and stir in the cucumber, runner beans and sugar. Crush the garlic in the salt and stir this in as well. Bring the mixture up to simmering point again, cover and cook for a further 5 minutes. The vegetables should still all be slightly crisp – so don't go away and forget them.

Now set a large colander over a large bowl and pour the contents of the saucepan into it. Leave everything to drain, reserving the vinegar. Mix the mustard powder, turmeric and flour together in a bowl. Gradually work in the additional 5 tablespoons of vinegar and the water to make a fairly loose paste. Next add a ladleful of the hot vinegar liquid drained from the vegetables, stir and transfer the blend to a saucepan.

Bring to the boil, whisking with a balloon whisk, and gradually add the remaining hot vinegar. Boil gently for 5 minutes, then transfer the vegetables from the colander to the large bowl and pour the sauce over the top. Stir well to mix before spooning the piccalilli into washed, dried and warmed screw-top jars. Keep for three months before eating.

Note: If you get lumps in the sauce, whisk with a rotary whisk to disperse them.

Makes about five 1 lb (350 ml capacity jars)

2 oz (50 g) mustard powder
½ whole nutmeg, grated
½ teaspoon ground allspice
1 oz (25 g) ground turmeric
2 medium cauliflowers, divided into 1 inch (2.5 cm) florets
1 lb (450 g) small onions, quartered and cut across
1 cucumber, peeled, cut into ¼ inch (5 mm) rounds, then each round quartered
1 lb (450 g) runner beans, cut into largish pieces
2 pints (1.2 litres) malt vinegar, plus 5 extra tablespoons
12 oz (350 g) caster sugar
2 cloves garlic, crushed with 3 teaspoons salt
6 level tablespoons plain flour
3 tablespoons water

You will also need a large saucepan; and five 1 lb (350 ml capacity) jars, all sterilised (see page 561).

Giardiniere Pickles (Italian Gardener's Pickles)

I had a spell of work in Italy when I was 21, and one of my abiding memories of all those Italian meals was that Sunday lunch always began with a plate of salamis, prosciutto and mortadella served with pickled vegetables. I loved the way the pickles cut through the richness of the meats. So, here is another recipe Lucy Crabb used to make when she was chef at the football club, where it's known as Italian Gardener's Pickles.

Makes four 17½ fl oz (500 ml) preserving jars

8 oz (225 g) red onions, peeled
8 oz (225 g) courgettes
12 oz (350 g) aubergine
9 oz (250 g) trimmed fennel bulb
1 medium red pepper
1 medium yellow pepper
4 oz (110 g) button mushrooms
4 oz (110 g) cherry tomatoes
(or small vine tomatoes)
6 cloves garlic, thinly sliced
7 tablespoons olive oil
1¼-1½ pints (725-850 ml) good-quality white wine vinegar
8 fresh bay leaves
8 small sprigs each fresh rosemary and thyme
16 black peppercorns
6 oz (175 g) sea salt

You will also need four 17½ fl oz (500 ml) preserving jars, sterilised (see page 561).

This has to begin the night before with the normal salting process. Work your way through the list of vegetables until they are all prepared: cut each onion into eight wedges through the root; next, cut the courgettes and aubergine into thick matchsticks, and the fennel bulb into wedges; lastly, core and deseed the peppers and cut them into 2 inch (5 cm) chunks. Now layer all the vegetables, except the tomatoes and garlic, in a non-metallic bowl, and as you pile them in, sprinkle salt between the layers. Now pour over 3 pints (1.75 litres) of water, cover with a plate with a weight on it to submerge the vegetables, and leave the bowl in a cool place overnight.

Next day, drain the vegetables in a colander, then rinse them well under cold, running water. Now shake off the excess water, dry them in a clean tea cloth, and leave them spread out for about 3 hours on another clean tea cloth to thoroughly dry off.

After that, tip the vegetables into a bowl and stir in the garlic, along with the tomatoes and olive oil. Next, pour a thin layer of vinegar into the bottom of the hot, sterilised jars and add a bay leaf, a sprig of rosemary and a sprig of thyme. Then pack in the vegetables, adding the remainder of the herbs and peppercorns as you go, and pour in enough vinegar over each layer to ensure the vegetables are covered completely. Now swivel the jars to make sure the air is expelled and really press the vegetables down under the liquid before you cover with vinegar-proof lids. Label when cold and store the pickles in a cool, dry, dark place to mellow for a month before eating. They will keep for up to 6 months.

Pickled Okra

This is one of my most favourite pickles. The recipe was given to me by a very talented artist, Deborah MacMillan, whose paintings (I have three) I am very attached to. When I bought my first one, Night Swimmer, she offered me a glass of wine and some pickled okra, then, as I was so taken with it, kindly gave me the recipe.

Makes two 17½ fl oz (500 ml) jars
1 lb (450 g) small okra
4 cloves garlic, peeled
1¼ pints (725 ml) distilled vinegar
4 oz (110 g) light soft brown sugar
1 tablespoon sea salt

You will also need two 17½ fl oz (500 ml) preserving jars, sterilised (see page 561).

Begin this the night before. First of all, wash the okra, put it into a colander and sprinkle it with the salt. Cover with a clean tea cloth, put a large bowl underneath it to catch the juices and leave it overnight.

Next day, rinse the okra, then press them to get rid of the excess moisture and dry them with the cloth. Then leave them spread out on it to thoroughly dry off. After that, pack the okra into the hot, sterilised jars, along with the garlic. Next, in a saucepan, slowly bring the vinegar to the boil with the sugar, boil for 3 minutes, then pour it over the okra and garlic, covering them completely. Now swivel the jars to make sure the air is expelled and really press the vegetables down under the liquid before you place waxed discs on top. Seal tightly with vinegar-proof lids, label when cold and store in a cool, dry, dark place to mellow for 3 months before eating.

Pickled Peppers and Courgettes

This is adapted from an old Cordon Bleu recipe for pickled cucumber. It's one of the best, in my opinion, for serving with pâtés, as it provides a bit of crunch and acidity to cut through the richness.

Begin this the night before. First, deseed the peppers, cut out any pith and slice them into 2 inch (5 cm) strips. Next, trim and slice the courgettes into diagonal ½ inch (1 cm) slices. After that, halve the onions and cut them into ¼ inch (5 mm) slices. Now pack the vegetables into a large colander in layers, sprinkling each layer with salt, put a dish underneath it to catch the juices and another with a weight on it on top, and leave them overnight.

Next day, rinse the vegetables under cold, running water, really press them to get rid of any excess moisture, and pat them dry with a clean tea cloth. Then leave them spread out on the cloth for about 2 hours to thoroughly dry off.

After that, place the vinegar, sugar and spices, including the chillies, in a saucepan and stir them together over a medium heat until the sugar has completely dissolved. Let it all simmer for about 3 minutes and then add the vegetables, simmering for another 3 minutes. Then divide the pickle between the hot, sterilised jars, packing it right up to the top. Swivel them to make sure the air is expelled and really press the vegetables down under the liquid before you place waxed discs on top. Then seal tightly with vinegar-proof lids, label the jars when cold and store the pickles in a cool, dry, dark place. They are supposed to be kept for 3 months to mellow before eating (if you are patient), but I've found them to be very good in about a month.

Makes four 17½ fl oz (500 ml) preserving jars
2 large red peppers
2 lb 8 oz (1.15 kg) courgettes (no need to peel)
12 oz (350 g) red onion (about 3 onions), peeled
1½ pints (850 ml) good-quality white wine vinegar
8 oz (225 g) demerara sugar
1 oz (25 g) mustard seeds
1 teaspoon celery seeds
1 rounded teaspoon ground turmeric
½ teaspoon ground mace
2 medium-sized red chillies, deseeded and thinly sliced
1½ oz (40 g) sea salt, lightly crushed

You will also need four 17½ fl oz (500 ml) preserving jars, sterilised (see page 561).

Sour Dill
Pickles

Supermarket dill-pickled cucumbers are always a bit on the sweet side for me, so this is my attempt at capturing that lovely sour New York deli-type pickle.

Makes two 17½ fl oz (500 ml) preserving jars
¾ oz (20 g) fresh dill, stalks removed, broken into sprigs
1 lb (450g) ridge cucumbers (small cucumbers)
4 shallots
1 pint (570 ml) good-quality white wine vinegar
1 heaped teaspoon coriander seeds
1 heaped teaspoon black peppercorns
1 oz (25 g) sea salt

You will also need two 17½ fl oz (500 ml) preserving jars, sterilised (see page 561).

You need to begin this the night before. First of all, cut the cucumbers in half lengthways and then in quarters lengthways, then cut them on the diagonal into 1 inch (2.5 cm) chunks. After that, peel and slice the shallots in half through the root, then into three. Next, you need to place the cucumbers and shallots in layers in a non-metallic colander and sprinkle with the salt between each layer, making sure they are fairly evenly coated. Then place a plate over them, press it down with a scale weight, or something equally heavy, and leave them overnight so the salt can draw out the excess moisture. Put a dish underneath the colander to catch the drips.

Next day, rinse the vegetables under cold, running water and dry them in a clean tea cloth, then spread them out on the cloth for about an hour to thoroughly dry off. After that, pack them into the hot, sterilised jars.

Now place the vinegar and spices in a saucepan, along with the dill, bring it up to the boil and simmer for about 30 seconds, then pour the whole lot over the vegetables, covering them completely. Swivel the jars to make sure the air is expelled and really press the vegetables down under the liquid before you place waxed discs on top. Then seal tightly with vinegar-proof lids, label when cold and store the pickles in a cool, dry, dark place to mellow for 3 months before eating.

25

Waist watchers

This chapter is included by overwhelming popular demand. On my website it is the most requested subject. There are, it seems, millions of waist watchers out there asking for help: please can we have recipes that taste good but are not fattening; can you help us to eat well but stay slim? I've never been one to turn down a challenge and, I have to say, it is a subject that has occupied my thoughts and a great deal of my time for ages. I have concluded that what we need to do first is stand back, rid ourselves of the myths and confusion, and focus on what the basic problem is.

Let me say from the outset that I am not a qualified nutritionist; I can only offer you my own views and thoughts, and what has been helpful to me personally over the years.

The problem. Simply that we eat too much and do too little. During the war and for a while afterwards we had fewer food choices than today and didn't have cars, so we did a hell of a lot of walking or cycling to get around. Nowadays, we ride everywhere and consume far more snack-type foods and chocolate bars. If sweets and crisps and snacks are a regular part of your daily diet, then me offering you low-fat recipes won't help one bit.

The myth of healthy foods. I'm thoroughly fed up of hearing about 'healthy' foods. It's an absolute con. What we have to grasp is there's *no* such thing. *All* food, if it is pure and natural, is good for you: it provides pleasure, comfort, community – all that's important in life. Imagine Mother Nature saying, here are all the good things of the earth to give you pleasure, and then rapping you on the knuckles, saying, but don't eat this or that – it's bad for you!

What *is* unhealthy is too much of something. I know it's not sexy advice, but it does boil down to one thing, and that's balance. A doughnut is not unhealthy, neither is a KitKat or a steak-and-kidney pudding or even half a pint (275 ml) of double cream. If you're not eating too much, you can eat anything. Those things (if they existed at all) were treats during the war, not something available every hour of every day. Cookery presenters like me are always in the firing line. How, people ask, can you be using all that butter, all that cream? But the point is, I'm not saying, eat roast buttered chicken every day or even every week. I'm saying, if I'm not eating butter the rest of the week, why not have some on Sunday? I have always had an uphill struggle with my own weight, and what's helped me is treating Sundays or dinner with friends as a feast day. I will always make a dessert or a cake for weekends, but I very rarely eat sweet things on other days – it also gives me something to look forward to!

The big fat question. Just as we've been duped into thinking some foods are unhealthy, so we are also victims of the commercial low-fat lobby. Yes, we may well need to cut down our fat intake overall (and if we're not getting any exercise, we certainly do), but buying so-called low-fat products containing a load of other undesirable ingredients is sometimes not the way to do it. There is too often an unhealthy obsession with fat that regards it as poison. Spare me from egg-white omelettes, for instance, in which we are not allowed even the relatively small amount of fat contained in an egg yolk – it's bordering on madness. So, despite what you might have heard, fat isn't all bad, and we do need some in our diet.

The other culprit. Cutting down on *excessive* fat is one way to lose weight, but there's another ingredient that is often hidden away in all those manufactured low-fat foods and recipes. Carbohydrates, once consumed, are themselves converted into sugar, so any *added* sugar is going to be extra to that. (Also, lots of sugary foods contain lots of fat, too.) Not that having extra is necessarily a bad thing, but think about it – are you a person who *needs* sweetness every day? Really enjoying something sweet is different to actually *needing* it. That need may not be a problem if you're not overweight, but, if you are, it could be. Enjoying sweet things now and then is part of the joy of eating. But if you need to lose weight, they have to be restricted, and sometimes it's helpful to use a sweetener, but, again, not every day. Some of our weight problems can be put down to this addiction to unnatural sweetness.

Sugar is a highly refined, concentrated form of sweetness and if you were to remove it (along with artificial sweeteners) from your diet, a minor miracle would happen: you would eventually cease to be an addict. In fact, in about six weeks, you would begin to discover how wonderfully sweet an apple or a glass of milk is. When I gave up adding sugar to tea and coffee I hated it for weeks, but when I put it back I hated it more, and understood how the sweetness had been masking the real flavour. Once you've managed to kick the habit, you'll find most commercial products too sweet and you won't want them. (It's my theory that chocoholics may not be addicted to cocoa, but simply to sweetness.)

Getting the right balance. The now famous advice to eat five portions of fruit and vegetables every day is a sound one, and should also lessen the desire for sugary snacks – an excellent way of beginning to cut down on the wrong sorts of food. It's also important to remember that you can have something of everything, but not too much of anything. As a seasoned dieter myself, I now feel that one of the best ways to achieve that balance and lose weight sensibly is the Weight Watchers™ programme. I like the fact that with the points system no foods are taboo, and several of my friends – even if they're not continuing to diet – have been helped to re-educate themselves into a much more sensible pattern of eating.

The recipes. The question remains, what can the home cook do to make losing a few pounds more interesting? What I have attempted to do here is provide recipes that contain the minimum amount of fat and hardly any sugar. In some cases, there may be a minimal quantity of sweetener, and I'm aware of the controversy surrounding its use, but soft drinks and most yoghurts contain it and I would be far more worried about those being consumed on a daily basis than I am about its appearance in the occasional, once- or twice-a-week dessert.

You'll find that cooking non-fattening dishes is a lot easier if you stock up on a number of basic ingredients. Some of these have been mentioned in earlier chapters, but, in addition, you'll find the following useful.

Diet products

Fromage frais: The best low-fat versions I've found are one from Isigny in Normandy (a version with 8 per cent fat), and La Faisselle, the strained fromage frais. Both are divine eaten just as they are, or with fruit, or even spread on bread instead of butter – you'll be amazed how this can give you a real dairy taste without all the fat. I also use fromage frais a lot in cooking in place of cream. There is, if you are seriously cutting down, an Isigny fromage frais with virtually no fat at all.

0 per cent Greek yoghurt: A brilliant product – still thick and 'creamy', with no fat, no sugar and no artificial flavour. This, together with fresh fruit, is a delight for breakfast.

Natural low-fat yoghurt: Although I prefer the Greek yoghurt for eating, I have found natural low-fat yoghurt is sometimes better for cooking.

Quark: A soft, white, skimmed-milk, very low-fat cheese. For an instant snack, try it spread on sesame Ryvitas with Marmite, or add it to scrambled eggs or mashed potato.

Cottage cheese: The slimmer's friend, sprinkled with chives and served with a salad, or in low-fat Cappuccino Cheesecakes (see page 610).

Buttermilk: Since embarking on this chapter, I have discovered that buttermilk makes a wonderful marinade ingredient. Both fish and chicken respond beautifully to it, becoming moister and more luscious.

Semi-skimmed milk: I'm afraid I can't cope with skimmed milk, so I opt for semi-skimmed, which still has some residual creaminess. When I've really needed to cut down, I have allowed myself 5 fl oz (150 ml) per day.

Light evaporated milk: Great for cooking, as it's the nearest thing to cream without all the fat (see Slimmers' Wild Mushroom Risotto on page 603).

Half-fat crème fraîche: Useful, but do add it sparingly, as it contains more fat than the ingredients above.

Oriental ingredients: In my recipes I have included Japanese soy sauce, mirin (Japanese sweet rice wine), Shaosing (Chinese brown rice wine) and Thai fish sauce (make sure you buy an authentic one, as some of the fish sauces available are over-salty). All these are really helpful as you can add lots of flavour with little or no fat. Even toasted sesame oil, though it *is* an oil, is so strong and assertive you need only a minimal amount.

Oil, butter and cheese: Not, as you might have thought, banned totally, but to be used in minute quantities – I've confined myself to using no more than a teaspoon of oil or butter per person when creating the diet recipes in this chapter. Strong-flavoured cheeses, such as Parmesan and Pecorino, give a fair amount of cheese flavour without too many calories.

Bloody Mary Soup with Vodka Tomato Salsa

More of a Virgin Mary really, but there's nothing to stop you adding a shot of vodka if you have the mind to. Honestly, though, it won't need it because it has a lovely spicy kick of its own, and the very best news is it must easily be the fastest soup to make on record, although it tastes as though it took hours!

First place the tomatoes (including the one for the salsa) in a heatproof bowl, pour boiling water over them and count 60 seconds. After that, pour off the water and slip off their skins (protecting your hands with a cloth if the tomatoes are hot). Reserve the tomato for the salsa and chop the others very finely, adding them to a medium-sized saucepan. Bring them up to a gentle simmer and let them cook for about 3 minutes.

Meanwhile, make the salsa. Cut the reserved tomato in half, then squeeze out the seeds and dice the flesh. Now mix the tomato and the celery with the remaining ingredients.

Next, pour the tomato juice and the rest of the soup ingredients into the saucepan and season. Taste and add more Tabasco or lime, if needed. Now bring everything back up to simmering point. Then ladle the soup into hot bowls and spoon half the salsa on to each one before serving.

Serves 2
3 large ripe tomatoes (weighing about 6 oz/175 g)
18 fl oz (510 ml) fresh tomato juice
1 tablespoon Worcestershire sauce
1 tablespoon balsamic vinegar
juice 1 lime
4 drops Tabasco sauce
salt and freshly milled black pepper

For the salsa:
2 teaspoons vodka
1 medium-sized ripe tomato
3 inch (7.5 cm) piece celery, destringed and diced
¼ teaspoon celery salt
2 dashes Tabasco sauce

Marinated Chicken Brochettes with Green Couscous

Buttermilk makes a superb marinade – so much so you'll wonder why you ever needed oil. The chicken will be luscious and tender and, with all the other wonderful flavours, you'll forget this is in any way a diet recipe. This is also good served with the Coriander Chutney on page 209.

Serves 2
2 x 6 oz (175 g) boneless chicken breasts, skin removed
6 fresh bay leaves, cut in half
½ medium red onion, peeled, halved and separated into 8 layers
½ large yellow pepper, deseeded and cut into 8
1 teaspoon groundnut or other flavourless oil
salt and freshly milled black pepper

For the marinade:
1 clove garlic
1 teaspoon peeled, grated fresh root ginger
1 medium-sized green chilli, deseeded
1 tablespoon fresh coriander leaves
1 teaspoon ground turmeric
6 fl oz (175 ml) buttermilk
salt and freshly milled black pepper

For the couscous:
5 oz (150 g) couscous
9 fl oz (250 ml) boiling chicken or vegetable stock
4 spring onions, including the green parts, finely chopped
2 tablespoons chopped fresh coriander
1 oz (25 g) rocket, leaves finely chopped
2 limes: juice of 1, 1 cut into wedges, to garnish
salt and freshly milled black pepper

You will also need two wooden skewers, about 10 inches (25.5 cm) long.

First of all, you need to make the marinade. To do this, use a pestle and mortar to crush the garlic with about ½ teaspoon of salt until it becomes a purée. Next, add the grated ginger. Then chop the chilli and coriander and mix these with the garlic and ginger, along with the turmeric and some freshly milled black pepper. After that, pour the buttermilk into a bowl and whisk the other ingredients into it.

Now cut each chicken breast into five pieces, add them to the bowl and give everything a good stir. Then press the chicken down well into the marinade, cover the surface with clingfilm and pop the bowl into the fridge for a few hours or, preferably, overnight.

When you are almost ready to cook the chicken, soak the skewers in hot water for 30 minutes (to prevent them burning). Pre-heat the grill to its highest setting for at least 10 minutes and line the grill pan with kitchen foil.

Next, dry the skewers in a clean tea cloth and thread half a bay leaf on to each one, then a piece of chicken, a piece of onion and a piece of pepper. Carry on alternating the bay leaf, chicken, onion and pepper until you have threaded five pieces of chicken on to each skewer, finishing with half a bay leaf on each. Make sure you pack everything together as tightly as possible, then season with salt and freshly milled black pepper and brush the vegetables with a minute amount of oil. Lay the brochettes on the grill rack and place them under the grill, about 4 inches (10 cm) from the heat source. Brush liberally with some of the remaining marinade and grill them for 10 minutes, before turning them over and grilling them for a further 10 minutes, brushing them with more of the marinade as they cook, and watching them carefully so they don't burn.

While the chicken is cooking, place the couscous in a largish bowl, then pour the boiling stock over it, add some salt and freshly milled black pepper and stir it with a fork. Then leave it on one side for 5 minutes, by which time it will have absorbed all the stock and softened. After that, fluff it up by making cutting movements across and through it with a knife. Then stir in the remaining couscous ingredients and season to taste.

When the chicken is ready, pop the brochettes on top of the couscous and serve straight away on warmed serving plates, garnished with the wedges of lime.

PER SERVING
CHICKEN: 260 kcal, FAT 4.2 g, SATURATES 1 g, PROTEIN 46.3 g, CARBOHYDRATE 10.3 g
COUSCOUS: 178 kcal, FAT 0.9 g, SATURATES 0 g, PROTEIN 4.9 g, CARBOHYDRATE 39.5 g

Swordfish Ceviche

Ceviche is a dish in which fish is 'cooked' in lime or lemon juice with lots of other gutsy flavours. I love to serve it on a hot summer's day, but it's good at any time of year when you want something really interesting that doesn't contain any added fat.

Serves 4

1 lb 4 oz (570 g) skinned swordfish, cut into ½ inch (1 cm) cubes

8 oz (225 g) tomatoes, preferably yellow

6 oz (175 g) red onion (about 1 medium onion), peeled and very thinly sliced

1 fat clove garlic, finely chopped

½ oz (10 g) chopped fresh coriander leaves, plus 1 tablespoon coriander leaves to garnish

1 tablespoon chopped fresh mint leaves

juice 6 limes (about 6 fl oz/175 ml)

1 teaspoon black peppercorns, crushed

1 teaspoon sea salt

You will also need a shallow serving dish with a base measurement of 6½ x 8 inches (16 x 20 cm).

Begin by skinning the tomatoes. Place them in a heatproof bowl and pour boiling water on to them. After exactly a minute (or 15-30 seconds if the tomatoes are small), remove them from the water and slip off their skins (protecting your hands with a cloth if they are hot). Then cut them in half, squeeze out the seeds and cut them in half again to make quarters.

Next, layer the swordfish, tomatoes, onion, garlic, and chopped coriander and mint leaves in the serving dish, sprinkling with the salt and freshly crushed black pepper. Now simply pour over the lime juice and press down with your hands so that everything is well covered with juice. Then cover the dish with clingfilm and refrigerate for 12 hours, turning the fish over once during that time.

Serve with salad leaves and garnished with the remaining coriander.

PER SERVING: 187 kcal, FAT 6.2 g, SATURATES 1.3 g, PROTEIN 27 g, CARBOHYDRATE 6.2 g

This is probably the most difficult challenge in low-fat cooking (apart from creating a low-fat chocolate dessert). If I'm watching the fat content in my diet, I often just squeeze lemon or lime juice over my salad, or sometimes, particularly with tomatoes, I use balsamic vinegar. However, that can become boring, so here are three very low-fat dressings to enliven your salads and, hopefully, help you forget the word 'diet'.

A low-fat version of a classic dressing.
Crush the garlic and salt with a pestle and mortar until creamy, and then work in the mustard and some freshly milled black pepper. Next, add the oil, wine and vinegar and blend well with a small whisk. Whisk again before dressing the salad.

PER SERVING: 29 kcal, FAT 2 g, SATURATES 0.3 g, PROTEIN 0.6 g, CARBOHYDRATE 0.5 g

This is popular in America, but normally mega-calorific!
You'll need to start off by making the Almost Mayonnaise on page 590 and then chill it for a couple of hours in the fridge. All you do now is mix all the remaining ingredients into the mayonnaise, whisk the whole lot together until well blended and sprinkle with the cayenne pepper.

PER SERVING: 56 kcal, FAT 1.5 g, SATURATES 0.4 g, PROTEIN 3.4 g, CARBOHYDRATE 7.5 g

Yes, it does contain cheese, but very little gives a lot of flavour!
This one's even speedier! Just whiz everything together in the small bowl of a food processor, or in a small mixing bowl, using an electric hand whisk (in which case, you'll need to crush the garlic first). Sprinkle with the chives and it's ready to serve.

PER SERVING: 34 kcal, FAT 2.7 g, SATURATES 1.6 g, PROTEIN 2.1 g, CARBOHYDRATE 0.7 g

Clockwise, from left: Almost Vinaigrette, Thousand Island Dressing and Blue-Cheese Dressing

Almost Vinaigrette

Serves 2

1 teaspoon olive oil
1 small clove garlic
1 teaspoon wholegrain mustard
1 tablespoon wine (any colour)
1 tablespoon balsamic vinegar
¼ teaspoon sea salt
freshly milled black pepper

Thousand Island Dressing

Serves 2

2 tablespoons Almost Mayonnaise (see page 590)
2 tablespoons tomato-and-chilli relish
1 cornichon (baby gherkin), finely chopped
a pinch of cayenne pepper
salt and freshly milled black pepper

Blue-Cheese Dressing

Serves 3-4

1 oz (25 g) Gorgonzola Piccante, at room temperature
5 oz (150 g) 0 per cent Greek yoghurt
1 small clove garlic
1 tablespoon semi-skimmed milk
a few freshly snipped chives
salt and freshly milled black pepper

Almost Mayonnaise

This is adapted from Eliza Acton's recipe for English Salad Sauce, written in the 1840s. While hers used double cream, the recipe below uses 8 per cent fat fromage frais. The vote from the team when we were testing this is that it's every bit as good as the original.

Serves 4-6
3 large eggs
1 tablespoon cold water
2 pinches cayenne pepper
5 fl oz (150 ml) 8 per cent fat fromage frais
4 teaspoons white wine vinegar
¼ teaspoon salt

First, place the eggs in a saucepan and cover completely with plenty of cold water. Bring the water up to simmering point and give them exactly 9 minutes from the time it starts boiling. Then cool them under cold, running water to stop them cooking any further. Now peel away the shells, cut the eggs in half and place the yolks only in a mixing bowl.

Add the tablespoon of cold water and pound the yolks to a smooth paste with a wooden spoon. Then add the cayenne pepper and salt, and stir in the fromage frais, bit by bit, mixing it smoothly as you go. When it's all in, add the vinegar, check the seasoning and add more if it needs it. If you think the mixture's far too runny at this stage, don't worry. Cover the bowl and leave it for a couple of hours in the fridge, after which time it will have thickened. (It should, in any case, have the consistency of thickish cream, rather than mayonnaise.)

Note: To make a low-fat Tartare Sauce, after chilling the Almost Mayonnaise, add 1 small garlic clove, chopped; ½ teaspoon mustard powder; 1 dessertspoon lemon juice; 1 tablespoon chopped fresh flat-leaf parsley; 1 heaped tablespoon salted capers and 4 cornichons (baby gherkins), both chopped; and mix together.

PER SERVING: 65 kcal, FAT 3.7 g, SATURATES 1.1 g, PROTEIN 6.1 g, CARBOHYDRATE 1.8 g

Sea Bass with Puy Lentil Salsa

This is an extremely fast supper dish for two people that is full of colour and flavour. Some small new potatoes would make a good accompaniment, but for serious waist watchers, I don't think it really needs it.

Serves 2

2 sea bass fillets (each weighing
7-8 oz/200-225 g)
1 teaspoon olive oil
½ lime, cut into wedges
salt and freshly milled black pepper

For the lentil salsa:
1½ oz (40 g) Puy lentils (no need
to soak), rinsed
4 fl oz (120 ml) water
1 large tomato
¼ medium red onion, peeled
1 small red chilli, halved and deseeded
2 tablespoons fresh coriander leaves
juice 1 lime
salt and freshly milled black pepper

Begin by making the lentil salsa. Place the lentils in a small saucepan with the water and some salt. Next, bring them up to simmering point and gently simmer without a lid for about 30 minutes, or until they are tender but still have some bite and retain their shape, by which time, most of the water will have been absorbed.

While the lentils are cooking, skin the tomato. Do this by placing it in a heatproof bowl and pouring boiling water on to it. After exactly a minute, remove it from the water and slip off the skin (protecting your hands with a cloth if the tomato is hot), then halve it and squeeze out the seeds. Now chop it into small pieces. After that, chop the onion and chilli very small, add the tomato and coriander, and keep all this aside, covered in clingfilm, until needed.

When the lentils are cooked, empty them into a bowl and while they are still warm, toss them in the lime juice. Now taste to check the seasoning and add the rest of the prepared salsa ingredients. Mix well and leave aside in a cool place.

To cook the fish, you need to pre-heat the grill to its highest setting for at least 10 minutes. Next, line a grill tray with kitchen foil, brush the fish fillets on both sides with the oil and place them on the tray flesh-side up. Season with salt and freshly milled black pepper, then grill for 5-6 minutes, turning halfway through, or until just cooked through. Serve straight away with the salsa and some lime wedges to squeeze over.

Note: Sometimes farmed sea bass fillets are very small, in which case, use two per person.

PER SERVING: 311 kcal, FAT 7.5 g, SATURATES 1.2 g, PROTEIN 47 g, CARBOHYDRATE 14.9 g

Chinese Steamed Trout with Ginger and Spring Onions

As with salmon, trout is slightly higher in fat, but still very low compared with meat. The fat in both trout and salmon is the good kind we all need to include in our diets. If you're wondering what the pink bits are in the photograph, they're pink spring onions, which looked very pretty the day we took the picture!

Serves 2
2 whole trout (each weighing about 8 oz/225 g), gutted
1 inch (2.5 cm) piece of fresh root ginger, peeled and cut into thin strips
4 spring onions
1 clove garlic, sliced thinly
1 dessertspoon crushed sea salt

For the sauce:
1 teaspoon peeled, grated fresh root ginger
1 clove garlic, chopped
3 tablespoons Japanese soy sauce
3 tablespoons Shaosing (Chinese brown rice wine)
1 teaspoon toasted sesame oil
½ teaspoon dark soft brown sugar

You will also need a steamer.

First of all, rinse the trout and dry it with kitchen paper, then sprinkle the outside of the fish with salt and leave aside for half an hour to help firm up the flesh. Meanwhile, place all the sauce ingredients in a small saucepan, then bring them up to simmering point and simmer for 5 minutes.

Next, the spring onions should be cut in half where the green and white parts meet, and the very green part cut in diagonals (making diamond shapes when opened out). The rest should be thinly shredded lengthways.

When you're ready to cook the trout, wipe the salt away with some more kitchen paper and place the fish in the steamer, with the ginger and garlic scattered inside and all over. Place it over boiling water and steam with a lid on for exactly 15 minutes.

Serve the trout with the re-heated sauce poured over and garnished with the spring onions. Plain basmati rice would be a good accompaniment.

PER SERVING: 319 kcal, FAT 13.3 g, SATURATES 2.7 g, PROTEIN 45.5 g, CARBOHYDRATE 4.8 g

Eggs and Leeks en Cocotte

This can be a starter or a light snack for one person, providing something very special for the bored dieter. You can ring the changes, too – instead of leeks, use steamed asparagus tips or lightly cooked, chopped spinach. For a low-fat accompaniment, serve with wholemeal bread spread with a little Greek yoghurt instead of butter.

First of all, cut the leek vertically, fan it under cold, running water to get rid of any dirt, then chop it quite finely. Now place a small pan over a medium heat, add the leeks and some seasoning, stir, then turn the heat down to low. Cover and let them cook gently in their own juices for about 5 minutes, shaking the pan and stirring two or three times. After that, use a draining spoon to transfer them to the ramekin (or dish).

Next, carefully break the egg in on top of the leeks and add some seasoning. Then gently spoon the yoghurt over, spreading it out with a knife so it covers the egg completely. Finally, sprinkle with the Parmesan.

Now pour about 1 inch (2.5 cm) of boiling water into the roasting tin, place the ramekin (or dish) in it and pop the whole lot in the oven to bake for 15-18 minutes, depending on how you like your egg cooked (bearing in mind it will go on cooking after it has been removed from the oven).

Serves 1
1 large egg
2 oz (50 g) leeks (about 1 medium leek), trimmed
2 rounded tablespoons 5 per cent Greek yoghurt
½ teaspoon freshly grated Parmesan (Parmigiano Reggiano)
salt and freshly milled black pepper

You will also need a ramekin 1½ inches/4 cm deep, with a base diameter of 3 inches/7.5 cm (or a small, round ovenproof dish), smeared with a trace of butter from a butter paper; and a small roasting tin.

Pre-heat the oven to gas mark 4, 350°F (180°C).

Turkey
Saltimbocca

This is a variation on the famous Italian recipe made with thin escalopes of veal – but turkey is usually easier to find. However, you can ring the changes by using veal, or even slices of pork fillet.

Serves 2

2 turkey steaks (weighing about
10 oz/275 g in total – choose fairly
equal-sized steaks)
6 slices Parma ham (weighing
about 3 oz/75 g in total)
8 large fresh sage leaves
8 fl oz (225 ml) dry Marsala
1 teaspoon olive oil
salt and freshly milled black pepper

You will also need a medium-sized
frying pan and eight cocktail sticks.

First of all, prepare the turkey steaks, which need to be flattened out. So, place one of them between two large pieces of clingfilm and gently pound it using a rolling pin, being careful not to break the meat. It needs to be flattened out to a shape measuring about 6 x 7 inches (15 x 18 cm), ⅛-¼ inch (3-5 mm) thick. Repeat this with the second turkey steak, between two fresh pieces of clingfilm. Then cut each flattened steak into four pieces measuring about 3 x 3½ inches (7.5 x 9 cm).

Next, you need to separate the slices of Parma ham, trim away the fat and cut a 1½ inch (4 cm) strip off the end of each slice. (You'll need these smaller pieces of ham to finish off two of the turkey pieces.) Now place a piece of ham on each slice of turkey, folding and creasing it up to fit, if necessary, then divide the six smaller pieces of ham between the last two turkey slices. Finally, top each one with a sage leaf and secure the whole thing together with a cocktail stick. Then season each piece on both sides with salt and freshly milled black pepper.

Next, measure the Marsala into a small saucepan and heat it gently until it begins to bubble. While that's happening, cook the turkey: heat the oil in the frying pan over a fairly high heat and when it's really hot, put in half the pieces of turkey, sage-side down, reduce the heat to medium and fry for 2-3 minutes, until crisp and golden. Then turn them over and give the other side about a minute before removing them to a warmed serving dish. Do the same with the remaining pieces and when they're done, keep them warm with the others. Now pour the warmed Marsala into the frying pan, turn the heat right up again and let it bubble and reduce to a syrupy sauce, which should take 4-5 minutes. Return the turkey pieces to the pan and turn in the sauce. Serve on warmed plates (not forgetting to remove the cocktail sticks!) with the syrupy sauce poured over.

PER SERVING: 352 kcal, FAT 7.5 g, SATURATES 2.3 g, PROTEIN 44.1 g, CARBOHYDRATE 7.3 g

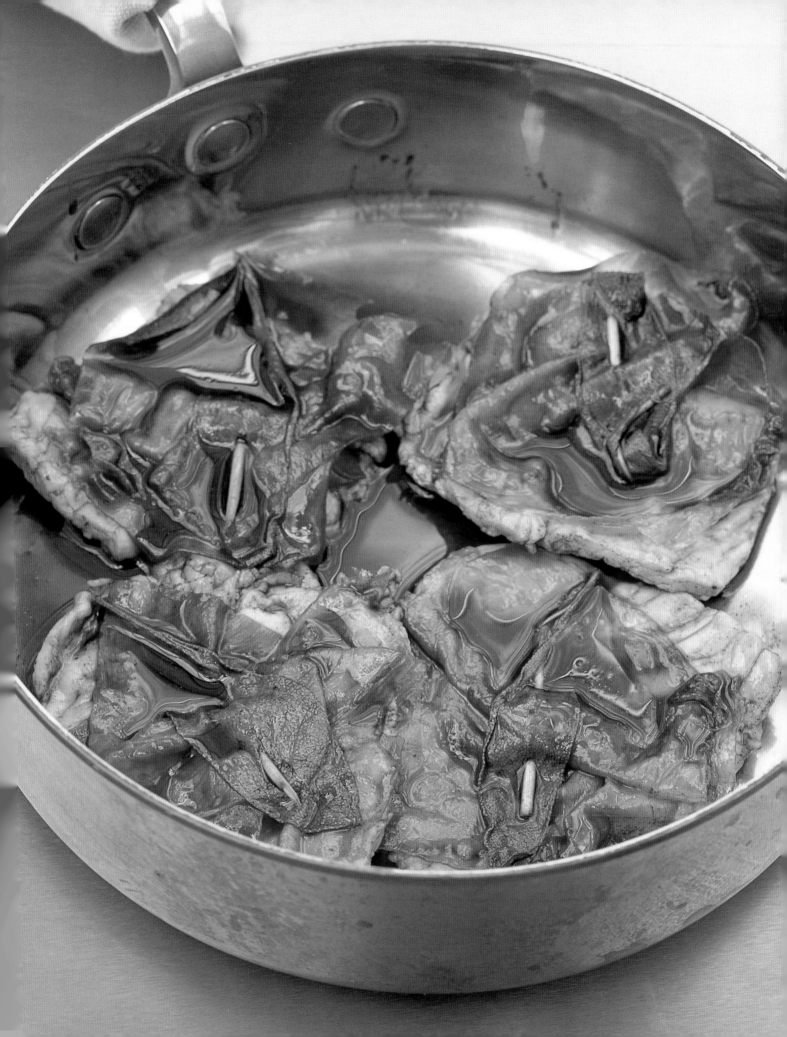

Oriental Chicken

It's hard to believe something so simple and easy can, firstly, be low-fat and secondly, taste so very good. I guarantee that once you've made this once, you'll go on making it forever.

Serves 2

4 plump free-range chicken thighs
5 fl oz (150 ml) Shaosing (Chinese brown rice wine)
3 fl oz (75 ml) Japanese soy sauce
2 fl oz (55 ml) water
1 heaped teaspoon peeled, grated fresh root ginger
4 cloves garlic, crushed
5 whole star anise
1 teaspoon toasted sesame oil

To garnish:
1 small red chilli, deseeded and cut into fine shreds
1 spring onion, cut into fine shreds

To serve:
5 fl oz (150 ml) rice, cooked

You will also need a small flameproof casserole.

Pre-heat the oven to gas mark 6, 400°F (200°C).

I'm afraid you're first going to have to remove the skin from the chicken, but because of all the lovely flavours, you won't miss it. Then place the skinned chicken thighs in the casserole. Now mix the rest of the ingredients together in a bowl and pour this mixture over the chicken, place the casserole over a medium heat and bring the liquid to the boil. Now transfer it to the oven (no need to cover) and bake on the centre shelf for 40 minutes, turning the chicken halfway through the cooking time.

Serve the cooked chicken on a bed of plain rice with the sauce poured over and the shreds of chilli and spring onion sprinkled on top.

PER SERVING
CHICKEN: 146 kcal, FAT 4.5 g, SATURATES 1.1 g, PROTEIN 22.8 g, CARBOHYDRATE 4.5 g
RICE: 287 kcal, FAT 2.7 g, SATURATES 0.7 g, PROTEIN 5.5 g, CARBOHYDRATE 64.3 g

Oriental Green Beans with Red Chillies and Toasted Sesame Seeds

This is a vegetable dish that will accompany any oriental recipe, or can be served with a bowl of rice or noodles all on its own.

First toast the sesame seeds. Place a small saucepan over a medium heat to heat through, then add the sesame seeds. Shake and keep them on the move until they have turned golden and begin to splutter – about a minute. Then remove the pan from the heat and allow it to cool. After that, add the rest of the sauce ingredients, return the pan to the heat and simmer for 5 minutes.

All this can be done well in advance, then, when you're ready to cook the beans, steam them over simmering water for about 6 minutes, or until tender, then toss them quickly in the sauce just before serving.

Serves 2, or 4 as an accompaniment
8 oz (225 g) dwarf beans (or fine green beans), topped, but tails left on

For the sauce:
1 small red chilli, deseeded and very finely chopped
1 heaped teaspoon sesame seeds
2 tablespoons Japanese soy sauce
2 tablespoons Shaosing (Chinese brown rice wine)

You will also need a steamer.

Steamed Cod with Nori and Soba Noodle Salad

This is a wonderful combination of flavours and textures – and only contains half a teaspoon of oil between two people! In the photograph, we used green tea soba noodles – buckwheat noodles made with green tea – but if you find these difficult to get, ordinary soba noodles are fine. Most of the other ingredients are readily available in all supermarkets.

Serves 2

10 oz (275 g) skinless cod fillet
2 sheets toasted nori seaweed
1 tablespoon Japanese soy sauce
1 tablespoon Thai fish sauce
2 tablespoons cold water
2 tablespoons Japanese pickled ginger, to serve

For the noodle salad:

7 oz (200 g) dried soba noodles
3 tablespoons Japanese soy sauce
3 tablespoons lime juice
½ teaspoon toasted sesame oil
about 6 sprigs watercress
a pinch salt

You will also need a Chinese bamboo steamer or a fan steamer.

First of all, cut the cod into eight equal pieces measuring about 1½ x 2 inches (4 x 5 cm), then mix these with the soy sauce, fish sauce and water in a medium-sized bowl. Now stir the cod around, cover it with clingfilm and leave it to marinate in the fridge for about an hour, stirring it around once or twice more in that time.

While the fish is marinating, make the soba noodle salad. What you do here is – as for pasta – have plenty of water boiling in a largish saucepan with a little salt added. Boil the noodles for exactly 3 minutes, then drain them in a colander and let the cold tap run on them while you lift and shake them with your hands. (They need to be cooled down quickly, otherwise the heat makes them sticky.) After that, shake off all the excess water and place the noodles in a bowl. Now whisk the soy sauce, lime juice and sesame oil together and pour this over the noodles, mixing well so they are all coated in the dressing.

Now for the fish. Towards the end of the marinating time, place the steamer over a pan of boiling water. (Pre-heating it will prevent the nori sticking.) When you're ready to cook the fish, cut each of the nori sheets into quarters, then take one of them and lay it, shiny-side down on a clean, flat surface. Now take a pastry brush, dip it into the fish marinade and brush the nori. Then place a piece of cod in the centre, First fold in two opposite sides, then brush the two remaining flaps with a little more of the marinade and wrap them over the fish, too, to form a tight parcel. (Don't worry if some of the fish is not covered.)

Then repeat this with the remaining seven pieces of fish and quarters of nori. To cook them, place all the parcels seam-side down in the steamer, put a lid on and steam them for 5 minutes. Then serve them with the noodles, garnished with the watercress, and hand the pickled ginger around separately.

After brushing the surface of the nori with the fish marinade, fold the sides around the fish to form a tight parcel.

PER SERVING: 545 kcal, FAT 8 g, SATURATES 0 g, PROTEIN 42 g, CARBOHYDRATE 81 g

Slimmers' Wild Mushroom Risotto

This is an oven-baked risotto with the deep, fragrant flavour of mushrooms. It's extremely creamy and luscious but – can you believe it? – it contains no cream, no butter and, what's more, no cheese. The secret of all this lies in one simple ingredient – low-fat evaporated milk. Hard to believe, I know, but try it and see.

First of all, give the dried mushrooms a quick rinse in a sieve under cold, running water, then place them in a heatproof bowl and pour 1 pint (570 ml) boiling water over them. Then just leave them to soak and soften for about 30 minutes. Meanwhile, chop the fresh mushrooms into chunks – not too small, about ½ inch (1 cm), as they shrink quite a bit in the cooking. Now pre-heat the oven to gas mark 2, 300°F (150°C).

Next, put the shallots and the Madeira into a medium-sized saucepan, bring it up to simmering point and simmer gently for 10-15 minutes, until the shallots have softened and the Madeira has reduced down to about 2 tablespoons. Then remove the pan from the heat, add the fresh mushrooms, stir well and then leave the pan on one side.

When the dried mushrooms have softened, line a sieve with a double layer of absorbent kitchen paper, place it over a bowl and strain them, reserving the liquid. Squeeze them to remove any excess liquid, then chop them fairly finely.

Next, put the rice into the baking dish, along with the dried and fresh mushrooms and shallots, then season well with salt and freshly milled black pepper. Now whisk the evaporated milk into the reserved mushroom-soaking liquid, pour it over the rice and give it all a good stir. Place the dish on the centre shelf of the oven without covering, set a timer and give it exactly 20 minutes.

After that, gently stir and turn over the rice grains. Put the timer on again and give it a further 20-25 minutes' cooking – when ready, the risotto should be very slightly soupy, and the longer you leave it to stand, the thicker it will get, so, immediately it is ready, remove it from the oven and serve as soon as possible.

Serves 2-3

½ oz (10 g) dried porcini mushrooms
8 oz (225 g) fresh mixed mushrooms, such as dark-gilled open-cap, chestnut or girolles
6 fl oz (175 ml) carnaroli rice (use a measuring jug)
2 shallots, peeled and finely chopped
7 fl oz (200 ml) dry Madeira
7 fl oz (200 ml) Carnation Light (evaporated semi-skimmed) milk
salt and freshly milled black pepper

You will also need a 2½ inch (6 cm) deep baking dish, with a diameter of 9 inches (23 cm).

Thai Crab Salad with Mango

This is a low-fat variation of the Thai Grilled Beef Salad with Grapes on page 384. In Thailand they serve it with pomelo, which is very similar to grapefruit. When they're not available, I use mango, but you could ring the changes with grapes or small segments of pink grapefruit.

Serves 4 as a light lunch or 6 as a starter
12 oz (350 g) each white crab meat and brown crab meat (or 2 medium-sized, ready-dressed crabs in the shell)
grated zest 1 lime (juice reserved for dressing)
3 tablespoons chopped fresh coriander
3 tablespoons chopped fresh mint

For the salad:
1 large mango, peeled and sliced into strips (see page 418)
1 teaspoon sesame seeds
4 oz (110 g) rocket leaves, stalks removed
3 stems lemon grass, ends trimmed and tough outer layer discarded, then very finely sliced
6 kaffir lime leaves (if available), rolled into a cigar shape and very finely shredded
1 teaspoon freshly snipped chives

For the dressing:
2-3 medium-sized red chillies, halved and deseeded
2 cloves garlic
1 inch (2.5 cm) piece fresh root ginger, peeled
6 sprigs fresh coriander
1 sprig fresh mint
1½ tablespoons Thai fish sauce
juice 2 limes (about 3 tablespoons)
1 teaspoon light (or dark) soft brown sugar

First pre-heat a small frying pan over a medium heat, then add the sesame seeds. Keep them on the move until they're golden and begin to splutter – about a minute. Then remove the pan from the heat and allow it to cool.

Meanwhile, make the dressing. Blend the chillies, garlic, ginger, and sprigs of coriander and mint in a food processor or blender until finely chopped, then add the fish sauce, lime juice and sugar and whiz again.

Next, put the crab meat into a bowl and pour over three-quarters of the dressing, then add the lime zest and most of the chopped coriander and mint (saving some to sprinkle over later), and toss so it's well coated.

Now put the rocket leaves into a large serving bowl, toss them in the remaining dressing and pile the crab meat on top, along with slices of mango here and there. Then sprinkle over the lemon grass, lime leaves (if using), remaining coriander and mint, chives and sesame seeds.

Pasta with Pepper Relish

The great thing about this is that, because the flavour of the peppers and garlic is so intense, the pasta honestly doesn't need any cheese.

First dry-roast the cumin seeds in the frying pan for about a minute, until they become fragrant. Now add the oil and when it's hot, stir in the peppers, garlic and chillies and turn the heat down as low as possible. Then cover and cook slowly for about 40 minutes, stirring from time to time, until the peppers are really soft.

After that, add the tomatoes and the sun-dried tomato paste to the softened peppers. Season and continue to cook, uncovered, over a highish heat, until the mixture is reduced and thickened slightly – about 5 minutes.

Next, keep the sauce warm and cook the pasta – for a minute less than the pack instructions advise. Then drain it and quickly return it to the hot pan, along with the sauce, and place it over a gentle heat. Stir, and continue to cook for about another minute, to allow the pasta to absorb the sauce. Serve straight away in hot bowls, garnished with the basil.

Serves 4

1 lb (450 g) pasta: rigatoni or spaghetti

For the relish:

1 lb (450 g) mixed red and yellow peppers (about 3 peppers in total), quartered, deseeded and cut into ¼ inch (5 mm) strips
1 rounded teaspoon cumin seeds, lightly crushed
1 dessertspoon olive oil
5 cloves garlic, chopped
2 medium-sized red chillies, deseeded and chopped
4 medium-sized ripe tomatoes, skinned (see page 585) and roughly chopped
2 tablespoons sun-dried tomato paste
4 sprigs fresh basil, to garnish
salt and freshly milled black pepper

You will also need a lidded frying pan with a 10 inch (25.5 cm) diameter.

Teriyaki Grilled Marinated Salmon with Marinated Cucumber and Sesame Salad

Serves 4

4 x 5 oz (150 g) skinless salmon fillets
½ teaspoon groundnut or other flavourless oil for greasing
a few freshly snipped chives, to garnish

For the marinade:

4 tablespoons each Japanese soy sauce, sake (Japanese rice wine) and mirin (Japanese sweet rice wine)
1 teaspoon golden caster sugar
1 tablespoon peeled, grated fresh root ginger
2 fat cloves garlic, crushed

For the salad:

1 cucumber
2 tablespoons sesame seeds
3 tablespoons Japanese soy sauce
2 teaspoons each sake, mirin and rice vinegar
1 teaspoon golden caster sugar

You will also need a large baking tray.

Like Chinese Steamed Trout (see page 594), this has a slightly higher fat content than the other Waist Watcher recipes because I'm using salmon, which works best, but it can be made with other fish, such as cod or haddock fillet, too.

To begin with, make the marinade. All you do is whisk together the soy sauce, sake, mirin, sugar, ginger and garlic. Next, place the salmon fillets in a small, shallow dish and pour the marinade over. Now cover them and leave in a cool place for two hours, turning them once, halfway through the marinating time.

To make the cucumber salad, begin by toasting the sesame seeds. Do this by pre-heating a medium-sized, heavy-based frying pan over a medium heat, then add the sesame seeds, moving them around in the pan to brown evenly. As soon as they begin to splutter and pop and turn golden, they're ready. This will take 1-2 minutes. Then remove them to a plate.

Next, cut the cucumber in half, then into quarters and then into eighths (all lengthways). Remove the seeds, then chop each piece on the diagonal into 3 inch (7.5 cm) strips and place them in a bowl.

After that, measure the soy sauce, sake, mirin, vinegar and sugar into a screw-top jar, shake them together thoroughly, then pour this mixture over the cucumber wedges and leave them to marinate for about an hour – again, giving them one good stir at half-time.

When you're ready to cook the salmon, pre-heat the grill to its highest setting for at least 10 minutes. Brush the baking tray with the oil and put it under the grill to pre-heat as well. When the grill is really hot, remove the tray, using a thick oven glove. Now take the salmon steaks out of the marinade (reserving it) and shake them slightly before placing them on to the baking tray. (They should sear and sizzle as they touch the hot metal.) Then position the tray about 3 inches (7.5 cm) from the heat source and grill them for 6 minutes exactly. I advise you to use a kitchen timer here, as the timing is pretty crucial.

Meanwhile, pour the marinade into a small pan and bring it up to simmering point, allowing it to bubble, until the mixture has reduced by about a third, or until it is syrupy. Strain this sauce through a sieve.

Serve the salmon with the sauce poured over, garnished with the chives. Sprinkle the sesame seeds over the cucumber salad and hand it round separately on a plate.

PER SERVING: 334 kcal, FAT 20.3 g, SATURATES 3.4 g, PROTEIN 32.6 g, CARBOHYDRATE 5.4 g

Grilled Venison Steaks with Red Onion, Grape and Raisin Confit

Venison steaks are very lean and tender and, so, perfect for a low-fat supper dish. A confit to serve with them is, I think, far nicer than a sauce containing lots of cream and butter. Having made the confit once, you might want to serve it again with other meats, such as lean gammon steaks or low-fat, very meaty sausages.

Begin by making the confit. You can make it at any time – even the day before. What you do is put all the ingredients together in a medium-sized saucepan, bring everything up to a very gentle simmer, then let it cook as gently as possible, without a lid, for 45-60 minutes – you'll need to give it a gentle stir from time to time – until all the liquid has reduced to a lovely sticky glaze.

When you are ready to cook the steaks, season them with freshly milled black pepper. Then pre-heat the grill to its highest setting for about 10 minutes. Brush the steaks lightly on both sides with the oil and grill them for about 4 minutes on each side if you like them medium-rare, otherwise for a little longer. Meanwhile, gently re-heat the confit. Serve the venison on warmed plates with the confit and a crisp salad.

Serves 4
4 venison steaks (each weighing about 5 oz/150 g)
2 teaspoons groundnut or other flavourless oil
a few salad leaves, to garnish
freshly milled black pepper

For the confit:
1 medium red onion, chopped, but not too small
6 oz (175 g) black grapes, halved and deseeded (no need to peel)
3 oz (75 g) raisins
10 fl oz (275 ml) red wine
2 fl oz (55 ml) red wine vinegar
1 teaspoon dark soft brown sugar

Baked Apple Meringues with Orange-Soaked Raisins

This is the perfect dessert for someone watching their waistline. I'm quite proud of the fact this tastes so sublime without any fat or sugar, but, depending on you and what you're trying to cut down on, you could use sugar instead of sweetener.

Serves 4

2 medium Bramley apples, washed and cored (no need to peel)
4 large egg whites
grated zest and juice 1 orange
4 oz (110 g) raisins
2 tablespoons granulated sweetener
a little butter for greasing

You will also need a small baking tray, lightly buttered.

Pre-heat the oven to gas mark 5, 375°F (190°C).

First mix the raisins and the orange zest and juice in a bowl and then leave them to soak for about 30 minutes.

Meanwhile, using a sharp knife, cut each apple in half horizontally, arrange the halves on the baking tray and pop them on to the centre shelf of the oven for 30 minutes. After that, slide the shelf half out, spoon the soaked raisins over each apple half and bake for another 15 minutes.

Towards the end of that time, place the egg whites into a grease-free bowl and, using an electric hand whisk, whisk them until they form soft peaks that just tip over when you lift the whisk. Then whisk in, bit by bit, all but a teaspoon of the sweetener. Now pile up the fluffy egg white on top of each baked apple, sprinkle with the remaining sweetener, and return them to the oven for another 10-15 minutes, until the egg white has just set and is tinged golden brown.

PER SERVING: 113 kcal, FAT 0.2 g, SATURATES 0 g, PROTEIN 3.7 g, CARBOHYDRATE 25.8 g

Tropical Fruit Jellies

This is a cheat's recipe. The tropical fruit juice comes freshly squeezed – in a bottle from the supermarket. And, what's more, this really beautiful dessert contains virtually no fat.

First of all, put ¼ pint (150 ml) of the tropical fruit juice into a shallow dish. Add the gelatine, pressing it down so the liquid covers it, and set it aside to soften – about 10 minutes.

Now put another ¼ pint of the fruit juice into a small saucepan and bring it up to simmering point. Then remove the pan from the heat and add the softened gelatine, squeezing it first and reserving the liquid, and begin to whisk the gelatine in until it is completely dissolved. Pour the remaining juice into a large jug, along with the lime juice and the liquid from the squeezed gelatine, add the dissolved gelatine mixture and give it all another good whisk. Then pour the whole lot into the glasses, cover, and chill for at least 3 hours or, preferably, overnight.

Just before serving, halve each passion fruit and scoop out the seeds and juice to spoon on top of the jellies – the fruit will seep down as you eat.

Serves 8

1¾ pints (1 litre) freshly squeezed tropical fruit juice
12 g leaf gelatine
6 large passion fruit
juice 4 limes

You will also need eight serving glasses with a capacity of about 6 fl oz (175 ml).

Cappuccino Cheesecakes

These are so lovely, no-one will know they're low-fat. You do need to make them the day before as they're much easier to remove from the cases if they've had a chance to become firm.

Serves 8

3½ fl oz (100 ml) freshly made hot espresso (can be made up using instant coffee powder)
6 oz (175 g) Ricotta
6 oz (175 g) cottage cheese
8 biscuits, such as low-fat chocolate-chip cookies or ginger biscuits
½ oz (10 g) powdered gelatine
2 large egg yolks
1 tablespoon granulated sweetener
5 oz (150 g) 5 per cent Greek yoghurt

For the topping:

1 large egg white
2 tablespoons 8 per cent fat fromage frais
2 teaspoons granulated sweetener
½ teaspoon cocoa powder, for dusting

You will also need sixteen muffin cases, and eight 1½ inch (4 cm) deep ramekins with a base diameter of 3 inches (7.5 cm).

First of all, put two of the muffin cases into each ramekin – we find using two gives you firmer sides. Next, put a biscuit into the base of each ramekin. Now make the filling. Sprinkle the gelatine into the espresso and whisk until it has completely dissolved.

Now put the Ricotta, cottage cheese, egg yolks and sweetener into a food processor and process for about a minute, or until smooth. Then pour in the coffee-and-gelatine mixture through a strainer and blend again until everything is thoroughly mixed and absolutely smooth.

After that, transfer the mixture to a bowl and, using a balloon whisk, whisk in the yoghurt until it's all well blended. Now carefully spoon this mixture over the biscuits in the ramekins, cover with clingfilm and chill them overnight.

When you are ready to serve the cheesecakes, remove them from the ramekins and arrange them, in their paper cases, on serving plates. (Because it looks so pretty, I like to serve them like this – the paper can be peeled away before eating.) Then whisk the egg white to soft peaks in a grease-free bowl and fold in the fromage frais and sweetener. Spoon this mixture on top of the cheesecakes and dust each with a little cocoa powder, just like a cappuccino.

Note: This recipe contains raw eggs.

PER SERVING: 130 kcal, FAT 5.8 g, SATURATES 2.9 g, PROTEIN 9.1 g, CARBOHYDRATE 10.9 g

Marmalade Soufflés

You're simply not going to believe this until you taste it – no fat, no sugar, not even any sweetener, and yet you have one of the easiest and most fragrantly lovely soufflés in the world.

First, what you need to do is have the egg whites ready in a grease-free bowl. Then place the marmalade in another, largish bowl and, using a fork, whisk it around to break up any lumps. After that, add a pinch of salt to the egg whites and, using an electric hand whisk, whisk them until they reach the stiff-peak stage. Now take a large kitchen spoon and first fold a spoonful of the egg whites into the marmalade to slacken the mixture, then quickly fold in the rest a spoonful at a time. Next, divide the mixture between the ramekins, piling it up as high as possible – it won't collapse.

Now place them on the baking tray on the centre shelf of the oven and cook them for 10-12 minutes, or until the tops are nicely browned. Serve immediately, but don't worry – they hold up extremely well.

Serves 6
6 oz (175 g) thick-cut, sugar-free orange marmalade
5 large egg whites
½ teaspoon unsalted butter for greasing
salt

You will also need six 2 inch (5 cm) deep ramekins with a base diameter of 2½ inches (6 cm) and a top diameter of 3 inches (7.5 cm), very lightly buttered; and a medium-sized baking tray.

Pre-heat the oven to gas mark 4, 350°F (180°C).

Squidgy Chocolate Cakes with Prunes in Marsala

Serves 4
½ oz (10 g) cocoa powder, plus a little extra for dusting
3 large eggs
1 tablespoon granulated sweetener
a little groundnut or other flavourless oil for greasing

For the filling:
12 ready-to-eat vanilla prunes
1½ fl oz (40 ml) Marsala
2 rounded tablespoons 8 per cent fat fromage frais
1 teaspoon granulated sweetener
1 teaspoon chocolate extract

You will also need four 1½ inch (4 cm) deep ramekins with a base measurement of 3 inches (7.5 cm), very lightly greased; and a small baking tray.

When I had dinner with a friend from New York while writing this book, he asked me how the low-fat recipes were coming along and gave me a challenge: 'If you can come up with a low-fat, low-sugar chocolate dessert that tastes really good, you'll have broken new ground.' So, here follows the ground-breaking recipe!

First of all, deal with the prunes by placing them in a small saucepan, together with the Marsala, then just bring them up to simmering point and leave to cool. Transfer them to a small, lidded plastic box and leave to soak for as long as possible, turning them now and then. (I always try to let them soak overnight.)

When you're ready to make the cakes, pre-heat the oven to gas mark 4, 350°F (180°C). Then separate the eggs, placing the yolks in a medium-sized bowl and the whites in a large, grease-free one. Next, whisk the yolks and the sweetener together quite briskly for about a minute, then sift the cocoa powder on to the yolks, whisking briefly until it's well blended in.

Now, using an electric hand whisk, whisk the egg whites to the soft-peak stage. (They need to be standing up in peaks that just nod over when you lift the whisk.)

After that, thoroughly stir a tablespoon of the egg white into the chocolate mixture, then quickly but carefully fold in the rest. Divide the mixture between the ramekins – it will pile up quite high – then place them on the baking tray and bake them for 12-15 minutes, or until they feel springy but still a bit wobbly to the touch. Remove them from the oven, and don't be alarmed to see them shrink because that's quite normal. When they're cool enough to handle, slide a small palette knife around the edges and turn out first on to the palm of your hand, then right-side up on to a cooling rack.

While they're cooling, make the filling. Drain the prunes, reserving the liquid. Next, measure the fromage frais into a bowl, together with the sweetener and chocolate extract, then add the prune-soaking liquid and whisk everything together. Now transfer the prunes to a board, reserving four of them for the tops of the cakes, and roughly chop the rest, before folding them into the fromage-frais mixture.

Finally, slice the chocolate cakes in half horizontally, fill with the prune mixture and sandwich the two halves together again. Pop a whole prune on top of each one and dust lightly with cocoa powder before serving.

Note: If you want to make these in advance, you can cover them loosely with clingfilm and store in the fridge until needed.

PER SERVING: 155 kcal, FAT 6.2 g , SATURATES 1.9 g, PROTEIN 9.5 g, CARBOHYDRATE 14 g

26
Pâtés and starters

In our modern vocabulary, the rather old-fashioned word 'hors-d'oeuvre' has been replaced by another – starter. But there is another word for both, and that is appetiser – something that arouses the appetite. I think this is the best description of what a first course should be: something that begins to draw you into the fullest pleasure of eating.

So often, and particularly on holiday, I have groaned about how I'm ever going to face dinner after I've had a rather splendid lunch. Then, when I start to eat the first course, suddenly it's as if the brain has switched back into eating mode, and I end up eating more than anyone!

When I'm cooking, I always choose the first course carefully, and my advice to beginners is to keep it very simple indeed. A rich, over-elaborate starter can have the opposite effect: instead of arousing the appetite, it can kill it completely. I was recently served a first course of quail with a very rich stuffing, sitting on a croûte of fatty bread, with nothing, bland or sharp, to eke out the richness. Although I only ate half of it, I simply didn't want to eat anything after, apart from plain bread!

How to keep it simple

Don't be afraid, is the answer. We can sometimes be dazzled by the grandiose, aspirational cooking we encounter in all areas of the media. But we mustn't be deflected from grasping the virtues of simplicity. If you find some soft, ripe, buttery avocados, make a really good vinaigrette and serve them with some crusty bread and you have a simply beautiful starter.

The same applies to another great first course that's gone missing from most modern menus – in early summer, a plain, boiled globe artichoke (see page 627), from which you strip the leaves and dip the fleshy parts in vinaigrette, savouring all the flavour, until you finally reach the prized part at the end: the heart. Or, at the same time of year, what could possibly be better than English asparagus, simply steamed and served with Foaming Hollandaise (see page 626)?

In the autumn, when tomatoes are ripe and full of fragrance, a plain tomato salad garnished with fresh basil leaves and the fruitiest olive oil you can find, plus bread to soak up all the sweet juices, makes an outstanding start to a meal (and why not serve a few slices of buffalo Mozzarella with them as well?). I know a pub in Norfolk that serves old-fashioned, half-pint tankards filled with fresh-boiled prawns, which you peel yourself, dip into mayonnaise and eat with brown bread and butter. Heaven. And just think of fragrant, juicy melons with slices of Serrano or Parma ham, or, in late autumn, with some fat, squidgy figs…

Smoked fish

Now farmers' markets are springing up all round the country, search them for some good smoked fish, which always makes a fine start to a meal. For me, the best of all are fillets of smoked eel, moist and vivid, served with a sharp horseradish sauce. Smoked wild salmon is a real luxury, but less expensive – and still a treat – are smoked trout and mackerel.

Eggs and salads

I have to confess, my most favourite starter of all is Eggs Mayonnaise (see page 630): boiled eggs with creamy centres and a home-made garlic mayonnaise that stands proud and wobbles, garnished with a few sliced cornichons (baby gherkins) and small black olives. Eggs en Cocotte (see pages 37 and 595) taste indulgent but are really simple to prepare. So are salads: in summer, perhaps Salade Niçoise (see page 383), and in winter, Tunisian Aubergine Salad (see page 358) or White Bean and Tuna Fish Salad (see page 378), or Hummus (see page 542).

Soups

'A meal without soup is like a palace without a portico' wrote the famous French chef Carême. I wouldn't go quite that far, but a soup certainly makes a fine entrance to a meal and I have included several of my best-loved ones here: Carrot and Artichoke (see page 514), Ajo Blanco (see page 515), The London Particular (see page 546) and Tuscan Bean and Pasta (see page 548). They are all winners, and now that we can buy ready-made stocks and Marigold Swiss vegetable bouillon powder, soupmaking has become so much easier.

Pâtés

In France, pâtés and terrines are a great tradition and regularly served at the beginning of a meal. At one of my favourite restaurants, the Auberge de la Mole in Provence, their splendid meals invariably begin with four lovely, lived-in earthenware or porcelain terrines, each filled with a different variation, a tall jar of cornichons and pickles, complete with tongs to help yourself, and chunks of char-grilled country bread.

Provided the main course is not too heavy, pâtés are perfect for a first course; they're a real blessing when you have a house full of people wanting snacks; or they can be served for lunch, with cheese to follow.

While the French have their pâtés and terrines, we in England have our own tradition of potted meats, fish, game and even cheese. I would love to see a revival of these, so have included my special English Potted Crab (see page 620), a very popular starter in our restaurant at Norwich City Football Club, where we are sometimes having to make enough for 400!

Friends come first

Just to sum up: what I'm offering here is a selection of first courses that are easy to prepare ahead. In fact, the most important aspect of a meal is the relaxed sharing of time with family or friends, and if the food dominates and distracts the host all the time, it's not going to be half as pleasurable. Everything here will taste really good, but will involve you in the minimum amount of last-minute fuss and bother.

Coarse
Country Pâté

If you long to eat some of the rough country pâté available all over France but in short supply here, why not make some? You won't believe how blissfully easy it is, and using a food processor instead of buying the meat ready-minced makes it coarser and chunkier. Serve it for lunch with a side salad or watercress, some crisp cornichons (baby gherkins) and char-grilled or toasted country bread, and, if you close your eyes, you're in France!

Serves 10-12

12 oz (350 g) boned shoulder of
British veal
1 lb (450 g) streaky pork slices, with
as much fat as possible
10 oz (275 g) dry-cured, smoked
streaky bacon
8 oz (225 g) pork liver
20 juniper berries, plus a few extra
to garnish
20 black peppercorns
¼ rounded teaspoon ground mace
2 fat cloves garlic, crushed
1 heaped teaspoon chopped fresh thyme
4 fl oz (120 ml) dry white wine
1 fl oz (25 ml) brandy
a few fresh bay leaves, to garnish
1 heaped teaspoon salt

You will also need an oval or
rectangular terrine with a capacity of
1.75 litres/3 pints (or a 900 g/2 lb
loaf tin).

You'll find it's best to process the meat one type at a time (finishing with the pork liver, as it is the messiest). Begin by cutting the meat into rough pieces, then place them in the food processor and process until quite finely chopped.

Next, tip each meat in turn into a large mixing bowl and mix them together very thoroughly. Then coarsely crush first the juniper berries and then the peppercorns with a pestle and mortar and add these to the meat, along with the salt, mace, garlic and thyme. Now you need to mix again even more thoroughly to distribute all the flavours evenly. After that, add the wine and brandy and give it a final mix, then cover the bowl with a clean tea cloth and leave it in a cool place for a couple of hours to allow the flavours to be absorbed.

Now pre-heat the oven to gas mark 2, 300°F (150°C). Then pack the mixture into the terrine (or loaf tin) and decorate the top with the bay leaves and the extra juniper berries. Place the terrine (or tin) in a roasting tin, half filled with hot water, on the centre shelf of the oven and leave it there for about 1¾ hours.

By the time it has cooked, the pâté will have shrunk quite a bit. Remove it from the oven and allow it to cool without draining off any of the surrounding juices; once the pâté has cooled, the surrounding fat and jelly will keep it beautifully moist.

When the pâté is cold, place a double strip of kitchen foil across the top and put a few scale weights on to press it down for at least a few hours – this pressing isn't essential, but it helps to make the pâté less crumbly if you want to serve it in slices. If you don't have weights, use any heavy object: a brick, a tin of food, or any other innovation you can think of. If you don't weight it, you can serve it in chunks rather than slices. Place the pâté, weights and all, into the fridge overnight.

To serve the pâté, you need to take it out of the fridge at least 30 minutes ahead to return it to room temperature, then turn it out of the terrine (or tin), remove the surrounding jelly and any fat and cut into slices.

Note: You can use raw, minced pork or veal, if this is available, but don't be tempted to buy lean meat – the presence of fat is essential.

What happens is that as it cooks it dissolves and surrounds the pâté, and although you won't be eating it, its presence is essential for keeping the pâté moist.

To char-grill bread, pre-heat a cast-iron ridged griddle for about 10 minutes so it is really hot. Cut the bread into fairly thick slices, then lay them on the griddle. Turn them over when they have dark stripes (after about 40 seconds, if the pan is really hot) and repeat on the other side.

Coarse Country Pâté baked in a terrine, left; to make the pâté, it is best to buy the meat in a piece, to chop in a food processor, above.

English Potted Crab

It's sometimes a real treat to take a break from modern, global cooking and return to something purely and simply British or, in this case, English. For centuries in this country there has been a great tradition of potting meat, fish, game and even cheese, and the results could hold their own among any collection of Continental pâtés and terrines. This particular recipe for potted Cromer crab is adapted from one given to me by one of my favourite chefs of all time, Michael Quinn. It's brilliant as a first course for a summer meal for six people, but two or three could easily polish off the whole lot for lunch. Either way, I like to serve it with toasted Irish soda bread, and mustard and cress.

Serves 6 as a starter or 2-3 for lunch
5 oz (150 g) each white crab meat
and brown crab meat (or you can use
2 dressed Cromer crabs instead)
1 oz (25 g) shallots (about 1 medium
shallot), peeled and finely chopped
2 tablespoons manzanilla sherry
a good pinch each cayenne pepper,
ground mace, freshly grated nutmeg
5 oz (150 g) unsalted butter, cut into
small cubes
1½ teaspoons anchovy essence
1 teaspoon lemon juice, plus extra
if needed
1 large lemon, cut into wedges,
to serve
salt and freshly milled black pepper

You will also need six 1¼ inch (3 cm)
deep ramekins with a base diameter
of 2¼ inches (5.5 cm), or one
larger dish.

Begin by placing the shallots, sherry and spices in a small saucepan. Bring the whole lot up to simmering point, then boil quite briskly until the liquid has reduced to about a generous dessertspoon – it should only take 1-2 minutes.

Next, stir in the cubes of butter and, when they are melted, turn the heat down to very low and let it all simmer as gently as possible for 15 minutes, giving it a stir from time to time. After that, remove it from the heat and leave it to cool for about half an hour.

Towards the end of that time, you'll need to assemble a nylon sieve over a bowl, and another, larger bowl filled with ice cubes and a little cold water. Then pour the spicy butter through the sieve and press well to extract all the juice from the shallots. Now set the bowl over the iced water and, using an electric hand whisk, whisk until the butter becomes thick and creamy without becoming hard.

Next, mix in the crab meat, anchovy essence, teaspoon of lemon juice and a really good seasoning of salt and freshly milled black pepper. Taste and check the seasoning – you might like to add a little extra lemon juice. Then spoon the mixture into the ramekins or the larger dish. Cover with clingfilm and chill for 3 hours.

Remove the potted crab from the fridge about half an hour before serving and serve with the lemon wedges.

Note: If you want to make this a day or so ahead, cover the surface with melted butter to seal off the air. To do this, melt 2 oz (50 g) of butter and divide it between the ramekins, pouring a bit over the potted crab in each one, or pour it all over the potted crab in the larger dish.

Smoked Mackerel Pâté with Ricotta and Capers

This is quite simply the easiest pâté I've ever made. All the ingredients are placed together in the food processor and, with one little whiz, it's made! It also has an utterly sublime flavour – brilliant! Serve it with hot, toasted wholemeal bread.

First you need to skin the mackerel fillets, which is no trouble, as the flesh can be lifted away very easily. Next, place the fish into the bowl of a food processor, then add the Ricotta, soured cream, lemon juice, some freshly grated nutmeg and a good seasoning of salt and freshly milled black pepper. Then switch on and blend until completely smooth, stopping the motor to scrape the mixture down the sides of the bowl halfway through. Now taste and add a spot more lemon juice or seasoning, if you think it needs it, then pack the mixture into the ramekins or the larger dish, cover with clingfilm and chill for several hours before serving.

Lastly, place about half a teaspoon of the capers in the centre of each ramekin (or the whole tablespoonful in the middle of the larger dish), sprinkle with a pinch of cayenne pepper and serve with the lemon wedges.

Serves 8 as a starter or 3-4 for lunch
3-4 smoked mackerel fillets (weighing about 10 oz/275 g in total)
4 oz (110 g) Ricotta
5 fl oz (150 ml) soured cream
juice ½ large lemon, plus extra if needed
whole nutmeg
salt and freshly milled black pepper

To garnish:
1 heaped tablespoon miniature capers (nonpareilles)
cayenne pepper
1 large lemon, cut into wedges

You will also need eight 1¼ inch (3 cm) deep ramekins with a base diameter of 2¼ inches (5.5 cm), or one larger dish.

Chicken Liver Pâté with Cognac, with Sweet-and-Sour Red Onion Salad

This is smooth and velvety and also works well with duck livers, if you can get them. The salad helps to cut through the richness. I like to serve this with toasted multi-grain bread.

To make the pâté, take a medium-sized, heavy-based frying pan, melt about 1 oz (25 g) of the butter in it and fry the chicken livers over a medium heat for about 5 minutes. Keep them on the move, turning them over quite frequently. Then remove them from the pan using a draining spoon and transfer them to a blender or food processor.

Now, in the same pan, gently melt 5 oz (150 g) of the remaining butter and add this to the blender or food processor. Then pour the Cognac on to the juices left in the frying pan (to capture all the lovely flavours), and pour that over the livers. Now add the mustard, mace, thyme and garlic, season well with salt and freshly milled black pepper, and blend until you have a smooth, velvety purée.

Next, divide the mixture between the ramekins (or pots). Then melt the remaining 2 oz (50 g) of butter, pour a little over each one to seal, press in a sprig of thyme, and leave them to get quite cold. Cover with clingfilm and leave them in the fridge till needed.

To make the red-onion salad, all you do is heat the oil in a medium-sized saucepan, add the onions, turn the heat down to low and let them cook gently for 5 minutes, stirring now and then. Next, add the sugar and water, stir well, then pop a lid on and let it continue cooking gently for another 10 minutes. After that, add the vinegar, mustard and some salt and freshly milled black pepper, and give everything another really good stir. Then spoon the onions into a serving bowl and cool until needed.

Don't forget to remove the chicken liver pâtés from the fridge about an hour before serving, as both the pâté and the salad need to be served at room temperature.

Serves 6
8 oz (225 g) chicken livers, rinsed and trimmed
2 tablespoons Cognac
8 oz (225 g) butter
2 teaspoons dry mustard powder
¼ teaspoon ground mace
1 teaspoon chopped fresh thyme, plus 6 small sprigs to garnish
2 cloves garlic, crushed
salt and freshly milled black pepper

For the salad:
3 medium red onions, peeled and cut into 8 wedges through the root
3 tablespoons olive oil
1 heaped teaspoon light soft brown sugar
3 tablespoons water
3 tablespoons red wine vinegar
¾ tablespoon wholegrain mustard
salt and freshly milled black pepper

You will also need six 1¼ inch (3 cm) deep ramekins with a base diameter of 2¼ inches (5.5 cm) (or six similar-sized pots).

Souffléd Sole Creams with Champagne Sauce and Salmon Caviar

Serves 6

8 oz (225 g) boneless, skinless lemon sole fillets
2 oz (50 g) jar salmon caviar
whole nutmeg
2 large eggs, lightly beaten
10 fl oz (275 ml) double cream
a little butter for greasing
salt and freshly milled black pepper

For the sauce:

6 fl oz (175 ml) Champagne
¾ oz (20 g) butter
1 large shallot, peeled and finely chopped
¾ oz (20 g) plain flour
5 fl oz (150 ml) double cream
6 sprigs fresh chervil, to garnish
salt and freshly milled black pepper

You will also need six 1½ inch (4 cm) deep ramekins with a base diameter of 3 inches (7.5 cm), well buttered; and a shallow roasting tin measuring 10 x 14 inches (25.5 x 35 cm).

This recipe is blissfully easy and all of it can be prepared in advance. In fact, I find it works best if you prepare the purée the day before. Dry white wine can be used instead of Champagne, but if you place an upturned teaspoon in the bottle of Champagne, it will keep its fizz stored in the fridge till your guests arrive.

Begin by cutting the lemon sole into pieces about 1½ inches (4 cm) square and placing them in a blender or food processor, along with the lightly beaten eggs, some freshly grated nutmeg and a little salt and freshly milled black pepper. Now blend until the mixture has turned to a smooth, even purée. Then transfer it to a bowl, cover with clingfilm and leave it in the fridge for at least 6 hours or, preferably, overnight.

When you're ready to cook the fish creams, pre-heat the oven to gas mark 5, 375°F (190°C). Fill the roasting tin with about an inch (2.5 cm) of boiling water and place it on the centre shelf of the oven.

Next, make up the sauce. Melt the butter in a medium-sized saucepan and cook the shallot in it over a gentle heat for 5-6 minutes, until softened and golden, but not browned. After that, add the flour to the buttery shallot juices, stir it in and cook for 1-2 minutes more. Now gradually add the Champagne to the pan, a little at a time, then blend in the double cream, whisking until the sauce is smooth. Let it come up to simmering point and cook for a further 1-2 minutes, then taste and add some seasoning. (The shallot can be strained out, if you like.) Now transfer the sauce to a heatproof bowl set over a pan of barely simmering water to keep warm, without letting the bottom of the bowl touch the water.

About 40 minutes before your guests sit down to eat, return the fish mixture to the blender or food processor, together with the cream, and blend them together thoroughly. Then fill each ramekin three-quarters full with the mixture, place all the ramekins in the tin containing the hot water and cook for exactly 30 minutes.

When the time is up, you need to turn out the creams on to warmed serving plates. Do this by holding each ramekin with a cloth, sliding a small palette knife round the edge and tipping the creams very briefly upside down on to the palm of your hand (they will very hot), then straight on to a plate, the right way up.

Serve as soon as possible, with a little of the sauce spooned over, a teaspoon of salmon caviar on top and garnish with chervil. Hand the rest of the sauce around separately in a warmed jug.

Souffléd Arbroath Smokies in Smoked Salmon with Foaming Hollandaise

This is another version of Sole Creams on page 624 – a very old favourite that never fails to delight. It's easy, can be prepared in advance and fulfils all the criteria of a really good first course.

Serves 8

12 oz (350 g) Arbroath smokies, skin and bone intact
8 oz (225 g) sliced smoked salmon
¼ whole nutmeg
2 large eggs, lightly beaten
10 fl oz (275 ml) double cream
8 sprigs watercress, to garnish
salt and freshly milled black pepper

For the foaming hollandaise:
2 large eggs, separated
1 dessertspoon lemon juice
1 dessertspoon white wine vinegar
4 oz (110 g) butter
salt and freshly milled black pepper

You will also need eight 1½ inch (4 cm) deep ramekins with a base diameter of 3 inches (7.5 cm), well buttered, and a large roasting tin.

Begin by carefully skinning the Arbroath smokies – you'll find the flesh will part very easily from the bones. (You should have about 8-10 oz/ 225-275 g of flesh after this.) Flake the fish and place it in a blender or food processor, along with a little salt, freshly milled black pepper and a good grating of nutmeg. Blend until the fish has turned to a smooth, even pulp, then blend in the lightly beaten eggs. Transfer the mixture to a bowl, cover it with clingfilm and leave it in the fridge for at least 6 hours or, preferably, overnight.

After that, pre-heat the oven to gas mark 5, 375°F (190°C). Fill the roasting tin with about an inch (2.5 cm) of boiling water and put this on to the centre shelf of the oven.

Next, return the fish mixture to the blender or food processor, together with the cream, and blend them together thoroughly. Now line the base and sides of each ramekin with smoked salmon – don't worry that you're doing this in pieces and patches as it won't show when they're finally turned out. Fill each ramekin three-quarters full with the fish mixture, then place them in the roasting tin. Cook for exactly 30 minutes.

Meanwhile, make the Foaming Hollandaise. Place the egg yolks into a food processor or blender and season with salt and freshly milled black pepper. Blend together for one minute. Now heat the lemon juice and vinegar in a small saucepan until they start to bubble and simmer. With the food processor or blender running, slowly pour the hot liquid on to the egg yolks in a steady stream, then switch off the machine.

Next, gently melt the butter in the same saucepan and when foaming, with the food processor or blender running again, pour in the butter in a thin, steady, slow trickle. When it is all blended, use a spatula to scrape down any that remains on the sides. Give the sauce one more quick pulse before transferring to a roomy bowl. In another, grease-free bowl, whisk the egg whites to soft peaks and fold them into the sauce. The sauce can be kept warm over a saucepan of simmering water, but make sure the base of the bowl does not touch the water.

Serve the fish creams as soon as possible, either in the ramekins or turned out on to plates, which looks attractive. Do this by holding each ramekin with a cloth, sliding a small palette knife round the edge and tipping the creams upside down very briefly on to the palm of your hand (they will be very hot) then straight on to a plate the right way up. Pour over the sauce and garnish with a sprig of watercress.

Note: This recipe contains raw eggs.

Globe Artichokes with Shallot Vinaigrette

An artichoke is, without doubt, a work of art – dark and pale green leaves with purple edges forming a perfectly shaped bud. There's something extremely satisfying about leisurely peeling off the leaves, dipping them into vinaigrette and biting into the fleshy part at the base of each leaf. Then, of course, the prize – the heart at the very centre, providing a kind of grand finale to the whole affair.

First prepare the artichokes. Remove about four of the toughest outer leaves, then place the artichoke at the edge of a table so that the stalk overhangs the edge. Grasp the artichoke and snap away the stalk, removing some of the tough fibres running up into the base. Now with a large serrated knife, carefully slice off the top quarter of each artichoke and discard. Then, with a pair of scissors, trim away the tips of all the leaves.

Don't boil artichokes in iron or aluminium pans as this can discolour them. Have your chosen large pan ready filled with salted, boiling water, with the tablespoon of lemon juice (or white wine vinegar) added. Simmer the artichokes, uncovered, for 30-40 minutes, or until one of the outer leaves pulls away easily and the bases feel tender when tested with a skewer. Then drain upside down, shaking them to get rid of excess water.

Now remove the hairy 'choke': carefully spread the leaves until you come to the central cone of thinner, lightly-coloured leaves – pull these out and underneath you'll find the choke. Pull it out in clumps – it will come away very easily.

Finally, make up the vinaigrette. Begin by crushing the salt quite coarsely in a mortar, then add the garlic. As it comes into contact with the salt, it will break down into a purée. Next, add the mustard powder and work it in with circular movements. After that, add some freshly milled black pepper. Now work in the vinegar in the same way. Then add the shallot and the oil, switch to a small whisk and whisk thoroughly.

Serve the vinaigrette in a bowl to dip the artichoke leaves into, and on the table, have a finger bowl, napkins, a separate plate for the discarded leaves, and a knife and fork each to eat the heart – wonderful!

Serves 2
2 large globe artichokes (each weighing about 14 oz/400 g)
1 tablespoon lemon juice (or white wine vinegar)

For the vinaigrette:
1 shallot, peeled and finely chopped
1 clove garlic
1 rounded teaspoon mustard powder
1 tablespoon good-quality red wine vinegar
5 tablespoons extra virgin olive oil
1 rounded teaspoon sea salt

Roasted Red Pepper and Tomato Tart

In the summer, one of my favourite starters is Piedmont Roasted Peppers (from the Summer Collection*). What I have done here is try to capture all those brilliant flavours and make them into a warm tart more suitable for a winter starter.*

Serves 8
For the pastry:
4 oz (110 g) plain flour
1½ oz (40 g) softened butter, cut
into smallish lumps
½ oz (10 g) softened lard, cut
into smallish lumps
½ oz (10 g) Parmesan (Parmigiano
Reggiano), finely grated
1 teaspoon chopped fresh thyme
a little cold water
a pinch of salt

For the filling:
4 medium red peppers
12 oz (350 g) ripe, red tomatoes
2 tablespoons olive oil
1 large clove garlic, chopped
2 oz (50 g) anchovy fillets in oil
1 tablespoon tomato purée
1 teaspoon finely chopped fresh thyme
2 large eggs and 2 large egg yolks
1 teaspoon sweet pimentón (smoked
paprika)
salt and freshly milled black pepper

You will also need a 9 inch (23 cm)
loose-bottomed, fluted tart tin, 1 inch
(2.5 cm) deep; and two baking trays
measuring 11 x 16 inches (28 x 40 cm).

Pre-heat the oven to gas mark 4,
350°F (180°C).

Begin by preparing the filling. First skin the tomatoes. To do this, place them in a heatproof bowl and pour boiling water on to them. Leave them for exactly a minute (or 15-30 seconds, if the tomatoes are small), then remove them, slip off their skins (protecting your hands with a cloth if they are hot) and cut them in half.

Next, prepare the peppers. Halve them, then remove the seeds and slice each half into three strips. Place the peppers and tomato halves in a bowl and add a tablespoon of the oil, the garlic and some seasoning (going easy on the salt because of the anchovies). Give it all a good mix, then spread everything out on one of the baking trays and roast in the top part of the oven for about 50 minutes.

Now make the pastry. Sift the flour and salt into a large mixing bowl, first cutting in the fats with a palette knife and then rubbing lightly with your fingertips, lifting everything up and letting it fall back into the bowl to give it a good airing. When the mixture reaches the crumb stage, sprinkle in the Parmesan and thyme. Then sprinkle in a tablespoon of cold water to bring it together to a smooth dough that leaves the side of the bowl absolutely clean, with no crumbs left, adding a few more drops, if needed. Place the pastry in a plastic food bag in the fridge to rest for 30 minutes. Meanwhile, pre-heat the second baking tray.

Next, transfer the pastry to a flat, lightly floured surface, roll it out to a circle and line the tin with it. Now prick the base with a fork (to prevent it rising) and brush it with a little of the egg for the filling. Bake the tart base on the pre-heated baking tray, at the same temperature as the peppers and tomatoes, for about 20 minutes, or until lightly golden.

Allow the peppers and tomatoes to cool before placing them in a food processor or blender, along with the anchovy fillets and all their oil. Next, add the tomato purée and thyme and blend until everything is reduced to a thick, smooth mixture. Then, in a large bowl, whisk the eggs and yolks together, along with the pimentón, then stir in the pepper-and-tomato mixture and the other tablespoon of olive oil.

When the tart base is cooked, turn the oven temperature up to gas mark 5, 375°F (190°C), then spoon the mixture into it and bake in the oven on the centre shelf for 35 minutes, or until it is firm and set in the centre. Leave the tart to rest for about 10 minutes before serving.

Eggs Mayonnaise

Serves 6
9 large eggs
18 medium cornichons (baby gherkins),
sliced lengthways
about 18 small black olives

For the mayonnaise:
2 large egg yolks
1 clove garlic, crushed
1 heaped teaspoon mustard powder
10 fl oz (275 ml) groundnut or other
flavourless oil
1 teaspoon white wine vinegar
freshly milled black pepper
1 teaspoon salt

Not the kind you get in help-yourself salad bars and cafés – this is the real thing. Eggs, boiled – not hard, but with a bit of squidge at the centre – anointed with a shimmering, golden emulsion laced with a little garlic. I have to admit, this is probably my most favourite starter. I like to serve it with sliced cornichons or pickled cucumbers and tiny black Provençal olives.

First, place a medium-sized mixing bowl on a damp tea cloth so it will remain steady and leave you both hands free to make the mayonnaise – one to drip the oil, the other to hold an electric hand whisk.

Next, measure out the oil into a jug. Now put the egg yolks into the bowl, adding the garlic, mustard powder, salt and a little freshly milled black pepper and mix all of these together well. Then, holding the jug of oil in one hand and the whisk in the other, add just a drop of oil to the egg mixture and whisk this in. However stupid it may sound, the key to a successful mayonnaise is making sure each drop of oil is thoroughly whisked in before adding the next drop. It won't take all day, because after a few minutes – once you've added several drops of oil – the mixture will begin to thicken and go very stiff and lumpy. When it gets to this stage, you need to add the vinegar, which will thin it.

Now the critical point has passed, you can begin pouring in the oil in large drops, keeping the whisk going all the time. When all the oil has been added, taste and add more salt and freshly milled black pepper, if it needs it. If you'd like the mayonnaise to be a bit lighter, add 2 tablespoons of boiling water and whisk it in.

Mayonnaise only curdles when you add the oil too quickly at the beginning. If that happens, don't despair. All you need to do is put a fresh egg yolk into a clean basin, add the curdled mixture to it drop by drop, then continue adding the rest of the oil as though nothing had happened.

Now place the eggs in a pan in cold water. Bring them up to the boil and boil for 6 minutes, then cool them rapidly under cold, running water and leave them in the cold water for about 2 minutes. Next, remove them from the water, peel off the shells, cover the eggs with clingfilm, and leave them in a cool place until needed.

Now cut the eggs in half, arranging three halves on each plate, top with a heaped tablespoon of the mayonnaise and garnish with the cornichons and olives.

Any leftover mayonnaise should be stored in a screw-top jar in the fridge, but for no longer than a week.

Note: You could also serve this with a couple of anchovies per person draped over the mayonnaise in a criss-cross pattern.

As well as being a brilliant starter, this can also be made into bite-sized canapés to serve with drinks, if you stamp out small rounds and distribute the toppings in small portions.

First of all, make the polenta. To do this, pour 1 pint (570 ml) boiling water from the kettle into a large saucepan and allow it to come back to simmering point. Then add the polenta in a long, steady stream, along with half a teaspoon of salt, stirring all the time with a wooden spoon. Place the pan on a low heat and allow the polenta to cook for 5 minutes, continuing to stir, until thickened – it should look like yellow porridge.

As soon as the polenta is ready, season it generously with freshly milled black pepper, then stir in the Parmesan and butter. Taste to check the seasoning and add more salt and pepper, if necessary. Then, as quickly as you can, spoon the polenta into the lined baking tin, smooth the top with a palette knife and allow it to get quite cold.

When the polenta is cold, lift it out of the tin, cut it out into six circles with the cutter and place these on the baking tray. Next, pre-heat the grill to its highest setting for 10 minutes. Measure the olive oil into a saucer and brush each piece of polenta with some of it, then season generously again with salt and freshly milled black pepper. Now place the baking tray under the grill, about 4 inches (10 cm) below the heat source. Grill the polenta for 3 minutes on each side until it becomes golden and toasted at the edges, then remove it from the grill.

Next, loosely fold the pieces of ham and place one on top of each polenta round. Then arrange a slice of cheese on top of the ham and, finally, dip the sage leaves into the remaining olive oil and lay two on top of the cheese on each one. All this can be done in advance if you allow the grilled polenta to get cold before you put the topping on.

When you are ready to serve the polenta, put them back under a hot grill for another 3-4 minutes, or until the cheese has melted and the sage leaves are crisp. Serve with warm ciabatta bread and extra virgin olive oil to dip the bread into.

Serves 6
4 fl oz (120 ml) easy-cook polenta
1 oz (25 g) Parmesan (Parmigiano Reggiano), finely grated
1 oz (25 g) softened butter
salt and freshly milled black pepper

For the topping:
3¼ oz (85 g) Parma ham (about 6 slices)
3 oz (75 g) Fontina (or Gruyère), cut into 6 slices
12 small fresh sage leaves
2 tablespoons olive oil
salt and freshly milled black pepper

You will also need a baking tin measuring 6 x 10 inches (15 x 25.5 cm), 1 inch (2.5 cm) deep, lined with silicone paper (parchment); a 3 inch (7.5 cm) pastry cutter; and a small baking tray, lightly oiled.

Char-grilled Squid with Chilli Jam

One of my favourite Norfolk chefs is Alison Yetman, who has kindly given me the recipe for this brilliant starter.

Serves 4

1 lb (450 g) small squid (cleaned weight)
1 dessertspoon groundnut or other flavourless oil
salt and freshly milled black pepper
rocket leaves, to serve

For the chilli jam:

1½ medium-sized red chillies, deseeded and roughly chopped
1 lb (450 g) very ripe tomatoes
2 cloves garlic, roughly chopped
1 inch (2.5 cm) piece fresh root ginger, peeled and roughly chopped
1 tablespoon Thai fish sauce
8 oz (225 g) demerara sugar
2 fl oz (55 ml) red wine vinegar
1 tablespoon balsamic vinegar

You will also need a cast-iron ridged griddle; and a 1 lb (350 ml capacity) jar, sterilised (see page 561).

Firstly, make the chilli jam. This can be done well in advance. First of all, you need to roughly chop the tomatoes. (You can leave on their skins.) Then put half of them into a blender, along with the chillies, garlic, ginger and fish sauce, whiz everything to a fine purée and pour the mixture into a large saucepan. Now pulse the remaining tomatoes in the blender until just chopped, but this time not puréed. Add these to the purée in the saucepan, along with the sugar and vinegars, and slowly bring the mixture up to boiling point, stirring all the time.

When the mixture reaches the boil, turn the heat down to a gentle simmer. Skim off any foam from the surface and cook gently, uncovered, for 30-40 minutes, stirring every 5 minutes to prevent the chopped tomato settling at the bottom. You will also need to scrape down the sides of the pan during the cooking so that everything cooks evenly. The mixture should reduce to half its volume. Now pour it into the hot, sterilised jar, allow it to cool and then cover and store it in the fridge. (You will need about a third of the chilli jam for this recipe.)

Next, pre-heat the griddle over a high heat. Meanwhile, prepare the squid. Slit it on one side and open it out to give two flaps (retaining the tentacles). Pat dry with kitchen paper. (It's important that you dry the squid properly, otherwise it will stew in the pan, rather than fry.) Now, using a small sharp knife, lightly score it on the inside – if you score it on the outside, it won't curl properly. Score diagonally in one direction, then do the same in the other direction, to give little diamond shapes, taking great care not to cut right through the squid.

When the pan is searing hot, lightly brush the squid and the tentacles on both sides with the oil, then season with salt and freshly milled black pepper. Only season the squid the moment it goes into the pan – if you do it in advance, the salt will draw out all the moisture. Now add the squid and tentacles in batches to the hot pan and cook for 1-2 minutes, turning halfway through, until lightly charred. (Be warned – the tentacles will look as though they're coming alive!) Use tongs to transfer the first batch to a warmed plate while you cook the rest. Serve warm or cold on a bed of rocket leaves, with the chilli jam drizzled over.

Note: The chilli jam will keep in the fridge for up to 3 months, and is also wonderful with sausages.

27

Hot puddings

Young cooks of Britain, I have a question to ask you. Are you aware of our unmatched reputation – dating back to the 17th century – for making and serving a multitude of baked, boiled and steamed puddings? Our history of pudding-making is a joyous tradition of marrying and blending simple ingredients into a unique miscellany of tastes, textures and sweetness. But what will happen to our glorious puddings now we are in the grip of an obsession with so-called healthy eating? Do we really want to write off this wonderful tradition that we have excelled at for centuries?

Long live puddings, is my message – a voice crying in the low-fat wilderness of the 21st century saying, please don't stop making and eating them! The pleasure we derive from our food is a gift and we mustn't turn our backs on what is superior in favour of the vastly inferior – I'd swap you a ton of over-sweet, short-on-cocoa-solids chocolate bars and a lorry-load of artificially flavoured supermarket yoghurts for one glorious, home-made British pudding.

Puddings are not wicked. My lifelong friend, chef John Tovey, once wrote a wonderful book called *Wicked Puddings*, a title that serves to remind us of our modern mind-set: puddings are naughty, puddings mean guilt. But it's all a big deception. The truth is, my grandfather never ate a supper in his entire life that did not include a pudding, and he died at the age of 87, a little but not greatly overweight. Such a scenario would be unheard of now. The reason for his long good health is he never owned a car – he walked everywhere – and his work was far from sedentary either.

Today we drive everywhere, have mostly static jobs and lack exercise, so we couldn't possibly live like my grandfather (who also invariably had bacon and eggs for breakfast, too). But what I am saying is, instead of pudding every day, why not treat yourself once a week? I'm always being ticked off by people who say, oh Delia, all that butter and cream! What I have failed to communicate is that recipes containing butter and cream are not for every day, but for *special* occasions. So, by all means, don't eat *too* much pudding but, please, have one now and then.

The health issue. Fat is fat is fat. Butter, margarine, vegetable fat, lard, suet, olive and other oils are all fats, and if you eat too much fat, you get fat. Animal fats (as I said in Chapter 17) also came under fire because it was thought they increased cholesterol in the blood, which, in turn, blocked arteries and caused strokes and heart disease. But the evidence is by no means conclusive and some scientists believe that stress and other factors are the real culprits. Be that as it may, eating large amounts of fat, animal or otherwise, is not wise. What *is* wise is balance, and in a balanced diet, a pudding once a week is absolutely *not* unhealthy, and let's not be duped into thinking it is.

A final word before we embark on our recipes – a wonderful quote from a French visitor to London at the beginning of the 18th century, M. Misson: 'Blessed be he that invented pudding, for it is a manna that hits the palates of all sorts of people.' So say I.

A note on puddings. Suet puddings have a somewhat undeserved reputation for heaviness, but they can always be lightened up by replacing some of the flour with breadcrumbs, as in the recipes in this chapter.

Steamers are described on page 484, but there are two important points to remember: (i) Don't let the water under the steamer ever come off the boil – this *can* make a pudding heavy. (ii) You must make sure the water is topped up out of a boiling kettle. The advantage of the old-fashioned, double-pan, deep, lidded steamer is that the saucepan can be filled almost to the brim, and may not need to be topped up as frequently.

Pudding basins have caused something of a problem with regard to their size – a bit of confusion that needs to be unravelled. If you pour water right up to the brim of a so-called 40 fl oz (2 pint) basin, it actually takes 2½ pints! The measurements for this standard size are as follows: 3½ inches (9 cm) base diameter, 6½ inches (16 cm) top diameter and 4½ inches (11.5 cm) deep. This is the one you need for our Steamed Panettone Pudding on pages 98-9 and Old English Apple Hat on page 646.

Canary Lemon Sponge Puddings with Lemon Curd Cream

Canary Pudding is an old English steamed sponge pudding with jam. Because our football team is called the Canaries, I have adapted it to become a lemony version, so as to add a little canary colour. It's very popular at our restaurant in Norwich City Football Club. If you haven't got time to make the Lemon Curd (see page 567), use jam and serve with custard.

Serves 6

For the sponge pudding:
4 oz (110 g) self-raising flour
4 oz (110 g) softened unsalted butter, at room temperature, cut into small cubes, plus a little extra for greasing
2 large eggs
4 oz (110 g) golden caster sugar
1 teaspoon baking powder
grated zest 1 lemon and 1 tablespoon lemon juice

For the lemon curd:
a half quantity of lemon curd
(see page 567)

For the lemon curd cream:
the remainder of the lemon curd
5 fl oz (150 ml) hot water
5 fl oz (150 ml) double cream

You will also need six mini pudding basins with a capacity of 6 fl oz (175 ml); some kitchen foil and silicone paper (parchment); and a steamer.

Begin by making the lemon curd for the puddings. After that, butter the basins well and place a round piece of well-buttered silicone paper (parchment) in the bottom of each one. Then take a large mixing bowl and sift the flour and baking powder into it, holding the sieve high to give the flour a good airing. Next, add the butter, eggs, sugar, lemon zest and juice. Then, using an electric hand whisk, beat the mixture for about a minute until it is thoroughly blended.

After that, fill the base of each basin with a dessertspoon of lemon curd and then spoon in the sponge mixture, dividing it equally between the basins and levelling the tops. Then place a piece of kitchen foil over each one, making a pleat in the centre and twisting the edges all round.

Now place a saucepan over the heat and add boiling water from the kettle. When it comes back to the boil, arrange the puddings in the steamer (you'll have to stack them on top of each other) and fit it over a saucepan. Pop a lid on and steam them for about 25 minutes, keeping the water at a steady simmer. They are ready when the centres spring back when pressed lightly.

While the puddings are cooking, you can make the lemon sauce. All you do is place the remaining lemon curd in a saucepan, add the water and the cream, and then heat very gently, stirring all the time, until hot but not bubbling. Then pour it into a warmed serving jug and keep warm. When the puddings are cooked, remove the kitchen foil and loosen them all round with a small palette knife. Then turn them out on to warmed serving plates, remove the paper discs and hand the sauce round separately, or pour a little over each one.

Spiced Bread Pudding with Brandy Cream

Sometimes this gets confused with bread-and-butter pudding, but it's quite different. It was invented, I think, to use up stale bread, which is still a good reason for making it – however, it has developed into something so wonderful, it's worth letting the bread go stale on purpose.

Serves 6
For the bread pudding:
8 oz (225 g) white or brown
bread, crusts removed
2 teaspoons mixed spice
whole nutmeg
4 oz (110 g) sultanas
1 oz (25 g) currants
1 oz (25 g) raisins
2 oz (50 g) whole candied lemon
or orange peel, chopped
3 tablespoons brandy
10 fl oz (275 ml) milk
2 oz (50 g) butter, melted, plus a
little extra for greasing
3 oz (75 g) dark soft brown sugar
1 large egg, beaten
grated zest ½ orange
grated zest 1 lemon
1 tablespoon demerara sugar

For the brandy cream:
1 dessertspoon brandy
5 fl oz (150 ml) double cream
1 oz (25 g) golden caster sugar

You will also need a baking dish with
a base measurement of 6¼ x 8 inches
(15.5 x 20 cm), 1¾ inches (4.5 cm)
deep, buttered.

Begin by placing the sultanas, currants, raisins and candied peel in a bowl. Pour over the brandy and leave aside to marinate. Then, in a large bowl, break the bread into ½ inch (1 cm) pieces. Add the milk, then give the mixture a good stir and leave it for about 30 minutes so the bread becomes well soaked. Pre-heat the oven to gas mark 4, 350°F (180°C).

Next, mix the melted butter, dark soft brown sugar, mixed spice and beaten egg together and then add to the second bowl. Now, using a fork, beat the mixture well, making sure there are no large lumps, then stir in the marinated fruits, with any brandy remaining, and also the orange and lemon zest.

After that, spread the mixture in the baking dish and sprinkle the sugar over it, along with some freshly grated nutmeg. Bake on the centre shelf of the oven for about 1¼ hours. Meanwhile, whisk together the ingredients for the brandy cream and serve it with the pudding warm from the oven.

Individual Queen of Puddings with Morello Cherry Conserve

This is another great English classic, yet when you look at the recipe, you can hardly believe such simple ingredients could be transformed into such wonderfully light lusciousness. It is a movable feast because the conserve can be whichever you prefer. Our home-made Dark Apricot and Almond Preserve on page 566 would be a star choice. It works divinely with marmalade, cranberry jelly, or even lemon curd. Definitely one of my top puddings of all time.

First, pour the milk into a saucepan and bring to the boil. Remove from the heat and stir in the butter, breadcrumbs, 2½ oz (60 g) sugar and the lemon zest, and leave for 20 minutes to allow the breadcrumbs to swell.

Now separate the eggs. Put the whites into a large, grease-free bowl and the yolks into a small bowl. Then beat the yolks and whisk them into the breadcrumb mixture. After that, divide the mixture between the ramekins, smoothing the tops with a palette knife. Now place on the baking tray in the centre of the oven and bake for about 25 minutes until set.

Meanwhile, in a small saucepan, melt the conserve over a low heat and, when the puddings are ready, remove them from the oven and spread it carefully and evenly all over the tops.

Next, use an electric hand whisk with clean, dry beaters to beat the egg whites to the stiff-peak stage, then whisk in 1½ oz (40 g) sugar. Now divide this meringue mixture between each ramekin, piling it up into high peaks. Finally, sprinkle the teaspoon of sugar over the tops of the puddings and bake them on the baking tray on the centre shelf for a further 10-15 minutes, until the tops are golden brown.

Don't worry if the puddings are ready before you've finished the main course – they won't mind waiting in a warm place.

Note: If it's easier, you can make one large pudding, using an oval baking dish measuring 10 x 7 inches (25.5 x 18 cm), 2 inches (5 cm) deep, generously buttered. The initial baking time will be 30-35 minutes and the meringue will take the same time as above: 10-15 minutes.

Serves 6

6 dessertspoons (about 5 oz/150 g)
Morello cherry conserve
1 pint (570 ml) milk
½ oz (10 g) butter, plus a little extra
for greasing
4 oz (110 g) fresh white breadcrumbs
4 oz (110 g) golden caster sugar, plus
1 extra teaspoon
grated zest 1 small lemon
3 large eggs

You will also need six 2 inch (5 cm) deep ramekins, with a base diameter of 2½ inches (6 cm) and a top diameter of 3 inches (7.5 cm) (or six similar-sized heatproof glass dishes), generously buttered; and a medium-sized baking tray.

Pre-heat the oven to gas mark 4, 350°F (180°C).

Warm Chocolate Rum Soufflés with Chocolate Sauce

These are very light and chocolatey, and made even more wonderful by the addition of chocolate sauce and cream. They're also reasonably well-behaved and though they may shrink a little, they won't collapse.

Serves 6
For the soufflés:
4 oz (110 g) dark chocolate
(75 per cent cocoa solids)
2 tablespoons rum
2 tablespoons double cream
4 large egg yolks
6 large egg whites
a little melted butter for greasing
a little golden caster sugar for dusting

For the sauce:
3 oz (75 g) dark chocolate
(75 per cent cocoa solids)
2 tablespoons double cream

To serve:
10 fl oz (275 ml) double or single cream
a little icing sugar for dusting

You will also need a medium-sized baking tray; six 2 inch (5 cm) deep ramekins, with a base diameter of 2½ inches (6 cm) and a top diameter of 3 inches (7.5 cm) (or six similar-sized heatproof dishes).

Pre-heat the oven to gas mark 6, 400°F (200°C).

First of all, pop the baking tray into the oven to pre-heat. Now break the chocolate into a heatproof mixing bowl, add the rum and cream, and place the bowl over a pan of barely simmering water, making sure the base of the bowl doesn't touch the water. Leave it until the chocolate is just soft, which will take about 6 minutes, then remove it from the heat and beat with a wooden spoon until it's smooth and glossy. Allow it to cool. In the meantime, brush the ramekins with melted butter and dust with golden caster sugar.

Now, in a small bowl, whisk the egg yolks thoroughly and stir them into the chocolate mixture. Then, in another, large, grease-free bowl – and making sure the beaters of your electric hand whisk are clean and dry – whisk the egg whites until they form stiff peaks. Then, using a metal spoon, fold a quarter of the egg white into the chocolate mixture to loosen it and then fold in the rest gently and carefully.

Next, pour the whole lot into the ramekins and bake on the baking tray for about 10 minutes, or until the soufflés are puffy and springy to the touch.

Meanwhile, make the chocolate sauce. Break the chocolate into another heatproof mixing bowl and add the cream. Place it over a pan of barely simmering water, once again making sure the base of the bowl doesn't touch the water. After about 6 minutes, remove it from the heat and beat it with a wooden spoon until smooth. Pour the sauce into a warmed jug and keep warm.

Serve the soufflés straight from the oven, dusted with the icing sugar. Hand around the chocolate sauce and the cream in jugs – then the surface of the soufflés can be gently divided using a teaspoon, and the sauce and cream poured into the space.

Spotted Dick Rides Again

This was once a very famous pudding, but it's now sadly forgotten – except by a certain supermarket that has a problem with its name! Just the thing to serve for Sunday lunch after a freezing cold, wintry walk. The ultimate comfort pudding.

Serves 4-6
For the suet pastry:
4 oz (110 g) self-raising flour, plus a little extra for dusting
2 oz (50 g) fresh white breadcrumbs
3 oz (75 g) shredded suet
2 fl oz (55 ml) water
2 fl oz (55 ml) milk
salt

For the filling:
6 oz (175 g) raisins
1 medium cooking apple (weighing about 6 oz/175 g), washed, cored and roughly chopped (no need to peel)
3 oz (75 g) dark soft brown sugar
grated zest ½ lemon

You will also need a sheet of kitchen foil measuring 10 x 14 inches (25.5 x 35 cm), and a steamer.

First of all, mix the filling ingredients together in a bowl. After that, make the suet pastry: sift the flour into a bowl, add the breadcrumbs, suet and a pinch of salt, and mix to combine. Mix the water and milk together and add a little to the dry ingredients, sprinkling it here and there. Now, using a flat-bladed knife, begin to mix, adding a little more liquid until the mixture looks as it is coming together. Finish off using your hands, adding drops of liquid until you end up with a smooth, elastic dough that feels moist.

Next, transfer the dough to a flat, lightly floured surface, roll it out to a rectangle roughly measuring 8 x 12 inches (20 x 30 cm) and dampen the edges with water. Then spread the filling evenly over it and roll it up gently and carefully from the narrow end. Now wrap the pudding in the kitchen foil, twisting it at each end to form a seal.

After that, fit a fan steamer (unscrew the central spindle) in a saucepan, add boiling water from a kettle and as soon as it comes back to the boil, pop the pudding in. Put a lid on and steam for 2 hours, keeping the water at a steady simmer, and making sure it is topped up if it needs it. Serve the pudding in warmed bowls, cut in thick slices, with Traditional English Custard (see page 62) – an absolutely essential accompaniment.

Old English Apple Hat

If it's true there's 'a time for everything under Heaven', then midwinter is quite definitely the most appropriate time to make an old-fashioned steamed pudding. There's nothing wrong with a cold, grey month in the calendar when it can justify such wonderful culinary indulgence. Here, I am offering you the real thing – a soft, steamy suet crust encasing fragrant and luscious apples, with a hint of cloves. It's no trouble at all to make, and you can leave it gently steaming away while you go for a brisk walk in the wintry chill, knowing all that soothing, comforting pleasure is awaiting you on your return.

Serves 6-8

For the suet pastry:
8 oz (225 g) self-raising flour, plus a little extra for dusting
4 oz (110 g) shredded suet
cold water
a little butter for greasing
salt

For the filling:
1 lb (450 g) Bramley apples (weight after coring), washed (no need to peel)
8 oz (225 g) Cox's apples (weight after coring), washed (no need to peel)
2 oz (50 g) golden caster sugar
6 cloves

You will also need a large pudding basin (see page 637), very well buttered; some kitchen foil and string; and a steamer.

To make the suet pastry, all you do is sift the flour into a bowl, add the suet and a pinch of salt and mix them together. Now start to add a little cold water, sprinkling it here and there. Then take a flat-bladed knife and begin to mix with it, still adding water, until the mixture looks like it is coming together. Finish off using your hands, adding drops of water until you get a smooth, elastic dough. There's no need to rest the dough, so you can straight away reserve a quarter of the pastry (for the lid) and then roll the rest out on a flat, lightly floured surface to a 10 inch (25.5 cm) round, giving it quarter turns as you roll to keep the round shape.

Now transfer the pastry to the pudding basin and arrange it to form a lining, using your hands to press it round as evenly as possible. If you have some pastry above the rim, just squeeze it down to form a neat edge.

Next, cut the apples into quarters. Now slice them into ½ inch (1 cm) chunks and, as you add them to the basin, sprinkle in the sugar and tuck in a clove here and there. Pack the apples down as you go and don't worry if they rise a bit above the top, as they will shrink in the cooking.

Now roll out the reserved pastry to form the lid, dampen the edge all round with water, then place it over the apples. Press the edge all round to weld it to the edge of the pastry lining the basin.

After that, take a double sheet of kitchen foil, about 10 inches (25.5 cm) square, make a pleat in the centre and cover the top of the pudding with it. Then tie it securely with string around the top of the basin, and make a string handle (to help you lift it into the steamer) by attaching a length of string to both sides. Now boil a kettle and pour the boiling water into a saucepan to about halfway, place it over a medium heat and when it comes back to the boil, fit the steamer over the top.

Pop the pudding in, put the lid on and steam the pudding for exactly 2 hours, keeping the water at a steady simmer. After an hour, check the water level in the saucepan and, if necessary, top up with boiling water.

To serve the pudding, remove the string and kitchen foil, loosen the pudding all round with a palette knife, then turn it out on to a warmed plate. Serve cut into slices, with the apples strewn around the pastry and – it has to be said – lots of proper custard.

Bread-and-Butter Pudding

This traditional English recipe, which I have made for years, has, I'm afraid, suffered from foreign chefs who have adapted it into 'modern' concoctions. This version is fragrant, soft, moist, wobbly beneath and toasted and crunchy on top. I would go the whole hog and serve it with some chilled, untreated Jersey cream.

First of all, cut each slice of buttered bread in half and then into quarters, leaving the crusts on. Now arrange one layer of bread over the base of the dish, sprinkle over the candied peel and half the currants, then cover with another layer of bread and the remainder of the currants.

Next, in a measuring jug, measure out the milk and add the double cream. Stir in the sugar and lemon zest, then whisk the eggs, first on their own in a small bowl and then into the milk mixture.

Now pour the whole lot over the bread, grate some nutmeg over the surface, then bake on the centre shelf of the oven for 30-40 minutes, or until the top is golden brown and crusty. Remove it and leave for 5 minutes before serving.

Serves 4-6
8 slices bread (from a small
loaf), buttered
½ oz (10 g) whole candied lemon
or orange peel, finely chopped
2 oz (50 g) currants
10 fl oz (275 ml) milk
2½ fl oz (60 ml) double cream
2 oz (50 g) golden caster sugar
grated zest ½ small lemon
3 large eggs
whole nutmeg
butter for greasing

Pre-heat the oven to gas mark 4,
350°F (180°C).

You will also need a rectangular baking
dish with a base measurement of 7 x 9
inches (18 x 23 cm), well-buttered.

Individual Sussex Pond Puddings with Lemon Butter Sauce

Serves 6
For the suet pastry:
4 oz (110 g) self-raising flour, plus a
little extra for dusting
2 oz (50 g) fresh white breadcrumbs
grated zest 1 lemon
3 oz (75 g) shredded suet
2 fl oz (55 ml) water
2 fl oz (55 ml) milk
a little butter for greasing

For the filling:
1 lemon
6 oz (175 g) butter
6 oz (175 g) demerara sugar

You will also need six mini pudding
basins with a capacity of 6 fl oz
(175 ml), very well buttered; some
kitchen foil; and a steamer.

This is one of the truly great English puddings, which has, sadly, fallen victim to the health lobby. Originally, a whole lemon was placed inside, along with butter and sugar, and when the pudding was opened, all the buttery juices spilled out, creating a 'pond' all around it. I have converted it to small individual puddings and it's still truly wonderful.

First of all, sift the flour into a bowl, then sprinkle in the breadcrumbs, lemon zest and suet and just mix everything lightly with your hands to distribute it evenly. Next, mix the water and milk together and sprinkle about 3 fl oz (75 ml) of this liquid into the flour. Begin mixing with a round-bladed knife, and then use your hands at the end to bring it all together to a smooth, elastic dough that leaves the bowl clean. If the mixture seems a little dry, add more of the liquid.

Next, transfer the dough to a flat, lightly floured surface, give it a light kneading and then divide it into six equal portions, slicing off a small piece from each for a lid. After that, roll out the large pieces into rounds big enough to line each basin. Now transfer the pastry to the basins and arrange it to form the lining, using your hands to press it round as evenly as possible. If you have some pastry above the rim, just squeeze it down to form a neat edge.

After that, cut the lemon into thin slices and divide the slices equally between the basins. Next, put 1 oz (25 g) butter and 1 oz (25 g) sugar into each basin. Finally, roll out the extra pieces of pastry into rounds and use these as lids, dampening the edges with a little water and pressing to seal them firmly all round. Now cover each basin with a double sheet of kitchen foil, pleated in the centre and twisted at the edges, and place in a steamer fitted over a saucepan filled with boiling water. Pop the lid on and steam for 2 hours, keeping the water at a steady simmer, and making sure it is topped up if it needs it.

When the puddings are ready, turn them out into warmed bowls, sliding a small palette knife around the edges to loosen them, and serve with some chilled pouring cream to mingle with the juices.

28

Parties and gatherings

Parties and gatherings so often present problems, beginning with where you are going to hold the event. You look for a venue, find one at the right price and then – what do you know? – you can't find a free date because the venue has been booked up months ahead. So, this is where I come in, hoping to encourage you to throw open your own doors, welcome your family and friends, and have a go yourself.

Although there will be a certain amount of hard work involved, it's not going to be difficult and it can also be enormous fun – and I'm sure you can rope in a few friends to help. The huge plus is going to be the quality of the food because, however inexperienced you are, proper home-made food is usually streets ahead of what's on offer from caterers – with the exception of Norwich City Football Club, of course!

Here, I've planned two types of buffet party: one hot and one cold. Both serve twelve people but can be increased to serve eighteen or twenty-four by making one-and-a-half times or twice the amounts specified in the recipes. Before embarking on the recipes themselves, I thought it would be helpful to give you a running order to show what can be prepared ahead, what on the day itself and what should be left until the time of serving.

The other two menus – one perfect at any time of the year, the other especially good in summer – are for eight people, but can likewise be increased to serve sixteen or twenty-four.

Finally, I have included some recipes for pre-dinner nibbles suitable for absolutely any occasion.

A Hot Middle Eastern Buffet

Why Middle Eastern, you're thinking? Let me explain. I sometimes think buffet food can be rather bland – a quiche served straight from the oven may be an absolute delight, but cold or re-heated, it loses much of its charm. The combination of lively flavours and contrasting textures in Middle Eastern cooking, though, makes for perfect buffet fare. A nice addition to this would be to include some warm Pitta Bread (see page 518) and a double quantity of Hummus (see page 542). Serves 12.

> *Menu*
> *Spiced Lamb Koftas Braised in Tomato Sauce*
> *Stuffed Yellow Peppers with Pilau Rice, Currants*
> *and Toasted Pine Nuts*
> *Courgette and Potato Cakes with Mint and Feta Cheese*
> *Mixed Vegetable Salad à la Grecque*
> *Greek Orange and Honey Syrup Cake with Yoghurt and Pistachios*
> *Pistachio Ice Cream with Pistachio Wafers*

Two days before

Vegetable Salad à la Grecque | Make the salad and store in a lidded container in the fridge.
Pistachio Ice Cream | Make the ice cream and freeze in a lidded plastic container.
Greek Orange Cake | Make the cake, drizzle with the syrup and store in a cool place in an airtight tin.

652

The day before

Make the koftas, simmering them in a covered saucepan for 30 minutes only, then cool, transfer them to a lidded plastic container and store in the fridge.

Roast the peppers for the rice, then cool and store them in a lidded container in the fridge.

Make the courgette cakes so they are ready to bake, arrange in layers on a tray, separated by silicone paper (parchment), cover well with clingfilm and then refrigerate.

Make the wafers and store in an airtight container in a cool place.

Lamb Koftas

Stuffed Peppers

Courgette Cakes

Pistachio Wafers

On the morning of your party

Weigh out the pilau rice ingredients. Chop and cook the onions in the oil, add the garlic and cook for a few minutes more. Remove the pan from the heat, cover and leave on one side until later. Chop the mint to garnish the rice, cover and store in the fridge until needed.

Chop the parsley and spring onions for garnishing the salad, cover and refrigerate until needed.

Transfer the ice cream from the freezer to a cool place to stand, then put a baking tray lined with silicone paper (parchment) into the freezer. After about 30 minutes, shape the ice cream into balls using a scoop, put them on to the chilled baking tray and return them, uncovered, to the freezer. Arrange the pistachio wafers on a plate and cover with clingfilm.

Stuffed Peppers

Vegetable Salad à la Grecque

Pistachio Ice Cream

Pistachio Wafers

Two hours before your guests arrive

Put the butter and oil for the courgette cakes into a small saucepan ready to melt.

Put the salad into two serving dishes, drizzle with the oil and sprinkle with the prepared parsley-and-spring-onion garnish, and cover with clingfilm.

Place the cake on a serving plate, spread with the yoghurt and sprinkle with the pistachios. Then push five cocktail sticks into the cake to stop the cover touching the topping. Cover loosely with clingfilm and refrigerate.

Courgette Cakes

Vegetable Salad à la Grecque

Greek Orange Cake

When your guests begin to arrive

Pre-heat the oven to gas mark 7, 425°F (220°C), with a baking tray on the top and middle shelf.

50 minutes before serving the buffet

Put the koftas into a large saucepan, cover and bring to a simmer over a medium heat, then remove the lid and allow to simmer for 30 minutes to reduce the sauce and heat the koftas thoroughly. Transfer to one or two warmed serving bowls and cover with kitchen foil.

Lamb Koftas

40 minutes before serving the buffet

Courgette Cakes   Melt the butter-and-oil mixture and brush the courgette cakes, then arrange them on the pre-heated baking trays and bake for 25-30 minutes (turning them over once after 15 minutes, and at the same time, swapping over the baking trays). Transfer to a warmed serving dish once heated through and cover with kitchen foil.

30 minutes before serving the buffet

Stuffed Peppers   Warm the cooked onions and garlic for the rice, stir in the pine nuts, currants and cinnamon, then the rice, add the boiling stock, stir once and then cover. Cook on the lowest setting for 15 minutes. Remove the lid and cover with a clean tea cloth.

20 minutes before serving the buffet

Stuffed Peppers   Place the cooked peppers on a baking tray and warm through in the oven for 10 minutes. Then fill them with the cooked rice and serve the remaining rice in a warmed serving bowl. Cover with kitchen foil and keep warm.

Before calling your guests to the buffet

Vegetable Salad à la Grecque, Courgette Cakes, Lamb Koftas and Stuffed Peppers   Uncover the vegetable salad, courgette cakes, koftas and rice. Garnish the stuffed peppers with the prepared mint.

When you're ready for dessert

Pistachio Ice Cream   Remove the ice cream from the freezer.
Pistachio Wafers   Uncover the wafers.
Greek Orange Cake   Remove the clingfilm and cocktail sticks from the cake and drizzle with the honey.

Clockwise, from top right: Spiced Lamb Koftas Braised in Tomato Sauce; Mixed Vegetable Salad à la Grecque; Courgette and Potato Cakes with Mint and Feta Cheese; Stuffed Yellow Peppers with Pilau Rice, Currants and Toasted Pine Nuts; and extra Pilau Rice

Spiced Lamb Koftas Braised in Tomato Sauce

This is a great buffet recipe, but it's also extremely good for smaller numbers – cut all the ingredients by a third and it will serve four.

Serves 12 (makes 48)
For the koftas:
3 lb (1.35 kg) minced lamb
3 teaspoons coriander seeds
3 teaspoons cumin seeds
3 small onions, peeled and cut into chunks
3 tablespoons fresh mint leaves
3 tablespoons fresh coriander leaves
5-6 tablespoons olive oil
salt and freshly milled black pepper

For the sauce:
3 lb (1.35 kg) tomatoes
12 oz (350 g) onions (about 2 medium onions), finely chopped
3 cloves garlic, crushed
1½ sticks cinnamon
salt and freshly milled black pepper

You will also need a lidded, flameproof casserole with a capacity of 7 pints (4 litres).

First of all, you need to dry-roast the coriander and cumin seeds to draw out their flavour: place them in a small frying pan over a medium heat and toss them around for 2 minutes until they begin to jump and pop, then crush them as finely as possible with a pestle and mortar.

Next, place the lamb in a large mixing bowl. Put the onions in a food processor, along with the mint and coriander leaves, then pulse everything until the onion is finely chopped. Transfer all this to join the meat in the bowl, add the spices and a good seasoning of salt and freshly milled black pepper, then mix everything thoroughly and evenly together with your hands (easiest) or a large fork (takes longer). Then take small amounts of the mixture and roll them with your palms into little rounds slightly larger than a walnut.

Now heat about a tablespoon of the oil in a large frying pan over a medium to high heat and when it's hot, begin to brown the koftas, about six at a time, turning them to get brown on all sides. As they cook, transfer them to a plate and add more oil when needed as you continue browning all the others.

Meanwhile, skin the tomatoes for the sauce. Place them in a heatproof bowl and pour boiling water on to them. After exactly a minute (or, if the tomatoes are small, 15-30 seconds), remove them from the water, slip off their skins (protecting your hands with a cloth if they are hot) and chop them into small pieces.

After that, place the casserole over a high heat, add another tablespoon of oil and when it's hot, soften the onions, stirring them around now and then and keeping the heat highish so they turn golden brown, which should take about 6 minutes. Next, add the garlic to the onions and cook for about a minute more. Now add the tomatoes and cinnamon, stir well, then add the koftas, stir once more, turn the heat down to low and let them simmer slowly for about 30 minutes with the lid on. Then remove the lid to allow the sauce to reduce, continuing to simmer for a further 30 minutes before serving.

Stuffed Yellow Peppers with Pilau Rice, Currants and Toasted Pine Nuts

The beauty of these peppers is that they can be made well in advance, then warmed through and filled with the pilau rice just before serving.

All you do is cut the peppers in half lengthways through the stalk, then scrape out the seeds and place the halves on the baking tray. Now sprinkle a little of the garlic into each one and follow that with a teaspoon of oil. Brush a little more oil around the edges of the peppers, add a seasoning of salt and freshly milled black pepper, then bake them on a high shelf in the oven for 50-60 minutes, or until they are well browned at the edges.

Meanwhile, prepare the rice. Heat the oil in the frying pan over a medium heat. Add the onions and pine nuts and fry for 10 minutes, or until everything is golden. Then add the currants, cinnamon and garlic. When you are ready to cook the rice, stir it into the pan and turn the grains over until they are thoroughly coated in the oil. Then pour in the hot stock and season with salt. Stir once only, then put the lid on, turn the heat down to its lowest setting and let the rice cook for exactly 15 minutes. After that, take the pan off the heat, remove the lid and cover the pan with a clean tea cloth until the rice is needed.

When the peppers are cooked, transfer them to a warmed dish and fill each one with the rice, adding the mint at the last moment. Serve the remaining rice in a warmed bowl to accompany the peppers.

Serves 12

For the roasted peppers:
6 large yellow peppers
2 cloves garlic, chopped
4-5 tablespoons olive oil, including a little for greasing
salt and freshly milled black pepper

For the pilau rice:
1 pint (570 ml) basmati rice (use a measuring jug)
4 oz (110 g) currants
4 oz (110 g) pine nuts
3 tablespoons olive oil
2 medium onions, peeled and finely chopped
3 cinnamon sticks, halved
2 cloves garlic, crushed
2 pints of hot stock made with Marigold Swiss vegetable bouillon powder
12 sprigs fresh mint, to garnish
salt and freshly milled black pepper

You will also need a baking tray measuring 11 x 16 inches (28 x 40 cm), greased, and a large, lidded frying pan.

Pre-heat the oven to gas mark 4, 350°F (180°C).

Courgette and Potato Cakes with Mint and Feta Cheese

These quite brilliant little courgette cakes used to have to be fried, which is tiresome when you have much to prepare for a party. However, we have tried baking them in the oven, which works a treat.

Serves 12 (makes 16 cakes – one per person, plus a few extra)

6 medium courgettes (weighing about 1 lb 8 oz/700 g in total)
4 medium Desirée potatoes (weighing about 1 lb 8 oz/700 g in total)
4 tablespoons chopped fresh mint
1 lb (450 g) Feta, crumbled
4 spring onions, finely chopped
2 large eggs, beaten
2 tablespoons plain flour
2 oz (50 g) butter
1½ tablespoons olive oil
salt and freshly milled black pepper

You will also need two baking trays, each measuring 10 x 14 inches (25.5 x 35 cm).

First you need to coarsely grate the courgettes – a food processor is good for this – and put them into a colander. Then sprinkle them with 2 teaspoons of salt to draw out some of their excess moisture and leave them to drain for about an hour, with a plate or bowl underneath to catch the juices.

Meanwhile, scrub the potatoes and place them in a very large saucepan, with a little salt. Pour just enough boiling water over them to cover them, then simmer gently with a lid on for 8 minutes to parboil them. After that, drain them and leave them aside until they're cool enough to handle. Then peel them and, using the coarse side of a grater, grate them into a large bowl and season with more salt and some freshly milled black pepper.

When the hour is up, rinse the courgettes under cold, running water, squeeze out as much moisture as possible with your hands, then spread them out on a clean tea cloth and roll it up to wring out every last drop – this is very important, so the cakes are not wet.

Now, add the courgettes to the grated potatoes, along with the spring onions, mint, Feta and beaten eggs, and using two forks, lightly toss it all together. Next, divide the mixture into 16 and shape into rounds about ½ inch (1 cm) thick, pressing them firmly together to form little cakes. They don't have to be very neat – it's nice to have a few jagged edges. Then lightly dust the cakes with the flour.

To cook them, first pre-heat the oven to gas mark 7, 425°F (220°C) and also pre-heat the baking trays. Meanwhile, melt the butter and oil in a small saucepan, then brush the cakes on both sides with it. When the oven is up to heat, place the cakes on the trays, returning one to the top shelf and the other to the middle shelf for 15 minutes. After that, carefully turn the cakes over using a palette knife and a fork, swap the positions of the trays in the oven and cook them for a further 10-15 minutes. Serve hot.

Mixed Vegetable Salad à la Grecque

This is not a new recipe, but one I've always loved to serve at buffet parties. It has lots of gutsy flavours, can be made well in advance and doesn't need any last-minute attention.

First of all, you need to dry-roast the coriander seeds. To do this, place them in a small frying pan over a medium heat and stir and toss them around for 1-2 minutes, or until they begin to look toasted and start to jump in the pan. Now crush them quite coarsely with a pestle and mortar, along with the peppercorns.

Next, finely chop the onions, heat the oil in the saucepan and soften the onion in it for 10 minutes. Meanwhile, skin the fresh tomatoes, if using. Place them in a heatproof bowl and pour boiling water on to them. Leave them for exactly a minute (or 15-30 seconds, if they are small), then remove them and slip off their skins (protecting your hands with a cloth if they are hot). Now quarter them and add them (or the tinned tomatoes) to the pan. Then add the crushed coriander seeds and peppercorns, garlic, vinegar, oregano, lemon juice, water and tomato purée, and a teaspoon of salt. Bring everything up to the boil, stir in the shallots, cover the pan and simmer for 20 minutes.

Next, break the cauliflower into 1 inch (2.5 cm) florets, halve the mushrooms and add them both, along with the beans, to the pan. Cover it again and simmer for a further 20 minutes, stirring the vegetables around once or twice during the cooking time. After 20 minutes, test them with a skewer – they should be tender but still firm. Now taste to check the seasoning. Then pour the contents of the pan into the serving dishes and leave to cool. I think this is best left covered in the fridge overnight to allow the flavours to develop, so it can be made up to two days ahead.

To serve, remove the dishes from the fridge an hour in advance, drizzle the vegetables in each serving dish with half the oil, then scatter over the chopped parsley and spring onions.

Serves 12

3 medium onions, peeled
3 lb (1.35 kg) ripe, red tomatoes, (or 3 x 400 g tins Italian chopped tomatoes)
18 shallots, peeled
12 oz (350 g) cauliflower
12 oz (350 g) small to medium open-cap mushrooms, wiped
2 tablespoons coriander seeds
24 black peppercorns
5 fl oz (150 ml) olive oil
3 fat cloves garlic, crushed
7 fl oz (200 ml) red wine vinegar
1 tablespoon chopped fresh oregano (or 2 teaspoons dried oregano)
juice 3 medium lemons (about 4 fl oz/120 ml)
6 fl oz (175 ml) water, mixed with 1½ tablespoons tomato purée
6 oz (175 g) dried butter beans (or judion beans), pre-soaked (see page 536), cooked and drained
salt and freshly milled black pepper

To serve:
5 fl oz (150 ml) olive oil
1½ oz (40 g) chopped fresh flat-leaf parsley
6 spring onions, finely chopped, including the green parts

You will also need a saucepan with a capacity of 7 pints (4 litres), and two large, shallow serving dishes.

Pistachio
Ice Cream

This is so many people's favourite ice cream – pale green and fragrant, with lovely bits of frozen pistachio to bite into. Lovely on its own or served with the Pistachio Wafers (see opposite), the ice cream is also delicious with the Greek Orange and Honey Syrup Cake (see page 662).

Serves 12
8 oz (225 g) unsalted, shelled pistachio nuts
1 pint (570 ml) each double and single cream
4 oz (110g) golden caster sugar
8 large egg yolks
1½ tablespoons custard powder

You will also need an ice-cream maker (pre-frozen according to the manufacturer's instructions); and two lidded plastic boxes measuring 6 x 8 x 3 inches (15 x 20 x 7.5 cm).

First of all, whip the double cream until it reaches the 'floppy' stage but isn't too thick, then pop it into the fridge to chill. Then take 4 oz (110 g) of the pistachio nuts, place them in a food processor with the sugar and process until very fine. After that, roughly chop the remaining nuts.

Next, pour the single cream into a medium-sized saucepan, along with the finely ground pistachios, and gently heat to just below boiling point. While that is happening, in a large bowl, beat together the egg yolks and custard powder until smooth. Now pour the hot cream on to this mixture, whisking as you go. After that, return the pistachio custard to the pan and continue to whisk it over a medium heat until it has thickened and just come up to boiling point again. (Ignore any curdled appearance, which may come about if you don't keep whisking and have the heat too high; the custard powder will stabilise it, provided you beat it off the heat, and poured into a bowl, it will become quite smooth again.) Now pour the custard into a bowl and place it in a larger bowl of chilled water, stirring it now and then until cold.

Meanwhile, fold the double cream into the ice cream mixture. Now place half the mixture into the ice-cream maker, add half the remaining nuts and freeze-churn for about 30 minutes, until it has the consistency of soft-scoop ice cream. Then transfer it to one of the plastic boxes and place in the freezer. Repeat with the other half of the mixture.

Note: If you make a smaller quantity, not for a party, remember to remove the ice cream from the freezer 20 minutes before serving.

If you don't have an ice-cream maker, instructions for making ice cream without one are on page 527.

Pistachio Wafers

These pretty little triangular wafers are the perfect accompaniment to the Pistachio Ice Cream (see opposite). Their irregular shape is part of their charm.

First mix together the pistachios, icing sugar and cinnamon. Next, take a sheet of filo, covering the others with a clean tea cloth, and butter it generously, using a brush. Then sprinkle it with a sixth of the nut-and-sugar mixture. Now place another sheet on top, butter it and sprinkle with the same amount. Repeat with a third sheet and more of the mixture, pressing down the layers. Now begin again, so you end up with two stacks. Next, take each stack, cut it into four equal-sized rectangles, then take each rectangle and cut it into three haphazard triangles. Place half the triangles on the baking tray and bake them on the middle shelf for 10-12 minutes, or until they are crisp and golden brown. Then transfer the first batch to a wire rack and allow the tray to cool before baking the second. Allow this batch to cool, too. When the wafers are cold, store them in an airtight plastic box and sprinkle with a little icing sugar just before serving.

Serves 12

4 oz (110 g) unsalted, shelled pistachio nuts, finely chopped
3 oz (75 g) unrefined icing sugar, sifted, plus a little extra for dusting
½ teaspoon ground cinnamon
4 oz (110 g) fresh authentic Greek filo pastry (6 sheets)
4 oz (110 g) unsalted butter, melted, plus a little extra for greasing

You will also need an 11 x 16 inch (28 x 40.5 cm) baking tray, buttered.

Pre-heat the oven to gas mark 4, 350°F (180°C).

Greek Orange and Honey Syrup Cake with Yoghurt and Pistachios

The sharp acidity of the orange in this cake combines beautifully with the sweetness of the Greek mountain honey. Because the cake is soaked in syrup, you can make it well ahead and just whip it out when you're ready to serve.

Serves 12

For the cake:

2 small oranges (weighing about 9 oz/250 g)

4½ oz (125 g) ground almonds

6 oz (175 g) well-softened butter, plus a little extra for greasing

6 oz (175 g) golden caster sugar

3 large eggs, beaten

9oz (250 g) semolina

4½ teaspoons baking powder

For the syrup:

8 fl oz (225 ml) Greek mountain honey

5 tablespoons water

5 tablespoons orange juice

1½ tablespoons lemon juice

1½ inch (4 cm) cinnamon stick

For the topping:

7 oz (200 g) Greek yoghurt

1½ oz (40 g) unsalted, shelled pistachio nuts

2 tablespoons Greek mountain honey

You will also need a 10 inch (25.5 cm) springform cake tin, lightly greased and the base lined with greased silicone paper (parchment).

Pre-heat the oven to gas mark 6, 400°F (200°C).

First, cut the oranges into chunks, removing the pips. Then tip the whole lot – flesh, pith and zest – into a food processor and whiz it to a thick purée. Now all you do is simply put all the other cake ingredients into a large bowl and, provided the butter is really soft, just go in with an electric hand whisk and whisk everything together until you have a smooth, well-combined mixture. After that, fold in the orange purée, spoon the mixture into the prepared tin and smooth the top with the back of the spoon.

Now place the cake on the centre shelf of the oven and bake it for an initial 10 minutes. Then lower the temperature to gas mark 4, 350°F (180°C) and bake for a further 40-45 minutes, or until it is golden brown, springy in the centre and has shrunk slightly from the sides of the tin.

Meanwhile, make the syrup. To do this, simply combine the honey and water with the cinnamon stick in a small saucepan, place it over a gentle heat, bring it up to simmering point and let it simmer gently for about 5 minutes. After that, take the pan off the heat, remove the cinnamon stick and stir in the orange and lemon juices.

Leave the cake aside to cool for 5 minutes, then remove it from the tin to a wire rack to cool, with a large plate underneath. Make a few holes all over it with a skewer before pouring the syrup over it. (It will look like there is far too much, but don't worry, the cake will absorb more than you think, and any that is not absorbed can be poured from the plate back over the cake.) Then, when the cake is absolutely cold, place it on a serving plate, cover it and leave it in a cool place overnight.

Just before serving, spread the top of the cake with the Greek yoghurt, sprinkle over the pistachios, drizzle with the honey and serve cut into chunky slices.

Note: This cake can also be made to serve 8-10, in an 8 inch (20 cm) tin, using 1 orange, 3 oz (75 g) ground almonds, 4 oz (110 g) each softened butter and sugar, 2 large eggs, 6 oz (175 g) semolina and 3 teaspoons baking powder. For the syrup, use 5 fl oz (150 ml) honey, 3 tablespoons each water and orange juice, 1 tablespoon lemon juice and 1 inch (2.5 cm) cinnamon stick. For the topping, use 7 oz (200g) Greek yoghurt, 1 oz (25 g) pistachios and 1½ tablespoons honey. Bake the cake for 10 minutes at the higher temperature and 25-30 minutes at the lower temperature.

A Cold Buffet

What I've done here is devise a cold buffet menu that can all be prepared in advance – but I do think that in winter, particularly, it's essential to have just one hot item, so I've included some crunchy jacket potatoes. It's a truly delightful feast of flavours and textures that is bound to please – and still leave you blissfully free to join in the party yourself without ending up a nervous wreck. Serves 12.

> *Menu*
> *Curried Turkey Salad with Dried Fruits*
> *Mini Yorkshire Puddings with Rare Beef and Horseradish-and-*
> *Mustard Crème Fraîche*
> *Caramelised Onion Tartlets with Goats' Cheese and Thyme*
> *Brown and Wild Rice Salad with Dried Cranberries*
> *Gruyère Potato Halves with Chives*
> *Thai Pork Satays with Thai Peanut Sauce*
> *Lemon Roulades*
> *Chocolate Ricotta Cheesecake*

Mini Yorkshire Puddings

Up to a week ahead

Bake the Yorkshires, cool and freeze in a lidded container.

Curried Turkey Salad

The day before

Prepare all of the ingredients for the salad, then put the spring onions into a small plastic food bag and store in the fridge. Put the toasted almonds into a small lidded container and store in a cool place. Mix together the turkey, apricots, raisins and dressing and refrigerate. Prepare the coriander leaf garnishes, put them into a small plastic food bag with a wet piece of kitchen paper and pop in the fridge.

Mini Yorkshire Puddings

Seal and roast the beef for the Yorkshires, cool and refrigerate on a plate, covered. Prepare the watercress garnishes, put them into a plastic food bag with a piece of wet kitchen paper and chill. Mix together the sauce ingredients and store in the fridge, too.

Caramelised Onion Tartlets

Make the pastry for the tartlets and allow it to rest. Pre-heat the oven, then line the patty tins, prick the bases and brush with beaten egg. Bake, then cool, cover with a clean tea cloth and store in a cool place overnight. Prepare and cook the onions, then cool and refrigerate. Whisk together the egg, cream, mustard and some seasoning and chill in a small plastic box. Prepare the 24 thyme sprigs, mix them with the oil and chill in a plastic food bag.

Make the rice salad, mix with the dressing and dried cranberries only, then cool, cover and refrigerate. Prepare the cucumber, tomatoes and pepper and refrigerate. Put the spring onions into a small plastic food bag and pop in the fridge, too (separated from those for the turkey salad). Toast the walnuts, put into a lidded container and store in a cool place.

Brown and Wild Rice Salad

Wash the potatoes and leave in a cool place to dry. Grate the Gruyère, snip the chives and refrigerate separately from each other.

Gruyère Potato Halves

Make the marinade/sauce for the satays. Pour half into a large bowl for the pork, then add the peanuts to the remainder in the food processor and pulse the mixture once. Transfer the sauce to a lidded box and chill. Refrigerate the reserved coriander in a small plastic food bag. Cut the pork, add it to the marinade in the bowl and stir well, before transferring to a suitable container in the fridge.

Thai Pork Satays

Make the sponge bases and roll them up in silicone paper (parchment), as in the recipe. Then, when cool, wrap them in clingfilm and keep them in a cool place. Make the Mascarpone cream filling and the lemon curd and chill separately in lidded containers in the fridge.

Lemon Roulades

Make the cheesecake, cover and chill overnight. Make the chocolate curls and store in a box in the fridge.

Chocolate Ricotta Cheesecake

On the morning of your party

Assemble the turkey salad, arrange on the salad leaves, cover and keep in the fridge.

Curried Turkey Salad

Prick the potatoes and rub with sea salt.

Gruyère Potato Halves

Mix the salad with the prepared cucumber, tomatoes and pepper, add two-thirds each of the spring onions and walnuts, cover and refrigerate.

Brown and Wild Rice Salad

Soak the skewers for the satays. Chop the reserved coriander, add to the sauce and refrigerate until later. Pre-heat the grill and line the grill pan with kitchen foil, then thread the pork on to the dried and oiled skewers. Place the pork skewers on the grill rack and brush with some of the marinade. Grill for 15-20 minutes, turning the skewers over and brushing them with some more marinade halfway through cooking. Cool the satays, then arrange them on a serving dish, cover and store in the fridge until later.

Thai Pork Satays

Spread a third of the Mascarpone and a third of the lemon curd on to each of the sponges, then roll them. Arrange them on serving dishes.

Lemon Roulades

Make the icing and decorate the roulades. Push 5 cocktail sticks into each of the roulades to stop the clingfilm touching the topping. Cover and refrigerate. Mix together the remaining Mascarpone and lemon curd, put into a serving bowl and chill this, too.

Chocolate Ricotta Cheesecake Unmould and plate the cheesecake, decorated with the curls, then cover with clingfilm and keep in a cool place.

Two hours before your guests arrive

Pre-heat the oven to gas mark 4, 350°F (180°C).

Mini Yorkshire Puddings Crisp the Yorkshires in the oven (from frozen) for a couple of minutes, or until heated through. Slice the beef ready to top the Yorkshires, cover and store in the fridge.

Caramelised Onion Tartlets Slice each of the goats' cheeses into 12 slices for the tartlets. Divide the cooked onion between the pastry cases, then the egg mixture and then the cheese slices. Top each one with the prepared sprig of thyme, sprinkle with cayenne pepper, then bake, then cool. As soon as the tartlets are ready, increase the oven temperature to gas mark 5, 375°F (190°C), ready to bake the potatoes. When the tartlets are cool, arrange them on a serving plate and cover.

While guests are having drinks on arrival

Gruyère Potato Halves Put the potatoes in the oven and bake for 1-1¼ hours.

Before calling your guests to the buffet, finally garnish and arrange the food on the buffet table:

Mini Yorkshire Puddings Top the Yorkshires with the sauce, beef and watercress.

Thai Pork Satays Garnish the satays with the lime wedges and put the sauce into a bowl.

Curried Turkey Salad Uncover the turkey salad. Sprinkle with the remaining spring onions, almonds and coriander.

Brown and Wild Rice Salad Mix in the apple and garnish with the spring onions and walnuts.

Lemon Roulades Allow the roulades to return to room temperature.

Gruyère Potato Halves Split the potatoes, top with the Gruyère and return them to the oven 15 minutes before serving, then sprinkle with chives.

When you're ready for dessert

Lemon Roulades Remove the clingfilm and cocktail sticks from the roulades and serve with the lemon curd/Mascarpone cream from the fridge.

Chocolate Ricotta Cheesecake Dust the cheesecake with a little of the cocoa powder and pour the cream to accompany it into a jug.

From top to bottom: Mini Yorkshire Puddings with Rare Beef and Horseradish-and-Mustard Crème Fraîche; Curried Turkey Salad with Dried Fruits; Caramelised Onion Tartlets with Goats' Cheese and Thyme; and Brown and Wild Rice Salad with Dried Cranberries

Curried Turkey Salad with Dried Fruits

This is also a great recipe for leftover turkey on Boxing Day and if you're short of time, you can make it with ready-cooked chicken.

Serves 12 as part of the buffet
2 lb (900 g) cooked turkey (or chicken or 2 medium ready-to-eat chickens)
1 tablespoon Madras curry paste
3 oz (75 g) each raisins; ready-to-eat dried apricots, quartered; and whole blanched almonds
5 fl oz (150 ml) mayonnaise
3 fl oz (75 ml) natural yoghurt
2 tablespoons mango chutney
1 bunch spring onions, chopped, including the green parts
5 oz (150 g) baby leaf salad
1 tablespoon fresh coriander leaves
salt and freshly milled black pepper

You will also need a small baking tray.

Begin by pre-heating the oven to gas mark 4, 350°F (180°C). Next, spread the almonds out on the baking tray and toast them in the oven for 8 minutes, using a timer so they do not burn. Let them cool for a couple of minutes, then roughly chop them.

Next, cut the turkey (or chicken) into bite-sized pieces and place it in a large bowl. (If using ready-to-eat chickens, strip all the meat from the carcasses, discarding the skin and bones.)

Then, in a small bowl, mix the mayonnaise and yoghurt with the curry paste and chutney (finely chop any bits of mango), and pour this sauce over the meat. Now add the raisins, apricots, three-quarters of the spring onions and two-thirds of the almonds. Mix everything together thoroughly, taste and season, then cover and chill until needed.

When you are ready to serve, place the salad leaves in the base of one or two serving dishes and spoon the turkey (or chicken) over the top, heaping it up to give it some height. Then scatter the reserved spring onions and almonds and the coriander leaves over the top.

Gruyère Jacket Potato Halves with Chives

I always like to serve one hot dish with a cold buffet, and jacket potatoes are great in winter. In summer, I would serve hot new potatoes with butter and chives.

Serves 12 (makes 12 halves)
6 medium-sized Desirée potatoes (each weighing about 4 oz/110 g)
3 oz (75 g) Gruyère, finely grated
a little olive oil
2 tablespoons freshly snipped chives, to garnish
sea salt, crushed

You will also need a medium-sized baking tray.

Pre-heat the oven to gas mark 5, 375°F (190°C).

First scrub the potatoes, dry them with a clean tea cloth, then leave them aside to dry thoroughly for as long as possible. If they are already washed, all you need do is wipe them with damp kitchen paper. Next, prick their skins a few times with a fork, then put a few drops of oil on to each potato and rub it all over the skin. After that, rub on some crushed sea salt.

Place the potatoes straight on to the centre shelf of the oven and let them bake for 1-1¼ hours, until the skins are really very crisp.

Now cut each potato in half lengthways and score the flesh in a diamond pattern to break it up a bit. Then place the potatoes on the baking tray, and while still hot, divide the grated Gruyère between them. Return them to the oven for 15 minutes, until the cheese is melted and golden. Sprinkle with the chives just before serving.

This recipe is from Lindsey Greensted-Benech, who helped me to create the catering operation at the football club. I found it hard to believe at first: could a cold Yorkshire taste good? All I can say is, as you live, you learn – it is one of the most ingenious buffet-party recipes I've ever come across, and disappears like lightning.

You need to start this by making the batter, so sift the flour into a bowl, make a well in the centre, break the eggs into it and add salt and freshly milled black pepper. Begin to whisk the eggs with an electric hand whisk and as you beat them, the flour around the edges will slowly be incorporated. When the mixture becomes stiff, simply add the milk-and-water mixture gradually, keeping the whisk going. Stop and scrape the sides of the bowl with a spatula so that any lumps can be pushed down into the batter, then whisk again until all is smooth. Now the batter is ready to use.

Next, place the muffin tin on the baking tray and brush the cups generously with the dripping. Now pop the tin on the tray into the oven to pre-heat for 10-15 minutes. After that, use a thick oven glove and remove them from the oven, placing the baking tray over direct heat, and quickly spoon a tablespoon of batter into each cup. Immediately return them to the middle shelf of the oven and bake for 15-20 minutes, until well risen and very crispy. Then remove the Yorkshires to a wire rack to cool. Now repeat the whole process with the remaining batter.

For the beef, turn the oven up to gas mark 8, 450°F (230°C). In the meantime, pre-heat a large, heavy-based frying pan on the hob, brush it with a little dripping and, when that's hot, seal the beef on all sides, but don't move it around until each side has sealed properly. Remove the meat to a roasting tin, season with freshly milled black pepper and roast in the oven for 18 minutes for rare beef, or up to 25 minutes, if you like it less rare. After that, allow it to cool, then cover and chill thoroughly in the fridge to make it easier to slice.

When you are ready to serve the Yorkshire puddings, thinly slice the beef into 24 slices and arrange a fold of beef in each one. Mix together all the sauce ingredients, then add a teaspoon of the sauce and a sprig of watercress to each Yorkshire.

Makes 24

1 lb 8 oz (700 g) piece trimmed fillet of British beef
6 oz (175 g) plain flour
2 large eggs
6 fl oz (175 ml) milk mixed with 4 fl oz (120 ml) water
about 2 tablespoons beef dripping, melted
salt and freshly milled black pepper

For the sauce:
2 rounded tablespoons hot horseradish sauce
2 teaspoons wholegrain mustard
1 heaped tablespoon crème fraîche
salt and freshly milled black pepper

To garnish:
24 sprigs watercress

You will also need a 12-hole muffin tin with cups measuring 2 inches (5 cm) at the base and 3 inches (7.5 cm) at the top, 1¼ inches (3 cm) deep; and a large baking tray.

Pre-heat the oven to gas mark 7, 425°F (220°C).

Caramelised Onion Tartlets with Goats' Cheese and Thyme

When we made these tartlets for the photography, we couldn't stop eating them! Crisp, light pastry with such a luscious filling – and also lovely as a first course at a supper party.

Makes 24

For the pastry:

6 oz (175 g) plain flour
3 oz (75 g) butter, at room temperature, cut into smallish lumps, and a little extra for greasing
1½ oz (40 g) Parmesan (Parmigiano Reggiano), finely grated
½ teaspoon mustard powder
cayenne pepper
about 1½ tablespoons cold water
1 large egg, beaten

For the filling:

2 large Spanish onions, peeled and finely chopped
2 x 4 oz (110 g) Welsh goats' cheese logs
24 small sprigs fresh thyme, dipped in olive oil
1 oz (25 g) butter
1 large egg
4 fl oz (120 ml) single cream
¼ teaspoon mustard powder
cayenne pepper
salt and freshly milled black pepper

You will also need a 3¼ inch (8 cm) pastry cutter; and two 12-hole patty tins with cups measuring 1¾ inches (4.5 cm) at the base, 2½ inches (6 cm) at the top, ¾ inch (2 cm) deep, well greased.

First make the pastry. Sift the flour into a large bowl, then add the butter. Take a knife and begin to cut it into the flour until it looks fairly evenly blended, then add the Parmesan, mustard and a pinch of cayenne pepper, plus just enough cold water to make a smooth dough, before discarding the knife and bringing it together with your fingertips. Then place the dough in a plastic food bag and put it into the fridge to rest for 30 minutes. In the meantime, pre-heat the oven to gas mark 4, 350°F (180°C).

After that, roll it out as thinly as possible, use the cutter to stamp out twenty-four rounds and line the tins with them. (The pastry will stand proud of the rim of the cups to allow for shrinkage.) Then prick the bases and brush with the beaten egg. Now bake on the middle and top shelves of the oven (swapping them over halfway through to ensure even browning) for about 10 minutes, or until the pastry is just cooked through, then cool them on a wire rack.

Meanwhile, for the filling, melt the butter in a large frying pan and cook the onions very gently, uncovered and stirring often, for about 30 minutes, or until they have turned a lovely golden brown caramel colour. Then leave them to cool and set aside until needed.

Now whisk the egg with the cream and mustard in a jug and add some seasoning. Next, spoon a little of the onion mixture into each pastry case, spread it out evenly and pour the egg mixture over. Cut each cheese log into 12 thin slices (wiping the knife between slices to cut more cleanly; the cheese is quite soft, so you may have to reshape a few slices into rounds). Place a slice on the top of each tartlet, then top with a sprig of thyme and a sprinkling of cayenne pepper. Bake for 20 minutes, or until puffy and golden, swapping the tins again halfway through cooking.

Brown and Wild Rice Salad with Dried Cranberries

Good old rice salad is an absolute must at a buffet party. This one, made with wild rice, looks very pretty with the jewelled colours of the dried cranberries and nuts.

Begin by heating half the groundnut oil in the smaller frying pan, then add the wild rice and toss it around to coat the grains. Now pour over 8 fl oz (225 ml) of boiling water and add a little salt. Give it one stir, put the lid on and cook over a gentle heat for 50 minutes. Meanwhile, repeat the process with the brown rice, this time adding 16 fl oz (450 ml) of boiling water – it will take 40-45 minutes for the water to be absorbed and the rice to become tender.

While the rice is cooking, you can make the dressing. Pound the garlic and salt to a creamy paste with a pestle and mortar. Next, work in the mustard powder, then switch to a small whisk and add the vinegar and olive oil. Season with plenty of freshly milled black pepper.

Now you'll need to toast the walnuts, so spread them out on a baking tray and place them in the oven for 8 minutes, putting a timer on so you don't forget them. Meanwhile, place the tomatoes in a heatproof bowl and pour boiling water on to them. After exactly a minute, remove them from the water and slip off their skins (protecting your hands with a cloth if the tomatoes are hot), then halve them, squeeze out the seeds and chop them into small pieces.

When both amounts of rice are cooked, mix them together in a serving bowl and add 3-4 tablespoons of the dressing. Toss the rice around in the dressing and then leave it to cool.

When it's cool, mix in the cucumber, tomatoes, diced pepper, apple, cranberries, two-thirds of the spring onions and two-thirds of the walnuts. Drizzle with the remaining dressing and mix again so that everything is thoroughly combined and coated in dressing. Finally, just scatter the remaining spring onions and walnuts over the surface of the salad.

Note: I have tried to make this salad by cooking the two sorts of rice together, but I've found I can't get the timing right, as the wild rice takes a little longer, so you do need to cook them separately.

Serves 12 as part of the buffet
8 fl oz (225 ml) brown basmati rice
(use a measuring jug)
4 fl oz (120 ml) wild rice
(use a measuring jug)
2 oz (50 g) dried cranberries
1 dessertspoon groundnut or other
flavourless oil
2 oz (50 g) walnuts, roughly chopped
3 medium-sized ripe, red tomatoes
3 inch (7.5 cm) piece cucumber, cut
into small dice (no need to peel)
1 small red (or yellow) pepper,
deseeded and diced
1 red-skinned dessert apple, washed,
cored and finely chopped (no need
to peel)
3 spring onions, finely chopped,
including the green parts
salt and freshly milled black pepper

For the dressing:
1 clove garlic
1 teaspoon mustard powder
3 tablespoons Champagne vinegar
(or good-quality white wine vinegar)
6 tablespoons extra virgin olive oil
freshly milled black pepper
1 teaspoon sea salt

You will also need one small and one large heavy-based frying pan with tight-fitting lids.

Pre-heat the oven to gas mark 4, 350°F (180°C).

Thai Pork Satays with Thai Peanut Sauce

My thanks to John Curtis, formerly Head Chef at Norwich City Football Club, for this brilliant recipe. It has all the exotic fragrances and flavours of the East, yet it's very simple to make.

Makes 12

1 lb 4 oz (570 g) British pork tenderloin, trimmed
6 oz (175 g) smooth peanut butter
2 oz (50 g) salted, roasted peanuts
3 freeze-dried kaffir lime leaves
1 stem lemon grass, ends trimmed and tough outer layer discarded, roughly chopped
1 medium-sized red chilli, deseeded
1 clove garlic, crushed
½ tablespoon peeled, chopped fresh root ginger
grated zest 1 lime
juice 2 limes
1 tablespoon Thai fish sauce
¾ oz (20 g) fresh coriander
7 fl oz (200 ml) tinned coconut milk
1 oz (25 g) light soft brown sugar
a little groundnut or other flavourless oil, for brushing
lime wedges, to garnish

You will also need twelve wooden skewers.

You need to start by making the sauce, half of which is used as a marinade for the pork, the other half as a dipping sauce. Start off by placing the lime leaves in a small bowl, cover with boiling water and leave to soak for 5 minutes. Then, remove them, roll them up very tightly and shred finely.

Place the lime leaves in a food processor with the lemon grass. Now add the chilli, garlic, ginger, lime zest and juice, and fish sauce. Next, separate the leaves from the coriander stalks, and reserve them until later. Pop the stalks into the food processor and process until everything is very finely chopped. Now add the peanut butter, coconut milk and sugar and whiz again until everything is thoroughly blended. Then pour half the sauce (about 8 fl oz/225 ml) into a large bowl for the pork marinade.

Next, add the peanuts and reserved coriander leaves to the remaining sauce in the processor and pulse once again until coarsely chopped. (The chopped peanuts add a bit more texture.) Now pour the sauce into another bowl, cover and keep stored in the fridge until about an hour before you are ready to serve for the buffet.

Next, to prepare the satays, cut the pork into bite-sized cubes measuring about ¾ inch (2 cm). (You're aiming for 36 pieces.) Now add them to the marinade in the large bowl and mix well, then cover and leave aside for a minimum of an hour. Meanwhile, put the wooden skewers in a shallow dish, cover with hot water and leave to soak for a minimum of 30 minutes. (This helps to prevent them from burning under the grill.)

When you are ready to cook the satays, pre-heat the grill to its highest setting for at least 10 minutes and line the grill pan with kitchen foil. Remove the skewers from their water bath, dry them in a clean tea cloth, then brush them with the oil to prevent the pork from sticking. Thread three cubes of pork on to each skewer, keeping the pieces slightly spaced apart, and arrange the kebabs on the grill rack. Brush liberally with some of the remaining marinade and place under the grill, about 3 inches (7.5 cm) from the heat source. They will take 15-20 minutes to cook, and during that time, you need to turn them and brush them with the remaining marinade as they cook.

When the satays have cooled, cover and refrigerate until needed. Then serve with the sauce, garnished with the wedges of lime.

Lemon Roulade

This is very light, fresh and lemony, with a lovely squidgy centre and it always looks very pretty. And rolling up a roulade is much easier than you think!

Serves 12-16 (makes 2 roulades)
grated zest 2 lemons (juice reserved for the lemon curd)
4 oz (110 g) softened butter, plus a little extra for greasing
8 oz (225 g) golden caster sugar
4 large eggs
8 oz (225 g) self-raising flour, sifted
2 tablespoons hot water
a little icing sugar, sifted, for dusting

For the lemon curd:
grated zest 2 lemons
juice 4 lemons (half from the cake base)
4 large eggs
6 oz (175 g) golden caster sugar
4 oz (110 g) softened unsalted butter, cut into small cubes
1 dessertspoon cornflour

For the Mascarpone cream:
1 lb 2 oz (500 g) Mascarpone, chilled
14 oz (400 g) fromage frais, chilled
1½ tablespoons golden caster sugar

For the icing:
juice and zest 2 lemons
2 oz (50 g) icing sugar, sifted

You will also need two shallow baking tins measuring 9 x 13 inches (23 x 32.5 cm) and ½ inch (1 cm) deep, lightly greased and lined with silicone paper (parchment); and two 18 inch (45 cm) long sheets of silicone paper (parchment).

Begin by making the lemon curd ahead of time, as it needs to be well chilled (for method, see page 567). When the curd is ready, allow it to cool, then cover it with clingfilm pressed over the surface and chill it in the fridge. Meanwhile, pre-heat the oven to gas mark 6, 400°F (200°C).

When you're ready to make the sponge base, place all the ingredients except the icing sugar and hot water in a large mixing bowl and whisk, preferably with an electric hand whisk, for about a minute, then add the hot water and whisk briefly again. Next, divide the mixture between the two prepared baking tins, smooth it out and bake in the oven on the middle shelf for 8-10 minutes. (Don't be tempted to open the oven door until 8 minutes have elapsed, or the sponges may sink.) When the sponges are ready, they should feel springy in the centre when lightly touched with your little finger. Remove them from the oven and let them cool in the tins for 5 minutes.

Meanwhile, lay the sheet of silicone paper for each sponge on a flat surface and dust it all over with the icing sugar. Then, taking each sponge in turn, carefully turn them out on to the silicone paper and gently strip away the paper lining the bases. Cover them with a clean, damp tea cloth and leave for another 5 minutes (but no longer, as they should still be warm, to make the rolling easy).

Now, don't panic – this next part really is quite easy: just lift the paper along the shorter edge and fold it over, then gently roll each sponge up with the paper tucked inside as a lining. If cracks appear, don't worry – they can look very attractive. Now leave the sponges to get cold.

When you're ready to fill them, carefully unroll them and spread each with a third of the lemon curd all over. Now whisk the Mascarpone, fromage frais and sugar together and spread a third of that over each roulade. Then roll each roulade up carefully, but much more loosely.

For the finishing touch, place the zest of the two lemons (removed with a zester, so you get nice curly strands) in a saucer and mix with about a tablespoon of the lemon juice. Next, in a bowl, mix the icing sugar with 2 tablespoons of the lemon juice to make a thin glaze. Drizzle this with a spoon, using sweeping movements back and forth across the top of each roulade. Then drain the lemon zest and scatter half over the icing on each cake.

Combine the leftover Mascarpone mixture with the lemon curd and serve the roulades cut into slices, with the extra lemon Mascarpone cream handed round separately.

Chocolate Ricotta Cheesecake

This cheesecake is not intensely 'in-your-face' chocolatey, but more subtle. The texture and the slight acidity in the Ricotta give it an unusual edge and this, combined with the pure chocolate on top, is what makes it a very classy dessert. One thing is essential, though, and that's lots of chilled pouring cream to go with it.

Serves 12 as part of the buffet
For the base:
2 oz (50 g) unblanched whole almonds
6 oz (175 g) dark chocolate
oatmeal biscuits
1 oz (25 g) Grape-Nuts cereal
2 oz (50 g) butter, melted
a little groundnut or other flavourless
oil for greasing

For the cheesecake:
5 oz (150 g) dark chocolate
(75 per cent cocoa solids), broken
into small pieces
12 oz (350 g) Ricotta, at
room temperature
7 fl oz (200 ml) half-fat crème
fraîche, at room temperature
2 large eggs, separated
2 oz (50 g) golden caster sugar
7 g leaf gelatine
2 tablespoons milk

For the chocolate curls:
4 oz (110 g) dark chocolate
(75 per cent cocoa solids), broken
into small pieces
a little cocoa powder, sifted, for dusting

You will also need an 8 inch (20 cm) springform cake tin, the sides and base lightly oiled; and a plate with a diameter of about 4 inches (10 cm) not including the rim.

Pre-heat the oven to gas mark 6, 400°F (200°C).

First of all, spread the almonds out on a small baking tray and toast them in the oven for 7 minutes, using a timer. After that, chop them quite finely. Next, place the biscuits in a plastic food bag and crush them, using a rolling pin. Then tip the crumbs into a mixing bowl and add the nuts and Grape-Nuts. Now add the butter to bind it all together, then press the mixture into the base of the tin, pop it into the oven and bake for 10 minutes. After that, remove it and leave it to cool.

Meanwhile, melt the chocolate for the cheesecake in a heatproof bowl over a pan of barely simmering water, making sure the bowl doesn't touch the water, then remove it from the heat and let it cool as well. Next, in a large mixing bowl, whisk together the Ricotta, crème fraîche, egg yolks and sugar until smooth and well blended.

Now soak the leaves of gelatine in a small bowl of cold water for about 5 minutes, and while that's happening, heat the milk in a small saucepan up to simmering point before taking it off the heat. Squeeze the excess water from the gelatine, then add it to the milk and whisk until it has dissolved. Now stir the gelatine and milk, along with the cooled chocolate, into the Ricotta mixture, until it's all thoroughly blended.

Now, in another, grease-free bowl and using clean beaters, whisk the egg whites to the soft-peak stage. Then, first fold a tablespoon of egg white into the cheesecake mixture to loosen it, and after that, carefully but thoroughly fold in the rest of the egg white. Next, pour the mixture on to the cheesecake base, cover with clingfilm and chill in the fridge for at least 4 hours or, preferably, overnight – the longer the better.

To make the chocolate curls, melt the chocolate as before, then pour it on to the base of the plate to form an even layer about ¼ inch (5 mm) thick. Place the plate into the fridge for 45 minutes to chill and set. (The chocolate should be hard enough so that, if you press the surface, it doesn't leave an indentation, but not rock hard.) Then, using a large-bladed knife held carefully at either end with both hands (or a cheese slice), pull the blade across the chocolate, pressing down slightly. As the blade comes towards you, the chocolate will form curls. (If it is too hard, it will be brittle and will break rather than forming curls, in which case, leave it at room temperature for 5 minutes before trying again.) Store the curls in a sealed container in the fridge until you are ready to use them. You probably won't need all this chocolate to make enough curls to top the cake, but as the layer of chocolate gets thinner, it will be harder to form nice curls, so the remaining chocolate can be lifted off the plate and melted again for another recipe (or simply eaten!).

To unmould the cheesecake, first run a palette knife around the edge of the tin, then release the spring-clip and remove it. After that, carefully lift it off the base of the tin and transfer it to a serving plate. Decorate it with the chocolate curls and give them a light dusting of sifted cocoa powder.

Note: This recipe contains raw eggs.

An Italian Lunch or Supper

Once again, this menu leaves you perfectly free to enjoy your guests' company, as absolutely everything can be prepared ahead and be ready to go when you want. All you will have to do is pre-heat the oven and pop in the lasagne 45-50 minutes before you want to serve it, and dress the salad just before you eat. Serves 8.

Menu
Antipasti
Traditional Lasagne al Forno
Zabaglione Torta

Antipasti

Serves 8
16 slices Mortadella (12 oz/350 g)
16 slices Parma ham (6 oz/175 g)
24 slices salami (10 oz/275 g)
1 lb (450 g) Mozzarella
16 each olives, cornichons and radishes
4 tablespoons olive oil
freshly milled black pepper

This is my favourite Italian first course. If you can buy the meats and cheese from a specialist Italian deli, so much the better; alternatively, counters at supermarkets will cut you the correct quantities. You could serve it with some of the sharp Giardiniere Pickles on page 574. Then all it needs is some warm Italian bread and good, creamy butter.

All you need to do is divide the meats and cheese equally between eight plates, garnish with the olives, cornichons and radishes, and just before serving, drizzle the cheese with the olive oil and season it with freshly milled black pepper.

My first lasagne recipe is clearly in need of an update and that's simply because we are now able to buy more authentic ingredients. I have also discovered from an Italian friend that the long, slow cooking of the ragù really does develop all the flavours in a wonderful way. Lasagne has suffered greatly from being anglicised, factory made and served as cheap nosh, its authenticity obliterated – all the more reason to reinvent this great classic dish in all its original glory.

First of all, begin by making the ragù. Heat a tablespoon of the oil in your largest frying pan over a medium heat and gently fry the onion for about 10 minutes, moving it around from time to time. While it is softening, chop the pancetta: the best way to do this is to roll it into a sausage shape, then, using a sharp knife, slice it lengthways into four, then slice the lengths across as finely as possible. After the 10 minutes is up, add this to the pan, along with the garlic, and continue cooking the whole lot for about 5 minutes. Now transfer this mixture to the casserole.

Next, add another tablespoon of oil to the pan, turn up the heat to its highest, then add the minced beef and brown it, breaking it up and moving it around in the pan. (A wooden fork is really helpful here.) When the beef is browned, tip it into the casserole to join the onion mixture, then heat another tablespoon of oil and do exactly the same with the minced pork.

While the pork is browning, trim the chicken livers, rinse them under cold, running water and dry them thoroughly with kitchen paper. Pull off any skin and snip out any tubes or odd bits of fat with kitchen scissors, then chop the livers minutely small. When the pork is browned, transfer it to the casserole, too. Finally, heat the remaining tablespoon of oil and cook the pieces of chicken liver, adding these to the casserole as soon as they have browned nicely.

After that, you need to remove the pan and place the casserole over the direct heat, and give everything a really good stir. Then add the contents of both tins of tomatoes, the tomato purée, red wine, a really good seasoning of salt and freshly milled black pepper and about a quarter of a nutmeg, grated. More stirring now, then allow this to come up to simmering point. While that happens, strip the leaves from half the basil, tear them into small pieces and add them to the casserole. Then, as soon as everything is simmering, place the casserole on the centre shelf of the oven and leave it to cook slowly, without a lid, for exactly 4 hours. It's a good idea to have a look after 3 hours to make sure all is well and to have a good stir, but what you should end up with is a thick, reduced, concentrated sauce, with only a trace of liquid left in it. When that happens, remove the casserole from the oven, taste to check the seasoning, then strip the remaining leaves off the basil, tear them into small pieces and stir them in.

Traditional Lasagne al Forno

Serves 8

1 lb (450 g) green no-cook dried lasagne sheets (about 24 sheets)
14 oz (400 g) Mozzarella, diced
4 oz (110 g) Parmesan (Parmigiano Reggiano), freshly grated or shaved

For the ragù:
4 tablespoons extra virgin olive oil
1 large onion, peeled and finely chopped
7 oz (200 g) sliced pancetta
2 fat cloves garlic, chopped
12 oz (350 g) minced British beef
12 oz (350 g) minced British pork
6 oz (175 g) chicken livers
1 x 400 g tin Italian chopped tomatoes
1 x 230 g tin chopped tomatoes
6 tablespoons tomato purée
6 fl oz (175 ml) red wine
¼ whole nutmeg
⅓ oz (15 g) fresh basil
salt and freshly milled black pepper

For the cream sauce:
6 fl oz (175 ml) double cream
2½ pints (1.5 litres) milk
6 oz (175 g) butter, plus a little extra for greasing
4 oz (110 g) plain flour
¼ whole nutmeg
salt and freshly milled black pepper

You will also need a flameproof casserole with a capacity of 4½ pints (2.6 litres); and a roasting tin (or ovenproof dish) measuring about 10 x 12 x 3 inches (25.5 x 30 x 7.5 cm), well buttered.

Pre-heat the oven to gas mark 1, 275°F (140°C).

Now, to make the cream sauce, place the milk, butter, flour and some seasoning in a large, thick-based saucepan. Place this over a gentle heat and whisk continuously with a balloon whisk until the sauce comes to simmering point and thickens. Then, with the heat as low as possible, continue to cook the sauce for about 10 minutes.

After that, sieve the sauce into a bowl, beat in the cream, taste and season if it needs it, and grate in another quarter of the whole nutmeg. Now spread about a quarter of the ragù over the base of the roasting tin (or dish). Cover this with one fifth of the sauce, followed by a quarter of the Mozzarella, then arrange a single layer (about six sheets) of the lasagne. (I find you need four placed side by side lengthways and the other two halved and spread along the gap that's left.) Repeat this process three more times, finishing with a final layer of sauce, then cover the whole lot with the grated Parmesan and the lasagne is ready for the oven. All this can be done well in advance. Then, when you're ready to bake the lasagne, pop it on to the top shelf of the oven, pre-heated to gas mark 4, 350°F (180°C) for 45-50 minutes, or until it's bubbling and turning slightly golden on top.

Zabaglione Torta

This is my version of a truly wonderful dessert cake, which I first ate in Harry's Dolci, my favourite Venetian restaurant. The original recipe is in Harry's Bar Cookbook.

Serves 8

For the cake:

4 oz (110 g) self-raising flour

½ teaspoon baking powder

2 large eggs, at room temperature

4 oz (110 g) well-softened butter, plus a little extra for greasing

4 oz (110 g) golden caster sugar

¼ teaspoon pure vanilla extract

a little icing sugar, sifted, to decorate

For the filling:

3 large egg yolks

3 oz (75 g) golden caster sugar

1½ oz (40 g) plain flour, sifted

9 fl oz (250 ml) Marsala

12 fl oz (340 ml) double cream

You will also need an 8 inch (20 cm) sponge tin, 1½ inch (4 cm) deep, lightly greased and the base lined with silicone paper (parchment).

First of all, make the zabaglione filling. Using an electric hand whisk, beat the egg yolks for a minute in a medium bowl, then add the sugar and beat again until the mixture is thick and pale yellow – about 3 minutes.

Next, whisk in the flour a tablespoon at a time, mixing it in really well, then gradually whisk in the Marsala. Now tip the mixture into a medium-sized heavy-based saucepan and place it over a medium heat. Stir constantly until it has thickened and is just about to boil – this will take about 5 minutes. (Don't worry if it looks lumpy, just tip it into a clean bowl, then whisk until smooth again.) Now let it cool, whisking it from time to time to stop a skin forming. When it is cold, cover with clingfilm and pop it into the fridge for at least 2 hours.

Now pre-heat the oven to gas mark 3, 325°F (170°C). Meanwhile, make the cake. First sift the flour and baking powder into a large mixing bowl, holding the sieve high to give them a good airing as they go down. All you do next is simply add the other ingredients and just go in with the electric hand whisk. Whisk for about a minute, until you have a smooth, well-combined mixture that drops off a spoon when you give it a tap on the side of the bowl. If it seems a bit stiff, add a little water and mix again.

Now spoon the mixture into the tin, level it out with the back of the spoon and bake on the centre shelf for 30-35 minutes – don't open the oven door before 30 minutes have elapsed. To test, touch the centre lightly: if it leaves no impression and the sponge springs back, it is ready. Remove it from the oven, but wait about 5 minutes before turning it out on to a cooling rack. Carefully peel off the base paper by making a fold in it first, then pull it gently away without trying to lift it off too quickly. Now leave the sponge to cool completely.

To assemble the torta, whip the cream in a large bowl until stiff, then add the zabaglione and whisk again until thoroughly mixed. Now place the cake flat on a board and, holding a serrated palette knife horizontally, carefully slice it into two thin halves. Next, reserving 2-3 heaped tablespoons of the zabaglione to decorate the sides, spread the rest of it over the bottom half, easing it to the edges. Place the other half on top and press down very gently. Before you spread the zabaglione on the sides, brush away any loose crumbs, so they don't get mixed up in it. Now, using a small palette knife, spread the sides evenly with the reserved mixture. Finally, dust the top with the icing sugar before serving. If the cake is made and decorated ahead of time, store it, covered, in the fridge (to keep it firm), but remove it half an hour before serving.

Note: This recipe contains partially cooked eggs.

A Summer Lunch or Supper

Because of the vagaries of the British summer, this menu has been designed with sun *or* rain in mind. If you find the weather's not that good, it helps to serve a hot watercress soup and, as the main course is served cold, you could also serve the potato salad warm, if you prefer. On the other hand, if it's a lovely, hot, sunny day, then the soup can be served cold, in chilled bowls with ice cubes. There is nothing, but nothing quite like serving a whole salmon on a summer's day. Because the salmon is cooked slowly in kitchen foil, with bone, skin and head intact, the flavour will be far superior to cooking it any other way. Serves 8.

Menu
Watercress Soup
Baked Whole Salmon with Sauce Verte
Anya Potato Salad with Shallots and Vinaigrette
Chunky Green Salad
Gooseberry Crème Fraîche Tart

Watercress Soup

Serves 8
9 oz (250 g) watercress, destalked
and chopped, a few leaves reserved
for garnishing
4 oz (110 g) butter
the white parts of 5 leeks (weighing
about 14 oz/400 g), cleaned
and roughly chopped
4 medium potatoes (weighing
about 1 lb 8 oz /700 g), peeled
and roughly chopped
3 pints (1.75 litres) hot stock made
with Marigold Swiss vegetable
bouillon powder
4 heaped tablespoons crème fraîche
salt and freshly milled black pepper

Watercress is a star performer in so many ways. I love the fat, green leaves in salads, sprinkled with rock salt in sandwiches, in a sauce and perhaps most of all, in this soup, which is always a joy to make and eat.

First of all, melt the butter in a large, heavy-based saucepan, then add the leeks, potato and watercress and stir them around so they are coated with the melted butter.

Next, sprinkle in some salt, then cover with a lid and let the vegetables sweat over a very gentle heat for about 20 minutes, giving the mixture a good stir about halfway through.

After that, add the stock, bring everything up to simmering point and simmer, covered, for 10-15 minutes, or until the vegetables are quite tender. Then remove the pan from the heat and when the soup has cooled a little, liquidise it in batches, then return it to the saucepan.

Now stir in 3 tablespoons of crème fraîche, season to taste and re-heat the soup very gently, without letting it boil. Serve it in hot bowls and garnish each one with the reserved watercress leaves and an extra swirl of crème fraîche. Alternatively, cool the soup and serve chilled, garnished in the same way.

Baked Whole Salmon with Sauce Verte

Serves 8
4 lb (1.8 kg) fresh whole salmon,
cleaned and gutted
2 oz (50 g) butter, plus a little extra
for greasing
1 small onion, peeled and thinly sliced
3 bay leaves
4 sprigs chopped fresh tarragon
salt and freshly milled black pepper

For the sauce:
2 large eggs
2 teaspoons mustard powder
1 fat clove garlic
½ pint (275 ml) groundnut or other
flavourless oil
2 dessertspoons white wine vinegar
3 oz (75 g) spinach
1½ oz (40 g) watercress, tough
stalks removed
1½ oz (40 g) fresh flat-leaf parsley
2 tablespoons chopped fresh tarragon
1 tablespoon freshly snipped chives
1 tablespoon (or more) lemon juice,
to taste
salt and freshly milled black pepper

You will also need a baking tray
measuring 11 x 16 inches (28 x
40 cm), and some kitchen foil.

With summer in mind, when, if the weather allows, there can be all kinds of outdoor celebrations, nothing is nicer on a buffet table than a whole salmon. I wouldn't say I was the last of the big spenders foodwise, but I am very happy to fork out once a year and buy a wild salmon – the king of fish – and cook it to perfection to enjoy one of the best feasts of summer. The best accompaniment is a sweet Sauce Verte, flavoured with summer herbs, which I think is best made the day before, if possible, to allow the flavours to develop.

The way I cook a salmon is extremely slowly, wrapped in kitchen foil in the oven. I cannot recommend this method highly enough. Unfortunately, the gas equivalent of 250°F (130°C), which used to be gas mark ½, no longer exists. So, if you use a modern gas cooker that begins at gas mark 1, give the fish 25 minutes less cooking time.

First make the sauce. Break the eggs straight into your blender or food processor, then sprinkle in the mustard powder and add the garlic clove and a teaspoon of salt. Next, measure the oil into a jug, switch the machine on and pour in the oil in a thin, steady trickle with the motor running. (You must be very careful here: too much oil too quickly and the sauce will curdle.) When all the oil is in, blend in the vinegar.

Now rinse the spinach, watercress and parsley under a little cold, running water and put them into a saucepan. Then, with the heat turned to medium, stir them around until everything has just wilted. Next, tip them into a colander and rinse them again under cold, running water to keep their colour. Squeeze out the excess moisture very carefully, thoroughly pressing with a wooden spoon. Then transfer the leaves to the blender or food processor, along with the tarragon and chives, and whiz until the sauce is smooth and green. (There will be some fine specks, but that's okay.) Now taste and season with the lemon juice and freshly milled black pepper, and some more salt, if it needs it.

When you are ready to cook the salmon, pre-heat the oven to 250°F (130°C). (For the gas mark, see introduction). Start by wiping the fish with some damp kitchen paper, then place it in the centre of a large, double sheet of kitchen foil that you've generously buttered. Put 1 oz (25 g) butter, the onion slices, bay leaves and tarragon into the centre cavity, along with a seasoning of salt and freshly milled black pepper. The rest of the butter should be smeared over the top of the fish. Now wrap the kitchen foil over the fish to make a loose but well-sealed parcel and place it diagonally on the baking tray, so that it fits in the oven. If it's still too long, bend the tail end upwards. Bake in the centre of the oven for 2½ hours.

After that, remove the salmon from the oven and allow it to completely cool in the kitchen foil before serving. The skin will peel off very easily now the salmon is cooked. Slit the fish down the middle, following the backbone, and ease the fillets away. Serve with the sauce, crisp, dressed salad leaves (such as Cos lettuce), cucumber, and some hot, buttered new potatoes, or potato salad.

Note: For other weights of salmon, the cooking times are as follows: for 2 lb (900 g), 1½ hours; for 3 lbs (1.35 kg), 2 hours; for 5 lb (2.25 kg), 3 hours.

This recipe contains raw eggs.

Anya Potato Salad with Shallots and Vinaigrette

I love the consistently good flavour of Anya potatoes, which we use all the time at our catering functions at Norwich City Football Club, buying them direct from the grower. If you can't get them, try to buy other good-flavoured salad potatoes for this.

Serves 8

2 lb (900 g) Anya or other new potatoes, washed
6 shallots, peeled and finely chopped
4 tablespoons freshly snipped chives

For the vinaigrette:
2 cloves garlic
1 rounded dessertspoon mustard powder
1 tablespoon balsamic vinegar
1 tablespoon sherry vinegar
10 tablespoons extra virgin olive oil
freshly milled black pepper
1 rounded dessertspoon sea salt

You will also need a steamer.

Steam the potatoes over a pan of boiling water, sprinkled with salt and covered with a lid, for about 20 minutes until they are tender.

Meanwhile, make up the dressing. Begin by crushing the salt quite coarsely with a pestle and mortar, and then add the garlic. As you begin to crush it and it comes into contact with the salt, it will quickly break down into a purée. Next, add the mustard powder and really work it in, giving it about 20 seconds of circular movements to get it thoroughly blended. After that, add some freshly milled black pepper. Now add the vinegars and work these in in the same way. Then add the oil, switch to a small whisk and give everything a really good whisking.

As soon as the potatoes are cooked, cool them in a mixing bowl for 10 minutes, then stir in the vinaigrette and the shallots while they are still just warm. Now add the chives and give everything a good toss to distribute any dressing that has collected in the base of the bowl and transfer the salad to a serving bowl.

Chunky Green Salad

This is a simple salad of leaves with a bit of bite to them.

Serves 8

1 round lettuce and 1 head chicory, outer leaves removed
2 oz (50 g) rocket and watercress, stalks removed
½ cucumber, peeled and sliced thinly
3 spring onions, finely chopped

For the vinaigrette:
As above

First of all, tear the lettuce and chicory leaves and place them in a large serving bowl, along with the rocket and watercress. Now scatter in the cucumber and spring onions and toss well.

Next, make the vinaigrette as for the potato salad, above. Just before serving, whisk the dressing again, add half of it to the salad leaves and toss them, then add the remaining dressing and toss again, so that everything gets a good coating. Serve immediately.

Gooseberry Crème Fraîche Tart

This one disappeared in seconds when we were photographing the book. It's simple – just thin, crispy pastry and a layer of gooseberries set in custard. Delicious with or without some thick, yellow Jersey cream.

Serves 8
For the pastry:
5 oz (150 g) plain flour
1¼ oz (30 g) softened butter, cut into smallish lumps, plus a little extra for greasing
1¼ oz (30 g) softened lard, cut into smallish lumps
about 1½ tablespoons cold water
salt

For the filling:
1 lb (450 g) gooseberries, topped and tailed
3½ fl oz (100 ml) crème fraîche
2 large egg yolks
1½ oz (40 g) golden caster sugar
1 teaspoon balsamic vinegar

You will also need a 9 inch (23 cm) loose-based fluted tart tin, 1 inch (2.5 cm) deep, lightly greased; and a medium-sized baking tray.

First of all, make the pastry. Sift the flour and a pinch of salt into a bowl from a height to ensure it gets a good airing. Then take a knife and begin to cut the fat into the flour. Go on doing this until it looks fairly evenly blended, then rub in the fat using your fingertips only and with as light a touch as possible. As you do so, lift it up high and let it fall back into the bowl, which means that, all the time, air is being incorporated – and air is what makes pastry light. Speed is what's needed here, so don't go on rubbing all day – just long enough to make the mixture crumbly, with a few odd lumps here and there.

Next sprinkle a tablespoon of the water over the mixture, then start bringing the dough together, using the knife to make it cling. Now discard the knife and finally bring it together with your fingertips. When enough liquid is added, the pastry should leave the bowl completely clean. If this hasn't happened, then keep adding a spot more. (Sometimes it only needs your fingers dipped into water.) Place the pastry in a plastic food bag and rest it in the fridge for about 20 minutes. Meanwhile, pre-heat the oven to gas mark 5, 375°F (190°C) and pre-heat the baking tray at the same time.

Next, transfer the pastry to a flat, lightly floured surface and roll it out to a circle the diameter of the tin. Line the tin with the pastry, press it up about ¼ inch (5 mm) above the rim of the tin all round, then prick the base all over with a fork. Now brush the base and sides with some of the egg white left over from the eggs for the filling.

After that, place the pastry-lined tin on the hot baking tray and bake for 20 minutes until the pastry is just beginning to turn golden. Then remove it and reduce the heat to gas mark 4, 350°F (180°C).

Next, whisk the crème fraîche, yolks, sugar and vinegar together for the filling. Arrange the gooseberries in the pastry case, pour the crème fraîche mixture over them and return the tart to the oven for 40-45 minutes, or until it is a light golden brown. Then remove it from the oven and allow it to settle for about 20 minutes before serving. It also tastes extremely good served cold.

Savoury Mini Muffins with Two Flavourings

Makes 24
For the muffins:
10 oz (275 g) plain flour
1 tablespoon baking powder
2 large eggs
8 fl oz (225 ml) milk
a little butter for greasing
1 teaspoon salt

For the goats' cheese, red onion and rosemary flavouring:
2 oz (50 g) goats' cheese, cut into
¼ inch (5 mm) cubes
2 oz (50 g) red onion, peeled and finely chopped
2 teaspoons chopped fresh rosemary, plus 12 small sprigs for garnishing
½ oz (10 g) butter

For the Gruyère, sage and onion flavouring:
2 oz (50 g) Gruyère, grated
2 teaspoons chopped fresh sage, plus 12 small leaves for garnishing
2 oz (50 g) spring onions, finely sliced
2 teaspoons Parmesan (Parmigiano Reggiano), grated

You will also need two 12-hole mini-muffin tins, lightly greased; or two 12-hole mini-muffin tins, and 24 mini-muffin cases that have been lightly greased.

For a fresh approach to party nibbles, I offer you these magic little savouries that can be served warm from the oven or, if made in advance, frozen, defrosted and re-heated. First some simple muffin mathematics: the basic muffin recipe makes 24, and after that there are two flavourings – each for half that quantity – which should be prepared first. They can be made with or without muffin cases.

First, you need to prepare the two muffin flavourings. To make the goats' cheese, red onion and rosemary muffins, begin by melting the butter in a small saucepan and softening the onion in it for about 5 minutes. Then allow it to cool. Next, prepare and set aside the ingredients for the Gruyère, sage and onion muffins. Now pre-heat the oven to gas mark 6, 400°F (200°C) while you make the basic muffin mixture.

First of all, sift the flour, baking powder and salt on to a large plate, then take a large mixing bowl and sift the mixture again, this time into the bowl, holding the sieve up high to give the flour a good airing.

Now, in a jug, beat one egg, then whisk it together with the milk. Next, fold all this into the flour, using the minimum number of folding movements. (Ignore the unpromising look of the mixture at this stage and don't overmix.) Divide the mixture equally between two bowls in order to add the two different flavourings.

Now return to the first flavouring and gently mix the onion into the muffin mixture in one bowl, along with the goats' cheese and chopped rosemary, folding in, as before, with as few strokes as possible. Next, add the prepared ingredients for the second flavouring to the muffin mixture in the other bowl and fold them in in the same gentle way.

After that, if you are using muffin cases, arrange them in the tins and spoon the mixture into them; alternatively, spoon the mixture straight into the greased tins. You can pile the mixture quite high. Beat the second egg and brush the surfaces with it, then top the goats' cheese muffins with a sprig of rosemary, and the Gruyère muffins with the Parmesan and a sage leaf. Then bake them for about 20 minutes, or until well risen and golden. Remove the muffins from the tins to a rack and eat as warm as possible.

Bloody Mary Tomatoes

Serves 6
9 oz (250 g) baby plum tomatoes
(or cherry tomatoes), stalks removed
7 fl oz (200 ml) vodka
1 tablespoon sherry
1 tablespoon Worcestershire sauce
a few drops Tabasco sauce
½ teaspoon celery salt

To serve:
1 teaspoon celery salt, ¼ teaspoon
cayenne pepper, 2 tablespoons sea salt,
all mixed together

You will also need a small lidded
plastic box.

These look quite deceptive – I mean, what harm is there in a bowl of little tomatoes? But once swallowed, never forgotten! All the kick of a bloody Mary in one bite. Don't forget you need to start this two days in advance.

All you do is score a little cross on the base of each tomato, then place them in the plastic box cross-side up. Then whisk together the vodka, sherry, Worcestershire sauce, Tabasco and celery salt, and spoon it over them. Put the lid on the box and leave it in the fridge to allow the tomatoes to marinate for two days.

Before serving, drain the tomatoes and let them come back to room temperature. (You can keep any leftover marinade to use as a base for future batches.) Then arrange them on a plate with a bowl containing the salt mixture and invite your guests to dip in a tomato before eating.

Quails' Eggs with Cracked Pepper and Salt

Peeling boiled quails' eggs is not my favourite job so I usually rope in some help, but it's worth it because they look so pretty and taste wonderful dipped in cracked pepper and salt.

Serves 6
24 quails' eggs
1 tablespoon mixed peppercorns,
crushed in a mortar
1 tablespoon sea salt

To cook the eggs, put them into plenty of boiling water, bring them quickly back to the boil and using a timer, give them one minute and 45 seconds.

Next, run cold water over them to stop them cooking and peel them while they are still slightly warm, reserving a few with the shell on, to garnish. Then, to serve, arrange them on a platter with the unpeeled eggs and a little dipping pot containing the pepper and salt, which have been mixed together.

Chocolate Fudge with Roasted Nuts and Raisins

All the chocolates we serve with coffee at the football club are home-made. Over the years this fudge recipe has been a strong favourite, and here it provides a sublime and sweet ending to the book.

Makes 60 squares

14 oz (400 g) dark chocolate (75 per cent cocoa solids), chopped quite finely

3 oz (75 g) mixed nuts, such as hazelnuts and almonds

3 oz (75 g) raisins

1½ oz (40 g) unsalted butter

3½ fl oz (100 ml) liquid glucose

12 fl oz (340 ml) whipping cream

9 oz (250 g) golden caster sugar

For the top:

4 oz (110 g) milk chocolate

You will also need a small baking tray; a wide, heavy-based saucepan with a capacity of 6 pints (3.5 litres); a sugar thermometer; and a baking tin measuring 6 x 10 inches (15 x 25.5 cm), lined with silicone paper (parchment).

Pre-heat the oven to gas mark 4, 350°F (180°C).

Begin by roasting the nuts. Spread them out on the small baking tray and roast them for 8 minutes, using a timer so you don't forget them. Then remove them from the oven to a chopping board, let them cool a bit and chop them roughly. Now place them, along with the dark chocolate, raisins and butter in a large, heatproof bowl.

Next, measure out the glucose. (A hot spoon will be useful here – just dip it in boiled water for a few seconds, then wipe it dry.) Place the glucose, cream and sugar in the saucepan over a high heat. (It does need to be a large, wide pan as the mixture will come to a really fast, rolling boil.) Stir everything together until it gets really hot, and then stop stirring because the mixture does tend to catch on the bottom of the pan and you'll stir scorched bits into the fudge.

What you need to do now is insert the sugar thermometer (protecting your hands with thick oven gloves and being really careful not to splash yourself). When the temperature of the mixture reaches 225°F (110°C) – after about 5 minutes – the mixture will look like dark condensed milk. Now remove it from the heat and pour it over the nuts, dark chocolate, raisins and butter, and stir with a wooden spoon until the mixture is well blended, smooth and glossy. (Don't be tempted to add the chocolate to the hot pan – it will simply burn.) Now all you do is pour the whole lot into the lined tin. Then soak the saucepan in hot water immediately.

When the fudge is absolutely cold, cover it with clingfilm and chill it in the fridge for at least 6 hours or, preferably, overnight.

The next day, melt the milk chocolate in a heatproof bowl over a saucepan of simmering water, making sure the base of the bowl doesn't touch the water. Then turn the fudge out on to a chopping board, discarding the silicone paper, and use a palette knife to spread the melted chocolate over the top. Use a serrated palette knife or a fork to make a ridged pattern across the topping and allow it to set before cutting the fudge into 1 inch (2.5 cm) cubes.

Party Checklist

Item	Notes
In advance	
Plastic boxes and food bags; kitchen paper and foil; and clingfilm	Assemble the equipment you'll need to store party food cooked in advance. Lidded plastic boxes of varying sizes are invaluable for keeping prepared ingredients separate in the fridge to prevent flavour tainting, and plastic food bags are useful when space is limited. A piece of wet kitchen paper popped into a box or bag helps keep herbs and salad leaves damp and fresh. Kitchen foil and clingfilm are handy for covering both ingredients and made-up dishes
Ice	If you need to chill your bottles with ice, you will need about 1 lb (450 g) per person. Make it in batches and store it in bags in the freezer, or, if space is tight, ask your supermarket or off-licence to reserve you some bags of ice and collect it a few hours in advance (taking a cooler box with you)
Flowers	Order and collect
Menus, seating plan and place settings (if required)	Write, or design them on the computer
Music	Plan your playlist or choice of CD
On the morning of your party	
Napkins	Tie or fold. Assemble cocktail napkins, if required
Table	Lay a cloth and assemble main, starter, side, cheese and dessert plates; cutlery; salt and pepper mills; a bread basket; butter dishes; napkins; and menus, a seating plan and place settings, as required
Glasses	Polish and set out on trays, ready to be filled
Flowers	Arrange around the room and on the table
Candles or nightlights (if required)	Put in place around the room and on the table
Ashtrays (if required)	Put in place around the room
Tea cloths	Make sure you have plenty of clean cloths for kitchen tasks
Serving dishes and cutlery	Assemble in the kitchen
Coats	Clear coats from coat hooks, or decide on a bedroom where they can go
Guest cloakroom	Assemble toilet paper, hand towels, tissues, a scented candle and flowers
Before your guests arrive	
Drinks	Chill bottles in the fridge, if you have space, or on ice, if not – put them into a large plastic container (or a couple of washing-up bowls) an hour before the party, pour over the ice and add some cold water
Wine buckets or coolers	Assemble or chill, as appropriate
Rubbish bins	Empty all bins for the final time
Dishwasher	Empty and put away the contents
Music	Set up your playlist or put on a CD
Lighting and heating (if appropriate)	Adjust to suit
Candles or nightlights	Light
Cushions	Plump up
Shower, dress, pour yourself a cool drink or a glass of wine and relax!	Enjoy!

Suppliers and stockists

Delia's website

www.deliaonline.com
Includes information about
ingredients and where to get them,
recommended food shops and
equipment suppliers, Delia's
recipes, culinary advice and
techniques, and live
on-line chats with Delia

Kitchen equipment

Divertimenti
www.divertimenti.co.uk
Telephone 020 7823 8151
info@divertimenti.co.uk

Lakeland
www.lakeland.co.uk
Telephone 015394 88100
net.shop@lakeland.co.uk

Ingredients

Beef, lamb, pork and game

Donald Russell
www.donaldrussell.com
Telephone 01467 629666
order@donaldrussell.com

Cheese

La Fromagerie
www.lafromagerie.co.uk
Telephone 020 7359 7440
highbury@lafromagerie.co.uk
For European cheeses

Neal's Yard Dairy
www.nealsyarddairy.co.uk
Telephone 020 7500 7520
mailorder@nealsyarddairy.co.uk
For British and Irish cheeses

Chicken

Kelly Turkey Farms
www.kelly-turkeys.com
Telephone 01245 223 581
linda@kellyturkeys.com

Fish

Alex Spink & Sons
http://alexspinkandsons.com/
Telephone 01241 879056
aspink@fastfish.co.uk

Matthew Stevens & Son
Traditional Fishmongers
www.mstevensandson.co.uk
Telephone 01736 799392
shop@mstevensandson.co.uk

Springs Smoked Salmon
www.springs-post.co.uk
Telephone 01903 815066
julie@springs-post.co.uk

Italian foods

Fratelli Camisa Ltd
www.camisa.co.uk
Telephone 01992 763076
camisafood@aol.com

Smoked Suffolk pork, bacon and sausages

Lane Farm Country Foods
www.lanefarm.co.uk
Telephone 01379 384593
ian@lanefarm.co.uk

Spices

Seasoned Pioneers
www.seasonedpioneers.co.uk
Telephone 0800 0682348
feedback@seasonedpioneers.co.uk

Delia's Canary Catering

www.deliascanarycatering.com
www.yellowsdiner.com
For more information on Delia's
restaurants and Canary Catering:
Telephone 01603 218704

Index